MW00872576

ATAN

...this is going to hurt!

Kole Eremos

CONTENTS

****

To all who love the Lord Jesus; His Truth, and His appearing.

"Beware lest any man spoil you through philosophy and vain deceit, after the traditions of men, after the rudiments of the world, and not after Christ." (Col.2:8)

PREFACE

For some two thousand years the Body of Christ has been under relentless attack. At times by way of violent, bloody persecution from without; but alas, all too often by far more insidious predators from within! (See *Acts 20:29-30, Phil.3:2*)

Today's "Lions, tigers, gladiators and horsemen" may not be tormenting Christians in the arena, but they are nevertheless working just as hard to destroy the faith which is built upon,

> *"The foundation of the apostles and prophets, Jesus Christ Himself
> being the Chief Corner stone." (Eph.2:20)*

Just who these enemies are, and how they seek to undermine, weaken, and destroy the spiritual fabric and testimony of the *true* Church is the theme of this entire volume. Its pages will disclose many of the age-old weapons their leader has manufactured, including those he continues to employ so successfully in this "end-time" global struggle!

Currently, Satan is beguiling the whole religious world, and especially the *"Bride of Christ"* with the soothing strains of,

"God is All ~ All is One ~ so All share the Divine, and the Oneness that is God!"

Such New Age "mantras" are being spewed out by an endless array of self-styled, media-friendly gurus, who in turn have been glowingly endorsed by many of today's leading Talk-Show hosts!

****

For the record: not long ago on national television, New-Age-champion Oprah Winfrey swept away any possible confusion regarding her spiritual position by stating categorically, **"Jesus couldn't** *possibly* **be the only way to God!"**

(A video clip of that show is currently available online at http://www.watchman.org/oprah.htm)

****

Other more obvious end-time manifestations would have to include –

Increasingly violent and perverted entertainment being regarded more and more as the "norm" for television, movies, and of course the *Inter-net!* (Doesn't something called the *"World Wide Web"* speak for itself?)

Homosexuality promoted seemingly everywhere, and also accepted as normal. "*As it was in the days of Lot.*"(*Gen.19, Luke17:28*) – Who dares (publicly) to call homosexually an abomination today? (*Rom.1:24-28*)

Religious leaders echoing the New Age cry, "**All faiths are valid**" ~ "**All paths lead to God!**" (Satan may have more men in pulpits than God does?)

Foul streams of erroneous, even dangerous Bible translations, that are bent on watering down the Word of God in order to lead the undiscerning further and further down the ever-widening New Age road!

Mediums, psychics and other occult practitioners multiplying like bacteria! (Over 50,000 registered witches in the U.S. alone!)

Corrupt political leaders who cannot balance their petty cash (let alone countries' budgets), but know well how to legislate against righteousness!

No lions, tigers, or horsemen today – right?

Since time began, Satan (originally called Lucifer), and a horde of rebellious fallen angels (also known as evil spirits or demons) have delighted in pulling huge amounts of "spiritual wool" over the eyes of believers and non-believers alike. Hence the well-known saying,
"The devil's greatest achievement has been to convince the world he does not exist!"
Surely such an evil, supernatural, and egomaniacal genius (that no one believes in) could get away with just about anything! ... Any questions?

Needless to say, multitudes still live with their own version of the devil; a sweet, fictitious little character complete with horns, red suit, pitchfork and spiked tail! Truth is, the *real* devil loves it that way! Ignorance, unbelief, plus total misconceptions regarding this loathsome enemy of God and man form an integral part of Satan's strategy. He is after all, "*The father of lies!*" (*John 8:44*)
The inescapable reality is this. –
The devil has hurt every single one of us. (Some much more than others.)
He has made victims of us all. (Some much more willing than others!)

Equally true is the fact that only God's people really know what it means to "*fight a good fight,*" (*2Tim.4:7*) and "*overcome the world.*" (*1John 5:4-5*) Yet even they must be equipped and battle-ready if they want to rise up and hurt the devil right back! ...And don't we all?

The moment a person is "*born again,*" (*John 3:3*) he or she becomes a vital part of, "*the army of the Lord.*" (*Rev.19:14-19*) This book is simply an attempt to supply God's spiritual "soldiers" with some real, straightforward, and workable ammunition! First, by piercing and exposing demonic darkness with the light and truth of God's Word; and second, by pointing the reader to the liberty, victory, power and peace found only through complete and utter dependence upon God the Holy Spirit!

Above all however, may it be for the lifting up of God's Divine, Glorious and Ever-Risen Son; the only *True* Lord and Savior, Jesus Christ!

****

INTRODUCTION

"The heart is deceitful above all things, and desperately wicked: who can know it?" (*Jer.17:9*)

Deceptions have formed like strands in a vast evil net, which demonic spirits (fallen angels led by Satan himself) have been drawing around the world since the beginning of time. The ministry or work of deception is so widespread, varied and complex, that no one with the fallen nature of Adam could possibly avoid its influence. Anyone who claimed to would obviously be deceived!

According to the Word of God, deceptions (*"works of darkness"*) are in fact false doctrines, teachings, or evil acts inspired and promoted by demons, and subsequently passed on to and through any person willing to embrace them. (See *1Tim.4:1-3, Col.2:8*)

By the grace of God, it is now every believer's privilege and responsibility to *"reprove"* or expose such *"works ..."* wherever they may be found! (*Eph. 5:11*) In order to do this however, we must first humbly and sincerely ask the Holy Spirit to open the eyes of our hearts, and reveal them to us in the only safe light of Biblical truth!

****

Deception begins and ends with Lucifer. It began in Heaven when through pride he lifted himself up, and sought to rule over the kingdom of God. It will finally end after the coming *"one thousand-year"* reign of the Lord Jesus Christ on earth! (The Millennium)

Then and *only* then will the devil and his rebellious angels find themselves cast forever into *"the lake of fire;"* followed by *"Death and hell ... and whosoever was not found written in the book of life."*

(*Rev. ch. 20*)

****

In the eternity before God created time, and *"laid the foundations of the earth,"* (*Job 38:4*) an amazing and dreadful rebellion took place in Heaven. A rebellion, which would determine the course of history (not yet written), and eventually make deception and sin the enemies each and every one of us would have to reckon with!

The tragic details of that conflict are now a matter of public record.

"... And there was war in Heaven: Michael and his angels fought against the dragon; and the dragon fought and his angels, and prevailed not; neither was their place found any more in Heaven." (Revelation 12:7)

But God had already spoken with Sovereign authority.

"How art thou fallen from Heaven O Lucifer, son of the morning! How art thou cut down to the ground, which didst weaken the nations! ...Thou sealest up the sum, full of wisdom and perfect in beauty. Thou hast been in Eden, the Garden of God...Thou art the anointed cherub that covereth...Thou wast perfect in thy ways from the day that thou wast created, till iniquity was found in thee. By the multitude of thy merchandise they have filled the midst of thee with violence, and thou hast sinned: therefore I will cast thee as profane out of the mountain of God: and I will destroy thee, O covering cherub, from the midst of the stones of fire. Thine heart was lifted up because of thy beauty, thou hast corrupted thy wisdom by reason of thy brightness (splendor): I will cast thee to the ground, I will lay thee before kings, that they may behold thee...For thou hast said in thine heart, I will ascend into Heaven, I will exalt my throne above the stars (angels) of God: I will sit also upon the mount of the congregation, in the sides of the north: I will ascend above the heights of the clouds; I will be like the most High. Yet thou shalt be brought down to hell, to the sides of the pit. All they that know thee among the people shall be astonished at thee: thou shalt be a terror (horror), and never shalt thou be any more."
(From *Isaiah 14* and *Ezekiel 28*)

*"... And the great dragon was cast out, that old serpent, called the Devil, and Satan, which deceiveth the whole world: he was cast out into the earth, and his angels were cast out with him ...Therefore rejoice, ye heavens, and ye that dwell in them. Woe to the inhabiters of the earth and of the sea! For the devil is come down unto you, having great wrath, because he knoweth that he hath but a **short time**." (Rev.12:9 and 12)*

****

In His infinite wisdom, and for very specific reasons, God is allowing satanic forces to operate on the earth for a designated period (commonly referred to as history). As we travel through the chapters ahead, we will examine and hopefully better understand many of the devil's tactics, and the extraordinary events taking place within this "*short time:*" including some still waiting to unfold at its spectacular, earth-shaking, and totally God-ordained conclusion!

May these pages be as challenging and rewarding to read, as they were to write.

The victory of deception is the unawareness of our defeat.

PART ONE

THE UNCOVERER

CHAPTER ONE

BEFORE THE BEGINNING

Omnipotent (all powerful); Omniscient (all knowing); and Omnipresent (everywhere present); God is, was, and always will be The Eternal *"I AM."* (*Ex.3:14*)

"From everlasting to everlasting, Thou art God." (*Ps.90:2*)

"For Thine is the Kingdom, and the power, and the glory, for ever. Amen." (*Matt.6:13*)

"I am the first, and I am the last; and beside Me there is no God." (*Is.44:6*)

Like precious stones discovered near the surface of the earth, those and many other wonderful Bible verses are relatively easy for us to gather or understand. However, anyone wishing to leave the surface, and explore the fathomless treasuries of God more deeply – must be prepared to dig!

(*Pr.2:3-5*)

Back in the distant timeless past, and certainly before ever creating a physical heaven and earth below; the Trinity (Three in, or as One) of God the Father, God the Son (The Lord Jesus Christ), and God the Holy Spirit reigned over an idyllic, and sinless spiritual Kingdom.

(See *Matt.3:16-17, John 1:1, 1John 5:7*)

For His glory and pleasure, God would create *all* things; (*Rev.4:11*) including a myriad of angelic beings with varying rank and purpose. One of those perfect beings was a cherub whose ministry was literally to cover the Throne of God! *"Thou art the **anointed cherub that covereth**."* (*Eze.28:14*) The name of that anointed cherub was *"Lucifer, son of the morning."* (*Is.14:12*) Also translated, "light bearer." Now, if someone asks, "How can we be sure it was God's Throne that Lucifer was covering?" My response would be, "Grab your shovel, and let's go to the only place in the Word of God where we can find the answer!"

We must open the book of Exodus, and delve into the Tabernacle that God commanded Moses and the children of Israel to build while dwelling in the wilderness.

The Tabernacle (or tent) of the congregation, and everything in it was to be a *"pattern"* (an exact model or replica) of the Heavenly original. (See *Ex.25:8-9,40 and Hebrews 8:5*)

The most holy place in the Tabernacle (the Holy of Holies) would contain the *"Ark of the Covenant."* The ark itself was built to hold the Ten Commandments, but for a time it also held the *"rod of Aaron,"* and a *"golden pot of manna."* (See *Heb.9:1-5*) On top of the Ark was placed a lid, or cover of pure gold called the "*mercy seat*," above which, God would appear and dispense justice and mercy to the people of Israel. Read now as God describes the mercy seat in detail…

> "*And thou shalt make a mercy seat of **pure gold**: two cubits and a half shall be the length thereof, and a cubit and a half the breadth thereof. And thou shalt make **two cherubim of gold**; of beaten work shalt thou make them, in the two ends of the mercy seat. And the cherubim shall stretch forth their wings on high, **covering the mercy seat with their wings**, and their faces shall look one to another; **toward the mercy seat shall the faces of the cherubim be**. And there I will meet with thee, and I will commune with thee from above the mercy seat, from **between the two cherubim** which are upon the **Ark of the Testimony**, of all things which I will give thee in commandment unto the children of Israel.*"

(*Ex.25:17-20, 22*)

Scripture reveals that although the two cherubim faced each other from each end of the mercy seat, their faces were in fact toward the mercy seat itself. In other words, their eyes looked down and their heads were bowed in an attitude of worship while their wings reached out on high completely covering the "*ark of the testimony.*"

Notice also that the mercy seat was made of "*pure gold*" (type of heavenly perfection): the cherubim were not! (*vs. 17-18*) Lucifer had already fallen from Heaven, so that type (pure gold) was not upheld. "*Behold, He* (GOD) *put no trust in His servants; and His angels He charged with folly.*" (*Job 4:18*)

Last but not least, the cherubim were made, "*even of the mercy seat,*" (*Ex.25:19*) which means of one piece, formed with, or as a permanent part. This lets us know that the *real* heavenly cherubim were never meant to be separated from their glorious and blessed position –

covering the actual Throne of God!

NOTE: No measure of height (nor depth) is given for the mercy seat. This may well be an expression of God's unlimited mercy, forgiveness, and grace!

At this point, let's pause and review.

The Tabernacle, and everything in it, was an earthly copy (a type or shadow) of the Heavenly original (the substance). The Ark of the Covenant (with the mercy seat as its lid) was therefore a humble reproduction of God's Throne. The two golden cherubim were then merely figures representing the *real* and *living* cherubim that covered God's Throne in Heaven: and although the name of one is not given, the name of the other can be revealed with scriptural authority as,

"*Lucifer, the anointed cherub that **covereth**.*" (*Eze.28:1*)

Finally: because of his great beauty, Lucifer's "*head*" was lifted up in prideful rebellion. He exalted himself from the place of submission and worship, **uncovered** the Throne of God, and sought to reign in God's place! (*Isa.14:13-14*)

THAT WAS THE "ORIGINAL SIN!"

Prior to that rebellion, Lucifer, who would later become known as "*the great dragon, … that old serpent, called the Devil, and Satan …*" (*Rev12:9*) had managed to persuade one third of the "*stars of Heaven*" (angels) to follow him! (*Rev.12:4*)

Right about now, someone else may be asking, "Does all this really matter to us today?"

My answer? "More than you could possibly imagine! Stay with me, and let's discover what happened next."

Once upon a time ...

Having failed in their attempt to overthrow God in Heaven, Satan and his angels were cast down to the earth. (*Rev.12:7-9*) Now although the intense, supernatural hatred consuming these exiled criminals would be beyond the measure of any human being, there are scriptural glimpses of their state; and the dreadful consequences of such rebellion and sin!

God the Son said, "*I beheld Satan **as lightning fall from Heaven**.*" (*Luke 10:18*)

God the Father said, "*Thou hast defiled thy sanctuaries by the multitude of thine iniquities, by the iniquity of thy traffic;* (dealings) **therefore will I bring forth a fire from the midst of thee, it shall devour thee**, and I will bring thee **to ashes upon the earth** in the sight of all them that behold thee.*" (*Eze.28:18*)

And so it came to pass, that beaten, banished, and cast down upon the earth, Satan's burning and devouring rage (once aimed solely toward Heaven) would now begin to turn in a completely new direction. If he could not overthrow God on high, he would surely attempt to do anything and everything within his limited, yet still formidable power – to destroy God's creation here below!

"*...Woe to the inhabiters of the earth and of the sea! For the devil is come down unto you, having great wrath, because he knoweth that he hath but a **short time**.*" (*Rev.12:12*)

That "*short time*" would encompass the longest, and most devastating spiritual war in history!

THE BEGINNING

Knowing full well that finite human beings living in time and physical space would have no real concept of eternity (until death that is), God narrowed down the account of creation from infinity to a starting point we *could* relate to.

"*In the beginning, God created the heaven and the earth. And the earth was without form, and void; and darkness was upon the face of the deep. And the Spirit of God moved upon the face of the waters. And God said, Let there be light: and there was light. And God saw the light, that it was good: and God divided the light from the darkness. And God called the light Day, and the darkness He called Night. And the evening and the morning were the **first day**.*" (*Gen.1:1-5*)

No one knows exactly how long the earth was "*without form and void*," or how long the "*Spirit of God moved upon the face of the waters*." No one knows if Satan was watching the whole creative process, but it is entirely possible. One thing *is* certain, "*... the evening and the morning were the first day*," and that "*short time*" (the count-down to Satan's *ultimate* destruction) had begun!

With beginnings in mind, and for the glory of God, please allow me to share this short but treasured revelation I received from the Holy Spirit many years ago.

The Gospel according to Genesis

In the beginning, my life was without form (lost without substance), and void (empty and completely meaningless); and darkness (selfishness and sin) was upon the face of the deep (my soul, and my whole being!) Then the Spirit of God moved upon my life. And God said, "*Let there be Light; and there was light;*" and Jesus Christ, "*The Light of the world,*" and "*The Lord of Glory*" came into my life. And God saw that the Light was good! And God saved me by His grace, and called me a "*child of the day.*" (*1Thess.5:5*) He forgave *all* my sins; divided (separated or delivered) me from "*the night*" (the power of darkness), and "*translated me into the Kingdom of His dear Son.*"

(*Col.1:13*)

Praise God, I was "*born again.*" "*... And the evening and the morning were the first day*" of my glorious new, and eternal life!

That revelation is surely for *all* believers, and I pray it blesses you as it did me.

With the countdown under way, one can well imagine the devil feverishly plotting a vile and terrible revenge: but apparently, during the initial phase of God's Divine project, Lucifer saw little he could dig his teeth into.

"*... days, nights, firmaments, seas, herb yielding seed, fruit trees yielding fruit after their kind; lights, great whales, winged fowl, cattle, creeping things, beasts of the earth after their kind. ...*" (*Gen.1: 6-25*)

Nothing of any *real* interest there ... so he waited!

Having completed the first five days of His miraculous creation, "*God saw that what He had made was good.*" But then suddenly, on the *sixth* day, the Heavenly Trinity Satan detested so much began forming creatures of a totally unexpected, and altogether different "*kind!*"

Just how badly this once perfect cherub reacted to seeing the first of these strange, earthly creatures (fashioned out of what appeared to be nothing more than dirt) remains a mystery. But what may have been even *more* odious to him was the fact that these brand-new arrivals were actually being made in the "*image and likeness*" of God! Immortal beings that at God's command would begin to take dominion over the earth, and everything in it (*Gen.1:26-28*) – including Satan himself!

Finally, (as if to add insult to injury); after creating "*man*" on that truly loathsome day ...

"*God saw everything that He had made, and it was VERY good.*" (*Gen.1:31*)

Surely the blaze of hatred within Lucifer could not have burned more fiercely than at that very moment!

Gradually however, as those inflamed, murderous thoughts cooled, and his mind began to ponder this bizarre new development, it became increasingly, then even deliciously clear, that the couple presently residing in "*the garden of God, eastward in Eden*" might be all that stood between him and his total domination of the earth!

If he could only persuade them to submit to him, and hopefully *serve* him, he might be able, not only to conquer and control subsequent generations, but eventually (with mankind's help of course), to realize the most glorious possibility of all! That he could somehow use these otherwise useless humans to tip the balance of *Heavenly* power, and bring God down as well! ... Brilliant! But how? It was clear that God loved these abnormal, inferior hybrids; and so would not allow them to be overwhelmed by an angel's supernatural power. That would be far too easy! Therefore Satan would have to use a power equal to, or less than the humans themselves.

Obviously *he* could not become a human being; neither could he create one – nor anything else for that matter – No! Creation was God's privilege alone!

It appeared his only option (as repulsive and degrading as that might be) was to use a lesser, and even more revolting creature than man himself! The only problem would be finding one?

Earlier in the garden

> *"And the Lord God commanded the man, saying, Of every tree of the garden thou mayest freely eat. But of the tree of the knowledge of good and evil, thou shalt not eat of it: for in the day that thou eatest thereof thou shalt surely die." (Gen.2:16-17)*

Having created man (Adam) from the dust of the earth, God spoke directly to him and gave him absolute freedom to enjoy all the goodness of the Divine garden, including the fruit from every tree; even from the tree of life itself! The one and only exception being the fruit from *"the tree of the knowledge of good and evil."* This then was to become a simple yet profound test of man's obedience. To eat or not to eat? *...That* was the question!

Stepping aside just briefly here, let's consider two other questions (The answers may be helpful, especially to those influenced by the "Theory of Evolution.")

1. "How old was Adam the moment he was formed or created?"
Trick question of course: Adam was a moment old – the same as any baby newly born!

2. "How old do you think Adam *looked* the moment he was formed?"
Naturally answers vary, but the average estimate is somewhere between 20 and 33.

The point is this: if God Almighty, Creator of the universe could create a fully grown man who was actually a moment old, could He not also create the heavens and the earth in **SIX DAYS** and make them appear to be a great deal older? *(Gen.2: 1-4)*

The question the Bible asks is will we believe Darwin, our senses, and what we *think* we know, or will we believe **GOD'S WORD?**

The "wisdom" of this world believes the earth is billions of years old. Only a foolish person would believe it was made in six days and is therefore quite young!

> *"But God hath chosen the foolish things of the world to confound the wise, and God hath chosen the weak things of the world to confound the things that are mighty." (1Corinthians 1:27)*
>   (I simply delight in being one of God's *"foolish, weak things!"*)

Without doubt, Evolution is one of the most powerful deceptions Satan has woven around the world; and he still loves making monkeys out of men!

As we return to Eden, remember that Adam is still without a wife ...

> *"And the Lord God said, it is not good that the man should be alone; I will make him an help* (helper) *meet* (suitable) *for him. And out of the ground the Lord God formed every beast of the field, and every fowl of the air; and brought them to Adam to see what he would call them: and*

whatsoever Adam called every living creature, that was the name thereof ... but for Adam there was not found an help meet for him." (Gen.2:18-20)

This is important because it shows that Adam spoke to the animals, and interacted with them. Scripture reveals that the animals also talked, and had limited fellowship with him. However, when the animals departed, Adam was still alone.

The Lord was saving the ideal *"Help meet for him"* until last!

*"And the Lord God caused a deep sleep to fall upon Adam, and he slept: and He took one of his ribs, and closed up the flesh thereof, and the rib, which the Lord God had taken from man, made He a woman, and **brought her unto the man**." (Gen.2:21-22)*
    Some lighter spiritual insight from this passage may well be a word to the wise.

Adam fell into a *"deep sleep."* (God knew he would need the rest!) Just kidding! Any couple knows that a marriage takes hard work from *both* partners! But, if you're a single man who seriously desires a wife, seek the Lord earnestly first with *specific* prayer, and then wait! God's principle is to bring the woman to the man! No need to fret or run around! God's choice will be the best. Many have rushed in, made the wrong decision, and regretted it! (You don't need me to give you today's divorce statistics.) *"Delight thyself in the Lord, and He shall give thee the desires of thine heart. Commit thy way unto the Lord; trust also in Him, and He shall bring it to pass." (Psalm 37:4-5)*

Once we've found the way of obedience (in *any* given situation, test or trial), we'll find there is nothing quite like the peace and spiritual calm of knowing we are in the center of God's will. The alternative?

Learning the hard way!

Remember the storm on the lake? (*Luke 8:22-25*) Throughout the entire storm, Jesus was right there on board – in the midst! The disciples completely forgot that earlier, God had said,

*"Let us go **over** to the other side of the lake." (v.22)* ... **Not under!**

There is something else here we need to grasp. Some of the disciples were professional fishermen, and as such must have fought their way through many storms. They obviously tried to handle this one with their natural abilities as usual, but could not! This was no ordinary storm! To make matters worse, Jesus was asleep! (He alone knew they were going over!)

The fact is, those men could have called on the spiritual power they already had in His Name. They could have rebuked the storm by faith! Instead, they exhausted themselves in futile fleshly effort; became completely overwhelmed, and finally cried out to the Lord in terror for their lives!

Jesus was their last resort!

And think about this: the actual storm was *not* of God. (Why do men so often blame God for violent acts of nature?)

If the storm *had* been of God, Jesus would never have rebuked it.

Satan was behind it. – He came to destroy. (*John 10:10*) This particular storm was much more than the "natural man" could handle! This is why Jesus gave us **His** *"power over all the power of the enemy." (Luke 10:19)* If was impossible or wrong for the disciples to calm the wind and raging waves

22

themselves, the Lord would never have rebuked them saying, *"Why are ye fearful, O ye of little faith?"* (*Matt. 8:26*) They were in the center of God's will; they just didn't know it!

So today, in order to avoid heavy weather stress, it's vital for us to learn that though negative physical and spiritual storms may come our way, these things will never overwhelm us if we speak to them, and rise above them by faith!

Let's call upon the Name of Jesus *before* the storm clouds are gathered; not when we're going down for the third time in the flesh! We *can* do what Jesus did, ***"Because as He is, so are we in this world."*** (*1Jn.4:17*) Over the years, Satan has convinced many Bible preachers and teachers that verses like this (and hundreds of others in the Word of God) are not for today. All I can say is the devil is a liar, and he also comes to steal!

Light looks good on you

Back in the garden, Adam was speaking. *"This is now bone of my bones, and flesh of my flesh: she shall be called Woman, because she was taken out of man. Therefore a man shall leave his father and his mother, and shall cleave unto his wife: and they shall be one flesh. And they were both naked, the man and his wife, and were not ashamed."* (*Gen.2:23-25*)

One of the many wonderful aspects of their creation was that the man and woman were *"naked and not ashamed."* To understand their condition more fully, we must again "dig" into God's priceless Word: this time from the book of Psalms.

"O Lord my God, Thou art very great; Thou art clothed with honour and majesty. **Who coverest Thyself with light as with a garment:** *who stretchest out the heavens like a curtain."* (*Ps.104:1-2*)

Created *"in the image and likeness of God,"* there is no doubt in my mind that Adam and his wife were also covered with wondrous garments of light! Light which would reflect the honour, majesty, and purity of their Divine Father, and show forth God's Glory upon the earth over which they now ruled. No wonder they were not ashamed!

Meanwhile, in another part of that garden paradise, Satan had found a vessel suitable for his evil purpose,

"Now the serpent was more subtle than any beast of the field which the LORD GOD had made..." (*Gen.3:1a*)

NOTE: The serpent could have easily been Lucifer's physical counterpart on earth – crafty, cunning, sly, and probably of great beauty – all reasons why the devil would deign to use it; and we know it moved or walked uprightly before being cursed and *"cast down to the dust."* (*Gen.3:14*)

Be that as it may, three things will become evident.

1 Satan somehow knew the key to his success lay in persuading the humans to disobey the Lord God and eat the forbidden fruit.
2 He had discovered a way to enter or use the serpent for that specific purpose.
3 His attack would be directed towards the woman!

"And he (the serpent) said unto the woman, Yea, **hath God said, Ye shall not eat of every** *tree of the garden?"* (*Gen.3:1b*)

In this one verse (with revelation from the Holy Spirit) we can see Satan's foul strategy from beginning to the end of time.

In restating His creation, i.e., *"the generations of the heavens and of the earth;"*(Gen.2:4) God introduces us to the title, *"**LORD GOD**."* The importance of this cannot be overstated! It tells us that the Lord Jesus Christ was (with the Holy Spirit) actively involved in every phase of the creative process!

With one deceitfully loaded question, Satan (through the serpent) omits the whole counsel of God, thereby casting doubt on the integrity of God Himself. At the same time he cleverly evades the Lordship of Jesus Christ altogether! ...

"Hath God said?"

In the entire history of mankind, the devil has had no greater success than with that one question!

Today, in countless churches, the whole counsel of God is routinely omitted, and the Lordship of Jesus Christ is rejected by billions of lost souls!

The woman (who incidentally was not the slightest bit surprised by a talking snake) may have learned of the forbidden fruit from her husband, and not from the Lord God directly. Either way, she follows the serpent's leading.

*"We may eat of the fruit of the trees of the garden: but of the fruit of the tree which is in the midst of the garden, **God hath said**, Ye shall not eat of it, **neither shall ye touch it, lest ye die**."* (Gen.3:2-3)

The woman also avoids the title, *"Lord,"* but in her reply she actually manages to add to the Word of God! (Is she trying to convince herself?) Regarding the fruit; the words, *"neither shall ye touch it"* were never spoken by God! She also changes, *"...thou shalt **surely** die"* (Gen.2:17) into, *"...**lest** ye die."* (Satan must have loved that one!) Adding to, or taking away from God's Word gives us more or less to do (or believe) than God requires, and has become the foundation of every false religious cult known to man!

When it comes to *GOD* or *LORD GOD*, the following becomes clear.

The title *"GOD"* is vague enough that anyone can use it without causing offence, i.e. "There are many ways to God;" "God Bless you;" "We are *all* God's children;" "One nation under God;" "All religions lead to God;" "In God we trust;" "Oh my God!" ... You get the picture.

But of course, very few ask the question, "Which *God* are we talking about?" For the vast majority, it simply doesn't matter! Take away *"LORD"* and everyone's happy!

On the other hand, dare to insist that **JESUS CHRIST** is the **LORD GOD**, and the **ONLY WAY** to the Father in Heaven, and Satan's "fiery darts" will begin to fly!

Sensing she is about to take the bait, the serpent becomes bolder.

*"And the serpent said unto the woman, Ye shall not surely die: For God doth know that in the day ye eat thereof, then **your eyes shall be opened, and ye shall be as gods, knowing good and evil**."* (Gen.3:4-5)

Satan reassures his prey with a blatant lie, *"Ye shall not surely die…"* and sets the hook!

****

"Buy the truth, and sell it not." (*Prov.23:23*)

Everything so far points to this. If we allow the enemy to cause us to question God's Word, we may well begin to doubt God Himself. Once we doubt God, disobedience is only a "bite" away!

This has always been Satan's number one tactic: just listen to the serpent today …

"If God *really* loved you, why would He allow such terrible things to happen? After all, you're not a bad person. Haven't you always tried to do the right thing? Why look to God for help? He doesn't seem to care at all! Perhaps it's time to take things into your own hands. Be your own boss! Make up your own mind! Hasn't He given you free will? Go your own way; nothing bad will happen. It's *your* life! Deep down you know it's up to you. …"

There are thousands of variations, but all are based on the same old line, *"Hath God said?"* Never forget that Satan will use *any* willing vessel! Hollywood, the media, politicians, doctors, friends, family members and yes – even Christians may offer "reasonable doubt," so beware!

Serpents still speak, and they are lurking everywhere!

****

*"And when the woman saw that the tree was **good for food**, and that it was **pleasant to the eyes**, and a tree to be **desired to make one wise**, she took of the fruit thereof, and did eat, and gave also unto her husband with her, and he did eat."* (*Gen.3:6*)

Well it took a while, but here it is: the act that changed the course of history, and brought more misery into the world than all the poets, philosophers and artists combined could ever begin to express.

The fall of man came from eating just one piece of fruit. (Incidentally, nowhere does Scripture say it was an apple.) The temptation leading to that fall however was threefold.

*"**Lust of the flesh**."* (The tree was good for food) *"**Lust of the eyes**."* (The woman saw that the tree was pleasant to the eyes) *"**Pride of life**."* (It was desired to make one wise)

The Holy Spirit through the Apostle John spells out the tragic confirmation.

"For all that is in the world, the lust of the flesh, and the lust of the eyes, and the pride of life, is not of the Father, but is of the world." (*1John 2:16*)

Every deception and sin known to man continues to be fueled by those three selfish desires, but right now I want to concentrate on exactly what happened in those moments between the last few words of the temptation: *"Your eyes shall be opened, and ye shall be as gods, …"* and the sin itself. *"… She took of the fruit thereof, and did eat, and gave also unto her husband with her, and he did eat."*

25

Heads up again!

By the Word of God we've seen that Lucifer, *"lifted up his head"* and sought to reign as a "god" in Heaven. Now we may see clearly that the man and the woman (as much as lay within them) would do exactly the same thing on the earth!

The woman had already lifted up her head from the place of submission (under the covering of Adam), and had been speaking to the serpent on her husband's behalf. Now *both* their heads rise up as the temptation takes hold!

Do you see the excitement and expectation in the woman's face as she gives the fruit to Adam, and encourages him to eat with her?

Do you see their eyes growing wider and wider at the prospect of becoming "gods?"

Do you see as they eat, those same eyes suddenly opening to the dreadful reality of what has just happened?

Do you see the glorious covering of pure "light" departing from them, and leaving only the humiliating awareness of their sin, their shame, and the darkness of their defeat?

"And they knew that they were naked." (*Gen.3:7*)

Where on earth was Adam?

From my earliest childhood I remember being told (mostly by men of course) that the whole "sin thing" was the woman's fault! I even heard this comment quite recently,

"Well, Eve ate the stupid apple and got us into this mess didn't she?"

Although wrong on both assumptions (apple *and* mess!), and whether spoken in jest or not; that statement sums up the huge amount of ignorance and deception still affecting people of all ages and walks of life.

The key to understanding the truth behind the greatest tragedy ever recorded, comes with the last few words of *Gen.3: 6*, "*... she took of the fruit thereof, and did eat, **and gave also unto her husband with her;** and he did eat.*"

As an unbeliever, I was convinced that the man was somehow miles away. That the woman acted alone, and was therefore entirely responsible for our downfall! Wasn't that what the "battle of the sexes" was all about? "Poor old Adam; women really are to blame." – Bla! Bla! Bla!

I'll never forget the first time the Holy Spirit opened *my* eyes, and I "saw" Adam standing right there eating with her! It was one of many spiritual eye-openers the Lord would show me as He began to separate light from darkness, and the precious from the vile!

With all that in mind, let's go back to the original "Ground Zero."
Yes, Eve was out of order; but Adam allowed it! They uncovered each other, but –

SATAN UNCOVERED THEM BOTH!

Adam should have stepped right in and rebuked the serpent, but he wouldn't!

He should have been thinking, "We don't need this fruit to become gods; we already rule the earth in the image and likeness of Almighty God," but he wasn't!

He should have obeyed the direct Word of God, "*Thou shalt not eat of it,*" but he didn't!

So the only gods man *would* become like, were Satan and the fallen angels who, (to their everlasting shame) already bore the dreadful cost of knowing the difference between good and evil.

Yes, Eve was deceived, but Adam rebelled. And all to become something less than they already were!

Satan wins – Humans lose … But!

The uncoverer had worked his *"wiles"* to perfection. Satan could now (through Adam's sin) (*Rom.5:12*) hold the *"power of death,"* (*Heb.2:14*) and **uncover the entire human race!**

He could now boast of his great victory on earth, and claim such titles as, *"ruler of darkness,"* (*Eph.6:12*) *"god of this world,"* (*2Cor.4:4*) and, *"prince of the power of the air."* (*Eph.2:2*)

What he could *not* do however, was to understand that even before anything else existed, the Lord, the Everlasting God had actually seen and orchestrated it all: and for a purpose more magnificent and glorious than the devil, his rebellious angels, or the whole of fallen mankind could possibly imagine!

CHAPTER TWO

ONE SIN LEADS TO ANOTHER

Before we go any further, let me ask you this:

"What was the very first religious act performed on earth?"
(Does it help if I say, "man-made religious act?")

Having asked many fellowships, assemblies, and Bible study groups this same question, surprisingly, only a hand full of believers were able to give the correct response!

You may judge the importance of the question however, when I say that the most powerful and lasting deception **of all time** is actually found hidden in the answer!

One last trip to the garden

To check the answer, and to see more clearly how this particular deception operates in the world today, we must once again journey back to where it all began.

"And the eyes of them both were opened, and they knew that they were naked; and they sewed fig leaves together, and made themselves aprons. And they heard the voice of the Lord God walking in the garden in the cool of the day: and they hid themselves from the presence of the Lord God amongst the trees of the garden. And the Lord God called unto Adam, and said unto him, Where art thou? And he said, I heard Thy voice in the garden, and I was afraid, because I was naked: and I hid myself." (Gen.3:7-10)

Most of us are familiar with the old saying, "One thing leads to another." (An expression which suggests that one action or event may well become a catalyst for the next, and so on.) Unfortunately, in the case of deception, there is no mistaking the fact that *all* the "anothers" come from just "one thing." That thing is **SIN!**

Having first tasted of the fruit and become *aware* of their sin, Adam and his wife immediately and instinctively began trying to *cover* it up!

Together, they provide the answer …

"Sewing fig leaves" would be the very first religious act performed on earth!

Did you manage to get it right? Don't feel badly if you didn't. Praise the Lord, this isn't a Game Show!

But in all seriousness, that one simple yet enormously significant act of sewing fig leaves together announced the birth of what we now know as **false religion!**

Let me explain.

Once they ate the fruit and lost their supernatural covering from God, the couple resorted to natural, man-made coverings in order to, *"hide the shame of their nakedness."*

This of course was a useless, counterfeit attempt to hide the *real* issue: the shame and guilt of their underlying sin!

A "working" definition.

Fig leaf coverings are nothing more than self-righteous efforts (*"dead works"*), driven by guilt, fear or pride, which seek to hide sin, justify it, or win approval from God (or men) in spite of it!

(See *Is.64:6, Eph.2:8-9*)

This then is the essence of false religion – and the world is full of it!

NOTE: there is only one scriptural definition of true or *"pure religion,"* and it is found in the book of James.

"Pure religion and undefiled before God and the Father is this, to visit the fatherless and widows in their affliction, and to keep himself unspotted from the world." (*James 1:27*)

As stated already, false or man-made religion is the oldest and most powerful deception in the world. Every vile thing known to man has grown out of that one pathetic act in the garden, but thankfully, in spite of its consequences, God would not leave man without hope.

"And the Lord God said unto the serpent, ... I will put enmity between thee and the woman, and between thy seed and her seed; it (He) *shall bruise thy head, and thou shalt bruise His heel."* (*Gen.3:15*)

Guaranteed hostility between the children of darkness and children of light is coupled with God's glorious promise that the *"Seed"* of the woman (the Lord Jesus Christ) would one day deliver His people from Satan's dominion by *"bruising* (overwhelming or breaking) *his head"* (his power and position). By that same promise, Satan would be allowed to bruise Christ's *"heel."* (His walk, or life in human form up to and including His crucifixion.)

"Unto Adam also and to his wife did the Lord God make coats of skins, and clothed them." (*Gen.3:21*)

Having made clear to Adam the dreadful penalty for disobedience (*"Thou shalt surely die"*), God did not immediately take away the man's *physical* life. (Adam would go on to live a total of 930 years.) It was *spiritual* death that came upon Adam and Eve, and separation from God was to be a part of its fearful curse!

The end of their intimate fellowship with God inspired one of the saddest verses in the entire Bible.

"Wherefore, as by one man (Adam) *sin entered into the world, and death by sin; and so death passed upon all men, for that all have sinned." (Rom.5:12)*

Physical death (passed on to the whole human race) would be the sure sign that spiritual death had already occurred! *"The wages of sin is death." (Rom.6:23)*

Nevertheless, the penalty of *immediate* physical death (the wages demanded by God's Righteousness) would still be required! Only now (and purely by God's grace) that penalty would not be paid by Adam or Eve, but by an altogether different creature!

The greatest love: the greatest gift!

"God is Love." (1 John 4:8)
(God's love is as infinite as God Himself!)

In view of that revelation, I would like to share just three ways in which God's amazing love for mankind was demonstrated when He took away Adam and Eve's unacceptable *"fig leaf"* coverings, and (Personally) replaced them with, *"coats of skins." (Gen.3:21)*

His mercy. As much as God so loved the world, and *all* His creation, He was willing to sacrifice a still pure and innocent animal in order to spare the fallen couple, and provide them with an *acceptable* covering!

His loving-kindness. Once banished from the garden, God knew they would need a warmer and more durable form of clothing. Also important was the fact that before sin, Adam, Eve, and all the animals in Eden had been vegetarian. *(Gen.1:29-30)* Soon, in addition to the *"green herb,"* God would allow mankind the use of *any* animal for food. (See *Gen.9:2-3*) Henceforth, every creature's death would serve to remind them of Adam's fall, and God's mercy, covering, and provision.

His grace. Although the name of the first animal to make an atonement for sin is unknown, we may be sure that as a type, its identity is forever linked to the One who would become God's Final Sacrifice, and the ultimate expression of His Grace!

In the twenty-second chapter of Genesis, a great drama unfolds as God seeks to prove the obedience of a man named Abraham.

And God said, *"Take now thy son, thine only son Isaac, whom thou lovest, and get thee into the land of Moriah; and offer him there for a burnt offering upon one of the mountains which I will tell thee of." (v.2)*

This extraordinary command would certainly test Abraham's faith to the very limit, but he obeyed! After arriving at the appointed place (the eventual site of Solomon's Temple), Abraham built an altar and laid his beloved son Isaac upon it.

*"And Abraham stretched forth his hand, and took the knife to slay his son. And the Angel of the Lord called unto him out of Heaven, and said, Abraham, Abraham: and he said, Here am I. And He said, Lay not thine hand upon the lad, neither do thou any thing unto him: for now I know that thou fearest God, seeing thou hast not withheld thy son, thine only son from Me. And Abraham lifted up his eyes, and looked, and behold behind him **a ram caught in a thicket by***

*his horns: and Abraham went and took the ram, and offered him up for a burnt offering **in the stead of his son.***" (*vs. 10-13*)

Here again the Holy Spirit reveals some beautiful things for our edification, even though the "glass" is still somewhat dark. (*1Cor.13:12*)

The Greatest Offering!

Much earlier, God had promised Abraham that he would become a "*father of many nations*;" (*Gen.17:5*) and that the promise was to be fulfilled through his descendants, beginning with his son Isaac. (*Gen.17:19*)

Now, after waiting so long for this "child of promise" (Abraham's own seed born miraculously to his barren wife Sarah), God was telling him to sacrifice the precious boy. It made no sense at all!

The only possible explanation was that God had an even greater plan, and would reveal it in His own time.

Whatever Abraham was thinking, ultimately he believed God!

As the deadly knife rose in Abraham's hand, the Angel of the Lord was satisfied. It was enough! Abraham had been tried and found faithful! Wonder of wonders; Abraham turned to see a ram held in a thicket by his horns.

Here, in place of Abraham's son, God gives us a foretaste (type or shadow) of the most magnificent gift mankind would ever receive!

The Holy Spirit shows us the "*Ram*" (the king of sheep) as a type of Jesus Himself. The "*thicket*" as the cross or tree. "*Caught by his horns*" as the strength of Christ's love for fallen mankind, coupled with His perfect obedience to the Father in Heaven. Obedience which not only took Him to the cross, but held Him there!

Books have been written concerning the many animal sacrifices offered to God by man, so it is not my purpose to detail them here. Suffice it to say that every animal offered correctly was again, merely a "type" or "shadow" pointing toward the supreme offering made for the sins of mankind by the sacrifice of God's beloved Son, the Lord Jesus Christ!

Obviously no *one* animal type could possibly fulfill all the perfect characteristics, or aspects of Christ's magnificent atoning work.

Throughout the Old Testament, He is seen as the bullock; the male sheep or goat; and the turtledoves or pigeons in the "*Burnt Offering*."

As the fine flour, frankincense, and anointing oil in the "*Meal offering*."

As the male or female from the herd, and the male or female from the flock in the "*offering for peace*."

As the animals and fine flour in the "*offering for trespass and sin*." (See *Lev.1-9* for much more detailed treasure.)

Regardless of which sacrifice was to be offered however, one characteristic was emphatically required. Every single animal was to be "***Without spot or blemish***." (*Lev.1:3, Num.19:2*)

That then would be as high as any animal type could rise in foreshadowing Christ's fulfillment of the whole sacrificial system!

Our brothers recording the New Testament, soared far beyond the confines of Mosaic law to bring us these beautiful words:

"*Forasmuch as ye know that ye were not redeemed with corruptible things, as silver or gold ... neither by the blood of goats and calves ... **but with the precious Blood of Christ, as of a lamb*** *without blemish and without spot ... For if the blood of bulls and of goats, and the ashes of an heifer sprinkling the unclean, sanctifieth to the purifying of the flesh: How much more shall the Blood of Christ, who through the eternal Spirit offered Himself without spot to God, purge your conscience from dead works to serve the living God?"* (See 1 Pet.1:18-19 and Heb.9:12-14)

As we begin to gather up these heavenly *"fragments"* (that nothing may be lost), we will see in scripture that of all the animal types wherein God reveals Christ to us, His most frequent choice was that of a "lamb."

"Behold the Lamb of God, which taketh away the sin of the world." (*John 1: 29*)
"And lo, in the midst of the throne and of the four beasts, and in the midst of the elders, stood a Lamb as if it had been slain ..." (*Rev.5: 6*)
And even in the New Jerusalem, *"There shall be no more curse: but the throne of God and of the Lamb shall be in it ..."* (*Rev.22: 3*)
From His perfect life on earth, to His Eternal Glory in Heaven, Jesus will forever remain,
"The *True* Lamb of God!"

Is it so hard to imagine therefore (for that is all we may do), that the first pure and spotless sacrifice which the Lord God made in the garden long ago would be a natural, *four* legged lamb pointing the way to God's last and greatest Sacrifice.
The *two* legged Lamb – Jesus the Christ – Son of the Living God?

Let this be *"proclaimed from the house tops"* (*Luke 12: 3*)
GOD HIMSELF MADE THE FIRST AND LAST SACRIFICE FOR SIN:
AFTER CHRIST, THERE WOULD BE NO OTHER!

Another powerful truth should be mentioned here:
GOD DID NOT FORGIVE OUR SINS!
When Jesus offered Himself on the cross, it was to take God's full punishment for each and every one of them!
The sinless Christ fulfilled *all* of His Father's demands for righteousness and *paid* for our sins!
Then (and only then) was God prepared to forgive us!
Through the sacrificial blood of Jesus (His finished atoning work), God's forgiveness is now extended to His people on a daily basis.
"If we confess our sins, He is faithful and just to forgive us our sins, and to cleanse us from all unrighteousness." (*1 John 1:9*)

As this glorious revelation dawns on us, we can begin to understand the utter abomination of satanically inspired, man-made religions, which seek to find, reach, or satisfy God by any other means!
Our sins separated us from God. Jesus paid the full price for them by bearing the judgment the rest of us deserved. He then became the *Only* Way we could ever be reunited with (or reconciled to) the Father in Heaven! (*John 14: 6*)

Sadly, after scaling such lofty spiritual heights, we must once again return to man's desperate plight on earth long before Christ came.
We are about to discover that once Adam and Eve sold out to sin, and began to multiply, it would not be at all difficult for Satan to find a plentiful supply of enthusiastic, but boringly similar customers!

CHAPTER THREE

ALL SIN LEADS TO A NOAH!

Many years ago, I saw a western movie in which one of the characters (a villain) spoke the following line,

"The first time I killed a man, it was hard. After that it just got easier!"

How perfectly those words describe sin! The fall of Adam actually set in motion a "wheel" of sin, which, like the river in the famous old song, "… just keeps on rollin' along."

"And the Lord God said, Behold, the man is become as one of us, to know good and evil: and now, lest he put forth his hand, and take also of the tree of life and live forever:

Therefore the Lord God sent him forth from the garden of Eden, to till the ground from whence he was taken." (Gen.3:22-23)

There was no way back. God placed *"Cherubim and a flaming sword"* at the east of the Garden of Eden to keep Adam and Eve from reaching the tree of life *(Gen.3:24)*.

For them to eat of that fruit now would mean living forever in a sinful condition!

The very thought of that appears to be so horrifying, God will not finish His sentence!

Can you imagine Stalin, Hitler, Chairman Mao (or *any* member of the human race for that matter) living forever with unrestrained sin? God forbid!

So Adam and Eve were forced to take up residence outside the garden where they would bring forth sons.

Cain and Abel

*"In the process of time it came to pass, that Cain brought of the **fruit of the ground** an offering to the Lord. And Abel, he also brought of the firstlings of his flock and of the fat thereof. And the Lord had respect unto Abel and to his offering: But unto Cain and to his offering He had not respect. And Cain was very wroth* (extremely angry) *and his countenance fell." (Gen. 4:3-5)*

Surely Adam, or perhaps even the Lord Himself had spoken to the boys about the dreadful consequences of disobedience; and the fact that along with the pain of child bearing and death, God had *"cursed the ground for man's sake." (Gen.3:14-19)*

They must also have known the significance of the skins they now wore, and that animal sacrifices to the Lord (and for food) were to be constant reminders of God's Grace. (His Mercy, Provision, and Promise.)

There are at least two "gems" we can gather from Cain's offering.

1. As a result of sin, the Lord now decreed the labor of raising of crops in order to supply man's legitimate needs. Nevertheless, the fact that these crops came directly from a now cursed earth would make them totally unacceptable as offerings to God Himself!

*"In the **sweat of thy face** shalt thou eat bread, till thou return unto the ground."* (Gen.3:19)

God does not want anything from his people that comes with sweat!

Much later, Levitical priests would be forbidden to wear wool while ministering to the Lord because it caused them to *"sweat"* (Eze.44:17-18). Only linen garments were allowed to be worn before the Lord!

Sweat has always been a type of "fleshly works" and therefore anything that causes sweat is rejected! That's why God's angels are, *"Clothed in pure and white linen, and having their chests girded with golden bands."* (Rev.15:6)

To His people, the Lord also gives *"Fine linen, clean and white: for the fine linen is the righteousness of saints."* (Rev.19:8)

2. Knowing full well that God had already rejected *"fig leaf"* coverings (i.e. plants) would make Cain's offering an even greater insult; and one performed in willful disregard for God's wishes!

(1John3:12)

He could have consulted his father to see what was right – but he wouldn't!
He could have been thinking, "Let me pray and ask the Lord" – but he wasn't!
He could have traded grain for one of Abel's flock – but he didn't!
Doesn't that remind you of someone?
In this case, who could argue with the old saying, "Like father like son?"
Cain's offering was but a religious act: that is to say, he went through the motions while his heart was far from God. *(See Is.29:13, Matt.15:8)*

Today, all over the world in religious establishments, spiritually dead people still sit covered with fig leaves, and use *"vain repetition"* (endless hymns, chants, offerings and prayers – especially the so called, "Lord's prayer") while going through the motions of archaic rituals and form.

(See Matt.6:7)

Alas, countless numbers following directly in the footsteps of Cain!

****

NOTE: The prayer that begins, *"Our Father which art in Heaven"* is *NOT* the Lord's Prayer! Jesus gave that prayer to His disciples as a model or pattern on which to base their *own* prayers, but certainly not as one to be spoken repetitiously (word for word) every Sunday!

The *real* Lord's Prayer, known as His "High Priestly" Prayer (the most beautiful prayer ever spoken, and offered on our behalf) is found throughout the whole of *John, chapter 17.*

****

What is so magnanimous about the Grace of God however, is that in spite of rejecting Cain's offering, and being fully aware of his evil heart; God still spoke directly to him with words of encouragement and warning.

"And the Lord said unto Cain, Why art thou wroth? and why is thy countenance fallen? If thou doest well, shalt thou not be accepted? and if thou doest not well, sin lieth at the door. And unto thee shall be his desire, and thou shalt rule over him." (Gen. 4:6-7)

SIN! Rule over, or grovel under!

Let's cut to the chase. If Cain repents (changes his mind), and gets his attitude right (which he *could* have done), God will accept him. If not, the spirit of sin will lie in wait knocking continually at the door of his heart until sooner or later, he's invited in!

Tragically for both boys, it would be sooner ...

"And Cain talked with Abel his brother: and it came to pass, when they were in the field, that Cain rose up against Abel his brother, and slew him. And the Lord said unto Cain, Where is Abel thy brother? And he said, I know not: Am I my brother's keeper?" (Gen. 4:8-9)

We are back to Satan's favorite work; causing us to "rise up" and uncover! This time it would be against a natural brother, with murder being the ultimate act of uncovering!

When Cain "*talked*" with Abel, was he openly hostile, and raging like a "*dragon*" (enjoying the fear he was creating before destroying a life), or was he perhaps smooth and charming like the "*serpent*" (inwardly smiling and proud of a clever deception) in order to throw his brother off guard?

Whatever the conversation, the outcome would be the same.

Filled with resentment toward God, and bitter jealousy toward Abel, Cain had backed himself into a corner from which there was now no escape. Cain "*slew him.*"

In lying blatantly to God after the crime, and questioning Him defiantly at the same time, Cain showed utter disregard for God, life, or virtue! He could well have asked, "**Am I my brother's coverer?**"

The answer God gives to all of us is an emphatic "**YES!**"

Love covers (*1Pet.4:8*) therefore – hate uncovers!

The New Testament makes it clear that we don't have to physically murder a brother or sister to be guilty of such a heinous crime.

"He that loveth not his brother abideth in death." And, *"Whosoever hateth his brother is a murderer: and ye know that no murderer hath eternal life abiding in him."* (See 1 John 3:11-18)

In any confrontation, the believer must immediately allow the Holy Spirit to take away any unrighteous anger, thereby quenching "Satan's anointing" (fuel on the fire), which so often causes anger to blaze out of control. We all know what the results can be!

*"**A soft answer turneth away wrath: but grievous words stireth up anger.**" (Pr.15:1)* (See also, *Pr.14:29, 19:19, 27:3-4, 30:33* and *Eph.4:26*)

Cain's Legacy

And God said, *"What hast thou done? The voice of thy brother's blood crieth unto Me from the ground ...thou art cursed from the earth ...a fugitive and a vagabond shalt thou be in the earth. And Cain said unto the Lord, my punishment is greater than I can bear. Behold, Thou hast driven me out this day from the face of the earth ... and it shall come to pass, that everyone that findeth me shall slay me. And the Lord said unto him, Therefore whosoever slayeth Cain, vengeance shall be taken on him sevenfold. And the Lord set a mark upon Cain, lest any finding him should kill him. And Cain went out from the presence of the Lord, and dwelt in the land of Nod, on the east of Eden."* (Excerpts from *Gen.4:10-16*)

To dwell on Cain's punishment is not my intention at this time, but as alluded to earlier, Cain is still "out there" in the form of those lost religious souls who throughout history have remained *"fugitives and vagabonds;"* living and dying separated from God's presence *"in the land of Nod."*
(Heb. Wandering.)

NOTE: The actual "mark of Cain" remains in the realm of *Deuteronomy 29:29*.
"The secret things belong unto the Lord our God: but those things which are revealed belong unto us and to our children forever, that we may do all the words of this law."

Although the mark is one of those *"secret things,"* Satan has long enjoyed using its mystery as a means of deceiving the gullible. For example: hear the lies that Mormons are "buying and selling."
"Those who, less valiant to God in "pre-existence," who therefore had certain spiritual restrictions placed upon them during mortality, are known to us as Negroes. The mark put upon Cain for his rebellion against God and murder of Abel, being a black skin." [1]

That disgusting garbage was quoted in the name of God!
And also this:
"Negroes in this life are denied the Priesthood ... Cain was cursed with a dark skin; he became the father of the Negroes, and those spirits who are not worthy to receive the (Mormon) Priesthood are born through that lineage. [2]

In 1978 (after some 140 years), it seems that political pressure on the Mormon leadership caused God to change His mind, so this vicious lie was abandoned. (At least publicly!)

"If a house be divided against itself, that house cannot stand." (Mark 3:25)

Don't think for one moment however, that their attitude toward the black race has changed. "Sacred" Mormon doctrine still teaches that they wear the black skin and curse of their "ancestor Cain!"
What is lost on the entire Mormon membership is that a fallen, demonic *"angel of light"* named "Moroni" (see *2Cor.11:14*) gave "glass-looker / diviner / fortune hunter / convicted felon, Joseph Smith

Jn., the bogus blueprint for building his entire "Moronic" house of cards! [3] Needless to say, that "house" is built on nothing more than spiritual sand! (*Matt.7:24-27*)

Perhaps one other example will express something of Mormonism's dreadful plight as it continues to teach such gross deceptions. Mormons are actually taught that, "God the Father has a body of flesh and bones, as tangible as man's." [4]

Now why would anyone believe that when Jesus Himself said,

"GOD IS A SPIRIT?" (*John 4:24*)

The answer is not far away ...

"For this cause God shall send them strong delusion, that they should believe a lie: that they all might be damned who believed not the truth, but had pleasure in unrighteousness."

(See *2Thess.2:11-12, and Rom.1:18*)

Moving on from Mormonism, we come to another interesting challenge regarding Cain.

Who exactly did Cain marry?

After going out from the presence of the Lord to live in the land of Nod, *"Cain knew his wife; and she conceived"* (*Gen. 4:16-17*)

Just whom Cain married on the *"east of Eden"* has probably been the subject of debate (and argument) for as long as man has read and discussed the Holy Scriptures!

Unbelievers often throw this issue up with the increasingly arrogant claim, "The Bible contradicts itself!" Even some Study Bibles won't comment on the marriage of Cain, which recently seems to be more of a hot potato than ever. But despite all that, there really are only two possibilities. (Apart from God creating an especially troublesome wife just to suit him!)

And they are,

A. Cain married someone from a "pre-Adamic" race or group of people that God had already created in *Gen.1:26-28*.

Or,

B. He married an unnamed sister.

Here's the argument in support of **A.**

"Eve was the mother of all living." (*Gen. 3:20*) (Referring to those who continued to live in the presence of God.) So the woman Cain married belonged to a "pre-existing," fallen tribe which was already "spiritually dead," and had therefore been living outside the presence of God for some time. This reasoning falls short on the following grounds:

Genesis chapter one is the overview of God's creative process, whereas Genesis chapter two goes on to give specific detail of man's creation. There is no Scripture to suggest that those two chapters relate to two separate groups of people. Further more, after sin, Adam and Eve were *also* "spiritually dead," so let's not forget to ask the really pertinent question,

Who did Seth (their *third* son) marry?

He obviously stayed with his parents in the presence of the Lord. (*Gen.4:26*) Therefore in spite of *Lev.18* prohibiting incest (written much later of course), all observations point to,

B. Cain and Seth married their sisters!

The most viable reason for believing this would be that Adam and Eve's blood and natural reproductive systems were still so clean and free from later defects (God would surely have made them so), that the multiplication of the human race did in fact begin with the first married couple on planet earth!

Finally: the Scriptures say it was *Adam's* sin, (not some pre-existing sin) that came upon all men! (See *Rom.5:12-19*)

Calling all Demons!

Much to Satan's delight, it wasn't long before rebellion and murder became a way of life (make that death) on the earth!

> *"And Lamech* (a descendant of Cain) *took unto him two wives; the name of the one was Adah, and the name of the other Zillah ... And Lamech said unto his wives ... hear my voice ye wives of Lamech ... for I have slain a man to my wounding* (merely for bruising me), *and a young man to my hurt* (merely for striking me). *If Cain shall be avenged sevenfold, truly Lamech seventy and sevenfold."* (See *Gen. 4:16-24*)

Within just five generations of Cain, men would begin to routinely demonstrate a satanical disregard for the sanctity of marriage, life, and the Word of God!

Lamech takes up the practice of bigamy contrary to *Gen.2:24*, and who knows if our modern word "lame" (referring to something stupid or foolish) didn't come from his pathetic excuse to commit murder?

In justifying his crime, Lamech adds to, and mocks God's Word from *Gen.4:15*; but as such men groped their way along in ever increasing blindness and sin, they couldn't possibly have been aware of the devastating judgment which was to come.

> *"Be not deceived; God is not mocked: for whatsoever a man soweth, that shall he also reap!"*
> (*Gal.6:7*)

> *"And it came to pass, when men began to multiply on the face of the earth, and daughters were born unto them, that the **sons of God** saw the **daughters of men** that they were fair; and they took them wives of all which they chose. And the Lord said, My Spirit shall not always strive with man, for that he also is flesh: Yet his days shall be an hundred and twenty years. There were **giants in the earth in those days; and also after that,** when the **sons of God** came in unto the **daughters of men,** and they bare children to them, the same became **mighty men** which were of old, men of renown."* (*Gen. 6:1-4*)

First Adam and Eve, then Cain, then Lamech: but as we continue the theme of Satan's uncovering work, we arrive at a passage of scripture that makes the teaching on all of *them* seem positively 5th grade!

To begin with; if you should find a copy of the "Nelson, King James' Study Bible" (notes copyrighted 1975), you will see something quite interesting. In reference to *Genesis 6:1-4*, the teaching notes (written by various "Contributing Editors") deny emphatically that the "*sons of God*" are fallen angels. They make the following statement,

"Sons of God (Heb. bene elohim) refers to the godly line of Seth, which intermarried with the daughters of men, the ungodly line of Cain." They then state, "While the term sons of God refers to angels in *some* passages (e.g., Job 1: 6), this is certainly *not* the case here." (Emphasis added)

Their notes on Jude v.6 however, will make an amazing contradiction!

The verse reads, "*And the angels which kept not their first estate*, (proper domain) *but left their own habitation*, He (God) *hath reserved in everlasting chains under darkness unto the judgment of the great day.*"

Here, different note writers (I assume) refer us directly back to the "*sons of God*" in *Gen.6:1-4*. This is total confusion! It appears that some men refuse to believe that demonic beings (fallen angels) had sexual relations with certain women on earth, and produced a race of physical giants.

Do they think they were simply "giants of sin," as many others believe? (Either way they deny the Word of God)

Do they seriously think that natural "sons of Seth," (types of believers) marrying natural "sons of Cain" (types of non-believers) could actually produce giants standing anywhere between thirteen and fourteen feet tall? (*See Deut.3:11*)

Let's remember that in Deuteronomy, the warning Moses gave concerning marriage between God's people and the pagan nations of Canaan was not that giants would be born, but that the Israelites would be turned away from following the Lord! (*Deut. 7:1-5*)

For exactly the same reason, The Holy Spirit warns us through Paul,

"Be ye not unequally yoked (married) *together with unbelievers*" (2Cor.6:14-18)

And no one could miss a similar meaning behind the famous line from "Fiddler on the Roof"

"A bird may love a fish; but where would they build their nest together?"
(It likewise had nothing to do with bearing giants!)

Let's face it, if believers marrying non-believers produced 13-14 foot offspring, then basketball nets would certainly be a whole lot higher; not to mention the headroom in motor vehicles!

The fact is those angels responsible for such atrocities (before, and for some time after the flood, see *Gen.6:4*) were placed in,
"... *everlasting chains under darkness unto the judgment of the great day.*" (*Jude v.6*)
(That's why there are no *Biblically* sized giants around today!)

NOTE: It's well known that Goliath was one of the last and smallest of the giant race. He was only nine feet nine inches tall! (See *1Sam.17:4*)
In addition; the overwhelming evidence of demonic activity in the world today makes it clear that relatively few fallen angels were actually bound in "*everlasting chains.*"

In bringing this chapter to a close, let me stress that before any fallen angel (demon spirit) could enter a human being, sufficient "ground," or access must be given. In the case of Genesis 6:1-4, that "ground" was **supreme** wickedness!

"*And God saw that the **wickedness of man was great** in the earth, and that **every imagination of the thoughts of his heart** was only evil continually. And it repented the Lord that He had* *made man on the earth, and it grieved Him at His heart. And the Lord said,* **I will destroy man whom I have created from the face of the earth ... But Noah found grace in the sight of the Lord.**" (*Gen.6:5-8*)

NOTE: To help the reader gain more awareness of demonic activity, I have written chapter four as a brief overview. Much of what is contained there is controversial (to say the least) even among Christians! (Thankfully more and more are coming to recognize and acknowledge the presence of demonic entities, and are learning how to deal with them!)

If you happen to be reading these things for the first time, and receive them as truth, you may become extremely hurtful to Satan (and to his cause); so be sure to approach this "mind-field" with prayer and the "*Whole armor of God.*" (*Eph.6:10-18*)

CHAPTER FOUR

ANOTHER DAY AT THE DEMONIC OFFICE

Today, multitudes do not believe in demons: they do not believe that demons can (and do) possess human beings. Satan is delighted with such deluded souls! After all, remember that one of the devil's all-time favorite deceptions has been to convince the world that he and his evil spirits do not exist!! (Just ask any secular psychiatrist about demons.)

Sadly, many believers still refuse to accept that Christians can also have demons. If you're one of them, Satan obviously wants you to stay that way!

As a new believer, I also fell under that same lie. Spirits of pride (demons of course) tell us that Christians could not possibly play host to demonic entities. How could evil spirits be "squatters" in the Temple of the Holy Ghost? (*1Cor.6:19*)

This is exactly what evil spirits want us to believe!

In reality, every unredeemed person on the planet is possessed (controlled or ruled over) by their "*father*" Satan (*John 8:38-44*). Like it or not, we were *all* born under his dominion!

NOTE: True "*born again*" believers cannot be possessed by demons! Being born again means that our quickened spirits are indwelt by the Holy Spirit, and possessed by the Lord Jesus Christ Himself!

However, believers being oppressed or even demonized is a completely different story!

To use a simple and well-worn analogy: a Christian's "house" may be free of vermin in the living room but could well have infestations in the kitchen, bedroom, hallway closet, etc. Although demons can attack the re-born spirits of believers, they cannot *dwell* there! It is our minds and bodies that are vulnerable, and can be affected, or taken over by evil spirits!

(Consistent sin or deception will certainly open the door to demonization.)

Physical *and* mental oppression are constant threats to Christians; especially those seriously involved in spiritual warfare. (See *2Cor.10:3-5, Eph.6:10-18*) Now for the really great news!

"*... at the Name of Jesus every knee should bow*, *of things in heaven, and things in earth, and things under the earth.* (*Phil.2:10*) "*God anointed Jesus of Nazareth with the Holy Ghost and with power: who went about doing good, and healing all that were oppressed of the devil; for God was with Him.*" (*Acts 10:38*) Jesus said, "*He that believeth on Me, the works that I do shall he do also; and greater works than these shall he do; because I go unto My Father.*" (*John14;12*) And, "*Behold, I give unto you power to tread on serpents and scorpions,* (demons) *and over all the power of the enemy:* (Satan himself) *and nothing shall by any means hurt you.*

*Not withstanding, in this **rejoice not** that the **spirits are subject unto you**; but **rather rejoice, because your names are written in Heaven**."* (*Luke 10:19-20*)

Key phrases are highlighted in the verses above to show exactly how our victory over Satan and all demonic spirits is obtained; and also the wisdom to keep us in balance!

God has given us Jesus, *"the Name which is above every name;"* and it is the **power of His Name spoken in faith**, which makes evil spirits bow or submit!

NOTE: Before casting out certain strong or long abiding spirits, a time of prayer and fasting may be required. (*Matt.17:14-21*) After deliverance, deeper physical and emotional wounds may take considerable time to heal.

Deliverance, healing, victory and freedom are all found in the Name of Jesus!

This brief guide to reaching natural and spiritual freedom is written with the hope of benefiting new believers who do not yet know the truth regarding demonology, and those older in the Lord who are still not clear on the subject. The Holy Spirit glorifies Jesus by taking the wonderful things that are His, and revealing them to us. (*John 16:13-15*)

"For the Spirit searcheth all things, yea, the deep things of God." (See *1Cor.2:9-11*)

THE WORK OF DEMONS

Background - *Matt. 8:28-34, Mark 5:1-15, Luke 8:26-35*

No living person on earth has ever been free from demonic influence!

Although the exact number is unknown, (*Rev.12:4*) demons obviously form a huge multitude, and vary greatly in type and purpose. (See *Mark 5:9*) A single Roman "legion" consisted of up to 6000 men!

They can lend supernatural strength. (*5:3-4*) They sometimes encourage the self-mutilation of their victims. (*v.5*) They are also territorial; (*v.10*) and if all else fails (*vs..11-12*) they will settle for animal possession!

Once their animal hosts were destroyed, (*v.13*) the demons (who will never die) were forced to seek new victims! They delight in deceiving, uncovering and humiliating. (*Luke 8:27*) Be aware, evil spirits are eternal beings, so those that possessed the "Gadarene demoniac" are still very much at large today! (Only after the millennium will they be cast into the lake of fire, i.e. gone forever!)

Ideally, demons seek people to inhabit. People whose natural characteristics are already congenial to their own such as "unclean spirits." (*Mark5: 2 and 8*)

"Familiar spirits" (from the word family) inhabiting fortune-tellers, astrologers, mediums, psychics, etc., are often passed on from one generation to the next. Then of course there are stronger spirits such as drunkenness, jealousy, control, anger, perversion, hate, murder, etc., etc.

Some primarily attack the body, some the mind, and others the spirit of man. Those attacking the spirit (in believers only) are known as *"angels of light."* (*2Cor.13-15*)

Because evil spirits identify with the personality of their host, their detection can be most difficult. A vital resource to aid in the discovery of demons is found among the nine gifts of the Holy Spirit (listed in *1Cor.12: 8-10*). ***"Discerning of spirits"*** (the ability to identify or name them) is an extremely important gift, especially in these *"latter times"* where *"seducing spirits, and doctrines of devils"* abound! (*1Tim.4:1*)

Flesh or Spirit?

A simple way to discern between flesh (the old nature) and demonic influence is to note whether a person's emotions and behavior are normal (balanced or natural): i.e. under control most of the time with perhaps an occasional loss of temper (for example) in a particularly trying situation.

Now although "unrighteous" anger is still sin (*Eph.4:26-27*), it is not **abnormal**; and can be considered a *"work of the flesh."* (See *Gal.5:19-21*) This leads us to Romans chapter 6.

"For in that He (Christ) *died, He died unto sin once: but in that He liveth, He liveth unto God. Likewise **reckon ye also yourselves to be dead indeed unto sin, but alive unto God** through Jesus Christ our Lord. **Let not sin therefore reign in your mortal body,** that ye should obey it in the lusts thereof."* (*Rom.6:10-12*)

It is the responsibility of the saint to *"mortify the deeds of the body."* (*Rom.8:13*) (Easier said than done of course) but we do this by faith through the Holy Spirit.

Reckoning ourselves dead to sin is a *daily* commitment to obedience, therefore,

*"**Work out your own salvation with fear and trembling**."* (*Phil.2:12*)

Strong's Concordance renders *"work out"* as "finish," (as in *2Tim.4:7*) i.e. to "finish the course of our salvation by faith! (*Not* by working to keep it!) Remember; *"The **fear** of the Lord, that is **wisdom**."* (*Job 28:28*) Godly fear does not mean being afraid of God! (See *Heb.10:19-22* for balance)

In Strong's, the word *"trembling"* is translated "reverence;" so a lovely way of seeing *Phil. 2:12* would now be,

"Finish the course of your own salvation with Godly wisdom and reverence!"

Oppressed or Demonized?

The Lord Jesus was *"oppressed"* (Heb. "taxed, harassed, tyrannized" see *Is.53:7*) more than any man! He was *never* demonized! Read His awesome and totally unique confession ...

*"**The prince of this world cometh, and hath NOTHING IN ME**."* (*John14:30*)

"Demonization" is the demon within, and concerns *only* the believer.
For the unbeliever, that state is called "possession."
"Oppression" is the demon "against us" attacking from without, trying to get in!

Unlike rare outbursts of "fleshly" temper, the demon within promotes uncontrolled outbreaks on a regular basis! One of the saddest examples of this is found in the book of Samuel.

The Spirit of the Lord departed from Saul (Israel's first king) *and an evil spirit from the Lord troubled him."* (*1Sam.16:14*)

As mentioned earlier, God will only allow an evil spirit to enter a person, if enough "ground," or access is given. In Saul's case the ground was multiple acts of disobedience, culminating in rebellion, stubbornness, and rejecting the Word of the Lord. (*1Sam.15:23*)

Saul was already an angry man who walked much in the flesh, and blamed others for his shortcomings. (*1Sam.15:24*) There came a time in his life however, when he "crossed the line," and moved from fleshly anger to regular, and sometimes violent fits of rage! It was here that a young shepherd, and musician named David first entered Saul's miserable life.

> *"And it came to pass, when the evil spirit from God was upon Saul, that David took an harp, and played with his hand: so Saul was refreshed, and was well, and the evil spirit departed from him." (1Sam.16:23)*

After a time though, even the soothing music failed to pacify the troubled king; and Saul; who (without the help of a demon) had already threatened the life of his son Jonathan (*1Sam.14:44*); now tries to destroy David as well! (*1Sam.18:10-11*) The Scriptures declare that God finally killed Saul for his transgression against the Word of the Lord (he fell on his own sword rather than be captured by the Philistines), and for seeking the counsel of a medium (one with a familiar spirit).
(*See 1Sam.28:7-25, 1Chr.10:13-14*)

Although the Scriptures help us to gain overall knowledge of Saul's condition; it is the phrase, **"crossed the line"** which is critical to our understanding of demonic activity.
There are four sure ways in which human beings can cross the line from the natural or fleshly realm to actual demonic subjection.

1. **Consistent sin.** This usually invites in a spirit with the same name as the sin itself; i.e. Spirit of lust, greed, drunkenness, gluttony, anger, jealousy etc.
2. **A weak or yielded will:** e.g. man fearing or man pleasing. Usually inviting in a spirit of bondage. (Wrongful submission to a cult leader's influence for example.)
3. **Ancestral sins.** Especially occult involvement. Possibly handed down through several generations: (*Ex. 20:6*) often producing a "crossed line" of demonic entry even before birth. (Familiar spirits are frequently passed on this way.)
4. **Personal occult involvement.** This is a "gold-plated" invitation for demonic entry! Ignorance is no excuse (ask any judge), and will not prevent access. Long standing occult children's games such as "Dungeons and Dragons," "Ouija" (popular with adults also), and many of today's Video games have been equally useful for demonic infestation.

By the way; "Pokemon" is certainly demonically inspired, and can easily put your children in bondage!

NOTE: An addiction can be described as the inward demonic control of what was once a consistent sinful habit. Because the "victim" had some measure of control prior to the addiction, he or she believes that that control still exists. "I can quit anytime I want to!" is the frequent reply when an addict is challenged. Most addicts do not know they have "crossed the line" and are addicted; let alone that they are under the control of an evil spirit!
A simple yet profound test, or proof of an addiction is the question,
> **"Can you give up permanently, the habit you think you are not addicted to?"**

Object of attack

The object of any demonic attack or influence is to,

1. Prevent the unbeliever from coming to salvation. (*Matt.13:19, 2Cor.4:3-4*)
2. Keep Christians from entering into the fullness of the Spirit filled life. (*Gal.5:1-7*)
3. Destroy the witness of believers and bring the church into humiliation. (*1Cor.5*)
4. Hinder the will and purpose of God in the heavenly *or* earthly realm.
    (*Dan.10:12-13 and 20, Matt.16:21-23, 2Thess.2:3-10*)
5. Rob believers of the fruit and gifts of the Spirit, along with their joy and victory.
6. To destroy physically if at all possible. (*John10:10, 1Cor.11:29-30*)

Most dangerous to the believer

1. **Religious** demons such as spiritual pride, or ambition. (*3John 9-10*) (Answer with *Phil.2:3*)
2. **Seduction** and false doctrine. (*Jer.5:31, Matt.24:24, 1Tim.4:1*) (Ans. with *1John4:1-6 and Acts17:10-11*)
3. **Accusation** – criticism leading to condemnation. (*Rev.12:10*) (Ans. with *Rom.8:1, 28-39*)
4. **Isolation** – often due to an unteachable spirit. (*Jude18-19*) (Ans. with *Heb.10:24-25*)
5. **Legalism** – ministering bondage. (*Mark 7:1-13*) (Ans. with *Heb.7:19, Gal.5:18, Rom.4:14*)
6. **Division** – partisan spirit. (*1Cor.1:11-12*) (Ans. with *vs. 10 and 13*)
7. **Heresies** – to preach or teach contrary to the Word of God. (*2Tim.2:17-18, 2Pet.2:1-3*) (Ans. with *2Tim.2:14-15, 22-26, and 2Pet.1:5-10*)

Deceptions

The nature or work of demonic deception is tailored to fit our level of maturity.

***All* unredeemed people are deceived!**

Mature believers are rarely urged to fornicate, gamble, drink, steal etc., as are young or "carnal" Christians; but are more often seduced and betrayed by false teaching and doctrines. I.e. the Word mixed with men's traditions, or extra-biblical revelations. (*Col.2:8, 2Cor.11:3-4*)

Of the three counterfeit revelations mentioned in *1Cor.11:4*, "another Jesus," "another spirit," and "another gospel," it is "another spirit" which I believe to be the most seductive and difficult to discern. Deceived teachers are often "good men" who are believed for that reason alone!

(Always seek truth by searching the Scriptures as the Bereans did in *Acts17:10-11*)

NOTE TO THE CHURCH: Women who are teaching men, or taking authority over them (as in a pastoral role for example) are operating contrary to the will of God, and are therefore hindering and deceiving the men "under their ministry." If this is "*an hard saying*" (*John 6:60*); remember– men did not inspire the Word of God, and that includes the Apostle Paul! (*2Tim.3:16*) It must therefore be God Who says,

> **"*I do not allow a woman to teach, nor to usurp* (supplant or take) *authority over a man, ...*" (*1Tim.2:12*)**

After hearing me explain that there was not one example of a female pastor to be found in the entire Word of God, a young pastor (whose wife also acts as a pastor) replied, "Well, that may be so, but we can't put God in a box." Sadly, this response will allow for of all sorts of error based on man's reasoning.

The truth is, God *has* put Himself in a box! That box is "Genesis to Revelation," and outside that box is a world of trouble! I'll say here what I said to that young brother, "When something is confirmed by the *Word* of God, we know that it is *of* God: we can then agree and say Amen. If not, we risk bringing error into the church!"

There are wonderful gifts and anointings poured out upon women in terms of ministry (including the prophetic and evangelical); the pastoral role is just not one of them!

(See *Titus 2:3-5, 1Tim.5:14, Acts* 21:8-9, *Matt.28:5-8* for scriptural examples of female ministries)

Scriptures which bring more deceptions into the light ...

Being hearers of the Word and not doers. (*James1:22*) Saying we have no sin. (*1John1:8*) Thinking ourselves to be something. (*Gal.6:3*) Using Worldly wisdom. (*1Cor.3:18*)

Speaking with an unbridled tongue. (*James1:26*) Believing we do not reap what we sow. (*Gal.6:7*)

Believing sin won't contaminate, (*1Cor.15:33*) or that one sin is worse than another. (*James2:10-11*)

Some Demonic influences which always hinder growth ...

Unforgiveness (*Matt.6:12-15, and 18:21-35, Luke17:3-4*) **Pride** (*Pr.8:13, 16:18*) **Bitterness or resentment** (*Eph.4:31-32, Heb.12:14-15*) **Rebellion** (*1Sam.15:23*)
Man-fearing (*Pr.29:25*) **Man-pleasing** (*James2:1-9*) **Ignorance** (See *1Cor.1:18-30*) **Worldliness** (*1John2:15-16*) **Subjectivity** (1Cor.4:3-5) **Passivity** (*Pr.19:15*)
Compromise (*2Cor.6:14-18, Eph.5:11*) **Hyper Activity** (*Dan.7:25, Luke10:38-42*) **False Trust** (*John2:23-25*) **Fear** (*1John4:18*) **All Sin** (*Pr.5:22, Rom.14:23*)

All this leads us to bring out the "Big Guns" ... *Luke10:19, Mark16:17-18, 2Cor.10:3-5, and Eph.6:10-18*. Carefully reading and applying these Scriptures (and others like them) will prove invaluable in this ever-increasing "last days" conflict!

NOTE: Only when the Word of God is spoken with the anointing or empowering of the Holy Spirit will believers cause Satan and his minions to tremble and flee!

Detection
Anything forced (unnatural or false) in thoughts, words, and actions will help to discern the presence of evil spirits. Again, even a believer may be tormented with strange abnormal behavior, which is out of proportion to their character in general.

Deliverance
*Ridding ourselves of demonic influences (inward or outward) requires great humility and honesty before God. We must ask the Holy Spirit to reveal any and all ground given over to the enemy as a result of sin, false teaching, or other deceptions. Then by faith, reclaim and take back that ground in the Name, and by the Blood of Jesus! (*Phil.2:10, 1John1:5-10, Rev.1:5*)
Finally: STAND (protect), and HOLD (keep) that ground! (*Deut.1:8, Eph.6:13*)
V.I. Once deliverance is obtained, the evil spirit(s) will invariably try to re-enter by tempting individuals to fall back into the same patterns, or fleshly habits of sin, which gave access to begin with. This temptation must be fought *at all costs* to avoid further bondage!

To stay free, the spirit must win the "battle of the mind." (*Rom.12:1-2*)

As with all things pertaining to the Lord, deliverance is by faith. Sometimes a believer is delivered instantly, and sometimes it is a more gradual manifestation. The walls of Jericho fell miraculously, and the city was taken immediately, but other cities took much longer to fall! There are times when the enemy must be "starved out" as in a time of siege. (*James 4:7, Eph.4:27*) If faith is present (*Luke5:20*), and deliverance (or healing) does not come straight away; we must consider that God has a purpose and plan which is even better for the individual in the long run. We must continue to believe (*Mark11:22-24*), and not be discouraged!

In all cases, the Holy Spirit must lead and guide.

*A more complete checklist concerning occult involvement is given in the addendum along with further information, and specific prayers to aid in personal deliverance. (See page 423)

Derek Prince used to say, "Nothing has been taught until something has been learned."

Here are two precious truths concerning deliverance that are easy to teach, but (believe me), so very difficult to learn!

1. God delivers us from our enemies, *not* our friends!
2. A weakness that remains a weakness becomes a strength, or stronghold!

The children of Israel were told by the Lord, "*to utterly destroy*" the evil nations of Canaan.

(*Deut.7:2*)

Failure to do so would cause those nations to become, "*Thorns in Israel's side, and a snare.*"

(*Judg.2:1-3*)

Instead of destroying them all, Israel made them **servants.** (See *Jos.ch.9*)
Later they became **friends** and began marrying them; making them **partners.** (*1Kings 11:1-8*)
Finally, the People of God were overwhelmed and **conquered** by them! (*2Chr.36:11-21*)

People who are holding on to a "favorite sin" and think they can control it, should learn from old Israel! (*1Cor.10:11*) Ask the Lord to show you that your "friend" (alcohol, tobacco, drugs, gambling, lust, etc.) is nothing more than an enemy that is waiting to destroy you, and perhaps the family around you! The longer we refuse to acknowledge and deal with a sinful weakness, the stronger it becomes, and the harder it will be to get rid of. Ultimately it could kill us!

Years ago, a dear friend and brother in Christ would often joke with me about how fast he drove. He was always in a hurry! Also, he was inclined to park anywhere he wanted, with little regard for "lines or signs."

He once told me, "The Lord and I have an understanding." (Meaning that it was alright for him to do such things.) He laughed off my counsel several times, and continued to rush on his way.

He was such a great guy, and so young; but some time later (while overtaking another car at high speed) he was killed instantly in a head-on smash! Anyone who has lost a close friend or relative in such circumstances may well have experienced the same kind of "angry sorrow" that I did!

Because of his faith in Christ however, I will know the joy and consolation of seeing him again in Heaven: but in the mean time, what a tragic waste of an earthly life!

Truly, some ongoing sins "bite" harder (and quicker) than others, but all are set to destroy us sooner or later.

Make sin your enemy NOT your friend!

Now a brief word about deliverance for unbelievers.

It is quite fruitless to minister deliverance to unbelievers without them first coming to a knowledge of Salvation in Christ.

Jesus said,

*"When the unclean spirit is gone out of a man, he walketh through dry places, seeking rest, and findeth none. Then he saith, I will return to **my house** from whence I came out; and when he is come, he findeth it empty, swept, and garnished. Then goeth he, and taketh with himself **seven other spirits** more wicked than himself, and they **enter in and dwell there**: and the **last state** of that man is **worse than the first**, even so shall it be also unto this wicked generation."*

(Matt.12:43-45)

Unless a person receives the Lord, and the indwelling of the Holy Spirit, there is nothing to stop an expelled demon from returning with others, as the "door" is still open. This would simply create more torment and chaos than before.

With notable exceptions (such as the Roman centurion, *Matt.8:5-13* and the woman of Canaan, *Matt.15:21-28* – note that *both* came to Jesus) the Lord's ministry of healing and deliverance was to God's chosen people. (*Matt.10:5-6*)

****

What we learn from the Canaanite woman's story is extremely significant.

"Then Jesus went thence, and departed into the coasts of Tyre and Sidon (Gentile cities).
*And behold, a woman of Canaan came out of the same coasts, and cried unto Him, saying, Have mercy on me, **O Lord, thou son of David**; my daughter is grievously vexed with a devil* (demon possessed). *But He answered her **not a word**. And His disciples came and besought Him, saying, Send her away, for she crieth after us. But He answered and said, **I am not sent but unto the lost sheep of the house of Israel**. Then came she and worshiped Him, saying, **Lord, help me**. But He answered and said, It is not meet* (fit or good) *to take **the children's bread**, and to cast it to **the dogs**. And she said, Truth Lord: yet the dogs eat of the crumbs which fall from their masters' table. Then Jesus answered and said unto her, O woman, **great is thy faith**: be it unto thee even as thou wilt. And her daughter was **made whole** from that very hour."*
(*Matt.15:21-28*)

A gentile woman approached Jesus with a religious cry, "*Son of David!*" No doubt she had heard the Jews (God's people) using that title legitimately, (*Mark10:46-48*) and thought that by copying it (as in vain repetition) she would get His attention, but ...

"***He answered her not a word.***" Only when she fell before Him with the cry of sincerity, "*Lord help me*," did Jesus respond with a test. He made it perfectly clear that deliverance is the "*children's bread*" (a gift to God's people), but her God given faith, wisdom, and humility (*John 3:27, Luke 7:1-10*) moved Jesus to act on her behalf!

NOTE: We do well to remember that this woman, and *all* gentiles in the flesh were once considered "dogs." However, those of us now saved (by the grace of God) have been lifted, seated, and wonderfully provided for at our Master's heavenly table! (See *2 Sam.9* and *Eph.1:3-6, 2:11-22*)

****

To conclude this brief overview of demonology; I would like to share two personal testimonies involving deliverance. They are taken from my earliest experiences in order to reveal how gently (and patiently) the Holy Spirit can bring us to understand and embrace this vital aspect of Christ's ongoing ministry.

"Mom, I want cake!"

One day, a young couple who attended our fellowship, invited me to dinner. The wife was a committed Christian, but her husband (by his own admission) had not yet made a decision for Christ. When I arrived at the house the table was already laden with good things to eat, including a number of sumptuous deserts.

I noticed the couple's six-year-old son staring longingly at the cakes and puddings; but when his mother entered he withdrew. She told me immediately that her child (I'll call him Peter) was extremely allergic to dairy products and was never allowed to eat the "good stuff." Sadly, for the whole of his young life, he had been forced to put up with a diet of dairy substitutes, which at that time were expensive and inconvenient.

Shortly after our main course, the cake tray was handed round, and I saw just how miserable Peter looked at not being included. (This time, no alternatives had been prepared for him.)

Apparently the boy's allergy was so bad, that within half an hour of eating dairy, his skin would blotch, and his face would blow up to nearly twice its normal size!

Something inside me was yearning to help the boy, but as his father was unsaved I didn't want to push. All I could do was offer up a silent prayer, "Lord if you are wanting to move here, please cause his father to accept your help." After that I took a deep breath and said, "I believe God can deliver Peter from his allergies: would you like me to pray for your son?"

Expecting a polite "No," I waited. (O ye of little faith!) ..."Yes; by all means," came the firm reply! – Now I was in trouble! Suppose I pray and nothing happens! The enemy was busy ... "You'll have egg on your face, and His father will think you're a religious idiot who doesn't know what he's doing!" (No pride there!) – "Get behind me Satan!"

I slowly began praying over the boy while he sat on his dad's lap. Suddenly; Peter began squirming and kicking, and trying desperately to wriggle out of his father's grasp. The more I prayed, the more violent the boy became. (For a six year old, he was giving his father quite a hard time!) I reached out; laid my hand gently on the child's head, and commanded a spirit of allergy to come out of him!

All at once little Peter broke wind very loudly! Both parents laughed with surprise (or perhaps embarrassment!) I on the other hand, could only wait in silence and hope.

Moments later, a still small voice inside me seemed to be saying, "He's free now, it's over."

(Later with understanding and experience, I would recognize the "*gift of faith*" as a supernatural emptying of doubt; and be more comfortable with it; but at that time the gifts of the Spirit were still very new to me.) I took another deep breath; looked at the boy's father, and repeated calmly, "He's free now, it's over." Before all the words had left my mouth, Peter jumped up; grabbed some cake; looked at his mother (who nodded her approval), and started munching as if there were no tomorrow!

His father asked nervously, "Do you think he'll be alright?" To which his wife replied, "Well, we'll know in half an hour!" Thirty minutes came and went: the spirit was gone, and we were all praising the Lord!

P.S. Peter was delivered (had lots more cake), and Peter's dad made a commitment to Christ and was "*Born again.*" (*John 3:3-8*)

JESUS 2 Satan 0 – God is so good!

"Who am I?"

Some time later, a young man in his early twenties came for help. He had grown up in a non-Christian home, but at the age of thirteen he attended a young people's Gospel rally, and received the Lord Jesus Christ as his Savior and Lord.

Over the years, this young man (I'll call him Rodger) developed a "gift" of mimicry and could impersonate almost anyone. The problem was; in discovering and accepting this occult gift, he had opened the door to demonic activity. Gradually, and with each new impersonation, other demons would gain access. Unfortunately, the gift lent popularity to him, which only increased his desire to keep it! (Incidentally; impersonators, ventriloquists, magicians etc., are all demonically inspired!)

What began as a blessing for this young man, slowly turned into a curse! (As always with Satan's "gifts.") After years of mimicking others, he had absolutely no idea who he was himself!

He had no normal or genuine personality whatsoever. Everything he did or said came from someone else. He knew he was in a mess, but, praise the Lord, he knew Jesus!

(Needless to say, he had never impersonated the Lord.)

The deliverance session took over ten hours! (Those of us participating had so much to learn, and the Holy Spirit guided us step by step.) There were so many mimicking spirits hiding behind one another, it was like going through a series of revolving doors!

Amongst other things, it became clear we were ministering to a victim of schizophrenia (meaning "two [split] minds;" often with multiple personalities). Demons would keep switching places and using different voices to confuse the issues and maintain a hold, but fortunately; those of us involved had recently learned about "*Binding the strong man.*" (*Matt.12:29*)

The "*strong man*" in this case was the spirit of rebellion, fed or supported by rejection and insecurity. Rejection was actually the first spirit to enter through "ground" given up [before birth] by his parents due to an unwanted pregnancy: and was followed closely by insecurity, thereby opening the door to everything else. Rebellion *always* works with rejection and insecurity, which is why it is such a strong demon. – It is also the driving spirit of mankind!

We are *all* born with the nature of sin, so the spirit of rebellion becomes more or less powerful, depending on the circumstances of our birth and upbringing. Only God's gift of salvation through Jesus Christ can prevent that spirit from taking every single one of us to hell! As we "*bound the strong-man,*" we moved forward and learned much more as time went on.

The Holy Spirit was again very gracious. We learned how "lying spirits" *had* to tell the truth when commanded to do so with the authority of Jesus' Name! We watched as certain spirits caused Rodger to writhe around on the floor like a snake, hissing out profanities. (We were very young; we wouldn't allow that now.)

After more than eight hours; in a moment of calm, (and gradually increasing victory) Rodger asked for a drink. (We *all* learned deliverance can be thirsty work!) We gave him a large glass of orange juice with much pulp, and continued with the session. (I'll explain the mention of pulp in a moment.)

Some time later, the Holy Spirit revealed that several spirits still lingered in this young man; including the "*strong man.*"

Strangely enough at that point our brother became unwilling to give these spirits up!

The reason for this soon became clear. Without his "friends" to make him a "somebody," he was afraid that in the end, he would become, "just another nobody!"

His eventual willingness (after more prayer) to see these friends as real enemies (then to repent and give up the ground allowing such demonic control) enabled us to command the remaining spirits to leave.

NOTE: Ground lost or given up was due to an ever increasing desire for love, acceptance and recognition found on the human level; but when this was exchanged for the unconditional love, acceptance, and *true* recognition found only in our Father's Heavenly Kingdom; the battle was won!

It was then we learned why Jesus allowed the "legion" of demons to go into the herd of swine!

The Lord knew better than anyone of course, what kind of devastating effect the mass expulsion of demons could have on a human being; especially if they were to fight to the very end!

In his compassion for the possessed man, Jesus made it easier for those spirits to leave by giving them the alternative of entering swine. (*Mark5:12-13*) ...Wonderful lessons from the Master!

****

Last, but definitely not least, and with a good deal of physical stress on Rodger's part, the final group of spirits came out. During their departure, he vomited out a large ball of compacted mucus (golf ball sized), with not one drop of orange juice! – Not the tiniest piece of pulp to be seen! Just another indication to us that what was happening was in fact a true "*miracle,*" (See *Mark9:38-39*) with victory in Jesus' mighty Name!

CHAPTER FIVE

DON'T WALK LIKE AN "EGYPTIAN"

For this study, I'd like to bring back a word we're already familiar with. A word which virtually describes Satan's entire ministry, especially in our modern world.

That word is **uncover**, and to understand more of its meaning and importance, we should again turn to the Word of God.

> *"And the Lord spake unto Moses saying, … I am the Lord your God. … After the doings of the land of* **Egypt**, *wherein ye dwelt, shall ye not do: and after the doings of the land of* **Canaan**, *whither I bring you shall ye not do: neither shall ye walk in* **their ordinances**. *…None of you shall approach to any that is near of kin to him to* **uncover** *their nakedness: I am the Lord. The nakedness of thy father, or of thy mother shalt thou not* **uncover**: *she is thy mother; thou shalt not* **uncover** *her nakedness. … The nakedness of thy father's wife shalt thou not* **uncover**: *it is thy father's nakedness. … The nakedness of thy sister …the nakedness of thy son's daughter, or of thy daughter's daughter, even their nakedness thou shalt not* **uncover**: *for theirs is thine own nakedness*. (See all of Leviticus 18)

Of the twenty-five times the word "uncover" appears in Scripture, all but one are to be found in this chapter of Leviticus! Twenty-four times the word is used negatively, and *that* translates to a strong warning for the church today!

Some of the Hebrew renderings of the word uncover, read like Satan's resume!

"To spread self – to betray – to denude (or strip) – to set at naught – to leave destitute – to shamelessly show or tell – to take captive – to demolish or destroy!"

No wonder uncovering is the devil's favorite work!

The warnings God gave Israel in Leviticus chapter eighteen concerned the abominable sexual practices of the ancient Egyptians and Canaanites. "*Uncovering the nakedness of any that is near of kin,*" refers to incestuous relationships, and was one of the reasons God wanted the "*seven nations of Canaan*" utterly destroyed! (*Lev.18:24-25, Deut.7:1-5*)

As a result of disobedience, the Israelites failed to wipe out those nations in the Promised Land, which in turn led them to live with, and eventually adopt the same hideous pagan practices! These and other willful sins, uncovered the children of Israel, and brought God's judgment down upon them time, and time again. (See the book of Judges for the sad confirmation)

"Do not be deceived, evil communications (companionships) *corrupt good manners."* (Good habits or morals, *1Cor.15:33*)

A question now arises: if everything that happened to Israel was to be *"an example for us, and was written for our admonition"* (mild but serious warning, *1Cor.10:11*); what are we to learn from such terrible sins? Surely no Christian would ever uncover the *physical* nakedness of a family member incestuously; so what could Leviticus ch.18 possibly be saying to us today?

Three golden nuggets will help us find the answer.
Jesus said, *"It is the Spirit that quickeneth; the flesh profiteth nothing: the words that I speak unto you, they are Spirit, and they are life."* (*John 6:63*)

Paul wrote, *"Howbeit that was not first which is spiritual, but that which is natural; and afterwards that which is spiritual."* (*1Cor.15:46*)

Lastly: we should know that parables are natural, earthly stories, (easily understood) which have spiritual, or heavenly meaning. (Some explanation required)

NOTE: Much of the Old Testament comes in parable form, and so contains many hidden types and shadows, or "keys;" the loveliest of course being those which help us to "see" Jesus, Who is the New Covenant substance or fulfillment.

Now place these three nuggets alongside the Hebrew meanings of the word "uncover," and we will readily understand the "parable" of Leviticus eighteen, and just how easy it is to *"uncover someone's nakedness"* today! ...

The true Church of Christ is a "Royal Family:" (*Eph.3:15, 1Pet.2:9, Rev.1:6*) therefore everyone who is *"born again"* is eternally related to God through Jesus by the Holy Spirit, and to each other as members of Christ's Body. There are spiritual fathers and mothers (mature believers); brothers and sisters (those growing strong in the Lord); children (those growing up in the Lord); and babes (new believers just beginning their spiritual walk with the Lord).

Special reminder: God has no grand children – only sons and daughters!

Because only this New Covenant spiritual family can receive the things of the Holy Spirit, or be taught and admonished by the Word of God, (*1Tim.3:16-17*) we can now address one of the most serious and relevant issues within the Body of Christ today!

Any member of God's family who *judges* (criticizes or finds fault); *gossips* (shamelessly shows or tells); *belittles* (sets at naught); *betrays* (cheats or deals deceitfully); *puts in bondage* (preaches legalism for example); *leaves destitute* (does not care for his or her own); *creates a stumbling block* (smokes, drinks alcohol, dresses provocatively etc., in front of weaker brethren especially); *demolishes or destroys* (tears down or hurts for any reason); *spreads self* (is proud, puffed up, or self-seeking with fleshly ambition). The one who does these things is guilty of uncovering others and themselves!
They walk (or behave) **like an "Egyptian!"**

This is by no means a complete list, but in today's world *all* of those sins are acceptable!

The *"Egyptians"* and the *"Canaanites"* (types of unbelievers) are constantly uncovering themselves! On secular television many of those things are considered admirable, some funny, and some even exciting and fashionable!

It doesn't take much to see how well Satan has done his job – even in the church!

The great blessing for believers however is that when the Holy Spirit convicts us of doing any of those evil things, (we all have) we can by faith, and through the Blood of Christ (*"by a new and living way"*) enter directly into the *"Holiest,"* (God's presence) there to confess our sins, and find God's forgiveness and cleansing! What an incredible gift that is! (*Heb.10:19-20*)

"If we confess our sins, He is faithful and just to forgive us our sins, and to cleanse us from all unrighteousness."
"...God is Light, and in Him is no darkness at all."
"If we walk in the light, as He is in the light, we have fellowship one with another, and the Blood of Jesus Christ, cleanses us from all sin." (See 1John1:5-9)

We can stop the "Uncoverer" in his tracts, but to do so we must be vigilant! Remember that we too lived as "Egyptians" and "Canaanites," even as they are now! Satan still has a tremendous hold on the men and women of *"this world,"* (*2Cor.4:4*) and uncovering is as natural to them as barking is to a dog! The most powerful weapon in destroying those *"nations"* (sinful practices) is of course, *"Walking in the Spirit, and not in the flesh."* (*Rom. 8:1*) But keep in mind, this is not often a swift victory, but rather a *"long war"* against the *"works of the flesh"* as we now know them! (See *2Sam.3:1* for another great type.)

Help for the battle comes from reading God's Word, being in fellowship, and from praying to be more sensitive to the leading of the Holy Spirit on a day-to-day basis!

Walking in the Spirit is essentially walking while covered with, or bearing spiritual fruit. That is to say, bearing the inward and outward expression of, *"Love, joy, peace, long-suffering, gentleness, goodness, faith, meekness, temperance: against such there is no law."* (*Gal. 5:22*)

In other words, these things cannot be uncovered! As this fruit ripens in our lives, it will fall in every direction; and never forget, *"Charity* (love) **shall cover** *the multitude of sins."* (*Prov.10:12, 1Pet. 4:8*) Covering our brother, sister, father or mother, and loving our neighbor as ourselves is to show forth the love and compassion of a certain Samaritan revealed in what may well be the best known of all the Lord's parables. (*Luke10:25-37*)

NOTE: Jesus did not call the Samaritan good. Men added the "good" because among the *"Egyptians,"* and many others, the actions of *this* man were so exceptional. Nevertheless, the Lord made it clear that for us, those actions should be the absolute norm! Of course, as we look at the *"Samaritan,"* it becomes impossible not to see Jesus; and in revealing to us the deeper truths of the parable itself, the Holy Spirit gives glory to Christ in a very special way!

The Wonder of it all!
"A certain man went down from Jerusalem to Jericho, and fell among thieves, which stripped him of his raiment, and wounded him, and departed, leaving him half dead."

God "dwelt" in the city of Jerusalem. He chose it above all others, and placed His Name there. (*2Chr.12:13, Ps.46:4-5*) Jericho on the other hand was a cursed city, and one almost entirely destroyed by God during the days of Joshua. (*Josh.ch.6*) The man and both cities are types.

"*A certain man*" can be seen as Adam, and in him, all mankind. His journey began in Jerusalem (in fellowship with God in the garden of Eden), but he **went down to Jericho** (down under sin to live in its curse).

> Along his *own* way (*Is.53:6*) **he fell among thieves** (demonic powers who came to steal, kill, and destroy), **who stripped him of his raiment, and wounded him** (stole his righteous covering, and did everything they could to destroy him, which is exactly the ministry of "*serpents,*" "*scorpions,*" and "*fowl of the air*" to this day!) **And departed, leaving him half dead** (God graciously did not permit Satan to kill him). "*... And the Lord said unto Satan, Behold, he is in thine hand; but save his life.*"
>
> (*Job.2:6*)

> "**And by chance there came down a certain priest that way: and when he saw him, he passed by on the other side. And likewise a Levite, when he was at the place, came and looked on him, and passed by on the other side.**"

No one could doubt that here the priest and Levite were representatives of the "*Old Covenant*" or the "*Law of Moses.*" The continued well-being of Israel's social, political, and religious life depended entirely upon keeping its precepts. Failure to do so would cause severe judgments to fall upon the nation.

The Word of God declares that, "*The Law is holy, just, and good,*" (*Rom.7:13*) but when looking upon the plight of mankind's fallen, sinful, naked, wounded, and utterly lost condition, the Law could do nothing! The Law (like a thermometer) merely tells us how sick we are: it can do nothing to cure the sickness! The priest and the Levite "*passed by.*"

> "**But a certain Samaritan, as he journeyed, came where he was: and when he saw him, he had compassion on him, and went to him, and bound up his wounds, pouring in oil and wine, and set him on his own beast, and brought him to an inn, and took care of him.**"

How could we fail to see the wonder of God's Love and Grace? Jesus left the glory of Heaven and came down to where we are! He saw us, and had compassion on us. "*He saw us in our own blood.*" (pollutions) (*Eze.16:6*) He came to us, bound up our wounds, bore our sorrows and our grief, and carried the iniquity of us all! "**With His stripes** (wounds) **we were healed.**" (See the whole of *Is.53*)

"**He poured in oil and wine.**" He gave us His anointing of Spirit, and joy. *Ps.45:7, Ps.105:43.*

"**He set him on His own beast.**" "*God hath raised us up together, and made us sit together in heavenly places in Christ Jesus.*" (*Eph.2:6*)

"**He brought him to an inn,**" may refer to salvation itself, or perhaps the Church. In any event, it was certainly the place of rest. (*Heb.4:10*)

"**He took care of Him.**" Are we not told to "*Cast all our cares upon Him, for He careth for us?*" (*1Pet.5:7*) Can we not say, "*Surely goodness and mercy shall follow me all the days of my life?*" (*Ps.23:6*)

"And on the morrow when he departed, he took out two pence, and gave them to the host, and said unto him, Take care of him; and whatsoever thou spendest more, when I come again, I will repay thee."

To understand the last part of this amazing parable, we must first hear from the Lord in another place ...

"Nevertheless I tell you the truth; It is expedient (better) *for you that I go away: for if I go not away, the Comforter will not come unto you; but if I depart, I will send Him unto you."* (*John16:7*)

"When he departed ..."
Jesus had to go, but how wonderful to know that His Divine provision would cover and keep us while He was away.

"He took out two pence ..."
A penny was a day's wage (*Matt.20:2*) and, *"One day is with the Lord as a thousand Years, and a thousand years as one day."* (*Ps.90:4, 1Pet.3:8*)

Is it reasonable to suggest that the *"two pence"* refers to the Church Age (some two thousand years), and that we are surely living in the last days?

Let me share something from the book of Joshua that may confirm this.

When traveling through the wilderness, the children of Israel were told to follow the Ark of the Covenant as it was borne upon the shoulders of the Levites. The people were told very clearly that there should be a space between them and the Ark of *"two thousand cubits."* (Many modern Bible translations have ruined this, and other beautiful types. Be watchful!)

The officers said to the people, *"Come not near it, that you may know the way by which you must go: for ye have not passed this way heretofore."* (*Jos.3:3-4*)

We who are saved, certainly know THE WAY, (*John14:6*) but not one of us has passed *this* way or lived *this* life before! Let me take this opportunity to say that **reincarnation** is an age-old, judgment-avoiding, **satanic lie!** A lie that has ruthlessly deceived and led millions of sincere but unsuspecting people into a Christless eternity. (See *Heb.9:27* for the truth)

To continue: The Ark (Jesus), and we the people of God have not yet finished our journey together, but praise God the end is most definitely in sight!

"And gave them to the host, and said unto him, take care of him ..."
I must admit there has been some disagreement as to the identity of this particular type. Some see the host or innkeeper as a type of pastor or elder; some think of an individual believer; others believe he represents the whole church.

While I can understand the reasoning behind each of these opinions, I am forced to disagree. With the utmost respect to pastors, elders, and *all* believers, I cannot rely on any man to take care of me, or be responsible for my spiritual walk with the Lord. (*John 2:24-25, Ps.118:9*) Therefore I am drawn overwhelmingly to conclude that the "Host" to whom Jesus has given the task of caring for His whole Body is none other than God the Holy Spirit Himself!

Apart from the wonder of His presence within us, the Holy Spirit has watched over, loved, kept, strengthened, enlightened, guided, protected, provided, nourished, equipped, instructed, convicted, comforted, reproved, chastened and *put up with* – every single member of the Body of Christ throughout the entire Church age!

"And whatsoever thou spendest more ..."

Here we see why man knows *"neither the day, nor the hour"* when Jesus will return. (*Matt. 25:13*)

For like the *"great and costly stones"* that were gathered, and then silently raised up to build the Temple of Solomon, the Holy Spirit has been quietly gathering *"living stones"* from all nations (*1Pet. 2:5*) to build God's *spiritual* house! And even though our preparation requires much hewing, chipping, grinding, cutting, and sanding in the "quarry," the people of this world have absolutely no idea that God is working on a living Temple! (The sound of a tool was not to be heard on the Temple site; see *1Kings 5:17-18, and 6:7*)

Not one of us here knows when God will put the last miraculous stone in place, but when He does, His Church will rise gloriously, and the scripture will be fulfilled!

"The whole of creation groans and travails in pain, waiting for the manifestation of the sons of God." (See *Rom. 8:19-23*)

If the time should seem overly long to us, the finished result will nevertheless be exactly according to God's will and purpose; determined in Christ before the foundation of the world!

"When I come again, I will repay thee."

The Greek word for repay is "apodidomi," and can also be taken to mean render, which agrees more with *Rom.2:6*. This means of course that God gives; not because He is indebted to anyone, but rather because, *"It is more blessed to give than to receive."* (*Acts20:35*) Any rewards or loses pertaining to the five fold ministry of Apostles, Prophets, Evangelists, Pastors, Teachers, or to the Body of Christ as a whole, must be seen in that light. God is no man's debtor: everything that we are, have, receive, or lose is by His Grace!

At the "rapture," or "catching away" of the church, the Holy Spirit will gather the "saints" (*the "Israel of God"Gal.6:16*), and we will *"all appear before the judgment seat of Christ."* (*2Cor.5:10*)
There, all the works of the Holy Spirit will be revealed – as well as our own!

"For other foundation can no man lay than that is laid, which is Jesus Christ. Now if any man build upon this foundation gold, silver, precious stones, wood, hay, stubble; Every man's work shall be made manifest: For the day shall declare it, because it shall be revealed by fire; and the fire shall try every man's work of what sort it is. If any man's work abide which he hath built thereupon, he shall receive a reward. If any man's work shall be burned, he shall suffer loss: but he himself shall be saved; yet so as by fire." (1 Cor. 3:11-15)

"Therefore judge nothing before the time, until the Lord come, who both will bring to light the hidden things of darkness, and will make manifest the counsels of the hearts: and then shall every man have praise of God." (1 Cor.4:5)

Man made or God breathed?

Another study opens up at this point, which is well worth our consideration.
To avoid life long deception, God shows the believer six materials that can be used to build on Christ's Foundation. "...***Gold, silver, precious stones, wood, hay, and stubble.***"

These materials provide us with an opportunity to discern our ministries and lives in light of that which will, or will not be burned! Obviously wood, hay, and stubble are extremely combustible; which tells us that these are the types of works done by man in the *"flesh."*

The Hebrew word for man is "Iysh" (often translated "Ish"), so this means that everything done in the flesh can now actually be seen as self-**ish**-ness or self-**man**-ness!

When Adam sinned, he ceased to be God-centered and became self-centered, so in other words, Adam's sin was man's first independent act! These independent acts (though often morally good) are still all *"works of the flesh;" (Gal.5:19-21)* making it abundantly clear that (without repentance) it is entirely possible for a believer to spend his or her whole life gathering materials (or doing works) which will eventually be burned!

V.I.P. (Very Important Promise!) Before we go any further, let's put this in our spiritual "bank."

Believers may lose their rewards, but *never* their salvation!
"He shall suffer loss: but he himself shall be saved; yet so as by fire."
(Or as is sometimes described ... by the "skin of his teeth!")

Stay out of the woods!

When most of us think of wood, we are not so much thinking of a living tree, but of something already cut by man and formed into something useful, i.e. planks or beams to build houses, barns, fences etc. Wood is also turned into beautiful (and often expensive) furniture, and even works of art such as statues or figurines. Strictly speaking the tree is dead the moment it is cut down: Spiritually speaking, everything made from it automatically becomes a *"dead work!"*

Sadly, even a wooden sailing yacht (in my opinion the loveliest of all man's creations) will still burn!

"For that which is highly esteemed among men, is abomination in the sight of God." (Luke 16:15)

The best the "old nature" can offer (even with good intentions) is only fit for the fire!

An elderly sister in Christ came to see me one day, and in the course of our conversation she spoke several times of visiting, and ministering to the sick in several local hospitals.

"But," she said sincerely; "I never tell anyone that I do it." – **Wood is no good!** (*See Matt.6:1-8*)

Let the animals keep the hay!

Webster's dictionary defines hay as, "herbage (grass) mowed and cured for fodder."

Fodder is defined as, "coarse, dry food (corn stalks) for livestock."

Mr. Webster – we get it! Hay is for animals (good for them) but not good for us!

This takes us to more obvious works of the flesh (*Is.10:15, Matt.6:1-4,16-18*), such as public displays of giving or doing. Having one's name announced on radio or television for contributions to a particular ministry; or being put on a plaque in a church or community building. How about an evangelist, (or anyone else) putting *this* kind of bondage on their audience? – "$100 will help *us* save 100 souls. If you can afford $100, but you only give $50, then 50 souls will be lost!"

Now listen to one of Jesus' disciples.

"Master, see what manner of stones and what buildings are here! (Mark 13:1)

Here we have men actually boasting to *God* about their good works! These are only a few examples, there are so many more. You may have heard them, I certainly have. Let's face it, hay *"rejoices in boastings, and all such rejoicing is evil."* (*James 4:16*) Boasting should not be heard among the saints. **- Keep the hay at bay!** (*Eph.4:22*)

Don't even think about stubble!

When all the trees are gone and all the grass is cut, what we have left is neither fit for man nor beast. Stubble is frequently burned or plowed under at the end of the harvest to provide natural fertilizer for the next year's crop. Which ever way you look at it, stubble is a type of spiritual *"dung"* (the most deplorable of a believer's fleshly works) as seen for example in the first Corinthian letter.

> *"It is reported commonly that there is fornication among you, and such fornication as is not so much named among the Gentiles, that one should have his father's wife."* (See all of *1Cor.5*)

This was fornication unconcealed and unrepented of, and it uncovered the nakedness of the whole church! Today, sins of that nature would include brothers and sisters in Christ, living openly together outside of marriage, and attending a Fellowship or Church where there was full knowledge of that sin.

This is why the Word of God thunders, *"Abstain from all appearance evil."* (*1Thess.5:22*)

Marriage displaces the brother-sister relationship, putting an end to wrongful unions, and their bad testimony! Marriage covers: two become one in the Lord, and therefore ...

> *"Marriage is honorable in* (among) *all, and the bed undefiled: but whoremongers and adulterers* (uncoverers) *God will judge."* (*Heb.13:4*)

The appearance of evil, and addictions or demonic strongholds such as gluttony (over-eating), drunkenness (alcoholism), homosexuality (vile affections, *Rom.1:26* – those three especially are signs of "end time" behavior, *Luke 17:26-30*), along with smoking, gambling, tattoos, piercings, illegal drug use, etc., etc., are for the most part harder to conceal than say addictions to pornography (lusting and consenting to adultery), fetishes (idolatry), masturbation (self-gratification), and so on, which are nearly always more secretive. To emphasize the seriousness of a difficult verse, I have taken the liberty of writing it in modern form.

> "Some people's sins are clearly seen now, and those sins are leading them to judgment: some people's sins however, will not appear *until* the judgment!" (*1Tim.5:24*)

> Therefore, *"Be sober, be vigilant; because your adversary the devil, as a roaring lion, walketh about, seeking whom he may devour."* (*1Pet.5:8*)
> **Stubble is BIG trouble!** (*Gal.5: 16-21,Col.3:5-9*)

To summarize

All works of the flesh (from the best to the worst) are for burning!

Ministries or lives motivated by pride, ambition, greed, competition and self-interest, which on the surface may have looked so good down here: on *that* day will be seen going up in smoke! It's a sobering thought for all of us. Surely none of us would want to be *"naked and ashamed"* before the Lord! (*Rev.3:17-18, 16:15*) Praying for the Holy Spirit to reveal such sins in our lives is the first step to freedom!

The glorious truth is that through confession and repentance, God can and does deliver us from *"wood, hay, and stubble;"* then, as always by His amazing grace, helps us gather materials of a completely different kind!

GOLD, SILVER, AND PRECIOUS STONES

Once we've discovered the kind of works these precious materials speak of, we should encourage one another to start "building" immediately!

Let's go for the gold! Physical or natural gold is first revealed to us in *Havilah. (Gen.1:11-12)* *"And the gold of that land is good."* What do you think God is saying here? That we should all buy plots, and go prospecting in Havilah? – Definitely not! But we do know that natural gold differs greatly in quality (10, 14, 22kt etc.), and that the Bible speaks of gold and *pure* gold (as we've already seen). Further more, we know gold has always held tremendous value; and that using it would be much more convenient than trading goats for furniture, or putting camels in the bank!

As a result, gold was destined to become man's primary currency, while at the same time testing his integrity in a way few possessions would ever do.

*"For the **love** of money is the root of all evil." (1Tim.6:10)*

The deception of loving gold (*"mammon"*), and serving or worshipping it (*Matt.6:24*) has led countless souls to perdition; so quite obviously, physical gold (money) reveals a great deal about the condition of human hearts! But flip a gold coin over (so to speak), and we will see that its spiritual value far outweighs any natural worth! (Just look at the New Jerusalem!)

"The city was pure gold, like unto clear glass ... And the street of the city was pure gold, as it were transparent glass." (Rev.21:18, and 21)

On earth, "streets of gold" have always been pure fantasy. In Heaven they are pure reality!
We may now see God's Word revealing gold as a type of **FAITH**.

"That the trial of your faith, being much more precious than of gold that perisheth, though it be tried with fire, might be found unto praise and honor and glory at the appearing of Jesus Christ." (1Pet.1:7)

We may also see, that any work done by the believer in faith speaks of the gold that will *not* burn on that day! Therefore A *"good work"* in the Christian life could well be described as an act of faith!
*"... **Without faith, it is impossible to please God.**" (Heb.11:6a)*
Faith or "Spiritual gold" *here* will always help us to reflect and focus on our eternal home *there!*
(Not only in our hearts, but also in the way we build throughout our lives.)
I pray this will help those who are caught somewhere between *"dead works"* and the outright bondage of legalism; i.e. knowing that we are saved by grace, but trying to *stay* saved by works! Trying to keep this law or that rule is a treadmill God does not want His people walking on!

"Therefore we conclude that a man is justified by faith without the deeds of the law." (Rom.32:8)

Another thought here: the book describing the early church is nearly always called "The Acts of the Apostles," but the Apostles would never have named it so. To be more accurate, the book should be called, "The Acts of the Holy Spirit," for without question, all the "spiritual gold" recorded in those wonderful pages came exclusively from Him!

Now for the silver

Though considered a lesser prize than gold, silver remains one of the most noble metals.

It has among other attributes, the highest thermal and electric conductivity of any substance known to man. Silver can be highly polished, and so from earliest times it has been used for mirrors, fine eating utensils, and tableware. The Bible speaks of silver as a type of **HOPE.**

In the Old Testament, silver shekels were used as "redemption money" (*Lev.27*), and in Psalms, King David likened silver to the "Words of God." (*Ps.12:6*)

Silver is therefore an integral part of every New Testament believer's redemption (*Rom.8:24*): for the "Word of God (the Lord Jesus Christ), is most certainly our Blessed and Only Hope!"

(See *1Tim.1:1,Titus 2:13,Heb.6:19*)

Like silver, hope is highly conductive (spiritually contagious), and is spoken of by Peter as that which motivates us to share the Gospel.

"But sanctify the Lord God in your hearts: and be ready always to give an answer to every man that asketh you a reason of the hope that is within you with meekness and fear." (1Pet.3:15)

Polished silver (as a type) shows that we may look into the "mirror" of God's Word, and see not only His perfect Beauty and Holiness, but also those areas of our lives that need to be sanctified and cleansed (brought into obedience) by the washing of that very same Word. (*2 Chr.20:21, Eph. 5:26*)

Finally: when crafted into fine eating utensils, silver can remind us that Jesus (the Word of God) is our perfect spiritual food, i.e. the *"Bread of Life"* (*John 6:33, 51*) which, like the manna God gave to His people in the wilderness, sustains us while we sojourn in this world.

"Hope is a consolation, a refuge and an anchor of the soul, both sure and steadfast." (*Heb.6:18-19*)

It is also part of our spiritual armor ...

"Putting on the breastplate of faith and love; and for a helmet, the hope of salvation." (*1Thess.5:8*)

"Now the God of Hope fill you with all joy and peace in believing, that ye may abound in hope, through the Power of the Holy Ghost." (*Rom.15:13*)
Alleluia – *"**We rejoice in hope!**"* (*Rom.12:12*)

"Gold and silver abide,

but the greatest of these is ..."

There are no prizes for guessing that "*precious stones*," the most valuable of all the materials given as types of believer's works, would be used to create a wonderful picture of Love! Looking briefly at a natural diamond for instance, will reveal so many parallels as to be unmistakable.

Like all gemstones, the diamond is forged in the bowels of the earth under tremendous pressure and heat, to be brought forth as a rough, often unattractive and worthless looking object. Only when placed in the hands of an expert craftsman (where it is painstakingly scrutinized, cut, ground and polished) does the stone take on its true character. Stones are then rated from D-Z, with D being the most pure and valuable. A diamond is a crystallized and transparent form of pure carbon, and has the hardest surface known to man. (Only a diamond can cut a diamond!) Carbon, the "building block" of all life is so complex and diverse, that an entire field of organic chemistry is devoted to this one element! (Indeed, *"We are fearfully and wonderfully made." Ps.139:14*)

For the longest time diamonds have been regarded as symbols of purity, strength, and "never ending love." They are given primarily at engagements, and 75th wedding anniversaries.

"Diamonds are forever" is a well-known catch phrase.

The strength and endurance of the diamond comes from the carbon atom's unique ability to bond readily with others (as hydrogen, oxygen and nitrogen), but no two stones are ever alike. Finally in this overview, it takes an amazing 250 tons of mined and processed ore to produce just one carat of diamond! (1/5 gram) Jesus said, *"For many are called, but few are chosen." (Matt.22:14)*

Every phase of a diamond's life is a mirror of our own: from the pressure and heat of trials and tribulation (*John 16:33*), to the glorious finished result of being like Christ! (*1John 3:2*)

Only the perfect, brilliant, and flawless One is worthy of the letter **D**. Jesus is our **D**ivine Savior, and all other stones are pale by comparison!

In spite of ourselves, the Holy Spirit bonds us together, which is the strength of His Body,
"rooted and grounded in love." (Eph. 3:17)
Our Heavenly Father spoke these beautiful words to us through the prophet Jeremiah.
*"Yea, I have loved thee with an **everlasting love**: therefore with loving-kindness have
I drawn thee." (Jer.31:3)*

Through Isaiah He said, *"I have chosen thee in the furnace of affliction." (Is. 48:10b)*

And through Moses, *"The Lord did not set His love upon you, nor choose you, because ye were more in number than any people; for ye were the fewest of all people: but because the Lord loved you, and because He would keep the oath which He had sworn unto your fathers, that the Lord brought you out with a mighty hand, and redeemed you out of the house of bondmen, from the hand of Pharaoh king of Egypt." (Deut.7-8)*

"God *is* Love!" He chooses us *by* love. He redeems us *through* love. He keeps us *in* love and He crowns us *with* love! *"If God be for us, who can be against us?" (Rom. 8:31)*

From the bowels (the furnace and affliction) of "Egypt" (the world), God the Father draws us to Jesus (*John 6:44*); Who in turn commits us to the hands of the "Master Craftsman!" The Holy Spirit then lovingly scrutinizes each marred, unattractive, worthless looking creature; and begins to patiently (sometimes painfully) cut, grind and polish each and every facet of our lives, gradually conforming us to the image of Jesus Himself! (*Rom.8:28-30*)

The flesh must die so Love can live. (*Gal. 2:20*)
We walk and work by **faith**, we abound in **hope**, we grow in grace; but we must walk, work, abound, *and* grow – all in and by **love!**

"By this shall all men know that ye are My disciples, if ye have love one to another." (John 13:35)

Any work (thought, word or deed) inspired by, and manifested through God's love is a precious stone that will abide the hottest fire on that day of accountability before the judgment seat of Christ!

"Then they that feared the Lord spoke often one to another: and the Lord heard ... And they shall be mine, saith the Lord of hosts, in that day when I make up my jewels."(Mal. 3:16-17)

"Love is patient and kind; love is not envious; love is not proud or arrogant; love is not rude or selfish; love is not easily provoked, and thinks no evil; love hates wickedness but rejoices in the truth; bears all things, believes all things, endures all things. Love never fails ... and now abideth faith, hope, love, these three; but the greatest of these is love."(1Cor. 13:4-8, 13)

CHAPTER SIX

MEET THE NEW WORLD – SAME AS THE OLD WORLD

Almost as soon as the great flood was over, Satan's uncovering work would begin again! As far as the flood itself is concerned, (*Gen.7-8*) there are so many beautiful types and shadows to share, but only so much paper! (*John 21:25*)

May these few be a blessing.

The Ark of Noah would forever be a "type of Christ." He is the *True* Ark of refuge, and the *only* shelter (salvation) from the coming judgments of God! (*Acts4:12*)

NOTE: Although there will not be another flood, (*Gen.9:11*) God has shown us that Hell and the Lake of Fire are both real, and waiting for those who are not saved *in* Christ Jesus! (See *Rev.20:13-15*)

Someone once asked me, "How did Noah get all those animals into the ark without them tearing each other to pieces?"

Answer: God changed their natures!

How did Jesus get Matthew (a tax collector for Rome), Simon (a political zealot, who *hated* Rome), not to mention James and John whom Jesus called *"Boanerges"* (lit. "sons of thunder" because of their tempers) to follow Him as disciples? Answer: He changed their natures! (Once we're in Christ, isn't it amazing how He does that?)

As the time of the flood drew near, the wicked people (type of the unsaved) living alongside Noah and his family (type of those in Christ) had no idea what was about to happen. (See *Matt.24;36-44*) They had time to repent, but didn't!

Today in this "age of grace," the gospel is being preached around the world, and mankind is living just as carelessly! "Eat, drink and be merry; tomorrow (hopefully) we *won't* die!"

The vast majority give no thought whatsoever to God's impending judgment, but time is running out!

God's Love is infinite; His patience is not!

If you should be reading these words without assurance of your own salvation in the Lord Jesus Christ (the "Ark" of God); know that He is reaching out to you at this very moment! ...
"Behold now is the accepted time; behold, now is the day of salvation." (2Cor.6:2)
"If thou shalt confess with thy mouth the Lord Jesus, and shalt believe in thine heart that God hath raised Him from the dead, thou shalt be saved." (Rom.10:9)
Come into the Ark now, and be safe from the judgment to come!

When released by Noah the raven did not return, but *"Went to and fro until the waters were dried up from off the earth." (Gen.8:7)* We may well catch a glimpse of Satan here. (See *Job1:7* and *2:2*) As the raven thrives on carrion it would have no difficulty landing and feeding on the carcasses of floating, dead, and rotting creatures! Don't you think that fits Satan perfectly?

The first time Noah sent forth a dove however, she *"Found no rest for the sole of her foot,"* and so returned to the ark. *(Gen.8:9)* The dove becomes a lovely type of the Holy Spirit; Who likewise could find no place to rest until ...

*"He descended in a bodily shape like a dove, **and lighted and abode** (remained) **upon Jesus!"***
(Matt.3:16, Mark1:10, Luke3:22, John 1:32)

"For He whom God hath sent speaketh the words of God: for God giveth not the Spirit by measure unto Him." (John 3:34)

In all of time, only one man (the perfect, sinless Jesus) could receive the Spirit without measure. Only He could be trusted to carry the unfathomable burden and responsibility of drinking the ultimate "cup of suffering," *(Matt.26:39,42)* and becoming *"The Lamb of God that taketh away the sin of the world." (John1:29)* Only He could die the perfect, sacrificial death for our sins, and become *"The First-Born* (first in rank) *among many brethren,"* and *"Of* (over) *every creature."*

(Rom.8:29, Col.1:15)

In awe the disciples cried out, ***"What manner of Man is this?"*** *(Luke8:25)*

And now because of Him we also cry, ***"Behold what manner of love the Father hath bestowed upon us, that we should be called the sons of God?"*** *(1John3:1)*

The second time the dove was sent (after seven days), she returned with an *"Olive leaf in her mouth." (Gen.8:11)* The olive tree has always been a precious type of Israel, (see the whole of *Rom.11*) with God's loving-kindness continually reaching out to them as His natural and beloved people. It would then apply so graciously through Christ, to any and all who would become partakers of, *"the root and fatness of the olive tree." (Rom.11:17, Luke2:10-11)*

****

"...And, behold, the face of the ground was dry." (Gen.8:13)

Having temporarily lost access to mankind, Satan couldn't wait to get his "claws" into the survivors! Demons do not remain in, or possess the *physically* dead; just the ones who are *spiritually* dead! (see *Eph.2:1-10*)

But first, immediately after the flood, God had some very important things to say.

1. *"Be fruitful and multiply" (Gen.8:17).*

Mankind was to replenish the earth and once again take dominion, but this time, not just over the other creatures, but over himself as well! (*Gen.9:4-6*) This then would be the era or dispensation of human government: men would now be accountable to men for their misdeeds! Before the flood, no *man* had arrested Cain and Lamech, or punished anyone else for their crimes!

2. *"I will not again curse the ground any more for man's sake; for the imagination of man's heart is evil from his youth; neither will I again smite any more every thing living, as I have done" (Gen.8:21).*

Two separate issues come into focus here. If taken literally, the first would involve a lifting, or partial lifting of the curse of *Gen.3:17*. But don't worry; later man would have no trouble in cursing the earth himself! (*Is.24:3-6*) (You can always count on man!) Wars, toxic waste, acid rain, pollution of oceans, lakes, and rivers; destruction of Rain Forests and other eco-systems.

Let's face it, God really didn't need to curse the earth!

The second (as also recorded in *Gen.9:15*), emphasizing that God would never again destroy the earth with a flood and kill every living thing that breathed. With respect: what would be the point? That judgment would have to be poured out over and over and over again!

"For the imagination of man's heart is ... EVIL from his youth." (Gen.8:21)

Why do foolish people still hang on to the concept that man is inherently good?

This has always been an obvious, satanically inspired "New Age" deception! (You'd think that by now, even die-hard Humanists would recognize the truth!)

"As it is written, There is none righteous, no, not one: there is none that understandeth, there is none that seeketh after God. They are ALL gone out of the way, they are together become unprofitable; there is none that doeth good, NO, NOT ONE." (Rom.3:10-12)

We are *ALL* evil from our youth!

Hello, humanistic New Age person; where do you keep *your* gold, silver, jewelry, or life savings? Let me guess: in your car – no? Perhaps in your garage? No wait – I've got it! Under the kitchen table – right? Why would anyone even bother to lock their doors in this "inherently good" world of ours? (I just pray sincerely that your "wake up call" isn't too loud!)

Recently, there has been a growing number of vandalistic crimes reported in neighborhoods across the United States. For instance, teenagers (or younger) slashing the tires of parked cars; even in private driveways! Listen to the reaction of one victim – who incidentally needed $400-$500 worth of replacement tires! – "Oh, they're probably good kids; just bored, and getting up to a few pranks." All I can say is, "Good kids? Pranks? A prank is pouring iced water over the coach! WAKE UP PEOPLE! These "kids" are already criminals; and if parents don't do something soon, it's going to get a whole lot worse!

If we were so "good," why did Jesus have to die for us?

Parents who have ears to hear (Christians especially) need to read and *act on* scriptures like *Ecclesiastes 8:11* ...

"*Because sentence* (punishment) *against an evil work* (crime or disobedience) *is not executed speedily, therefore the heart of the sons of men is fully set in them to do evil.*"

And,

"*The rod and reproof give wisdom: but a child left to himself bringeth his mother to shame.*"

(*Pr.29:15*)

One of the most painful of all prophetic Scriptures concerning families reads as follows,

"*Thou shalt beget* (father) *sons and daughters, but thou shalt not enjoy them; for **they shall go into captivity**.*" (*Deut.28:41*)

The "captivity" of physical, emotional, and spiritual bondage is brought on by such sins as disobedience, rebellion, and violence: leading to all manner of injury, property damage, and even death! (Especially in schools.) Younger and younger illicit sex; leading to pandemic diseases such as syphilis, gonorrhea and aids. Greater involvement (escapism) with alcohol, drugs, pornography, gambling, etc., has simply added more strength to that bondage!

Teenage poker is presently in vogue, promoted by "celebrity" games and contests on the internet and television. "Street" or "drag racing" on public highways is also gaining in popularity; indirectly promoted by satanic puppets who make a fortune creating high-speed car chases (and lots of other visual garbage) for virtual reality and electronic video games!

NOTE: Parents, you *can* take authority over these rebellious evil spirits operating so freely in our children's lives today; but it won't be by listening to Freud, Spock, Ruth, Phil., or a host of other motley characters currently spewing forth from New Age television!

It will be by reading, knowing, and obeying, THE WORD OF GOD!

"*The people that DO KNOW their GOD* (by His Word) *will BE STRONG and DO EXPLOITS.*"
That means, **take action!** (*Dan.11:32*) But on the other hand, the implication is –
They that do not will be weak and **do nothing!**

One more thought here After God was voted out of the school-system back in the early 60's, it fell mostly into the hands of evolutionary atheists. We also know He allowed that to fulfill His Word. (See *2Tim.3:1-9*)

But how long do you think it will be before Washington's brilliant New Age governmental decision makers figure out exactly *who* it was that took God's place?

3. "*Every moving thing that liveth shall be meat for you; even as the green herb have I given you all things.*" (*Gen.9:3*)

Here is the official and dramatic departure from vegetarianism. The Lord's will and purpose in this matter can be traced from the garden of Eden right through to the glorious manifestation of the New Jerusalem, the eternal home of the saints of God.

In the beginning there was no sin, therefore there was no death! When sin entered, death reigned, and God commanded that "*Every moving thing that liveth* **shall be meat for you.**"

Mention of this was first made in chapter 2 under the heading, **The greatest love: the greatest gift.**

For some, what follows may be an extremely hard pill to swallow, but ...

VEGETARIANISM IS ABSOLUTELY NOT OF GOD!

Vegetarianism is another strong satanic deception, intended to rob men of –
- **A)** The knowledge of God's Grace, Mercy, and Provision.
- **B)** The reality and need for the ultimate atoning blood shedding sacrifice of Jesus Christ, the *True* Lamb of God!

Christian vegetarians please take note,
> "*Now the Spirit speaketh expressly, that in the latter times some shall depart from the faith, giving heed to **seducing spirits**, and **doctrines of devils**; speaking lies in hypocrisy; having their conscience seared with a hot iron; forbidding to marry, and **commanding to abstain from meats**, which God hath created to be received with thanksgiving of them which believe and know the truth. For **every creature is good**, and **nothing to be refused**, if it be received with thanksgiving: for **it is sanctified by the word of God and prayer**.*" (*1Tim.4:1-5*)

Gen.9:3 sanctifies *all* meat; and for Gentiles, that Word has never been rescinded!

Jesus said,
> "*And into whatsoever city ye enter, and they receive you, **eat such things as are set before you**.*"

(*Luke10:8*)

If "*such things*" include meat, how can a Christian vegetarian possibly obey the Word of the Lord?

By way of balance, the Scriptures declare,
> "*Him that is weak in the faith* (still held by the law) *receive ye, but not to doubtful disputations.* (Splitting hairs) *For one* (free from the law) *believeth that he may eat all things: another, who is weak eateth herbs. Let not him that eateth despise him that eateth not; and let not him which eateth not judge him that eateth: for God hath received him.*" ... "*One man* (weaker in faith) *esteemeth one day above another;* (due to the law) *another* (free from the law) *esteemeth every day alike. Let every man be fully persuaded in his own mind.*" (*Rom.14:1-3, 5*)

Clearly, the only Scriptural reason preventing a believer from eating "*all things*" would be his fear of breaking Jewish dietary laws. (See *Lev.11*) We are to be sensitive to such weakness, and must avoid causing such a brother or sister to stumble. (See all of *Rom.14*) But what is also important is that we seek the Holy Spirit for wisdom to help such a one find the "***perfect law of liberty***." (*James1:25*) For we are no longer under law, but under Grace! (*Rom.6:14*)

NOTE: Not eating certain meats for medical reasons, or because one simply doesn't like the taste is a valid choice; and not a "legal" issue! Once again; refusing to eat meat or *any* food strictly for **religious** reasons is what makes for legalism, demonic deception, and bondage!

4. "*And I will establish My covenant with you; neither shall all flesh be cut off any more by the waters of a flood ... I do set My bow in the cloud, and it shall be for a token of a covenant between Me and the earth.*"(*Gen.9:11,13*)

The rainbow which God set in the clouds was to be a covenant reminder to Him, and also to us that He would never again destroy the earth with a flood. (*Gen.9:15-16*) This covenant would later become on of Satan's special targets for corruption. Notice that rainbow symbols have sprung up all over the world, and are used profusely by the homosexual community. They are never made up of the seven colors of God's original design, but vary mostly from just four to six! This occult rainbow symbol is used by the New Age Movement to signify their building of the bridge between man and Lucifer, whom they believe to be the "Great Universal Mind," or "Over-soul."

In a moment (and continuing our theme), we shall see Satan once again taking great delight in his uncovering work; this time on God's almost new, post-diluvial race! But first a word concerning,

Food, drink and other motives

The deal was done. Gary left the showroom and headed home in his brand new Ford automobile.

He had worked hard, saved "every penny," and was thrilled to be finally driving the fruit of his labor. Unfortunately by mistake, someone had placed a Chevrolet manual in Gary's glove compartment.

With much enthusiasm, and not even a glance at the cover, Gary opened the manual and began a self-maintenance program to keep his Ford in perfect running order. – Poor old Gary!

A silly little story: surely no one could be that foolish. So why are there millions of people in the world called "Gary?" And why has dieting become a multi-billion dollar industry?

Simple: millions of People eat too much! And other people who don't know the truth (but like making money) sell diet programs to those people who don't know any better. – Over and over and over again!

Low carb., high carb., high fat, low fat. How about this one? ... "Eat whatever you like: if you buy *my* diet book, you can *still* lose weight!" (Often the only significant weight loss is from your wallet!)

People want to lose weight; they want to look better; they want a great life, but like Gary, they're reading the wrong manual!

Our bodies are "*Fearfully and wonderfully made.*" (*Ps.139:14*) God is the designer and Creator, and wants us to maintain them in perfect order. For that purpose He has given us *His* "**Manual;**" or (even better) His "***Immanuel.***" (*Is.7:14*) His "Living Word!"

After receiving Christ, (*John1:12*) the Bible offers a "limited warranty" on all our physical parts in this life, (*Is.53:5*) but an "eternal (spiritual) warranty" in the life to come! (*John 6:47*)

All this by reading His Word, and (by faith), following the instructions contained within it.

Don't let Satan void your warranty! (*John10:10*)

Sometimes, wrong thinking can do as much harm as sin itself.

A believer once said to me, "We're not allowed to drink or smoke, so I love to eat: it's about the only thing I can do without feeling guilty!"

Although this brother was holding the wrong end of the Christian "stick," most of us can understand his point of view. It's true that if we buy Satan's portrayal of our Heavenly Father as the great "Party Pooper," (always trying to spoil our fun) we will see Christianity only as a negative system of rules and regulations, i.e. "Don't do this!" – "Don't do that!" With a scary God waiting to beat us if we do! This is *such* a lie!

The glorious truth is, God knows us perfectly, (*Heb.4:13*) and wants to give us His absolute best!

(*1Cor.2:9*)

Anything contrary to His will and desire is in fact harmful and hindering; not only to our physical lives, but also to our spiritual walk with Him. This is why the *"Fruit of the Spirit"* includes *"Temperance"* (*Gal.5:22-23*), which is moderation or self-control. (*Phil.4:5*)

Statistics vary of course, but most show that between 50% and 60% of all Americans are overweight!

"Be not among winebibbers; among riotous (over) eaters of flesh: for the drunkard and the glutton shall come to poverty: and drowsiness shall clothe a man with rags." (Pr.23:20-21)

Continued wrongful eating is an invitation to all manner of problems; from straightforward gluttony (becoming heart-threatening obesity), to the extreme demonic addictions of anorexia and bulimia! These demons work together to encourage starvation in the **anorexic** (often leading to a shame filled death); and seesaw bingeing and purging which destroys internal organs *and* mental health in the **bulimic!** Strangely enough, both conditions are brought on by spirits of gluttony, though they work to torment their victims in opposite ways.

To gauge the seriousness of the food issue, just pause and consider the following:

Adam fell by wrongful eating: Jesus overcame by fasting! (*Luke4:1-14*)

While multitudes follow Adam, and persistently fall to food; countless numbers follow Noah, and fall to drink!

*"And Noah began to be an husbandman, and he planted a vineyard. And he drank of the wine, and was **drunken**; and he was **uncovered** within his tent. And **Ham**, the father of Canaan, **saw the nakedness** of his father, and told his two brethren without. And Shem and Japheth took a garment, and laid it upon both their shoulders, and went backward, and **covered** the nakedness of their father; and their faces were backward, and they **saw not** their father's nakedness. And Noah **awoke from his wine**, and **knew what his younger son had done unto him**. And he said, **Cursed be Canaan**; a servant of servants shall he be unto his brethren." (Gen.9:20-25)*

There can be little doubt that before the flood, wine and perhaps even strong drink was available in great quantities: now it was all gone. The knowledge and means of producing it once again however, was not! God had given permission for man to eat every living thing that moved, as well as plants, fruits, and crops.

With all the wonderful choices available to replenish and build a "brave new world," Noah chose to make alcohol!

Now come the questions

Why would this godly man need to plant a vineyard?
Did he take cuttings from a grapevine into the ark, to make sure of his supply after the flood, or did he salvage the plants from the ground once the waters were abated?
Did he already have a weakness for the "fruit of the vine," and so needed to maintain his habit?
Was there an emptiness or lack in his life, character, or marital relationship, which gave him a reason or an excuse to drink?

There are of course, no definite answers here; and certainly no pointed fingers either!

But this much is certain: if a man plants a vineyard, he will be used to drinking wine. But one glass of wine does not make a vineyard owner drunk!

According to the Bible, anyone who gets drunk is a drunkard! (*Nah.1:10, Pr.23:20-21*) And that's how Satan gets in!

*"Who hath **woe**? Who hath **sorrow**? Who hath **contentions**? Who hath **babbling**? Who hath **wounds without cause**? Who hath **redness of eyes**? They that tarry long at the wine; they that go to seek mixed wine ... At the last it **biteth** like a serpent, and **stingeth** like an adder ...They have beaten me, and I felt it not: when shall I awake? I will seek it yet again."* (From *Pr.23:29-35*)

Alcohol is one of the most powerful uncoverers of all time!

With only eight people on the planet (Noah, his wife, their three sons and daughters in law), the concentration of evil forces against them must have been incredible!

The sadness of God in judging man for his wickedness would surely stand in sharp contrast to the triumph and jubilation coming from the enemy's camp! In Satan's perverted mind, he had succeeded in destroying God's creation even sooner than expected. What a push over mankind was! Yet the battle was not completely over; for as long as any human lived, there would still be a threat from that "**seed of the woman**."

Noah was uncovered by his *own* drunkenness, but Satan was right there; and ready to encourage even more wickedness!

Naked, and in a drunken stupor, Noah was not aware of Ham's presence. When he awoke however, he "**Knew what his younger son had done unto him**." (*Gen.9:24*)

Before commenting on this situation, it might be helpful to look at a similar story (occurring much later) regarding Abraham's nephew Lot. Particularly after God destroyed the cities of Sodom and Gomorrah.

Lot had all but lost his testimony. At least two of his daughters had married Sodomites, who in turn treated his warnings with contempt. (*Gen.19:14*) Prior to its destruction, Lot needed to be "man handled" out of the city by angels. – He was in no hurry to leave! (*Gen.19:16*)

Having seen his wife turned into a "*pillar of salt*" (*Gen.19:26*) for looking back (longingly and disobediently) at her cursed, but beloved home; Lot took his two remaining daughters up into the hills and dwelt in a cave.

Afraid that there were no men left alive to give them children, the girls hatched a vile scheme to become pregnant by their father! (No doubt they were much influenced by their culture's incestuous and homosexual lifestyle.)

*"Come, let us **make** our father drink wine, and we will lie with him, that we may preserve seed of our father. And they **made** their father drink wine that night: and the first-born went in, and lay with her father, and **he perceived not when she lay down, nor when she arose**."* (see *Gen.19:30-38*)

The following night, the younger sister did exactly the same thing!

Lot's daughters had their way, and uncovered their father's nakedness by making him "blind drunk!"

What made it so easy for Satan to work there, was the fact that Lot had been steadily giving away "ground" to him whilst living in Sodom. (*1Cor.15:33*)

The result of this illicit union between father and daughters was that two sons were born, who would become fathers of the Moabite and Ammonite tribes. *Both* would become a curse and snare to Israel further down the road! (*Num.25:1-4, Judg.10:4*)

If we needed any more evidence regarding the negative effects of alcohol, remember that Jacob, who so loved Rachel, and was about to marry her (after 7 years of waiting), actually had to marry her sister Leah first. – Why? Because after a drinking feast the night before his wedding to Rachel, he slept with the wrong woman (Leah), and didn't know until the next morning!

(*Gen.29:15-30*)

Now the questions surrounding Noah's drunken state are these:

1. If Ham had entered Noah's tent, and accidentally seen his father naked and then simply left, how could Noah have known "*what his younger son had **done** unto him?*"
2. How was it possible for Noah to identify Ham immediately upon waking?
3. If there was nothing seriously wrong and inappropriate with Ham's actions, why would Noah place such a dreadful and lasting curse upon Ham's son, Canaan?
4. After Ham told his brothers, Shem and Japheth what had happened; why did they feel the need to walk backward into Noah's tent, and take such pains to cover his nakedness with a garment instead of just leaving him alone to "sleep it off?"
5. Why was homosexuality (along with idolatry) one of the most commonly practiced abominations among the Canaanites?

Satan is not satisfied with mere drunkenness. His interest lies in what that drunkenness can produce! In Noah's case, excessive drinking gave ground for violation and curse!

Clearly nothing has changed, but let's also remember that as Satan's time runs out, his anger, hatred, and destructive desires toward mankind will become even stronger! (*Rev.12:12*)

Jesus said, "*As it was in the days of NOAH, and LOT ... so shall it be also in the days of the Son of man.*" (*Luke17:26-30*) In other words, the characteristics of the "*last days*" would be **gluttony, drunkenness**, **homosexuality**, and **worldwide wickedness**! (If anyone needed proof of that, just turn on the TV!)

The Tower of Babel and beyond ...

After Noah, that "wheel" of sin would begin to turn faster and faster!

"*And the sons of Ham; Cush, and Mizraim, and Phut, and Canaan ... And Cush begat **Nimrod**: he began to be a **mighty one** in the earth ...a **mighty hunter before the Lord** ... And the beginning of his kingdom was **Babel** ... And Canaan begat Sidon his first-born, and Heth, and the Jebusite and the Amorite and the Girgashite and the Hivite ... and afterward were the families of the Canaanites spread abroad.*" (From *Gen.10:6-20*)

Ham, Cush, and then Nimrod: just three generations before man (led by Nimrod) began building the most evil city on earth! The meaning of Nimrod's name was a true indication of his character: "Let us revolt!" Whereas, *"Mighty hunter before the Lord,"* denotes him as a satanically driven hunter of men's souls in the very face of God! His exploits as a dictator and builder of Babel would attract God's attention in a way not seen since *Gen.6:5-7.*

The city and its tower was at that time, the most blatant expression of man's rebellion and disobedience. "Babel" means confusion, and is associated with the Hebrew word "Balal" meaning to mix, or confound. God had told Noah to *"Multiply and replenish* (fill) *the earth,"* (*Gen.9:1*) but by Genesis chapter 11 we read,

> *"And the whole earth was of one language, and of one speech. And it came to pass, as they journeyed from the east, that they found a plain in the land of Shinar; and **they dwelt there**. And they said one to another, Go to, let us **make brick**, and **burn them thoroughly**, And they had **brick for stone**, and **slime** (pitch or tar) had they for mortar. And they said, Go to, let us build us a city and a tower, **whose top may reach unto heaven; and let us make us a name, lest we be scattered** abroad upon the face of the whole earth."* (*Gen.11:1-4*)

Here the vanity, disobedience, and rebellion of man are manifested in three outstanding ways.

1. Refusing of spread out and replenish the earth as God had commanded, they chose to huddle together in one place and make a "name" for themselves.

2. Calling God a liar! God had said, *"The waters shall no more become a flood to destroy all flesh,"* (*Gen.9:15*) but they deliberately built a **waterproof** tower using baked bricks instead of porous rock, and pitch (tar) for mortar! (Can you read the mentality here? If they weren't intending evil, why would they be worried about another flood?)

3. Building a tower that was meant to *"reach unto heaven"* for at least three demonically inspired reasons. (The first already mentioned; in case God sent another flood!)
   The second to make the supremely arrogant statement that man was now at least equal with, and therefore capable of replacing God.
   The third as an occult monument to Satan who chose to place his *"seat"* or throne there, and would again try to use mankind's pathetic rebellion to renew his efforts to overthrow God! (Although *"Satan's seat"* has certainly moved around over the years, [*Rev.2:13*] we'll see later why he has never forsaken "Babylon!")

NOTE: *"Mystery Babylon," "Babylon the Great," "The Whore,"* and *"Mother of Harlots"* are all titles given in Scripture for the same One World religious system emanating from that original, malignant city! Although *Physical* Babylon means little or nothing to Satan today, part two of this book we will reveal why *spiritual* Babylon continues to have such an effect or hold on the entire unsaved world!

> *"And the Lord said, Behold, the people **is one**, and they have all **one language**; and this they begin to do: and now **nothing will be restrained from them, which they have imagined to do**. Go to, **let us go down**, and there confound their language, that they may not understand one another's speech. So the Lord **scattered them abroad** from thence upon the face of all the earth: and they left off to build the city."* (*Gen.11:6-8*)

Interestingly enough, no matter how high man builds his "Babel towers" – they're getting taller every day – God still has to "come down" to take a look! (*Gen.11:5*)

Man will never top God!

Taking advantage of the common language, Satan had gathered mankind together, and inspired them to build a colossal edifice for his glory. Doubtless he was still gloating over his masterful stroke of uncovering a whole civilization, and perhaps planning his next triumphant move; when suddenly ... God came down and spoiled it all!

Ah Satan, so smart, so proud, so *stupid*. When will he ever learn?

The enemy of mankind will never be allowed to go beyond the bounds of God's perfect plan and purpose for creation. The truth is –

SATAN STILL WORKS FOR GOD!

How he must loathe being told that! Of course, he should also be considered the world's number one "bottom feeder!" That's right! He has always done so much of the necessary dirty work, like "*sifting*," and separating the "*flesh from the spirit*;" the "*wheat from the chaff*."

(See *1Cor.5:1-5, Luke22:31*)

Despite many rumors to the contrary, he is only allowed to do this work in believers as God ordains; (see *Job 1and 2*) and guess what? It's *all* for our good! (*Rom.8:28*)

But I'm getting ahead of myself.

"*Let US go down*," indicates once again that Father, Son, and Holy Spirit are vitally and intimately concerned in every phase of history (His-story). Nothing escapes Their attention!

God puts an end to man's first unified rebellion simply by confounding their language, and causing them to do what they would never have done willingly: "*Replenish and fill the earth.*" I'm told that there are now over three thousand languages and dialects around the world, making it extremely difficult for us to "huddle" in one place. However, clever and determined people (with a lot of help from you know who) are doing their very best to overcome this barrier. Have you been to the United Nation's Headquarters lately? Speeches are simultaneously translated into the languages of all the delegates in a forlorn attempt to reverse the judgment of Babel, and bring the nations together!

This of course is nothing new; the enemy has for a long time been successfully manipulating Governments, and uniting world organizations like the U.N., until they are now quite literally "hell bent" on bringing in their "One World," or "New World Order!"

Take a quick look at the back of any dollar bill.

Left and right you will find the two sides of the "Great Seal of the United States."

On the left, (above the Egyptian pyramid) the Latin words, "Annuit Coeptis," meaning, "Announcing the birth," and underneath, "Novus Ordo Seclorum," or "New World Order." The date on the base of the pyramid in Roman numerals is 1776: the birth year of the Illuminati and American independence!

On the right, look for the words, "E Pluribus Unum" meaning, "One out of many."

This also is nothing new. The Seal was quietly introduced to Americans back in the "thirties," and perfectly timed with the "Great Depression," when all people really cared about was *earning* a dollar, and very little about what was printed on it!

It doesn't take a rocket scientist to figure out that the "Seal" is just one aspect of a well-orchestrated, worldwide plan to unify governments, religions, armies and financial institutions, thereby preparing the planet for Satan's last Hurrah: a "golden New Age" – courtesy of it's long awaited "Messiah," a.k.a. the Anti-Christ!

By the way, if you're asking, "What is an Egyptian pyramid (with the "Eye of Horus") doing on the American dollar bill?" The answer and much more will be found in chapters twenty-three and twenty-four!

All that needs be said at this point is that the whole hideous New-Age-New-World-order deception is nothing more than a giant demonic vacuum cleaner, constantly working to seduce, enslave, and ultimately destroy anyone foolish enough to be sucked in!

Running for cover!

As we continue our journey through the ancient world, it appears more and more obvious that the human race had no real answer to (nor any lasting measure of success against) the uncovering work of its ruthless foe.

We see Abraham's wrongful union with Hagar resulting in the birth of Ishmael: a wild man and forefather of the Arab nations. Nations that without contradiction would be made up of the most anti-Semitic people on earth! (See *Gen.16 and 21:9-21*) However, just as Satan will never succeed in overthrowing God, the Arab nations will never succeed in overthrowing God's natural people Israel! (No matter how hard they try!) Nor will they defeat God's *New* Covenant people who are the chosen among Jews *and* Gentiles, and have together become, *"The Israel of God,"* (*Gal.6:15-16*) or *"The Body of Christ – His Church!"* (See *Eph.1:10-23*, and *ch.2*)

Just one look at the devil's uncovering work involving Judah and Tamar; (*Gen.38*) the continual, sinful marriages between Israelites and pagans, (*1Kings11:1-3, Ez.9:1-2, Hos.5:7, Mal.2:11*) and we will see clearly that by now, the only true Jews are those described by Paul in his letter to the Romans.

"For he is not a Jew, which is one outwardly; neither is that circumcision, which is outward in the flesh: But he is a Jew, which is one inwardly; and circumcision is that of the heart, in the spirit, and not in the letter; whose praise is not of men, but of God." (*Rom.2:28-29*)

Paul is saying that natural circumcision (once a valid expression found exclusively in God's Old Covenant with Israel) has been replaced by inward spiritual circumcision of the heart!

This *true* separation from sin and the world is brought about by a new spiritual birth, and is now the only way into the New Covenant established by Christ's precious blood.

Making the believer an eternal member of the Kingdom of God, and a *true* Jew!

What an amazing and wonderful transformation the Grace of God wrought in that brother's life. **From bondage under law,** (*Gal.4.:25*) **to Liberty in the Holy Spirit!** (*2Cor.3:17*)

Paul threw off his boastful *"fig leaf"* coverings of religion, legalism, fleshly zeal and self-righteousness (counting them all *"dung"* *Phil.3:3-9*); and ran to the righteous covering of the Blood of Jesus: *"The Lamb of God which takes away the sin of the whole world!"*

NOTE: If we are praying for *"the peace of Jerusalem,"* (*Ps.122:6*) we must do so with the understanding that Israel's one and only hope for true and eternal peace will also be found by running to (acknowledging and receiving) the One and Only Savior, Jesus Christ!

Uncovered by prosperity!

As Satan increased his hold on the human race, it became evident that his main objective lay in corrupting and tormenting God's Old Testament people. (He already had the pagan nations, so corrupting them was nowhere near as much fun!) To lead the children of Israel astray, and to separate them from God (mostly through idolatry and perversions, *1Kings14:22-24*) must have been the devil's most pleasurable task! To weaken, humiliate, and ultimately destroy them had been his number one priority even before God brought them forth as a nation! (Remember this was still God's way of using Satan to "sift.")

As a young Christian, I had often wondered how Israel could possibly have fallen from such a high place of privilege and blessing in Egypt (thanks to God's Grace upon and through Joseph) to the humiliating depths of abject slavery and bondage!

> *"Now there arose a new king over Egypt, which knew not Joseph. And he said unto his people, Behold, the people of the children of Israel are **more and mightier** than we: come on, let us deal wisely* (shrewdly) *with them; lest they multiply, and it come to pass, that, when there falleth out any war, **they join also our enemies, and fight against us**, and so get them up out of the land."* (*Ex.1:8-10*)

Why should any Pharaoh feel remotely threatened by the people of God?
Why would he believe, that they would turn on the Egyptians, and "knife them in the back?"
I had read the book of Ezekiel several times over the years, but one day – there it was! (It pays to keep reading God's Word)

> *"Thus saith the Lord God; In the day when I chose Israel, and lifted up Mine hand unto the seed of the house of Jacob, and made Myself known to them **in the land of Egypt,** when I lifted Mine hand unto them, saying, I Am the Lord your God ... Then said I unto them, Cast ye away every man the **abominations of his eyes**, and **defile not yourselves with the idols of Egypt**: I Am the Lord your God. **But they rebelled against Me**, and would not hearken unto Me: they did not every man cast away the abominations of their eyes, neither did they forsake the idols of Egypt: then I said, **I will pour out My fury upon them**, to accomplish My anger against them **in the midst of the land of Egypt**."* (From *Ez.20:5-8*)

While in a blessed and prosperous state, the children of Israel ignored the warnings of the Lord. They grew "soft," and turned to the practices of the Egyptians (the unsaved); becoming more and more like them! An Egyptian could knife you in the back at any time, so why wouldn't these so-called people of God?

No wonder Pharaoh was afraid! No wonder the Israelites became his slaves: they were already serving his gods!

Take heed Church

The things that happened to them were written as, *"examples for our admonition* (warning), *upon whom the ends of the world are come!"* (*1Cor.10:11*) If we fail to hear and obey God's warnings today (*Come out from among them and be ye separate, saith the Lord, And touch not the unclean thing! (2Cor.6:17)* If we lose *our* spiritual edge through "prosperity," "easy believism," and other such comfortable (compromising) doctrines; we too will find ourselves going down in the *"midst of the land of Egypt"* (falling into the deceptions and darkness of this world), and losing our testimony and blessed position as the *"Light of the world, and a city set on a hill!"* (*Matt.5:14*)

"Be sober, be vigilant; because your adversary the devil, as a roaring lion, walketh about, seeking whom he may devour." (1Pet.5:8)

And be careful: when the church isn't being persecuted, she is often found persecuting herself! *(2Cor.12:20)*

Natural or spiritual?

I'd like to step back here for a moment and reinforce the truth concerning the new (spiritual) birth. Speaking to Nicodemus (a ruler of the Jews), Jesus made it clear to Israel (and to all mankind) that natural birth in no way qualifies a person to enter the Kingdom of Heaven!

"Verily, verily, (truly, truly) I say unto thee, except a man be born of water (natural birth) and of the Spirit (supernatural birth), he cannot enter the Kingdom of God. That which is born of the flesh is flesh; and that which is born of the (Holy) Spirit is spirit. Marvel not that I said unto thee, ye must be born again." (John3:5-7)

In the simplest of terms, anyone truly chosen of God, will have TWO birthdays. One natural, and one spiritual. One birth from their mother's womb; a second by God's regenerating Holy Spirit! This glorious New Covenant truth or substance is unmistakably foreshadowed in the Old Testament, and is also readily compared to the wonder of human birth.

Whilst in the "womb" of Egypt (type of the world), the Hebrew (type of believer) was in bondage and slavery (type of sin and death). We've already seen why!

Nevertheless, solely by God's Grace and Sovereign choice, He sent His *"Seed"* (His Word) by Moses, and commanded Pharaoh (type of Satan) to *"Let My people go!"*

As Pharaoh hardened his heart and refused, God sent "labor pains" upon Egypt in the form of plagues, which would grow more and more powerful until the time of Israel's "delivery!"

Before the final plague (death of first born Egyptian males), God's people were told to sacrifice a Passover Lamb (type of Christ), and strike its blood upon the doorposts of their houses. This was to cover them, and spare them from God's judgment. (Speaking of our salvation, and the true covering of Christ's Blood over our lives.) That night there arose a great cry throughout all Egypt,

"For there was not a house where there was not one dead." (Ex.12:30)

So it was that Pharaoh's son(s) came under judgment for the murder of God's first-born Hebrew son(s) who had been cast into the river Nile *(Ex.1:22)*. After that, Pharaoh couldn't wait to get rid of them! At last, Israel was free to go! But even as God's people made their way across Egypt to the shore of the Red sea, Pharaoh's heart was hardened yet again! This time he sent all his chariots, and a huge army after them. (Satan of course, hates anyone escaping from his kingdom, and does everything he can to get them back!)

Trapped by Pharaoh behind, and by the sea in front, the Israelites began complaining to Moses!

"This is all your fault!" (my translation) *"Were there so many graves in Egypt that you had to bring us out here to die? Leave us alone! Better to serve the Egyptians then die in the wilderness!" (Ex.14:11-12)* (Type of whining Christians!)

It was here that Moses uttered some of the greatest words ever recorded in Scripture.

"Fear ye not, stand still, and see the salvation of the Lord, which He will show to you this day: for the Egyptians whom ye have seen today, ye shall see them again no more for ever. The Lord shall fight for you, and ye shall hold your peace." (Ex.14:13-14)

Our Salvation is of the Lord! From start to finish! Only a fool would now dare to *"touch the Ark of God,"* and try (like "Uzzah") to give God a helping hand! (*2Sam.6:6-7*) Yet remarkably, Uzzah has untold numbers of descendants still guilty of this very crime! Some are known as "Arminians," but many more are recognized by their original name, *"Dead Works!"* (*Heb.6:1*)

Millions of these family members have been persuaded to spend their lives in Rome or Canterbury; and although there are a few differences in their religion, (the Pope being head of one family, and the reigning English monarch being head of the other) those differences are rapidly disappearing! This is due primarily to high level "religious dialogue," helped along by cozy little get togethers within an abominable organization known as the W.C.C. (World Council of Churches).

Now although the Word of God commands true believers to separate themselves from anyone bearing those names and addresses, (*2Cor.6:17, Rev.18:4*) it also commands us to reach out earnestly to any and all who are willing to hear the truth! Sadly, though many letters and invitations have been sent, only a few have chosen to reply. (*Matt.22:14*)

"For by Grace are ye saved through faith; and that not of yourselves: it is the gift of God: not of works, lest any man should boast." (Eph.2:8-9) "For by the works of the law, shall no flesh be justified." (Gal.2:16)

"So then it is not of him that willeth, nor of him that runneth, but of God that showeth mercy. For the Scripture saith unto Pharaoh, Even for this same purpose have I raised thee up, that I might show My power in (over) thee, and that My Name might be declared throughout the whole earth. Therefore hath He mercy on whom He will have mercy, and whom He will He hardeneth." (Rom.9:16-18)
"The Egyptians whom you have seen today, ye shall see them again no more for ever."

The Assurance of our salvation is sounded out, loud and clear! No matter how much the "chosen ones" whined and complained (sometimes we do), and wanted to return to Egypt (sometimes we try) … God never let them go back!

WE ARE OUT FOR GOOD!

If anyone (having been truly born again) doubts the absolute certainty of their salvation, then read and enjoy once more the wonderful confirmation of God's Eternal Word.

*"Blessed be the God and Father of our Lord Jesus Christ, who hath blessed us with **all** spiritual blessings in heavenly places **in** Christ: according as **He** (God) **hath chosen us in Him** (Christ) **before the foundation of the world**, that we should be **holy and without blame** before Him in love: **having predestinated us** unto the adoption of children by Jesus Christ to Himself, **according to the good pleasures of His will**, to the praise of the Glory of His Grace, wherein He hath **made us accepted** in the Beloved." (Eph.1:3-6)*

How could a person read that passage, and many others like it, (*Rom.8:28-39, 1John5:4-13 John5:24, 6:37-40,47*) without recognizing that God has taken care of every single detail: not just of our salvation, but of our whole lives! BEFORE CHRIST – TO CHRIST – IN CHRIST, and all the way to the very Throne of God in Heaven itself! (*Phil.1:6*)

Let me drive this home with a comparison.

Under the terms of the Old Covenant, God was saying, **I will, if you will!**

IF Israel (as a nation) would keep God's Commandments and obey His Statutes, then God would lift them up above all people. He would fight for them, provide for them, be faithful to them, prosper them, and cover them under the shadow of His Wings! (*Deut.28:1-14, Ps.91*)

When Israel failed to uphold *their* end of the covenant, God allowed them to be overwhelmed and punished by surrounding nations. (*Jdg.2:11-14*) These often repeated judgments (chastenings) upon Israel however were of little effect in bringing the nation to lasting repentance.

There would come a time when enough was enough! (*2Chr.36:14-16*)

Having found fault with the first covenant, (*Heb.8:7-10*) God's purpose was to create a brand new one! However, this New everlasting Covenant would be not be placed in the hands of fallen men with their inability to keep it; but would be limited exclusively to the Godhead of Father, Son and Holy Spirit! (*Heb.9:14, 13:20*)

IF Jesus (as a man) would keep God's commandments and obey His every statute – thereby totally fulfilling the law of righteousness (*Mt.3:15, 5:17*) – He would then be able to offer Himself "*without spot to God*" (*Heb.9:14*) as the perfect atoning Sacrifice for the sins of the whole world! God would then raise up His Son on high, and give Him a "*Name above every name!*"

(*Phil.2:9-10*)

With all this wonderfully fulfilled in His life, and on the cross of Calvary, the Blood of Jesus became the substance of the New Covenant, and God was able to do an amazing thing! He would begin to gather all those He had chosen "*Before the foundation of the world,*" and put them into this New Covenant (into Christ) without them having to "work" (continually trying and failing) to fulfill God's Righteousness themselves! (*Eph.1:4-12*)

The problem with every member of the "Dead Works" family is that they just cannot accept that man has nothing to do with this New Covenant: that it has all been done for us by God's Son! Salvation is by God's Grace alone, through the faith God has already given to those that are chosen in Christ! Under the terms of the New Covenant, God is in fact saying,

I will … you can't, and don't have to … "*It is finished!*" (*John19:30*)

"And Moses stretched out his hand over the sea; and the Lord caused the sea to go back by a strong east wind all that night, and made the sea dry land, and the waters were divided. And the children of Israel went into the midst of the sea upon the dry ground: and the waters were a wall unto them on their right hand, and on their left." (Ex.14:21-22)

Seeing Old Testament types and shadows fulfilled in our lives today can be a source of constant joy, and Israel's journey is certainly no exception. Before Israel could be delivered, the waters of the Red Sea had to part! (Before a baby is born into the world, the water must break, or part.)

Before a person can be "born again," he or she must be born of "*water and of the Spirit.*"

The Spirit of God parted (broke) the waters of the Red Sea, and the People of God were "birthed" as His chosen nation. The water that brought life to the people of God would bring death to the Egyptians who tried to follow! (See *1Cor.1:18*)

Only when supernaturally delivered by the mighty hand of God could the children of Israel be freed and brought forth out of the land of Egypt! In this present world, only that same mighty hand can free a man from the bondage of sin and death, and *"deliver him from the kingdom of darkness, ... into the Kingdom of His Dear Son!"* (*1Pet.2:9, Col.1:13*)

CHAPTER SEVEN

THE (NOT SO) GOOD, THE BAD, AND THE REALLY UGLY!

The Biblical account of Israel's natural and spiritual battles has taken up almost the entire volume of Old Testament Scripture (and more than a little of the New), but we can be certain that the rise and fall of Israel, followed by her inevitable and glorious "rising again" will one day be seen among God's greatest triumphs! (See *Zech.14*) More over, God would allow (and use) the nation's many failures to teach the Church some of her greatest lessons!

After all that God had done for His people, they were still not satisfied!

They complained at Marah because of the bitter water (look for a type of the cross which is hidden there. *Ex.15:22-26*)

In the "*wilderness of Sin*" they complained and wanted to return to Egypt in order to satisfy the flesh. (We already know the type there!) Be careful what you pray for – you might just get it!

God gave them quail (flesh) to eat until it came "*out of their nostrils; and they loathed it!*" (*Num.11:18-20*) Lusting after, and then fulfilling the desires of the flesh brought a plague upon the people, and still does! (See *Num.11:33, James 1:14-15*) Today a plague (even if not physical) still causes a lack of spiritual life in the believer, which may be harder to spot, but no less serious!

Always remember; in spite of inflation, the wages of sin is still death! (*Rom 6:23*)

When the people pitched their tents in Rephidim there was no water, so (naturally) they complained.

God commanded Moses to "*Smite the rock*" with his rod there in "*Horeb*" (Mt. Sinai), and as he did, water came forth for the people to drink! (*Ex.17:1-7*) What makes this so interesting is that when the people cried out for water again (this time in the "*wilderness of Zin*"), God's instructions were that Moses (with Aaron) should merely "*Speak to the rock*" to bring forth the water!

(Num.20:7-11)

It was there that Moses and Aaron made two devastating, and life-changing errors.

First: in an angry outburst Moses said to the people, "*Must we fetch you water out of this rock?*"

Second: Moses did not speak to the rock, but "*smote it twice*" with his rod instead!

Now although water came forth abundantly, God was not pleased, and said to the two men,

"Because ye believed me not, to sanctify Me in the eyes of the children of Israel, therefore ye shall not bring this congregation into the (promised) *land which I have given them."* (*Num.20:12*)

If you're anything like me, you've wondered why God would punish Moses and Aaron so severely for what at first glance seems like a minor infraction. Once again, I read those passages many times before the Holy Spirit opened my eyes. If you're still not sure why God was so angry, please consider this.

Moses presumed (perhaps not deliberately, but in the heat of the moment) to think that he and Aaron could bring water out of the rock. (Only God could do that!)

But secondly (here comes the crunch); that rock was a type of Christ! (*1Cor.10:4*)

It was God's will that Christ *"The Rock"* **be smitten once!** – One death for all time for our sin.

(*Heb.7:27, and 9:26*)

The next time "water" (now eternal life or salvation) was required, Moses (now mankind) was only to speak, and God would give it!

In striking the rock a second time, Moses and Aaron challenged God's eternal Word concerning the gift of salvation, which is received simply by asking with the voice of faith. – *That's* why it was so serious!

When the people were gathered together at Mt. Sinai to receive the Law of God, things got much, much worse.

"And when the people saw that Moses delayed to come down out of the mount, the people gathered together unto Aaron, and said unto him, Up, make us gods, which shall go before us; ...And all the people brake off the golden earrings which were in their ears, and brought them unto Aaron ...And he fashioned it with a graving tool, after he had made it a molten calf ...And Aaron built an altar before it ...and said, tomorrow is a feast to the Lord ...and the people sat down to eat and drink, and rose up to play." (From *Ex.32:1-6*)

Obviously it's one thing to get God's people out of Egypt, but quite another to get Egypt out of God's people! In view of how life-draining, de-humanizing, and humiliating slavery in Egypt really was, isn't it remarkable how quickly the people ran back there in their hearts!

What were the Israelites guilty of doing in Egypt? – Worshipping idols!

What was the most obvious idol to lead them back there? – A golden calf!

****

At the age of twenty-one (some eleven years before being saved), I made a very brief visit to India. After landing in Bombay, an airline bus took us to stay in one of the city's "better" hotels until our connecting flight arrived the following morning.

As we approached the hotel, the driver began making short but regular stops so that large, free-roaming, and extremely healthy looking cows could walk safely across the main highway!

Each cow had what looked like a golden bell around its neck, and when one of the passengers asked the driver to explain, he answered proudly, "Cows are sacred to Hindus, and have right of way in any situation! They are worshipped, and even their dung and urine is holy. It is eaten and drunk to bring favor and blessing, and is also smeared over bodies to protect the wearers from evil spirits. The bells sound out to warn any and all, especially the lowest caste (class) to make way for the passing animals."

While trying to comprehend the incomprehensible, I saw numbers of pathetic, emaciated and almost naked Indian men lying on straw mats along the side of the road begging. I was told that some had deliberately made themselves blind in order to beg more successfully! Most were diseased and in a dreadful condition. It was truly a pitiful sight to see well-fed and pampered cows "lording" it over these desperate people! I also learned that this horrifying spectacle was by no means limited to Bombay, but was common across the entire country!

After spending an hour or so in my hotel room (the air conditioner was a block of ice in front of a fan!) I decided to take a short walk. Within minutes I found myself on the outskirts of a shanty town (most of the houses were nothing more than sheds), and surrounded by a group of begging children. The only Indian money in my wallet was a five-rupee note (at that time worth less than one U.S. cent), so I offered it to a little girl who by now was holding on to my sleeve. As she eagerly took hold of the note, another hand suddenly flashed out from behind me and grabbed the almost worthless piece of paper!

As I let go, an incredibly old-looking woman (the owner of the other hand), and the young child began a very careful "tug-of-war" so as not to damage this amazing windfall! Within moments it seemed that the whole village had gathered together in noisy support of one or the other, and as the situation grew more and more intense, I became completely overwhelmed, and fled!

My only purpose in presenting this story is to reveal first hand the kinds of hardship, poverty, and spiritual blindness infesting this and other nations given over to such gross idolatry!

Shortly after my visit, the Beatles went to India, and entered into a "spiritual" relationship with one of the countless gurus or "holy men" found there. In turn, they encouraged multitudes of people around the world to look for "light" in one of the darkest countries on earth!

That was then, but praise God for all He's doing in that land now!

******

Having made the "molten calf," Aaron announced, "*a feast to the Lord.*" – Nice try Aaron!

Satan had things going just the way he wanted. Take any idol (religious icon, relic, or compromise from Egypt), offer it up in the name of worshipping God, and bingo, you have a "feast" to the devil!

Now there's an insult to God he could really enjoy! Let's see what else could he get away with.

"*And the people sat down to **eat** and **drink**, and rose up **to play**.*" (*Ex.32:6*)

Definitely not your average family lunch followed by horse-shoes in the garden! No, this meal had Satan's trademark all over it!

Gluttony, drunkenness, followed by pagan style singing and dancing (sexual orgies, and perversions.) What a great "brew" to wipe out the people of God!

"*And when Moses saw that the people were **naked**; for Aaron had made them **naked unto the shame among their enemies** ...*" (*Ex.32:25*)

As we've seen many times already, to uncover, shame and ultimately destroy God's people has been the enemy's favorite and most consistent work. As we dig deeper into this sorry tale, we will find that it was invariably the "*mixed multitude*" (*Ex.12:38, Num.11:4, Ps.106:35-39*) that caused Israel to lust after the things of Egypt (the world); so that once again the Scripture is fulfilled,

"*Be not deceived: evil communications* (company) *corrupt good manners.*" (Habits or lifestyle)

(*1Cor.15:33*)

Lamech himself could not have offered a more pathetic excuse than Aaron did for the whole molten-calf-mess! For Aaron had said to the people,

*"Whosoever hath any gold, let them break it off. So they gave it me: **then I cast it into the fire, and there came out this calf.**"* (*Ex.32:24*)

God has heard *all* the excuses for sin, *"There is no new thing under the sun."* (*Ecc.1:9*)

FOR SIN, OR AGAINST IT?

Only the fervent intercession of Moses prevented God from destroying the whole nation right there and then!. (*vs.11-14*) But in spite of the Lord's mercy overall, His righteous hand would still fall.

*"Then Moses stood in the gate of the camp, and said, Who is on the Lord's side? Let him come unto me. And all the son's of Levi gathered themselves together unto him. And he said unto them, Thus saith the Lord God of Israel, put every man his **sword** by his side, and go in and out from gate to gate throughout the camp, and **slay** every man his **brother**, and every man his **companion**, and every man his **neighbor**. And the children of Levi did according to the word of Moses: and there fell of the people that day **about three thousand men.**"* (*Ex.32:26-28*)

It must have been incredibly hard for the Levites to take swords and destroy their nearest and dearest, even though they were guilty of such gross sins. Yet spiritually, this is exactly what God is saying to His people today!

The sins or demonic influences that are "nearest and dearest" to us are surely the most difficult to eliminate from our lives! These are the *"brothers, companions and neighbors"* who will bring us down unless we are prepared to be ruthless! Our "sword" is the Word of God, but Remember, "friends" must first be seen as enemies before we can hope to be delivered! The Levites were shown a *physical* revelation of this truth, and responded in obedience. How much more should we today?

They might have said, "Couldn't we kill some of those further away on the outskirts of the camp that don't mean as much to us?"(Surely that would have been a whole lot easier.) But they didn't!

They dealt with those who were "up close and personal." Always the harder choice!

When facing these issues today, the question, *"Who is on the Lord's side?"* simply means, where do we stand regarding sin and demonic activity? Time is running out Church, so let's stop playing games! How can we help others, if we ourselves remain in bondage to sin and willful disobedience?

Jesus said,

"He that is not with Me is against Me; and he that gathereth not with Me scattereth abroad."
(*Matt.12:30*)

Willful sins, walking in the flesh, and demonic bondage *"scatter;"* and are all *"against Christ!"*
No Christian should be caught living with *those* "brothers!"

The price of rebellion was twofold,

"And Moses took the calf which they had made, and burnt it in the fire, and ground it to powder, and strawed it upon the water, and made the children of Israel drink of it." (*Ex.32:20*)

The sins that not long ago had tasted so sweet would now become bitter and humiliating as they were forced to drink and literally reap what they had sown!

"Bread of deceit is sweet to a man; but afterward his mouth shall be filled with gravel." (*Prov.20:17*)

In spite of the severity there (and elsewhere) in dealing righteously with His old testament people, God still shows us those situations as precious types and shadows if we are willing to look.

*"But we see Jesus, who was made a little lower than the angels for the suffering of death, crowned with glory and honor; **that He** by the grace of God **should taste death for every man.**"* (*Heb.2:9*)

To the everlasting glory of God, the sins of the whole world were laid upon the Lord Jesus Christ, God's Son, Who drank the bitterest cup of all and,

*"Who His own self bare our sins in **His own body** on the tree!"* (*1Pet.2:24*)

Because of Him, the saved will not "drink" of their sins in eternal judgment! Thank you Jesus!

Under the Law, *"There fell of the people that day **about three thousand men.**"* (*Ex.32:28*)
But under Grace, *"When the day of* Pentecost was *fully come,"* about three thousand souls were saved! (*Acts2:1*and *41*)
How our Father loves to speak of this blessedness,
    "But if ye be led of the Spirit, ye are not under the law." (*Gal.5:18*)

"Wherefore then serveth the law? It was added because of transgressions (sins), ***till the Seed*** (Jesus) ***should come*** *to whom the promise was made. (Gal.3:19)*

*"Stand fast therefore in the **liberty** (freedom from sin and law) wherewith Christ hath made us free, and **be not entangled again** in the **yoke of bondage**."* (The captivity of sin and legalism. *Gal.5:1*)

*"For **Christ is the end of the law** for righteousness to every one **that believeth**."* (*Rom.10:4*)

****

From this high-light of uncovering Israel with a lowly cow, Satan slithered on through history weaving his deceptive cords around as many as would open the door to him.
The Scriptural record of his work contains a long and sobering list: may the following few examples continue to warn, humble, and above all – keep us on guard!

Never forget: Satan works only when God allows!

Miriam (Moses' sister) and Aaron criticized their brother, then rose up against his God given authority. For this Miriam would face the shame of leprosy (type of revealed sin), and be shut out of the camp (ostracized or dis-fellowshipped) for seven days. (*Num.12*) (Criticism always keeps us from God's presence.)

Korah, Dathan and Abiram rose up against Moses and Aaron, and challenged their positions of leadership. God made His choice and all those in the rebellion died! (*Num.16:1-35*) Many churches today have been divided, or have even "died" (ceased) for exactly the same thing!

When the people complained that Moses and Aaron had killed those men, the Lord smote nearly fifteen-thousand more with a plague! (vs. *41-50*) "*It is a fearful thing to fall into the hands of the Living God.*" (*Heb.10:31*)

Samson's life (*Judg.13-16*) is a tragic type of the unstable strengths and weaknesses of believers.

Evidently it was not his long hair that made Samson so incredibly strong, for there were many who entered into the covenant of separation as "Nazarites," and did not cut their hair. (*Numbers 6:1-8*) There is no record of them possessing such strength.

Who gave Samson his phenomenal power? The Holy Spirit of course! (*Judg.15:14*)

It was He who enabled the man to fulfill God's purpose, and all by God's sovereign choice! Samson's uncut hair symbolized an unbroken covenant, or a total commitment to God.

It was through consistent disobedience, impurity (touching a carcass; attending a drinking feast etc.), sexual lust (marrying a Philistine; visiting a prostitute; living with Delilah) that the covenant was finally broken!

His hair was cut by the enemy, and he became, "**As weak as any other man.**" (Judg.*16:17*)

As Christians, we too are in a "Covenant of separation," (*John15:19, Heb.8:6*) and must always rely on the only true strength we have – "*Christ in us*" by the power of His Holy Spirit!

(*Phil.4:13, Zec.4:6*)

In the flesh we become "*as weak as any other* (unsaved) *man.*"

Lose our testimony: lose our strength!

For me, the most heartbreaking moment of Sampson's entire life is described in just ten poignant words.

"**He wist** (knew) **not that the Lord was departed from him.**" (*16:20*)

Thank God, in Jesus Christ, there can *never* be a broken covenant!

Thank God Jesus said, "*Lo, I am with you alway, even unto the end of the world.*" (*Matt.28:20*) Thank God, "*He will never leave us, nor forsake us.*" (*Heb.13:5*)

But Sampson paid a dreadful price for his transgressions (and so can we!) *Judges 16: 21* reads,

"*The Philistines* (type of demons) *took him, and **put out his eyes** (type of lost spiritual vision), and **brought him down to Gaza** (type of fall from Grace), and **bound him with fetters of brass** (type of demonic bondage through sin), and he did grind in the prison house.*" (Type of Christian held captive by the world, or a life squandered on fleshly, carnal activities, i.e. works of "*wood, hay, and stubble.*")

It's easy to see why Samson has been called, the "prodigal son" of the Old Testament!

By the Grace of God, Samson's repentance was marked by the re-growth of his hair (renewal and restoration), but most importantly, by the sincere cry of his heart!

"*O Lord God, **remember me**, I pray Thee, and **strengthen me**, I pray Thee, only this once, O God, that I may be at once avenged of the Philistines for my two eyes.*" (*16:22-28, Luke 23:42*)

Wonder of wonders! God renewed His covenant with Samson; gave him back his strength, and in the end, allowed him the privilege of becoming an altogether different, and totally magnificent type!

With his hands on two central pillars supporting the temple of the Philistine god Dagon, Samson, *"Bowed himself with all his might; and the house fell upon the lords, and upon all the people that were therein. (About three thousand men and women.) **So the dead which he slew at his death were more than they which he slew in his life**."* (29-30)

(We'll be rejoicing in the fulfillment of that scripture, later in the book!)

Despite Samson's brave farewell, the book of Judges closes with the sad chronicle of Israel's descent into an abyss of sin, degradation and death. From the mockery of Micah's idolatry (an expose of religious men for sale to the highest bidder) to the most abominable and disgusting acts ever recorded in Scripture. (On which I respectfully decline to comment, except to say that in the reading of those last chapters, you will discover the very essence of Satan; his unspeakably vile character, and his absolute loathing of the human race!)

But that was just the beginning ...

*"The thing that hath been, it is that which **shall be**; and that which is done is that which **shall be done**: and there is no new thing under the sun."* (*Eccl.1:9*)

In recent history, monstrous individuals like Mao, Stalin, Hitler, and, closer to home, Manson, Dahmer, Bundy, etc., have all been used by Satan to make *Judges 19* look positively tame!

And (sorry Reconstructionists) – **it's going to get worse!**

In retrospect however, it appears that the most complete and honest summary of this disastrous, yet profoundly helpful book is recorded in the very last verse. *"In those days there was no king in Israel: every man did that which was right in his own eyes."* (*Judg.21:25*)

Could we find a better verse to describe the spirit of our own rebellious age?

Look back at Michal, who despised her husband David for *"leaping and dancing before the Lord."* (A joyful expression of praise and thanksgiving.) As a direct result of her attitude, Michal was barren (fruitless) for the rest of her life! (*2Sam.6:16-23*)

Look now at many religious institutions and their ministers, who also *"despise David in their hearts."* Hear them insisting, "No dancing, clapping, or Hallelujah-ing in *this* church!" Truly, Michal would be at home in any one of them!

Vashti the queen, rebelled, and disobeyed the king's command to appear before the court. She was put off the throne, and replaced by Esther. (Types here of Vashti as Old Testament Israel, and Esther as the new bride, or the *"Israel of God."Esth.1-2, Gal.6:16*)

Disobedience will always prevent us from *"reigning in life by one, Christ Jesus."* (*Rom.5:17*) Without repentance, Christians can certainly lose their "throne," i.e., the privilege of place, service, responsibility, or ministry. As well as the blessing of knowing His best for their lives!

There is no substitute for obedience.

Samuel told King Saul, (who also lost his throne) *"Hath the Lord as great delight in burnt offerings and sacrifices, as in obeying the voice of the Lord? Behold, to obey is better than sacrifice, and to hearken than the fat of rams. **For rebellion is as the sin of witchcraft, and stubbornness is as iniquity and idolatry.** Because thou hast rejected the Word of the Lord, He hath also rejected thee from being King."* (*1Sam.15:22-23*)

Some of the greatest examples of failure and recovery are found throughout the life of King David. Under Satan's influence, and contrary to the Word of God, (*Deut.17:17*) David married several women. This act of disobedience came to full bloom in the life of his son Solomon, who would eventually take seven hundred wives, and three hundred concubines! (*1Kings11:1-8*)

These "*strange* (pagan) *women*" turned Solomon's heart away from the Lord by persuading him to build "*shrines*" (places of occult worship) for their gods; which in turn led the people of Israel into the realm of darkness and idolatry. (Satan loves the ripple effect of one sin leading to another)

David obviously failed to discipline his sons (*1Kings1:5*): as a result, both Adonijah and Absalom rose up in rebellion against him, and Amnon committed a grievous sin against his own half sister, Tamar. All these "ripple effect" events ended in sorrow and death.

At a time when "*Kings go forth to battle*," David remained behind in Jerusalem.

With "idle time" on his hands (you know the proverb), he took a stroll on the palace roof and (surprise, surprise) saw a beautiful woman "*washing herself.*" (It all started with looking ... remember *Gen.3:6?*) Looking with lust is sin! (*Matt.5:28*) The sin that followed looking was adultery: the sin that followed adultery was murder! (See all of *2Sam.11*)

Now although God forgave him (David did not die), the illegitimate child would still be taken, and for the rest of his life there would be wars against his kingdom, and strife within his own house! It's clear that *all* wars and strife come from walking in the flesh, i.e. "*the works of the flesh*," i.e. selfishness, i.e. SIN! (*Gal.5:19-21*)

For the King of Israel, his sin with Bath-sheba culminated in personal shame and defeat. It also led to blasphemy, gloating and cursing from his enemies; the (temporary) loss of his throne, and Absalom fornicating openly with David's concubines on the roof of the palace where it all began! (See *2Sam.12 and15*) ... Talk about "ripples!"

Later on, when his kingdom was established (see *1Chr.21*), David was "*moved by Satan to number Israel.*" (A census of pride.) It was wrong because God did not order it!

The modern version of David's sin goes something like this. "Wow, God is really blessing; just how many do I have in my congregation these days? Let's have everyone fill out a card."

Of course it may be more subtle than that, but the principle is very much the same!

Well, that prideful trip of David's became very costly. God gave him three choices. Three years of famine, three months of being destroyed by enemies, or three days of, "*The Sword of the Lord, even the pestilence.*" (Plague) David chose to, "*Fall into the hand of the Lord.*" (Wise choice, because man doesn't know when to stop!)

"*So the Lord sent pestilence upon Israel: and there fell of Israel seventy thousand men.*"
(*1Chr.21:14*)

David was guilty, so why did the Lord smite the men of Israel and not him?

Because God deemed Israel guilty as well!

"*For all have sinned and come short of the Glory of God.*" (*Rom.3:23*) "*Let God be true, but every man a liar ...*" (*Rom.3:4*)

David was forgiven because (by God's Grace alone) he had a heart after God. He was quick to repent, and took responsibility for his actions (unlike Saul, and so many others who blame everyone but themselves!) God spared David time and time again because he humbled himself and acknowledged his sins with Godly sorrow. Of course, that doesn't mean we should do what David did just because (by the same Grace) we can also be forgiven!

THERE WILL NEVER BE A LICENCE (reason or excuse) TO SIN!

I'd like to close this chapter, with a brief look at what may well be the most controversial example of Satan's work in the entire Bible. The sufferings of Job!

Countess sermons and books have been written seeking to explain the difficulties and apparent contradictions of this often misunderstood book. Titles such as, "Why do bad things happen to good people?" and, "Why do the righteous suffer?" often prove there is little understanding of the book's bottom line...

NO ONE IS GOOD BUT GOD! (*Mk 10:18*)

Chapter one presents Job as,
"A ***perfect*** *man and* ***upright****, and one that feared God, and eschewed* (shunned or avoided) *evil.*"
"*Perfect*" as in sincere: "*upright*" as in just, but certainly not without sin as we shall see.

Here was a man of great substance, with a large and loving family (for whom he interceded on a regular basis), who was also protected and blessed by God. Not a bad start, but – "*There came a day when the sons of God* (angels) *came to present themselves before the Lord, and* ***Satan came also among them****. And the Lord said unto Satan, Whence comest thou? Then Satan answered the Lord, and said, From going* ***to and fro in the earth****, and from* ***walking up and down in it.****"* (*1:6-7*)

Two "gems" are given here which will be explored more fully in part two, but from these verses we know that,
1 Satan still had access to the Throne of God.
2 The earth was very much under his control. (Bearing in mind he still works for God!)

God does not argue with the devil's boastful claim (neither did God the Son! *Matt.4:8-10*), but mentions Job as someone who has remained faithful to Him, and as one not directly or willingly under Satan's influence.
God actually praises Job in front of His arch-enemy!
"*There is none like him in the earth.*" (*v.8*)
To Satan, this was nothing less than "red rag to a bull;" for God would say nothing better of any man until Jesus!
"*This is My Beloved Son, in Whom I Am well pleased.*" (*Matt.4:17, Luke3:22*)
In view of what happened to Job, may we all in "awesome wonder" behold the sufferings that Jesus would one day endure for our sakes? (Worthy, worthy, worthy is the Lamb!)

Job's testing comes as the result of a satanic challenge, so no wonder people have a problem with it! Satan maintained that the only reason Job was faithful, was because God had put a "*hedge*" (wall) of protection around him, and blessed him in everything he had.
Satan went on to say to God, "*But put forth* ***Thine hand*** *now, and touch all that he hath, and he will curse Thee to Thy Face.*" (*v.11*)
The Lord replied, "*Behold, all that he hath is in* ***thy power****; only upon himself put not forth thine hand.*" (*v.12*)
There can be no doubt that Satan was allowed to bring severe trials or testings upon Job, but God always remained in complete control, and drew a clear line beyond which the devil would not be permitted to go!

ROUND ONE *(1:13-19)*

The devastating loss of his children by a *"great wind."* (Remember the "storm on the lake" and who brought the wind?) *"The fire of God"* (now we know which "god") destroyed what was left of his livestock after the Sabeans had plundered and killed his servants.

Although naturally overwhelmed and probably very confused, Job continued to walk in obedience and gave God the glory. *(vs. 20-22)*

ROUND TWO *(ch. 2)*

Realizing that Job is not about to *"curse in the Face of God"* *(1:11)*, Satan seeks and receives permission to take it up a notch.

*"And Satan answered the Lord, and said, Skin for skin, yea **all that a man hath will he give for his life.** (The devil knows a thing or two about the fallen nature.) But put forth Thine hand now, and touch his bone and his flesh, and he will curse Thee to Thy face. And the Lord said unto Satan, Behold, he is in thine hand; **but save his life.** So went Satan forth from the presence of the Lord, and smote Job with sore boils from the sole of his foot unto his crown. And he took a potsherd to scrape himself withal; and he sat down among the ashes."* (2:4:8)

To bring home how things actually work in the spiritual realm, (even to this day) it's vital to look at chapter 2 and verse 3. Not only does God allow Satan to act against believers, He takes responsibility for those acts!

"Although thou movedst Me against him, to destroy him without cause."

This is why Paul can write with absolute confidence,

*"And we know that all things work together for good **to them that love God,** (not for everyone!) **to them who are the called** according to His purpose."* *(Rom. 8:28)*

Don't sit down among the ashes!

God will only allow what in the end becomes the very best for us; so there is never a reason to complain, or be in despair, or run away from our trials and circumstances.

Again it is written, *"**In everything give thanks,** for this is the will of God in Christ Jesus concerning you."* *(1Thess.5:18, Eph.5:20)*

We are *over* our circumstances in Christ, not under them as those without hope! *(1Thess.4:13-14)*

Many believers have been through as much as Job, (and some even more) but from testimonies such as those found in "Fox's Book of Martyrs," great numbers went home to the Lord joyfully (in spite of horrible deaths) with songs of praise and thanksgiving!

HOLD ON CHRISTIAN: THE BEST IS ALWAYS YET TO COME!

If Satan gets to work on Job, it could only be because God knew there was a work to be done!

By the way, there are times when God tells a man to listen to his wife, *(Gen.21:12)* but this certainly wasn't one of them!

*"Then said his wife unto him, Dost thou still retain thine integrity? **Curse God and die.**"(2:9)*

Satan speaks through the woman in a desperate attempt to make Job *"curse God to His face."*

(The devil would love it if *all* believers did just that!)

Job rebukes his wife *(2:10)* and accepts what he thinks is God dealing directly with him.

NOTE: Did you know that the word "devil" is found nowhere in the Old Testament?

It seems from men's reactions, he was as good at hiding his identity then as he is now!

In spite of everything, and without nearly as much revelation as we have today, Job remained faithful. However, as time went on, Satan started to wear him down, and he began to defend himself in terms of his own goodness. (see *ch.13*) (Of course, the company of Job's three "wonderful friends" didn't exactly help!)

The crunch comes in *verse 15*.

"Though He slay me, yet will I trust in Him ..."

Having read that much, the contributing editors in my King James Study Bible made the following comment.

"This verse, expresses the unquenchable faith of one who lives by faith, not by sight. Even when it appears that God Himself has turned against Job, he will still trust in God."

At that moment, they closed the Book (so to speak), and seemingly walked away; as if the second half of the verse didn't exist!

"... but I will maintain mine own ways before Him."

Yes, we may trust God; yes, we may be born again; yes, we may go to fellowship with the other saints; yes, we may be on our way to Heaven. BUT! if we continue to *"maintain our own ways"* before Him, we are simply maintaining *"Wood, Hay and Stubble."*

God allowed Job to see his sin, and be truly broken (*42:1-6*) before delivering him from that subtle, but awful root of self-righteousness which every one of us possesses!

"Maintaining our own ways" is guaranteed to hinder the Holy Spirit's work in our lives. "Closing the book" or avoiding the whole counsel of God's Word may rob us of Job's "double blessing," (*42:10-17*) and leave us standing before the *"Judgment Seat of Christ"* both naked and ashamed! (See *Rom.14:10, 2Cor.5:3, 1John2:28, Rev.3:18*) – God forbid!

The Word of God is able to ***"transform us by the renewing of our minds."*** Jesus is the ***"Open Door,"*** and the ***"Only Way"*** to the Father in heaven. The Holy Spirit is willing to ***"lead us, and guide us into all truth."***

So in the glorious light of all that –

HOW FAR ARE WE WILLING TO GO?

"Brethren, I count not myself to have apprehended: but this one thing I do, forgetting those things which are behind, and reaching forth unto those things which are before, I press on toward the mark for the prize of the high calling of God in Christ Jesus." (Phil.3:13-14)

*"Looking unto Jesus the Author and Finisher of our faith, who for the joy that was set before Him endured the cross, despising the shame, and is set down at the right hand of the throne of God. For **consider Him** that endured such contradiction of sinners against Himself, lest ye be wearied and faint in your minds." (Heb.12:2-3)*

"For as many as are led by the Spirit of God, they are the sons of God ... And if children, then heirs of God, and joint heirs with Christ; if so be that we suffer with Him, that we may be also

glorified together. For I reckon that the sufferings of this present time are not to be compared with the glory which shall be revealed in us." (From *Rom.8:14-18*)

CHAPTER EIGHT

GOD'S MYSTERIOUS MASTERPIECE

Over the years, Satan had worked for, and brought about (God ruled over, and allowed) the many defeats and failures of God's people. But to see the whole nation devastated by pagan conquerors and then removed to foreign lands would surely be one of the devil's proudest moments: not to mention the glorious possibility of Israel's total destruction!

First the "Northern tribes" carried away to Assyria, (see the whole of *2Kings17*) and later the "Southern tribes," Judah and Benjamin carried away to Babylon where they would remain for seventy years! (see *2Kings 24 and 25*) Satan must have been ecstatic!

In truth it was only a matter of time before the prophecies of God's men such as Moses, (*Deut.28;36*) Jeremiah, (*Jer.22;24-25*) Hosea, (*Hos.9:3*) and Amos (see the whole book!) would be fulfilled!

"Moreover all the chief of the priests, and the people, transgressed very much after all the abominations of the heathen; and polluted the House of the Lord which He had hallowed in Jerusalem. And the Lord God of their fathers sent to them by His messengers, rising up betimes (early and often) *and sending; because He had compassion on His people, and on His dwelling place; but they mocked the messengers of God and despised His words, and misused His prophets, until the wrath of the Lord arose against His people,* **till there was no remedy**."

(2Chr.36:14-16)

The Land of Israel was so infested with idolatry and pagan practices, that God finally decided put His "adulterous wife" away for a season in order to chasten her for her sins! (*Eze.16:15-43*)

Yet, in spite of His anger, God's Heart still yearned for His people.

"Yea, I have loved thee with an everlasting love: therefore with loving kindness have I drawn thee … And there is hope in thine end, saith the Lord, that thy children shall come again to their own border." (*Jer.31:3,17*)

God's purpose now was to gradually prepare the nation of Israel (and eventually the whole world) for the most astonishing event that would ever occur on planet earth!

(True to form, Satan's *futile* plan would be to prevent God's *eternal* plan from being realized!)

Once again, it's essential to remind ourselves, that the number one reason for the devil's relentless war upon God's Old Testament people was to destroy the "*Seed of the woman*" who would one day "***bruise his head.***" (*Gen.3:15*) To stop that "Seed" from ever being born, Satan would settle for nothing less than the total destruction of the entire Jewish race!

For example: in the book of Esther, the Holy Spirit reveals Haman as a type of Satan bent on annihilating every Jew in the kingdom of Ahasuerus (*Est.3:1-6*) simply because Mordecai would not bow the knee to him!

After the seventy years of captivity in Babylon, the Israelites returned to their land, and began the slow and painful process of rebuilding the nation. (Seen in the books of Ezra, and Nehemiah)

Although idolatry continued to manifest itself among the people (old "friends" are never easy to give up!), it would never again reach the level of obscenity found during the reigns of kings like Ahab and Manasseh. Things in Israel were certainly changing; and soon would never be the same again!

God at work in Jacob,
The Potter with the clay,
In His Hands to mould him,
For a glorious brand-new day!

You must know that when a master craftsman is engaged in creating a monumental work of art, there is often no fanfare; no media coverage; and therefore from the public's point of view, not the slightest awareness of the masterpiece being brought forth. So it was with God!

Between the final words of the Old Testament –

"Behold, I will send you Elijah the prophet before the coming of the great and dreadful day of the Lord: and he shall turn the heart of the fathers to the children, and the heart of the children to their fathers, lest I come and smite the earth with a curse." (*Mal.4:5-6*) – and that glorious new day when His Masterpiece would be revealed …

there was silence!

For some four hundred years God did not speak an inspired Word through prophet, priest, or king, but during this "gap" between the Old Covenant and New … Satan was extremely busy!

NOTE: For those interested in historic details of this period, there are many accounts worthy of study, but although the Ptolemies, Seleucids, Maccabees, Hasmoneans, Essenes etc., provide colorful background regarding the ongoing political and religious struggles of Israel, I have chosen to stay with the overview of Scripture revealed in the vision of Daniel (written here in shortened form) from the time of the Babylonian captivity to the distant crushing weight of Roman occupation, and the actual unfolding of God's mystery!

*"Daniel spake and said, I saw in my vision by night, and, behold, the four winds of Heaven strove upon the great sea. (Mediterranean) And four great beasts came up from the sea, diverse one from another. The first was like a **LION**, (Babylon) … And behold another beast, a second, like to a **BEAR**. (Medo-Persia) … After this I beheld, and lo another, like a **LEOPARD**. (Greece) … After this I saw in the night visions, and behold a **FOURTH BEAST**, (Rome) dreadful and terrible, and strong exceedingly; and it had great iron teeth: it devoured and brake in pieces, and stamped the residue with the feet of it: and it was diverse from all the beasts that were before it; and it had ten horns."* (From *Dan.7:2-7*)

Babylon, Persia, Greece, and Rome were (in that order) all conquerors of the ancient world (including Israel), and would become major influences on God's people. Not so much as a result of military domination (God gave Satan permission to punish Israel, *not* to utterly destroy her), but due to the cultural, philosophical, and spiritual pollutions that accompanied each world power. None more so than Greece!

When Alexander (I refuse to call *any* human being "great") conquered Persia around 333 B.C., he traveled through Palestine, and brought with him the "great" curse of Hellenism! (Israel was losing her identity even then; for the word Palestine comes from the same root as the word Philistine!)

Any description of the Hellenistic culture would have to include, "The devotion to, or imitation of ancient Greek thought, customs, or styles." Also; "Pagan joy, freedom, and love of life in contrast with the morality and Monotheism of the Old Testament." In other words, "anything goes!" Just think; a pagan feast *"unto the Lord"* every day, with your very own "personalized golden calf!" Thank you Alexander!

Did God's people buy it? Of course they did! The Pantheon in Athens contained the statues of gods from all the earliest Greek cultures, so people could literally worship what ever they wanted! "Something for everyone!" (Proving once again that there's nothing new about the New Age Movement!) Hellenism also includes astrology and divination, which seek to gain knowledge or learn the future from the stars or gods. And Animism (nature worship), with its belief that all natural objects in the universe have souls. (The Greek word "anima" meaning mind or soul.)

The multitude of Greek gods (male and female) became known as "Olympians." (Did you know that these "gods" are now celebrated and venerated every four years in little gatherings called the Olympic Games?) The gods' supernatural powers however, were restricted by a concept of fate known as "Moira," or the "relentless force of destiny"(a kind of Greek karma). All these ancient heathen practices (and many more) are contained within the N.A.M., so we have knowledge of where the world has been, and more importantly, where it's going!

NOTE: Such was the seductive, demonic influence of ancient Greece, that today practically the whole world is affected by it – especially western civilization. From our language to the buildings we erect: from entertainment to government; from science to philosophy; from birth even to the grave.

The stage is set!

Knowing the hearts of His people would become harder and harder due to pagan influence, God spoke these piercing words through the prophet Isaiah some seven hundred years before the birth of Christ.

> *"Who hath believed our report? and to whom is the arm of the Lord revealed? For He shall grow up before Him as a tender plant and as a **root out of a dry ground:** He hath **no form nor comeliness;** and when we shall see Him, there is **no beauty** that we should desire Him.*
> *He is despised and rejected of men; a man of sorrows, and acquainted with grief: and we hid as it were our faces from Him; He was despised, and **we esteemed Him not.**" (Is.53:1-3)*

Centuries later, as the mighty hammer of Rome came down upon the known world, the nation of Israel was still holding onto much of the pagan philosophy and idolatry of Greece. Beauty was everything to the Greeks, and especially beautiful people were often elevated to the stature of gods! (Does that ring a loud enough bell today?)

Jesus was a "plain Jew" so there was nothing about His outward appearance that was attractive to a shallow "Vogue" and "Cosmopolitan" mentality. *Of course* He would be despised!

But as in the days of Elijah, (*1Kings19:18*) God had a faithful remnant who by His Grace had not forsaken Him. A remnant who waited for the *"consolation of Israel,"* (*Luke2:25*) and whose prayers for a deliverer had been heard and answered!

It was to them that God would speak, and manifest His immutable will.

"Now the birth of Jesus Christ was on this wise: When as His mother Mary was espoused to Joseph, before they came together, she was found with child of the Holy Ghost. Then Joseph her husband, being a just man, and not willing to make her a public example, was minded to put her away privily (secretly). *But while he thought on these things, behold the angel of the Lord appeared to Joseph in a dream and said, Joseph, thou son of David, fear not to take unto thee Mary thy wife: for that which is conceived in her is of the Holy Ghost. And she shall bring forth a Son, and thou shalt call His Name Jesus: for **He shall save His people from their sins**. Now all this was done, that it might be fulfilled which was spoken of the Lord by the prophet, saying, **Behold, a virgin shall be with child, and shall bring forth a Son, and they shall call Him Immanuel, which being interpreted is, God with us**."* (*Matt.1:20-23*)

The Angel of the Lord also spoke to shepherds and said,
"Fear not! For, behold I bring you good tidings of great joy, which shall be to all people. For unto you is born this day in the city of David a Savior, which is Christ the Lord. And this shall be a sign unto you; ye shall find the babe wrapped in swaddling clothes lying in a manger." (*Luke2:10-12*)

Not a gorgeous bed in the palace of a demonically inspired "Greek god," but a lowly feeding trough in a borrowed stable inspired by *"Almighty* God!"

The sign of the manger would show forth the Divine love and humility of the One who would descend from highest Heaven to dwell with the lowliest of men! This then was Jesus, Who in His maturity called for that same measure of humility from all those who would follow Him.

"Take My yoke upon you, and learn of Me; for I AM meek and lowly in heart: and ye shall find rest unto your souls." (*Matt.11:29*)

And again,

"Verily I say unto you, except ye be converted, and become as little children, ye shall not enter the Kingdom of Heaven. Whosoever therefore shall humble himself as this little child, the same is greatest in the Kingdom of Heaven." (*Matt.18:3-4*)

Now although the prophets wonderfully foretold the coming of the *only* "Great One," they could not possibly have known the vast, and eternal implications of His Divine Birth!

"For unto us a child is born, unto us a Son is given: and the government shall be upon His shoulder: and His Name shall be called Wonderful, Counselor, The Mighty God, The Everlasting Father, The Prince of Peace." (*Is.9:6*)

ONE LIFE – FOR ALL MEN – FOR ALL TIME!

As colossal as Rome's size and power was, she was merely a speck of dust in the hand of God! To fulfill His Word, He simply allowed Satan to move Caesar Augustus to tax the *"whole world"* (nations Rome had conquered); thus causing Joseph and Mary to leave Nazareth and travel to Joseph's ancestral home of Bethlehem.

"Because he was of the house and lineage of David." (*Luke2:1-4*)

So it was, that a corrupt emperor's greed would pave the way for God's most magnificent and gracious gift!

Unable to prevent the Messiah's birth, Satan, in vicious hatred, moved Herod to destroy all the children (aged **two years** and under) in Bethlehem and the surrounding districts. (*Matt.2:16-18, Jer.31:15*) *"According to the time which he had diligently inquired of the wise men."*

NOTE: "Christmas" has always been a lie. Suffice it to say here that the *"wise men"* were nowhere near the birth of Jesus in Bethlehem! And there was no star of Bethlehem either!

"The star, which they (number unknown) *saw in the east, went before them, till it came and stood over where the* ***young child*** *was. ... And when they were come into the* ***house***, *they saw the young child with Mary His mother ..."* (See *Matt.2:9-11*) If you love the truth, then please know this; the star led the wise men to a **house in Nazareth!** Jesus was already a young child of about **two years old!**

Joseph and Mary had returned to Nazareth after **40 days**, which were the days of her purification according to the Law. (*Luke 2:39*)

Before Herod killed the children, Joseph was told to take Jesus to safety in Egypt, (*Matt. 2:13-14*) so that another prophecy could be fulfilled. *"Out of Egypt have I called My Son."* (*Hos.11:1, Matt.2:15*)

Just as God called his son Jacob (Old Israel) out of Egypt, so God would call His Only Begotten Son Jesus, and then call the "New Israel" (the church) out too! In recording the Lord's early life, God in His wisdom breathed just one beautiful and all encompassing verse, which was written down for us by our brother Luke.

"And the Child grew, and waxed strong in Spirit, filled with wisdom: and the Grace of God was upon Him."(*Luke 2:40*)

I have often been asked, "When do you think Jesus really knew who He was?" And the truth is, no one knows. Certainly He knew by the time He was twelve!

Returning home from the feast of Passover, Joseph and Mary were unable to find Jesus among their friends and relatives, so they went back to Jerusalem. After three days, found Him at the temple, sitting among the doctors (teachers), and amazing them with His understanding and answers. (From *Luke2:41-47*) When challenged by His worried "parents," Jesus replied,

"How is it that ye sought Me? Wist ye not (didn't you know) *that **I must be about My Father's business?**"* (*Luke2:49*)

A deeper question – "When did Jesus begin to suffer for us?" – was answered for me in a dream.

I saw the Lord in Heaven, surrounded by angels, and the most glorious music imaginable.

In perfect love, joy, peace, and tranquility He moved and had His Being: King of kings and Lord of lords! ...Then He came here!

I saw Him lying in a dirty, foul-smelling cattle trough with nothing but the coarse, guttural sounds of fallen creatures (both man and animal) surrounding Him. It was clear, that from the very beginning and for the rest of His life, He would suffer all the trials, provocations, and temptations of humanity in far greater measure than we could possibly comprehend. And He did so without sin! (*Heb.4:15*)

We know now that just one sin would have disqualified Him from becoming the perfect, atoning sacrifice for the sins of mankind. (A sinner cannot save a sinner!) Make no mistake: Jesus suffered **His whole life** for us! And He did it all (including His death on the cross) purely for love, and for "*the joy that was set before Him!*" (*Heb.12:2*)

No movie ever made, nor book ever written by man could possibly portray the real "Passion" of this wondrous "God-Man" – Jesus The Christ!

Truly, every single one of us should immediately bow down in awe before Him; and one day (like it or not) everyone will! (*Rom.14:11*)

As I began this chapter, the Holy Spirit made me aware of something I hadn't really seen before, and I share it with you now in celebration of our amazing Savior!

Whilst pondering the four hundred year gap between the Old and New Covenants, He brought to my mind, Israel's four hundred years of bondage under the Pharaohs of Egypt. (See *Acts7:6* and *Gen.15:13* and remember the types and shadows) Well: it wasn't exactly four hundred years …

"*Now the sojourning of the children of Israel, who dwelt in Egypt, was **four hundred and thirty years**. And it came to pass at the end of the four hundred and thirty years, even the selfsame day it came to pass, that all the hosts of the Lord went out from the land of Egypt.*" … "*And **He saved them** from the hand of him that hated them, and **redeemed them** from the hand of the enemy.*"(See *Ex.12:40-42* and *Ps.106:10*)

If the gap between the Old and New Covenants might represent the four hundred years of bondage and the "great darkness" of captivity, (*Gen.15:12*) then how do we account for the extra thirty years it took for God to deliver them and bring them to Himself?

"*Now when all the people were baptized, it came to pass, that Jesus also being baptized, and praying, the Heaven was opened, and the Holy Ghost descended in a bodily shape like a dove upon Him, and a voice came from Heaven, which said, Thou art My Beloved Son; in Thee I am well pleased. … And Jesus began to be about thirty years of age.*"

Luke3:21-23 tells us by inspiration of the Holy Ghost, that Jesus began His ministry of redemption and deliverance at the age of thirty, and we find him in the synagogue at Nazareth, reading from the book of Isaiah, and proclaiming there, just who He really was!

"*The Spirit of the Lord is upon Me, because He hath anointed Me to preach the Gospel to the poor; He hath sent Me to heal the broken-hearted, to preach **deliverance** to the captives, and recovering of sight to the blind, to **set at liberty** them that are bruised, to preach the acceptable year of the Lord. … And He began to say unto them, **This day is this Scripture fulfilled in your ears**.*" (*From Luke4:18-21*)

Four hundred and thirty years for God to begin to deliver Israel from the bondage and captivity of Egypt. Four hundred and thirty years for God's Beloved Son to begin to deliver us from the bondage of this world, and the captivity of sin and death!

However, before God the Son could utter the immortal words, "*Repent: for the Kingdom of Heaven is at hand.*" (*Matt.4:17*) He would have to face the "*god of this world*" – head on!

The battle for the souls of men would be fought on equal terms, just as it had been in the Garden. Drawing from his intimate knowledge of mankind, Satan would use everything at his disposal to bring Jesus down in sin, and therefore under his dominion. Jesus would not take unfair advantage by using His Divine power and glory, but would limit Himself to total reliance upon the Holy Spirit, and fight as a man!

Even in His darkest hour He refused to call upon angels for help. (*Matt.26:53-54*)

The Lord, as the "*Last Adam,*" (*1Cor.15:45*) came to win back all that the "*first Adam*" had lost to Satan through rebellion and sin, but Christ's victory could now only be accomplished through prayer, fasting, and absolute obedience to His Father's will!

With angelic hosts (from both sides) standing by; and the whole of fallen creation at stake, the opening round of history's greatest contest would be fought in absolute solitude.

*"And Jesus being full of the Holy Ghost returned from Jordan, and was led by the Spirit into the wilderness, **being forty days tempted of the devil**. And in those days He did eat nothing: and when they were ended, He afterward hungered"* (*Luke4:1-2*)

By now (if not before reading this book), you will be familiar with some of the lovely "types and shadows" the Holy Spirit is constantly revealing to glorify the "substance" of our Lord and Savior, Jesus Christ.

From Genesis to Malachi God has graciously invited us to see glimpses of His Son; undeniably veiled, but nevertheless manifested through the eyes of faith!

Without doubt, one of the most powerful and profound of all the types I have ever seen (the one describing Christ's monumental victory over Satan in the wilderness) is found in what has become for many Christians, just a Sunday school story for children.

Please join me now as we turn back the pages of the Old Testament, and feast on one of the most significant "parables" of all time!

I have called this God given treasure,

THE FIVE SMOOTH STONES. (*1Sam. Ch's 8 - 17*)

First some Background.

*"Then all the elders of Israel gathered themselves together, and came to Samuel unto Ramah, and said unto him, Behold, thou art old, and thy sons walk not in thy ways: **now make us a king to judge us like all the nations**."* (*1Sam.8:4-5*)

Young Saul stood "head and shoulders" above every man in Israel. (Forever a type of human wisdom and strength) (*1Sam.9:1-2*) He was a tall, good-looking "hunk" of a man, and the people's perfect choice to "*Judge them, and lead them into battle.*" (*1Sam.8:5, 19-20*)

In their carnal desire for a king, the sons of Jacob were actually rejecting God, and seeking to become like all the pagan nations around them. God warned them of what would happen in *1Sam.8:11-18*, but still they insisted.

King Saul was to become the visible, "nominal head" of Israel in terms of the nation's religious and political life. But God was very displeased, and eventually rejected the "people's choice," providing them with a better king (David) who would be, "*a man after God's own heart.*" (See *1Sam.13:14, 15:26-28*) Already we can see David as a type of Jesus.

Now take a good look at the nominal "head and shoulders" religious and governmental leadership in our world today, and take notice. Like Saul, God has rejected it! The great buildings and man-made religious movements, which to the undiscerning may look like the "Church," are in fact loathed by God, and will one day come crashing down in ruins!

(See *Rev. ch's 17* and *18*)

God rejected (and destroyed) Saul because "*he rebelled,*" (akin to the sin of witchcraft, *1Sam.15:22-23*) and consulted a medium (one with a familiar spirit. *1Chr.10:13*)

As I write this, worldly religious organizations are becoming increasingly polluted with all manner of witchcraft or other New Age corruptions; and the devil who leads them is desperately trying to seduce true believers into their midst – especially the young ones, so let's be vigilant!

As time went on, Saul (also a type of Adam or self; and therefore all of us!) began to demonstrate just why God had rejected mankind in favor of someone infinitely better!

"*But the Spirit of the Lord departed from Saul, and an evil spirit from the Lord troubled him.*" (*1Sam.16:14*) (If that doesn't describe the human race, I don't know what does!)

There came a day when God spoke to Samuel and said,

"*How long wilt thou mourn for Saul, seeing I have rejected him from reigning over Israel? Fill thine horn with oil, and go, I will send thee to Jesse the Beth-lehemite: for I have provided me a king among his sons.*" (*1Sam.16:1*)

Isn't it comforting to know that God anointed His new king long before the old fleshly regime finally fell? The house of Saul continued to rule Israel in name only; for God had already chosen David, the son of Jesse, to reign over His people for ever! (*1Chr.22:10*) These "pictures" of Saul and David show us that long before Adam fell (and brought the human race down with him), God had chosen His Only Begotten Son, Who in human form would also be a descendent of Jesse.

Jesus was revealed to Israel as, "*The* Son of David" (born in Bethlehem, which means, "House of Bread") in order to fulfill prophecy, and to perfectly describe Him as the "*Bread of Life.*"

(*John 6:48*)

This same Jesus will ultimately redeem, and reign over His people for ever in righteousness and peace. Praise God!

To appreciate even more of what the Lord has done for us (as seen in the life of David), we must look at the greatest single episode ever (by type), not only in the history of Israel, but of creation itself!

"*Now the Philistines gathered together their armies to battle ... And Saul and the men of Israel were gathered together ... And the Philistines stood on a mountain on the one side, and Israel stood on a mountain on the other side: and there was a valley between them. And there went out a champion out of the camp of the Philistines, named Goliath, of Gath, whose height was six cubits and a span.*" (Approx. 9 feet 9 inches. From *1Sam.17*)

Let me set the "spiritual players" in place – again by type.
The Philistines (demons) stood on one side of the valley.
Saul and Israel (the old order or anointing) stood on the other.
Goliath (Satan) came out and began to defy Israel.

*"Why are ye come out to set your battle in array? Am not I a Philistine, and ye servants to Saul? Choose you a man for you, and **let him come down to me**. If he be able to fight with me, and to kill me, then **we will be your servants**: but if I prevail against him, and kill him, then **shall ye be our servants and serve us**. And the Philistine said, I defy the armies of Israel this day; **give me a man that we may fight together**. When Saul and all Israel heard those words of the Philistine, they were **dismayed** and **greatly afraid**. ... And the Philistine drew near morning and evening, and **presented himself forty days**."* (From *1Sam.17*)

This arrogant and supremely self-confident challenge of Goliath went on for *"forty days,"* during which time no one from the camp of Saul was remotely capable of accepting the giant's terms! (What member of our fallen race could offer any hope of victory against Satan's domination?) The "old anointing" was of course completely inadequate, but then God (Who has always been a few million steps ahead) gives us another opportunity to bathe in the light of His superb handiwork, and to explore a few more treasures from His "revelation chest!"

Earlier, the Lord had sent Samuel to Bethlehem, where he commanded Jesse to bring forth his sons so God could choose His new King from among them.

"And it came to pass, when they were come, that he (Samuel) *looked on Eliab* (the eldest), *and said, Surely the Lord's anointed is before Him. But the Lord said unto Samuel, Look not on his countenance, nor on the height of his stature; because I have refused him: for the Lord seeth not as man seeth; for **man looketh on the outward appearance, but God looketh on the heart**. ... Again, Jesse made seven of his sons to pass before Samuel. And Samuel said unto Jesse, The Lord hath not chosen these. And Samuel said unto Jesse, Are here all thy children? And he said, There remaineth yet the youngest, and, behold, **he keepeth the sheep**. And Samuel said unto Jesse, Send and fetch him: **for we will not sit down till he come hither**."* (see *1Sam.16:4-13*)

The Holy Spirit reveals at least four beautiful truths here to magnify the Lord Jesus.

1. Only Jesus would possess the perfect heart in the sight of God. (*Matt.3:17*)
2. His outward (human) appearance had *"No form nor comeliness* (beauty) *that we should desire Him."* (*Is.53:2*) His Divine (spiritual) appearance is truly glorious! (See *Rev.1:13-16*)
3. Jesus alone is the Chief Shepherd, Who would lose none of His Father's sheep. (*John17:12, 1Pet.5:4*)
4. Not one member of the Kingdom of God (including the Bride or Body of Christ) will *"sit down"* (spiritually speaking) till Jesus *"comes hither!"* (*Luke12:37, 13:29*)

When David (the eighth son) arrived, the picture of Jesus as the "New Beginning" is clearly seen (for that is what the number eight stands for), and is so wonderfully confirmed by God's Word.

"And the Lord said, Arise, anoint him: for this is he. Then Samuel took the horn of oil (type of the Holy Spirit), *and anointed him **in the midst of his brethren: and the Spirit of the Lord came upon David from that day forward**."* (*1Sam.16:12-13*)

The anointing of Jesus was also in the *"midst of His brethren,"* as the Holy Spirit (like a dove) came upon Him after His baptism at the Jordan River. (*Luke 3:21-22*)

"And Jesus, being full of the Holy Ghost, returned from Jordan, and was led by the Spirit into the wilderness. … And Jesus returned in the power of the Spirit into Galilee: and there went out a fame of Him through all the region round about." (Luke4:1and 14)

"For He Whom God hath sent speaketh the Words of God: for God giveth not the Spirit by measure unto Him. *(John 3:34)*

CHAPTER NINE

THE MYSTERY REVEALED!

In chapter five, I wrote briefly about King Saul's angry and violent demonic condition, and how it was soothed for a time by David's musical skills. Right now I'd like to enlarge on that situation a little, and bring it right up to date.

Saul's servants knew what was happening to him (*1Sam.16:15*), and one of them also knew that there was a man called David …

> "*Cunning* (skillful) *in playing, and **a mighty valiant man**, and **a man of war**, and prudent in matters,* (speech) *and **a comely** (lovely) **person, and the Lord is with him**." (1Sam.16:18*
>
> … Anyone see Jesus?

By the way; how many have been taught that when David fought Goliath he was a little boy? Most think of the rhyme; "Five foot two, eyes of blue, etc., etc. Well don't believe the lie!

David was a tall, strapping young "*man of war!*" (If you still don't believe that, I'll give you confirmation in a few moments.)

First though, remember that David's playing soothed Saul for a season, but after a time the evil spirit overcame him and he tried to kill David – and went on trying – over and over again! (Look at *1Sam.19:8* and beyond.)

Now look at Jesus. For a while He was loved by the people, but was then rejected and crucified by the same crowd! (Saul loved David to begin with; see *1Sam.16:21*)

Next, take a look at this scripture, and be prepared!

> "*Now we, brethren, as Isaac was, are the children of promise. But as then, he that was born after the flesh* (Ishmael) *persecuted him that was born after the Spirit,* (Isaac) **even so it is now**."
>
> (*Gal.4:28-29*)

NOTE: Saul appeared as the first nominal "head and shoulders" leader of government under the Old Testament; but by type he surely represents any of the world's dead religious organizations and denominations today!

Like David, some of us have been into those lifeless religious places. We have played our guitars, and sung our spiritual songs for them (and still do when given the opportunity). We have soothed them, and they loved us ... to begin with! But sooner or later they turn, and the scripture is fulfilled "... *even so it is now.*" Let's be sure we are not caught unawares –

Satan's worldly inspired religion will always persecute God's Heavenly inspired faith!

When David arrived at the battlefield, (he was bringing supplies to his three eldest brothers and their commanding officer) he saw and heard the challenge of Goliath. He watched the men of Israel flee from him, and heard the promise of Saul to the man brave enough to fight and defeat the giant.

> "*And it shall be, that the man who killeth him, the king will enrich him with great riches, and will give him his daughter,* (as a bride) *and make his father's house free in Israel.*" (*1Sam.17:23-27*)

David's angry conversation with his eldest brother regarding the "*uncircumcised Philistine who insulted the armies of the Living god*" was reported to King Saul, and Saul sent for him. (See *1Sam.17:26-39*)

After granting this "little boy" permission to fight Goliath, **Saul offered David his very own armor** (including helmet, sword, and coat of mail) to wear for the one-on-one conflict; but after trying them on David's response was,

> "*I cannot go with these; for I have not proved* (tested) *them. And David put them off him.*"

I'd like to emphasize two things here, the first with a question.

Why would Saul, who stood "head and shoulders" above every man in Israel (perhaps at least six foot six) offer his armor to a "little boy?"

David had already killed a "*lion and a bear*" – not cubs! David didn't say, "This armor is huge, it's drowning me!" And he wasn't tripping over the edge of the chain mail coat as it dragged along the floor!" He simply said, "*I have not proved them.*" Meaning of course, that he hadn't fought in restrictive armor before.

So much for the "little boy" theory; and please bear in mind, it's always the "*Little foxes that spoil the vine.*" (*S. of S. 2:15*) Believing enough "little lies," is how the "New Age Movement" was formed in the first place!

The second truth is revealed when David put off Saul's armor because he had absolutely no use for it! The New Anointing (the liberty and power of the Holy Spirit) could never be contained in the Old Order's restrictive garments!

Jesus put it this way, "*New wine must be put into new bottles?*" (*Luke 5:38*)

Don't let anyone try to put "Saul's armor"(legalistic bondage) on a New Testament Believer!

David would fight under the anointing of the Holy Ghost, and in the Name of the Living God.

So would Jesus!

(And for the record, Jesus was the mightiest, and most valiant warrior of all time!)

We come now, to the "**Five smooth stones.**" (It took awhile, but I hope it was worth the wait.)

> "*And he* (David) *took his staff in his hand, and chose him five smooth stones **out of the brook**, and put them in a shepherd's bag which he had, even in a scrip; and his sling was in his hand: and he drew near to the Philistine. ...And the Philistine said unto David, Am I a dog, that thou comest to me with staves? ...Then said David to the Philistine, Thou comest to me with a sword, and a spear, and with a shield: but I come to thee in the Name of the Lord of hosts, the God of*

*the armies of Israel, whom thou hast defied. This day will the Lord deliver thee into mine hand; and I will smite thee, and **take thine head from thee** ... that all the earth may know that there is a God in Israel. And all this assembly shall know that the Lord saveth not with sword and spear: **for the battle is the Lord's** and He will give you into our hands.*" (From *1Sam.17:40-47*)

Revelations contained in those few verses will bring us close to the climax of Old Testament history. They remain my all time favorite pictures of the Lord Jesus Christ. (To Him be the Glory, for ever and ever!)

The stones which David chose and placed in his shepherd's bag were worn smooth: polished by the water of the brook. (That water is a type of the Holy Spirit)
We will see that Jesus also chose from five well-worn and polished "stones" when He confronted the strongest and deadliest enemy known to man!

Goliath tempted Israel for forty days, seeking to gain victory over God's nation.
Satan tempted the Lord Jesus for forty days in the wilderness, seeking to gain the ultimate victory over all mankind!
There was no one else to represent Israel, but David.
There was no one else to represent mankind, but Jesus.
If Goliath beat David, Israel would serve the Philistines!
If Satan beat Jesus, mankind would serve demons!

The five smooth stones available to Jesus were the five books of the Law:
Genesis, Exodus, Leviticus, Numbers, and Deuteronomy!

David used just one stone to hurl at Goliath.
Jesus used just one book to hurl at the temptations of Satan. (The fifth Book of Deuteronomy)
With one stone, David would overcome the giant.
With one book, Jesus would overcome the devil!
David had no sword. Remember he said, "*The Lord will give you into our hands.*"
Jesus had no sword. Remember He said to Peter, "*Put up again your sword into his place.*"
(Matt.26:52)

David took Goliath's own sword, and smote off the giant's head.
Jesus took Satan's own "sword" (the cross), and with it He would finally "cut off" or "*Crush the serpent's head!*" (*Gen.3:15*)
Once David had destroyed Goliath, Israel would rise up to chase the Philistines, and slaughter them all the way back to Gath (Goliath's home).
Once Jesus had destroyed the power of the devil, (*Heb.2:14, 1John3:8*) He commanded His Church (the New Israel, *Rom.2:29, Gal.6:16*) to rise up and cast out demons, and take complete dominion over the "*works of darkness,*" exposing them in the Light and Truth of God's all powerful Word!

In the wonder of Christ's glorious finished work, let's not forget a second revelation of the five stones, which concerns each and every believer on a very personal level.
As we have seen, the stones that David chose were all made smooth by being *in* the water of the brook. (I say again, this water is a type of the Holy Spirit, see *John4:14*)
Clearly he could have used any one of them for God's purpose!

NOTE: Stones along side the brook were *not* chosen, because they would have been too rough and poorly shaped for use in a sling. They would not fly true! – They would not find the mark!

Scripture tells us that believers are "***Lively*** (living) ***stones***" (*1Pet.2:5*), and that we should be "*Sanctified* (separated, washed, polished) *and meet* (fit) *for the Master's use* (His sling?), *and prepared unto every good work.*" (See *2Tim.2:19-21*)

After being "born again," there is a tremendous need for believers to be baptized with (in or by) the Holy Spirit (*John1:33*) in order to receive the fullness of His anointing and power. (*Acts1:8, 2:4*)
     The gift or baptism of the Holy Spirit is *not* automatic.
     Jesus said, "*If ye then being evil, know how to give good gifts unto your children: how much shall your Heavenly Father **give the Holy Spirit to them that ask Him?**" (Luke11:13*)

NOTE: The whole of chapter twelve is dedicated to this enormously controversial yet vital subject. As you will see there is nothing the devil fears more on earth than a Christian who has embraced God's promise, and is standing by faith in the power and anointing of the Holy Ghost!

****

In the garden, Satan had gained the ongoing right to uncover and control mankind because of Adam's sin.
     Remember that during His wilderness temptations, Jesus did not argue when Satan claimed to own, "*All the kingdoms of the world.*"
     The devil said, "*All this power* (authority over them) *will I give Thee, and the glory of them: **for that is delivered unto me**; (by Adam) **and to whomsoever I will, I give it.**" (Luke4:5-6*)

However, in persuading the crowd to crucify Jesus, Satan (who could not have understood the parable of David and Goliath) crossed the line, and for the first time in history uncovered a totally innocent, sinless man!
     Satan's ignorance of the "*mystery*" (inner workings) of God's eternal redemptive plan gave rise to the most devastating mistake of his evil career, and is revealed by the Holy Spirit through Paul.

"*For I determined not to know any thing among you, save Jesus Christ, and Him crucified ...But we speak the wisdom of God in a mystery, even the hidden wisdom, which God ordained before the world unto our glory: **Which none of the princes** (including principalities, powers and rulers of the darkness, Eph.6:12) **of this world knew: for had they known it, they would not have crucified the Lord of Glory.**" (1Cor.2:2,7-8*)

At long last: desperate, insanely angry, and having utterly failed in his attempts to make Jesus sin by any means – even by betrayal, desertion, an illegal trial, and torturous death – Satan's doom was sealed!
     The great uncoverer would soon learn how it feels to be stripped of all his power and authority before God, the holy angels, and the Church!

Christ Crucified, and "*raised again for our justification.*" (*Rom.4:25*)
     Nothing in creation will ever eclipse that Divine achievement, and God's promise of the glory to come! (See *Rom.5:1-11*)

The Mystery Revealed in Christ

SEVEN TIMES Jesus spoke whilst on the cross!

There, hanging in naked agony before the world and the demonic powers of darkness, He would leave mankind with a Royal declaration of love, forgiveness and grace sufficient for all of us to remember Him by ... until His return!

"FATHER FORGIVE THEM; FOR THEY KNOW NOT WHAT THEY DO." (*Luke 23:34*)

Even as the crowd jeered, and the gruesome spikes of ignorant, sin-hardened men were penetrating His flesh, the Lord carried for them in His heart that Divine love and forgiveness, which characterized not just His ministry, but His entire life!

This imperative prayer of intercession was spoken not just for those who were physically responsible for His crucifixion, but for *all* men: for *all* time! Our combined sins would be laid upon the Son of God, making the whole human race spiritually responsible for His sacrificial death! (*Is.53, 1John2:2*) But as much as Jesus paid the full and total price for every sin, it is still necessary to ask for His forgiveness (remember we must "*speak to the Rock!*") and by faith "*receive Him*" into our lives as Savior and Lord. (*John1:12*)

Today, the vast majority of people, with all their pride and selfishness, remain lost even within the very sound of the gospel message. Near and yet so far from God's great gift!

"*The wages of sin is death; but the gift of God is eternal life through Jesus Christ our Lord.*"
(*Rom.6:23*)

Alas, another Scripture is fulfilled, "**Many are called, but few are chosen.**" (*Matt.22:14*) May we reach out to them while there is still time! (*2Cor.6:1-2*)

NOTE: By way of contrast, for those who are saved, there is no longer an excuse for sin. We are faced with a sobering reality – "Father forgive us; for we *do* know what we do!"

****

"VERILY I SAY UNTO THEE, TODAY SHALT THOU BE WITH ME IN PARADISE"
(*Luke 23:32-43*)

Two thieves were crucified with Jesus; one on His left, and one on His right. Thereby fulfilling the prophecy of Isaiah who wrote, "*He was numbered with the transgressors.*" (*Is.53:12*)

One robber, whose heart was hardened, blasphemed and said, "*If Thou be the Christ, save Thyself and us.*" Showing that even while facing an agonizing and certain death, men without the "*gift of repentance*" (*2Tim.2:24-25*) will still "spit" in God's Face!

In rebuking him, the other thief acknowledged his sins, and spoke a prayer of God given faith to Christ, "*Lord, remember me when Thou comest into Thy kingdom.*" (*Lk.23:42*)

Responding favorably and with the utmost grace, Jesus revealed that no one who sincerely turns to Him before death (no matter how late) will ever be refused!

****

"WOMAN, BEHOLD THY SON! ... BEHOLD THY MOTHER!"
(John19:26-27)

Spoken in compassion to Mary (wife of Joseph), giving her shelter under the wing of His disciple John; then in turn to John regarding Mary. As a result ..."*From that hour, that disciple took her unto his own home.*" *(John19:27)* Although the Gospel writers call Mary the "*mother of Jesus,*" the Lord Himself never once referred to her as such. (See *John 2:4* for example.) Exactly why remains in the realm of conjecture, but I offer this possibility. Jesus knew better than anyone, the kinds of hideous acts and corruptions which would later be perpetrated in the name of the "Mother of God," and did nothing to promote those errors! (I have no desire to hurt or offend any member of the Roman Catholic church, so should there be offence in speaking out against the erroneous doctrines of Catholicism – may it be that of the Gospel only!)

"ELI, ELI, LAMA SABACHTHANI? *that is to say,* MY GOD, MY GOD, WHY HAST THOU FORSAKEN ME?" *(Matt.27:46)*

In Spirit, and quoting directly from the first verse of Psalm twenty-two, Jesus cried out in reaction to the crushing weight of "*bearing in His own body on the tree*" every sin the world had ever known! *(1Pet.2:24)*

Part of the inexplicable act of paying for our redemption was to somehow suffer the eternal separation from God's presence that all of us deserved! However, because the Lord's experience of actual "*hell*" and the "*lake of fire*" *(Rev.20:14-15)* is so incredibly hard for us to grasp, very few are even aware of that aspect of His torment!

The amount of suffering, and how long he endured it (in terms of eternity) while hanging on the cross may never be fully known to us; but one undeniable truth soars above them all.

He did it! Every "*jot and tittle*" He fulfilled! *(Matt.5:18)*

Every last drop from the "*cup of God's wrath*" (meant for us) He drank! *(Matt.26:39)*

And then (while conquering death) He destroyed its spiritual power over believers; took back the "*keys of death and hell,*" which the devil had held for so long, and totally destroyed his power in the process! *(Rev.1:18, Heb.2:14, 1John3:8)*

His sinless sacrifice was clearly accepted by God the Father in that He rose again from the dead!

David beat Goliath: Jesus triumphed over Satan!

That without doubt is the *only* reason the human race exists today, and the "*chosen*" are on their way to Glory!

****

"I THIRST" *(John19:28)*

Quoting again from Psalm twenty-two, (which together with Isaiah fifty-three, contains some of the greatest Messianic passages ever written) Jesus fulfills yet another prophecy.

"*I am poured out like water, and all My bones are out of joint:* (speaking of bodily dislocations during crucifixion) *My heart is like wax; it is melted in the midst of my bowels. My strength is dried up* *like a potsherd; and **My tongue cleaveth to My jaws;** and Thou hast brought Me into the dust of death."* (*Ps.22:14-15*)

In an act of mockery, Roman soldiers, who had already fulfilled prophecy by casting lots for Christ's garments (*Ps.22:18, Matt.27:35*) filled a sponge with vinegar, (gall or sour wine) put it on a reed, and offered it up to Him. (See *Luke23:36-38*) They also mimicked the words of the chief priests, scribes and elders who had mocked and tempted Jesus earlier.

"If Thou be the King of the Jews, save Thyself ... He trusted in God; let Him deliver Him now, if He will have Him: for He said, I am the Son of God." (*Matt.27:43*)

How could any of them have known or understood that a thousand years before, the Holy Spirit (through David) had foretold these things exactly!

"Reproach hath broken My heart; I am full of heaviness: and I looked for some to take pity, but there was none; and for comforters, but I found none. They gave Me also gall for My meat; and in My thirst they gave Me vinegar to drink." (*Ps.69:20-21*)

"All they that see Me laugh Me to scorn: they shoot out the lip (shout with contempt), *they shake the head, saying, He trusted on the Lord that He would deliver Him: let Him deliver Him, seeing He delighted in Him."* (*Ps.22:7-8*)

One day, Israel and the whole world will know that Jesus (*"Joshua," "Messiah," "Immanuel"*) is truly the *"Christ, and Son of the Living God."* (*Matt.16:16*)
The One Who,
    "Came unto His own, and His own received Him not." (*John1:11*)

"But Isaiah is very bold and saith, I was found of them (Gentiles) *that sought Me not; I was made manifest unto them that asked not after Me. But to Israel He saith, All day long I have stretched forth My hands unto a disobedient and gainsaying people."* (*Rom.10:20-21, Is.65:1-2*)

"Seeing then that we have such hope, we use great plainness of speech: and not as Moses, which put a veil over his face, that the children of Israel could not steadfastly look to the end of that which is abolished; but their minds were blinded: for until this day remaineth the same veil untaken away in the reading of the old testament; which veil is done away in Christ. But even unto this day, when Moses is read, the veil is upon their heart. Nevertheless, when it shall turn to the Lord, the veil shall be taken away." (*2Cor.3:12-16*)

"For blindness in part is happened to Israel, until the fullness of the Gentiles be come in."
    (*Rom.11:25*)

*"In that day ... I will pour upon the house of David, and upon the inhabitants of Jerusalem, the spirit of grace and of supplications: and **they shall look upon Me Whom they have pierced,** and they shall mourn for Him, as one mourneth for his only son, and shall be in bitterness for Him, as one that is in bitterness for his first-born."* (*Zech.12:10*)

"For dogs have compassed Me: the assembly of the wicked have enclosed Me; they pierced My hands and feet." (*Ps.22:16*)

****

"*FATHER, INTO THY HANDS I COMMEND MY SPIRIT.*" (*Luke23:46*)

Jesus came to earth to accomplish all that His Father required of Him.

"*Then said I, Lo, I come (in the volume of the Book it is written of Me) to do Thy will, O God.*" (*Heb.10:7*)

Having experienced the immense physical pain of crucifixion, and the horror of separation from God, (*Matt.27:45*) the Lord now speaks to fulfill His own words from an earlier time.

"*And He that sent Me is with Me: the Father hath not left Me alone; **for I do always the things that please Him.**" (John8:29)*

No one else ever had such a testimony! It is also evident that even when the Lord was subject to the white-hot fire of His father's wrath against our sin, He was still pleasing to God, and in the center of His perfect will!

"*Surely He hath borne our griefs,* (pains) and c*arried our sorrows: yet we did esteem* (reckon) *Him stricken, smitten of God, and afflicted. But **He was wounded for our transgressions, He was bruised** (crushed) **for our iniquities:** the chastisement of our peace was upon Him; and **with His stripes we are healed.** All we like sheep have gone astray; we have turned every one to his own way; and the Lord hath laid on Him the iniquity of us all ... **Yet it pleased the Lord to bruise Him;** He hath put Him to grief: when Thou shalt make His soul an offering for sin, He shall see His seed, He shall prolong His days, and **the pleasure of the Lord shall prosper in His hand. He shall see of the travail of His soul, and shall be satisfied:** by His knowledge shall My Righteous Servant justify many; for He shall bear their iniquities.*" (*Is.53:4-7, 10-11*)

Isn't it the absolute longing of every believer to, "***do always the things that please Him?***"
Even though, "*the spirit indeed is willing, but the flesh is weak,*" (*Matt.26:41*) God knows the desire of our hearts, and the Holy Spirit is always there to encourage us.

"*Forgetting those things which are behind, and reaching forth unto those things which are before, I press toward the mark for **the prize** of the high calling of God in Christ Jesus.*"
(*Phil.3:13-14*)

That "prize" is so profoundly summed up by the Holy Spirit, as Paul faced his final days.

"*I have fought a good fight, I have finished my course, I have kept the faith: henceforth there is laid up for me a crown of righteousness, which the Lord, the righteous Judge, shall give me at that day: and not to me only, but unto all them also that love His appearing.*" (*2Tim.4:7-8*)

If a man like Paul, who claimed to be the "*chief of all sinners*" (*1Tim.1:15*) can end his life with that kind of testimony, surely the witness of the Spirit throughout the whole redeemed community is – SO CAN WE!
May we live seeking the Lord's testimony of always pleasing our Father, so that if we die before the "catching away," (*1Thess.4:17*) those same words of faith and confidence will be on *our* lips.

"Father into Thy hands I commend my spirit."
Surely this is the desire of all that follow after the One Who for love alone, laid aside His Crown (and everything else) to deliver us out of darkness, and into His marvelous Light!

****

"IT IS FINISHED." (*John19:30*)

The world could not contain the books
Eternity the time
To rightly tell the whole account
Of those three words sublime!

Although the poem is true, there are still some wonderful things that *can* be told of those final three (world-changing) words spoken by the Lord before bowing His Head and giving up the Ghost (His Spirit).

Not long ago while listening to the radio, I heard a nationally known pastor speaking about the death of Christ. During the program he declared rather emphatically, "Immediately after giving up His Spirit, the lord went straight into the presence of the Father!"

At that point there was an uncomfortable check in my spirit, as certain scriptures came to mind which seemed to contradict his teaching. As a result, I called the brother's ministry, and left a message sharing my concern. A few days later, I received a letter from one of the church's assistant pastors who obviously agreed with what had been taught on the air. My response to that letter forms the basis of what I now share with you.

For the Glory of God I have titled this argument,

THE THREEFOLD WORK OF CHRIST
(Concerning His death.)

1. THE CROSS

"For by ONE offering He hath perfected for ever them that are sanctified." (*Heb.10:14*)
"This is the New Covenant in My Blood." (*Luke22:20*)
"Without shedding of blood is no remission." (*Heb.9:22*)
"Christ Jesus came into the world to save sinners." (*1Tim.1:15*)

Clearly, the sacrifice of Jesus was to pay for all sin – past, present, and future!
Which is why, when unbelievers stand before the Great White Throne, they will be judged according to their works, *not* their sins! (*Rev.20:11-13*) There is a *huge* difference!
If men were yet to be judged for sin, the death of Christ would have been a complete and utter failure: of no effect whatsoever! He could never have said, *"It is Finished*!" His resurrection would be a lie, and Christians would still be in their sins!

*"But now **is** Christ risen from the dead, and become the First fruits of them that slept."* (*1Cor.15:20*)

Stripes – Many or Few?

Based on the knowledge they had of God's will however, there will certainly be degrees of punishment for the wicked! (See *Luke 12:45-48*)

For example: the person who "knew God's will" i.e. sat in church for twenty years listening to the Gospel message, and still died in sin rejecting Christ, "will be beaten with many stripes!" Logically this means he or she will suffer far more in hell (and eventually the lake of fire) than the man or woman who also "committed things worthy of stripes," but died without knowing God's will, or hearing of Christ! They as such, "will be beaten with few!"

"More knowledge increases sorrow." (*Ecc.1:18*)

After dying without Christ, the *judgment* of say Hitler and that of the average person will be exactly the same, i.e., eternal separation from the presence of God, which is the "second death," or "lake of fire."

But the *punishment* they receive there will be vastly different!

NOTE: Some Christians believe that there are as many levels of punishment in the lake of fire, as there are levels of blessing in the New Jerusalem! That belief however comes with no scriptural confirmation, and we would do well to leave such matters to the Lord, Who will judge all things in righteousness and truth on that Great Day!

2. PRISON

The assistant pastor who wrote to me, provided me with endless quotes from **"The Bible Knowledge Commentary: New Testament Edition,"** (such books explain in detail, why Jesus didn't really say what He said here, and didn't really mean what He meant there!)

I wish these men would send scripture to prove their case, instead of passing on some professor's regurgitated interpretation of what he *thinks* the Scripture says!

Men are teaching that after His death; "Christ went straight into the presence of the Father," but what does the Bible teach?

"For Christ also hath once suffered for sins, the just for the unjust, that He might bring us to God, being put to death in the flesh, but quickened (made alive) *by the Spirit."* (*1Pet.3:18*)

No problem so far, but here come verses 19 and 20 ...

*"**By which also He went and preached unto the spirits in prison**; which sometime were disobedient, when once the longsuffering of God waited in the **days of Noah**, while the ark was a preparing, wherein few, that is, eight souls were saved by water."*

There is no honest way of rendering the word *"prison"* (holding place) as hell, or Hades; so prison it is!

Also; to understand, *"The days of Noah,"* we need help from other Scriptures.

"Wherefore, as by one man (Adam) *sin entered into the world, and death by sin; and so death passed upon all men, for that all have sinned. For until the law, sin was in the world: **but sin is not imputed** (reckoned with, or judged) **when there is no law**. Nevertheless death reigned from Adam to Moses, even over them that had not sinned **after the similitude of Adam's transgression**, who is the figure* (type) *of Him* (Jesus) *that was to come."* (*Rom.5:12-14*)

Seeing all this in the Spirit is one thing, putting it down on paper, is quite another!

We may, or may not see the *"days of Noah"* as the days between Adam and Moses, but certainly those who died then had received neither the Law nor the Gospel. They died because of sin, (its "wages") but there was no basis for judgment!

They had not *"walked in the garden with God."* They had not been warned by God directly. They *"had not sinned after the similitude of* (in the same way as) *Adam."*

For that reason, they were kept in prison – not hell!

NOTE: The *"rich man died,"* (*Luke16:19-31*) and went to hell (under the Law! *v.29*). Lazarus died, and went to *"Abraham's bosom."* (*v.22*) Souls in hell could not be reached; **neither was there any way out.** *"There is a great gulf fixed!"* (*v.26*) This was *not* a parable!

On the other hand, let's remember these two things.

A Those in prison can be set free!
B If a pastor, evangelist or any believer goes to a prison to preach the Gospel, he or she is in the prison, but not *in* prison!

    If the gift of salvation is offered to *every* prisoner, how many would receive Christ?
    "... Many are called, but few are chosen."

Is it so hard to believe that the Spirit of Jesus went into the "prison" realm, and preached to those spirits (souls) who had not yet been eternally judged?

Those souls in prison did *not* have a second chance. They were given the same opportunity to believe as men living under the Law, or (as of now) the Gospel!

Trusting Christ would enable them to live unto God in the spirit ...

"For for this cause was the **Gospel preached** *also to them that are dead, that they might be judged according to men* **in the flesh,** *but live unto God in the spirit."* (*1Pet.4:6*)

Unsaved people walking around in a mall today don't know they're in "prison," so how many will ask Jesus to free them?

The souls preached to in that "spiritual prison" (*1Pet.3:19*) had to be in a similar condition.

Finally: what would be the purpose of preaching the Gospel of salvation to souls who were incapable of being freed by it? – Absolutely none!

Therefore Christ would take from prison those who *accepted* Him, along with all those in Abraham's bosom who were *waiting* for Him, so that these scriptures could be totally fulfilled

"Wherefore He saith, When He ascended up on high, **He led captivity captive,** *and gave gifts unto men. Now that He ascended, what is it but that* **He also descended first into the lower parts of the earth"** (*Eph.4:8*)

"Your father **Abraham rejoiced to see My day:** *and he saw it and was glad. ...*
Verily, verily, I say unto you, before Abraham was, I AM." (*John8:56, 58*)

Did I mention that while Jesus was doing all that, He also had time to, *"Spoil principalities and powers, making a show of them openly; and in His victory, completely triumphed over them all."*

        (From *Col.2:15*)

Now think back to Samson (who killed more physical enemies in his death than in his life) as a last act type of our Lord Jesus, Who in *His* death brought down every spiritual enemy known to man! Now we have added wonderful (revelation) color to Christ's already glorious picture, making Him even more beautiful to look upon!

LET NO MAN LESSEN WHAT JESUS ACCOMPLISHED IN HIS DEATH!

3. HEAVEN

On the Day of Atonement, Aaron alone took, *"the blood of the bullock, and sprinkled it with his fingers upon the Mercy Seat ... SEVEN times."* (*Lev.16:14*)

"It was therefore necessary that the patterns of things in the Heavens should be purified with these; (the blood of bulls and goats) *but the Heavenly things themselves with better sacrifices than these ... Once in the end of the world.* (*Heb.9:23-26*)

The sins of the entire nation of Israel were atoned for (covered or reconciled) when the High Priest entered the Holy of Holies once a year with a censer or container of burning incense, and the blood of a bullock. The blood would be sprinkled *seven times* on the Mercy Seat, (type or symbol of God's Heavenly Throne) and later on the horns of the Golden altar, which was before the veil in the Holy Place.

If you're already "seeing" revelations of Christ here, just look at what follows:

"And there shall be no man in the tabernacle of the congregation when he goeth in to make an atonement in the Holy Place, until he come out" (*Lev.16:17*)

The verse ends with Aaron leaving the Holy Place, having made atonement for himself, and for his household, and for all the congregation of Israel.

If Aaron is one type of Jesus, our Great High Priest, then so is incense and the blood sprinkled seven times on the earthly copy of God's Heavenly Throne!

Hebrews 9:23-26 tells us that the copies of Heavenly things were purified with the blood of bulls and goats, but that the Heavenly things themselves would have to be purified with a better sacrifice than these!

See how the Holy Spirit puts all these things together in Christ! ...

When Jesus was arrested, all of His disciples fled in fear. (*Matt.26:56*)

He was alone! (*"No man shall be in the Tabernacle"*)

SEVEN TIMES Jesus sprinkled His Blood on the cross. From His head, His back, His hands, His feet, and His side!

Now let us see what sets our Eternal High Priest, so far above, and apart from every other!

Unlike Aaron, or any human priest, Jesus needed no incense to cover the smell of His flesh: His Flesh was without sin!

Unlike Aaron, Jesus needed to make no atonement for Himself: He was forever pure!

Unlike Aaron, Jesus would not need to make atonement for His people year after year with animal offerings that could never take away sins. (*Heb.10:1-4*)

Because,

"Once in the end of the world," He sacrificed Himself, (*Heb.9:26*) and dealt with sin for ever!

"For By one offering He hath perfected for ever them that are sanctified!" (*Heb.10:14*)

Unlike Aaron, Jesus entered once into the Heavenly Holy of Holies (made without hands) with the *"Better sacrifice"* of His precious Blood, and there, *"Appeared in the presence of God for us."*

(*Heb.9:24*)

On the morning of the *"third day"* after His death, Mary Magdalene went to the tomb, but Jesus was gone! She saw a *"gardener,"* and asked Him where he had taken the Lord's Body. When she heard Him speak her name, her eyes were opened, and she knew then that the gardener was Jesus! Instinctively she must have reached out to touch Him as she uttered the word *"Rabboni;"* but instead of embracing her, Jesus said,

"Touch Me not; for I am NOT YET ASCENDED to My Father ..." (See *John 20:11-18*)

Yet later, on that same "third day" (the first day of the week), Jesus would return and invite His disciples to "touch, handle, and even eat with Him!" (See *Luke24:13-43, Jn. 20:19*) Why?

Because in order to present His Blood, pure and undefiled before the Father; Jesus could not allow Himself to be defiled by the touch, smell, or stain of sinful, human flesh. Therefore He would not let Mary touch Him!

"No man (or woman) would be in the tabernacle – UNTIL HE CAME OUT!"

A man tells us that immediately after His death on the cross, Jesus went straight to the Father in Heaven. – Jesus Himself tells us He did not!

The word of a man, or the Word of God? ... Choose this day whom you will believe!

Finally: one more succinct, but splendid "picture" (taken from a different angle) confirms Christ's vicarious sacrifice. This time "shot" from *Lev.16*.

On the day of Atonement, a bullock, a ram and two goats were brought to the tabernacle.

The bullock for a sin offering, the ram for a burnt offering; one goat for a sin offering, and one which would become the "scapegoat." The goat chosen by lot to be the sin offering was killed, and its blood (along with the bullock's) was sprinkled on and before the Mercy Seat, as well as the golden altar.

After cleansing the Holy Place and the tabernacle, Aaron laid his hands on the head of the scapegoat, confessing over it the iniquities of the children of Israel; and putting them upon the head of the goat. A *"fit"* (prepared) man then led the goat away (bearing all their sins), and released it in, *"a land not inhabited"* i.e. the wilderness.

Next: Aaron changed his clothes (leaving his high priestly garments inside the tabernacle); washed his flesh in the Holy Place, and put on his own garments. He then offered the ram as a whole burnt offering.

Last but certainly not least, another man carried away the skins, flesh, and dung of the sin offerings, and burned them outside the camp. Both men had to wash their clothes, and bathe their flesh before returning.

Believe it or not, every single thing here glorifies Jesus!

As I've shared already, no one type could possibly fulfill all the amazing aspects of Christ's character and ministry; these then are just a few more among so many.

The goat for the sin offering signified that Jesus would die for *all* men. The sheep *and* the goats; the Israelite and the Canaanite; the believer and the non-believer. – That goat *paid the price* of sin!

The scapegoat also speaks of Jesus, Who bore our sins to a place where God would never remember them again. – That goat *took away* the sin!

Incidentally, there's a vast difference between forgetting, and not remembering.
If God simply "forgot" where He put our sins, He might (one day) find them again ... God forbid! But God has said,

"I WILL REMEMBER THEIR SIN NO MORE!" *(Jer.31:34)*
(He has chosen never to find them again - Alleluia!)
"As far as the east is from the west, so far hath He removed our transgressions from us."
(Ps.103:12)

To emphasize this truth, one more extremely important revelation is needed.
God did not forgive our sins: He judged them all in His Only Begotten Son, so He could then forgive us!

The ram would point to Jesus as our whole (complete) burnt offering.
"Who gave Himself for us an offering and a sacrifice to God for a sweet-smelling savor." *(Lev.1:13, Eph.5:2)*
The "burnt offering" was not typically made for sin, (see *Lev. ch's 1-6*) but for dedication, or as an act of devotion to God. Which is why (after we have been saved) the Holy Spirit beseeches us, *"Present your bodies as living sacrifices, (whole burnt offerings) holy, acceptable unto God, which is your reasonable service."* *(Rom.12:1)*

The two men speak of Jesus being separated (cut off) for a season. The one who took the scapegoat away, and the one who burned the skins, flesh, and dung of the sin offerings outside the camp. Both washed their clothes and bathed their flesh before returning to the camp.

Although Jesus was cut off outside the camp, He did not need to wash His clothes or bathe His Flesh; for He was never soiled or defiled by sin!

These types are yet again confirmed by the Word of God.

"Behold the Lamb of God, which taketh away the sins of the world." *(John1:29)*

"For the bodies of those beasts, whose blood is brought into the sanctuary by the high priest for sin, are burned without the camp. Wherefore Jesus also, that He sanctify the people with His own Blood, suffered without the gate." *(Heb.13:11-12)*

"For we have not a High Priest which cannot be touched with the feeling of our infirmities; but was in all points tempted like we are, yet without sin." *(Heb.4:15)*

"... And He was clothed in a vesture (robe) dipped in Blood: and His Name is called - The Word of God." *(Rev.19:13)*

Remember that after listing his natural human credentials as a *"Hebrew of the Hebrews; of the tribe of Benjamin; a Pharisee; blameless under the law"* etc., Paul went on to say,

"I count them but dung, that I may win Christ." *(Phil.3:5-8)*

It follows that if man's best (self-righteous) works "are as "*filthy rags*," (*Is.64:6*) then what is "*dung,*" if not his worst!

Trying to please God with self-effort, qualifications, or pedigree is altogether "*skin, Flesh, and Dung!*" All of it was "burned in Christ" on the cross, so we wouldn't burn in the Lake of Fire!

Can you imagine people standing before God, completely covered in "dung," and still trying to tell Him how nice they smell? ... **Thank God for Jesus!**

Finally: "*Aaron took off his garments.*"

When Jesus came to earth, He "took off" His Heavenly garments; left them in Heaven's Holiest Place, and "put on" the most humble of rags (human form).

"*Who, being in the form of God, thought it not robbery to be equal with God: but made Himself of no reputation, and took upon Him the form of a servant, and was made in the likeness of men: and being found in fashion as a Man, He humbled Himself, and became obedient unto death, even the death of the cross.*" (*Phil.2:6-8*)

Even without the music, these choruses make great reading.

****

There could never be a song to great to praise Him,
Nor the words that lift too high His Holy Name,
There could never be a song to great to praise Him,
So just love Him and you'll never be the same!

****

It is finished it is done!
Jesus rose from the dead
And now the battle is won
Finished and done
Finished and done
Once I was a sinner
But now I am a son!

****

NOTE: sinners are separated from God by sin. Christians are not sinners! They may sin, but when they do, they are disobedient sons or daughters. – There is an enormous difference!

Once again, let it be said with total scriptural authority that after His death, Jesus did *not* go immediately to His Father. To say that He did, robs Him of the glory He deserves for His total victory!

"***Wherefore God hath highly exalted Him, and given Him a Name which is above every name: that at the Name of Jesus every knee should bow, of things in Heaven, and things in earth, and things under the earth; and that every tongue should confess that Jesus Christ is Lord, to the glory of God the Father.***" (*Phil.2:9-11*)

My letter of response to the pastor who wrote me, consisted of just two pages (an outline of what you have just read), and I closed with the following:

I realize that none of this may change your beliefs, but as brothers in Christ we can at least agree to disagree agreeably! In any event, I would rather be guilty of giving Christ too much glory (impossible of course) than too little!

———————

To tie all these things together, and to prepare for that which follows later in part two, I'd like to share some revelations concerning David and Solomon.

WAR AND PEACE

Having confirmed his throne in Israel, king David yearned to build a great house for the Lord. God refused his request, telling him his son Solomon would build the temple, and that in so doing the throne of David would be established forever. (See *2Sam.7:1-16*)

> *"And David said to Solomon, My son, as for me, it was in my mind to build a house unto the Name of the Lord my God: but the Word of the Lord came to me, saying, Thou hast shed blood abundantly, and hast made great wars: thou shalt not build a house unto My Name, because thou hast shed much blood upon the earth in My sight. Behold, a son shall be born unto thee, who shall be a man of rest; and I will give him rest from all his enemies round about: for his name shall be Solomon* (peaceful), *and I will give peace and quietness unto Israel in his days. He shall build a house for My Name."* (See*1Chr.22:6-10*)

Earlier David had said,

> *"Solomon my son is young and tender, and the house that is to be builded for the Lord must be exceeding magnificent, of fame and of glory throughout all countries: I will therefore now make preparation for it. So David prepared abundantly before his death."* (*1Chr.22:5*)

In bringing these verses to us, God not only manifests His unfailing love towards the Old Testament nation of Israel, but continues to demonstrate that same perfect love towards His New Covenant people as well!

Keep in mind that in righteousness, David often becomes a type of the Lord Jesus, but in sin he becomes a type of any believer!
David's desire to build a house for the Lord was certainly righteous, but there was still a problem.
"He was a man of war who had shed much blood in the sight of God."

King David would have to die (go away) before Solomon could begin to build the temple of God. Before his death however, David *"prepared abundantly"* for the enormous task ahead, and gave his son specific instructions from the *"pattern"* which God had already given him. (*1Chr.28:19*)
Now all we need to do is convert this O.T. "treasure" into today's N.T. "spiritual currency!"

The Lord Jesus Christ desired with all His heart to build a temple unto God His Father, but He too was a man of war! (*Luke 22:15*)

"Think not that I am come to send peace on earth: I came not to send peace, but a sword."

(Matt.10:34)

Jesus would shed much blood on the earth in the sight of God.
"This is My Blood of the New Testament which is shed for many for the remission of sins."

(Matt.26:28)

Jesus, like David, had to go away. Only then could the Holy Spirit begin to build the temple of the Living God. (Fulfilling Solomon's type.)
Jesus said,

"Nevertheless I tell you the truth; it is expedient (beneficial) *for you that I go away: for if I go not away, the Comforter will not come unto you: but if I depart, I will send Him unto you."* (*John16:7*)

After the abundant preparations of Jesus, *"through the Blood of the everlasting covenant,"* (*Heb.13:20*) the Holy Spirit Himself would ultimately build the "temple" of the living God: His Body, and Church!

"Know ye not that ye are the temple of God, and the Spirit of God dwelleth in you?" (*1Cor.3:16*)

"Ye also, as lively (living) *stones, are built up a spiritual house, a holy priesthood, to offer up spiritual sacrifices, acceptable to God by Jesus Christ."* (*1Pet.2-5*)

Speaking in regard to Jews and Gentiles becoming one in Christ, the Holy Spirit tells us that all believers, *"Are built upon the foundation of the apostles and prophets, Jesus Christ Himself being the Chief Corner Stone; in whom all the building fitly framed* (joined) *together groweth unto a holy temple in the Lord: in whom ye also are builded together for an habitation of God through the Spirit."* (*Eph.2:20-22*) – In the habitation of the Holy Spirit, everything fits!
So at last, each brilliant facet of God's masterpiece was in place.
Jesus had perfectly prepared the way. He finished His work, and later would ascend into Heaven to sit down at the right hand of the Father in total, triumphant victory!

*"He that descended is the same also that ascended up **far above all heavens**, that He might fill all things."* (*Eph.4:9*)

The Word tells us again that, *"God Raised Christ from the dead, and **set Him at His own right hand** in the Heavenly places, **far above all principality**, and **power**, and **might**, and **dominion**, and **every name that is named**, not only in this world, but also in that which is to come: and hath put **all things under His feet**, and gave Him to be the **Head over all things** to the church, which is His Body, the fullness of Him that filleth all in all."* (*Eph.1:15-23*)

The Holy Spirit was sent to fulfill the task of building, or raising up that *"Living Temple; the Bride and Body of Christ; the fullness of Him"* for the Eternal Glory of God!

"That in the dispensation of the fullness of times, He might gather together in one, all things in Christ, both which are in Heaven, and which are on earth; even in Him." (*Eph.1:10*)

In the glorious and eternal light of Christ's resurrection, the devil's earthly reign ended!

He had no choice but to lick his wounds; nurse his permanently injured pride, and somehow figure out what to do with the little he had left! After all, Jesus had just conquered death; destroyed his power, and reduced his mighty army of fallen angels to the equivalent of wretched little *"serpents and scorpions!"* It was another nightmare! To Satan it was like being in the Garden of Eden *before sin*, when Adam was still in charge! He was right back where he started, only now it was much worse. Now even *new* believers would be able to tread on him and his demons! (*Luke 10:19*) That is once they became empowered with the Holy Spirit, learned how to move in His gifts, and walk in the victory of Christ by faith!

Needless to say, the powers of darkness would be determined to stop *that* from happening ...
at all costs!

At this point however, about all the evil one could hope and scheme for, was that these soon to be called Christians – and what a loathsome name *that* was! – would buy his standard pack of wiles, and fall for well-worn deceptions like fear, compromise, discouragement, false doctrines, and especially his all time favorite ~ *"Hath God said?"*

Long ago Satan recalled, God *did* say, *"I will cast thee to the ground, I will lay thee before kings, that they may behold thee."* (*Eze.28:17*)

Now, suddenly, those words rained down on him like dreadful, unquenchable fire!

If being *"cast down"* wasn't humiliating enough (the serpent was never the same again), Satan realized with mounting horror that these contemptible little people with *"Christ in them,"* were to be the very *"kings"* God would lay him before!

For the first time in history there was to be a special and chosen group of people: a *"royal priesthood;"* *"an holy nation;"* a terrible army of "little-Christs," who could not only see the devil, but (with the spiritual eyes of faith) could see him "under their feet!"

Faced now with insurmountable odds, and very little time, the devil would be forced to change his strategy! On the plus side, he still had control over the vast numbers of "spiritually dead" humans who had always *"loved darkness rather than light;"* (*John3:19*) and who, in their prideful rebellion remained delightfully unattached to Christ.

He would simply begin to poison these unbelievers with suspicion, fear, and hatred; and use them to somehow salvage his already devastated plans, and his totally (though never-to-be-admitted) lost cause!

****

For forty days after His resurrection, Jesus played a kind of spiritual "hide and seek" with His disciples. (*John 20:26, 21:1*) He was gently preparing them for the time when He would no longer be with them in physical form, but would ascend to the Throne of His Glory and sit at the right hand of the Father in Heaven. (*Eph.1-20, Col.3:1*)

"For He must reign, till He hath put all enemies under His feet. The last enemy that shall be destroyed is death." (*1Cor.15: 25-26*)

During those forty days, He *"showed Himself alive after His passion by many infallible proofs, and spoke of things pertaining to the Kingdom of God."* (*Acts1: 3*)

Just before His departure, Jesus gathered His apostles together, and told them not to depart from Jerusalem, but to wait for the promise of the Father.

"Which, saith He, ye have heard of Me. For John truly baptized with water; but ye shall be baptized with the Holy Ghost not many days hence." (Acts1:4-5)

When asked if He would restore the kingdom to Israel there and then: Jesus replied,

"It is not for you to know the times or the seasons, which the Father hath put in His own power. But ye shall receive power, after that the Holy Ghost is come upon you: and ye shall be witnesses unto Me both in Jerusalem, and in Judea, and in Samaria, and in the uttermost part of the earth." (Acts1: 7-8)

At that moment, an amazing and wonderful thing happened: the disciples actually saw The Lord of Glory rise before them, and watched until a cloud received him out of their sight!

Whilst looking, *"steadfastly toward Heaven as He went up"* (who wouldn't?); two men stood by them in white clothing and said, *"Ye men of Galilee, why stand ye gazing up into Heaven? This same Jesus, which is taken up from you into Heaven, shall so come in like manner as ye have seen Him go into Heaven." (Acts1: 9-11, Matt.24:30)*

After that, the disciples returned to the upper room in Jerusalem, where they had eaten the last Passover meal with the Lord ... and waited!

It would not be long

The second greatest event in the history of mankind was about to be manifested on earth; and in accordance with God's Divine nature and perfect will, it would occur in another humble, unknown, and completely unexpected place!

CHAPTER TEN

LIFE'S A FEAST

The waiting would soon be over!

In an upper room, the apostles and disciples were gathered together with the women, (the number being about one hundred and twenty), and throughout the land of Israel, the *"Feast of Pentecost"* was about to begin.

> *"And when the day of Pentecost was **fully come**, they were all with one accord* (mind) *in one place." (Acts 1:12-14, 2:1)*

To understand why the words, *"fully come"* are so important, we must return to the Old Testament and take a look at the original, *"Day of Pentecost"* (fiftieth day) as revealed within the setting of,

"THE SEVEN FEASTS OF THE LORD"

Deeper meaning of Israel's Feasts can be found in a three-fold revelation.

1. **NATURAL AND HISTORIC** – Old Israel's actual Feasts.
2. **PROPHETICAL** – seen as types, and all fulfilled in the Lord Jesus Christ.
3. **EXPERIENTIAL** – to be embraced now, and enjoyed spiritually by faith!

The seven feasts are recorded in *Leviticus 23, Numbers 28:16-31*, and *Num. ch. 29.*
The first two are also described in *Exodus 12*, and a careful reading of that chapter will bring forth spectacular treasure!

THE FEAST OF PASSOVER *(Ex.12:1-14, 43-49)*

This great feast was first celebrated while the children of Israel were still in Egypt (their last night). It was to be so incredibly significant for them, that God literally "stopped the clock," and introduced a brand-new calendar the very next day!
Believe it or not, these Feasts can be used as a time frame for the entire "church age!"

> *"This month shall be shall unto you the beginning of months: it shall be the first month of the year to you." (Ex.12:2)*

After all but destroying Egypt with nine miraculous plagues, God gave instructions to Moses and Aaron and said,

> "*Speak ye unto all the congregation of Israel, saying, In the tenth day of this month they shall take to them **every man a lamb**, according to the house of their fathers, **a lamb for a house** ... every man **according to his eating** ... Your lamb shall be **without blemish**, a male of the first year: ye shall take it out from **the sheep or from the goats**. And ye shall keep it up until the fourteenth day of the same month: and the **whole assembly** of the congregation shall kill it in the evening. And they shall **take of the blood**, and strike it on the two **side posts**, and on the **upper door post** of the houses, wherein they shall eat it.*" (From *Ex.12:3-7*)

The long awaited day of Israel's deliverance was at hand! God's Old Covenant people knew well that this Passover feast was to be celebrated and remembered as the day of freedom from their "natural" captivity in Egypt under Pharaoh.

What they could *not* have known however, was that everything contained in it would speak of the ultimate freedom bestowed upon God's New Covenant people: i.e., deliverance from their *spiritual* captivity in this world under Satan's dominion, and obtained by none other than,

> "***The Lamb of God***, (Christ Jesus) *which taketh away the sin of the world.*" (*John1:29*)

Entering into the realm of spiritual revelation, we will see that Jesus fulfills every single aspect of the Feast of Passover, as summed up in *1Cor.5:7.*

> "***For even Christ our Passover is sacrificed for us.***"

Understanding how the Holy Spirit has used the natural Passover lamb to picture the Lord Jesus Christ will wondrously explain the prophetic words of Jesus Himself!

> "*Verily, verily, I say unto you, except ye the Flesh of the Son of Man, and drink His Blood, ye have no life in you.*" (*John6:53*)

Everyone who is saved in the Church Age and brought into the Body of Christ has partaken spiritually of the Passover Feast, and therefore has also eaten spiritually of our Passover Lamb; Jesus the Savior!

Special note: Eating or drinking *natural* blood was forbidden to anyone; not just God's people!

> "*But flesh with the life thereof, which is the blood thereof, **shall ye not eat**.*" (*Gen.9:4*)

> "*Only be sure that thou **eat not the blood**: for the blood is the life; and **thou mayest not eat the life with the flesh***." (*Deut.12:23*)

Here is proof that we do not eat the *literal* flesh, nor drink the *literal* blood of Jesus Christ (as is taught in Catholicism) **for that would make us CANIBALS!**

(I have given more Scriptural proof of this argument in chapter 26, in the section on Roman Catholicism.)

Jesus was in no way referring to His *physical* flesh and blood, for He would never have encouraged the people to disobey His Father's commands!

Jesus also said,

"*It is the Spirit that quickeneth;* (gives life) ***the flesh profiteth nothing:*** *the Words that I speak unto you,* ***they are Spirit, and they are life.***" *(John 6:63)*

In addition:

The bread He broke for the disciples, and the wine He gave them to drink were tokens, or symbols of His broken Body and shed Blood! They could not have been His *actual* Body and Blood for He was still alive when He ordained the communion! (See *Luke22:14-20*)

Clothed with that knowledge, let us now "feast" on the glories of Jesus ("our Passover") in the Spirit and Life of God's Holy Word.

The Passover lamb, without spot or blemish was slain

God's message to Israel (and to the whole world) is this:

"Redemption will never come through corruptible things such as gold and silver, or the vain religious traditions of men, but through "***the precious Blood of CHRIST, as of a lamb without blemish and without spot.***" *(1Pet.1:18-19)*

And again,

"*How much more shall the* **Blood of Christ***, Who through the Eternal Spirit offered Himself without spot to God, purge your conscience from dead works to serve the Living God.*" *(Heb.9:14)*

"*And I beheld, and, lo, in the midst of the Throne and of the four beasts, and in the midst of the elders, stood* **a Lamb as if it had been slain**" *(Rev.5:6)*

"*And all that dwell upon the earth shall worship him*; (the beast, or anti-Christ) *whose names are not written in the Book of Life of* **the Lamb slain** *from the foundation of the world.*" *(Rev.13:8)*

The blood of the lamb was struck with hyssop (a humble weed) on the doorposts of the houses,

"*And the blood shall be to you for* **a token** (sign) *upon the houses where ye are: and when I see the blood, I will* **pass over** *you, and the plague shall not be upon you to destroy you, when I smite the land of Egypt.*" *(Ex.12:13)*

"*And being found in fashion as a man,* **He** (Christ) **humbled Himself***, and became obedient* **unto death***, even the death of the cross.*" *(Phil.2:8)*

"*He was oppressed, and He was afflicted, yet he opened not His mouth: He is brought* **as a lamb to the slaughter***, and as a sheep before her shearers is dumb, so He openeth not His mouth.*" *(Is.53:7)*

Only the Blood of Christ, "*struck*" or "*sprinkled*" on our hearts (received by faith) can protect us from the coming judgment of God! When God "*sees the Blood*" covering our lives ("door posts"); He passes over us (spares us), and delivers us out of this world and into the Kingdom of Heaven! And so it is written,

*"Let us draw near with a true heart in full assurance of faith, **having our hearts sprinkled** (by His blood) from an evil conscience, and our bodies washed with **pure water**."* (By the Word of God, *Heb.10:22, Eph.5:26*)

*"Verily, verily I say unto you, He that heareth My Word, and believeth on Him that sent Me, hath everlasting life, and shall not come into condemnation; but **is passed from death unto life**."*
(John 5:24)

*"Who hath **delivered us** from the power of darkness, and hath **translated us into the Kingdom of His Dear Son.**" (Col.1:13)*

If the household was too *"little* (few) *for the lamb,"* neighbors would be allowed to share the feast together. *(Ex.12:4)*
What a privilege it is to "share the lamb" (the Gospel) today, and not just with neighbors!
For Jesus said again,

*"All power is given unto Me in Heaven and in earth. Go ye therefore, and **teach all nations**, baptizing them in the Name of the Father, and of the Son, and of the Holy Ghost: teaching them to observe **all things** whatsoever I have commanded you: and, lo, I am with you alway, even unto the end of the world. Amen." (Matt.28:18-20)*

It was taken out from the sheep or from the goats. *(Ex.12:5)*
This confirms that the sacrifice of the Lord Jesus Christ was for *all* men.

"We trust in the Living God, Who is the Savior of ALL men, especially of those that believe."
(1Tim.4:10)

"Christ Jesus came into the world to save sinners" *(1Tim.1:15)*

*"But **as many as received Him**, to them gave He power (the right) to become the sons of God, even to them that **believe** on His Name." (John1:12)*

The lamb was to be roasted with fire, and eaten that night with unleavened bread and bitter herbs. It was not to be eaten raw, or boiled in water! Everything was to be roasted; the legs, the head, and the entrails. *(Ex.12:8-9)* Jesus would feel the hottest fire of God's judgment! There would be no quick, easy way out for Him (as in *"raw"*). The truth of His sufferings should not be reduced or watered down (as in *"boiled"*).
The Lord gave Himself as a Whole Burnt Offering - *"Legs, Head, and Entrails"* (Bowels).
He did not have to! He could have walked away at any time from the scourging, the mockery; from the crown of thorns, and even the cross itself, **BUT HE DID NOT!**
His love, His devotion, and His obedience would triumph: so instead of leaving us, He prayed again and again saying,
*"O My Father, if this cup may not pass away from Me, except I drink it, **Thy will be done**."*
(Matt.26:42)
"And being in an agony He prayed more earnestly: and His sweat was as it were great drops of blood falling down to the ground." (Luke22:44)

NOTE: In this day and age of easy believe-ism; unscrupulous ministers tell the unsaved to come to Christ, and all their troubles will be over! Accepting Jesus will make everything all right!
"No need for blood or crosses in this church; but make sure you bring your wallets!" (See *2Pet.2:1-3*)

"Another Gospel" is being preached (see *2Cor.11:1-4*) and it's *"raw!"*

The *real* Jesus says to His followers,
   "In the world ye shall have tribulation, but be of good cheer; I have overcome world."
                                        (*John16:33*)
   "Whosoever will come after Me, let him deny himself, and take up his cross, and follow Me."
                                        (*Mk.8:34*)

Bible translations like the N.I.V., the Message (Msg), and so many others have been flooding into bookstores all over the world. They water down not only the Word of God, but the Blood of Jesus; His Lordship, and some even deny the Fatherhood of God! (These neutered versions are often referred to as "gender" or "consumer friendly!")

The Lord Jesus Christ: *"The Word, and Lamb of God"* is being *"boiled!"*

As for "Unleavened Bread:" its true meaning is best shared in our next feast, but you can be certain that this "Bread" will glorify the Lord in a unique and wonderful way!
   "Bitter herbs" would forever signify the dreadful bitterness of our captivity to sin and death, and just what it would cost our Savior to set us free!

With no time to wait for their bread to rise, *natural* unleavened bread was eaten by the children of Israel to remind them of the haste in which they were to leave Egypt. Bitter herbs would remind them of the bondage of enslavement under Pharaoh.
   Today, Christians must not loiter in this world. We must go ... and stay gone!
   May the Holy Spirit remind us of the bitterness of our bondage under Satan, so that our hearts never turn back! Jesus said, *"Remember Lot's wife!"* (*Luke17:32*)

"No uncircumcised person would be allowed to eat of the Passover lamb." (*Ex.12:48*)
   We know that back then, in order to gain access to God, the stranger would first have to become a part of the nation of Israel. (*Gen.17:9-14, Lev.12:3*) A stranger (someone who was not home-born and was not automatically circumcised on the eighth day) would have to be physically circumcised (no matter what his age) in order to become part of God's congregation. Circumcision (the actual cutting away of the flesh to show separation unto God) was an absolute must! Those who would not submit to it were never allowed to eat of the lamb!
   We know that now, in order to gain access to God, every single one of us (Jew, *"natural branch"* or Gentile, *"wild branch,"* see *Rom.11:13-24*) has to become part of God's spiritual *"Olive Tree,"* (*vs.16-17*) also called *"The Vine;"* (*John15:1-8*) the *"Israel of God;"* (*Gal.6:16*) the *"Body of Christ;"* (*Eph.2:11-22, 5:30*) *"His Church."* (*Col.1:18*)
   Circumcision is still a must, but now of course it is of the heart and not of the flesh!

*"For he is not a Jew, which is one outwardly; neither is that circumcision, which is outward in the flesh: but he is a Jew, which is one **inwardly; and circumcision is that of the heart, in the Spirit**, and not in the letter; whose praise is not of men, but of God."* (*Rom.2:28-29*)

The legs of the lamb, MUST NOT BE BROKEN!

"***In the house*** *shall it be eaten; thou shalt not carry forth aught of the flesh abroad out of the house;* ***neither shall ye break a bone thereof***." *(Ex.12:46)*

"*In the house*" now speaks of those in Christ partaking of intimate communion or fellowship with Him, and with one another. This is not something to be shared with the "*uncircumcised*" (un-believers).

NOTE: Non-believers must be warned of the spiritual danger involved in assuming they are Christians simply because they attend a "church," and receive the bread and wine. Eating a wafer or a piece of bread will not save anyone! To trust in, or worship mere "elements" is deception and idolatry!

To close this study on the Feast of Passover, let me share with you a joyful yet sobering revelation given some years ago while sharing communion.

I had often wondered why it was so important that the bones of the lamb, or those of the Lord Himself should not be broken. Of this, God was very insistent!

"***Neither shall ye break a bone thereof***." *(Ex.12:46)*

"*They shall leave none of it unto the morning, nor break any bone of it*" *(Num.9:12)*

And of Jesus …"*He keepeth all His bones: not one of them is broken.*" *(Ps.34:20)*

"*Then came the soldiers, and brake the legs of the first, and of the other which was crucified with Him. But when they came to Jesus, and saw that He was dead already, they brake not His legs.*" *(John 19:32-33)*

Although I understood something of, "*not leaving any unto the morning,*" i.e. salvation is given by grace and received the very moment we receive Jesus Christ as our Lord and Savior. It is complete: there are no "left-overs!" But why, "*not a bone to be broken?*"

As the Holy Spirit dropped this word into my spirit, it was like rain from Heaven.

"*For we are members of His Body, of His Flesh,* ***and of His Bones***" *(Eph.5:30)*

"A broken bone is the worst form of separation within the body!"

The Body of Christ should not be divided! His words are truly "*Spirit and Life!*"

NOTE: Perhaps now we can see that every denomination (find one in Heaven, or in the Word of God) is a "broken bone" within the Body of Christ!

The unbroken bones of Jesus forever speak of our unity in the Holy Spirit!

Beseeching the Ephesians (and all Christians) to walk worthily before the Lord, Paul wrote,

"*With all lowliness and meekness, with long-suffering, forbearing one another in love; endeavoring to keep the unity of the Spirit, in the bond of peace.*" *(Eph.4:3)*

In Spirit, King David wrote,

"*Behold, how good and how pleasant it is for brethren to dwell together in unity.*" *(Ps.133:1)*

Strife or disputes producing schisms (splits or divisions) all come from pride.

"Only by pride cometh contention: but with the well advised is wisdom." (*Pr.13:10*)

Believers who will not submit to Godly counsel, or work out their differences humbly in the light of God's Word are forced to separate. The early church was no exception.

Ungodly separation

"Now this I say, that every one of you saith, I am of Paul; and I of Apollos; and I of Cephas; and I of Christ. Is Christ divided? was Paul crucified for you? or were you baptized in the name of Paul? ... For ye are yet carnal: for whereas there is among you envying, and strife, and divisions (dissensions), *are ye not carnal* (worldly or fleshly) *and walk as men?"* (As the unsaved) (*1Cor.1:10*, and *3:3*)

Earlier, even Paul and Barnabas had their share of broken bones!

"And the contention was so sharp (strong) *between them* (Paul would not take Mark with him), *that they departed* (separated) *asunder one from the other: and so Barnabas took Mark, and sailed unto Cyprus; and Paul chose Silas, and departed."* (See *Acts15:36-41*)
(Perhaps the seed of this contention, was sown in *Gal.2:11-13*.)

Who knows what damage was done there, but it does seem that later, Paul, Barnabas, and Mark were reconciled. (*1Cor.9:6, 2Tim.4:11*) One thing is certain, God healed (and goes on healing) all manner of painful wounds caused by broken bones within His Body, but this should not be so!

On the other hand, the Holy Spirit makes it clear that certain kinds of separation are absolutely necessary:

Godly separation
"Mark them which cause divisions and offenses contrary to the doctrine which ye have learned; and avoid them." (*Rom.16:17*)

These were not true Christians, but *"false brethren"* stirring up contentions within the church through their own greed and prideful ambition!

Godly Separation!
"Be ye not unequally yoked together with unbelievers: for what fellowship hath righteousness with unrighteousness? And what communion hath light with darkness? ...Wherefore come out from among them, and be ye separate, saith the Lord, and touch not the unclean thing; and I will receive you, and be a Father unto you, and ye shall be My sons and daughters saith the Lord Almighty." (See *2Cor.6:14-18*)

Speaking of *"Mystery Babylon"* (the world's religious system), God's Word thunders ...
"Come out of her, my people, that ye be not partakers of her sins, and that ye receive not of her plagues." (*Rev. 18:4*)

If we truly recognize Satan as the *"god of this world"* (*2Cor.4:4*) we will understand that any fellowship with the world is a form of fellowship with Satan himself!
Touch the world – touch the devil! (Not a bad way to remember a vital truth!)

"Ye adulterers and adulteresses, know ye not that the friendship of the world is enmity with God? Whosoever therefore will be a friend of the world, is the enemy of God." (James 4:4)

"Love not the world, neither the things that are in the world. If any man love the world, the love of the Father is not in him. For all that is in the world, the lust of the flesh, and the lust of the eyes, and the pride of life, is not of the Father, but is of the world. And the world passeth away, and the lust thereof: but he that doeth the will of God abideth for ever." (1John 2:15-17)

Summary:

Christ our Passover creates a brand new day (new birth, new life) for the one who receives Him and keeps this feast. Today Passover is a spiritual feast; and speaks of salvation i.e. being *"born again."* (*John 3:3*) Christians are now free to celebrate it every day as we remember being delivered from sin, the world, and damnation by the precious Blood of the Lamb - Jesus Christ our Lord! To continue to eat the natural Feast of Passover (every year) without ever desiring or receiving the One it represents, is to miss the very meaning of life itself; and to refuse the greatest gift mankind will ever know!

Truly, every thing we have is found in Him.

"For in Him we live, and move, and have our being."(Acts17:28)

Only by keeping this feast can we move on to the remaining six, and enjoy all the other blessings God has so graciously ordained for us.

THE FEAST OF UNLEAVENED BREAD (*Ex.12:15-20*)

Named as one with Passover (*Luke22:1*), this feast began the same night as the lamb was killed and eaten; and continued for seven days.

*"Seven days shall ye eat unleavened bread; even the first day ye shall put away leaven out of your houses: for whosoever eateth leavened bread from the first day until the seventh day, that soul shall be **cut off** from Israel." (Ex.12:15)*

The seriousness of keeping this feast is underscored in *Ex.12:17.*

*"And ye shall observe the feast of unleavened bread; for in this selfsame day have I brought your armies out of the land of Egypt: **therefore shall ye observe this day in your generations by an ordinance for ever**."*

To discover the beauty of this second feast, we must first grasp the meaning of "unleavened bread" as applied to the life of Jesus: then as it can, and should be applied to the Body of Christ as a whole.

With one notable exception in *Matt.13:33* (where a parable of Jesus proves there is nothing wrong with natural leaven), all references to leaven as a spiritual type are negative!

Natural leaven (often described as yeast) is actually a fungus which, when mixed with dough or batter, causes them to ferment and rise. Its most common use of course is in the making of bread.

Spiritual leaven on the other hand, speaks of corruption, hypocrisy, and compromise. In other words ... the old nature of sin!

For seven days during the Feast of Unleavened Bread, no leaven was to be found in or near the tents or (later) the houses of the Israelites. Failure to observe this law would mean being *"cut off"* or put away from God's people, and therefore from God Himself!

NOTE: Even today at Passover, many Hebrew fathers still take a candle and lead their families through every room in a traditional, albeit symbolic search for natural leaven! May God deliver Israel from such shadows; and bring her into His glorious substance and Light!

Regardless of tradition, the feast was originally meant to remind God's people of their hurried escape from Egypt; followed by their entrance into a new life of separation and holiness under the government of God. Sadly, the Old Testament is filled with examples of Israel returning to her "leavened," or sinful ways. (See *Amos 4:1-12*)

The ultimate and only example of *true* "Unleavened Bread" is to be found in the person of the Lord Jesus Christ, Who was born without spot or blemish, and remained that way throughout His entire Life!

Because of His sinless perfection (unleavened life), He alone is able to lead His New Covenant people out from the bondage of sin and death; into a life of holiness and separation from the world, and into the presence of God!

Today we do not throw *natural* leaven out of our houses, but we must certainly seek to throw any and all spiritual leaven out of our lives – and with all haste!

It is the work of the Holy Spirit (as we yield to the Lordship of Christ) to *"purge out the old leaven"* (sinful habits) and conform us to the *"image of Christ!"* (*1Cor. 5:7, Rom. 8:29*)

Again, just as those who would not put away leaven were *"cut off from Israel."* (*Ex.12:15*)

So today, Christians who are not prepared to put away sin will (sooner of later) find themselves *"cut off"* (disfellowshipped) from the true Body of Christ!

Another good old saying to commit to memory:
"Loving the Book, (the Bible) will keep you from sin: loving sin will keep you from the Book!"

Let's take a look now at *"leaven"* in the New Testament.

The leaven of the Pharisees (*Luke 12:1*)

Jesus said to His disciples first of all,
> *"Beware ye of the leaven of the Pharisees, which is hypocrisy."*

Some of the most vehement words ever spoken by the Lord were aimed at these religious leaders, and we would all do well to heed them!

"Woe unto you scribes, lawyers, Pharisees, for you ..."
Love to wear long, (religious) *robes* – to impress men.
Love to make known what you do (works) – to be seen of men.
Love to make public processions and prayers – to be exalted by men.
Love to put heavy (legalistic) *burdens on people* – to bind men.
Love to make a show of outward righteousness – to be praised by men.
Love to teach the doctrines, commandments, and traditions of man – to damn men!
Ask for signs – to tempt God.
Twist the Scriptures – to anger God.
Resort to worldly tactics (such as politics) – to reject the power of God.
Lead the blind into ditches – to miss God altogether!

Please! *"Search the Scriptures to see if these things are so."* (Acts17:11)
(See also *Matt. 6:1-7, 6:16-18, 15:1-20, 16:1-12, 22:15-46, 23:1-36, John 19:15, Acts23:8*)

"Jesus Christ the same yesterday, and today, and for ever." (Heb.13:8)

Jesus warns us today that judging (criticizing) our brother by pointing out his faults and not seeing our own is also hypocrisy, and is as ugly as any other kind of spiritual leaven! (See *"the mote and the beam,"* Matt.7:1-5)

The leaven of the Sadducees *(Acts 23:8)* was primarily **false doctrine** (through unbelief), and included
Denying the supernatural – to limit God.
Denying the resurrection – to insult God!

Those men actually denied the existence of angels (God's or Satan's), the spirit (God's or man's), and the resurrection (Christ's or ours!)

Today, so-called Christian professors continue to revive and promote this ancient leaven by denying the virgin birth or incarnation of Jesus: His atonement, His bodily resurrection, and His second coming.(Expect to hear that Christ is no longer the Only Way of salvation!)
Many of them refuse to believe in eternal damnation for the unrepentant, water baptism by full immersion, and (of course) in the gifts (Healing, Miracles, Tongues, Interpretation, Prophecy, etc.) of the Holy Spirit! Watch out for those Ssssaducees!

The leaven of Herod *(Mark 8:15)*

Herod (ruling at the time of Jesus' birth) was consumed with fear, insecurity, pride, deceit, and jealousy: all of which led to the heinous crime of murdering the infants in Bethlehem! (*Matt.2:16*)
Herod Antipas (Tetrarch, or ruler of a fourth part of a country) was a later king, and probably the one Jesus was referring to. His leaven was lawlessness, worldliness, man fearing, man pleasing, lust, rash promises, and (like his father before him) murder! (See *Matt. 14:1-11*)

Herod Agrippa (grandson of Herod the great) was guilty of murdering James (the brother of John), and later died under God's judgment for exalting and glorifying himself before men, which is to steal or accept the glory that is God's alone! (See *Acts 12:1-3, 20-23*)

Today, if we have hatred (resentment or unforgiveness) in our hearts, it is the same as murder!
(1John3:15)

Sooner or later, without repentance, we will find ourselves in *"prison"* (bondage) and in the hands of *"tormentors"* (demonic spirits, Matt. 18:21-35.)
These "tormentors" include spirits of bitterness, (hardening the heart and defiling others) worry, anxiety, jealousy, suspicion, depression, fear, guilt, migraine headaches, isolation, and many, many others!
Jesus warned us: *"Beware of the leaven of Herod."*

The leaven of the Corinthians (*1Cor. Ch. 5*)

Having already written of this matter in a different context, I will share briefly here that this leaven refers to the church failing to deal with sin. In this case, "open fornication." (*v.1*)
The attitude of the brethren overall was seen as follows:

1   They were puffed up. 2 There was no sorrow. 3 No action was taken. (*v.2*)
4   They stayed in fellowship with the guilty party. 5 They gloried in it all. (Considered themselves so spiritual that they could allow the sin to continue.) (*v.6*)

In his written statement of rebuke, Paul took them straight back to the Feast of Unleavened Bread.

"Your glorying is not good. Know ye not that a little leaven leaveneth the whole lump?
Purge out therefore the old leaven, that ye may be a new lump, as ye are unleavened. For even Christ our Passover is sacrificed for us: therefore let us keep the feast, not with old leaven, neither with the leaven of malice and wickedness; but with the unleavened bread of sincerity and truth." (*vs. 6-8*)

Paul's admonition, *"Not to keep company with fornicators"* (*v.9*) applies of course to those within the Church. Verses *10-13* however, make it clear that Christians must go out among sinners in order to reach them with the Gospel of Jesus Christ! The good news is that after being put out of fellowship (this chastening would lead to repentance), Paul urges the Corinthians to reinstate the brother, thereby allowing the church to move on into blessing! (*See 2Cor.2:5-11*)

The leaven of the Galatians (*Gal.5:1-9*)

A careful reading of the whole letter will bring into focus one of the most common and difficult to eradicate types of leaven found throughout New Testament history: **LEGALISM!**
Central and key verses regarding this problem, are given in chapter 3.

"This only would I learn of you, received ye the Spirit by the works of the law, or by the hearing of faith? Are ye so foolish? Having begun in the Spirit, are ye now made perfect by the flesh?" (*vs. 2-.3*)

Legalism is perhaps *the* greatest stumbling block of the entire church age, and is still very much "alive and well" (make that "deadly and sick") within the Body of Christ today!
Christians who would oppose any reference to "salvation by works," can still be found vainly "working" or trying to keep their salvation by misguided obedience to false doctrines (church rules spewed out by insecure leadership), or by the traditions of men, making void the Word of God!
(*Mark 7:1-23, Luke 16:15*)

You won't believe what some believers are "buying and selling" in an effort to hold on to their salvation! (More on the "fleshly circumcision" of the church up ahead!)
We must *"rightly divide* (understand or interpret) *the word of truth,"* (*2Tim.2:15*) and be continually on guard; (*Pr.4:23*) if not, this poisonous, legalistic leaven, may well seep in and corrupt our lives!
A wise old brother (now with the Lord) once said to me, "Little wonder Romans 7 comes after Romans 6." Implying of course, that it's easier to get rid of the **FLESH** than it is to get rid of the **LAW!**

SUMMARY:

Just as the Feast of Passover speaks of us being *"justified"* (just-if-I'd never sinned!) once and for all by faith (remember the lamb was eaten at one sitting); so the seven day Feast of Unleavened Bread speaks of us being *"sanctified"* (separated unto holiness) over a period of time!

At Passover (salvation), God immediately declares us righteous through (under the covering of) the Blood of Christ.

During Unleavened Bread however, the Holy Spirit begins the task of working that very righteousness into our lives until we become that which He has already declared us to be. Praise God!

The righteousness of Christ is available to us all; instantly given, and progressively learned.

I say learned, *not* earned! ... If we *"follow on to know the Lord."* (*Hos.6:3*)

Jesus said,

"If any man will come after Me, let him deny himself, and take up his cross daily, and follow Me." (*Luke 9:23*)

Obviously not all the work is done in seven *natural* days; but as we yield to the leading of the Holy Spirit, His work in us will most assuredly be done (sooner rather than later); for seven speaks of God's *spiritual* time!

As our lives become progressively infused with the fragrance of Christ's Love, Joy, Peace etc., (*Gal.5:22-23*) this "fruit" will be the most wonderful indication (to the unsaved) that we have been with Jesus! (*Acts 4:5-13*)

****

Can you imagine being in a room full of people; watching a woman pour a bottle of precious ointment over the Lord Who was sitting in our midst? (*John 12:1-3*)

Wouldn't the smell of that ointment permeate the clothes and hair of everyone present?

After a while, when we all left the room with Him, wouldn't the crowd gathered outside begin to say, "These people smell just like Jesus?" ... How beautiful would that be?

****

This seven day feast then, is the commitment of a lifetime: a commitment to the way of holiness, and to manifesting His fragrance from every fiber of our being.

"A new commandment I give unto you, that ye love one another; as I have loved you, that ye also love one another. By this shall all men know that ye are My disciples, if you have love one to another." (*John13:34-35*)

"But seek ye first the Kingdom of God, and His righteousness; and all these things (the needs of life) *will be added unto you."* (*Matt.6:33*)

"For the Kingdom of God is not meat and drink, but righteousness, peace and joy in the Holy Ghost." (*Rom.14:17*)

May God give us grace to keep the feast!

THE FEAST OF FIRST FRUITS (*Lev. 23:9-14*)
"When ye be come into the land" (*v.10*)

The Feast of First Fruits could not be physically celebrated until the children of Israel arrived in the Promised Land and saw the fullness of God's blessing on their crops. It was withheld from them for forty-one years! (I'll explain the extra year in a moment)

NOTE: They had a real taste of that blessing when the "twelve" (one from each tribe) returned from spying out the land. (*Num.13:1-25*) The spies cut down a branch containing just one cluster of grapes, and two men had to carry it between them on a pole! (*v.23*)

Someone may well ask, "If that was the size of one bunch of grapes, however did they carry the pomegranates and figs?"

Nevertheless, because of unbelief, a whole generation (twenty years and older) would die in the wilderness without ever experiencing those intended blessings, or seeing the promises of God fulfilled in their lives!

Of course God still took care of them. He kept their shoes and clothing from wearing out, (*Deut.29:5*) and fed them by providing "*manna*" every day. But even though that manna was a type of Christ, (*John 6:31-51*) it was still not God's ultimate provision for His people!

V.I. Leaving Egypt (type of being saved or born again) by crossing the Red Sea (type of baptism in water) is only the *first* step!
Crossing the Jordan River (type of Baptism in or with the Holy Spirit), and living in the Promised Land (type of walking in the fullness, power, and victory of the Spirit) is truly the perfect will of God for His New Testament people! All in and through Christ while we are still here on earth!

Peter said, "***Repent*** (get out of Egypt), *and **be baptized** every one of you in the Name of Jesus Christ for the remission of sins* (cross the Red Sea), ***and ye shall receive the gift of the Holy Ghost.***" (Cross the Jordan, and live triumphantly in the Promised Land!)

Remember Jesus said,
> *"How much more shall your Heavenly Father give the Holy Spirit **to them that ask Him?**"*
> (*Luke 11:13*)

We must *ask* Jesus to save us! God does *not* give His Spirit to the unsaved! Therefore Jesus is only referring to those who belong to Him!

Once again: if the baptism with the Holy Spirit comes automatically when we receive Christ as Savior and Lord ...

WHY WOULD JESUS TELL BELIEVERS TO *ASK* FOR HIM?

Question:
Why is Satan so desperate to keep us from the power (or "sign gifts") of the Spirit, and not nearly so much from the *"fruit?"*

BECAUSE WE WON'T HURT SATAN NEARLY AS MUCH BY BEARING FRUIT!

Spiritual fruit shows *human beings* who we are. (*John 13:35*)
Spiritual gifts show humans *and* demons who we are! (*Eph. 6:10-18*)

WE HURT SATAN WITH *SPIRITUAL* WEAPONS! (*2Cor.10:4*)

No demon wants to be identified and cast out! (*Discerning of spirits,* and *deliverance*)
Satan does not want people supernaturally *healed,* or brought to faith in Christ by *miracles.*
He doesn't want believers speaking in *tongues, interpreting* or *prophesying,* so God can *exhort, edify,* and *comfort* us. (*1Cor.14:3*)
Neither does the enemy want us to minister *words of wisdom* and *knowledge,* so God can bring people out of areas of darkness such as fear, unbelief, ignorance and deception. In short, the devil does not want *any* of us to believe the whole Counsel of God!
Let's never forget, *"Hath God said?"* was his favorite lie!

With that in mind, take a look at *Mark 16:15-18, 1Cor. ch's 12* and *14* (which is the *"Word of God, yesterday, today and for ever"*), then decide if it's Satan, or our Father in Heaven who is keeping believers from dwelling in the Promised Land!
Again, I had originally planned to include this in chapter12, but felt very strongly that this much was needed here. However it is received, I must be faithful to what I believe the Spirit is saying to the church!
May He also make the following real to you.
Even our use of the Word of God will not hurt the demonic realm unless it is quickened by the power and anointing of the Holy Spirit. The Word must come from the lips of a believer who by faith wields the *"Sword of the Spirit"* in right standing with God's Sovereign will!
Please read *James 5:14-18, and Heb. ch's 3 and 4* in light of what has just been written.
There is also no doubt that praising God strengthens our faith! Faith empowers the "Sword," which in turn defeats the enemy!

****

**With the High praises of God in our mouth
A two edged sword in our hand,
We'll bind their kings with chains
Their nobles with bands of iron,
With the high praises of God in our mouth
A two edged sword in our hand!**

(Words from a Chorus based on *Ps. 149: 6 and 8*)

****

Following directly after those powerful words, come these;
"To execute upon them the judgment written: this honor have all His saints. Praise ye the Lord."
(Ps.149:9)
The *"High Praises"* of God are nothing less than Spirit filled, anointed words of faith; spoken or sung *"with the Spirit"* (with tongues), or *"with the understanding"* (our own natural language.)
(1Cor.14:14-15.)

Naturally, there are many who will try to use other Scriptures to rob you of this great blessing, but, *"Let God be true, and every man* (and demon) *a liar!"* (Rom.3:4) Men make come, and men may go, but when it comes to using God's Spiritual gifts to bind, cast out, or gain victory over Satan, and the entire demonic host ...

"THIS HONOR HAVE <u>ALL</u> HIS SAINTS"

"I would (earnestly desire) *that ye **all spake with tongues**, but rather* (desire even more so) *that ye prophesied: for greater is he that prophesieth than he that speaketh with tongues, **except he interpret, that the church may receive edifying.**"(1Cor.14:5)*

I believe with all my heart that as you read these things (and are sincerely seeking the truth), you can ask the Holy Spirit to baptize you this very moment! Let Him take you out of the "wilderness" of nominal Christianity, and into the deeper walk and progressive victory of the Spirit filled life!

The Promised Land is waiting for *all* God's people!

NOTE: Once in the Promised Land (after the forty years), the children of Israel would wait still one more year (the "extra" year) for the first new harvest. The first year they would eat the old corn of the land. (See *Josh.5:11-12*)

Finally: on the day after the Sabbath, and before the new harvest could be gathered in,

*"The Lord spoke to Moses saying, ... Ye shall bring **a sheaf** of the first fruits of your harvest unto the priest: and **he shall wave the sheaf before the Lord, to be accepted for you: on the morrow after the Sabbath** the priest shall wave it. And ye shall offer that day when ye wave the sheaf, an **he lamb without blemish** of the first year for a burnt offering unto the Lord. And the meat* (meal) *offering thereof shall be **two tenth deals of fine flour mingled with oil**, an offering made by fire unto the Lord for a sweet savor: and **the drink offering thereof shall be of wine**, the fourth part of an hin. And ye shall eat **neither bread, nor parched corn, nor green ears, until the selfsame day that ye have brought an offering unto your God**: it shall be a statute **for ever** throughout your generations in all your dwellings." (Lev.23:9-14)*

Before the harvest, one sheaf was to be waved (offered) before the Lord! On the day after the Sabbath! (Three days after Passover)
Do not our hearts burn within us as we see, *"The Author and Finisher of our faith"* (Heb.12:2) raised on the third day as the *"Single Sheaf"* of the first fruits harvest: presenting Himself before His Father in heaven (on that "selfsame resurrection day") to be totally accepted on our behalf?
There could be no ingathering (harvest of souls) until this final act of redemption was fulfilled!
(Heb.9:11-15, 24)

*"But **now is Christ risen from the dead**, and become **the First Fruits** of them that slept."*
(1Cor:15:20)
"Of His own will begat He us with the Word of Truth, that we should be a kind of first fruits of His creatures." (James 1:18)

What Jesus did – He did for us!

Of course, we also see the Lord Jesus as our Burnt Offering Lamb without blemish: but wait! What have we here? ...
*"**Two tenth deals of fine flour mingled with oil.**" (v.13)*
Can we not see and celebrate this *new* picture; Jew and Gentile *"mingled"* (brought together) by *"oil"* (the anointing of the Holy Spirit) in Christ?

*"For He (Jesus) is our Peace, **Who hath made both one**, and hath broken down the middle wall of partition between us ... for to make in Himself of twain (two) **one new man**, so making peace." (see Eph.2:11-22)*

*"Therefore if any man be in Christ, he is a **new creature**: old things are passed away; behold, all things are become new." (2Cor.5:17)*

"For by one offering He hath perfected for ever them that are sanctified." (Heb.10:14)

*"**The drink offering thereof shall be of wine.**" (v.13)*
The wine speaks of joy, gladness and the abundant, or full life found in the Holy Spirit!
(See Ps.104:15, Acts 2:1-13)

The following Scriptures present important truth concerning *"First Fruits,"* and *"First Born,"* and make for a deeper study in the Word of God.
FIRST FRUITS - see *Rom.11 esp. v.16, Rom.8 esp. v. 23, 1Cor.15 esp. 20-23, James1 esp. v.18.*
FIRST BORN - see *Rom.8 esp. v.29, Col.1 esp.v.18, Heb.12 esp. v.23.*

With all these amazing verses in our hearts we may now see the beauty of *Psalm 126*, and in particular *verses 5* and *6*.

"They that sow in tears shall reap in joy. He (Jesus, the Single Sheaf) that goeth forth and weepeth, bearing precious Seed, (His Word) shall doubtless come again with rejoicing, bringing his sheaves (the redeemed) with Him."

SUMMARY:
To reap the blessings of the Feast of First Fruits (or any Feast), we must first *"See Jesus: Made a little lower than the angels for the suffering of death, crowned with glory and honor; that He by the grace of God should taste death for every man. For it became Him, for Whom are all things, and by Whom are all things, in bringing many sons (sheaves or first fruits) unto glory, to make the Captain (Author, First Fruit, and First Born) of their salvation perfect (complete, as the Gatherer of the whole harvest or Church) through sufferings. For both He that sanctifieth and they who are sanctified are **all of one**: for which cause He is not ashamed to call them brethren." (Heb.2:9-11)*

Jesus stands alone as the True and Perfect *"Passover Lamb:"* the Only Holy Life, and Fulfiller of the *"Feast of Unleavened Bread."*

By becoming *"The First Fruit"* accepted before God the Father; He paved the way for the great ingathering, or harvest of the redeemed in preparation for His Glorious return! Now we see the *"Feast of First Fruits"* fulfilled in Christ, and being fulfilled in these last-days in the completion of His Church!

When Jesus ascended up on high,

*"He gave gifts unto men ... some **apostles**; and some, **prophets**; and some, **evangelists**; and some **pastors** and **teachers**; for the perfecting* (equipping) *of the saints,* (believers) *for the work of the ministry, for the edifying of the body of Christ: Till we ALL come in the unity of the faith, and of the knowledge of the Son of God, unto a perfect man, unto the measure of the Stature of the fullness of Christ." (Eph.4:8-13)*

*"That in the dispensation of the fullness of times **He might gather together in one all things IN CHRIST**, both which are in Heaven, and which are on earth; **even in Him**." (Eph.1:10)*

But Jesus also said,
*"Every plant, which My Heavenly Father hath not planted, shall be **rooted up**." (Matt.15:13)*

...Gather ye together first the tares, (weeds resembling wheat) *and **bind them in bundles** to burn them: but gather the wheat into My barn."* (From *Matt.13:24-30, 36-43*)

..."So shall it be at the end of the world: the angels shall come forth, and sever (separate) *the wicked from among the just, and shall **cast them into the furnace of fire**: there shall be wailing and gnashing of teeth."* (See *Matt.13:47-50*)

THE FEAST OF PENTECOST (*Lev.23:15-21*)
*"And when the day of Pentecost was **fully come** ..." (Acts2:1)*

We began this chapter with about one hundred and twenty anxious followers of Christ waiting behind the locked the doors of an upper room (in fear of the Jewish authorities) for the promise of Jesus to be fulfilled! (see *John20:19*, and *Acts1:12-13*)

"Ye shall be baptized with the Holy Ghost not many days hence." (*Acts1:5*)

The feast of Pentecost began exactly fifty days after the priest waved the sheaf of the first fruits before the Lord; and the details are phenomenal.

*"And the Lord spake unto Moses, saying, ...Ye shall offer a **new meat*** (meal) ***offering** unto the Lord. Ye shall bring out of your habitations **two wave loaves of two tenth deals**: they shall be of fine flour; **they shall be baked with leaven**; they are the **first fruits** unto the Lord." (Lev.23:16-17)*

Like the candlestick with three branches either side (**seven lamps in total**), which was the central piece of Tabernacle furniture, God places Pentecost in the center of the seven feasts; making it an immensely important aid in our understanding of God's purpose for the church.

NOTE: Satan never stops working! He has modern Menorahs (candlesticks) routinely displaying five, eight or even nine lamps in a flagrant disregard of God's original and precious design of seven!

Those Menorahs remind me of his other favorites; today's reader-friendly Bible translations that have likewise added to, or taken away from the Word of God – what a coincidence!

But have you ever wondered why so many erroneous Bible versions have spewed onto the market in just the last thirty or forty years? Could they perhaps be demonically inspired tools to aid in the "*falling away*," and "*departing from the faith*" mentioned in *2Thess.2:1-3 and 1Tim.4:1?*

Could these things be playing their part in the great end time deception spoken of by Jesus in *Matt.24, Mark 13, and Luke 21?* ... Truly, the time is at hand!

Pentecost was a new meal (grain) offering, and would be in complete contrast to all others!

For the first and only time ever, leaven (type of sin) was included in an offering to the Lord!

Two wave loaves of two tenth deals (making them equal in every way) speaks of nothing less than Jew and Gentile being brought before God on exactly the same basis: BY FAITH!

"But without faith, it is impossible to please Him." (Heb.11:6)

In these two loaves we may see again a type of "*first fruits.*" Just as the High priest had waved the first sheaf before the Lord (foreshadowing Christ presenting Himself before the Father as our perfect "First Fruit Offering"), so on the day of Pentecost, the High priest waved the two leavened loaves, which were also first fruits.

"And the priest shall wave them with the bread of the first fruits for a wave offering before the Lord."
(Lev.23:20)

Only when the children of Israel celebrated Pentecost for the first time, did God begin to reveal His heart's desire for the chosen nation.

*"Ye have seen what I did unto the Egyptians, and how I bare you on eagle's wings, and **brought you unto Myself**. Now therefore, if ye will obey My voice indeed, and keep My covenant, **then shall ye be a peculiar** (special) **treasure unto Me above all people**: for all the earth is mine: and ye shall be unto Me **a kingdom of priests**, and **a holy nation**."* (Ex.19:4-6)

These beautiful, but conditional promises, were followed by,

SANCTIFICATION. The people washed their clothes (purification, *v.10*), and for three days refrained from marital intimacy. (Separation, *v.15*)

GOD DESCENDING upon Mt. Sinai in fire with thunder and lightning, thick cloud, and the voice of the trumpet so loud that the mountain shook, and all the people trembled! (*vs. 16-18*)

GOD SPEAKING to His people in a new way, and giving them the Law! (*Ex.20:1-17*)

Sadly, as we have already seen, the sons of Jacob were not yet ready to become a "*kingdom of priests*," and the "*holy nation*" God so yearned for them to be. Even as the revelation of God's Law was being given to Moses, rebellious people began corrupting themselves with the golden calf. As a result, **three thousand** of them would die at the hands of the Levites! (*Ex.32*)

Keep remembering that all the natural feasts (Old Testament types or shadows) pointed directly towards Christ (The Fulfiller); and through Him, to spiritual application by the Church. (New Testament substance)

By this we can measure something of God's patience, grace, and longsuffering; in that He allowed nearly fourteen hundred and fifty years of preparation before Jesus, *"our Passover Lamb and Unleavened Bread"* ascended on high as *"First Fruits;"* and sat down at the right hand of the Father in order to bring forth God's Pentecostal revelation!

Before and until that day arrived,

"... ye shall offer with the bread seven lambs without blemish of the first year, and one young bullock, and two rams: they shall be for a burnt offering unto the Lord, with their meat (meal) *offering, and their drink offering made by fire, of sweet savor unto the Lord. Then ye shall sacrifice one kid of the goats for a sin offering, and two lambs of the first year for a sacrifice of peace offerings ... And ye shall proclaim on the selfsame day, that it may be an holy convocation unto you: ye shall do no servile work therein: it shall be a statute for ever in all your dwellings throughout your generations."* (*Lev.23:18,19,21*)

We know that all these offerings were fulfilled in Christ; with this one very notable exception;

*"Ye shall bring ... **two wave loaves** of two tenth deals ... **baked with leaven** ...and wave them **before the Lord.**"* (*Lev.23:17,20*) (Loaves baked with leaven could never represent the Lord Jesus Christ!)

When the great Day of Pentecost finally dawned in Jerusalem, God had prepared a remnant of His people for a new and mighty revelation of His will and purpose. A revelation which would forever change the way He would deal with Israel, and ultimately the whole world!

As the high priest began to perform the ritual waving of two leavened loaves in the temple, God began to reveal His *true* desire for the chosen nation ... Jew *and* Gentile ... His Church!

*"But ye are **a chosen generation, a royal priesthood, an holy nation, a peculiar** (special) **people;** that ye should **show forth the praises of Him** who hath called you out of darkness into His marvelous light: **Which in time past were not a people, but are now the people of God: which had not obtained mercy, but now have obtained mercy.**"* (*1Pet.2:9-10*)

*"And from Jesus Christ who is the Faithful Witness, and the **First Begotten** of the dead, and the Prince of the kings of the earth. Unto Him that loved us, and washed us from our sins in His own Blood, and hath made us kings and priests unto God and His Father; to Him be Glory and Dominion for ever and ever. Amen!"* (*Rev. 1:5-6*)

Those beautiful but conditional promises of God (All fulfilled in Christ) must now be received by faith, and are followed by,

SANCTIFICATION. Our robes (lives) are washed (purified) in the Blood of the Lamb! (*Rev.1:5, 7:14*) In God's sight, the true Church is Christ's virgin bride separated from this world unto Him! (*John 17:9-17, Rev.19:7, 21:2*)

GOD DESCENDING from heaven upon the upper room in fire (cloven tongues), and as the sound of a "*rushing mighty wind*," which "*filled all the house where they were sitting.*" (*Acts2:2-3*)

GOD SPEAKING to and through His people in a new way by the Holy Spirit!
"*And they were all filled with the Holy Ghost, and began to speak with other tongues, as the Spirit gave them utterance.*" (*Acts2:4, 19:6, 1Cor.12:10,14:4-5*)
After the form and ritual of Old Testament tradition, here was the fire and reality of **New Testament life!**

So when the Day of Pentecost was "*fully come*," the Holy Spirit empowered the young church, giving men (believers already) the supernatural ability to, "*Turn the world upside down.*" (*Acts 17:6*)
If the early Church needed that power, then how much more does the end-time Church, which is asleep (for the most part) in a Laodicean bed?
(The times and spiritual condition of the Body of Christ throughout the church age, are clearly shown in the letters to the seven churches: *Rev.2 and 3*.)

NOTE: leaven as a natural fungus or bacteria, continues to grow until it is arrested (killed) by heat, i.e. fire! In the believer, spiritual leaven (sin) behaves in exactly the same way, and so the Holy Spirit often allows us to go through "the fire" of trials and tribulations in order to purge out the "*old leaven*" from our lives! (*1Cor.5:7*)

On the Day of Pentecost, the "*tongues of fire*" that sat upon the one hundred and twenty would fulfill the words of John the Baptist in a literal manifestation of *Luke 3:16.*

"*He* (Jesus) *shall baptize you with the Holy Ghost and fire.*"

The number one hundred and twenty represents, and is seen from God's gracious point of view as, "***The end of all flesh.***" (See *Gen.6:3*)
This throws revelation light on both the judgment of sin in Christ (for our salvation), and the ultimate judgment of mankind (all flesh), which will be by fire – *not* water!
This means that from the moment we are born again (redeemed), God sees the death of our "leavened" flesh through Christ's death, and the perfection of our new "unleavened" spiritual lives through Christ's resurrected Life!
Now the "*glass*" is a little clearer.

"*For ye are dead, and your life is hid with Christ in God.*" (*Col.3:3*)

"*For by one offering He hath perfected for ever them that are sanctified.*" (*Heb.10:14*)

"*And if Christ be in you, the body is dead because of sin; but the spirit is life because of righteousness.*" (*Rom.8:10*)

Once again: in Christ we are justified by faith. God immediately declares us righteous through the Blood of Christ. Then (in Christ) we are sanctified by the Holy Spirit, as God begins to change us into what He has already declared us to be!

"*Being confident of this very thing, that He which hath begun a good work in you will perform it until the day of Jesus Christ.*" (*Phil.1:6*)

146

*"For we are **His workmanship**, created in Christ Jesus unto good works, which God hath before ordained that we should walk in them." (Eph.2:10)*

Let me stress that our spiritual perfection is in **God's sight only!** That's how precious and powerful the covering of the Blood of Jesus really is!

Christ's Blood and CHRIST'S BLOOD ALONE stands between Mankind and eternal damnation!

(Let no one be afraid to declare that glorious yet sobering truth!)

Sadly, because of our flesh, one visitation of fire would not be enough!

One look through the book of Acts, and we see that although God's Fire brought immediate power, strength and effectiveness to the early church, it would take the constant attention and care of the Holy Spirit to deal with "leaven;" and to keep things on track!

Ananias and Sapphira lied to the Holy Ghost and died under the judgment of God. (*Acts 5:1-11*)

Disputes arose between Greeks and Hebrews concerning the daily ministrations (provisions) to widows in the church. (*Acts 6:1*)

Great arguments broke out over the need to circumcise the Gentile believers. (*Acts 15*)

Paul and Barnabas departed asunder as a result of contention. (*Acts 15:36-41*)

Peter was rebuked openly in Antioch, for refusing to eat with the Gentiles when James and others arrived from Jerusalem. (*Gal.2:11-21*)

I mention these things, not to criticize, but to reveal an important truth. You may have heard Christians lifting up certain ministers today as though they were "supermen." You may also have heard certain ministers lifting up the apostles (especially Paul) to the point of idolatry!

Yet the Word of God thunders, *"A man can receive nothing, except it be given him from Heaven." (John 3:27)*

At our best we are men with Jesus. At our worst – we are just men!

It should come as no surprise that the Bible's middle verse reads as follows:

"It is better to trust in the Lord than to put confidence in man." (Ps.118:8)

The book of Acts and the epistles are the best records (patterns) we have of Church government, conduct, and life; but men are still only men!

"All flesh is as grass, and all the glory of man as the flower of grass. The grass withereth, and the flower thereof falleth away: but the Word of the Lord endureth for ever." (1Pet.1:24)

*"**Therefore let no man glory in men**" (1Cor.3:21)*

OUR *POSITION* IS PERFECT IN CHRIST; OUR *CONDITION* IS ANYTHING BUT!

*"And ye shall proclaim on the selfsame day, that it may be an holy convocation unto you: ye shall do **no servile work** therein: it shall be **a statute for ever in all your dwellings** throughout your generations." (Lev.23:2)*

To keep the Feast of Pentecost we must first acknowledge our absolute need to be *"baptized with* (or in) *the Holy Spirit,"* and to rely upon Him on a day-to-day basis!

Only then will the words, "*No servile work*" find reality in our lives. God does not intend for us to "*walk (or work) in the flesh,*" but "*after the Spirit;*" (*Rom.8:1-14*) and that we should do everything, "*heartily, as to the Lord and not unto men.*" (*Col.3:23*)

This is why the Spirit confirms that Pentecost must be kept as, "**A statute for ever in all your dwellings.**" (In our hearts now, and throughout our entire Christian lives!)

Although we are in for a battle …

"*The flesh lusteth against the Spirit, and the Spirit against the flesh …*" (*Gal.5:17*)

…The battle is the Lord's!

"*There was a long war between the house of Saul* (flesh) *and the house of David:* (Spirit) **but David waxed stronger and stronger, and the house of Saul waxed weaker and weaker!**"

(2Sam.3:1)

So no matter what it may look like during any given moment of our lives, we can boldly confess by faith,

The Lord won the victory *FOR* us: is winning it *IN* us, and will share it *WITH* us –
FOR ALL ETERNITY!

Put that in your "spiritual bank" and stand fast Christian: Jesus will see us through!

SUMMARY:

Pentecost was at the very heart of the seven feasts; and its spiritual application is now the key to receiving every blessing God has called the Body of Christ to enjoy today!

The pouring out of the Holy Spirit when that day was "*fully come*" was by no means a one-time experience: since Acts, chapter 2, multitudes of believers have been blessed with the baptism of the Spirit, and continue to move in His anointing, gifts, and power!

In this feast, God confirms His love and calling to the Gentiles who are seen as one of the leavened loaves offered to Him on that day. His Word, spoken by James to the church in Jerusalem, rings down through the ages.

"*Men and brethren, hearken unto me: Simeon* (Peter) *hath declared how God at the first did visit the Gentiles, to take out of them a people for His Name. And to this agree the words of the prophets; as it is written, After this I will return, and will build again the **Tabernacle of David**, which is fallen down; and will build again the ruins thereof, and I will set it up: that **the residue of men** might seek after the Lord, **and all the Gentiles, upon whom My Name is called**, saith the Lord, Who doeth all these things.*" (*Acts 15:13-17*)

Having touched briefly upon Spiritual gifts and fruit in the "*Feast of First Fruits,*" I would like to share some additional thoughts with you here.

The balance of gifts and fruit (in type) can be found as far back as the book of Exodus. Describing the "*robe of the ephod*" (also with beautiful types of its own), God spoke to Moses and said,

"*Beneath upon the hem of it thou shalt make **pomegranates** (Spiritual fruit) of **blue**, (Heavenly) and of **purple**, (Royalty) and of **scarlet**, (Blood and suffering) round about the hem thereof; and **bells of gold** (Spiritual gifts) between them round about: **a golden bell and a pomegranate, a golden bell and a pomegranate**, upon the hem of the robe round about.*" (*Ex.28:33-34*)

Naturally: the ringing of bells would be softened by the pomegranates so God would hear Aaron's distinct sound when he went into the Holiest of Holies, ***"that he dieth not."*** *(v.35)*

Spiritually: the gifts (bells) are softened or balanced by the fruit (pomegranates), so the unique sound of Jesus will be heard before God in the Church, the world, and the heavenly realms.

Letting *everyone* know that the Body of Christ is alive and well!

NO GIFTS – NO POWER!   NO FRUIT – NO GROWTH!

Now here's an amazing coincidence.

Take a careful look at *1Corinthians; chapters 12, 13 and 14*. There you will actually find a *"Bell,"* a *"Pomegranate,"* and a *"Bell!"*

Chapter 12 involves **GIFTS** – *13* involves **FRUIT** – *14* involves **GIFTS.**

(With specific instructions on how to use the ones which can be misused in the "flesh" i.e. "Tongues," "Interpretation," and "Prophecy.")

Interestingly enough, no instructions come with the *"Word of Wisdom,"* the *"Word of Knowledge,"* the *"Gift of Faith,"* *"Gifts of Healing,"* *"Miracles,"* or *"Discerning of spirits."* **Why? ...**
Because the Holy Spirit alone has control of those!

Of course, other gifts are mentioned in addition to the nine in *1Cor.12:8-10*: (see *1Cor.12:28, Rom.12:6-9, and Eph.4:11*) making a grand total of twenty-two.

However, the Fruit of the Spirit is,
"Love, Joy, Peace, Long-suffering, Gentleness, Goodness, Faith, Meekness, and Temperance;"
(*Gal.5:22-23*) making a total of just nine!

So although we are not given the actual number of *"Bells and Pomegranates"* sown onto the hem of Aaron's robe, my observation (from the balance of Scripture, and to glorify the Lord Jesus) is that there may well have been – you guessed it!
Nine Bells, and **Nine Pomegranates!**

Obviously our salvation does not depend on that particular type of revelation (one day we'll know for sure), but isn't it fun exploring possibilities?

FOOT NOTE:

It needs be said that throughout our incredible Old Testament journey, the Gentiles (as a whole) stood *"afar off,"* and merely watched as the children of Israel came all the way from the bondage of Egypt, to their ultimate liberty (of the Spirit) in an upper room somewhere in the heart of Jerusalem.

For we Gentiles, *"were **aliens** from the commonwealth of Israel, and **strangers** from the covenants of promise, having **no hope**, and **without God** in the world: **BUT NOW IN CHRIST JESUS**, ye who sometimes were afar off are **made nigh** by the **Blood of Christ**. For He is our peace, Who hath made both one, and hath broken down the middle wall of partition between us ... for to make in Himself of twain* (two) *one new man, so making peace!" (Eph.2:12-15)*

For the eternal glory of God in Christ, Gentiles have become ONE with Jews! We are a NEW CREATION: *"old things have passed away, and ALL things are become new!" (2Cor.5:17)*

Purely as a result of God's amazing grace, Jews and Gentiles have been given the blessed privilege of reflecting the Light of His Glory into a world of gross darkness and sin, and can now proclaim together the Glorious Gospel of Christ as its only salvation and eternal hope!

Now in this present world, thanks to God's great gifts of *"Passsover," "Unleavened Bread," "First Fruits,"* and *"Pentecost"* (the last three feasts I'll share later), we can put on the *"Whole armor of God ... stand against all the wiles of the devil ... and wrestle* (to defeat) *the powers and principalities of this present darkness."* (*Eph.6:10-18*) The very spirits that even now rule over the unsaved *"children of disobedience;"* (*Eph.2:2*) those lost and still fallen sons of Adam!

In these last days, compromise and ungodly New Age doctrines are flooding into the Body of Christ like never before. We must take up the Mighty "Sword" of God's Word, stand fast, and slay the ungodly giants of worldliness and deception, bringing every dark thing into His Marvelous Light. Therefore ...

"Have no fellowship with the unfruitful works of darkness, but rather REPROVE THEM!" (*Eph.5:11*)

And reprove them we shall!

PART TWO

UNCOVERING THE UNCOVERER

"REPROVE" (Eph.5:11)

Strong's Concordance: To confute, correct, admonish, convict, convince, tell a fault, rebuke.

Webster's dictionary: To overwhelm by argument, warn, prove, persuade, reprimand, scold, and express disapproval of.

Nelson's King James Study Bible: Expose. (Bring into the light)

CHAPTER ELEVEN

ARE WE DECEIVED?

(In order to deceive, one must first be *deceived!)*

I have never heard anyone say, "I'm deceived!" Occasionally, "I *was* deceived;" but never, "I *am* deceived!" The pride of man makes it extremely difficult to admit to *present* deception, especially when it comes to spiritual matters such as long held beliefs, or knowledge gleaned from trusted teachers. To the Christian however, some deceptions are obvious.

1. **Every unsaved person on the planet is deceived!** (All true believers know this, and can freely admit to their own deception before coming to Christ)

2. **Anyone trusting in his or her own good works** (religious efforts) **to get them to Heaven is** *doubly* **deceived!** ("*For by grace are saved through faith and that not of yourselves, it is the* **gift** *of God,* **not of works,** *lest any man should* **boast.**" (*Eph.2:8-9*)

3. **Anyone who adds to, takes away from, contradicts, or corrupts the Word of God is deceived! Such a person who then influences others is a deceiver!** (A false prophet or teacher)

All right so far? Yes of course. If only *all* deceptions were that easy to discern – but wait! Look at number **3** again. Now read these prophetic words from Jesus Himself.

"For many shall come in My Name, saying, **I am Christ** *… And many* **false prophets** *… and* **false Christs** *… shall rise, and shall deceive many … insomuch that if it were possible, they shall deceive the* **very elect.**" (True believers) (From *Matt.24:5,11, and 24*)

Millions of people have been taught and are now believing that we *all* have the "Christ consciousness;" the "Divine light within;" or that "God is in all, so all is God!"

The "New Age Movement" also teaches that Jesus Christ was just one of a number of "enlightened souls" who reached an extraordinary level of "Divine consciousness" (along with Buddha, Mohammed, Confucius etc.,) and, as a result, became a "god." Therefore if those men achieved "god-hood," so can we! The fact is, millions of people are already saying, "I am Christ!"

(How can New Agers believe in the *real* Jesus Christ, if they are busy believing in themselves?)

HEAR THE TRUTH – DO THE TRUTH!

I'd like to repeat the statement I made in the opening pages of this book.

The victory of deception is the unawareness of our defeat!

It follows therefore, that the amount of victory we will gain over deception is in direct proportion to the amount of truth we are willing to embrace!

Many are familiar with Jesus' words, "***And ye shall know the truth, and the truth shall make you free.***" (*John 8:32*) Fewer realize that the "***And***" refers to an "***if***," which is a condition put forth in the previous verse. "***If ye continue in My Word, then are ye My disciples indeed; And ye shall know the truth, and the truth shall make you free.***"

So then, truth and freedom are progressively obtained by continuing in, and obeying the Word of God!

Jesus Christ is, "*The WAY, The TRUTH, and The LIFE*" (*John 14:6*)

Only His "*Sword*" (His Word) can cut away the cords of deception from our lives! (*Eph.6:17, Heb.4:12*)

But that is only the beginning!

Putting all this in the form of a question, the next vital issue becomes apparent.

If men and women are being deceived *within* the Church, how can they possibly minister truth, liberty and light to a world of darkness and deceit *without*?

In reality, our spiritual "freedom" does not come simply by acknowledging, or *knowing* the truth; but by *applying* it to every area of our lives!

"*But whoso looketh into the perfect law of liberty, and **continueth** therein, he being not a forgetful hearer, but a **doer** of the work, this man shall be blessed in his deed.*"

(*James 1:25*)

You might think that all Christians would be thrilled to hear, know, and apply God's Truth once they became aware of it, right? Wrong! – Why?

Because there is a price to pay!

Why else would Paul write to the Galatians saying,

"*Am I therefore become your enemy, because I tell you the truth?*" (*Gal.4:16*)

Let me give you an example.

Some thirty years ago (approaching my first Christmas as a believer), I saw with brand new "born again eyes," the worldliness and commercialism of the Christian tradition. Soon after, in prayer, I asked the Lord if Christmas was pleasing to Him.

A "*still small voice*" (*1Kings 19:12*) spoke to my heart and said,

"If the world hates Christ: why does the world love Christmas?"

I immediately checked my Bible to learn if that "voice" was indeed the *Spirit* of God; and found the verse where Jesus said,

"***If the world hate you, ye know that it hated Me before it hated you.***" (*John 15:18*)

The Word of God confirmed that the world hates Christ; so why *does* the world love Christmas?

Research into this "festival of lies" uncovered the "unholy spirit of Christmas," and led to the writing of a tract called, **"Christmas: the Truth Behind It."** (Did you know that the promotion of "Santa Clause" is one of the first lies parents teach their children?) Needless to say, the more I dug, the more lies I found! In the end, not one truth!

Since that first revelation of Christmas, it has pleased the Lord to give me many similar messages (reproving deceptions both in and out of the Church), which have been shared with people around the world. However, to say, "They were not always well received" is rather an understatement!

A brother who read the tract and heard the *real* story of Christmas, spoke for many when he said,

"I realize that's the truth, but my family and I love Christmas too much to give it up! Besides, we try to keep out all the bad stuff, and just concentrate on the good."

Later, this phrase, "keeping out the bad, and concentrating on the good" would evolve into, "It may be wrong, but we don't think of it like that!" (Parents also use this expression as an excuse for dressing up their young children as witches, zombies, ghouls or ghosts during Halloween!)

So then, part of the price we must pay to please God is to walk in the truth, and to separate ourselves and our children from religious corruption, and from the ways of a dead world still held in Satan's grip!

Many now know that Christmas, Halloween, and all other non-scriptural religious celebrations are nothing more than CONVERTED (Christianized) PAGAN FESTIVALS!

"Come out from among them, and be ye separate, saith the Lord, and touch not the unclean thing." (*2Cor.6:17*)

It may be the twenty-first century, but some things have *not* changed. **That is still the Word of God!** (Please understand, God loves you – that's why He has people writing books like this!)

V.I. The issue within the Body of Christ today is not; "**Are we** *saved?"* The real issue is, "**How saved** *are* **we?**"

Allow me to illustrate. Suppose we compare salvation to owning a portion of heavenly land.

The question *now* is, how much real estate would we possess? Sadly, some Christians don't have enough land to build a shed on – and that's not right! (I share these things to challenge myself as well as the reader!) Suppose God said we could have a thousand acres? Would we say, "Thank you Lord," and immediately move in and start to enjoy it? Or would we say (be honest now), "Well that's very nice of You Lord, but I'm really quite happy with the few square feet I already have.

I don't want to be greedy. Besides, taking on a thousand acres would demand so much more time, effort, and responsibility; not to mention the possibility of giants! Thanks, but no thanks; I think I'll stay were I am!"

No wonder the Israelites were called, *"The church in the wilderness!"* (*Acts 7:38*)

There are huge numbers of Christians sitting in "wilderness" churches and fellowships everywhere, going round and round *John 3:16*, who don't yet know that a "Spiritual Promised Land" exists, let alone how to go in and possess a thousand acres of it!

Three obvious reasons why believers are not entering, and living victoriously in the "Land" (the fullness of the Holy Spirit) are ignorance, unbelief, and the simple fear of moving in! (So often the fruit of bad teaching.) If we are willing to trust God and "follow the cloud" (acknowledge and obey the truth), God will lead us forward! But ...

"My people **are destroyed** (type of not growing, or living in victory) *for lack of knowledge. Because thou hast rejected knowledge,* **I will also reject thee**" (type of God leaving us where we are!)

(*Hos.4:6, Heb.6:1-3*)

We can become quite comfortable in our little corner of the wilderness: especially if the guides (leaders or teachers), who are supposed to take us into the Land, don't even know how to read the Map!

(Interpret the Scriptures) Bear in mind, that with every new, and increasingly flawed map (modern Bible translation), it becomes harder and harder for Christians to find the way in by themselves!

"Consider what I say; and the Lord give thee understanding in all things." (2Tim.2:7)

Let's put some common "wilderness teachings" to the test.

Have you been taught, and do you believe –

"WE ARE *ALL* BORN, OR CREATED IN THE IMAGE AND LIKENESS OF GOD?"

In gatherings where I have asked that question, at least ninety nine percent of the people raised their hands in affirmation! Many "guides" teach it; *vast* numbers of Christians believe it; but ...

IT'S AN ABSOLUTE LIE!

The truth is found in *Gen.5:3*.

*"And Adam lived an hundred and thirty years, **and begat a son in his own likeness, after his own image**; and called his name Seth."*

First: God does not create *sinful* beings! (Only sinners beget sinners!) Neither did He create beings in order that they should die!

Second: *"God is a Spirit"* (*John 4:24*) but had He chosen to manifest Himself as a human being, He would surely have looked a lot like Adam; His *first* human creation!

Third: Only three people in history were ever created (formed or made) in the image and likeness of God: **Adam, Eve,** (before sin!) and the **Lord Jesus Christ!**

The "image" is the *look* of; the "likeness" is the *nature* or character of.

Please put those things on one side for a moment, and allow me to build a scriptural foundation.

*"And God said, Let **Us** make man in **Our** image, after **Our** likeness"* (*Gen.1:26*)

There is no mistaking the plurality of that statement: God is Three in One: *Father, Son,* and *Holy Spirit!* (*Matt.28:19*)

NOTE: It's been said that, *1John 5:7* was added by those wishing to justify the doctrine of the "Trinity." (The word Trinity does not appear in scripture)

*"**For there are Three that bear record in Heaven, the Father, the Word, and the Holy Ghost: and these Three are One.**"* (*1John 5:7*)

Let me ask a question that will help ground a new believer in the faith.

Does the Holy Spirit witness with your spirit, that *1John 5:7* (like *all* Scripture) is *"inspired by God,"* (*2Tim.3:16*) and is indeed **THE WORD OF THE LIVING GOD?**

If so, simply stand on the Word!

So Adam and Eve were perfectly created (formed or made) as three-in-one beings in the image and likeness of the perfect Three-in-One God,

BODY – SOUL – SPIRIT!

Perhaps this will help:

GOD the FATHER relating to the SPIRIT of Adam.

GOD the SON (JESUS) relating to the BODY of Adam.

GOD the HOLY GHOST relating to the SOUL of Adam.

At that point, the couple had eternal life, but God told them they would lose that life if they sinned, i.e. ate the forbidden fruit.

*"For in the day that thou eatest thereof **thou shalt surely die**." (Gen.2:17)*

When Adam sinned, he obviously did not die physically: he went on to live a total of *"nine hundred and thirty years!" (Gen.5:5)* He died *spiritually*, and carried the nature of sin and spiritual death within him until he died *physically*! And so the scripture was fulfilled,
> ***"The wages of sin is death."*** Spiritual *and* natural! *(Rom.6:23, see Eze.18:4)*

When Adam begat (fathered) children (mankind), he did not pass on to us the perfect nature of God; he passed on to us his own fallen nature of sin!

"Wherefore, as by one man (Adam) *sin entered into the world, and death by sin; and so **death passed upon all men**, for that all have sinned." (Rom.5:12)*

Because of sin, mankind would no longer be created in the "Three in One" image of God, but in the "two in one" image (body and soul only) of fallen Adam!

Now here's the real heart of the matter.

    If all of us were born or created (naturally) in the image and likeness of God –

WHY ON EARTH WOULD WE NEED TO BE "BORN AGAIN?"

Think now! Who would want all men to believe they are created in the image and likeness of God? And why is the truth here so desperately important?

Remember the New Age teaching, "We all have the Christ Consciousness within." – "The Christ Light?" Well, they also teach, "There really is no sin, so there is no need to be born again." "We are all born with the Divine nature: We are all slowly evolving into gods!"

Christians who continue to believe and teach this "born in the image of God" lie are actually promoting the New Age Movement, and are aiding and abetting in their own deception!

Guess who loves that?

TRUTH: we must be *"Born again of the Spirit" (John 3:5)* in order to get back the spiritual life that was lost through Adam's sin!

Mankind must actually be **RECREATED** in order to be brought *back* into the image and likeness of God! ... Do you see it?

NOW WE CAN PREACH THE GOSPEL!

Look at it this way: there are only two kinds of people on earth: the "saved" who are now *back* in the image and likeness of God (three in one); and the "un-saved" (still two in one) who are not!
Another way: many "two in ones" are called, but few are chosen to be "three!"

I pray we're getting this, because if not, we will be preaching *"another Gospel!"* (*Gal.1:6-9*)

If (from our mother's womb) we were created in the image and likeness of God, WE ARE THE SAME AS JESUS WAS! Then of course we don't need Him! His death was for nothing!
We are (like all New Agers) evolving into what He, and others like Him have already become –
"gods!" (*Hath God sssss-said?*)

I cannot reveal this work of darkness more clearly than that!

But someone may say, "Didn't Paul and James teach that we *are* created in the image and likeness of God?"
To begin with, Paul and James were both writing to believers: people who had already become "three in one." But let's discount that for a moment, and consider the broader view. *1Cor.11:7* and *James 3:9* can best be seen in light of *Gen.9:6*: as referring to God's *original* creation.
The problems we have in using these verses to prove that we are all created in God's image and likeness are as follows:
In *1Cor.11:7*: Paul writes that only the man *"is the image and glory of God"* not the woman! Sorry ladies, but at least you are the *"glory of the man!"* Using that verse, someone could even teach that only Eve fell into sin! (How foolish would that be?)
James 3:9 also says that men are the only ones made after the *"similitude* (likeness) *of God!"* Whoops! Sorry again ladies: ONLY BROTHERS should know better than to *"bless God, and curse men"* with the same mouth! (I don't think so!) These verses must surely be read in the context of man's creation *before* sin.
*"For in the image of God **MADE** he man."*(*Gen.9:6*)
(I mean no disrespect to brothers, but in their walk with the Lord, Christian women often appear a lot closer to the image and likeness of God, than do many Christian Men!)
By the way:
Phil.2:7 says that Jesus was *"made in the likeness of men."*
Rom.8:3 says He was sent, *"in the likeness of sinful flesh."* … Did that make Jesus a sinner?
Of course not!
So then: since Adam and Eve, no one else but Jesus has been created in the *sinless* image and likeness of God!
David best summed it up when he said,
*"Behold, I was **shapen in iniquity**; and in sin did my mother conceive me."* (*Ps.51:5*)
David is not saying he was born out of wedlock; but that he was born (as all fallen men are) with the rebellious nature of sin! One of the more difficult truths to accept is that *all* of Adam's fallen children are born under the *"power of darkness:"* with *"one* (spiritual) *father, the devil."*
(See *Col.1:13* and *John 8:38-44*)

If we were automatically God's sons and daughters, there would be no need for the *"Book of Life:"* no *"Eternal judgment"* for the wicked in the *"Lake of Fire,"*(*Rev.20:14-15*) and no need to *"repent"* or *"receive Jesus Christ as Savior and Lord."* It's easy to see why the enemy loves this lie!

Some people think that Jesus had an advantage because He was born without sin. **Not so!**
Adam was created without sin, and it didn't help him one bit!
One strike and Adam was out!
Jesus Christ spent His entire life suffering every temptation known to man, (*Heb.4:15*) and died in agony on the cross without a single sin against Him! ... **NOT ONE SIN!**
A perfect, obedient, spotless life: all out of love for us!

"Neither is there salvation in any other: for there is none other Name under Heaven given among men, whereby we must be saved." (*Acts 4:12*)

We come now to another major deception: this one so deeply rooted in the true church and in religious communities everywhere, that it may never be completely weeded out!

TITHING

It would be difficult to find a false teaching that has pulled more "wolfish" wool over "sheepish" eyes throughout the church age than tithing!
The fervor, and so-called Godly zeal with which tithing is so often preached has to be seen to be believed!
It has reached the point where one well known pastor actually made the following statement:
"I don't see how anyone could get to Heaven without tithing!" [1]
Having spoken personally to the man, I know he stands sincerely behind every word.
However, when I challenged him to find one verse in the New Testament, which calls upon the Church to tithe – he could not!
He referred me to several Old Testament Scriptures: especially *Malachi 3:8-10,* but could offer not one single scripture under the New Covenant to support his erroneous position.
Of course he could always ask God to "adjust" His Word ...
"To as many as tithed, gave He power to become the sons of God."
Or this,
"Except a man be born of water, and of the Spirit, and tithes; he cannot enter into the Kingdom of Heaven!"
(Look again at the very beginning of this chapter for the definition of a deceiver!)

Now hear from leading "Christian Reconstructionists."
"The tithe is a royal tax ... to deny the tithe is to deny that God is Lord and King." [2]
Unfortunately these legalists are deadly serious! ("Deadly" being an appropriate word to describe *any* form of legalism!) They will destroy your spiritual life by robbing you of the liberty you should have in Christ Jesus! (*Gal.5:1*)
As we take an open and honest look at tithing throughout the Word of God; I pray we will discover truths upon which we can *"stand fast!"*
First the foundation
With two notable exceptions, all references to the *"tithe"* (the giving of a tenth) are found under the Law!
The first exception is found in *Genesis 14.*

159

After his battle with *"Chedorlaomer, and the kings that were with him,"* (*Gen. 14:17*) the victorious Abram (Abraham) *"brought back all the goods,"* i.e. spoils of war, (*v.16*) and gave *"Melchizedeck, (type of the Lord Jesus Christ, see Heb.7:11-17) King of Salem, and Priest of the most high God ...tithes of all."* (*Gen.14:20*)

The second is found in *Genesis 28*.

> *"And Jacob vowed a vowed, saying, If God will be with me, and will keep me in this way that I go, and will give me bread to eat, and raiment to put on, so that I come again to my father's house in peace; then shall the Lord be my God ... and of all that thou shalt give me I will surely **give the tenth** to thee."* (*Gen.28:20-22*)

Two important pieces of the tithing puzzle need to be locked in place here.

1. Both these examples occurred before the Law.
2. Abram and Jacob tithed voluntarily! Nowhere does it say in scripture that they were *commanded* to give!

It's unclear where the tithe originated: perhaps Abraham learned of it in Egypt, or from some other culture. Perhaps God spoke directly to him. Certainly God did not *insist* on the tithe until later; and then from His Old Testament people only!

The following can be stated with confidence.

Before the Law, tithing was very much a matter of free will. (*Gen.14:20, 28:22*)
Under the Law it was compulsory for Israel only! (*Deut.14:22-2, Eph.2:11-12*)
After the Law (which Jesus fulfilled), tithing was replaced altogether by voluntary giving: to be inspired or led by the Holy Spirit! (*Acts 4:32-37, 2Cor.9:7*)

> *"For **Christ is the end of the law** for righteousness to every one that believeth. For Moses describeth the righteousness which is of the law, that **the man which doeth those things shall live by them**."* (*Rom.10:4-5*)

In other words, if you live by (keep) one law, you must live by (keep) them all!

The *commandment* to tithe is found only under the law! So if you're going to tithe, be sure to keep *every other law* – OR ELSE!

That would include stoning someone to death for working on the Sabbath! (*Num.15:32-36*) (Which by the way is Saturday!)

Please understand.

According to the Holy Spirit, anyone who dares to put you in bondage to the tithe (or to any form of legalism) is preaching *"another Gospel"* by *"another Spirit,"* where Moses is upheld, *not* Jesus!

"Let them be accursed." (*Gal.1:6-9*)

If that wasn't enough.

The early church leadership flatly refused to put tithing upon Gentile believers!

This is how Peter and James put it,

*"Now therefore **why tempt ye God**, to put **a yoke** upon the neck of the disciples, **which neither our fathers nor we were able to bear?"** (Acts 15:10) "Wherefore my sentence is, that we trouble not them, which from among the Gentiles are turned to God: but that we write unto them that they abstain from*

pollutions of idols, and from fornication, and from things strangled, and from blood." (Acts 15:19-20)
(If tithing was for the Gentiles; surely they would have mentioned it!)

It's also interesting to note, that believers (Jews and Gentiles) would later be freed even from those early church laws regarding foods.

"For every creature of God is good, and nothing to be refused, if it be received with thanksgiving: for it is sanctified by the Word of God and prayer." *(1Tim.4:4-5)*

Let me ask this question.

Are we in sin because we eat a steak with the blood still in it? The apostle Paul gives an emphatic "NO!" We are free! In fact, he went so far as to say we can eat meat in *"an idol's temple,"* as long as it doesn't cause a weaker brother or sister to stumble! *(1Cor.8:4-13)*

To refuse any meat for religious reasons is to be deceived by a *"doctrine of demons"* *(1Tim.4:1-3)*. Whatever we eat (or don't eat) is unto the Lord! *(Rom.14:6)* Either way, we are free by faith!

Once again, beware of "tithe preachers:" after establishing our spiritual liberty, this same Paul pronounced a curse on anyone trying to bring us under the law!

Another question.

If the Word of God teaches that we are *"not under law, but under grace"* *(Rom.6:14)*, why do so many men still insist on promoting the tithe?

My observation is this:

Many are bound by legalism and tradition because they simply don't understand *true* grace.

Plus: many have absolutely no idea what it means to be led by the Holy Spirit!

As long as God's people continue to tithe, all sorts of ministries can count on a regular income, regardless of whether they are of God or not!

However, leaders like those of the Christian Reconstruction Movement are not merely satisfied with forcing the tithe and legalistic bondage on the Body of Christ: they want to put the whole world in the hands of Moses! (If you think I'm exaggerating, just wait until you get to chapter 16!)

According to brother Paul, men who teach tithing are *"false brethren."* They are under a curse, and are guilty of putting that curse on you! *(Gal.3:10)*

Once saved, we should understand that everything we have belongs to God!

"We are bought with a price, the precious Blood of Jesus." *(1Cor.7:23, 1Pet.1:19)*

To stay free, believers must seek to learn when, where, and how much to give, according to the leading of the Holy Spirit! *(Rom.8:14, Gal.5:18)* If this ever happens, we would soon discover which ministries were of God, and which were nothing more than leaky, carnal, man-made barges being kept afloat by the tithe!

If God orders the meal, *HE* will pick up the check! If not, men must find other ways to pay their bills. Emotional appeals (better known as begging), and tithing seem to be the most popular!

After hearing me speak on this subject, a brother in missions came to me and said,

"It would be great to simply trust God, but there's never enough money: I usually end up asking people for their financial support."

What could I say? What would you have said?

This is what David wrote,

"I have been young, and now am old; yet have I not seen the righteous forsaken, nor his seed begging bread." (Ps.37:25)

That tells us a lot about those who beg; and not just the ones standing in front of stores or by the roadside! (The worst possible testimony comes when the Body of Christ begs the world for help!)

Once and for all: TITHING IS NOT OF THE SPIRIT OF GOD!

"For where the Spirit of the Lord is, there is liberty." (2Cor.3:17)
"Am I therefore become your enemy, because I tell you the truth?" (Gal.4:16)

NOTE: Not once in *any* of his inspired letters to the churches, does Paul even hint at tithing!
If God had wanted tithing, do you not think He would have told the *"apostle to the Gentiles"* to tell us? (Can't the tithe pushers see that?) Paul does however, have plenty to say about giving! (*See 1Cor.9:7-14, 16:1-2, 2Cor.9, Eph.4:28*)
The sum of his teaching is this –

"If ye be led of the Spirit, ye are not under the law." (Gal.5:18)
And,
"Every man according as he purposeth in his heart, so let him give; not grudgingly, or of necessity (compulsion): *for God loveth a cheerful giver."* (2Cor.9:7)

Offerings: free will (voluntary) and even sacrificial giving if that's the way the Holy Spirit leads, or wants to teach us – **YES!** But never by *law* (compulsion, tradition or fear), which is what makes it a legalistic curse! (And tithing will never be anything else!)
One woman (a single mother) who came to our fellowship (there are many like her) was so burdened by the tithe, she often had no money left for her children's school lunches!
Praise God for setting her (and so many others) free!

First the bad news. Most hard-line tithe preachers won't budge an inch when it comes to a message like this. If they ever had to give up on the tithe, they would surely find a way to legalize and enforce the free will offering!
Now the good news. If just one person receives the truth, and shares it with another, it *will* make a difference! Don't be afraid; speak the truth in love, and help set the captives free!

To end this chapter, I would like to include three more of the devil's sweet deceits.
Although they are somewhat less pervasive than the first two, they still influence a multitude of believers and as such, need to be exposed.

Deception
"WATER BAPTISM IS NECESSARY FOR SALVATION."

Truth *"Believe on the Lord Jesus Christ, and thou shalt be saved."* (Acts 16:31)
Truth *"If thou shalt confess with thy mouth the Lord Jesus, and shalt **believe** in thine heart that God raised Him from the dead, thou shalt be saved."* (Rom.10:9)
Truth *"For by grace are ye saved **through faith**; and that not of yourselves: it is the **gift of God: not of works,** lest any man should boast."* (Eph.2:8-9)

If the physical act of water baptism is necessary for salvation, then baptism becomes a "work" and salvation is no longer by faith alone!

Remember: anything that adds to, or takes away from the requirements of God's Word gives birth to deception! (See *Rev.22:18-19* to appreciate the seriousness of that warning.)

Baptism (full immersion) *after* salvation is a really important step of obedience, and one that opens the door to other great blessings such as baptism with (and gifts of) the Holy Spirit! (see *Acts 2:38*) But if you're relying on it to get you to Heaven ... you are deceived!

Jesus gave a command to baptize in *Matt.28:19*, but in *Mark 16:16* He said something which has been grossly misinterpreted, and now lies at the very heart of the "salvation by baptism" deception .

> ***"He that believeth and is baptized shall be saved ...*** (perhaps someone who stopped there, brought forth the error) however, Jesus goes on to say, ... ***but he that believeth not shall be damned."***

Jesus doesn't add the words, **and is not baptized** after "*he that believeth not.*" Why?

Because He's telling us that failure to be baptized won't damn us: **only not believing will!**

NOTE: Certain man-made denominations gathered around this false doctrine, but now even those within them are divided over its significance. (Man-made denominations? – Yes, they *all* are! Jesus doesn't build denominations, He builds *HIS* church!) But while we're on the subject of denominations, please allow me to step on *lots* of toes! They'll be no Anglicans, Baptists, Charismatics, Catholics, Lutherans, Methodists, Pentecostals, Presbyterians, etc., etc., etc., in Heaven! Only blood-washed, redeemed ex-sinners will be there; who by God's grace through faith alone, repented of their sins, received Jesus Christ as their Lord and Savior, and became the sons and daughters of God!

Let me share a definition of true believer's baptism, in simple rhyme.

> **An obedient outward expression**
> **Of salvation from death and sin,**
> **Which by grace through faith alone**
> **Has already occurred within.**

After salvation, baptism is an important Godly step of faith in our "*spiritual walk.*"

(Gal.5:25, Heb.6:1-2)

Before (or as necessary for salvation), it becomes nothing more than a "*filthy rag*" (*Is.64:6*) and is as "dead" as any other vain religious effort!

Adding anything to the finished work of Christ is an insult to Him, and an offence to the Grace of God!

Jesus died *for* our sin, "*and was raised again for our justification.*" (*Rom.4:25*)

As believers, we must (by faith) die *to* our sin, that "*we should walk in newness of life.*" (*Rom.6:4*)

God wisely gives us the act of water baptism as a type or symbol of our *death to sin* in order to strengthen our faith in its spiritual reality!

As we rise up out of the water, we identify with Christ's resurrection, and move closer to fulfilling the scripture:

*"That we might **know Him,** and the **power of His resurrection,** and the fellowship of **His sufferings,** being made conformable unto **His death."** (Phil.3:10)*

If we receive the inner witness of these truths, the scriptures should open like a beautiful flower.

"What shall we say then? (As Christians) *Shall we continue in sin, that grace may abound? God forbid. How shall we that are dead to sin, live any longer therein? Know ye not, that **so many of us as were baptized into Jesus Christ were baptized into His death?** Therefore we are buried with Him by baptism into death: that like as Christ was raised up from the dead by the glory of the Father, **even so we also should walk in newness of life.** For if we have been planted together in the **likeness of His death,** we shall be also in the **likeness of His resurrection:** knowing this, that our old man* (sinful nature) *is **crucified with Him,** that the body of sin might be destroyed, that henceforth we should **not serve sin."** Therefore ... **"Reckon ye also yourselves to be dead in deed unto sin, but alive unto God through Jesus Christ our Lord."** (Rom.6:1-5, 11)*

To any *true* believer I say this: if for any reason (age, physical limitations, fear of water, false teaching etc.,) you should die without being baptized, you will *not* lose your salvation! Baptism should be seen as an opportunity to walk deeper into the revelation of the new life, which is the life crucified to sin, and to the world.

Victorious living is manifesting Christ daily, reigning over the flesh, the world, and Satan's entire demonic realm!

To live that life should be our heart's desire, our confession, and our continual fervent prayer!

> *"I am crucified with Christ: nevertheless I live; yet not I, but Christ liveth in me: and the life which now I live in the flesh I live by the faith of the Son of God, who loved me, and gave Himself for me."* (Gal.2:20)

Be very careful: My first days as a Christian were spent under the ministry of a man who taught the following:

"If you were christened as a baby, there is no need to be baptized as a born again believer."
This is pure deception, and should not be regarded by any one who names the Name of Christ!

There is neither truth, nor spiritual value of any kind to be found in christening! It is a loathsome practice, and one found mainly within the most deceived of all demonically inspired, pseudo Christian denominations; the Catholic and Anglican (Episcopal) churches! Christening is still one of religion's most deeply ingrained deceptions, in spite of this clear proclamation from the Word of God.

> ***"REPENT, AND BE BAPTIZED EVERY ONE OF YOU IN THE NAME OF JESUS CHRIST ..."*** (Acts 2:38)

In order to repent, we must be old enough to know (or acknowledge) that we are sinners before God! **How in the world can a baby REPENT?**

(There is no scriptural justification for infant baptism whatsoever!)

An infant freely dedicated to the Lord by *believing* parents? ... Yes, by all means. (*Luke2:22*)

But "sprinkling" merely to enter or join religious institutions? (more accurately described as "tombs") – **NEVER!**

Many years ago, after returning to England, I watched a "Vicar" (Anglican priest) sprinkle a baby boy in the baptistery. After making a "sign of the cross" on the tiny forehead, he turned to the whole congregation and said (I'll never forget those sickly sweet words), "After the service, don't forget to say hello to your new baby brother in Christ!" Even though I was saved, I still wanted to strangle the man! Not just for that lie, but for all the lies I had grown up with in the so-called "church." Lies that are still holding so many in the bondage of ignorance, deception, and spiritual death!

Well, I didn't strangle him! And I repented of wanting to! I did however share the truth with him, and gave him a straightforward, heart-felt Gospel message. His reply came as no real surprise.

"Well, I believe there are many ways to God; we should all choose our own path."

Some of the saddest words anyone could *not* wish to hear; especially from the lips of a blind shepherd, leading his "flock" down the *"broad way that leads to destruction."*

Deception
TO BE CALLED A "MESSIANIC JEW"

The erroneous title, Messianic Jew is another demonic "cord," which gains strength from ignorance, or disregard for the finished work of Christ! Once again, there is no scriptural foundation to support it.

Truth *"For He is our peace, Who hath made both* (Jew and Gentile) *one, and hath broken down the middle wall of partition between us." (Eph.2:14)*

Truth *"There is neither Jew nor Greek, there is neither bond nor free, there is neither male nor female: for ye are all one in Christ Jesus." (Gal.3:28)*

Truth *"For in Christ Jesus neither circumcision availeth any thing, nor uncircumcision, but a new creature." (Gal.:6:15)*

A love for the nation of Israel should be deep in the heart of every true Christian: a love equal to the desire of seeing Jewish people saved through faith in God's Son!

Those of natural Israel, who *are* redeemed, join with all other believers around the world in making up the true Church, ***"The Israel of God."*** *(Gal.6:16)*

Unfortunately that *"wall of partition"* between Jew and Gentile, which was broken down by Christ's death and resurrection (see *Eph.2:11-17*) has been kept in place through the Church age (by the flesh of course), and today in many places is as high, and as thick as ever!

The scriptures make it so clear.

When a Jew comes to Christ he is no longer a Jew! The Gentile is no longer a Gentile! The two have become one in the Spirit!

"Old things (including carnal divisions) ***are passed away; behold, all things are become new."***
(2Cor.5:17)

One can understand why natural Jews have a strong dislike for the word "Christian;" after all, a satanically inspired monster by the name of Hitler had the habit of calling himself one! Throughout history, the vast majority of persecutions against the Jews have come from *religious* enemies, and some from those falsely called Christians! (Not the kind of stuff from which good relationships are made!)

However, spiritual (born again) men and women must realize that in Christ, the wall of separation *has* to come down! To continue to call oneself a "Messianic Jew," or to refer to someone as such, only maintains a division within the Body of Christ.

(Just think how pointless *and* unscriptural the title **"Christianic Gentile"** would be?)

Perhaps even a *saved* Jew may not like the name Jesus, or Christ; but it's time to get over it! The truth is, "flesh" doesn't like *anything* concerning Christ; but the "spirit" must overcome, and say, "Father; *Thy* will be done?"

May we check *all* divisive labels at the door, and enter God's presence simply as BELIEVERS and BRETHREN!

Does any of this *really* matter?

Well; If we want to glorify Jesus and hurt the enemy it certainly does! God's will is to see Christ's Body *united* in the Holy Spirit; and anything that prevents that from happening is to Satan's advantage!

"A house divided against itself cannot stand." (Mk.3:25)

What will it take to bring *"new creatures"* together in the unity and freedom of the Spirit?

Prayer, first and foremost; but also a deeper desire to acknowledge, embrace, and then walk in the truth! (*John 8:32*)

Surely there can be no doubt in the minds of believers, that Jesus; Yeshua; Adonai *is* the Messiah: for He is *"King of kings, and Lord of lords."* But to give place to divisive errors which separate the brethren is to allow the devil to continue his work of hindering the ministry of the Holy Spirit; and particularly the High Priestly prayer of our Lord and Savior in *John 17:21.*

"That they all may be one; as Thou, Father, art in Me, and I in Thee, that they also may be one in Us: that the world may believe that Thou hast sent Me."

Unity among believers is vital (especially in these last days) if the true Church is to show (and give) Christ's love and truth to an unbelieving world. (*John 15:12, 1Cor.13:6*)

Wonderful things are happening among the Jewish people as the Holy Spirit moves among them; but where are the fellowships made up of new men and women (ex Jews and ex Gentiles) with all the old differences put away (buried under the cross): praising and magnifying Father, Son, and Holy Ghost, *together as one?*

Praise God for such places! Praise God for NO WALLS!

By the way; in addition to the fact that there'll be no denominations in Heaven, it's good to know there'll be no Jews nor Gentiles either! If it's God will for us to be one on earth (*"neither Jew nor Greek"*), how much more so in Glory?

True believer: if you are still determined to hang on to religious labels or titles, know that you will surely lose them after you fall "asleep." ... *"To be absent from the body is to be present with the Lord."* (*1Cor.5:8*)

Or alive when, *"Caught up together in the clouds to meet the Lord in the air!"* (*1Thess.4:17*)

So why not let go of them now?

Jesus is building *His* Church, one *"living stone"* at a time, (*1Pet.2:5*) and wants us *"fitly framed* (joined and growing) *together unto an Holy Temple in the Lord."* (*Eph.2:21, 4:16*)

The measure of God's desire for this is perfectly revealed in *1Kings 6 and 7.*

All the stones used for the Temple of God (and Solomon's house) were *"great and costly,"* (*7:9-12*) but once the Temple was finished, *"There was no stone seen."* (*6:18*)

THE WHOLE TEMPLE WAS OVERLAID WITH GOLD! (See *6:18-22*)

Brothers and sisters, we are not here to be seen! We are here to be "covered in Gold!" (The Divine Glory of the Lord Jesus Christ!) Only **HE** is to be seen!

Petty labels, titles, divisions, and especially sin within the Church, are preventing the world from seeing **HIS** Glory! When are we going to realize that? I say once more: if there's *anything* in our lives that does not agree with the Word of God ... WE HAVE GOT TO LET IT GO!

May God give us the grace, and a willing heart to do so!

Presumption

"ALL BABIES THAT DIE, GO TO HEAVEN."
Sadly, this claim often goes hand in hand with another deeply held belief, which is,
"BABIES HAVE NO SIN!"
Although neither statement is found in scripture, millions of people have (and without hesitation) received and believed both as though they were! My reason for approaching this extremely controversial subject therefore, is to prove how strongly human feelings can influence our beliefs; especially in the absence of a specific Word from God!

Let's explore the second statement first.

It has nearly always been through the vulnerable realm of mankind's fallen emotions that Satan has gained primary access, worked his greatest wiles, and brought so much deception and defeat into our lives. Nowhere is this more acutely demonstrated than in the powerful, and often unyielding position taken (even by believers) on the subject of babies and sin!

Truth David said, "*Behold I was shapen in iniquity; and in sin did my mother conceive me.*"
(*Ps.51:5*) (David was not born out of wedlock [see *1Sam.*16], but with a sinful nature!)
Truth "*The wicked are estranged from the womb: they go astray as soon as they be born, speaking lies.*" (*Ps.58:3*) (Who teaches a child to lie? Who plants weeds?)
Truth "*... For I knew that thou wouldest deal very treacherously, and wast called a transgressor from the womb.*" (*Is.48:8b*) (Lies like weeds, simply appear!)
Truth "*Wherefore, as by one man* (Adam) *sin entered into the world, and death by sin; and so death passed upon all men, for that all have sinned.*" (*Rom.5:12*)
Truth "*And Adam ... begat a son in his own likeness, after his image ...*" (*Gen.5:3*)
(All of us are sons and daughters of Adam. *All* of us inherited his fallen sinful nature!)
Truth "*For the wages of sin is death ...*" (*Rom.6:23*) (The very heart of our study!)

"Once upon a time" (after a teaching session) a Christian mother came forward; looked me right in the eye, and with almost frightening tenacity, announced a fairy tale!

"How could you teach that? My babies were certainly not born in sin! I don't believe any baby is!"

Compassion and truth were lost on her as she flatly refused to return to the scriptures with me. Such is the attitude of so many (not always that outspoken) when confronted with this volatile issue: but in spite of it sensitive nature – and the occasional intense reaction it provokes – we must never fail to address it in the light and truth of God's infallible Word!

For some two thousand years, the Word of God (together with the revelation of the Holy Spirit) has enabled Christians to discern the "*Spirit of truth, and the spirit of error.*" (*1John 4:6*)

So: as with all spiritual matters (including those equally challenging), we must continue to "*search the Scriptures*," (*Acts 17:11*) and find the help or correction we need through honest, unbiased, and especially prayerful study.

Let me begin by asking this all-important question.

Do you know a reason for death, other than sin?

A Christian needs little time to respond: the *true* answer has already been established.

"*The wages of sin is death.*" Sin is the *only* reason for death! God has given no other!

However, we know from earlier studies that God created man to live with Him eternally.

It follows therefore that someone *without* sin **WOULD HAVE NO REASON TO DIE!**

This is why only Jesus (who had no sin) could say,

"*Therefore doth My Father love Me, because **I lay down My life**, that I might take it again. **No man taketh it from Me, but I lay it down of Myself**. I have power to lay it down, and I have power to take it up again. This commandment have I received of My Father.*" (*John 10:17-18*)

I doubt Pontius Pilate had any idea of the profound and glorious truth now revealed to us in the statement he made during his examination of Jesus, "*... I have found **no cause of death** in Him.*"

(*Luke 23:22*)

"NO SIN – NO REASON FOR DEATH" is absolute truth!

Once again, only *sin* brings on the curse of death. As distinctly as the Holy Spirit had spoken to me about Christmas, He spoke again with a question,

"IF BABIES HAVE NO SIN, WHY DO BABIES DIE?"

Obviously the sin found in a baby is not the strong, willful, and openly rebellious sin manifested in later life! Nevertheless, it is still the same sinful nature that Adam passed on to *all mankind*, and which is rooted in each and every one of us – even from the womb!

This brief and common-place scenario may reveal just how quickly our inherently sinful nature is manifested.

The baby crying for a genuine reason (say want of a fresh diaper) is picked up, changed, comforted, and put back into the cradle or crib. Naturally the baby likes this comfort or attention, and soon realizes that in order to be picked up and comforted on demand, all that is needed (hopefully) is a counterfeit cry, and some good old "crocodile tears!"

Believe it or not, we are looking at deception! Of course this "game" of deceit develops as the baby grows, until it becomes full-blown sin; i.e. lying, cheating, stealing, manipulating, etc., etc., etc!

Welcome to the human race!

Acknowledging this truth regarding babies and sin is vital if we are to explore the absolute lack of scriptural evidence supporting the statement, "All babies that die go to Heaven."

There is not one solitary verse in God's Word, which gives credence to such a declaration!

There is no blanket salvation for *any* group of individuals; including babies!

When Jesus said,

"*Suffer the little children to come unto me, and forbid them not: **for of such** is the Kingdom of Heaven*," (*Mk.10:14*) He was rebuking anyone who would hinder or prevent a child from coming to Him in faith! He also meant that the Kingdom of God is made up of individuals with child-like faith! Not that every child or baby will be saved! Hence His statement to adults.

"*Except ye be converted, and **become as little children**, ye shall not enter the Kingdom of Heaven.*" (*Matt.18:3*)

Serious mistakes have occurred (including "*damnable heresies*") simply because God's Word is silent; but if every baby that died was automatically saved, it would make nonsense of verses that are both loud and clear!

"***For many be called, but few chosen.***" (*Matt.20:16b*)

While Esau and Jacob were still in Rebecca's womb, God made a Sovereign choice

"***As it is written, Jacob have I loved, but Esau have I hated.***" (See *Rom.9:10-13*)

(If Esau had died as a baby, would he have gone to Heaven automatically?)

If the wicked who are, "*estranged from the womb, and go astray as soon as they be born*" (*Ps.58:3*) die as babies ... are they automatically saved?

When the Israelites entered the Promised Land, God told them to "*utterly destroy*" the nations that were living there. They were commanded to destroy, "*every soul ... men, women, and little ones ... all that breathed.*" (See *Deut. 2:32-34, 20:16-17*, and *Josh. 10:29-40*) ...What of the babies killed in all *those* cities?

In the Lord's prayer (*John 17*) Jesus said, "*I pray **not for the world**, but for **them which Thou hast given Me; for they are Thine.**"(John17:9)*

Of course, we could always use certain verses to teach (as some erroneously do) that *everyone* will be saved!

1 God is ... "*not willing that **any** should perish, but that **all** should come to repentance.*" (*2Pet.3:9b*) Will they *all* come to repentance?

2 God is ... "*the Savior of **all** men, specially of those that believe.*" (*1Tim.4:10b*) Will they *all* believe?

Obviously not! The balance of scripture clearly shows,

"*Though the number of the children of Israel be as the sand of the sea, **a remnant shall be saved.**" (Rom.9:27)*

Jesus said,

"*Because strait is the gate, and narrow is the way, which leadeth unto life, **and few there be that find it.**" (Matt.7:14)*

"*So then, it is not of him that willeth, nor of him that runneth, but of God that showeth mercy. ... Therefore hath He mercy on whom He will have mercy, and whom He will He hardeneth.*"

(*Rom.9:16, 18*)

Let's look again at scriptures **1** and **2**, and the problem that many have struggled with.

"If God is the Savior of *all* men, and isn't willing for anyone to perish; why then does He harden men's hearts so they will not believe?"

People in New Testament times asked a similar question:

"***Why doth He yet find fault? For who has resisted His will?***" (*Rom.9:19*)

In other words, "How could God judge sinners for sinning, if they are only doing what He chose them to do?" The apostle Paul answered them with a whole series of other questions ...

"Who do you think you are to question God? *Shall the object created say to Him that created it, Why have You made me this way?*"

Doesn't the Potter have power over His own clay?

Can He not use the same lump to make one vessel for honor, and another for dishonor?

What if God, wanting to demonstrate His wrath (fierce anger against sin), *and to make His power known; patiently tolerated the people of wrath* (those with angry rebellion against God) *who were already prepared for judgment: that He might reveal the riches of His glory upon the people He would be merciful to: those who were already chosen for glory?* (See Rom.9:14-27)

Can God extend salvation's message to all men, yet limit that salvation to the few who are chosen to accept it? Will He righteously judge the many who are chosen not to?
YES HE CAN, AND YES HE WILL! (*Matt.22:1-14*)

"The Lord hath made all things for Himself: yea even the wicked for the day of evil." (Day of doom or judgment) (*Pr.16:4*)

All this teaches us that God is the total and absolute Ruler of His creation!
"Nevertheless, the foundation of God standeth sure, having this seal,
"THE LORD KNOWETH THEM THAT ARE HIS." (*2Tim.2:19*)

Millions of people are so attached to the idea that "God would surely not send a baby anywhere but to Heaven," that they forget (or just don't know) the balance of scriptural truth!

Before the *"foundation of the world,"* an infinitely wise and holy God had predestined (already chosen) all things for His own pleasure and glory. He knows the spirits and souls of *all* men (see *Eph.1:4, Ps.115:3, Rev.4:11, John 2:24-25*), and righteously chooses their final destination!

Once again, the real question becomes: if there is no evidence in the Word of God to support the phrase, *"All* babies that die go to Heaven," then why do so many believe it, and who above all would want them to?

One tragic aspect of this deception (rarely mentioned) is that in today's world especially, believing that all dead babies go to Heaven makes it that much easier to live with the mass-murder or wholesale slaughtering of them by legalized abortion!

Perhaps now we can understand why the devil would enjoy cultivating such a lie! (I know *"this is an hard word;"* but it needed to be said!)

SOUTH OF THE BORDER
The devil, who would like nothing more than to control mankind from cradle to grave (simply to get us into hell) often gives some of that control to useful religious men; who in turn would get their fleeting share of worldly power, glory, and money!

Such men taught that if babies died un-baptized, their souls would immediately go to a place called **"Limbo."** (Latin word, "Limbus" meaning "hem," or "border.")

Limbo was originally conjured up as a place of eternal separation from God (somewhere outside the "borders" of heaven, but not quite as far as hell!) As a result, millions of poverty-stricken parents would beg, steal or borrow to pay for a christening rather than risk their baby's eternal soul!

Not surprisingly, this vile doctrine of Limbo lives on, and has taken many superstitious forms. Even today there are people who believe that the souls of un-baptized babies are seen as fireflies in the evening air!

BLESSINGS FOR SALE!
Throughout time, corrupt religious leaders have often managed to capitalize on the ignorance, fear, or superstitions of others; and nowhere is this more clearly revealed, than in the devilish practices that follow.

Remember: whenever religion runs out of money, it is forced to use carnal or worldly schemes to make more. Back in the middle-ages however, religion came up with some of the most despicable fund raising methods imaginable!

Average people didn't have access to the Word of God, so officials in the "church" had no difficulty in, "*making merchandise of them*." (See *2Pet.2:1-3*) Desperate souls searching for a glimpse of God were allowed to see, or touch "holy relics" or "icons" – for a price!

"Would you like to look at a feather from the wing of the angel Gabriel? No? Well, for a few more pence you could see the chains of St. Peter? Perhaps you'd like to hold a vial containing Christ's blood? (You'll never know it's the blood of an animal) It's guaranteed to make you feel good, even holy, so where's the harm in that?"

Countless numbers of deceived human beings paid hard-earned money to touch a fake piece of the Cross of Christ, resulting in the worthless superstition of "**touching wood!**" (It's been said that the amount of wood being touched in churches across Europe could have built a railroad track across the United States!)

In the days of Martin Luther (1483-1546), the Pope and hierarchy of the Roman Catholic Church realized that the "Mass" (a fantasy involving sponsored prayers for the dead in "purgatory") was failing financially.

NOTE: PURGATORY remains "on the books" to this day; and is defined by the catholic church as a place of fiery punishment for sins not forgiven in this life! Of course, no one knows how long the dead must stay there, but more prayers offered for more money would certainly shorten the time!

There always seems to be a financial reason why the "finished work" of Christ is never quite finished!

Because Mass was not bringing in enough cash, a "BUL" (an infallible decree) was issued, which (for a little *more* lucre) granted the dead a reduced period of suffering in, or even a complete escape from purgatory, (a.k.a. "La-la Land!")

NOTE: Later, in "Reformation" England, a common (though impolite) phrase began linking the word "Bul" with three other words. "A load of — !" Not the subtlest of statements, but I think the point is well made! These worthless, money for blessing Buls were also known as "indulgences."
The expression, "**When a coin in the coffer rings, a soul from purgatory springs**" became a fund raising jingle of indulgence peddlers; but when Luther, who had spent years punishing himself and seeking God's forgiveness by works, heard them crying, "**Forgiveness for sale**" ... he went to war!
Like him or not (Luther was strongly anti-Semitic), he was used by God to spread the fire of the "Protestant Reformation." The rest as they say, is history!

GOD'S FINAL WORD? APPARENTLY NOT!

"The task of interpreting the Word of God authentically has been entrusted solely to the Magisterium (leadership) of the (Catholic) Church: that is, to the Pope and to the bishops in communion with him." [3] (Parenthesis added)

However, today's Magisterium, somewhat embarrassed by the public relations nightmare of "purgatory," "limbo," and "hell" has in various places changed or withdrawn such doctrines altogether, tailoring its teaching to suit modern public opinion! (I wonder what a twenty-first century Pope would say to the untold multitudes throughout history who paid protection money in order to "save" their dead loved ones and children?)

NOTE: In many Catholic churches, money is no longer required for a priest to baptize an infant, but only parents who are parishioners may apply.

Times "they are a changing," and so it appears is the "Word of God!" The "church" must adapt!

In other words: religious rogues must make it up as they go along!

Catholics all over the world may well be on the verge of seeing both hell and purgatory sink quietly into limbo!

What will religion think of next?

CHAPTER TWELVE

THE GREAT DIVIDE

It is an enormously blessed and sacred privilege to speak or write on behalf of God! Those who do so must weigh their words with utmost care, for the people of God are to be nourished and strengthened by their teaching! God's anger is revealed against shepherds (pastors) who do not feed their "flocks" correctly. To these men God says,

> *"As for My flock, they eat that which you have trodden with your feet; and they drink that which you have fouled with your feet." (Eze.34:19)*

Anyone ministering to the Body of Christ who knowingly (or unknowingly) rejects or hinders the whole counsel of God's Word, *"Limits the Holy One of Israel"* (*Ps.78:41, Matt.13:58*), and becomes an enemy of the truth! Such a person does God's people a terrible disservice by robbing them of light, liberty, and blessing; and automatically falls to the level of a deceiver.

It is therefore with great sadness (and not a little anger) that I quote the following statements made by pastors, and other spiritual leaders who are, or have been involved in radio and television ministries throughout the United States.

"The gifts of the Holy Spirit ceased at the end of the apostolic age." R.C. Sproul, Ligonier Ministries.

"Tongues are the least of the gifts." Steve Brown, Key Life ministries.

"Sign gifts and healings have ceased." Tim Munger, Friends of Israel.

"To see the gifts of the Holy Spirit operating, go to the parking lot after the service." Bob Davis, N. Country Chapel: from his book on Galatians, P. 146.

"The gifts of the Spirit are not operating today in the same sense as in the early church." Bill Welte, America's Keswick.

"The only tongues in *this* church are in shoes!" D. James Kennedy, (deceased) Coral Ridge Presbyterian Church, Florida.

These ministers, (and so many more like them who broadcast similar errors) are reaching, teaching, and *polluting* hundreds and thousands of believers and non-believers with the *"fouled waters"* of a limited and corrupted gospel!

No one doubts the sincerity of these men, but they are deceivers and false teachers nevertheless. One day (if they fail to repent), they will have to answer to God for leading so many astray!

Let me give you an absurd but true example of how this kind of false teaching can influence God's people.

In the course of ministering to a new patient, a Christian nurse noticed a Bible lying by the side of the woman's hospital bed. To her surprise, she saw that it was no thicker than an average magazine; and, upon lifting it up, discovered it weighed almost nothing! In bewilderment she flicked through its pages, only to find nearly all the Old Testament (and quite a lot of the New) completely missing! When asked the reason for this, the woman replied, "My pastor taught us that most of the Bible is irrelevant for today, so he encouraged us to tear out the parts we don't need, and this is what we have left!"

Hard to believe? Perhaps; but I saw that "Bible" with my own eyes!

Now comes an obvious question.

If that kind of gross spiritual error is being taught, believed and acted upon, how will the saints of God (true believers) ever be "***perfected*** (properly equipped) *for the work of the ministry?"*

(Eph.4:11-12)

Those who reject or ignore the *full* ministry of the Holy Spirit today will (sooner or later) fall into other errors along the way! I say to such men, "You quench and grieve the Holy Spirit; rob God of His Glory, and preach a "*boiled*" (watered down) version of His Word!

V.I. Pray for men like these, and where possible, confront them with the truth! If they continue to resist the Spirit, find a fellowship with "clearer waters" where God's people are being properly equipped, and can exercise spiritual gifts in liberty under the guidance of the Holy Spirit.

It has been well said that if the Holy Spirit had left the early church, ninety five percent of what was being done would have ground to a halt! Today if the Holy Spirit left the church, ninety five percent of what is being done would carry on as though nothing had happened!

In these last days, the Bible tells us that countless numbers of false prophets and teachers (thieves and liars) will come out of the "woodwork," but "*God is not mocked.*" (*Gal.6:7*)

In spite of them, "*God is pouring out His Spirit upon all flesh.*" (*Joel 2:28-29, Acts 2:17-18*)

God's people *are* prophesying, speaking with other tongues, interpreting, seeing miracles, speaking words of wisdom and knowledge, discerning spirits, casting out demons, *and* healing the sick! All for the Glory of God! (See *1Cor.12 and 14, and Mark 16:17-18* for the truth!)

"***Jesus Christ, the same yesterday, and today, and forever.***" (*Heb.13:8*)

SPIRITUAL OR CARNAL?

"*For the weapons of our warfare are not carnal, (worldly) but mighty through God to the pulling down of strongholds.*" (*2Cor.10:4*)

"*For we wrestle not against flesh and blood, but against principalities, against powers, against the rulers of the darkness of this world, against spiritual wickedness in high places.*" (*Eph.6:12*)

One of the most tragic results of erroneous Gospel preaching is the total lack of power in the area of spiritual warfare. Men who deny the "*Gifts of the Holy Spirit*" cannot possibly teach God's people how to fight demonic beings, i.e. "*principalities, and rulers of darkness.*"

In the "*Feast of First Fruits,*" I began to describe the need for an absolute reliance upon the Holy Spirit for victory in our day-to-day lives or ministries. At this time, I would like to explore in more detail, what has possibly become the single most divisive issue in the church today. The "Gifts" of the Holy Spirit; and in particular, "Speaking with other tongues!"

If you will carefully consider the following treatise, I believe it will help to explain why the devil has fought so long and hard to keep "tongues," and other spiritual gifts away from the people of God.

The title of this chapter, **The Great Divide**, points towards one central, and all important question.

ARE *ALL* THE GIFTS OF THE HOLY SPIRIT FOR TODAY?

In simple **YES** and **NO** columns, I have taken the liberty of listing gifts that are generally accepted by the vast majority of "main-line" (conservative) Christians today, and those that are not.

YES:	NO:
Ministry	**Word of Wisdom**
Teaching	**Word of Knowledge**
Exhortation	**Gift of Faith**
Giving	**Gifts of Healing**
Ruling	**Working of Miracles**
Showing Mercy	**Prophecy**
Helps	**Discerning of Spirits**
Governments	**Different Tongues**
	and Interpretations
Evangelists	
Pastors	**Apostles**
Teachers	**Prophets**

Again, these lists represent a broad view of beliefs held by Christians in England and the United States, and are based on many years of conversations, ministry, and plain old "tire and road" experience!

The twenty-two ministerial Gifts of the Holy Spirit can be found in *Romans 12:6-9, 1Cor.12:8-10 and 28*, and *Eph.4:11*)

PART A)
SHOULD CHRISTIANS SPEAK WITH OTHER TONGUES?

TRUTH "*Now there are diversities* (various types) *of gifts, but the same Spirit ... differences of administrations,* (ministries) *but the same Lord ... different operations* (activities) *but the same God which worketh all in all. But the manifestation of the Spirit is given to every man to profit withal.*" (*1Cor.12:4-7*)

To address this challenging subject, let me first quote a Bible verse at random.
Paul wrote, "***For the love of money is the root of all evil.***" (*1Tim.6:10*)
In over thirty years of ministry, I have never heard an argument between believers (or witnessed a division in the church) over that verse ... it is the Word of God!

Why then, would there be such confusion, ignorance, division, and loss to the church over the apostle Paul's statements found in *1Cor.14?*

TRUTH "*I would* (strongly desire) *that* **you all** *spoke with tongues, but rather* (even more so) *that you prophesied.*" (*1Cor.14:5a*)

TRUTH "*I thank my God I speak with tongues more than **you all**.*" (*1Cor.14:18*)

Question Are these verses given "*by inspiration of God*" (*2Tim.3:16*), or are they just Paul's ideas?

If they *are* from Paul (mere men), we can throw them out; along with others that we don't understand or agree with. But if they are from God, then we had better listen!

"*He that hath an ear, let him hear what the Spirit is saying to the churches.*" (*Rev.2:29*)

Question Do you believe that "*you all*" in (*1Cor.14:5*) refers to Christians living only in the first century A.D., or to **all of us** throughout the ages who belong to the church of our Lord and Savior, Jesus Christ?

Question Why is it that today, countless numbers of true believers are speaking with other tongues; interpreting; prophesying; as well as exercising other supernatural gifts of the Holy Spirit? (see *1Cor.12 and 14*) And could these gifts bring help and great blessing to you?

A word of testimony that might be helpful.

Although born in England, by the grace of God, I was "*born again*" in Ft. Lauderdale, Florida. Soon afterwards, I found myself in a large Bible-believing church where the Gospel was preached. Unfortunately, it was the very place where Dr. D. J. Kennedy first confirmed that,

"The only tongues in this church are in shoes!"

The man had a Ph.D., and a congregation of some five thousand – of course I believed him! Thus the error was planted, and when I returned to England, it was to "do battle" with anyone who dared to say, "Tongues are for today!"

Now as a brand new believer, it can be somewhat annoying when he or she first discovers that God is always right – right? (Later, that fact becomes the source of the most wonderful security we could ever know.) In the mean time, I just kept meeting beautiful Christians who spoke in tongues, believed in prophecy, miracles, healings, and all the other gifts!

Naturally I was very zealous with my "**No tongues; shoes only!**" argument, but each time I spoke, they simply smiled and said, "We're praying for you." Can you imagine how annoying *that* was? These people actually believed the **WHOLE** Bible!

So who was right? After many months I was still struggling!

If the "sign" gifts were *not* for today, how could so many sincere and Godly people be deceived into believing that they had them?

On top of that, if tongues *were* only in shoes, and Christians "**get it all**" the moment they are born again; I was forced to ask myself, "Were *is* it?" ... "Help!"

In my frustration I realized that the answer would have to come from God Himself. I began to pray, "Father, if tongues and the other gifts *are* for today, please open my heart, and let me receive them. If not, please protect me from the error. In Jesus' Name."

A few days later (during prayer) I was "baptized with the Holy Spirit," and began to speak with other tongues! No one else was there; no one laid hands on me; there was no outward pressure; just an inward desire to know God's grace and blessing. – God *will* have His way! (Of course, if we humble ourselves and are willing, it will be quicker and *much* less "painful!")

Twenty-five years later

Having returned to the U.S., I contacted the Ft. Lauderdale ministry again; only to discover that the message, "Tongues are in shoes" was still being preached by the very same pastor!

Again I mention the fact that in his lifetime he influenced hundreds and thousands of believers and non-believers through his television and radio ministries. Now sadly (even after his death) his recordings still do.

Yes, there must be righteous anger toward such teaching; but an even greater desire to take back the precious things the devil has stolen, and is keeping from God's people!

I recognize of course that not every believer will speak with other tongues. (*1Cor.12:30*)

This particular message is written for the encouragement of those who *do*, and those who *will*!

Some are so set against the gifts (for a variety of reasons), that they may *never* accept the truth; but for those who have not closed the door completely, I pray this will be an opportunity for light and revelation to come forth.

Let me ask one more question.

Just who exactly decided which gifts are not for today?

One thing is certain: If "*Jesus Christ is the same yesterday, and today, and forever,*" then it certainly wasn't *God*! A great clue is given in a now sadly familiar verse.

> "***Beware lest any man spoil you*** (rob you, or take you captive) *through philosophy and vain deceit, after the tradition of men, after the rudiments* (principles) *of the world, and not after Christ.*" (*Col.2:8*)

During the church age, the devil has influenced an awful lot of Christian leaders (I suspect through too many board meetings), and has caused them to vote out certain gifts which obviously didn't gel with their philosophies, vain deceits, or traditions!

(Some of Satan's best work has been done through the minds and pens of religious intellectuals!)

EXPOSING SATAN'S LIES!

Revealed now are some of the arguments the enemy has used to rob the church of her rightful blessings. Unfortunately, over the years, I have heard every one of them: perhaps you have too!

1. **"Tongues is the *least* of the gifts."**

2. **"*When that which is perfect is come*, (taken to mean the scriptures) *then that which is in part, shall be done away.*"** (Taken to mean supernatural gifts. A total misrepresentation of *1Cor.13:10*)

3. **"Tongues are for those who need an extra emotional boost. Christians get all they need the moment they are saved. There is no second experience."**

4. **"Supernatural gifts ceased at the end of the apostolic age."**

5. **"Tongues are of the flesh, or of the devil!"**
   These lies have been planted everywhere, so let's dig them out one by one!

Lie number 1

TONGUES IS THE LEAST OF THE GIFTS.

In answer

The apostle Paul exhorts us to, "*Covet* (desire) *earnestly the best gifts*" (*1Cor.12:31*), and above all to seek the gift of prophecy! (*1Cor.14:1*) The purpose of prophecy is to "*edify, exhort, and comfort.*" (*1Cor.14:3*)

Now although he says,

"*... For greater is he that prophesieth than he that speaketh in tongues ...*" (that's where Satan wants us to stop reading) Paul goes on to say, "*... EXCEPT (unless) he INTERPRET, that the church may receive EDIFYING.*" (See *1Cor.14:5*)

Do you see the equation?

Tongues + Interpretation = Edification = Prophecy!

Therefore, Tongues *with* Interpretation equals the gift Paul urges us to "*covet*" the most, i.e. Prophecy! ("*Edification*" could obviously include, "exhortation, *and* comfort!")

Some who claim that tongues is the least of the gifts, do so (they say) because, "Tongues is the last gift recorded in *1Cor.12:8-10*."

That statement is *also* incorrect! "*Interpretation of Tongues*" is actually mentioned last!

And just to put an end to such foolishness, if importance were based solely on a list, then the "*Word of Wisdom*" (which appears first) would be the best gift, and *not* Prophecy!

Let no one despise or reject tongues! And do not assume for one minute that it is the least simply because a mere man tells you so! (You should take a look at the Amplified version of *1Cor.12:8-10*)

Let someone dare to tell *GOD* which one of His gifts is the least!

Lie number 2

WHEN THAT WHICH IS PERFECT IS COME ...

To expose *this* error we must look at the verses surrounding *1Cor.13:10*.

"**Without love I am nothing**" is the sum of *verses 1-3*. Prophecy, knowledge, faith, giving, and the understanding of all mysteries mean nothing without love. The Holy Spirit (through Paul) goes on to define love in a very beautiful and challenging way, (*vs. 4-7*) but in *verse 8* a comparison is made.

"*Charity* (love) *never fails: but prophecies will fail ...tongues will cease, and knowledge will vanish away.* (Keep knowledge in mind) *For we know in part, and we prophesy in part, but when that which is perfect is come, then that which is in part shall be done away.*" (*vs. 9-10*)

Now it becomes a straightforward issue. If gifts such as tongues and prophecy have been "***done away***", then knowledge must be done away also. ("*For we know in part, and we prophesy in part*") So would *all* the supernatural gifts, including Ministry, Teaching, Exhortation, Giving, Ruling, Showing mercy, Helps, Governments, Evangelists, Pastors, Teachers and so on.

According to the Word of God, they are ALL supernatural gifts of the Holy Spirit!

How could the sign gifts have ceased, and not the others?

HAS KNOWLEDGE VANISHED AWAY?

The scriptures say that in the last days, "*... knowledge shall be INCREASED?*" (*Dan.12:4*)

Look now at *1John3:2*.

"Beloved, now are we the sons of God, and it doth not yet appear what we shall be: but we know that, when He shall appear, we shall be like Him; for we shall see Him as He is."

"For now we are looking (as it were) *into a mirror that gives only a blurred reflection* (as in a riddle or puzzle) *but then* (WHEN PERFECTION COMES) *we shall see face to face."* (*1Cor.13:12*)

It is evident that perfection has not yet come! In these last days we *need* the "Gifts!" We *need* the power of God! We need all the help we can get! Why would anyone not want that help? Could the answer be fear? Could the answer be pride?

Suppose we've spent most of our Christian lives believing or teaching this lie!
I'm sure it would take all the grace and humility we could find to admit it and embrace the truth!
Those who believe the *scriptures* to be "that which is perfect," often use *James 1:23-25* to support their view.

*"For if anyone is a hearer of the Word, and not a doer, he is like a man who looks at himself in a mirror, and leaves, then straight away forgets what he looked like. But whoso looketh into the **perfect law of liberty**, and continueth therein, he being not a forgetful hearer, but a **doer of the work**, this man shall be blessed **in his deed**."*

Clearly this passage speaks of obedience to the Word of God: *not* the coming of that which is perfect?

From Joel to Peter to ALL of us!

*"And it shall come to pass in **the last days**, saith God, I will pour out My Spirit upon all flesh; and your sons and daughters **shall prophesy,** (speak on behalf of God with power and authority) your old men shall dream dreams, your young men shall see visions: ..."* (See *Joel 2:28-32*)

These scriptures were quoted and confirmed for us by Peter on the Day of Pentecost!
(See *Acts 2:16-21*)
Will any knowledgeable Christian deny we are living in *"the last days?"* Yet the Word of God is being constantly denied by those who believe the gifts (especially sign gifts) have ceased!

Once and for all

CHRIST is the Perfect One! The gifts are still here; as are *all* the ministries of the Holy Spirit! Knowledge has obviously increased, but when **HE** is come, we will see *"face to face."* **When HE is come,** *"We shall know even as we are known."* **When HE is come,** *"We shall be like Him, for we shall see Him as He is."*
On *that* day prophecies will fail! On *that* day tongues will cease! On *that* day our little bit of knowledge (in this present world) will vanish away! We will no longer need the gifts we need in the church today! We will no longer look through a "blurred mirror!" We will need neither **Faith** nor **Hope**, for we will be in His Glorious Presence!
Only when Jesus returns will there be perfect love, joy and peace; and blessings forever more!

Lie number 3.
THERE IS NO SECOND EXPERIENCE.

A careful reading of Acts will reveal that being *"born again"* and *"baptized with the Holy Ghost"* are two separate, and distinct Divine experiences.

The first and most powerful example comes from Peter and the rest of the disciples.

Let's ask ourselves this question.
When were the disciples actually saved? i.e. Born again?

Peter and the others were called, and walked with the Lord for three and a half years. They may have been weak at times (who isn't?), but with the exception of Judas, they belonged to Christ, and were as *"chosen"* and *"saved"* as anyone could be!

Peter made this confession to Jesus in *Matt.16:16*.
"Thou art the Christ, the Son of the Living God."
Immediately Jesus answered him and said,
"Blessed art thou, Simon Bar-jona: for flesh and blood hath not revealed it unto thee, but My Father which is in Heaven." (Are we saved any other way?)
God revealed Jesus to him, and to those who were **"chosen"** and called Him **"Lord."**
(See *John 15:16, and Matt.26:20-25*)

Before ascending to Heaven, Jesus told the disciples to stay in Jerusalem, and wait for, *"the promise of the Father."*
This would *not* be for salvation – it would be for the *empowering* of the saved! (*Acts 1:4*)

In the Church Age, no *unsaved* person was ever *"sent"* anywhere by God! No unsaved person *ever* received the Holy Ghost!

During the forty days Jesus was with them (after He rose from the dead), the disciples' lives were purely nominal. At one point, Thomas, Nathanael, James, John, and two others, even went back with Peter to his old trade of fishing! (see *John 21:1-3*)

Yet on the Day of Pentecost, Peter (a man who had fled from Jesus' side, and denied Him three times) was baptized with the Holy Ghost, filled with power, and preached a message which brought three thousand souls into the Kingdom of God!

Jesus wasn't kidding! He said,
"Ye shall receive power, AFTER that the holy Ghost is come upon you." (*Acts 1:8a*)

In *Acts 19*, Paul asked a number of Christians (believers already),
*"Have you received the Holy Ghost **since you believed?"***
Earlier preaching had not given them a full revelation, so they answered,
"We have not so much heard whether there be any Holy Ghost."
After they were baptized in water, Paul laid his hands on them: *then* the Holy Ghost came upon them, and they spoke with tongues and prophesied! (See *Acts 19:1-7*)

In *Acts 8:5-16*, Philip preached the Word in Samaria; and, *"many believed on the Lord Jesus Christ, and were baptized in water."* (*v.12*) Much later, Peter and John came and prayed for them all that they might receive the Holy Ghost; for, *"As yet He was fallen upon none of them."*
After Peter and John laid hands on them, they received the Holy Ghost!

Question: Was Paul (then Saul) converted on the Damascus road?

In *Acts 9:5-6*, Jesus appeared to him, and *twice* Saul called Him Lord. Later in *verse15*, the Lord spoke to Ananias and said of Saul, *"He is a chosen vessel unto Me."* (Not *will* be!)

Then Ananias went to Saul, laid his hands on him and said, *"Brother Saul ... receive thy sight and be filled with the Holy Ghost."*

Saul went on to change his name, fight the good fight, and become the man who under the inspiration of the Holy Ghost would write,

"FORBID NOT TO SPEAK WITH TONGUES!" (1Cor.14:39)

Today from radios, televisions, and platforms far and wide, you will hear well-spoken preachers or teachers expounding the Word of God. Listen carefully, and you may hear what many of them learned in cemeteries (sorry) seminaries; where meticulous care is taken to explain the Greek meaning of a word or phrase, but where they continue to deny and quench the gifts of the Holy Spirit!

I offer them this testimony from Dr. Hobart Freeman (now present with the Lord) who said,

"I was born again, and preached the Gospel for fourteen years using every scripture I could find to prove that the Baptism with the Holy Spirit, and His sign gifts were not for today!

For fourteen long years, a brother in the church was praying that God would open my eyes to the truth. Finally God did! I was baptized with the Holy Spirit; spoke with other tongues, and then used the very same scriptures to preach the truth! I couldn't go back and wipe out all the tapes and radio messages that are still in circulation: I could only say to the people who heard them; I'm sorry!"

(Those of us who love and understand that testimony will simply say, Praise the Lord!")

Lie number 4

THE SIGN GIFTS CEASED AT THE END OF THE APOSTOLIC AGE.

It is widely believed that John was the last Apostle to die. That takes us back to somewhere around one hundred A.D., and to a truly remarkable scenario ...

Those close to the apostle watch sadly as he takes his final breath. Filled with grief, they leave John's side, and shout to the crowds outside still waiting to be healed, **"We're sorry; it's all over! John's dead! The apostolic age has ended! God can't or won't heal you any more! Go home! Go to the doctor, or learn to live with your sicknesses!"**

(As ridiculous as all that may sound, Satan has millions of Christians believing it!)

I mean no disrespect to John, but was he *really* God's be all and end all? God forgive us! Who in their right mind would teach such nonsense? Perhaps you know someone who does, although in a less obvious way. Pray for them; confront them with the truth; give them any biographical book on Wigglesworth, Koolman, or Bevington!

Listen as *GOD* speaks,
"These signs shall follow THEM THAT BELIEVE; in My Name they shall cast out devils; ... (Did you know that casting out a demon is a miracle? See *Mk.9:38-39*) *... they shall speak with new tongues;* (Heavenly *or* earthly, see *1Cor.13:1*) *... they shall take up serpents;* (not to *tempt* the Lord, but see *Acts 28:1-5* for context) *... and if they drink any deadly thing, it*

181

shall not hurt them; (again, not to tempt the Lord!) *... they shall lay hands on the sick, and they shall recover."*

(Mk.16:17-18)

Why receive teaching or ministry from anyone who claims these verses are not inspired, or are not for today?

JESUS SAID IT ... HOW LONG WILL WE DOUBT IT?

Lie number 5.

"TONGUES ARE OF THE DEVIL"

Very few will make that statement publicly. Most will say, "Tongues are of the flesh!"
Perhaps God is protecting them because,
   "Blasphemy against the Holy Ghost shall not be forgiven." (Matt.12:31-32)
In that passage, Jesus was accused of casting out demons by the power of Beelzebub (the devil) and not by the Holy Ghost. (Calling something or someone of God evil is a terrible – not to mention dangerous – thing to do!)

When we realize that tongues and the other sign gifts really *are* for today, it will begin to dawn on us just how many of God's people are being taught to *"Quench the Spirit,"* (1Thess.5:19) and even *"fight against God!"* (Matt.12:30, Acts 5:39)

I once heard a brother give a humorous but cynical answer to those who believe this monstrous "devil and tongues" lie; He said,

"Before I was born again, I did everything the devil wanted me to. If tongues were of the devil, why didn't I speak with them as well?" (Many true words have been spoken in jest!)

Let me say now with utmost seriousness.

If you have been taught that the wonderful Gifts and Graces of Almighty God are not for today; then I urge you to seek the Lord afresh; and with a sincere heart, ask the Holy Spirit to *"guide you into all truth."* (John 16:13)

Pray to find a fellowship where the Holy Ghost is welcomed; His gifts are encouraged, and operate freely as and when He leads!

I come now to the most joyful part of this message.

PART B)

WHY CHRISTIANS *SHOULD* SPEAK WITH OTHER TONGUES!

Here are five reasons for your prayerful consideration.

INTERPRETATION

Why did Paul write so many instructions to the Church about the vocal gifts, i.e. tongues, interpretation and prophecy; and so few about the others? Because those gifts of utterance are the ones *we* can control! (1Cor.14:32)

The Corinthian church was young and very zealous: everyone wanted to get involved!

It seems they all had gifts to share, but because of a lack of order, their meetings were getting out of hand. (*vs. 26-33*) It's important to remember that a tongue given in and for the assembly needs to be interpreted, or the church will not be edified (instructed or built up). (*14:5*) If a tongue is motivated by fleshly zeal (yes, Christians can get fleshly!), it may not be interpreted! If many try to speak at once, the unlearned or unbelievers will say we are "mad!" (*v.23*)

But in any Spirit filled assembly where unbelievers *are* present or not, it is safe to say that if the Holy Spirit inspires a tongue, He will also inspire the interpretation! – "***God is not the Author of confusion.***" (*v.33*)

Now, look at the equation again: **Tongues + Interpretation = Edification = Prophecy.**

It is certainly a somewhat smaller (no less important) step of faith to give a tongue. Because the interpretation carries with it the added responsibility of being God's Word spoken directly to the congregation (exactly the same as in prophecy) with everyone understanding and judging. That is, discerning whether or not the word spoken agrees with the written Word of God.

Simply stated, a tongue is often used by the Holy Spirit to stir up faith; causing His people to actively seek Him for the interpretation, which then brings prophetic "*edification, exhortation, and comfort,*" (*1Cor.14:3*) and blessing to all!

INTERCESSION

"*I will pray with the spirit* (with tongues) *and I will pray with the understanding* (my own language) *also.*" (*1Cor. 14:15*)

"*...For we know not what we should pray for as we ought: but the Spirit itself* (Himself) *maketh intercession for us with groanings which cannot be uttered. And He that searcheth the hearts knoweth what is the mind of the Spirit, because HE maketh intercession for the saints* (believers) *according to the will of God.*" (*Rom.8:26-28*)

Did you ever wonder why there is no mention of Jesus praying or speaking in tongues?
The answer is; He always *knew* the will of His Father! (*John 6:6, 8:29*)
Do *we* always know God's perfect will for ourselves, and everyone we pray for? Of course not! If we did, we wouldn't need the gift of tongues! So it's marvelous to know that when we pray in the Spirit (with tongues), the Holy Spirit will interpret those tongues, and use them to intercede in a way we could never hope to do with our minds or intellects.
Just think: prayer in the perfect will of God!
Any pride (to do with answered prayer) is removed, and remember this,
If your mind doesn't understand your prayer, the enemy cannot interfere with it either!
Can you imagine one day, people coming to you in Heaven and saying, "Thank you so very much; your prayers in the Spirit helped me through a very difficult time!"
(And you never even knew you were praying for them! – All glory to the Lord!)

SPIRITUAL WARFARE

In Ephesians chapter 6, Paul stresses the need to,
"*Put on the whole armor of God, that ye may be able to stand against the wiles* (schemes or attacks) *of the devil. For we wrestle not against flesh and blood,* (physical enemies) *but against principalities, against powers, against the rulers of the darkness of this world, against spiritual wickedness in high places.*" (*Eph.6:11-12*)

After describing the armor, he goes on to write (still in the context of warfare),
*"Praying always with all prayer and supplication **in the Spirit** ..."* (v.18)

As with intercession, so with spiritual warfare: if you *know* the names of all the demons affecting your life, your loved ones, your town, your city, or your country; you don't need to pray (fight or war) in the Spirit (with tongues). Need I say more?

PRAISE AND WORSHIP

"I will sing with the spirit (with other tongues) *and I will sing with the understanding* (my own language) *also."* (*1Cor.14:15b*) If the Holy Spirit intercedes for us as we pray or war with other tongues, how much more will He do so in praise and worship?

"God is a Spirit, and they that worship Him must worship Him in Spirit and in truth."
(*John 4:25*)

If you've ever heard a congregation of saints worshipping God in the Spirit, you might actually think angels were singing. There is often no rhythm at all, just a Divine flow, which seems to carry you to the very Throne of God! This is the Divine Will, and the Holy Spirit's longing for His saints.

Of course, singing with our understanding is also good, and many Godly songs and choruses have been written, which give praise and glory to Him. However, singing, speaking, or praying with the Spirit far exceeds anything we can do in our own understanding, and takes us to a level of intimacy with the Lord, which is way beyond our normal capabilities.

A young brother once said to me, "When I worship the Lord, I quickly run out of things to say, and I begin to repeat myself. You know, "Praise the Lord," "Hallelujah," "Thank you Jesus:" Surely there must be more." "Amen" I said, and began to share with him how God could give him a whole new worship and prayer language that is always fresh and inspired!
"Ask and it shall be given you" (*Luke 11:5-13*)

EDIFICATION

"He that speaketh in an unknown tongue edifieth himself" (*1Cor.14:4, Jude 20*)

So then, there is a tongue for interpretation (mostly in an assembly); a tongue for praise and worship (in or out of the assembly as the Spirit leads), and there is a more personal or private tongue for intercession, warfare, and edification. (Though in prayer meetings I have often seen believers interceding, warring, and being edified together) It should always be as the Holy Spirit leads.

To *"edify"* means to **instruct**; to **confirm**; to **build up**, and to **make bold ... all concerning our FAITH!**

No wonder the Holy Spirit said, *"I would that ye all spake* (spoke) *with tongues"* (*1Cor.14:5a*)
(No wonder the devil stops at nothing to prevent us from doing so!)

*"But ye beloved, **building up yourselves** on your most holy faith, **praying in the Holy Ghost**, keep yourselves in the love of God, looking for the mercy of our Lord Jesus Christ unto eternal life."* (*Jude 20-21*) Amen and amen!

THE LAKE

To more fully understand the difference between "*receiving*" the Holy Spirit (which we all do at salvation), and being "***baptized with***" the Holy Spirit, let me give you this simple analogy.

You are dying of thirst, so come with me to a vast, fresh water lake, and bring a glass.

Kneel by the water's edge; fill your glass, and drink. You have just received a glass full of the lake. You have some of the lake (so to speak), and that's a great start. Now jump into the water! Suddenly, the lake has *you*! Its power supports you and becomes known to you! The lake gives you *power*! You realize that drinking (when you are *in* the lake) is much easier; and so much more satisfying! You see and understand things you never did before. The lake is crystal clear, and so beautiful; you never want to come out. It's amazing!

Then all at once, a thought hits you: "Why doesn't *everyone* jump in?"

Ultimately of course, the answer to that question is in God's hands; but for now, please know that when we drink the glass of water (by faith), we receive the "*Spirit of Christ,*" and we are "*born again.*"

> "*But as many as received Him, to them gave He power to become the sons of God, even to them that believe on His Name.*" (John1:12)

To jump into the Lake is to be baptized in or with the Holy Spirit: Who then empowers our Christian lives, and calls and anoints us for the work of the ministry.

> "*But ye shall receive power, **after** that the Holy Ghost is come upon you: and ye shall be witnesses ...*" (Acts1:8)

> (Remember: Jesus spoke that to men who were already believers!)

Prayer and "drinking" God's word regularly in the Lake, fills us and *keeps* us empowered! But never forget; the "***Natural man*** (believer's carnal or worldly nature) ***cannot understand these things ... they are foolishness to him***" (1Cor.2:14)

Which is why so many stumble over this truly wonderful God given experience.

May it not be so with you, in Jesus' Name.

Christ ascended on high, and gave gifts to us: (*Eph.4:8*) **may God bless you as you move forward into them.**

****

Chapters 13-26 will focus on exposing other areas of deception and darkness in the light, truth and authority of God's infallible Word. Not merely those deceits which are preventing the Body of Christ from rising to its full and glorious potential, but also those that are hindering multitudes of lost souls from coming to know and enjoy a personal and eternal relationship with the Only Lord and Savior, Jesus Christ.

NOTE: Much of the following material is hard-hitting and quite intense, so I urge you to prayerfully put on the whole armor of God before reading, and especially before using any of it in the realm of spiritual warfare!

CHAPTER THIRTEEN

FICKLE FOLK ON SHIFTING SAND

Today more than ever before, people are trying to find spiritual answers to some of life's most difficult and meaningful questions.

"Why are we here?" "What happens when we die?" "Is there really life after death?" "Can I contact someone on the other side?" "Is reincarnation possible?"

To answer these questions, millions of seekers, encouraged by N.A. television shows, and a host of well-known "spook" movies such as "Ghost," "The Others," "Sixth Sense," etc., are turning to mediums (spiritists or spiritualists), and psychic power!

Around the world there are thousands upon thousands of mediums (channels for communicating with the "dead"); psychics (clairvoyants or fortune-tellers); astrologers (fortune-tellers using the stars and planets); Necromancers (fortune tellers aided by "spirits of the dead"); etc., etc., etc., and

THE OCCULT BUSINESS IS BOOMING!

Some time ago, before being exposed as a fraud, one leading American "TV psychic" (a certain Miss Cleo with nationwide "hot lines") was reportedly earning around $20 million a month for the company that employed her! Doesn't that tell you just how many gullible souls are searching? Medium Sylvia Browne is also well-known to television audiences, and of course Oprah Winfrey routinely invites psychics, occult authors and practitioners to be her guests!

Mediums James Van Praagh, and John Edwards currently have their own nationwide television shows. Van Praagh tells a tearful young woman who has lost her fiancé in a car crash, "Your fiancé will guide you; he will always be with you; he wants you to know it wasn't your fault."

A woman who has lost her husband and three sons in a tragic house fire is told, "Your husband is right beside you; he doesn't want you to worry; he says, you'll always be a mother."

The medium gives intimate details of the accidents (and of the dead) that only the grieving women would know, and as a result both are convinced they have heard the "truth."

These psychic sessions (known as "readings") are immensely popular, and bring a sense of emotional comfort and closure to many sincere, heartbroken souls; but without realizing it, they have willingly bought into a **VICIOUS LIE!**

They completely overlook the fact that there are **TWO** sources of hidden knowledge and power in the supernatural realm – God *and* the devil!

In their desperate search for answers, millions of people continue to ignore the loudest and clearest warning signals ever given for their safety and well-being. All of them found in the world's best selling (and least read) book, the Bible!

The bottom line is this:

A PERSON WHO IS SPIRITUAL IS NOT AUTOMATICALLY OF GOD!

Van Praagh closed one of his shows with the following words, "We are *all* created in God's image. We have nothing to fear from Him; so live your life as you see fit. Be happy, and don't worry about death: you need not fear the beyond."

This of course is exactly what the devil *wants* us to believe. "Don't fear God! – Don't fear death! Death is just a step beyond!" Also this favorite; "If you didn't like your life, you can always return (reincarnate) in another form, and try again!"

THIS IS WHAT GOD SAYS!

"There shall not be found among you, anyone who practices fortune telling, astrology, soothsaying, magic, sorcery, hypnotism, clairvoyance, psychic power, or necromancy.
For all who do these things, are an abomination to the Lord." (Deut.18:10-12)
AND THIS:
"As to the person who turns to mediums and spiritists (Spiritualists) *to play the whore after them, I will set My Face against that person, and will cut him off from among his people." (Lev.20:6)*

IF MEDIUMS AND PSYCHICS WERE OF GOD, WHY WOULD GOD'S WORD (THE BIBLE) CONDEMN THEM?

Why does God speak so vehemently against these occultists?

Because all of them are Satan's disciples (servants), and their work (though most do not know it) is to lead the living into the very deepest deception possible, which is to keep them from God's glorious Kingdom, and the true love, joy, and peace they could have for all eternity!

Let it be said in the strongest terms,

Reincarnation is a demonic myth! Contacting the dead is a demonic joke!

There are no "human" spirits wandering around on earth after their death! (See *Luke 16: 19-31*, and *Heb.9:27*) So where exactly do mediums, psychics, and all the others get their information from?

In four words ...

THE SERPENT STILL SPEAKS!

Certain demons, known as "familiar spirits" (from the word family) are able to impersonate or represent the dead, and "contact" the living through a mediumistic "channel." These evil spirits are active throughout our lives, and know us extremely well! When we die, they merely pass on as much intimate, personal information as is needed to complete the deception in the hope that enquiring loved ones will accept or receive the lies!

The bible says, *"Satan can appear as an angel of light,* (as an angel of God) *so is it any wonder that his ministers* (in this case, mediums and psychics) *can appear as ministers of righteousness?*
... But their end shall be according to their works." (2Cor.11:14-15)

Once again:

Mediums do *not* contact the dead! They contact demonic spirits who *impersonate* the dead!

For those sincere people who have searched for answers through occult practitioners (or have thought of doing so); here is sobering truth.

"There is a way which seemeth right unto a man, but the end thereof are the ways of death."
(Prov.14:12)

Mediums may offer short-term comfort, but in reality they are handing out "serpents," which sooner or later will bite, poison, and destroy all who are taken in by them!

NOTE: God destroyed Saul (Israel's first king) for rejecting His Word, and attending a séance! (Consulting a medium) (See *1Chr.10:13-14* Amp. Version)

Stay away from mediums, psychics, astrologers, etc., and *ALL* occult involvement: it is extremely dangerous!

Advertisements and web sites proclaim Spiritualism as "The essence of all religions," and although it claims to offer, "Love, and the oneness of all things," it conveniently forgets that,

"LOVE REJOICES IN THE TRUTH." (*1Cor.13:5*)

Love without truth really *is* the "**essence of religion**." It is the damnable, lying pill that multitudes have swallowed in their quest for life's meaning and hope!

If the truth should hurt, let this be remembered ...

"Faithful are the wounds of a friend; but the kisses of an enemy are deceitful." (*Pr.27:6*)

There is no oneness apart from Jesus Christ, *"The Only Way, Truth and Life."* All attempts to find meaning and hope without Him are absolutely futile, and will surely end in destruction!

Here now are the answers to those difficult questions which so many have asked at some point in their lives.

WHY AM I HERE?

God created us to live and enjoy fellowship with Him forever!

Adam and Eve's sin broke that fellowship, and brought the curse of death and spiritual separation from God upon all of us. ("*For that all have sinned.*" *Rom.5:12b*)

But God loves us, and has made a way (just *ONE* way) for us to be with Him again for all eternity. **We *CAN* be saved.**

IS THERE LIFE AFTER DEATH?

Absolutely yes! Everyone will live forever: the only question is WHERE?

Heaven and hell are real, and are waiting for us. We can only get to Heaven if we are saved from hell!

So we *NEED* to be saved.

WHAT HAPPENS WHEN WE DIE?

If we remain separated from God, and die in that condition; there are TWO deaths. The first is physical death, at the end of this life. The second is *spiritual* death, which is the punishment described as eternal separation from God in the *"Lake of Fire."* (*Rev.20:14-15*) This is God's judgment against those who reject His Beloved Son Jesus and die in their sins!

No purgatory; no second chance; no reincarnation; NO WAY OUT!

Now comes the most important question anyone will ever ask?

WHAT MUST I DO TO BE SAVED?

Knowing that all of us were lost in sin and could never save ourselves, God sent His Only Son Jesus Christ into the world to pay the enormous price that our salvation from sin would cost.

By shedding His precious Blood and dying on a cross, He somehow took the dreadful punishment that should have been ours. Punishment which every one of us deserved!

Jesus made it possible for us to avoid God's wrath, and to live with Him in Heaven itself!

Thank God, Jesus took our place, so we could avoid eternal fire!

Jesus is the ONLY WAY! ALL other ways are false and will end in tragedy!

God's Way through the Lord Jesus Christ, or Satan's way through mediums and psychic power?

"Choose you this day whom ye will serve." (*Josh.24:15*)

To compare Christianity with spiritualism (or any other false way), takes us immediately to the parable of the "two houses" spoken of by Jesus in *Matt.7:24-27*.

"Therefore whosoever heareth these sayings of Mine, and doeth them, I will liken him unto a wise man, which built his house upon a rock: And the rain descended, and the floods came, and the winds blew, and beat upon that house; and it fell not: for it was founded upon a rock. And every one that heareth these sayings of Mine, and doeth them not, shall be likened unto a foolish man, which built his house upon the sand: and the rain descended, and the floods came, and the winds blew, and beat upon that house; and it fell: and great was the fall of it."

Founders of modern spiritualism, Margaret and Kate Fox, both died of alcoholism, but not before one of them openly renounced their spiritualist cult.

At a New York gathering in 1888, Margaret Fox said, "I am here tonight as one of the founders of spiritualism, to denounce it as absolute falsehood, the most wicked blasphemy the world has ever known."

How then could such a false, blasphemous cult possibly grow and continue (especially in England) in the face of such a blatant renunciation by its founder?

"Those who are on their way to hell will be completely deceived, because they have refused to believe and love the truth, that it might save them. For this cause God will send them strong delusion that they should believe a lie. That they all might be damned..." (*2Thess.2:10-12*)

Spiritualism is simply another age old demonic lie, which does away with repentance toward God and faith in the Lord Jesus Christ as the only way to receive forgiveness of sins, and salvation from hell!

Spiritualists everywhere believe in ...

"Personal responsibility for every thought, word and deed."(Dying without Christ's forgiveness will make this the heaviest of all burdens!)

"Compensation, and retribution hereafter for all." (Without Christ, **all** will be judged according to their works! See *Rev.20:12*)

"Eternal progress open to every soul." (Without Christ, the only "eternal progress open to every soul" is the fearful journey from hell to the Lake of Fire! See *Rev.20:14-15*)

Spiritualists are trapped in a no-hope religion! The Christian mission is to pluck such burning brands out of the fire before they are devoured forever! (*Zech.3:2*)

Alas, spiritualism is but a small deceptive chord in Satan's overall (and rapidly closing) "net."

A net clearly identified by the Biblical titles of, *"Great whore;"* (*Rev.17:1b*) *"Mystery Babylon the great;"* (*Rev.17:5*) and *"Mystery of iniquity."* (*2Thess.2:7*)

Not surprisingly this ancient, highly camouflaged, incredibly diverse and abominable *"whore"* (Satan's counterfeit religious system) is now recognized by an altogether different, and far more socially acceptable name – a slimy but shiny showroom equivalent called,

"THE NEW AGE MOVEMENT"

Having already established that the term "New Age" is a fundamental lie, I will merely state that this wretched, false religious movement contains every filthy, festering, and poisonous ingredient known to the demonic mind!

In view of its complex nature I am forced to concentrate on key areas of the movement's history, teachings, involvements and goals. My desire is to alert the Body of Christ (or any interested person) to the subtle dangers of this repugnant growth, and to help combat its pervasive influence around the world.

A brief history.

The serpent changes its skin.

As old as sin and the fall of man, Mystery Babylon (the N.A.M.) began taking on its present form in 1875 with the founding of the "Theosophical Society" by Helena Petrova Blavatsky. Joining her in this endeavor was Colonel Henry Steel Olcott, who became its first president.

In 1867, Blavatsky (the first female Russian immigrant to be naturalized as an American citizen) began receiving telepathic communications from so called "ascended masters" (said to be spiritual beings or fortunate men who have "evolved" to a higher level than the common herd, such as Buddha, Mohammed, St. Germain, Confucius, etc.); and continued receiving them until her death in 1891.

These "ascended masters," a.k.a. fallen angels, or *"angels of light"* (*2Cor.11:14, Gal.1:8*) insisted on the "theory of evolution," and taught Helena that all world religions have common truths which transcend potential differences.

From the very beginning, she and her growing movement showed outright hostility and contempt towards Christianity, and (of course) the one and only Lord and Savior, Jesus Christ.

She wrote,

"The Christians and scientists must be made to respect their Indian betters. The wisdom of India; her philosophy and achievement must be made known in Europe and America, and the English be made to respect the natives of India and Tibet more than they do." [1]

Just how exactly England and America would "be made to respect their Indian betters," soon became frighteningly clear.

An overflowing flood of occult deceptions such as "Yoga," "Transcendental Meditation," Eastern philosophies and healing techniques has literally engulfed the west within the last fifty years!

How did Satan manage it?

Back in the early sixties, young Americans (in particular), disillusioned with the so-called "church," and then with the war in Vietnam, began experimenting with a plethora of psychedelic drugs, and heard the siren call of India!

In 1967, the most popular English musical group of all time met an Indian (not-so-holy-man) "guru" known as the **Maharishi Mahesh Yogi**, and brought India to the West! (More on M.M.Y., the Beatles, and the "Transcendental Meditation Movement" in chapter 17.)

The Beatles' "musical invasion" of America was but the tip of the iceberg: through them, the devil did more to draw the New Age net around western youth than with all his other influences combined! (I include this mainly for the benefit of those too young to have witnessed the events first hand)

EVE STILL DECEIVED!

Strangely enough; although Blavatsky is credited with bringing the "ancient wisdom of the east" to the modern west; her satanically inspired books, "Isis Unveiled: Secrets of the Ancient Wisdom Tradition," (1877-78) and, "The Secret Doctrine: The Synthesis of Science, Religion, and Philosophy" (1888) would actually become a testimony and tribute to the truth of Biblical Scripture!

Speaking to Lucifer – the once anointed cherub, and secret power behind the throne of the prince of Tyre – God said,

> *"Thou sealest up the sum, full of wisdom, and perfect in beauty.*
> *Thou hast been in Eden the garden of God;" (Eze.28:12-13)*

Giving her the false *"wisdom"* and *"beauty"* of the world's ancient religions (from the *"perfect"* demonic point of view), Satan's "ascended masters" led Blavatsky on an exhaustive magical mystery tour of deceptive *"garden"* sites. With a just enough accuracy thrown in to keep the old "poisoned pot" simmering. (*2Kin.4:40*)

Her books can be read on the Theosophical Society's web site, but having looked through them, I can honestly say, "A Christian could be less bored watching traffic lights!"

Both books can easily be summed up with just one solitary Bible verse.

> *"...Ever learning, and never able to come to the knowledge of the truth." (2Tim.3:7)*

Nevertheless, as far as "Unveiling Isis" is concerned, a glimpse into the past will help reveal just how successful these "ancient mysteries" have been in polluting today's unwary world!

Isis is known as the **"Egyptian goddess of 10,000 names"** – **"Virgin Mother"** – **"Queen of Heaven"** – **"Goddess of the Moon"** – **"Stella Maris / Star of the sea"** (Some of these titles will be household words to Catholics.) – **"Ankhet"** (producer or giver of life: Ankhs are symbols of eternal life or reincarnation.) – **"Goddess of fertility and motherhood"** and most offensive of all –

"FEMALE CREATOR" (Satan must love that one!)

Isis represents *all* feminine aspects: **"rebirth," "ascension," "intuition," "psychic abilities," "higher frequency vibrations"** (i.e. love and compassion), **"Higher *Chakra*"**(wheel in Sanskrit), which declares that the body has spinning energy centers that look like spinning wheels, and are called Chakras. Healing comes when Chakras are brought into cosmic harmony, alignment and balance, and … **BLA, BLA, BLA-vatsky!** (I always wondered where that expression came from.)

It follows that Isis is **"Yin energy,"** the **"Mother Nurturer,"** the **"High Priestess of the Tarot,"** and, **"Goddess of all Mythological Tales!"**

Is "Isis" still alive and well?

ABSOLUTELY EVERYWHERE!

Isis is the **iris** in the "**All seeing Eye of Horus**" (her son). Depicted with wings, she is the "**Phoenix**" (the female bird of reincarnation). Do those titles and images sound familiar?
They should: **they're on your dollar bill! ...**

The Phoenix and the Eye of Horus are favorite symbols of **Freemasonry**: but as masons couldn't get away with putting the actual image of Isis (the Phoenix) on the "Great American Seal," it was conveniently switched to an eagle. The eagle (symbol of pagan Rome) was obviously more acceptable and politically correct for a so-called "Christian founded" country!

Those worshiping the goddess Isis will automatically worship or revere nature.
Here is just one of many bizarre examples.
In a 2005 ceremony, wreaths were laid for nine oak trees cut down by mistake in Rome, Georgia. A short eulogy given by a retired Reverend (that's a man or woman using **God's Name** as a title! (See *Ps.111:9*) brought tears to the eyes of some of the forty-five mourners present. The service carried all the marks of a human funeral! The proceedings began with the solemn melody of "Taps" ringing out over the swishing din of passing motorists; and the nine departed leafy friends were praised for the shade their canopies had provided, and for their grace. [2]
Enough already! Respecting God's natural creation is one thing, but a memorial service for trees? *– Please!*

INCIDENTALLY: do you have any idea just how offensive it is to God to refer to NATURE (the creation of GOD THE FATHER, SON, and HOLY SPIRIT) as "MOTHER?"

Satan could not have been more insulting to the Trinity than in persuading millions of people to worship or revere Isis as the "**divine mother**" (now in the religious guise of Mary), or as "**mother nature**" (now in the pagan guise of environmentalism!) ...

"Professing themselves to be wise, they became fools ... who changed the glory of God into a lie, and worshipped and served the creature (creation and created things) *more* (rather) *than the Creator, who is blessed for ever. Amen."* (*Rom.1:22 and 25*)

The "Wisdom Tradition" given or dictated to Blavatsky includes **Occult Philosophy**, **Hermetica** (the teachings of an ancient Egyptian called Hermes Trismegistus), **Alchemy**, **Sacred Geometry**, **The Way of the Elders,** and **Labyrinths**.

In 1993, the social science laboratory at the university of Colorado in Boulder, switched to a unix-based operating system (whatever *that* means), and needed a theme for naming its machines. They decided on Egyptian gods! Their initial server became Osiris – brother *and* husband of Isis!
(According to Egyptian mythology, Osiris was murdered by his brother Seth, and his body was found in Phoenicia by a heart-broken Isis. After turning herself into a bird, Isis cradled Osiris in her wings, and raised him from the dead. Hence her title, "Phoenix." ... Ta-da!)

In 1879, Blavatsky and Olcott moved to India, where the Society spread rapidly, and became inundated with the religion and pagan philosophies of Hinduism. In 1882, the movement established its head quarters in Adyar (a suburb of Madras now known as Chennai where it remains to this day). For purely demonic reasons, the Theosophical society and its teachings (not its effects) were to be kept secret for one hundred years. This order was given by one of Blavatsky's "masters," and was carried out obediently until the appointed time of worldwide declaration in 1975.

During this period however, Helena's "crown" was passed onto two other deluded women, Annie Besant, and Alice Ann Bailey.

Besant, (second president of the Society) wrote a seductive little prayer, which has since become known as the "Universal Invocation." ...

"O hidden light, vibrant in every atom
O hidden light, shining in every creature,
O hidden love, embracing all in oneness.
May all who feel themselves as one with thee
Know they are therefore one with every other."

New Age Teachings
GOD – IN MAN'S IMAGE!

Besant and Alice Ann Bailey (considered by many to be the high priestess of the N.A.M.) taught that all men are divine beings, and strongly condemned the "narrow way" of Christianity.

"One life pervades and sustains the universe. Human consciousness, also called spirit or soul (they obviously don't know the difference) **is in essence identical with the one supreme Reality or "oversoul;" including each of our particular beings and uniting us with one another. The gradual unfolding of this latent divine Reality within us, takes place by the process of reincarnation."** [3] (parenthesis added)

Bailey's teachings came from an "ascended Tibetan master" called, Djwhal Khul, who gave her (along with demon possession) doctrines which,

"Oppose the materialism of science and every dogmatic theology, especially the Christian, which the chiefs of society regard as particularly pernicious." [4]

Also on the Society's web site, you will see the N.A.M. serpent (symbol of wisdom, as encircling the world) surrounding the interlocking triangles of the hexagram. (Often referred to as the **"Star of David."**) In the center stands the "Ankh" (symbol of Isis or reincarnation), and above it all rules the

loathsome, ancient, tilted swastika. (Some swastikas were reversed, and tilted to symbolize ongoing motion.)
Hitler adopted the swastika, and also used Blavatsky's teachings to justify the annihilation of so-called "inferior species," such as Gypsies, Christians, and Jews!

Let me state here that as much as the nation of Israel should be loved, supported, and prayed for by Christians: (*Ps.122:6*) Jewish people should know the truth! ...
THERE IS NO STAR OF DAVID!
(I challenge anyone to find such a star in Scripture.)

Biblical references to "*A Star out of Jacob*," (*Num.24:17*) and to "***His star in the east***" (*Matt.2:2*) pointed specifically to the coming of the Lord Jesus Christ.

The star used as Israel's national emblem however, is the "***Star of Remphan;***" (see *Acts 7:43*) also known as the "**Seal of Solomon**," and was "*taken up*" from the ancient Egyptians, and others who worshipped Remphan (a.k.a. Rephan); a god believed to have been associated with the planet Saturn. Some suggest that this **hexagram** (the most powerful symbol in the occult world) was re-introduced to Israel by Solomon as the result of his marriages to many "***strange*** (pagan) ***wives.***"

(See *1 Kings 11:1-8*)

NOTE: With such a hideous demonic symbol hovering over Israel's people (*any* occult image or emblem is an open invitation to demons); we may well understand why they have suffered so much oppression and destruction under the "*powers and rulers of darkness?*" (*Eph.6:12*)

The N.A.M. teaches that the human pilgrimage takes us from our source in the One, through experience of the many, back to the union with the One Divine Reality. Our goal is thus to complete the cosmic cycle of manifestation with full conscious realization of ourselves, no longer polarized between consciousness and matter, or divided into self and other, but unified within and united with all other beings through our common Source.

In other words we are all one; so what goes around comes around – even if it takes a thousand reincarnations!

Helena Blavatsky's Big Secret

"As God creates, so man can create. Given a certain intensity of will, and the shapes created by the mind become subjective ... Intense concentration creates a concrete, visible objective, and man has learned the secret of secrets ... he is a magician." [5]

Back in the early sixties (for me that's "B.C."), I was at a party in London, England. At 3am, lost souls were still sitting around talking, drinking, and some taking drugs. Suddenly, a young woman jumped up and shouted, "I know the secret of the universe!" Silence fell: everyone looked toward her; eagerly awaiting the announcement of some great revelation.

With tears streaming down her face she stood in the middle of the room and exclaimed,
"If I stand on my tip-toes, I can touch the ceiling!"
(That girl's name could have been Helena!)

"Ascended master" teachings

These teachings are said to contain keys to the kingdom of heaven that can only be accessed through the heart. The core of the ascended masters' teachings is that the one God individualizes humanity's I AM presence through a number of reincarnations as each individualization of the I AM presence gathers more experience around itself. Through self-effort and constancy, and through the assistance of ascended masters and the angelic host, mankind will eventually regain the memory of their own divine identity, and manifest the Christ.

New Agers say that the "ascended masters" are our big brothers and sisters who, through the victory of the **ascension**, are one with their own I AM presence. (The "ascension" here, refers to any and all who have reached the divine level of "Christ consciousness.") Believe it or not, garbage such as this is being dumped into the Body of Christ like never before; and is being eaten up by millions of undiscerning Christians! (Which is the main reason for exposing it in the first place!)

New Agers love "**Harry Potter**," "**Mary Poppins**," **Chronicles of Narnia**," and of course, "**Lord of the Rings**." Tributes to these (and others) by various authors can be found on their web site, and in "Quest magazine." You'll also find the Ascended Master Teachings, and the following N.A. goals. (Simply type in Theosophical Society on any search engine, and look around)

New Age Goals
To form a nucleus of the universal brotherhood of humanity without distinction of race, creed, sex, caste (Hindu term for class), or color.
To encourage the comparative study of religion, philosophy, and science.
To investigate the unexplained laws of nature, and the powers latent in humanity.

"At the dawn of every new age, the masters have sent forth an enlightened one to lead mankind into greater light. Such a one was Buddha; such a one was Jesus. The ultimate one however, is yet to come." (N.A.M. teaching) It has always been the goal of the New Age Movement to unify the world, and bring in the "ultimate one" who will lead and guide all men into their greatest hour!

NOTE: To the N.A.M. separation is evil; therefore Christianity is evil because it teaches separation!
(2Cor.6:14-18)

The devil wants the whole world to worship the "ultimate one" (better known as anti-Christ): however,
"those whose names are written in the Lamb's book of life" – will not! (See *Rev.13:2, 8 and 15*)

New Age Involvements
In 1982, a national English newspaper ran a full-page advertisement announcing the arrival and manifestation of the "**Lord Maitreya!**" This "ultimate one" would be "Christ to the Christians," "Buddha to the Buddhists," "Mohammed to the Muslims" etc., etc.
The ad went on to say that he would speak to the world "telepathically" and "simultaneously" at some great event in the near future. At that time, he would reveal his plans to introduce a "golden new age" of peace and tranquility. (Such full-page announcements were placed in leading newspapers around the world as preparations for this "great happening" began!) Some time later a much smaller ad appeared stating, "Regretfully (due to an apathetic world), the appearance of the Lord Maitreya would be delayed indefinitely!"
(Someone once said, "Apathy is a terrible thing; but who cares?")
The whole campaign was hatched, dispatched, and hoisted on the unsuspecting public by one Benjamin Crème: a leading "cog" in the New Age machine!
Although thwarted by widespread indifference in the eighties, the N.A.M. currently insists that the world is now almost ready for the "ultimate one." The following list will bring to light a few of the organizations engaged in preparing his way.

Lucis Trust and Publications (Widely regarded as the "head" of the serpent!)
L.T.P. was originally founded in 1920 by Alice Bailey and husband Foster Bailey (a 33rd degree Freemason) as the "**Lucifer Trust**," but shed its skin to "Lucis" in 1922. The Trust has since formed connections with powerful business, political, and religious leaders around the world who seek to usher in the Luciferian "Age of Aquarius" or "Maitreya;" and eventually (by way of their "master plan") – the "ultimate one," i.e. "anti-Christ" himself!

L.T.P's offspring, or co-conspirators include, but are not limited to –

The Rockefeller Foundation, The World Health Org., Habitat for Humanity (ex- presidents, and every one else be warned!) **Coca Cola Foundation, CHRISTIAN CHILDREN'S FUND (WORLDWIDE), World Wildlife Federation** (no surprise), **Green Peace, Triangles Publishing,** (more and more N.A. books are showing up in public schools *and* Christian bookstores!) **Planetary Initiative for the World we Choose. (P.I.), Network World Alliance, Club of Rome, The European Union (E.U.), N.A.T.O., Amnesty International, Women's Peace Movement, New World Alliance, International Co-operation Council, The (W)Holistic Movement, Friends of the Earth, COUNCIL ON FOREIGN RELATIONS, The Bilderbergers, The Trilateral Commission, Findhorn Foundation, Lorian Association, North American Interfaith Network, World Council of Churches (W.C.C.) New Religions Movement, The Tara Center, The Cathedral of St. John the Divine in N.Y., N.Y.** (spiritual headquarters for the whole deluded bunch!) **WORLD GOODWILL,** which is deeply entwined as an **N.G.O.** (non-governmental organization) within the Communistic/ Social Democratically controlled **U.N! (UNITED NATIONS)**

WAIT! Let's not forget **FREEMASONRY, and EVERY OTHER SECRET SOCIETY** on the planet!

"... for this cause God shall send them strong delusion, that they should believe a lie." (*2Thess.2:11*)

The list of occult based New Age organizations goes on and on, but I could not close this small portion without also mentioning a few demonic N.A. practices, such as **Yoga,** *All* **Martial arts,** (including Tai Chi) **Transcendental Meditation (T.M.), Bio Feed Back, Hypnosis, Hypnotherapy, Reiki** (pro. ray-key), **Psychic healing, Silva mind control, Acupuncture, Macrobiotics, Homeopathy, Telekinesis, Extra Sensory Perception (E.S.P.)**

More spring up every day, but involvement with *any* of these activities will harden the heart against the Truth (the Lord Jesus Christ), and will invariably lead a person down the *"broad way"* of deception, darkness, and death! (*Matt.7:13*)

NOTE: Research by any interested enquirer will reveal the occult origins of all organizations and practices mentioned here.

A "**WORLD GOODWILL**" promotion declares ...

"During both the full moon and new moon periods there is similar emphasis on the work of energy distribution in meditation ... we consciously align with the rhythmic pattern of energy flow every month: we become a part of a planetary meditative process carried forward at all levels of consciousness, and with great creative potential for anchoring the seeds of the coming civilization, and the germ of the new culture."

One of the most subtle and dangerous offshoots of "Lucis (Lucifer's) Trust" is "**Triangles Publishing**." Described in some detail here because of its corrupting effects on our children.
Among the goals of "World Goodwill" through its outreach called "Triangles in Education" is –
"The World Program for Soul Education."

This program apparently,
"Guarantees the conscious alignment of human education with the purpose which the masters know and serve."

Launched in 1994, "Triangles" is now operating in over 130 countries! (These people are not playing games!) It works to bring schoolteachers into "triangles" (groups of three), who then form a "cell" and sit quietly meditating for a few minutes each day.
                    (*Especially* of course, during full and new moons!)
This meditation is:
A) "To direct the soul's **ch'i** into educational service worldwide."
B) "To enhance our capacity to vision the extra planetary significance of the formation of triangles within human consciousness at the dawn of the Age of Aquarius."

During meditation, teachers are encouraged to pray or proclaim the **"Great Invocation,"** and to imagine themselves being linked together by a "golden thread."

Please bear with me as I uncover this "Invocation," and remember; people around the world are falling victim to this satanic lullaby, even as you read it!

The Great Invocation.
From the point of light within the mind of god
Let light stream forth into the minds of men
Let light descend on earth.
From the point of love within the heart of god
Let love stream forth into the hearts of men
May Christ return to earth. (Absolutely *NOT* Jesus!)
From the center where the will of god is known
Let purpose guide the little wills of men
The purpose which the masters know and serve.
From the center which we call the race of men
Let the plan of love and light work out
And may it seal the door where evil dwells.
(Evil is anyone who resists their "Plan!")
Let light and love and power restore the plan on earth. (Parentheses added)

The "Great Invocation" was given to Alice Bailey by her Tibetan master Djwhal Khul, but its real meaning comes with Triangles' own explanation.

"This invocation embodies the fundamental soul energies which Triangles in Education helps release into educational thought and practice worldwide. The daily use of this invocation imbues our work with spiritual purpose and power, and helps maintain the high keynote of our service as a group. Some educators, according to cultural background, prefer to substitute terms such as Messiah, Bodhisattva, Imam Mahdi, or World Teacher in place of the term Christ. The principle of the emergence of a spiritually exemplary teacher for the whole human race remains the same. The themes of this invocation have been found to be of use in orienting teaching and learning to a greater sensitivity to the Soul potential of teacher and student alike." [6]

Now for the clincher:

An ancient occult symbol called the "**CADUCEUS**," loosely resembling Moses' serpent on a pole (used by the medical profession, and found in *Num.21:4-9*) has been quietly slipping into schools everywhere.

The symbol is a circle with seven lines representing the sun god with its seven sacred rays: Power, Love, Intelligence, Harmony, Knowledge, Devotion, and Organization or order. The circle contains a triangle with the "all seeing eye" in its center, and sits on a pole which has wings and twin serpents entwined around it. The "pole" (teaching rod of Hermes or Mercury, god of communications) means the strength which comes from right discrimination and choice.

The "triangle" and "eye" speak of the "ageless wisdom;" the "wings" point to the liberation of "self-hood," and of movement into light and illumination. The "twin serpents" picture the cyclic expansion of knowledge and consciousness. The fact that they are entwined around the rod explains the concept of linear (logical), and non-linear (analogical) ways of learning: a key feature of (w)holistic education. ... And *that's* just for kids!

Now are you ready for this?

The Caduceus (root word in Sanskrit "Karuh," meaning singer or poet) is presented with all its imagery to 11 year olds at the commencement of their modern language courses!

(This whole Caduceus deception is being "sold" under the guise of a non-religious subject!)

Students are taught occult mysticism by being encouraged to draw the symbol at home as well as at school, and to use their own versions in "eyes closed exercises," i.e. prayer and meditation!

For children, the Caduceus outlines three fundamental principles of success.

1. Apply the light of your mind.
2. Develop your capacity for love.
3. Use your power (ch'i) to do your best. [7]

CADUCEUS

Finally: World Goodwill states,

"The light of humanity and the "SOLAR LOGOS" will emerge as a crowning achievement of education in the dawning age. The term Logos is used to represent Divine Reason for the solar system, and our existence. Logos is described by Christians as "God is love," and in the esoteric psychology as a "great Lotus" (from yoga) of love and wisdom - the Source of the OM." [8] (parenthesis added)

As of the year 2000, the "World Program for Soul Education" has adopted a twenty-five year project: "Project Sol." (Sol may stand for soul, but [wouldn't you know] it's also the name of the pagan sun god worshipped in ancient Rome!)

Project Sol involves group research into the use of "soul energy" (as if we don't have enough already!) to empower and facilitate the emergence of a spiritually enlightened, Solar Humanity!

Conclusion

THE COMING ONE

"**The Great Invocation**" (said to be one of the oldest prayers known) was revealed to the masses during the full moon of June 1945: the "Full Moon of the Christ!" (The full moon of May being that of the Buddha.)

This "prayer" (recited regularly by new agers) is believed to be the means of fulfilling "**The Plan**," or blue print for the divine purpose. [9]

"For decades, the reappearance of the Christ (the Avatar*) has been anticipated by the faithful in both hemispheres. Not only by the Christian faithful, but by those who look for Maitreya and for the Boddhisattva; as well as those who expect the Imam Mahdi."

"The reason he has not come again is that the needed work has not been done by his followers in all countries. His coming is largely dependent ... upon the establishing of right human relation. This the Church has hindered down the centuries and has not helped because of its fanatical zeal to make "Christians" of all peoples, and not followers of Christ. It has emphasized theological doctrine, and not love and understanding as Christ exemplified it. The Church has preached the fiery Saul of Tarsus, and not the gentle carpenter of Galilee, and so, he waited. But his hour has now come, because of the people's need in every land and because of the invocative cry of the masses everywhere and the advice of his disciples of all faiths and of all world religions," [10]

"There is an inner spiritual government on the planet, known under such different names as the 'Spiritual Hierarchy', 'The Society of Illumined Minds', or 'Christ and His Church'; according to various religious traditions. Humanity is never left without spiritual guidance or direction under The Plan ..." [11]

"The widespread expectation that we approach the 'Age of Maitreya' as it is known in the East; when the World Teacher and present head of the Spiritual Hierarchy - the Christ will reappear among humanity to sound the keynote of the New Age." [12]

NOTE: World Goodwill is an activity of the "Lucis Trust," which is on the roster of the U.N.'s Economic and Social Council!

To the Lucis Trust, the Theosophical Society, and every active, consciously aware member of the New Age Movement: the True Church of chosen, blood bought and redeemed saints belonging to the TRUE and ONLY LORD JESUS CHRIST has *this* to say to you,
> **"You *want* your New Age Christ – you'll *get* your New Age Christ!"**

But be very sure you know what you're letting yourselves in for!

According to Holy Scripture, which is the *only* "Word of God," this long awaited "lord Maitreya" (better known to Christians as, "anti-Christ" or "beast") will *definitely* come!

But: His coming will be exactly as prophesied in the book of *Daniel*, and in the second epistle to the *Thessalonians*. – Right on time, and *BEFORE* the return and second coming of
> **JESUS CHRIST, THE DIVINE SON OF THE LIVING GOD!**

And so there should be no misunderstanding, hear now what Almighty God has to say regarding *your* lord, and chief of the "ascended masters."

"*... And he* (anti-Christ Matitreya) *shall **exalt himself**, and **magnify himself** above every god, and shall speak marvelous* (blasphemous) *things against the God of gods, and shall prosper till the indignation is accomplished: **for that which is determined must be done.** Neither shall he regard the God of his fathers, nor the Desire of women (the true Messiah), nor regard any god: for he shall **magnify himself** above all. But in his estate (their place) he will honor (worship) the **god of forces**... and honor him with gold, and silver, and with precious stones, and pleasant things.*" (Dan.11:36-38)

*According to New Age teaching, an Avatar is one who has a peculiar capacity (besides a self-initiated task and a pre-ordained destiny) to transmit energy of divine power. Such a one was Christ. Avatars most easily known are Buddha in the East, and Christ in the West.

"Now we beseech you, brethren, by the coming of our Lord Jesus Christ, and by our gathering together unto Him, that you be not shaken in mind, or be troubled in spirit, nor by word, nor by letter as from us, as that the day of Christ is at hand. **Let no man** (nor a Tibetan demon named Djwhal Khul) **deceive you by any means:** *for that day shall not come, except there come a falling away first, and that* **man of sin be revealed, the son of perdition;** *who opposes and exalts himself above all that is called God,* (The Godhead of Father, Son, and Holy Spirit) *or that is worshiped; so that he,* **as God** *sits in the temple of God,* **pretending that he is God!** *... For the mystery of iniquity is already at work, only he who now restrains will do so, until he is taken out of the way. And then shall that* **wicked one** (anti-Christ) *be revealed, whom the Lord* (Jesus) *shall consume with the Spirit of His mouth, and shall destroy with the brightness of His coming.* **Even him, whose coming is after the working of Satan with all power and signs and lying wonders,** *and with all unrighteous deception among those that perish; because they would not accept or love the truth, that they might be saved. For this reason, God will send them* **strong delusion,** *that they should* **believe a lie:** *that they all might be dammed who would not believe the truth, but took pleasure in unrighteousness."* (2Thess.2:1-12)

And Jesus said,

"These things must surely come to pass ... Let no man deceive you by any means ... for they shall see the Son of Man coming in a cloud with power and great Glory. ... and what I say unto you I say unto all ... **WATCH!"**

**ENVIRONMENTAL UPDATE

In 1963, a study was commissioned by the Department of Defense (Def. Sec. Robert McNamara)

And produced by the Hudson Institute (director Herman Kahn). Both men were members of the Council on Foreign Relations. The sole purpose of this study was to discover the best way to sustain and perpetuate government, and to maintain maximum control over its citizens without rebellion. It was agreed that wars have always been the most effective means of subjugating the masses without complaint. ...

"War can be used to arouse human passion and patriotic feelings of loyalty to the nation's leaders. No amount of sacrifice in the name of victory will be rejected. Resistance is viewed as treason. But in times of peace, people become resentful of high taxes, shortages, and bureaucratic intervention ... they become dangerous. No government has long survived without enemies and armed conflict."

However, with the possibility of a World Government, war would be phased out, and a new means of "peaceful" population control would be needed. After seriously considering various options (blood games, poverty, alien invasion, etc.), it was decided that the best alternative to war (producing a similar effect on the masses) would be a scare tactic based on environmental-pollution!

It's credibility and likely success would hinge on the fact that such things as acid-rain, smog, water pollution, and ozone threats are already well established in the mass mentality. It would not be difficult therefore, to exaggerate existing threats, or to invent new ones in order to bring about the end result. It may even be necessary to create a secret program of deliberate environmental poisoning to accelerate the process! After all, what wouldn't the ignorant masses put up with to "save mother earth?"

CFR member Lester Brown said this, "The battle to save the planet will replace the battle over ideology as the organizing theme of the new world order."

(The pieces of Satan's scam-puzzles are certainly coming together!)

**Adapted from "The Creature from Jekyll Island," by G. Edward Griffin, (American Media, Ca), pp.516-527, and based on the "Report from Iron Mountain on the Possibility and Desirability of Peace," edited by Leonard Lewin. (New York: Dell Publishing, 1967), pp. 9-81.

CHAPTER FOURTEEN

THE WHORE RAISES HER CUP

*"And one of the seven angels said to me … Come, I will show you the judgment of the great whore that **sits upon many waters** … and upon her forehead was a name written, **MYSTERY BABYLON THE GREAT, THE MOTHER OF HARLOTS AND ABOMINATIONS OF THE EARTH** … and the woman sits on **seven mountains** … and is that **great city** which reigns over the **kings of the earth** … having a golden cup in her hand full of abominations and filthiness of her fornication."* (From *Rev.ch.17*)

Every Christian knows that the Lord Jesus has a "bride" or "wife." (*Rev.21:9*)

His bride is the *true* Church made up of *"born again"* believers, chosen and redeemed from all nations.
Very few know that Satan also has a wife!

IDENTIFYING THE WHORE

Satan's "wife" is no less than "***Mystery Babylon;***" the rebellious, counterfeit, world religious system originating in ancient Babylon, but fully manifested in this age as the "***Great Whore***" of *Revelation chapters 17 and 18.* …

"***She was clothed in purple and scarlet, decked with gold, precious stones and pearls***," and was so impressive that the apostle John (who saw and wrote down the vision) "***Wondered with great admiration***" (was tempted to worship her! *v.6*)

The "*Whore*" is described by John as "***that great city***" sitting on "***seven hills***" and "***many waters***," which reigns over the kings or rulers of the nations. The "*waters*" are described in *v.15* as "*peoples, and multitudes, and nations, and tongues.*"

Rome, with the all the power of her false catholic (universal) religion is the only city or system that could possibly fit such a description; (She still holds multitudes in religious bondage, and has influenced almost every nation on earth.) but as we shall see, Mystery Babylon is in no way limited to Roman Catholicism!

When Babylon fell in 536 B.C., Satan immediately began looking for a better "location – location – location!" So when Rome became the world's most powerful empire, and began assimilating the gods and religions from the various pagan countries she had conquered; Satan simply shifted his headquarters, and "set up shop" (his spiritual throne) behind the throne of Caesar!

Caesar the "prince" – Satan the "king!" (See *Eze. 28* for a perfect scriptural example!)

Mystery Babylon's spiritual "*fornication*" (union) with the devil (*Rev.17:4*) had already given birth to the "Ageless Wisdom" found in the New Age mystery religions of Egypt and India: since then she has spewed forth every religious "*harlot daughter*" on the planet! From Hinduism and Buddhism to the full-blown New Age Movement. From Islam to Mormonism and the Jehovah's Witnesses. From Catholicism to the entire W.C.C. membership. From Animism's nature and creature worship to today's environmentalism and the veneration of "Mother Earth," or "Mother Nature!"

"Something for everyone" said N.A.M. writer Mark Satin. You name it; Satan can offer it!
(Everything that is, except the truth!)

Like mother, like daughters!
Since every "*harlot*" is the offspring of Satan's "*Whore*," God's judgment upon them will be particularly severe. (*Rev.18:5-8*) In view of that, a direct warning goes out from Heaven which should speak to *all* believers.

"Come out of her MY PEOPLE, that ye be not partaker of her sins, and that ye receive not of her plagues." (*Rev.18:4*) (Compare this with *2Cor.6:17*)

This amazing verse reveals, and sadly confirms that many of God's people (true believers) are actually involved (in fellowship) with Mystery Babylon!

How could that be? All I can say is, "Please keep reading!"

It's vital to understand that the "Whore" and her "daughters" hate the Bride of Christ as much (if not more) than the nation of Israel itself! Throughout history they have never ceased to persecute (even to death) God's spiritual and natural people.

Not content with that, Satan is manipulating governments and organizations around the world to remove any trace of true Christianity from our societies!

Exposing the Whore
We must also understand that the whore is both "*mother of harlots and abominations.*"
Every perversion known to man comes from Mystery Babylon!
Jesus said, "*As it was in the days of NOAH ... and LOT ... thus shall it be in the day when the Son of Man is revealed*" (*Luke 17:26-30*)

These prophetic words of the Lord Jesus were based on *Genesis chapters 6, 18* and *19*, and must be fulfilled before His return. (Second Coming)

Noah lived in a time of worldwide wickedness. Lot lived in Sodom, a city filled with all manner of sin and iniquity, including rampant homosexuality. Today that particular abomination is becoming increasingly acceptable, due mainly to the almost constant promotion it receives from films and television programs. (Count on Satan using Hollywood to hasten the fulfillment of God's Word!)

Wars – Political corruption – Genocide – Abortion – Drug/alcohol addictions – Pornography – Gambling – Child abuse – Murder – Rape ... another seemingly endless list!

AND ALL FROM ONE MOTHER!
(No wonder God will judge her so severely!)

Now look at this remarkable verse.

"And in her (Babylon the Great) *was found the blood of prophets and of saints,* (true believers) *AND OF <u>ALL</u> THAT WERE SLAIN UPON THE EARTH." (Rev. 18:24)*

False religion (in one form or another) is responsible for every murder or wrongful death on earth!

Now we can understand why God hates it so much, and why Jesus gave us this powerful and comparative revelation.

"The thief cometh not, but for to steal, and to kill, and to destroy: I am come that they might have life, and that they might have it more abundantly." (John 10:10)

EXPOSING THE HARLOTS
To count all the harlot daughters of deception is like trying to count the lies of Lucifer himself!

THE W.C.C. and the ECMENICAL MOVEMENT
"Ecumenical" (from a Greek word meaning, "of the whole inhabited earth.") Also, ("relating to, or representing the whole of a body of churches, and to the promoting of unity or cooperation.")

Back in 1983, the sixth W.C.C. assembly in Vancouver began with North American Indians lighting a "Sacred Flame," and burning dried fish and tobacco as an offering to the "great spirit." This pagan fire was maintained throughout the entire proceedings and used to light the candles for other *"strange fire"* worship services. Purification rites involving a "sweat lodge" were featured with drums, tribal dancing, chanting, and singing. Indian spokesman Art Solomon said, "The tide goes out, the tide comes in." In other words, what was once called pagan idolatry, was now being applauded, and described by W.C.C. officialdom as "A great spiritual tradition."

Archbishop Ted Scott commented,
"The opening ceremony reflects their (the Indians') deep religious conviction as they focus their attention on the Creator; and that creation is unified. A reality we could learn from in our world today."
[1]

Dr Dirk Mulder, Moderator of the W.C.C. interfaith dialogue program said he did not believe people are lost forever if they are not evangelized, and that a Buddhist or Hindu could certainly be saved without believing in Christ. [2]

In May 1984, an ecumenical (interfaith) service was held at Newcastle Cathedral, England. During that little religious "carnival" (my apologies for the insult to carnival owners everywhere), worship was offered (with flowers) to a Hindu goddess; Allah was given praise in a reading from the Koran; a Sikh guru and deity were honored, and a great fuss was made over the Hindu god Rama. (Who incidentally was proclaimed lord and king!)

The W.C.C. virus began incubating officially in 1948 in Amsterdam: since then, this filthy, ecumenical sludge of false religious compromise has spread like the cancer it is throughout the entire apostate community – exactly according to Biblical prophecy! (see *2Thess.2:3*)

It has presently multiplied to more than 350 churches representing some 400 million people!

Today, its web-page list of member and associate member churches presents a sobering and distressing revelation; and the sad fact is, many people at local levels don't even know their churches are involved!

Check the full list on the W.C.C.'s website to see if your church is there. If it is, you can heed the Word of God (as a true believer), and *"Come out from among them."* (*2Cor.6:17, Rev.18:4*)

NOTE: Unbelievers involved with the W.C.C., or who follow such ecumenical *"blind guides"* are on their way to an eternal *"ditch."* (*Matt.15:14*)
Here I name but a few –

The Alliance of Baptist Churches.
The American Baptist Churches in the U.S.A.
Assemblies of God.
Christian Church (Disciples of Christ)
Church of Jesus Christ of Latter day Saints. (Mormons!)
Church of the Brethren.
Evangelical Lutheran Churches in the U.S.A.
International Bible Society
Moravian Church in America (Northern and Southern provinces)
National Baptist Convention.
Polish National Catholic Church.
Presbyterian Churches (U.S.A.)
Russian Orthodox Church.
Society of Friends (Quakers)
United Methodist Church, U.S.A.

In 1973, Dr. Emilio Castro (one time chairman of the W.C.C.'s Commission for World Evangelism) said, **"We are at the end of a missionary era and at the beginning of the world mission."**

A speech given in 2003 by the moderator of the World Council of Churches' Central Committee, Aram 1, Catholicos of Cilicia clarified what Dr. Castro really meant when he made the following statement.

> **"We should accept that religious plurality is God's gift ... and consider other religions as part of God's plan of salvation, and not mere mission fields."** [3]
> > (In other words, *any* religion will do – *any* way will satisfy God!)

His helliness (some say "holiness") Aram 1 goes on to quote Georges Khodr, Metropolitan of Mount Lebanon.
> **"We should seek to identify the Christic values in other religions, and awaken the Christ who sleeps in the other religions."** [4]
Someone should tell these thieves and liars that *"God neither slumbers nor sleeps,"* (*Ps.121:4*) nor has He ever been in the false religions of Mystery Babylon!

In his opening remarks at the W.C.C.'s Inter-religious conference in Geneva, Switzerland; June 7th 2005; Aram continued to play his seductive religious fiddle.

> **"The vision of one community is focal in all religions ... we are all part of God's household ... I propose therefore, that a Continuation Committee be formed at this conference with the following aim ...** (I have listed only the last two of his four aims)

4. **To ensure inter-religious collaboration on specific issues by creating local, regional, and global networks of collaboration and joint action.**
5. **To create at a later stage ... a global council of religious leaders."**

Mmmm ... I wonder who would head a "global council of religious leaders?"

The goal of the W.C.C. is to produce nothing less than a **One World Church**, but so far (much to the Council's great disappointment) the Catholic Church remains officially aloof from the *visible* game, and at this time merely slithers along the side lines in a consulting mode.

It is a fact however, that the Catholic Church already sits on the WCC's Commission on Faith and Order; along with Southern Baptists, Pentecostals, and Seventh day Adventists!

Soon I believe, she will take her chosen ecumenical place, (along with all the other religious harlots) and once there, the *"Great Whore"* will finally, *"Sit on the beast as a Queen."* (*Rev.17:1-5, 18:7*) ...

At least for the short season God allows until she is *"utterly burned with fire: for strong is the Lord God who judgeth her."* (*Rev.18:8*)

Logically enough, and up high on the "to do" list of recently installed W.C.C. General Secretary, Samuel Kobia, was a June 16th 2005 visit to the Vatican and new Pope, Benedict XV1. The main topic of conversation was a three point WCC. agenda for further collaboration.

1. Understanding the Church; **2.** Spirituality; and **3.** (Surprise, surprise) Ecumenical Formation!

Kobia invited the Pope to visit WCC headquarters as quote, "Yet one more concrete step in our long journey towards visible unity."

The Pope said, "The commitment of the Catholic church to the search for Christian unity is irreversible." [5]

The WCC has always been the sweetheart of communists, liberals, political radicals and the undiscerning alike. Any vague reference to the Gospel of Christ is simply a means of camouflaging their true agenda, and deceiving gullible Evangelicals. What they really want is total interfaith unity to create their "One World Church," and everywhere resistance is slowly crumbling! ...

"I think there will be a time when my church may join the World Council of Churches. ... There are already Pentecostal member churches, and my church is a full member of the National Council in Korea."

Those sad words are from Dr Yong-Gi Hong; Pentecostal scholar and senior mission executive of the Yoido Full Gospel Church in the Republic of Korea.

His statement comes from a WCC press release at the 13th conference on World Evangelism in Geneva, May 9-16 2005, and is extracted from an interview with Theodore Gill, senior editor of WCC publications in Geneva, and ordained by the Presbyterian Church in the U.S.A.

To understand more clearly the sorry course of events which will culminate in the "Whore's One World Church," we must go back to the early twentieth century.

A satanic flood of **Liberalism** (an updated version of *"Hath God said?"* – Also called Modernism) swept over Christianity, engulfing many unsuspecting and ill prepared churches. Those in leadership who refused to be swallowed up by the growing movement, left denominations according to the Word of God; (*2Cor.6:17*) formed new assemblies, and became known as "**Separatists**" or "**Fundamentalists**."

Sadly, as time passed, many of those Separatists (who naturally were accused of being "unloving," "uncaring," "critical," or "too narrow") became tired of the spiritual conflict; put off their uncomfortable Separatist labels, and put on a new one called, "**Evangelicalism.**"

Religious liberals were thrilled – Satan was *ecstatic*!

You may have heard the saying, "If Christianity had remained faithful to the truth, all those religious "isms" would now be "wasms!" Not so! let's remember that God is still allowing Satan to have his "***short time.***"

We must also bear in mind that although he's a complete loser, Satan is smart enough to know it takes a while to "fool some of the people some of the time:" so even with time running out, he continues to rely on one of his most effective "isms." – "Gradualism!"

If the water in the pot is heated slowly enough, the frog won't know he's being boiled to death!

Having orchestrated, and enjoyed two world wars, the devil waited until 1948 before officially introducing a special little "daughter" onto the world's already crowded religious stage.

This harlot's name would be,

"NEW EVANGELICALISM"

Supposedly coined by a Dr, Harold Ockenga at a rally in Pasadena, California; the term "New Evangelical" describes the spiritual flotsam and jetsam from all levels of apostasy. It is the slippery slope for any and all who forsake the truth of God's Word, and embrace the great ecumenical lie.

"WE ARE ALL GOD'S CHILDREN: HE WILL ACCEPT US IF WE ARE SINCERE, SO LET'S ALL JOIN HANDS AND FIND OUR WAY TOGETHER!"

Signs of the "gradual" sell out or move to New Evangelicalism will include any or all of the following errors.

Error 1 Believing that love is the unifying principle, or the basis of spiritual fellowship regardless of spiritual truth. (The Siren call of the WCC)

Truth GOD'S LOVE DOES NOT EXIST APART FROM TRUTH!

God's love can *only* be found in and through the Lord Jesus Christ, and is available to true (born again) believers by His Holy Spirit!

Jesus said,

> "*God is a Spirit, and they that worship Him must worship Him in spirit and in truth.*"
>
> (*John 4:24*)

And,

> "*I pray not for the world, but for those Thou hast given Me; for they are Thine.*" (*John 17:9*)
>
> "*Love rejoices in the truth.*" (*1Cor.13:6*)
>
> "*Sanctify* (separate) *them through Thy truth: Thy Word is Truth.*" (*John 17:17*)
>
> "*Now I beseech you brethren, mark* (note) *them which cause divisions and offenses contrary to the doctrine which ye have learned; and avoid them. For they that are such serve not our Lord Jesus Christ, but their own belly; and by good* (smooth) *words and fair* (flattering) *speeches deceive the hearts of the simple.*" (*Rom.16:17-18*)

Error 2 Acknowledging other faiths as being valid, and equal in God's sight; therefore supporting the New Age teaching that there are many ways to God.

Truth TO BELIEVE IN ANY WAY BUT *GOD'S* WAY AS REVEALED IN THE BIBLE IS ABSOLUTE FOLLY! (See *Prov.14:12*)

Jesus said, "*I am the Way, the Truth, and the Life: no man cometh unto the Father, BUT BY ME.*" (*John 14:6*)
"***Jesus Christ the same yesterday, and today, and for ever.***" (*Heb.13:8*)

"*Believe on the LORD JESUS CHRIST, and thou shalt be saved, and thy house.*" (*Acts 16:31*)

"*Neither is there salvation in any other: for there is none other Name under Heaven given among men, whereby we must be saved.*" (*Acts 4:12*)

Error 3 A willingness to compromise or even repudiate essential doctrines and foundational tenets of the Christian faith; and to teach or preach such compromises to others.

Truth THE MAN WHO WILL GIVE UP AN INCH OF GOD'S GROUND TODAY WILL GIVE UP A YARD TOMORROW!

"*A double minded man is unstable in all his ways.*" (*James 1:8*)

"*But there were false prophets also among the people, even as there shall be false teachers among you, who privily* (secretly or quietly) *shall bring in damnable heresies, even denying the Lord* (Jesus) *who bought them, and bring upon themselves swift destruction. And many shall follow their pernicious* (destructive) *ways; by reason of whom the way of truth shall be evil spoken of.*" (*2Pet.2:1-2*)

"*Beware lest any man spoil you* (take you captive) *through philosophy and vain deceit, after the tradition of men, after the rudiments* (basic principles) *of the world, and not after Christ.*" (*Col.2:8*)

Error 4 A live and let live attitude, which often accuses "straight and narrow way" preachers of being negative and judgmental. Typical New Evangelical comments would be, "Let's keep things positive!" – "Why can't we all just get along?" – "Didn't Jesus tell us to love everyone: so who are we to judge?" – "God called us to win souls, not to criticize other faiths." – "Other religions may not share some of our beliefs, but don't we all serve the same God?"

Truth ANY DEAD FISH CAN FLOAT DOWN STREAM: IT TAKES A LIVE ONE TO SWIM AGAINST THE CURRENT!

"*Be not unequally yoked together with unbelievers: for what fellowship hath righteousness with unrighteousness? And what communion hath light with darkness?*" (*2Cor.6:14*)

"*Beloved, when I gave all diligence to write unto you of the common salvation, it was needful for me to write unto you, and exhort you that ye should earnestly contend for the faith which was once delivered unto the saints.*" (*Jude 3*)

"*Whosoever transgresseth, and abideth not in the doctrine of Christ, hath not God. He that abideth in the doctrine of Christ, he hath both the Father and the Son. If there come any unto you, and bring not this doctrine, receive him not into your house, neither bid him God speed: for he that biddeth him God speed is partaker of his evil deeds.*" (*2John9-11*)

"Love not the world, neither the things that are in the world. If any man love the world, the love of the Father is not in him." (*1John2:15*)

"Ye adulterers and adulteresses, know ye not that the friendship of the world is enmity with God? Whosoever therefore will be a friend of the world is the enemy of God."

Error 5. Increasing involvement and emphasis on social reform, humanitarian causes, and political programs which, though often noble in appearance, will begin to draw a believer into the worldly realm of "self-satisfaction," "fleshly works," and the elevation of man instead of Christ!

Truth IF NOT EMPOWERED AND LED BY THE HOLY SPIRIT, ZEALOUS CHRISTIANS MUST ATTEMPT TO GAIN GROUND BY WORLDLY OR CARNAL MEANS.

"I have given them Thy Word: and the world hath hated them, because they are not of the world, even as I am not of the world." (*John 17:14*)

"For though we walk in the flesh, we do not war after the flesh: (For the weapons of our warfare are not carnal, but mighty through God to the pulling down of strongholds;) Casting down imaginations, and every high thing that exalts itself against the knowledge of God, and bringing into captivity every thought to the obedience of Christ." (*2Cor.10:3-5*)

"Ye are they which justify yourselves before men; but God knoweth your hearts: for that which is highly esteemed among men is abomination in the sight of God." (*Luke 16:15*)

"For they loved the praise of Men more than the praise of God." (*John 12:43*)

Error 6. Accommodating worldly or pagan beliefs, customs, and practices in an effort to get ahead or just to get along, i.e. conforming to the world so as to not "rock the boat!"
This list includes ... **Evolution** (some try to call it "Theistic evolution;" an easier pill to swallow!) **Christmas** (originally a plain old pagan festival, then a special Mass for Christ, now a "good time lie" that almost everyone loves.) **Halloween** (Satan's big night out!) **Psychiatry/Psychology**, (you'd be shocked to learn what worldly nonsense a Christian has to submit to in order to practice *those* trades!) **Vegetarianism, Humanism, Freemasonry, Yoga, Martial arts** are all just scratches on Mystery Babylon's surface!

Truth EACH WORLDLY DECEPTION, LIE, OR PRACTICE WE EMBRACE, DIMS OUR LIGHT; TAKES US AWAY FROM GOD'S PRESENCE, AND CASTS A SHADOW ON THE GOSPEL OF CHRIST!

The Old Testament (written for *our* admonition) provides a grim reminder of this.

"For it was so, that the children of Israel had sinned against the Lord their God ...and **walked in the statutes** *(customs)* **of the heathen** *... and they built high places ... images, and groves ... as did the heathen whom the Lord carried away before them. Yet the Lord testified against Israel, and against Judah, by all the prophets, and by all the seers, saying, Turn ye from your evil ways, and keep My commandments ... Nevertheless* **they would not hear,** *but* **hardened their necks,** *like to the neck of their fathers, that did not believe in the Lord their God. ... They became vain, and* **went after the heathen** *that were round about them. ... Until the Lord*

removed Israel out of His sight ... so they were carried away out of their own land to Assyria unto this day."

(See all of *2Kings 17*)

"For if God spared not the natural branches, take heed lest He spare not thee." (Rom.11:21)

*"And **be not conformed to this world**, but be ye transformed by the renewing of your mind, that ye may prove what is that good, and acceptable, and perfect, will of God." (Rom.12:2)*

Obviously there are degrees of apostasy: churches or individuals may not manifest *all* the erroneous characteristics of New Evangelicalism listed here, but even one is too many!

V.I. True believers must be ever watchful; speaking forth the Word of life; contending earnestly for the faith as originally delivered; not being entangled with the affairs of this life, but keeping themselves holy and separated unto God by the power of the Holy Spirit!

Finally: in order to appreciate the growing threat of New Evangelicalism, we should return to that sixth WCC assembly in 1983.

Gathered at Vancouver were many Evangelicals. They functioned as delegates, advisers, speakers, press representatives, and observers. Among them were between forty and fifty leading figures of the Evangelical movement, such as Dr. Waldren Scott (former Gen. Director of the World Evangelistic Fellowship), Robert Youngblood (an official of the W.E.F.), Dr. Richard Lovelace (Gordon-Conwell Theological Seminary), Dr. Orlando Costas (Eastern Baptist Seminary), Dr. Paul Schotenboer (Gen. Sec. of the Reformed Ecumenical Synod), Dr. Arthur Glasser (Fuller Theological Seminary), and well-known charismatic leader Dr. David duPlessis.

These men met several times (informally) during this 18-day fiasco of false worship and idolatry, and decided to draft an **open letter** in which they spoke of the "warm communal fellowship" they had enjoyed in the ecumenical meetings, and how they were impressed with the "rich diversity and complexity" of the WCC.

Although somewhat "troubled" by questionable statements, and "disappointed" by the lack of emphasis on Mission and Evangelism, their strongest words were used to condemn faithful believers who were there to expose the deceit of the ecumenical movement, and urge Christians to separate from it!

(Special thanks to the "Fundamental Evangelistic Association" for information on the WCC and "the letter!")

NOTE: For those interested, I have reproduced the whole "letter" in the addendum. It was entitled, **"Evangelicals at Vancouver."**

*"**Beware of wolves ...**" (Matt.7:15, Acts 20:29)*

End of Part 2

PART 3

SO MUCH DECEPTION: SO LITTLE TIME!

May the following studies encourage us to pray for, and reach out to all those who have yet to accept God's love, forgiveness and salvation through the Lord Jesus Christ.

"Beloved, believe not every spirit, but try (test) *the spirits whether they are of God: because many false prophets are gone out into the world."*

"They are of the world: therefore speak they of the world, and the world heareth them."
(1John4:1, 5)

CHAPTER FIFTEEN

MACROBIOTICS

Not a world-shaking cult by any means, but one that shows how easy it is to *"worship and serve the creature rather than the Creator, ..."* (*Rom.1:25*)
In this case the "creature" is **FOOD**!

"For The Kingdom of God is not meat and drink ..." (*Rom.14:17a*)

MACROBIOTIC is taken from the Greek words "MACROS," meaning great; "BIO," meaning life; "BIOTIC," also meaning view or techniques regarding longevity.

In short, "This Great View of Life" is described initially as a way of eating: sadly for its many devotees, their way of eating has become *the* way, *the* truth, and *the* life!

In his book "About Macrobiotics," author Craig Sams wrote, "It is a highly personal way of eating and living, yet it embraces everything."
And,
"A Macrobiotic is a person who seeks to become aware of his body's processes, and through an understanding of his living environment, to achieve harmony with the world around him."

Michel Abehsera, author of "Zen Macrobiotic Cooking" explains: "Zen Macrobiotic cooking is the ancient Zen art of selecting and preparing food to produce longevity and rejuvenation, formulated in language suitable for people living today."

The recognized founder of modern day Macrobiotics was Nyoiti Sakurazawa; better known as Georges Ohsawa of Japan, who combined the western tradition of Macrobiotics with 5000 years of oriental medicine. What is not widely known is that Macrobiotics originated in China not Japan, and has its roots firmly embedded in pagan philosophy and the occult!
The movement's main center in the west is known as the "Kushi Institute," (a division of the Kushi Foundation, Inc.) and was founded in 1978 by Michio and Aveline Kushi. Currently, the institute sits on approximately 600 acres in Becket, Massachusetts U.S.A.

Sacred Place
To bring Macrobiotics within clear spiritual confines (for Christians especially), it is important to grasp the following. To the Macrobiotic devotee, food will eventually become a "god," and the kitchen, the "Holy of Holies!"

If that sounds extreme, just read a little more from Mr. Abehsera.

"Georges Ohsawa was a man, yes a kind of magician, who moved the mountain into the sea by the marriage of philosophy and cuisine ... the kitchen is a sacred place where the man of tomorrow will be created."

In the same book, Abehsera wrote, **"Rice is the king of kings."**

The branch and the root

We must understand that the branch (Macrobiotics) cannot be separated from its root (Zen Buddhism). They are of the same tree! Buddhism was born from the failure of Hinduism. (In spite of what some Buddhists might say.) Reincarnation and the "Law of Karma" are common to both! Buddhism has four "elements" – Earth, Water, Fire, and Air. Macrobiotics adds a fifth – Metal. With these five elements, you will find **Oriental Astrology** high on their list of teaching as all are necessary in that form of occult practice.

Zen Buddhism also originated in China where it was known as **CH'AN** (meditation), and exercises to reach enlightenment (satori) are similar to pagan practices such as Yoga, Martial Arts, Kung Fu, T'ai Chi, Judo, Tang Lang Chuan, etc.

Macrobiotics and Buddhism insist on self-redemption, which of course is a total deception, and stands opposed to everything the Bible teaches. The growth of Macrobiotics and Buddhism in the west owes much to Christ's old enemy, the Theosophical Society, and so can immediately be discerned as part of the New Age Movement.

Macrobiotics is certainly no friend of Christianity!

Yin and Yang

Just as Homoeopathy (for example) has its roots deeply embedded in the occult realm (its founder Samuel Hahnemann was a Diviner, Freemason, and Hypnotist, who discovered Homoeopathy by means of divination), so also the occult origins of Macrobiotics are equally deceptive. Nowhere does this become more evident, than in the occult principle of "Yin and Yang."

The philosophical basis of Yin and Yang serves Macrobiotics with the belief that antagonistic forces are in fact complementary to one another, and need each other to sustain balance, i.e. Darkness –Yin; Light –Yang; Man –Yang; Woman –Yin.

When Yin and Yang are balanced there is said to be harmony, which gives rise to a state of well being and "at-oneness" with self and the universe (the desire of all New Age and Macrobiotic people).

Counterfeit

Sooner or later, a person entering Macrobiotics, will be encouraged to embrace such things as "Tao Yin Meditation," "Visualization," "Vegetarianism," "Palm Reading," "Oriental Astrology," "Numerology," "Guided Meditation," "Yoga," "Martial Arts," and "Acupuncture."

"Holistic lifestyle workshops" are dedicated to the "Transformation of Consciousness," and to getting in touch with "intuition," and the "healer within."

Macrobiotics teaches that nothing is absolute, save the laws of relativity and change, i.e. "everything changes."

Away with that! – *"Let God be true, but every man a liar."* (Rom.3:4)

God's Word is absolute, and thunders,

"FOR I AM THE LORD, I CHANGE NOT!"

Macrobiotics teaches, if your body is right, then your spirit will be right.
The Bible teaches, "*We are **spiritually dead** in trespass and sin, and must be born again.*"

Back to the "Force"

Here are some statements from an interview I did back in the early '80's with one-time student/ teacher of Macrobiotics, Vicky Bartlett, (now a Christian) who studied extensively under Michio Kushi in Massachusetts.

Question. "What kind of spiritual teaching did you receive from Mr. Kushi?"

Answer. "Michio referred to the help he received from masters such as Buddha, Lao Tsu, Jesus, Confucius etc., and said that with so much of their lives and works in written form, we could, with study and discipline, rise even higher than they did."

Q. "What were you taught to believe about God?"

A. "We were taught that God is an impersonal force, but Michio encouraged us to read the Bible: he said it was, 'Yin and Yang'. He also said that it was impossible to contain **total** Yin or Yang. Mostly though, we were left to believe pretty much what we wanted to."

Q. "What do Macrobiotic people believe regarding sin?"

A. "As far as I was concerned, sin was not an issue. Everything revolved around balancing Yin and Yang. All discord (including sickness and sin) could be eradicated if balance and harmony could be achieved."

Q. "So what was the point of Jesus **dying** for sin?"

A. "I was taught that Jesus didn't actually die on a cross, but that his twin brother Thomas took his place. I learned that Jesus traveled to Japan; lived a Macrobiotic lifestyle; had four children, and died at the age of 130."

Q. "If Mr. Kushi teaches that there is no total Yin or Yang, isn't he calling God a liar? The Scriptures state clearly, "God is Light, and in Him is **no darkness at all**." And Jesus said, "I am the First *and* the Last." – "I am Alpha *and* Omega, the Beginning *and* the Ending.""

A. "Before becoming a Christian, it never occurred to me to question my teachers; everything sounded so reasonable; I simply accepted it."

Her testimony is as follows:
"I had been a vegetarian for many years, but was still searching for truth. I wanted a total philosophy for my life, which would include, health, peace of mind, happiness, etc. When I came into Macrobiotics, I felt that this was it! It seemed to have everything I was looking for, and my commitment was total!

I learned that sickness, lack of peace and so on, were caused by imbalance (Yin and Yang), and as Macrobiotics provided that balance, my whole life became centered in food. After a while, I noticed that I was in total bondage to the kitchen; but that's not the expression I used then! "We are what we eat" became a mantra to me. It cost my husband and I thousands of dollars to stay and study at the Institute, and looking back, it's easy to see why we were so deceived.

Macrobiotics is a vanity, which so appeals to pride and the selfish nature within us. There is no teaching on man's true condition before God; that we are all sinners in need of forgiveness and salvation through faith in God's Son Jesus Christ. We were taught to save ourselves through what we eat and how we live. Truly we worshipped and served the creature more than the Creator!

In all my time at the Institute, I cannot remember seeing one person who didn't smoke or somehow look washed out! Michio himself was one of the unhealthiest looking people I ever saw. Men became weak, and the women became strong. As a Christian, I know now that vegetarianism is a deception, (*1Tim.4:1-4*) and I am so grateful to have the real meaning and freedom of life in Jesus Christ.

I was so afraid of bad health, but now I know that Jesus is my Healer – not Macrobiotics!

My husband and I have both received Jesus Christ as our Savior and Lord, and we say to anyone involved in anything that is not Christ centered, may you also know the truth, so that the truth might set you free."

Summary

Satan's methods – like those employed in Macrobiotics – are literally deceiving the "*whole world.*"(*Rev.12:9*) "You are what you eat" is a very reasonable argument, and one (of course) containing a measure of truth. No one would be too healthy if their diet consisted only of "junk food" and soda! There is need for moderation. However, when a person's natural lifestyle becomes dependent upon food and self-discipline, and not upon Christ, they enter a counterfeit realm, or the "*broad way*" of spiritual deception.

Multitudes are striving by their own efforts to find health and security in this sin-sick and despairing generation. They are running in every direction; looking, working, spending, hoping, but never attaining the goal!

I don't doubt that Michio Kushi, and his Macrobiotic followers are sincere, but sadly the Bible shows us they are sincerely wrong!

To them, and to anyone searching for the *real* food (truth and eternal life!), the Lord Jesus Christ reaches out with His unchangeable Word.

> "*Labor not for the food which perishes, but for that food which endures unto everlasting life, which the Son of man shall give unto you: for Him hath God the Father sealed. ... I AM the Bread of Life: he that cometh to Me shall never hunger; and he that believeth on Me shall never thirst.*" (*John 6:27* and *35*)

CHAPTER SIXTEEN

CHRISTIAN RECONSTRUCTIONISM

In a tract exposing *this* "tragedy of errors," I began tongue in cheek by presenting –

THE ALL NEW (not so new) TEN COMMANDMENTS
of "CHRISTIAN RECONSTRUCTIONISM."

As set forth by Rousas J. Rushdoony: Founding false prophet and teacher extraordinaire! With supporting cast of friends such as George Grant, Gary North, Gary DeMar, K.L.Gentry, Larry Pratt, Andrew Sandlin, Robert Parsons, D. J. Kennedy, and R. C. Sproul.

Although you may smile at the ludicrous nature of these commandments, be aware that they in no way exaggerate, or contradict the beliefs of committed Reconstructionists.

1. **Thou shalt not be led by the Holy Spirit, but by the Law.**

2. **Thou shalt take the law, and put it upon all men, their children, and their children's children.**

3. **Thou shalt subdue and dominate all nations by the Law.**

4. **Thou shalt totally ignore New Testament Scriptures regarding freedom from the Law. (Especially those written by the Apostle Paul)**

5. **Thou shalt not stand fast in the liberty wherewith Christ has made us free, but shalt be entangled once again in the yoke of bondage.**

6. **Thou shalt not look for the imminent return of Christ, but shalt build thine own New Jerusalem (the Developed Kingdom of God) here on earth.**

7. **Thou shalt try to "Reclaim America for Christ," by pretending that the Founding Fathers were "all good Christians," and not mostly religious, tobacco growing, slave owning, New Age, deistic thinking Freemasons!**

8. **Thou shalt endeavor to make anyone who disagrees with you, believe they are denying God's Word and His Sovereignty.**

9. Thou shalt lead everyone thou canst, into the wilderness –

They shall go directly to jail
They shall not pass Mt. Sinai
> **They shall not collect 200 shekels**

> **But if they ever do, they hadst better give 10% or else! Because ...**

10. THOU SHALT ENFORCE THE TITHE!

Legalism rears its ugly head – again!

Christian Reconstructionism, Dominion Theology, (Dominionism) and Theonomy (Greek for God's Law) are not names of denominations or individual churches, but beliefs held by a wide range of religious people throughout the entire Christian community.

Rising from conservative Presbyterianism in the early seventies, the movement has since taught that every area (in the world) dominated by sin must be reconstructed in terms of the Bible. In other words, **these so called Christians want to change the laws of the land, until they match the Old Testament scriptures!**

Widely recognized as the father of Reconstruction, Rousas John Rushdoony (1916-2001) left a sad legacy of lies and false teaching to many; including his son Mark R. Rushdoony, who (at this time of writing) is president of "Chalcedony," and "Ross House Publishing" (engine rooms of C.R.)

To label Reconstruction as a Christian movement is (I believe) a gross misrepresentation: a much more accurate title would be *Mosaic* Reconstruction!

C.R. is definitely not Christian in doctrine or purpose, but manifests all the characteristics of legalistic bondage!

Its declared goal is nothing less than world domination in the name of God, and if you think those "commandments" on the previous page are in any way extreme, please consider the following statements made by some of the movement's well-known leaders.

C. R. Deception
"World conquest. That's what Christ has commissioned us to accomplish ... the conquest of the land, of men, families, institutions, bureaucracies, courts and governments for the Kingdom of Christ. True Christian political action seeks to rein the passions of men and curb the passion of digression under God's rule. It is dominion we are after." George Grant [1]

TRUTH
Jesus said, *"Whosoever will be chief among you, let him be your servant."* (See *Luke 22:24-27*)

Deception
"Mosaic Law is still to be enforced, by the church or by the state or both, unless there is a specific injunction to the contrary in the New Testament," Gary North [2] – **(Specific injunction?)** ...

TRUTH
"YE ARE NOT UNDER LAW, BUT UNDER GRACE." (*Rom.6:14*)
> **...(Is *that* specific enough?)**

Deception

"The fulfillment of the covenant, broken in Adam – restored in Christ is our great commission. To subdue all things and nations to Christ and His Law-Word. The sacrament of the Lord's Supper is the renewal of the covenant … so that the sacrament itself, re-establishes the law, this time with a new elect group. **The people of the law are now the people of Christ**." R.J. Rushdoony [3]

(*Blue Ribbon award* for false teaching!)

TRUTH

"CHRIST HATH REDEEMED US FROM THE CURSE OF THE LAW." (Gal.3:13)

Deception

"We are determined to set the agenda in world affairs **for the next few centuries**." George Grant [4]

(All emphasis, comments and *awards* are mine!)

TRUTH

Jesus said, *"AS IT WAS IN THE DAYS OF NOAH … AND LOT,* (worldwide wickedness and rampant homosexuality) *EVEN THUS SHALL IT BE IN THE DAY WHEN THE SON OF MAN IS REVEALED."* (See *Matt.24:37, Luke 17:28-30*)

And,

"WHEN THESE THINGS BEGIN TO COME TO PASS, THEN LOOK UP, AND LIFT UP YOUR HEADS; FOR YOUR REDEMPTION DRAWETH NIGH."
(*Luke 21:28*)

"Buy the truth and sell it not." (Prov. 23:23)

Because, *"Many false prophets and teachers shall rise and shall deceive many … if it were possible, they shall deceive the very elect."* (True believers) (*Matt. 24:11 and 24*)

Contrary to the teachings of Reconstructionism, this present world will *not* be won for Christ! Neither will it be ruled over by Christians on His behalf! The cry of the citizens in Jesus' parable two thousand years ago is still the cry of the world today:

"We will not have this man to reign over us." (Luke19:14)

Jesus said, *"My Kingdom is not of this world." (John 18:36) "It is the Spirit that quickeneth; the flesh profiteth nothing." (John 6:63)*

In other words, during this dispensation Christ's Kingdom is a spiritual one of grace, not a natural one of law! It is within us, and comes not with outward observation. (*Luke 17:20-21*)

The Lord will not have His followers fighting in the flesh, or using the law to gain natural dominion over *this* world. (*John 18:36*)

Not until He returns in glory (the seventh trumpet heralds His Second Coming) will He reign in righteousness and peace; and all true believers with Him! (*Rev. 11:15, 20:6*)

Then, and *only* then will the world be ruled by His Law! (*Zech.14:16-21*)

Bondage

The more we explore C.R., the harder it will be to comprehend just how anyone could be snared by such nonsense; but as I've already explained, if zealous Christians are not empowered and led by the

Holy Spirit, they must endeavor to gain ground by some other means – even false doctrine! Sadly of course, there are always those with *"itching ears"* who are more than willing to listen!

At this point let me say without hesitation, I believe the word best suited to describe Rushdoony and "friends" is found in *Galatians chapter 2*, and *verse 4* ...

> *"For they are false brethren, unawares brought in, who came in privily* (by stealth) *to spy out our liberty which we have in Christ Jesus, that they might bring us into bondage."*

Reconstruct a curse

The early church had more than its share of enemies, within *and* without, but by far the most treacherous (according to the Apostle Paul) were those who sought to bring believers (especially converts from Judaism) back into bondage under the Law of Moses.

Paul fought these enemies of liberty at every turn, and even described them as satanic agents of witchcraft! ...

> *"O foolish Galatians, who has bewitched you, that ye should not obey the truth ... This would I learn of you, received ye the Spirit by the woks of the law, or by the hearing of faith?"*
>
> (From *Gal.3:1-2*)

He then uses a play-on-words to sum up his disgust with these troublesome peddlers of legalism (circumcision), and gets straight to the heart of the whole matter.

> *"I would they were even cut off which trouble you ... As many as desire to make **a fair show in the flesh**, they **constrain*** (try to compel) *you to be circumcised; only **lest they should suffer persecution** for the cross of Christ. For neither they themselves who are circumcised keep the law; but desire to have you circumcised, that they may **glory in*** (rule over) ***your flesh.**"*
>
> (See *Ex.8:9, Gal.5 and 6*)

Every motive of legalism is exposed here:

"A fair show in the flesh"

Self-righteous, legalistic religious works (*"filthy rags,"* Is. 64:6), or the New Testament equivalents of *"wood, hay and stubble"* (*1Cor.3:12*) are motivated (however sincerely) by the believer's old or fleshly nature. (Trying to keep the law makes the flesh look and feel *so* good!)

"Constrain or compel"

Reconstructionists claim they can dominate by serving, but God forbid they should ever have the *power* to serve! There would be stoning (or burning) to death for adultery, blasphemy, or gathering sticks on the Sabbath! Not forgetting death for witches, homosexuals, or anyone committing idolatry!

> *"Eye for eye, tooth for tooth, hand for hand, foot for foot."* (You get the picture)

NOTE: There are understandably some minor disagreements within the movement concerning these issues; but only (it appears) regarding methods of execution!

"Lest they should suffer persecution:"

Perhaps the main reason why C.R's are unwilling to believe and preach the *true* Gospel!

Let's face it; teaching Christians how to fight *human* enemies, and "reconstruct" the world with Old Testament Law is much less embarrassing and troublesome than being baptized with the Holy Ghost, and teaching them how to overcome the *real* enemy with God ordained New Testament weapons in the Spirit! (*2Cor.10:4, Eph.6:10-18*)

It will always be more comfortable and convenient to keep those (reputation destroying) gifts (especially tongues) – safely "in shoes!"

"Glory in your flesh:"
In this age, anyone who wants **"world conquest,"** and writes ..."**It is dominion we are after:"**
or ... "**Mosaic Law is still to be enforced**" has some serious issues! (Not to mention major conflicts with the New Testament Word, Will, and Grace of God!) The only way *any* of those statements could be fulfilled today is **in and by the "flesh!"** ... How glorious is *that*?
Ralph Reed (Executive Director of the Christian Coalition) described Christian Reconstruction as,
"An authoritarian ideology that threatens the most basic civil liberties of a free and democratic society."
Which Bibles did Rushdoony and company read to come up with these kinds of errors? –
"The goal of Reconstructionism is the developed Kingdom of God (the New Jerusalem) on earth."
And, once again, my own personal favorite ... "The people of the Law are now the people of Christ."
Rushdoony also makes it perfectly clear that Reconstructionists are not looking for the imminent return of Christ; i.e. the rapture of the Church, or His second coming. Nor in a *literal* New Jerusalem which comes "*down from God out of Heaven*" after the millennium! (See *Rev.20 and 21*) C.Rs' New Jerusalem is a fantasy kingdom where *they* eventually take over the earth and rule: which (though they'd never admit it) gives man the glory, and not Christ!
How could they have missed the fact that Gentiles were never *under* the Law of Israel! (*Eph.2:12*) So how could Gentile believers possibly be "a people of the Law?"
(Which Law even *Jewish* converts have been delivered from!)

"Know ye not, brethren, (for I speak to them that know the law,) how that the law hath dominion over a man as long as he liveth? For the woman which hath an husband is bound by the law to her husband so long as he liveth; but if the husband be dead, she is loosed from the law of her husband ... Wherefore, my brethren, ye also are become dead to the law by the Body of Christ; that ye should be married to another, even to Him who is raised from the dead, that we should bring forth fruit unto God ...But now we are delivered from the law, that being dead wherein we were held; that we should serve in newness of spirit, and not in the oldness of the letter." (See *Rom.7:1-6*)

Nowhere in N. T. Scripture are we commanded to subdue people or nations!
Jesus said, "*Teach all nations*" (*Matt.28:19-20*) **Not dominate them!**
The law, which C.R.s' love so dearly, was merely a "*schoolmaster*" to bring the Jews to Christ.
(*Gal.3:24*)

(Remember the Jews fell in love with the schoolmaster too!)
However: "*Once faith* (in Christ) *is come, **there is no more need for a schoolmaster** ... Christ has redeemed us from the curse of the law, being made a curse for us.*" (See all of *Gal.3*) "*If you are under the law, Christ is made of no effect to you.*"
SO: **why would anyone in their right mind want to be under the curse of the law?**
AND: **why would they want to take you with them?**

Reconstruct an agenda

By now we've seen that believing and promoting Reconstructionism makes a mockery of our freedom in Christ, and seeks to put God's people in legalistic bondage, (equivalent to circumcision) which the early church leadership categorically refused to do! (See *Acts ch.15*)

But remember; Reconstructionists are seeking *temporal* power; they are determined to rule *this* world with Old Testament law – even if it takes hundreds of years!

IT WILL NEVER COME TO PASS!

Let the word go forth to every Reconstructionist.

By seeking world dominion, you are merely swelling the ranks of all those who (motivated by the spirit of anti-Christ) have already tried! Among them of course, the "big three" ...

Catholicism .... "Submit to the Mother Church, or else!"
Islam .... "Submit to Allah, or else!"
Communism .... "Submit to the party line, or else!"
Reconstructionism .... "Submit to the Law of Moses – or else!"

Why not accept the truth?
THIS WORLD IS *NOT* GOING TO GET BETTER!

In *this* world, "*the wicked and all the nations that forget* (or reject) *God*" will not be ruled over by Christ, nor by God's people: neither will they be brought under God's Law.
"THEY WILL BE TURNED INTO HELL." (*Ps.9:17*)

"THIS WORLD IS PASSING AWAY" (See *1John2:15-17*)

Today, Christians are angry (justifiably so) about the way the world is going, and about the corruptions spewing forth on a regular basis. But instead of "*Walking* (and warring) *in the Spirit;*" (*Gal.5:16, Eph.6:12*) seeing the "*Signs of the times*" and "*Looking up;*" (*Luke 21:7-2*) many are being seduced into believing that changing worldly social and political systems will turn things around, and eventually create a better future.

Listen to the rising voice of "Christian" political activism.

"If we could only get more Christian Judges and lawyers."

"If we could only keep the Ten Commandments in our court houses."

"If we could only vote more Christian politicians into government, it would make all the difference in the world!" – **NO IT WOULDN'T!**

Listen again to Jesus.
"My Kingdom is not of this world: If My Kingdom were of this world, then would My servants fight, that I should not be delivered to the Jews: but now is My Kingdom not from hence."
(John 18:36)

Substitute natural weapons for those of the Holy Spirit, (*2Cor.10:3-4, Eph.6:10-12*) and you are immediately in opposition to Christ's purpose! (He did not allow His servants to take over the world then, and He certainly will not now!)

Also, the "*Blessed hope*" of Christianity is not centuries away, but soon to be fulfilled in the
"Glorious appearing of the Great God and our Savior Jesus Christ!" (*Titus 2:13*)

New Creatures

At this time, God is rebuilding the **Tabernacle of David**. (*Amos 9:11, Acts 15:14-17*)
NOT the Tabernacle of Moses!

The Tabernacle of David speaks of the Grace of God, and the liberty of the Holy Spirit moving upon **Jew** and **Gentile** alike. King David (as a type of Christ) was admired and loved by both!

(*1Sam.18:16, 1Kings 5:1*)

Around David's "tent," there was no outer court. Inside there was no veil – **NO SEPARATION!** The Ark of the Covenant stood in its very midst, and in the freedom of that same Holy Spirit. David (a man after God's own heart) "*... danced before the Lord.*" (See *2 Sam.6:14-17*)

Today in God's Church, ("the Israel of God" *Gal.6:16*) His people are also free! In the Spirit there is no longer Jew nor Gentile, but one "*new creature*" in the Lord Jesus Christ. (*2Cor.5:16-17, Eph.2:13-15*) (Spontaneous dancing in the Spirit is just *one* sign of our liberty!)

Let's be absolutely sure that, "*Old things are passed away; behold, all things are become new.*"

Together, the Body of Christ can worship the Lord in the beauty of holiness – in Spirit and in Truth – "*In the liberty wherewith Christ has made us free.*"

IN CONCLUSION

Reconstructionism is essentially preteristic, which means they believe that most of the scriptures have already been fulfilled: especially those in the Book of Revelation.

Dr. K.L. Gentry, teaching at a 1999 Ligonier conference in Orlando, Florida, (R.C. Sproul's Ministry) said,

"Satan was bound in the first century A.D. ..." (So just where do they think he is now?)

"The Battle of Armageddon was an Old Testament image applied to A.D.70, and the destruction of Jerusalem ..." (Did Jesus return on a white horse with all the saints in 70 A.D.? (*See Rev.19*)

"The Second Advent is not the literal return of Christ, but God's judgment upon Israel; again in A.D.70, based on *Rev.1:7*; These things which must shortly come to pass ..." (Unbelievable!)

"The Mark of the Beast is not literal; it is a metaphor for dominion and control ..." (That's especially interesting coming from a Dominionist!) (Parenthesis added.)

Reconstructionists are Post Millennialists

They don't believe Christ will return until much of the world (if not all) has been converted, and is living under the Law of Moses.

Reconstructionists reject antinomianism

True antinomianism is the freedom to live in righteousness *above* the law!

True Christians are saved by grace, and *stay* saved by grace!

C.R's salvation is maintained by works of the law, and by trying to live a moral life!

(They didn't *invent* the "tread-mill," but they'll sell you one in a heart-beat!)

Regrettably, as obvious as these errors are, more and more Christians are buying them!

According to Public Eye Magazine ... "Gary North claims that 'the ideas of the Reconstructionists have penetrated into Protestant circles that for the most part are *unaware* of the original source of the theological ideas that are beginning to transform them'. North describes the 'Three major legs of the Reconstructionist Movement as the **Presbyterian** oriented educators, the **Baptist** school headmasters and pastors, and the **Charismatic** telecommunications system'." [5] (Emphasis. added)

There is no way of knowing exactly how many Reconstructionists are out there, or how many other Christians are running on the tread-mills of fleshly works. I'm sure they're sincere, but nevertheless they are still trying to turn the words of Christ into a lie!

"WITHOUT ME YE CAN DO NOTHING." (*John 15:5*)

The "old nature" will *never* agree with that statement; but again, without total dependence upon the Holy Spirit we are forced to do something – *anything* – in our own strength!

"Are ye so foolish? Having begun in the Spirit, are ye now made perfect by the flesh?
... Ye did run well; who did hinder you that ye should not obey the truth?" (*Gal.3:3, 5:7*)

Reconstructionism tells us we don't have to keep **"ceremonial"** or **"dietary"** laws: only the **"moral"** law! **Are they so foolish?** We cannot separate the law for convenience!

THE LAW IS THE *WHOLE* LAW!

Keep one and we must keep them all! (*Deut.17:19, 31:12, Rom.10:5*)
Break one and we've broken them all! (*James 2:10*)

What say you? Without **LAW** or without **FAITH** is it impossible to please God?
(See *Heb.11:6*)

"Beware of dogs, beware of evil workers, beware of the concision." (*Phil.3:2*)

(Beware of *all* legalists!)

CHAPTER SEVENTEEN

TRANSCENDENTAL MEDITATION

First encounters

When I wrote the tract "**T.M.: the Truth Behind it**," England had already witnessed (some of us first hand) the Beatles' brief "love affair" with Maharishi Mahesh Yogi.

They met at one of his lectures in London back in 1967, and sang T.M.'s praises through a few songs, and television interviews.

In 1968 however, amidst rumors of manipulation and sexual misconduct by the Maharishi, the Beatles ended their meditational fling. England was mildly elated (not too many of us liked the silly, giggly little guru), but ten tears passed before I became a Christian, and began to understand just how dangerous Mahesh (that's his actual name), and his T.M. movement really were!

Written in the eighties, the original tract was intended for 3 groups of people.

1. **Those interested, but with little or no knowledge of the subject at all.**

2. **Those who were seriously considering T.M. involvement.**

3. **Those who were already involved.**

I was actually naïve enough to believe that someone deeply committed to T.M. might leave the cult after reading my message! These days I write for groups **1** and **2**, and pray that by any means, God will open the eyes of group **3!**

Maharishi Mahesh Yogi founded the T. M. Movement in 1955, and his promises (then and now) have been truly amazing!

"The T.M. program is the single most effective meditation technique available to gain deep relaxation, eliminate stress, promote good health, increase creativity and intelligence, and attain inner happiness and fulfillment … More then 6 million people of all ages, educational backgrounds, cultures and religions have learned the T.M. technique." [1]

To learn how this enviable state of "happiness and fulfillment" is arrived at, we must go to a typical T.M. initiation ceremony. Although this example is taken from the 1970's, very little has changed.

The "student" (initiate or recruit) arrives with **white cloth** or handkerchief, which stands for the offering of his or her soul. With **Flowers** to symbolize the blossoming presence of ascended Hindu master Guru Dev in the initiate's heart. (I smell Blavatsky already!) And with **Fruit**, which is an offering for all the fruits of future actions such as material wealth, success, happiness and so on.

The initiate enters a softly lit room and is told merely to watch, as it is the teacher who will be performing the "ceremony."

The teacher has already prepared an altar to Guru Dev with lighted candle and incense, and has placed camphor, sandalwood paste, rice, and other ritual offerings in the appropriate containers. Two comfortable chairs are directly in front of the altar, leaving room for teacher and student to stand before a photograph of the dead guru!

The initiation room is always prepared behind a closed door so that no student may see the altar before entering. Mahesh has said that the element of surprise is important for insuring a smooth and deep initiation experience.

When the initiate enters, the teacher accepts the fruit, flowers and handkerchief, (these items are usually carried in a wicker basket.) The teacher briefly glances at an initiation form to check the criteria for "**mantra**" selection.

T.M. recruits are given a mantra so secret that they are forbidden to disclose it to anyone, even a spouse.

****

The **mantra** (a repetitious sound with no *apparent* meaning) is to be repeated for 20 minutes each morning and late afternoon or evening to remove **stress** (blamed for every problem), enabling the practitioner to fulfill the T.M. promise of "perfect bliss".

In the 70's, recruits were assured that their mantras were carefully selected from thousands to fit their personalities. A skeptical investigator was puzzled when he joined the movement in three different cities (using three different names), and received the same mantra each time. It was later discovered that there were just 16 mantras, and all were given according to age or sex. [2]

Mahesh describes mantras in his own words.

"We do something here according to Vedic Rites, particular, specific chanting, to draw the attention of **beings or gods in the higher realms**." And … "For our practice, we select only the **mantras of personal gods**. Such mantras fetch us to the grace of personal gods and make us happier in every walk of life." [3] (Emphasis added)

****

NOTE: "Beings or gods in the higher realms" translates to demonic entities or "angels of light." Chanting *any* mantra (in this case the names of personal Hindu gods/demons) is guaranteed to invoke evil spirits, and bring about demon possession!

Before the ceremony is over, students will (usually) be bowing before the dead guru (an act of worship, knowingly or not), and inviting in said demons by means of the mantras they have now learned, and will chant **every day for the rest of their T.M. lives!**

The whole initiation (called "Puja") is nothing more than Hindu idolatry, which relies heavily on, **"Trance induction through suggestion**, applied unethically to implant very eccentric spiritual doctrines in unsuspecting recruits who happen to be susceptible to post trance indoctrination." [4]

Since the 70's, Mahesh has continually denied that T.M. is a religion, in spite of a U.S. Court ruling to the contrary. [5]

A partial transcript of that trial reads:

"In the Hindu religion, the supreme being is conceived in the forms of several cult deities. The chief of these, which stand for the Hindu Triad, are Brahma, Vishnu, and Shiva. Guru Dev is depicted in the teacher's chant as a Guru in the glory of the three major gods of Hinduism, and is said to be a personification of the Supreme Being of Hindu philosophy. Guru in the glory of Brahma, Guru in the glory of Vishnu, Guru in the glory of the great Lord Shiva, Guru in the glory of the personified transcendental fullness of Brahman. To him Shri Guru Dev adorned with glory, I bow down. ... The chant clearly invokes the spirit or 'deity' of Guru Dev."

"The teaching of the SCI/TM course in New Jersey public high schools violates the establishment clause of the First Amendment, and its teachings must be enjoined."

Summary Judgment
"Although defendants (Yogi et al) have submitted well over 1500 pages of briefs, affidavits, and deposition testimony ... defendants have failed to raise the slightest doubt as to the facts or as to the religious nature of the teachings of the S.C.I. and the Puja."
(Filed Dec. 12 1977)

NOTE: If you believe in karma, reincarnation, the existence of God everywhere and in all things, and the existence of beings that are on a greater evolutionary path than our own; you are by the Maharishi's definition, a Hindu. (You are also a member of the New Age Movement!)

Mahesh has tried to use names such as "Science of Creative Intelligence," and "School of the Age of Enlightenment" to cover his religious tracks, but there can be no denying the fact that at every slippery turn of T.M., the message of Helena Blavatsky is heard loud and clear!

"The Christians and scientists **must be made** to respect their Indian betters. The wisdom of India; her philosophy and achievement **must be made** known in Europe and America, and the English **be made** to respect the natives of India and Tibet more than they do." [6] (Emphasis added)

Look M.U.M. ... I'm Flopping!

Claims of "Vedic flying" (levitation) while meditating in the "lotus position" have never been verified. Dennis E. Roark (Ph.D., and former chairman of the physics department in what is now the Maharishi University of Management or **M.U.M.**) describes vedic flying as,

"Merely an energetic muscular hopping ... on the psychological level, something unusual and probably dangerous is happening during this and other advanced T.M. techniques."

Not "flying" but a counterfeit "muscular hopping!" This more than adequately describes the whole Mahesh T.M. deception!

NOTE: The only evidence of *real* flying found in the Movement was when the price of a basic T.M. course "flew" from $400 to $1000 in 1994!

Roark goes on to say,
"My belief is that T.M. is in its practice and in its theories, religious in nature and is based on a pantheistic Hinduism that has been reformulated to make it attractive to western minds. We in the west have great respect for science and often look to science and technology to explain our world and to solve our problems. (We probably have an over-reliance on science in fact, and it may turn into a religion itself.) By T.M. claiming to be scientific in a most fundamental way, it tries to demand of us a respect we reserve for things thought scientific, rational, efficient, and effective. Under the guise of this false scientific claim then, Hinduism seeks its entrance into our lives. Many innocent individuals who sought only for an effective (scientific) technique are then exposed to the real dangers of this technique, and to the misleading philosophy and meta physics claimed by its proponents." [7]

The demonic Effect

One of Mahesh's flamboyant promises concerning his new world reads as follows:

"There will be all good everywhere and non-good nowhere." [8]

Mahesh's "Heaven on Earth" program, and all the other make believe programs in T.M. are supported by what is known as the "**Maharishi Effect.**"
"The Maharishi Effect is the phenomenon of the rise of coherence in the collective consciousness of any community. Scientific research has clearly demonstrated that when one per cent of the population of a city or town practices Maharishi's Transcendental Meditation Program, the crime rate significantly decreases." [9]

A report by Germany's Institute for youth and society on T.M. however, reveals the Maharishi's *real* effect!

A substantial number of meditators developed anxiety, depression, physical and mental tension and other adverse affects.
76% of long-term meditators experienced psychological disorders, including 26% nervous breakdowns.
63% experienced tiredness and serious physical complaints.
70% recorded a worsening ability to concentrate.
52% suffered anxiety.
45% suffered depression.
43% had psychiatric or medical treatment.
20% expressed serious suicidal tendencies.

Researches found a startling drop in honesty among long-term meditators!
(The Study was ruled valid by the West German High Court on May 29 1989.) [(10)]

Of course, Satan takes care of his own (for a while that is) so in spite of law suites and mounting evidence of **FRAUD** and **WRONG DOING**, the T.M. movement marches on!

In 1986, an affirmation from Attorney Anthony D. DeNaro, equivalent to a sworn affidavit, was presented to Judge Gasch of the United States District Court for the District of Columbia as part of **Robert Kropinsky's** civil court action. (#85-2848.)

In this document, DeNaro alleges (with force of sworn testimony) "A very serious and deliberate pattern of fraud, designed ... to misrepresent the TM movement as a science (not as a cult), and fraudulently claim and obtain tax exempt status with the IRS."

Other quotes from the affidavit that highlight important themes: "A disturbing denial or avoidance syndrome, and even outright lies and deception, are used to cover up or sanitize the dangerous reality on campus of very serious nervous breakdowns, episodes of dangerous and bizarre behavior, suicidal and homicidal ideation, threats and attempts, psychotic episodes, crime, depression and manic behavior that often accompanied "roundings" or intensive group meditations with brainwashing techniques."

"The Movement, the defendants, Maharishi Mahesh Yogi, WPEC-US, and Maharishi International University (MIU) were so committed to advancing the organization and its ideology that they were, and are, very willing to violate the law and engage in criminal behavior."

"The consequences of intensive, or even regular meditation were so damaging and disruptive to the nervous system, that students could not enroll in, or continue with, regular academic programs."

Finally DeNaro clearly believed that the Maharishi personally knew of, and was therefore responsible for, the damage being done in the name of his organizations. He was aware, apparently for some time, of the problem, suicide attempts, assaults, homicidal ideation, serious psychotic episodes, depressions, inter alia, (among others) but his general attitude was to leave it alone or conceal it because the community would lose faith in the TM movement. Maharishi had a very cavalier, almost elitist, view about very serious injuries and trauma to meditators.

His basic attitude towards the concealment of the religious nature of TM was:

"When America is ready for Hinduism I will tell them." [(11)]

In his civil suit against the TM Organization, a Washington, D.C. jury awarded 39 year old Robert Kropinski, $137,890 to pay for his psychiatric treatment. Kropinski was an 11 year member of T.M., and was part of Maharishi's personal entourage.

According to the January 14 (1987) Philadelphia Inquirer, the jury in the precedent-setting case found that the TM movement "defrauded him with false promises of mental bliss and neglected to warn him about the possibility of adverse side effects."

After surveying hundreds of meditators, Leon Otis, a staff scientist at the Stanford Research Institute, concluded that "TM may be hazardous to the mental health of a sizable proportion of the people who take up TM." And Gary Glass, senior attending psychiatrist at the Philadelphia Psychiatric Center, testified that Kropinski's 11 years in T.M. triggered a "pathological state" that left him disoriented and depressed.

Kropinsky's "Shank" T.M. Bombshell!

In a series of interviews with Robert Kropinsky, Guru Dev's current successor, Shree **Shank**aracharya Swaroopanand Saraswati describes the Maharishi Mahesh Yogi as nothing more than an **unscrupulous fraud!**

Question: (R.K.) "We have heard that Mahesh Yogi instructs mantras himself, and some people believe in him as their teacher. He is a **kaaystha** (lower caste, not a Brahmin) by birth. Do you think it is appropriate for him to instruct like this?"

Answer: (Shank.) "In reality, preaching, initiating, guiding people engaged in spiritual pursuits is the duty of those who are born in a **Brahmin family**. If he is a follower of **Sanatan Dharma** (the Hindu religion), **he should not do what he is doing.** This is against the orders of his Guru. Moreover, **making others write "puujya"** (revered), **calling himself "Maharishi"** (a great seer) **is totally inappropriate.** No assembly of saints has either conferred upon him a title of Maharishi nor has announced him puujya (worthy of worship) In the ashram he was doing the work of typing and writing and translation. Then he became a sadhu. However, **he has never practiced yoga. ... T.M. is worldly Yoga ... Mantras are made up by Mahesh,** they were not given by Guru Dev. He (Mahesh) **was an ordinary clerk** (secretary).

He (Mahesh) went abroad. First to Singapore. The expatriate Indians there, thinking that he is the disciple of Shankaracharya, received him well and got him a ticket for the United States. After going to America, he brought the Beatles back here. It was rumored that he did inappropriate things with them and that's why they left him and went away. He later opened many camps and *pretended* that he could teach people to read minds and levitate. No one, however, succeeded in learning the things he promised.

He himself does not know or practice yoga. He does not know anything about those things. ... Anyone asking for money for a mantra shows he has nothing to offer ... Mahesh [is] charging minimum $10,000 for "sidhi (advanced) initiation." Mahesh Yogi should fly in the sky in front of everybody. It would be nice if he once flies from U.S. to India without an airplane. Then perhaps what he says can be accepted. Otherwise, he will be like those who entrap people in their net of forgery.

We want people like you to tell others that he (Mahesh) does not know anything about Yoga. Neither is he serving the American people nor Indian people. **He cheated millions of Rupees from people.** He knows that in the days ahead **he will be exposed.** Before that moment arrives, he wants to make sure that he will not have financial difficulty in life. **Mahesh has caused a severe blow to Indian culture."** [12] (Parenthesis and emphasis added)

NOTE:

T.M. is a relatively small (but growing) cog in the giant New Age machine. It is just one perverse offshoot from the already corrupt root of pagan Hinduism. Mantras (vehicles for self-hypnosis) are simply the means by which demons (in the guise of Hindu gods) are invoked, (remember; hypnosis will *always* invite demonic influence!) and even though some "victims" seem less affected than others, all are guaranteed some form of spiritual bondage. Not to mention the financial bondage of paying anywhere between $100,000 and $200,000 for the privilege! [13]

Leaving the movement does not automatically free a person from its demonic influence! Only the Lord Jesus Christ can truly free someone from this (or any other) satanic oppression. (See *Luke 4:18, Acts 10:38*)

(Incidentally, Satan doesn't care which words or mantras are used in Hindu meditation; they will eventually all cause the same dreadful effect as T.M.'s "one thousand dollar" kind!)

I close this segment with the words of Joe Kellet (in bold), former 13-year student/teacher of T.M., and for whose help and web site use (amongst others) I am extremely grateful.

"No matter what unpleasant effects you are experiencing from T.M., (called 'unstressing') **the parroted response of the T.M. teacher or 'checker' will be T.M.'s version of 'Catch 22', which is the phrase ... 'Something good is happening'."**

(This is designed to keep a victim falling further and further into what he calls, **"The T.M. Rabbit Hole!"**) Mr. Kellet also states,

"But there's nothing special about T.M. once you pull the curtain aside, and so
IT'S JUST NOT WORTH THE RISK!" [14]

"Little children, keep yourselves from idols." (*1John5:21*)

CHAPTER EIGHTEEN

$CIENTOLOGY

"**C**ome into my parlor," said the spider to the fly!
Is it possible that such a simple little nursery rhyme could hold the key to one of the most ruthless and greedy religious cults operating in the world today?

The answer is a resounding **YES!**

Meet the "Spider"

In 1949, a science-fiction writer by the name of Lafayette Ronald Hubbard was invited to speak at a Sci-Fi gathering in Newark, New Jersey. During that speech Hubbard said, "**Writing for a penny a word is ridiculous. If a man really wanted to make a million dollars, the best way would be to start his own religion.**" [1]

A few years later – he did!

L. Ron Hubbard was born on March 13th 1911 in Tilden Nebraska, U.S.A., and grew to become a home-spun philosopher, self-proclaimed scientist, interplanetary traveler, really *bad* film maker, and above all, founding father, and chief "*blind guide*" of the "Church of Scientology!"

Early in life Hubbard became interested in pagan philosophies, and gobbled up the teachings of Eastern religions, Gnosticism, the New Age Movement, and **Black Magic!**

His mentors included such notables as Aleister Crowley and Sigmund Freud, (both powerful tools in Satan's hands!)

Hubbard would later say,

"The magical cults of the 8th, 9th, 10th, 11th and 12th centuries in the Middle East were fascinating. The only modern work that has anything to do with them is a trifle wild in spots, but is a fascinating work in itself, and that's the work of Aleister Crowley – the late Aleister Crowley – my very good friend." [2]

In a 1983 interview; Hubbard's son, L. Ron. Hubbard Jr. declared,

"I believed in Satanism. There was no other religion in the house! What a lot of people don't realize is that Scientology is black magic that is just spread out over a long time period. To perform black magic generally takes a few hours, or at most a few weeks. But in Scientology it's stretched out over a lifetime, and so you don't see it. Black magic is the inner core of Scientology, and it is probably the only part of Scientology that really works. Also, you've got to realize that my father did not worship

Satan. He thought he *was* Satan. He was one with Satan. He had a direct pipeline of communication and power with him. My father wouldn't have worshipped anything. I mean, when you think you're the most powerful being in the universe, you have no respect for anything, let alone worship." [3]

NOTE: L. Ron Jr. changed his name to Ron De Wolf because he feared retaliation from the "Church!"

Mean while, back in 1950, our intrepid galactic adventurer L. Ron. Sr., equipped with satanic delusions and scientific mumbo-jumbo, committed his philosophical "pottage" to paper, and produced (no surprise here) a best selling book with the pretentious title of,
"Dianetics: The Modern Science of Mental Health."

Satan was pleased: over the years, vast numbers of "flies" have accepted the "spider's" invitation, and although 1986 saw Hubbard's death; his web of lies, witchcraft, and humanistic psychology continued to catch the unwary at a demonically inspired rate!

NOTE: The three strongest manifestations of witchcraft are,

DOMINATION, INTIMIDATION, and MANIPULATION!

These characteristics have always been the central pillars of Satan's domain, and they are certainly the ruling powers of Scientology! (see *Eph. 6:12*)

It should therefore come as no surprise to learn that American, Australian, Canadian, English, French, German, and Greek courts of law have unanimously denounced this awful sect!

For example:

October 1965: the Australian Board of Inquiry into Scientology, conducted by Kevin Anderson QC.

After 160 days, and hearing evidence from 151 witnesses, the Board vehemently condemned every single aspect of Scientology, and especially its founder!

"**Scientology is evil**; its techniques evil; its practice a serious threat to the community, medically, morally and socially; and its adherents sadly deluded and often mentally ill."

The report continued, "In many cases, mental derangement and a loss of critical faculties resulted from Scientology processing, which tended to produce subservience amounting almost to **mental enslavement**. Because of fear, delusion and debilitation, the individual often found it extremely difficult, if not impossible, to escape. Furthermore, the potentiality for misuse of confidence was great, and the existence of files containing the most **intimate secrets and confessions** of thousands of individuals was a **constant threat** to them, and a matter of grave concern."

Regarding Hubbard

"His sanity was to be gravely doubted. His writing, abounding in self-glorification and grandiosity, replete with histrionics and hysterical, incontinent outbursts, was the product of a person of **unsound mind**. ... He had a **persecution complex**; he had a great fear of matters associated with women and a prurient and compulsive urge to write in the most disgusting and derogatory way on such subjects as abortions, intercourse, rape, sadism, perversion and abandonment. His propensity for neologisms was commonplace in the schizophrenic, and his compulsion to invent increasingly bizarre theories and experiences was strongly indicative of paranoid schizophrenia with delusions of grandeur. "Symptoms," the report said, "Common to dictators." (Emphasis added)

Former Cult Awareness Network executive director Cynthia Kisser said, "Scientology is quite likely the most ruthless, the most classically terrorist, the most litigious and the most lucrative cult the country has ever seen." [4]

The first publication of "Dianetics" was in a **SCI - FI Magazine** released May 1950 (the same month as the book!) You'd think that by now, even die-hard "**SCI** - entologists" would be able to connect the dots!

Hubbard leaves no doubt as to his connections with the occult. In the same magazine, he describes his "research" by saying he used, "Automatic writing/speaking, and clairvoyancy to discover what the mind's memory banks were doing." [5]

$$\$\$\$\$\$\$\$\$\$\$\$$$

NOTE: "Automatic writing" simply means channeling the words of demonic spirits on to paper while in a trance-induced (hypnotic) state. "Automatic speaking" is when a medium or psychic relays vocal messages from these spirits by speaking on their behalf. Clairvoyants and Mediums possess the ability to communicate directly with certain demons who impersonate the dead!

$$\$\$\$\$\$\$\$\$\$\$\$$$

BLACK MAGIC

In spite of Hubbard's claims that "Dianetics," and subsequently "Scientology" were his own discoveries, it becomes increasing obvious that many (if not all) his ideas and theories were in reality stolen (plagiarized is too polite a term) from many existing sources. One of them being –

Aleister Crowley.
Self-proclaimed "anti-Christ;" "beast of Revelation – 666," and good friend of Hubbard Sr! Aleister Crowley wrote a book called "The Master Therion" (first published in London, England in1929, and later called "Magic in Theory and Practice:") the same book Hubbard so heartily recommended in his Philadelphia Doctorate Course, Lecture 18.

For several months, Hubbard was a member of Crowley's U.S. satanic cult, "Ordo Templi Orientis," and together with Jack Parsons (Crowley's disciple), conducted many disgusting black magic ceremonies. [6]

Crowley's writings and Hubbard's teachings bare a striking resemblance.
"Dianetics - Time Track," where every event in someone's life is fully recorded in the mind, and,
Crowley's "Magical Memory" gradually reawakens childhood memories long forgotten, as well as those from "past (or reincarnated) lives." [7]

Both Crowley and Hubbard hated psychiatry [8] [9] (not surprisingly, as they were both ridiculed and condemned by that profession!)

Both believed in a person's ability to leave the body by way of Astral travel. [10] [11]

L. Ron Hubbard, Jr. asserts that during the time when the Philadelphia course was given, his father would read Crowley's works "In preparation for the next day's lecture." [12]

Author Russell Miller gives us another short but revealing clue regarding the "originality" of Hubbard's works. ...

"Hubbard had finished [reading] a book and passed it on to a friend (Brian Livingstone) to read. He started reading it that night, but next day he heard Hubbard describing one of his past lifetimes where he had done the very same things (described) in the book that Brian was reading!" [13]

The facts concerning Hubbard's unscrupulous character, his lying disposition, and demonic involvements have been well documented: unfortunately, such details are critical when answering the questions,

WHAT IS SCIENTOLOGY? AND WHY IS IT CALLED A "CHURCH?"

"We've got some new ways to make slaves here." – L.R.H. [14]

For those (Christian or not) who lack the time or the inclination to sift through the vast amount of data available on this truly malevolent cult, I offer this synopsis.

Human beings *outside* "Scientology," are referred to as **"WOGS."** [15] (a despicable word used in England as a racial slur long before Hubbard borrowed it!) Those on their way into the "church" are labeled **"FRESH MEAT."** [16] (These expressions alone should confirm the movement's vile demonic nature)

Getting every penny from "Wogs" and "Fresh Meat" was (and still is) an absolute priority!

"Make money. Make more money. Make other people produce so as to make more money."

L.R.H. [16]

And again, with all of L.Ron's finesse and personal creativity ...

"Money! Repeat money! Repeat money! Repeat money! Repeat money!" [17]

A woman who quit Scientology after just one session said, **"It's the only church I've ever seen with a cashier's booth!"** [18]

Here now are some other fine uplifting "sermons" from "Reverend Ron" on the same "lrhquote" website. (See end note 17)

1. "People attack Scientology; I never forget it, I always even the score. People attack auditors, or staff, or organizations, or me. I never forget until the slate is clear." 2. "There are men dead because they attacked us." (Can't you just feel the love?)

3. "The only way you can control people is to lie to them. You can write that down in your book in great big letters. The only way you can control anybody is to lie to them.

4. "If anyone is getting industrious trying to enturbulate (Ron's self-made word) or stop Scientology or its activities, I can make Captain Bligh look like a Sunday-school teacher. There is probably no limit on what I would do to safeguard Man's only road to freedom against persons who seek to stop Scientology or hurt Scientologists."

5. "Scientology is not a religion!" [17] (Parenthesis added)

Hell-bound Hubbard speaks for the "serpent" on all counts: even number 5!

You see although he turned his Dianetic Sci-Fi into a church merely to gain tax-exempt status, and in vain hope of reducing criticism against the cult; Scientology is still a perfect example of religion!

MAN-MADE EFFORTS

L. Ron's Dianetic "fig leaves" have cost his victims millions of dollars, but in truth, Scientology is just another pathetic, counterfeit attempt to find salvation apart from the Lord Jesus Christ!

Sins (or "engrams" in Sci. terminology) are treated as merely painful, often subconscious memories from present or **"past lives,"** and can only be removed through a painfully expensive, and bogus counseling process called "auditing."

NOTE: Reincarnation is generously included, and taught at no extra charge!

Once Hubbard established his church, auditors became known as **"ministers;"** (some actually wear clerical collars) Dianetic franchises became **"missions;"** fees became **"fixed donations,"** and Hubbard became **"prophet," "savior,"** and ultimately Scientology's **"father god!"**

Over night his books (especially Dianetics) became **"scriptures!"**

His devoted followers believed (and many still do) that L. Ron was both the reincarnated Buddha, and Lord Maitreya, and would be the one to lead the world to enlightenment!

(EL Ron will just have to get in line!)

Scientology is packaged as "Man's only way to freedom," but (sooner or later) Scientologists will discover (as will all members of false religions) that when they open the lid, their package holds nothing but bondage and death! (*Prov.14:12*)

SPYING OUT THE LAND

A year or so after the death of L. Ron., I happened to be in Clearwater, Florida.

My tract, **"Scientology: The Truth Behind It"** had already been written, but Scientology's H.Q. ("Flag Land Base") was right there at the old Fort Harrison Hotel!

(Here was an opportunity not to be missed!)

I had read through Dianetics of course, and other books for and against Scientology; but no book could begin to describe the gross spiritual darkness permeating that place; nor the glazed expressions and "dead" looking eyes of the otherwise clean cut navy types who were scurrying in and out of the building like so many sea going ants!

(Scientologists really know how to live a "Purpose Driven Life!")

As I walked into the lobby, I immediately noticed a small group of people standing in front of a large, imposing portrait of L.R.H. The female group leader (tour guide, and navy officer look alike) was speaking in glowing terms about the "Founder," and their "Father Ron."

At the end of her speech, I watched with fascination as all of them raised their hands to the picture in an obvious show of worship and adoration. Moments later, the dead Hubbard received an enthusiastic round of applause!

Obviously these people were neither "Wogs" nor "Fresh Meat," but visiting church members on pilgrimage to Scientology's Mecca!

CHRIST ("clearly") IN US

After wandering around for some time, (surprisingly, no one challenged me or questioned who I was) a uniformed man sitting at a desk upstairs finally asked if he could help. Needless to say, our discussion went on for some time! When it was over, and without realizing it, (and completely contrary to Scientology's money grabbing philosophy) he glorified the Lord Jesus by saying, "I honestly don't think we can help you; you seem to be pretty clear already." "Praise the Lord!" I said, "That's what *Jesus* can do!"

NOTE: "Clear" is the illusive euphoric state that all Scientologists seek after, and pay such enormous sums to obtain! If they only knew that the **BLOOD of JESUS** could "clear" (cleanse) them from sin **FOR EVER ... AND FOR FREE!**

> *"For by **GRACE** are ye saved through **FAITH**; and that **NOT OF YOURSELVES**: it is the **GIFT OF GOD: NOT OF WORKS**, lest any man should **BOAST**." (Eph.2:8-9)*

Once again, the futile work, and goal of every Scientologist is to audit out "engrams." This is done with the help of an "**Electropsychometer**" or "**E-Meter**" for short!

This little "miracle" of "Hubbard science" (no more than two soup cans connected to an electrical box, and used by Scientologists as a kind of lie detector) is sold (today) for a "**fixed offering**" of over **four thousand dollars!**

The E-Meter registers galvanic skin response, which can vary by how hard the victim squeezes the cans held in each hand, or even by how much he or she is sweating!

Hubbard swears;

"**The E-Meter is never wrong. It sees all; it knows all. It tells everything.**" [19]

It is with the use of this "magical" devise, and under "**Dianetic Reverie**," (the trance induced state common to *all* auditing sessions, and similar to that of Transcendental Meditation. i.e. darkened room, soft lights etc.) that "Pre-Clears" go back to the womb and "past lives" to clear "engrams" away from the so called reactive mind (The "Dark Side" of the brain) and transfer them to the analytical mind (the good side) for proper storage. When all engrams are transferred, the "pre-clear" is pronounced "**CLEAR!**" [20]

Hubbard promised that Dianetic "Clears" would ...

$ **Have neither colds nor accidents.**
$ **Have soaring IQ's.**
$ **Have total recall of their entire lives from conception on.**
$ **Have cancer (possibly) and other physical deficiencies repaired.** [21]
$ **Be able to compute in seconds what the average person needs 30 or more minutes for.** [22]
$ **Be the first truly rational people.** [23]

He proclaimed, "We are dealing here with an entirely new and hitherto nonexistent object of inspection, the Clear." [24]

"This allegedly superhuman condition is the desired result of Dianetics, and the launching point toward the upper levels of Scientology training. Any individual not yet "clear" is known as an "aberrated" person (Ron's neologism for "low life"), and one incapable of full human potential." [25]

After using the infallible E-Meter and reverie on himself, the "prophet" Hubbard proclaimed, "**Christianity was an illusionary implant,**" and, "**Christ was a fiction!**" [26]

He also stated that this "fictional Jesus" was, "just a shade above Clear." [27]

"Well; I have been to heaven . . . It was complete with gates, angels and plaster saints, and electronic implantation equipment." (L.R.H.) [28]

"So there *was* a Heaven after all – which is why you are on this planet, and were condemned never to be free again – until Scientology" (L.R.H.) [29]

So, after the demons stopped laughing, and patting Satan on the back, the "father of lies" gave Hubbard even more "delightful revelations." – Truly, the devil had found his dunce!

L. Ron received the following dictation from a demon guardian; known to him as the "Empress."

1. "The most thrilling thing in your life is your love and consciousness of your Guardian. She materializes for you. You have no doubts of her. She is real. She is always with you."
2. "You can do automatic writing whenever you wish. You do not care what comes out on the paper when the Guardian dictates."
3. "You have no doubt about God ... some day you will merge with him and become part of all. When (his bidding) you have finished in these lives."
4. "You are psychic. You can let people in any world talk to you while you are wide awake."
5. "No matter what lies you may tell others, they have no physical effect on you of any kind."
6. "Your psychology is advanced and true and wonderful. It hypnotizes people. It predicts their emotions, for you are their ruler."
7. "Material things are yours for the asking. Men are your slaves. You are power among powers. Light in darkness, beauty in all."
8. "You use the minds of men. Your league with higher beings, your mighty Guardian and the all powerful, renders you beyond all human criticism."
9. "You are kind and love everything, even when you force it to do your will."
10. "You can be merciless when your will is crossed and you have the right to be merciless. You are merciless to any who cross your rule, but they do not affect you emotionally."
11. "God and your Guardian and your own power bring destruction on those who would injure you."
12. "You recall all your past times on earth. You have, and will live forever. You are part of God. You are a crown prince of your section of the universe. You are eternal. You are satisfied to live within God. Human death is not your death. You will never die."

NOTE: In the end; suspicious of everyone; Hubbard died in hiding; a sick, chain-smoking, morose, and fearful old man. – The usual satanic rewards for a lifetime of loyal service!

"For what is a man profited, if he shall gain the whole world, and lose his own soul?"
(*Matt. 17: 26*)

L. Ron built Scientology with statements like those, but it was his attitude toward women that would best reveal the sickening depravity of his nature.

13. **"It doesn't give me displeasure to hear of a virgin being raped. The lot of women is to be fornicated."**
14. **"You have no fear if they conceive. What if they do? You do not care."**
    (Numbers 1-14 are taken from "The Admissions of L. Ron Hubbard.") [30]

Surprise! – Surprise! – **Surprise!**

Having failed miserably to prove the existence of one single "Dianetic Clear," (in spite of the thousands who paid him a fortune to reach that exalted level) Hubbard simply introduced new and higher levels of deception to explain away their disappointment. (And to keep them coming back for more!)

"Today (at this time of writing), the church invents costly new services with all the zeal of its founder. According to the church's latest price list, new recruits ('Raw Meat' as Hubbard called them) take auditing sessions that cost as much as $1,000 an hour, or $12,500 for a 12 1/2-hour 'intensive'." [31] – What a deal!

Enter – The – **Thetan**

Thanks to more trance inducing "audits," L.R.H. convinced his **hypnotized** followers (hence the glazed looks and dead eyes) that "DIANETIC SCIENCE" only worked on the **BODY!**

Harmful *spirits* however; conveniently discovered and named "Thetans" by "Lie-Ron," which were so obviously preventing Clears from being *really* clear, could only be removed by – you guessed it – **MORE AND MORE COSTLY AUDITING – COURTESY OF $CIENTOLOGY!**

Let's hear it for Super-Ron. Faster than a speeding "bulletin!" (Hubbard's communications)
From science to religion to tall luxury buildings in a single bound!

Are – You – **kidding?**

To reach the *highest* realms of Scientology – beyond the level of "O.T." or Operating Thetan, (Sci. language for a free and finally clear "super- human being") Hubbard's **"Fourth Dynamic Engram"** must be "believed implicitly!" That is for any Scientologist who wishes to climb (pause for a yawn!) to the even *loftier* heights on Scientology's **"Bridge to Total Freedom,"** or Levels O.T. 1–15! (This is exhausting!)

(Incidentally, "mega buck" levels O.T. 9-15 have not been revealed to mere mortals at this time.)

Right now, those who were willing to spend years clambering up to level 8; (and Dishing out anywhere from $300,000 to $500,000 along the way!) will actually discover at level 3 on this

Bridge to Total Insanity, that $ci-Ron holds the secrets of the universe, and knows just why things are the way they are!

The ultimate lie, and absolute core of Scientology – the Fourth Dynamic Insult, a.k.a. **"The Legend of Xenu"** is (as far as we know) Da-Do-Ron-Ron's parting, and most expensive $ci-Fi "gift" to any and all who are foolish enough to purchase it!

Are – you – **ready?**

All right ~ ju$t relax now ~ you're feeling $leepy ~ **v e r y** $leepy. Ok then, let'$ begin ~

THE LEGEND OF XENU

Thus $aith El Ron ...

75 million years ago, (*give or take a year or two*) the alien ruler of this quadrant of the galaxy was someone called Xenu. He was lord over 76 planets, including Earth, which at that time was known as Teegeeack. (*Really, it was!*) Anyway, each planet was over-populated by an average of 178 billion, (*give or take a few*) so, with the help of **psychiatrists!** Xenu came up with a plan to get rid of the individuals who were over-crowding his turf!

Tax auditing demands were sent to all the objectionable folks. (*That's a lot of auditing!*) But as each one came to be audited, he, she (*or it?*) was grabbed, injected with a dose of alcohol/glycol, and frozen. Then, all 13.5 trillion of these frozen people (*give or take ...whatever!*) were put into spaceships that looked just like DC8 airplanes, except they had rocket engines instead of propellers! (*That's DC8 not OT-8*)

Xenu's entire fleet of DC8 spaceships then flew to planet Earth, where all the frozen folks were dumped into **volcanoes** in the Canary and Hawaiian Islands. (*Now we know why there's a volcano on the cover of "DIANETICS"*)

So when Xenu's Air Force had finished dumping the bodies into the volcanoes, hydrogen bombs were dropped in and the frozen space aliens were vaporized!

Unfortunately for Xenu, their **spirits** (*called "Thetans"*) were still in tact!

BIG Problem! Xenu now had to catch all the flying Thetans (*spirits/souls*) belonging to the dead space aliens!

NO problem! He simply invented electronic traps, (*that looked just like sticky fly-paper*) so as the 13.5 trillion spirits were being blown around the planet by nuclear winds, they gradually all stuck to Xenu's electronic flypaper!

Once captured, the spirits of the dead aliens were then taken to gigantic (*that's really, really big*) multiplex cinemas built by Xenu here on Teegeeack. In these movie theaters the spirits were forced to spend many days watching special 3-D movies, and for two very good reasons:

1) To indoctrinate them with a totally **"false reality,"** i.e. the things that "Wogs" on earth believe today; and other things that would keep them in line with Xenu's program.
2) To control these spirits for all eternity so that they would never again cause trouble for Xenu in this sector of the Galaxy.

After they were released from the cinemas, these now thoroughly evil little Thetans began to stick together in clusters and stayed that way until mankind started to inhabit the Earth!

Today, the spirits of these dead aliens have attached themselves to human bodies and are the root cause of everyone's false reality. All of us (*except Scientology's "Homo Novis" on level OT-8*) are stuck with these thetan /spirits, so it's the job of Scientology's elite to remove Xenu's false reality from the world by auditing each and every space alien from human beings until the entire planet is **CLEAR!** ... (*No more "Wogs!"*) It's so very simple – once you're clear of the aliens, you've made it! – *"YE SHALL BE AS GODS!"* And all for the bargain price of $360,000! (*Give or take a $1000*) – What a steal!

All right: last but by no means least, (*and before the hypnosis wears off*) ...

The evil Xenu was eventually brought to justice, imprisoned in a mountain fortress, (*somewhere over the rainbow*) and secured within a force field maintained by an **eternal battery!** (*It just keeps going, and going, and going!*)

The trouble is, some of Xenu's relatives are still on earth, and trying to keep Scientologists from accomplishing their grand humanitarian task. These relatives write books attacking savior EL RON, and have many websites, which inconveniently denounce and expose the C. of S. as a monumental **SCAM!** According to Sci. policy, these enemies will one day be,
"Terminated ...quietly and without sorrow." [32]

Now before I count to three and snap my fingers, let me remind you that every part of this "infallible scripture" must be taken **literally**, and believed **implicitly** if levels O.T. 4 ~ 8 ~ and beyond ~ are to be reached! Oh, and by the way, I have some ocean front property for sale in Arizona. ~ You're going to love it!

Start writing the checks as soon as you wake up: ~ One ~Two ~

Seriously though, and believe it or not.

Many Scientologists who fled from the highest levels of the cult have testified to being in rooms at **Sci's Satanic Space Station** (Fort Harrison Hotel) in Clearwater, Florida. – "For 5-7 hours per day for up to **15 years**, holding two asparagus cans together, attached to an E-Meter, and talking to EL Ron's dead space aliens!" [33] (emphasis added)

Book now, and take a trip to the world's most expensive nightmare!

Conclusion

To enjoy and even believe in Science fiction should be everyone's right. (No one disputes that) However, once Hubbard began to peddle "Sci-Fi" as the only means of salvation, Scientology became a vicious and damnable heresy that denies and rejects true Christianity and especially God's Son, the Only Lord and Savior, Jesus Christ!

The huge amount of time, effort and money wasted on the lies of Hubbard's "Church," (as tragic as that may be) could not begin to compare to the ultimate waste of God's priceless gift of forgiveness, and eternal life!

Money is replaceable; a precious human soul is not!

I applaud and am deeply grateful to all who have taken such tremendous risks in speaking out against the Church of Scientology over the years. Your books, website articles etc., have helped many of us gather the ammunition needed to fight the good fight in our own particular arenas. Thank you!

Finally:

To anyone interested in a more detailed study of the Church of Scientology, I recommend the following books and websites in addition to the ones already mentioned.

"The Scandal of Scientology," by Paulette Cooper

"The Road to Xenu," by Margery Wakefield. Both currently on line at http://clambake.org

http:/www.lisamcpherson.org/ (Lisa McPherson was a young woman killed at the hands of Scientology)

And finally, http://www.watchman.org (for a Christian perspective)

EXTRA EXTRA!

Scientologists are making much of the fact that Hollywood actor Tom Cruise has recently joined their Good Ship Crazy! Apparently, Tom has done so well in promoting the cult, they're actually promoting him as the next Messiah! (He may not walk on water, but he can certainly leap Oprah's *couch* in a single bound!) Of course his greatest challenge will come if he ever decides to look for honesty and truth in the works of L. Ron Hubbard; or for that matter, the whole Sci-Fi-entology movement! In that event, the intrepid Mr. Cruise would suddenly find himself starring in a *real* "M.I.!"

Stay tuned for breaking news.

CHAPTER NINETEEN

MARTIAL ARTS
(So wrong, for so long!)

M.A.

Between two and three million people are currently practicing Martial Arts in the United States. Forty per cent are said to be children between the ages of 7 and 14, [1] and the Martial Arts industry generates annual revenues of over one billion dollars!

According to Scott Conway, founder of the Christian Martial Arts Foundation, between 50 and 70 percent of all martial artists, and approximately 20 percent of all instructors in the U.S. call themselves Christians. [2]

DEFINITION

The word "**MARTIAL**" means "of warfare" (military) or "suitable for warfare." The word "**ARTS**" however, indicates that these are not merely forms of combat, exercise or self-defense, but expressions of Eastern spiritual philosophy and religion. With that firmly in mind, we must ask a Biblical question.

IS THE M.A. "TREE" GOOD OR CORRUPT? *(Matt.12:33)*

Most Christians who practice and promote Martial Arts, believe they can separate the "leaves and branches" (its visual physical aspects) from the "root" (its hidden spiritual source).

Could a tree survive without nourishment from its roots? Could Martial Arts function without the spiritual power that brought it forth and nurtures it still?

Jesus came *"to lay the axe at the root of the trees."* (*Matt.3:10*) In other words; to separate the holy from the profane (through a new spiritual birth), and to seek out a people who would be able to *"Worship God in spirit and in truth."* (*John 4:24*)

The question now becomes, Is M.A. found within the realm of God's "Spirit and Truth," i.e. acceptable and pleasing to Him; or part of what the Bible calls *"the Mystery of iniquity,"*(*2Thess.2:7*) and therefore an abomination in His sight?

LET'S EXAMINE THE ROOT

Although its origins have been lost in antiquity (the roots of M.A. go back thousands of years B.C.), it is widely accepted that the first Martial Arts system (or method) was practiced in India, and developed by a Zen-Buddhist monk named Bodhidharma. This monk is said to have traveled to a Shaolin temple in the Hunan province of Southern China during the 5th-6th century A.D., and taught his skills there.

Eventually, from the Shaolin temples came five schools of M.A., all using the following forms or techniques.

Dragon, Snake, Crane, Tiger and **Leopard**.
(For the record, two are identified directly with Satan! See *Rev.12:9*)

The tree's M.A. "branches," recognized in the West today, appeared only after centuries of Eastern rooting throughout India, China, Korea, Vietnam and Japan. Its full-blown arrival in the West did not come about until the mid twentieth century!

(Remember Blavatsky's promise to bring Eastern occult practices to the West?)
Here we see more of that promise fulfilled. ...

After the second world war, many servicemen stationed in Japan began training in M.A., but it was during the 50's and 60's that large numbers of U.S. Military personnel (who were taught Korean arts during the War with North Korea) brought their training home and continued to practice and teach it after their demobilisation. [3]

Today there is hardly a city or town that does not have one or more "Dojos." (M.A. centers.)

CAN THE ROOT BE AVOIDED?

There are countless forms of M.A., but here are some familiar examples.
From **Korea**: "Hwa Soo Do," "Tae Soo Do," "Hap Ki Do," **"Tae Kwondo."**
From **China**: **"Tai Ch'i Chuan,"** or Tai Ch'i. ("Kung Fu," or "Wu Shu" are terms for Chinese Martial Arts in general.)
From **Japan**: "Aikido," "Karate," **"Judo,"** "Kendo," "Jui Jitsu."

A translation of some of these names should give the parents of youngsters considering involvement in M.A., a better idea of just what their **"lil'** (little) **dragons"** (the name routinely given to very young M.A. students) will be getting into.

Tae Kwon Do. "Tae" – to kick or destroy with the foot. **"Kwon"** – to punch or smash with the fist. **"Do"** means "the way."
Tai Ch'i Chuan. (Tai Ch'i) – Supreme, boundless, or grand ultimate fist. Also used as a form of exercise known as "moving meditation."
Judo. – The **gentle way** of life (as expressed in Taoism: pronounced Dow-ism)
Aikido. – Harmony, energy way, or the way of the harmonious spirit. Also described as "Moving Zen," and the way of union or harmony with **"Ki"** (Chinese "Qi" or "Ch'I")

"The ability to harness one's **ki** or **ch'i** (translated "breath power," "energy," **"force,"** "spirit" or "soul") is essential in mastering many traditional M.A. techniques, especially Ai-**ki**-do."[4]

Although there is still much disagreement over the actual meaning of **"ki,"** Bob Orlando, Christian *and* M.A. instructor (he likes to separate the two) describes "ki" as, "A synergistic, near perfect union of mind body and spirit for the accomplishment of a specific task, which in our case is self-defense." [5]

Many traditional Martial artists however, believe "ki" to be "a type of metaphysical energy that sustains all living beings." [6]

NOTE: Many "traditional Christians" (myself included) believe "ki" is a demonically inspired counterfeit of the Holy Spirit!

"Most M.A. teachers claim to locate the ki in the body's center of gravity, situated in the lower abdomen, about two inches below and behind the navel. In training it is constantly emphasized that one should remain 'centered' so as not to 'lose' the ki. Very high ranking teachers sometimes reach a level of coordination that enables them to execute techniques with very little apparent movement, sometimes even without seeming to touch their opponent's body." [7] (This could be called "throwing the ki.")

No Christian could possibly avoid touching *"the unclean thing,"* (*2Cor.6:17*) i.e. using or embracing pagan ways and practices while performing M.A.: so how do believers justify their involvement?

CHRISTIAN (?) MARTIAL ARTS

Christian martial artist Patrick Zukeran says,
"I believe that the physical aspect of martial arts can be separated from the Eastern religious and philosophical teachings. Also, I believe the Bible teaches us that there is a time when we are called to use force, even deadly force to halt acts of evil." [8]
(The Gospel according to Bruce Lee?)

NOW THIS

"The Gospel Martial Arts Union exists for the sole purpose of enabling Christian martial artists to associate themselves with a **truly Christian** martial arts organization. Our purpose is to enable our members to associate, grow and flourish in an organization **without being unequally yoked with unbelievers and unbelieving philosophies.** We believe that Christians can study the martial arts, and do so **in holiness as unto the Lord. We do, however, recognize the strong occult powers entrenched in Asian practice and academies. We also understand that the martial arts predate the oriental martial arts and our goal is to reclaim the martial arts for Christ."** [9]
Splendid! Now we can see *Rev.1:13* in a whole new way ...

"The Son of Man was clothed in an **Hakama** down to the foot, and He wore a **black belt** around His waist!"

Next, with a lil' extra commentary, and *"mockery"* borrowed from Elijah (*1Kings 18:27*) ...

"Karate For Christ" teaches the traditional martial art of "Chutoku Ryu Budo Karate-Do," and states,
"This world martial arts system (you know, the one that Satan rules!) **trains students in the following techniques: personal devotions, Scripture memory, personal reading, writing and research. (And let's not forget Christ's personal favorites) ... Blocking, kicking, punching, ki/chi, tumbling, restraints, releases, nerve centers, throws, grappling, ground fighting, submission holds, street tactics, breaking wood and cinder blocks, competition sparring, stick and knife defense, as well as a variety of traditional weapons."**

(All this while gently sharing Jesus with "lil' dragons" of 4, 5 and 6 years old!)

Karate for Christ's founder goes on to say,

"Aikido is The Art of Reconciliation." (Silly me, I thought *Jesus* was our Reconciler!)
"Aikido is easily Christianized." (Don't you just love that one!)
"Applied properly, Aikido techniques leave no lasting injury." (That should make lil' dragon parents everywhere feel a whole lot better!)
"Taught from a strong Christian perspective, our Tai Chi program will be very God honoring." (Thou shalt "whup" thy neighbor before he "whups" thee!)
"We use quiet praise and worship music instead of the traditional flute and sitar." (Yes of course! That makes *all* the difference!)
"Students learn the traditional art divested of its historically pagan underpinnings." [10]
(Would someone kindly explain to these people that without the "historically pagan underpinnings" there *is* no "traditional art?")
Also, let's remember that Aaron tried to "honor" the Lord with a golden calf; (*Ex.32:2-5*) and that didn't exactly hit the mark either!

AT LAST:
Christian *and* Martial Arts instructor Bob Orlando finally says it like it is! ...

"Chinese kuntao is an aggressive, combat-oriented system of Chinese fighting arts as practiced in Indonesia and Malaysia. It is an art that defends by viciously attacking the attacker, destroying his weapons on the way in, and pounding him into submission." (Vengeance is mine, I will repay, saith Bob – M.A.Version!) ...

"In addition to the arts' combat principles and methods of execution, we teach and study two kuntao forms combined into a single kuen, received from Willem de Thouars as part of our curriculum." (You will *not* want to miss this.) ... **"Chinese kuntao is a punishing art, characterized by tearing and breaking. The opponent's extremities, for example, are attacked with devastating blows – punches and elbows to break down his defenses and open him up for an all-out assault. De Thouars often refers to this as 'torturing' your assailant."** (What better Christ-like example could there possibly be?) **"For some, this self-defense focus is difficult."** (Wait for it) ... **"A self-defense focus actually preserves the highest martial art tradition: self preservation. Everything else in one's training is secondary to that. ... How can anyone question, or worse discard, traditional training techniques, methods, and philosophies left us by great martial art masters of the past?** [11] (Parentheses and emphasis added.)

The answer is simple – **they cannot!** There is absolutely no Christian M.A. way of giving up, leaving out, or ever being separated from **the occult traditions of Martial Arts!**

If there should still be doubts as to whether the "branches" of M.A. belong to the same occult pagan "root;" or that the "Do" of M.A. is not *The* Way of the Lord Jesus Christ; let them be addressed by Black Belt, Kaleghl Quinn.

Quinn writes,

"The techniques of Martial Arts (including Judo) **have their origins in the spirits of animals**, such as Tigers, Cobras, Monkeys, Bears etc., and **the student is encouraged to take on the spirit** underlying the technique, i.e. become a Cobra, Tiger etc." [12] (Emphasis added)

M.A. author Fred Neff insists that, **"An understanding of both the physical and the philosophical principles is required of every Martial Arts student."** [13]

Those statements alone should be enough to warn any Christian that something is very, very wrong, so why be *"unequally yoked"* with any of it?

NOTE: warnings like these may have little to no effect on committed Christian martial artists (they have best "defense" in the Body of Christ). Such messages are best focused on those more recently involved, or on others who are still considering involvement with the M.A. deception.

From the beginning of time, God has separated "light from darkness;" "good from evil;" the "holy from the profane!" Is the Holy Spirit speaking in riddles when He says,

"Come out from among them and Touch not the unclean thing?" (2Cor.6:17)

Does He really mean, "Holding on to the branches is fine, but try your best not to touch the roots?"

PLEASE LOOK AGAIN

Chinese M.A. systems are all basically referred to as kung fu (meaning ability); a term used for any exercise that is performed well.

Overall, M.A. is divided into two main groups: **external** (hard), and **internal** (soft).

External, or hard M.A. (Karate for example) emphasizes physical aspects, i.e. foot, head, and hand strikes, together with concentrated body conditioning.

Internal, or soft M.A. (Tai Ch'i Chuan) focuses on inner spiritual development, control, form, and mental awareness. **Taoist** and **Buddhist** philosophical principles become increasingly important, and stress is placed on utilizing the ki /ch'i. Thus, through breathing and spiritual techniques, "internal" students and practitioners seek to gather, cultivate, and hold the ch'i force within. [14]

Taoism: deeply rooted with the ancient Eastern occult philosophy of **"Yin and Yang"** (see Macrobiotics), and the self-achievement of harmony or balance within. Taoism floats along with nature, and with the universe as a whole. (As in "dead fish" floating down stream!)

Buddhism: ("Zen" is its Chinese form) has no particular gods, but of course, no One True God either! Just another self-help, no-hope religion: this one is trying to reach **"Nirvana"** (salvation from suffering through meditation and ultimate enlightenment). A place of absolute nothingness where consciousness, and therefore all desire is forever extinguished.

NOTE: by refusing to believe in a literal *"hell"* or *"Lake of fire,"* cults like the Jehovah's Witnesses and Seventh Day Adventists have created a similar place of nothingness (for lost or wicked souls), referred to as the "cessation of existence."

With the root of M.A. so clearly exposed, it would be the height of folly to suggest that a Christian martial artist could avoid serious spiritual harm, or (at very least) the *"Wood, hay and stubble"* of counterfeit *"fleshly works"* by continuing to "Christianize" occult practices that are absolutely contrary to the Holy Spirit and the Word of God!

So ...

Why would sincere Christians choose to remain in martial arts after acknowledging,
"The strong occult powers entrenched in Asian practice and academies?" [15]

I believe one answer can be found in

THE PARABLE OF THE PUFFERFISH

There in his deep shadowy world of caves and towering coral heads, the Puffer's big, dark, "puppy-dog" eyes watched with nervous curiosity as this "alien invader" approached and quietly moved away. I kicked hard with my fins, and pointed my Hawaiian-sling (spear gun) towards safer and more desirable prey, such as snapper, barracuda or even shark! If threatened, the Puffer's only defense is to inflate with water or air, until he literally becomes a "ball." That way he is far less prone to being attacked and eaten by larger predators; hence his other names, "Balloon" or "Blowfish." In the Caribbean however, none of us wanted to catch this gentle and harmless looking creature. Why? Because its skin, and internal organs, contain a neurotoxin 1200 times more deadly than cyanide! (One Puffer has enough poison [tetrodotoxin] to kill up to 30 people!) Strangely enough, the Puffer's flesh is considered a delicacy in Korea and Japan; but due to its extremely toxic nature, only specially licensed chefs are allowed to prepare and serve them to the public! Not surprisingly, the most desirable of the species (the Tiger) is the most deadly of them all! There is no known antidote for Pufferfish poison, yet every year, and in spite of the danger, numbers of people die from eating them. Why? Because apparently, very small amounts of the poison give the tongue (and body) a very desirable sensation!

Tragically, those reckless and undiscerning people who perish, do so simply by miscalculating the amount of poison they are able to consume!

Could there be anything more straightforward?

For some, the Eastern "delicacy" of Martial Arts may "feel good on the tongue;" giving the body a great sense of confidence, well being and pride; which inevitably comes from mastering M.A. techniques and beating the competition. But no matter how carefully Christian "chefs" (M.A. instructors) prepare and present the "fish" (the edited Christian M.A. version), it is still part of a false, corrupt and poisonous system, which ultimately ministers death not life, and is best left well alone!

CLOSING THOUGHTS:

"He (God) *delighteth not in the strength of the horse: He taketh not pleasure in the legs of a man." (Ps. 147:11)*

Jesus said, *"It is the Spirit that quickeneth; the flesh profiteth nothing: the words that I speak unto you, they are Spirit, and they are Life." (John 6:63)*

Both Old and New Testaments make it very clear that we are to have *"No confidence in the flesh"* (*Phil. 3:3*), but once again, those that do not recognize, accept, or acknowledge the baptism, gifts, and power of the Holy Spirit (for whatever reason) must seek to overcome by alternative fleshly means. Nowhere is this more clearly demonstrated than in Christian Martial Arts!

To deliberately seek after (practice or rely on) natural, self-preservation techniques (even without the conscious addition of M.A.'s Eastern paganism) implies a lack of faith in God's sovereign ability to deliver and keep us by His supernatural power!

"For though we walk in the flesh, we do not war after the flesh. For the weapons of our warfare are not carnal, (natural or physical) *but mighty through God to the pulling down of strongholds." (2Cor.10:3-4)*

"For we wrestle not against flesh and blood, (human opponents) *but against principalities, powers, and rulers of the spiritual darkness of this world." (Eph.6:10-18)*

However, if as Born-again believers, our faith isn't strong enough to stand and overcome spiritually, *(1John 5:4)* and we feel the need to learn natural self-defense (no criticism intended): there are ways we can do so without stepping over into an *"unclean"* (hopelessly contaminated) Eastern martial arts system, ruled over by the *"god of this world!" (2Cor.4:4)*

In the end, freedom from any deception (in this case a false "Do") will come through prayer, and a deep desire for the Holy Spirit to *"guide us into all Truth!" (John 16:13)*
May the Grace of God prevent us from stumbling out of Christ's *"straight and narrow Way."*

"Truly my soul waiteth upon God
From Him cometh my salvation (deliverance) *He only is my Rock and my salvation; He is my Defense I shall not be greatly moved." (Ps.62:1-2)*

****

The "Dragon" has always been synonymous with Martial Arts.
It is a name given by God to describe the devil! *(Rev. 12:7-9)*
Why would anyone (especially a Christian) want to be associated with that hideous spiritual title?
Promoting the "Dragon" *anywhere* (and in *any* form) cannot possibly be honoring to God.
Business owners, venders, club members, football, soccer, and baseball teams beware!
It's black or white – in Christ there is no gray! You're either, *"With Him or against Him."*
(Matt.12:30)

Lift up the dragon, and you inevitably lift up Satan himself!

May it not be so among the Saints!

****

CHAPTER TWENTY

YOGA

"You will know the force when you are calm at peace
The Force is my ally and a powerful ally it is.
Life creates it, makes it grow.
Its energy surrounds us and binds us.
Luminous beings are we, not this crude matter."

(Yoda: 'The Empire Strikes Back')

The fool says in his heart, "There is no God."
Satan says, "There are many!"
(Ps.14:1) (Gen.3:5)

For thousands, if not millions of deceived adherents in Western civilization, (currently 10-12 million in the U.S. alone) Yoga is thought of and practiced merely as an attempt to gain self-control, relaxation, better health etc., through a series of different physical poses (called asana[s]) in which the body and mind, are brought into harmony. (Sadly, this is only a scratch on the surface!)

"Yoga" and the English word "yoke" are both derived from the same Indian Sanskrit root "Yuj," which means to **join**, **harness**, **discipline**, or **unite with**. Yoga is loosely applied to any discipline or technique that leads to a union with "god" or the divine.

Yoga is all about one's body, mind and spirit (soul or individual [little] consciousness) becoming one with the grand scheme of **"universal consciousness!"**

These elements of "god" (the divine), and "universal consciousness" will raise the curtain on the second oldest false religion known to man!

THE BIGGER PICTURE

Yoga devotee and author Mukunda Stiles makes two interesting statements:

1) **"The goal of Yoga is to merge the mind into the True Self, and thus be true to your Self, in all thoughts, words and deeds."**
2) **"Yoga is not a religion."** [1] ("True Self" and "Self" capitalized in the original.)

In answer to **1)**

"O Lord, I know that the way of man is not in himself: it is not in man that walketh to direct his steps." (Jer.10:23)

A man who is lost will never find the way by looking at himself!

The Word of God makes it abundantly clear that man's *real* nature (Mukunda's "True Self") is *"Dead in trespass and sin." (Eph.2:1)* ... He simply *cannot* help himself!

If there was any further doubt as to man's actual condition –

"The heart is deceitful above all things and desperately wicked: who can know it?" *(Jer.17:9)*

In answer to **2)**

Mr. Stiles calls down this lie upon himself when he admits that, "The first requirement in virtually all Yoga classes is to seek guidance from your inner teacher or Higher Power." [2] (Caps in original)

We soon discover that the "inner teacher" or "Higher Power" of Yoga has a lot to do with the well-known pagan expression for "god" – "OM" or "A-U-M."

(All false religions recognize higher powers; they simply refer to them by different names. Not one of them acknowledges that the Lord Jesus Christ is the ONLY WAY to salvation, and to the ONLY TRUE FATHER in Heaven! *John 14:6)*

Mr. Stiles also says, "The practice of Hatha Yoga can lead you to a deep understanding of the unity underlying all forms of life. The asanas (poses) of Hatha Yoga are named after animals, plants, legendary heroes, sacred geometric figures, and deities. As your body undertakes these various forms, you will come to realize the inherent life-force that exists in all creation." [3]

(This pagan belief or concept that "God is all" and "all is God" is known as Pantheism.)

SO JUST WHO (or what) IS YOGA'S "GOD?" – Swami Venkatesananda will introduce us to "it!" ...

"Discipline, observances, posture, exercise of the **life-force**, introversion of attention, concentration, meditation and illumination (at-onement) are the eight limbs of Yoga or the direct **realization of oneness."** [4]

Also,

"...That indwelling omnipresent sole reality is verbally alluded to as **OM**, which is the ever-new and eternal cosmic sound that is heard in all natural phenomena (thunderclap, roaring of the ocean, wind rustling trees in the forest, and the conflagration) and even in the reverberations of the musical instruments, the hum of engines, and the distant din of the carnival crowd.

How to utilize that OM in the adoration of god?

By **repeating it**, at the same time, inquiring into, contemplating and **saturating the whole-being with, the substance** indicated by it – that is, the **reality or god**, which is the real meaning of OM." [5] (All emphasis added)

NOTE: Through our study on Transcendental Meditation, we now know that the ultimate **"at-onement"** or **"oneness"** for any New Ager is to become one with the "god" (in this case "OM") within the "True-Self," i.e. the attaining of cosmic or divine consciousness.

Swami Vishnu-devananda gives us more detail ...

"The Supreme Being is one and is called OM. The highest mantra is OM: A-U-M.
All other mantras emanate from the OM: A-U-M. Every mantra that we can speak of, and every language in fact, is hidden in this one cosmic syllable OM." [6]

"We come to see that who we really are, is the consciousness itself, not the forms which arise. We declare with conviction, what the sages have said all along, **I am not my thoughts! I AM THAT I AM!"** [7] (Emphasis added)
(See that blasphemous deception in light of God's announcement to Moses in *Exodus 3:14*)

A summary of Vedantic (sacred Hindu) teachings looks like this ...

Brahma Satyam. Jagat Mithya. Jivo Brahmaiva Na Parah.
God only is real. The world is unreal. The individual is none other than God. [8]

"**You** and **Siva**, or **you** and **Krishna**, become one and the same. There is no difference in the last state; **the mediator and the meditated are one and the same.**" [9] (Emphasis added)

The Philosophy of Vedanta
Vedanta is a simple philosophy. It says that our true Self (what it calls the Atman) is God. "I am God" (Aham Brahmasmi) is the supreme truth. The same consciousness that resides at the core of our being pervades the entire universe. To know ourselves is to know God and to become one with all. Vedanta is a philosophy of Self-realization, and its practice is a way of Self-realization through yoga and meditation. [10]

There can be no possible mistake: **THE "GODS" OF YOGA are revealed as none other than our dear-old, lost-old, self-deluded SELVES!**
Remember Adam and Eve? Man's first disobedient act was **SELF–ISH** (man)**–NESS**, and the first *religious* act – his **SELF-MADE** covering of fig leaves!

Their eyes were opened and they became naked, self-righteous, fallen gods!

...WELCOME TO YOGA!

The bottom line? Yoga is really nothing more than the ultimate **exaltation of self!**
(Oh how Yogis deny that!) It is blatant **SELF-WORSHIP**; thinly disguised as **self-illumination** or **cosmic-consciousness.** (In short, Yoga is a love affair with self!)
Just listen to the late Swami Muktnanda ...
"Kneel to your own self. Honor and worship your own being. ...Meditate on your own self. God dwells within you as you." [11]
This man, thought by many to be a "god realized" master, ended his life in 1983 as a,
"...Feebleminded, sadistic tyrant, luring devout little girls to his bed every night with the promise of grace and self-realization." [12]
No one can afford to point a finger at the man; I only mention the ugliness to show that without the Lord Jesus Christ, sinners are still sinners no matter how enlightened they (or others) think they are!
Hell is waiting for all the self-deceived who finally become one with themselves!

Once again, and for the sake of "cosmic-ish-ness" ...

If we could become *"gods"* through self-realization, why on earth did Jesus have to die on a cross to *save us from ourselves?*

Spiritually speaking, practicing Yoga amounts to putting "band-aids" on terminal cancer, and spending the rest of your life hoping to be healed!

SO WHERE IS YOGA COMING FROM?

"He (Swami Vishnu-devananda) believed that mantra initiation was the necessary first step along the road to **God Realization**, and was always willing to help anyone who wanted to take that first step. In conjunction with mantra initiation he would also give you a spiritual name if you wanted one. This name was the name of a **HINDU DEITY**, an aspect of God usually related to your mantra." [13] (Parenthesis and emphasis added)

NOTE: Anyone wishing to "yoke" with the ancient deception of Yoga (especially Christians) should know that from the very beginning, they will be entering a pagan arena filled with demonic spirits in the guise of Hindu gods, or goddesses; and rituals and customs, the likes of which (for most people in the modern West) are totally incomprehensible!

Something we *must* understand however is that Yoga, Martial Arts, and Hinduism all share a common root; or to put it another way – all are cut from the same piece of highly deceptive, religious cloth!

HINDUISM

India's "Sanatana Dharma" (Eternal Faith) is known today as Hinduism, and comprises nearly a billion followers. It is a family of religions with four major denominations.

Saivism. **Shaktism.** **Vaishnavism.** **Smartism.**

YOGA has four major paths or "Margas"

Jnana. **Bhakti.** **Karma.** **Raja.**

I have taken the liberty of "joining" them together; only to show once again that the "branches" and "roots" will never be separated!

Saivism/Jnana Yoga
Saivite Hindus worship the Supreme God as Siva, the Compassionate One.

Saivites esteem **self-discipline** and **philosophy**. They worship in the temple and practice yoga, striving to be **one with Siva within**. [14]

Jnana Yoga (the Way of Wisdom) develops the **Intellect** or **self-will**. Disciples seek to identify with "Atman" or world soul and eventually the Eternal Spirit. (True self) [15]

Shaktism/Bhakti Yoga
Shaktas worship the Supreme as the "**Divine Mother**," Shakti or "**Devi.**" (In the West "Deva" is a title given to haughty or overbearing females.) She has many forms. Some are gentle, some are fierce.

SATAN ...this is going to hurt!

Shaktas use chants, real magic, holy diagrams, yoga and rituals to call forth cosmic forces and awaken the great kundalini power within the spine. [16]

Bhakti (Kama) **Yoga** (The Way of Love); the Yoga of **devotion** (more feminine), gently opening the heart. [17]

Vaishnavism/Karma Yoga

Vaishnavites worship the Supreme as Lord Vishnu and His incarnations, especially Krishna and Rama. Vaishnavites are mainly dualistic. They are deeply **devotional**. Their religion is rich in saints, temples and scriptures. [18]

Karma Yoga (the Way of Works) is the path of **action** of selfless **service**. [19]

Smartism/Raja Yoga

Smartas worship the Supreme in one of six forms: Ganesha, or Elephant god "thing" – you should see *that* guy! Siva, Sakti, Vishnu, Surya and Skanda. Because they accept all the major Hindu Gods, they are known as liberal or nonsectarian. (Hinduism's version of New Evangelicals!)

They follow a **philosophical**, meditative path, emphasizing man's oneness with god through **understanding**. [20] (These Smarties cover *all* their bases!)

Raja Yoga, (the Way of Mystical Experience); the royal or **psychological** path, which involves the **mind**. A branch of Raja Yoga is **Hatha Yoga**, which prepares the Yogi for the higher stages of Raja Yoga. [21] (Par. and emph. added)

Hindus all worship one Supreme Being, though by many different names. For Vaishnavites, Lord Vishnu is God. For Saivites, God is Siva. For Shaktas, Goddess Shakti is supreme. For Smartas (liberal Hindus), the choice of Deity is left to the devotee. [22] (Those guys have all the fun!)

Saivism makes a remarkable claim.

"Saivism is the world's oldest religion. Worshiping the God Siva (the compassionate one), it stresses potent disciplines, high philosophy, the guru's centrality, and bhakti-raja-siddha yoga leading to oneness with Siva within. Aum." [23] (Emphasis. added)

This being true, we have found a perfect match –

HINDUISM = ADAMISM!

Their eyes were opened, and Adam and Eve attained "cosmic consciousness!"
(The worst thing that ever happened on planet earth!)

Yoga is simply the path back to worldwide Adamic revival!

After that very brief look at Hinduism, two questions should be addressed.

1. Can a non-Hindu practice Yoga successfully?

2. Is there such a thing as "Christian Yoga?"

Regarding question one; let's hear from a teacher of the "ancient wisdom."

"Yoga is a broad system, emphasizing meditation for the purpose of Self-realization, but the tendency in the West is to reduce Yoga to its physical dimension ... Certainly anyone can practice the outer or physical aspect of Yoga regardless of one's religious orientation. ... One who does not accept karma, rebirth (reincarnation) and liberation **cannot practice deeper aspects of Yoga that are based upon a recognition of this process.**" [24] (P. and e. added)

In other words, Yoga (the "*Broad way*" *Matt.7:13-14*) will (more or less, and sooner or later) take anyone to the "*Ye shall be as gods*" realm of ever deepening self-deception; but the *more* you immerse yourself in Hinduism, the *sooner* you will get there!

So Yoga doesn't care who you are or what you believe: if you practice it sincerely (and follow through), you will eventually become "one" with all things, including Satan, the "*angel of light*" who inspired it! (*2Cor.11:14*)

2. "Christian Yoga?"
Christianity and Yoga are *diametrically* opposed! There is *no* middle ground! Yoga makes for compromise by aligning itself with *all* religions! *True* **Christianity stands alone in Christ!**

Yoga goes back to Hinduism and the ancient "Eastern mysteries" –
CHRISTIANITY GOES BACK TO THE CROSS!

Yoga (and every other false way) mocks the Word of God!
Listen to Swami (master) Vishnu-devananda. ...
"There is no such thing as sin. Sin is another word for a mistake" [25]

God says,
"ALL HAVE SINNED and come short of the Glory of God." (*Rom.3:23*)
"The soul that sinneth, IT SHALL DIE." (*Eze.18:4*)
"The wages of sin IS DEATH."(*Rom.6:23*)

If sin was just "**a mistake,**" why would God judge it so harshly?
Men can correct some mistakes ...**but only God can forgive sin!**
Sin is lawlessness and rebellion against God! It condemns us to hell!
That's why men need to repent:

SIN COULD NOT BE CORRECTED – IT HAD TO BE PAID FOR BY JESUS CHRIST!

Swami Rama says that grace is merely an "energy" or "force," and has to be earned. ...
"Grace is the impulse or the impetus of the energy to dispel darkness. How do we get this grace? It comes of its own when a seeker has made maximum effort. When all efforts have been made, and all efforts have been exhausted, then grace comes." [26]
God says,

"For by Grace are ye saved through faith; and that not of yourselves: it is the gift of God: not of works, lest any man should boast." (*Eph.2:8-9*)

"GRACE AND TRUTH CAME BY JESUS CHRIST." (*John 1:17*)
(Not by "maximum effort!")

**Grace is personally given, and comes by, from, and through One Person only –
God the Divine Son, The Lord and Savior Jesus Christ!**

Sadly, this is what Swami Rama thinks of Jesus.

"...One who has developed his or her own spiritual awareness to a very high level can guide others ... guru is not the goal. Anyone who establishes himself as a guru to be worshipped is not a guru. Christ, Buddha, and other great persons did not set up any such example. ...Guru (Jesus) is like a boat for crossing the river. ... The boat brings you across the river. When the river is crossed the boat is no longer necessary. You don't hang onto the boat after completing the journey, and you certainly don't worship the boat. ...Guru is a channel for spiritual knowledge." [27]

I am certain that Swami Rama is sincere, and has absolutely no intention of insulting God! Nevertheless, he still speaks for the serpent by calling God a liar!

GOD says,

"The Name of Jesus is above every name: At the Name of Jesus every knee should bow, of things in Heaven, and things in earth, and things under the earth." (*Phil.2: 9-10*)

And ...

"Let all the angels of God WORSHIP HIM!" (*Heb. 1:6*)

And,

"Unto the Son He (the Father) *said, Thy Throne O GOD is forever and ever."* (*Heb.1:8*)

"... And His disciples WORSHIPPED HIM." (*Matt.28:9, Luke 24:52*)

Jesus is God! *That's* why His disciples worshipped Him! And to the glory of God the Father! Make no mistake ...

Christians will worship, and "hang onto" *their* "BOAT" for all eternity!

Having compared Jesus to mere mortals like Buddha, and other "great persons," Swami Rama goes on to liken God the Father to an impersonal "stream of pure knowledge" and claims that Jesus, as an "enlightened (human) being" was merely "attuned" to that knowledge.

The Swami's final statement here in the face of God's Word.

Guru (Jesus) will "sustain, nurture, and guide a soul through lifetimes (reincarnations) to ultimate liberation." [28]

Having already expressed my view of reincarnation, (p.59) I simply quote God's Word of Truth again.

"And as it is appointed unto men ONCE to die, but after this the JUDGMENT: So Christ was ONCE offered to bear the sins of many; and unto them that look for HIM shall HE appear the second time without sin unto SALVATION." (*Heb.9:27-28*)

The most popular Yoga in the West is "Hatha Yoga" (the physical way of exercise), but don't be fooled; *every* part or purpose of Hatha Yoga, or *any* Yoga is spiritual!

References from the **"Hatha Yoga Pradipika"** (a reliable text on Hatha Yoga) should make its real nature very clear! ...

"The purpose of *Hatha* Yoga is to be a stairway to *Raja* Yoga, (ch.1:1-2) the higher Yoga Postures are the first *part* of Hatha yoga." (1:77)

"The energy of kundalini is the support of all the Yogas." (3:1)

"Kundalini opens the door to enlightenment." (3:105)

"Samadhi: meditation in its higher state, deep absorption of meditation, the state of perfected concentration." (3:3)

"The emphasis of Yoga moves from postures to breath, Kundalini, Raja Yoga, and Samadhi.

Samadhi leads one to the eternal and highest bliss." (4.2)

"Mind and the eternal merge like salt and the sea." (4.5)

"Those who do only *Hatha* Yoga without realization of *Raja* Yoga derive no fruits from their efforts." (4.79) (Emphases added)

NOTE: Kundalini means literally, **"coiled serpent power,"** and is said to be located at the base of the spine! (More on *that* little deception in chapter 21.)

Can Christians practice Yoga?

The immediate answer is, **"Yes, of course they can!"** God's people have *"liberty"* in Christ – they can do just about anything!

Sadly, the Old Testament is filled with examples (see *1Cor.10:11*) of God's people doing what "feels good," and yoking (make that "Yoga-ing") with the idolatrous pagan nations surrounding them. Today, thousands upon thousands of Christians are being seduced into all manner of false worship by pagan influences; and some are being promoted from within the Church itself!

First though, let's consider these two statements from *outside* the Church.

From an essay by Dr. Frank Gaetano Morales, Ph.D. (One of America's leading authorities on Hindu philosophy and religion.)

"The religious tradition of **Hinduism is solely responsible** for the original creation of such concepts and practices as **Yoga, Ayurveda, Vastu, Jyotisha, Yajna, Puja, Tantra, Vedanta, Karma,** etc. These and **countless other** Vedic-inspired elements of Hinduism **belong to Hinduism, and to Hinduism alone.** Though they are elements of Hinduism alone, however, they are also simultaneously **Hinduism's divine gift** to a suffering world. Thus, **so many of the essential elements of Hinduism are now to be found incorporated into the structures and beliefs of many of the world's diverse religious traditions."** [29]

From the late Swiss Psychiatrist, Carl G. Jung.

"There is good reason for Yoga to have many adherents. It offers not only **the much-sought way,** but also a philosophy of unrivalled profundity. Yoga practice is unthinkable, and would be also ineffectual, **without the ideas on which it is based.** It works the physical and the spiritual into one another in an extraordinarily complete way." [30] (Emphases added)

Now listen to a voice from *within* the Church ...

"The Outstretched philosophy is simple: we believe God will bless our sincere efforts at deepening a relationship with Him. He wants our fellowship and appreciates **creative approaches** to seeking his face. This is why Outstretched is dedicated to a Christ-centered pursuit of physical healing and spiritual growth through a practice of yoga." (Susan Bordenkircher, "Outstretched in worship: a Christian approach to Yoga.")

"Susan Bordenkircher disagreed with the emphasis on finding divinity in oneself, and achieving a higher level of spirituality by oneself as is espoused in some yoga classes. She says 'That's God's doing'. However, Bordenkircher says the movement and rhythm of Hatha (physical) yoga made her **more centered and reflective** and **more able to pray**. Hindus strive for wisdom, knowledge and inner concentration, which **clearly overlap with Christian goals**, Bordenkircher says. '**My feeling was; it's worked for them, why shouldn't we be able to do that?**' So Bordenkircher combined poses with Christian references. During the warrior pose, she talks about breathing in the Holy Spirit. She relates the child's pose to being at peace with God. And the balance poses are about finding spiritual balance. '**If it feels good for your body and soul, you should do it.**'" [31] (Emphases added)

That is without doubt, one of the most naïve and foolish (not to mention dangerous) invitations given to Christians during the entire Church age!

Remember again: Aaron's "*golden calf*" was a "*creative approach*" to the worship of God! Once the calf was made, Aaron built an altar for it, and uttered these immortal words ...

> "*Tomorrow is a feast unto the Lord... and the people said, **These be thy gods O Israel** ... and they offered burnt offerings, and brought peace offerings.* (That must have felt sooo – good!)
> *And the Lord said unto Moses, Go, get thee down, for thy people ...have corrupted themselves.*"
>
> *(Ex.32:4-6)*

There was only one calf, but the people said, "*These be thy gods O Israel.*"

One calf linked Israel to *all* the gods of Egypt: and if **one system** links someone to *all* the gods of the New Age today, that system is most certainly **YOGA!**

Can Christians walk before God with one hand holding the **LAMB,** and the other holding on to this demonic deceit? – **yes they can!**

Should they? – *NOT ON YOUR* (spiritual) *LIFE!*

Yoga wants an *empty* **mind: Christians want** *the mind of Christ!*

NOTE: "**Samadhi**" is a super-conscious state where *ultimate* oneness is experienced. This is the deepest and highest state of enlightenment where the body and mind are transcended, and the practitioner becomes one with the true-self, or "god!"

And here it is at last!
After years of meditation, dedication, (and who knows *what* medication?) **you'll actually become GOD!** ~ (Just as the "serpent" said you would!)

Sssh! ... Don't tell Swami: but if you prefer, you can "**play God**" immediately – simply by becoming a "**Humanist!**"

Truly, "*There is no new thing under the sun.*" *(Eccl.1:9)*

Food for thought:
Yogis spend their whole lives trying to *reach* the "**TRUE - SELF.**"
Christians spend their whole lives *CRUCIFYING IT! (Matt.16:24)*

For the believer, God's inspired Word (Scripture) is the final authority for *"doctrine, for reproof, for correction, for instruction in righteousness"* (2Tim.3:16); so I close this section with a profound, and amazingly relevant warning from God Himself.

"They know not, neither will they understand; they walk on in darkness: all the foundations of the earth are out of course. I have said ye are gods; and all of you are children of the Most High. BUT YE SHALL DIE LIKE MEN, and fall like one of the princes." (Ps.82:5-8)

May the grace of God keep us from Yoga, and *all* the deceptions yet to come!

CHAPTER TWENTY-ONE

ALTERNATIVE CHRISTIANITY

As I finished the previous chapter, the Holy Spirit brought a verse of Scripture to mind, which for me, made the threat of this next subject even more alarming for the Church today.

The verse began, *"Phinehas, the son of Eleazar ..."*

There is a remarkable story found in the book of Numbers; beginning at chapter 22.

Balak, son of Zippor, was king of a tribe known as the Moabites: a tribe incidentally whose founding father came by way of an incestuous relationship between Lot and his eldest daughter!

(See *Gen.19:30-38*)

King Balak had seen *"all that Israel had done to the Amorites,"* and was desperately afraid of them; believing they would defeat him and wipe out his whole nation. As a result, he hired a powerful false prophet and sorcerer named Balaam to curse God's people in the hope of gaining victory, and driving them away. (See *Ch's 22-24*)

In reading those chapters we discover that God sovereignly turned all Balaam's attempts at cursing Israel into blessings!

NOTE: research based on *Numbers 1-3*, suggests that the layout of Israel's camp took the form of a huge cross; so which ever hill Balaam looked down from, he faced God's eternal and blessed redemptive plan for His people!

In spite of his overall failure however, Balaam the "enchanter" still had a trick or two up his sleeve! His advice to King Balak (seen in *Rev.2:14*) can be summed up as follows:

"If I can't curse them, send in your women to seduce them! As far as these people are concerned, fornication and idolatry will prove as good if not better than any curse!"

"And Israel abode in Shittim, and the people began to commit whoredom with the daughters of Moab. And they called the people unto the sacrifices of their gods: and the people did eat and bowed down to their gods." (*Num.25:1-2*)

God's response through Moses (by the Law) was quick and severe.

"Say to the judges of Israel, Slay ye every one his men that were joined unto Baal-peor." (*v.5*)

Incredibly, in the midst of the slaughter, and in plain sight of Moses and many of God's people who were weeping before the tabernacle, a leading son of Israel brought a Midianitish woman right into the camp (*"unto his brethren"* *v.6*) and took her into his tent!

"When Phinehas, the son of Eleazar, the son of Aaron the priest, saw it, he rose up from among the congregation, and took a javelin in his hand; and he went after the man of Israel into the tent, and thrust both of them through, the man of Israel, and the woman through her belly. So the plague was stayed from the people of Israel. And those that died in the plague were twenty and four thousand."

(vs. 7-9)

The name of the Israelite executed by Phinehas was *"ZIMRI, son of Salu, a prince of a chief house among the Simeonites."* The name of the Midianitish woman who died with him was *"COZBI."* *(vs.14-15)*

At first glance, those disturbing events of long ago may not send a loud and clear message to the Body of Christ today; but as we delve deeper into their spiritual meaning, the Holy Spirit can again quicken types and shadows which give ample warning of the dangers facing every believer in these last climactic days!

As the Spirit reveals Old Testament Israel as a type of the Church, *(Acts8:38)* it becomes possible to see *Num.25:1-2* as a picture of true believers led astray by the *"seducing spirits, doctrines of devils, and false teachings and traditions of men"* in this *present* age! *(1Tim.4:1, Col.2:8)* The twenty-four thousand who died in that natural plague, surely represent innumerable saints who have been, and are being *"destroyed"* (weakened and made ineffective) through sin and *"lack of knowledge."* *(Hos.4:6)*

Because many are *"rejecting knowledge"* (refusing to heed the Word of God), an equally devastating "plague" of false and corrupting doctrine is flooding into the Church today!

Armed with that revelation, we can now focus on the main characters of this ancient tragedy, and through them (by the grace of God) be encouraged to *"fight a good fight; finish the course; keep* (and strengthen) *the faith"* in this critical hour! *(2Tim.4:7)*

King Balak: type of Satan, who, while facing defeat and utter destruction (fulfilled in Christ's resurrection, *Heb.2:14*), continues to offer temporal benefits to any willing puppet (false prophet or teacher) in an attempt to destroy God's people, and avoid the inevitable.

Balaam: prophet for hire, who represents every worldly religious deceiver or satanic mouth-piece ever used by the *"angel of light"* – Satan himself! *(2Cor.11:14-15)*

Cozbi: this one Midianitish woman readily becomes a type of *all* insidious false doctrines and pagan influences that seek to corrupt the Body of Christ!

Prince Zimri: type of deceived leader *within* the Church, who actually brings those false teachings, traditions, and philosophies *"unto his brethren:"* i.e., into the hearts and minds of God's people!

Phinehas: type of *any* faithful and zealous minister of God, who will not stand idly by while corrupt and compromising church leadership blatantly flaunts error in the face of Jesus Christ and His Blood-bought congregation!

"And when Phineas, the son of Eleazar, the son of Aaron the priest, saw it, he rose up..."

Let every Spirit-filled *"son of Eleazar"* rise up fearlessly with the *"javelin"* of God's truth! Let them pierce through the lies and deceptions facing Christianity in these prophetic times of *"falling away;"* *(2Thess.2:1-3)* and before that darkest *"hour of temptation comes upon all the world, to try them that dwell upon the earth."* *(Rev.3:10)*

Balaam, as we have seen, could not prevail against Israel from without. (External persecution has always made the "true" church stronger!) In thousands of years, Satan has learned that the most successful tactic against the "Army of the Lord" (Old *or* New Testaments) has been to soften, weaken, infiltrate, and corrupt from within!

(See the life and times of Israel's King Asa for a good illustration of this! *2Chr.14-16*)

Obviously one "javelin" will not stem the "*enemy's flood,*" but I believe with all my heart that the Lord's "*Standard*" (banner) will be lifted up on the points of many! (See *Is.59:19*)

So far, I have tended to expose the "works of Balaam," or *outside* influences; (see *Num.15-17*) the exceptions being, "Tongues are in shoes," etc., and "Christian Reconstruction." (Definitely *inside* jobs!) With "Christian Yoga" however, insider Zimri has to share equal billing with Balaam. ... You get the idea!

For the next few pages, I'd like to offer some exercises in "*trying* (or testing) *the spirits.*"
Decide if the following deceptions are the works of "outsider" Balaam, or "insider" Zimri, as I present a variety of their work in the form of quotes, questions, and hard-hitting answers.

To sharpen our "swords," and especially our discernment; we come to a study called,

WHO'S INFLUENCE IS IT?

First let's take a look at,

CONTEMPLATIVE (OR CENTERED) PRAYER

A man named Philip St. Romain wrote a book called, "Kundalini Energy and Christian Spirituality." In it, he says,

"Since the spring of 1986, I have been experiencing various psychological and physiological phenomena such as those attributed to kundalini (remember that's "coiled serpent power") in the Hindu and Taoist literature. Through the years, the process has intensified, bringing many positive and painful experiences. All this has happened to me in the context of Christian, contemplative prayer. ...

The purpose of this book is to describe the kundalini process as experienced by a Christian. As far as I know, this is the first book of its kind, which makes it significant in terms of the relationship between Christian and Eastern mysticism. ... I believe these reflections will be of interest to spiritual directors, pastoral counselors, contemplatives, New Age readers, and those interested in Christian-Eastern dialogue." [1] (Parenthesis added)

NOTE: In his introduction, Romain gives the meaning of the word Kundalini; not as, "coiled serpent power" (see p.260), but as, "Curl the hair of the beloved." (How sweet!)

Question

Why would any Christian work for "*Balak*" (Satan) by bringing "*Cozbi*" (New Age practices, and Eastern religions) into the Body of Christ?

Once again; does Romain have the spirit of "*Balaam*" or "*Zimri?*" Is he a non-believer trying to curse or influence the Body of Christ from *without*? Or is he an actual Christian, corrupting his brothers and sisters from *within*?

In the foreword of Romain's book, Thomas Keating claims that the author *is* a Christian.
He writes,

"Prior to the awakening of kundalini he (Romain) received the baptism in the Spirit and enjoyed the gift of tongues. While appreciating the immense value of kundalini, he sharply distinguishes it from the action of the Holy Spirit. He considers kundalini a **natural evolutionary energy** inherent in every human being. ... In order to guide persons having this (Kundalini) experience, **Christian spiritual**

directors may need to dialogue with Eastern teachers in order to get a fuller understanding." [2] (P. and e. added)

Question

Why would a Christian want to receive – then encourage others to cultivate – a "**natural evolutionary energy:**" or *any* power other than the Holy Spirit? Should believers practice Kundalini? Should righteousness embrace pagan Eastern religions? Does the darkness suddenly become light because it's "Christianized?" Has "*Christ*" made friends with "*Belial?*" ...

IS YOUR JAVELIN SHARP ENOUGH?

(Read *2Cor.6:14-18* again.)

KUNDALINI IS AN UNCLEAN THING: SO IS CONTEMPLATIVE PRAYER!

If Zimri had kept Cozbi outside the "camp," I'm certain Phinehas would not have risen up!

If Romain and others had kept this Contemplative New Age "harlot" away from the Body of Christ, God's servants might not be rising up to expose them!

PLEASE NOTE: I didn't buy Romain's book. (If I want garbage, I can get it from any dumpster!)

Some of it is currently on the Internet, and can be viewed by going to his website. Unfortunately, typing in Philip St. Romain will get you there!

All right, let's move on: here's a little more "fool's gold," which can still deceive the unwary.

"On an experiential level, kundalini energy is simultaneously pure ***libido**, pure **psychic energy**, and pure **spiritual consciousness**. ... Kundalini energy in its pure, undifferentiated form is experienced only after the personal and pre-personal dimensions of the unconscious mind have **emptied their contents**." [3]

(Emphasis added)

*****NOTE:** "Libido" is defined as the "energy of sexual desire or lust." (Oxford English Dictionary)
"Psychic energy" is the power or the ability to act as a Medium, Clairvoyant, or to be telepathic.
To the New Ager, "spiritual consciousness" means "At-One-Ness" with the "True-Self," and with all things, including "god."

Two other important definitions are needed here.

PANTHEISM: the pagan belief that "God is all, and all is God." Therefore animals, plants, and physical matter are all an equal part of the divine.

PANENTHEISM: the belief (also pagan) that "God is *in* all things" i.e. God is personal but is in all people; therefore ultimately, all people (and creation) will be saved, and become "One" with Him!

Based on those two definitions, Contemplative/Centered prayer is nothing more than Christianized, pagan centered Yoga! With a subtle twist ...

It invites (seduces) you to empty your mind in a form of self-hypnosis (using Christianized, Hindu styled mantras and breathing techniques); and then fools you into believing you are invoking the Spirit of Christ!

The techniques and teachings of repetitious, contemplative prayers are found nowhere in Scripture! They fall under deceptions clearly revealed by the Apostle Paul as,
"***Another Jesus, another spirit, and another gospel.***" (From *2Cor.11:4*)

They are uttered in total defiance of our Lord's own command and warning:
"***WHEN YOU PRAY, USE NOT VAIN REPETITION AS THE HEATHEN DO.***"(*Matt. 6:7*)
(If the "*heathen*" use "*vain repetition*" – you can be sure Satan is behind it!)

In his book, Romain shares many personal "*angel of light*" experiences; offering them in turn to anyone embarking on the soul trip to Kundalini! It would pointless to list them all, so here are the more obvious demonic manifestations. How could any true Christian get past the first of them without hearing the Holy Spirit's warning?

> "**Inner vision illuminated when the eyes are closed**, especially during times of prayer and meditation. Visual background turning blue, purple, ultraviolet, gold, silver, or white, sometimes forming circular, amoeboid, or tunnel-like patterns.
> **Sensations** of heat and or cold in different parts of the body, especially the shoulders and the top of the head.
> **Tingling sensations** in the brain, ears, forehead, spine, and other parts of the body.
> **Perception of inner sounds** – ringing, chirping or buzzing in the ears.
> **Strong compulsion** to be alone and to meditate very deeply.
> **Loss of affective memory**.
> **Sensations of electrical energy** rippling through the reproductive organs.
> **Compulsion** to move facial muscles and bodily limbs in yoga-like postures.
> **Disorientation** – a sense of fading, of not really being here.
> **Sense of an inner eye** seeing with the two sense eyes.
> **Drowsiness** when energy is pushing its way into the brain.
> **Pain** in the area of the heart and stomach …" [4] (Emphasis added)

Next, Romain explains exactly what to do when this dreadful state of demonic possession (in the unsaved), or demonization (in the saved) is occurring.
He says,
> "**Accept the process as a sign of growth**. Be grateful for the growth that is taking place within, painful though it may be.
> **Let the various states of consciousness** produced by kundalini come and go. Experience and explore them, but do not attach to them. The True-Self is not to be found in any particular state of consciousness.
> **Surrender yourself into the care of Christ, Whose Spirit is capable of guiding your kundalini energies toward a wholesome integration. Trust that a Higher Guidance is at work in the process. Ask for this Guidance when confused; listen for the answers.**
> **Accept the pains that come** and **willingly cooperate with asanas and compulsions to meditate.** These all pass away in time.
> **Practice yogic asanas** for at least **fifteen minutes a day** to help facilitate the movement of the energy. **Also consider using Tai Chi, massage,** and/or movement therapies, especially when the energy seems to be blocked.
> **Practice the mahabandha lock** under the supervision of an experienced guide. Tuck the chin into the chest, drawing the navel inward and upward during exhalation while gently contracting the

anal sphincter and perineal muscles. Keeping the chin tucked in, relax the muscles during inhalation drawing the navel outward to pull the diaphragm downward. **Gently repeat this pattern of contracting and relaxing muscles while exhaling and inhaling deeply, attaching a spiritually focused mantra (e.g., "Come, Lord") to the breathing pattern."** [5] (All emphasis added)

NO WONDER PHINEHAS PICKED UP A SPEAR!

Surely the spirit of any *true* believer is filled with sadness and righteous anger in reading such statements, but nevertheless we must move on. Here for now (as far as Romain's work is concerned) is one last hiss from another satanic source.

James Arras writes,

"The value of Philip St. Romain's book should not be sought first of all in the interesting hypotheses he advances ... rather it resides in the simple but remarkable fact that he now lives in two worlds that he has to struggle to bring together, not only for his own sake, but for all of us. It is the men and women who experience from within both Hinduism and Christianity, or Buddhism and Christianity, or Jungian psychology and Christianity, or modern physics and Christianity, and struggle to be faithful to each reality in the face of the temptation to give way to hasty identifications, that will lead the way to the creation of a true global culture." [6]

The "*falling away*" (*2Thess.2:3*) is in full swing! With voices such as these leading the way, be sure Satan's "One World, global culture" is just around the bend!

The following people are deeply involved in what could well be called, "**Romain's Syndrome.**"

THOMAS KEATING and BASIL PENNINGTON (Catholic monks)
Said to have actually birthed the term, "centering prayer:" together they have spewed forth all kinds of spiritual toxins, including some from a despicable little book called "**Finding Grace at the Center.**"...
"We should not hesitate to take the fruit of the age-old wisdom of the East and capture it for Christ. Indeed, those of us who are in ministry should make the necessary effort to acquaint ourselves with as many of these Eastern techniques as possible."
They go on to tell us that,
"Many Christians have been greatly helped by Yoga, Zen, T.M. and similar practices. Of course these Christians need ... reliable teachers, and a solidly developed Christian faith to find inner form and meaning to the resulting experiences." [7]

NOTE: That "age-old wisdom of the East" is just another "*satanic stronghold*," and needs to be "***PULLED DOWN BY THE SPIRIT OF GOD.*"** (*2Cor.10:4*) – Not "captured for Christ!")

THOMAS MERTON (Trappist monk, 1915-1968)
Merton said,
"At the center of our being is a point of nothingness, which is untouched by sin and by illusions; a point of pure truth ... this little point is the pure glory of God in us. It is in everybody."[8]
(Ooooh! Doesn't that make you feel warm and tingly all over?)

But *GOD* says, at the center of everyone's being *THERE IS NOTHING BUT SIN!*

"THERE IS NONE RIGHTEOUS, NO, NOT ONE." (*Rom.3:10*)
(Nothing is untouched by sin – not even a little self-righteous "point of nothingness!")

Let *any* descendant of fallen Adam dare to stand before The Almighty and Holy God, claiming that we have in or of ourselves ONE SPECK of purity or goodness to offer! – God forbid!

Paul and Jeremiah said it for *all* of us:

"For I know that in me, that is in my flesh, (fallen nature) *there dwelleth NO good thing ..."*
(*Rom.7:18*)
"The heart is deceitful above all things and desperately wicked: who can know it?"
(*Jer.17:9*)

CHRIST IS OUR *ONLY* RIGHTEOUSNESS! Please don't even *consider* any other kind!
(*Rom.3:21-27, 2Cor.5:21*)

There is no doubt that the primary influence or fuel for contemplative prayer came from those Merton described as, "Fourth century hermits who abandoned the cities of the pagan world to live in solitude." [(9)] (Having fled from secular society into the wildernesses of the near East, these hermits would later become known as the "Desert Fathers.")
Merton goes on to write,
"What the fathers sought most of all was their own true-self in Christ ... they sought a way to God that was uncharted and free chosen, not inherited from others who had mapped it out beforehand." [(10)]

Question: Where in all the teachings of Jesus does He tell Christians to "**abandon the world**" and live in solitude as "**Hermits?**"
Answer – *NOWHERE!*

Jesus said, *"Go ye into all the world, and preach the Gospel to every creature."* (*Mark 16:15*)
"Go ye therefore, and teach all nations ..." (*Matt. 28:19*)

"Ye shall be witnesses ...unto the uttermost part of the earth." (*Acts 1:8*)

The "Desert Fathers" were in error from the beginning! They disobeyed a direct command from the Lord Jesus Himself, so what do we *expect* would follow?

Justin O'Brien seduces Christians with this,
"Hesychasm, a spiritual tradition that dates back to the third century, uses **the Jesus formula** as one of its forms of inner prayer. A Hesychast is someone who **lets the memory of Jesus combine with their breathing**. As the monk Nicephorus suggests, 'Collect your mind, lead it into the path of the breath along which the air enters in, constrain it to enter the heart together with the inhaled air, and keep it there. Give it the following prayer: Lord, Jesus Christ, Son of God, have mercy on me. Let this be its **constant occupation**, never to be abandoned'. ...

For a Christian practicing Yoga, the above description is not merely similar to, but the same as *japa yoga*. The **constant intonation** of a sacred sound: ***mantram*** is commonly referred to as *japa*."[11] (Emphases added; italics in original)

There we have yet another example of "***vain repetition***", but can we see these "mantram / breath prayers" as God does? (Even apart from their satanic origin!)

An earthly father is delighted with his baby's first spoken word; let's say that word is "Dada." The baby says "Dada, Dada, Dada," and nothing could please the parent more. But, if at the age of sixteen, the grown boy or girl is still only saying the same word, "Dada" – over and over again – something is seriously wrong!

What kind of conversation could God have with someone who is constantly chanting, "Lord Jesus, Lord Jesus, Lord Jesus" or, "Come Lord, come Lord, come Lord?"

Having said that, the key to this deception can be found in the phrase, "**the Jesus formula.**"

The whole "contemplative/centered prayer" movement hinges on Eastern based **formulas** and **techniques** that are so completely contrary to sound doctrine, they can only result in shipwreck for anyone foolish enough to apply them!

Merton epilogue

"During his last years, Merton became deeply interested in Asian religions, particularly Zen Buddhism, and in promoting East-West dialogue. After several meetings with Merton during his trip to the Far East in1968, the Dali Lama praised him for having a more profound understanding of Buddhism than any other Christian he had known! It was during a conference on 'East-West monastic dialogue' (an ecumenical council of Catholics and Buddhist monks) that Merton died in Bangkok; the victim of accidental electrocution."[12]

Since then, Thomas Merton's Eastern mystical, and pagan influence has continued to grow steadily: currently it is found in Catholic, Protestant, and many so-called Evangelical churches as well! To my brothers or sisters in Christ whom I love dearly, and are reading this account, I say, "Beware! Serpents still whisper to any and all who will listen!"

I can only counsel you to reject any of the following names or book titles, if or when you should come across them!

RICHARD FOSTER

Foster's "**Celebration of Discipline**" was voted number three on Christianity Today's list of books having the most impact on Christian lives other than the Bible. [13] In it, he writes,

"Christian meditation is an attempt to empty the mind in order to fill it."[14]

In "**Prayer: Finding the Heart's True Home**," Foster encourages "breath-prayer," [15] which again is taking a single word or short phrase, and repeating it over and over while breathing systematically. He says that, "Thomas Merton's, **Contemplative Prayer** is a must book," [16] and that "Merton's works are filled with priceless wisdom for all Christians who long to go deeper in the spiritual life." [17] (How deep in satanic deception do you want to get?)

M. SCOTT PECK

His book, "**The Road Less Traveled**" has been walked on by millions (including Christians), but does anyone remember its blasphemous statements?

"The ultimate goal of spiritual growth is for the individual to become as one with God." [18]
And,

"It is for the individual to become totally, wholly God." [19]

Peck's form of counterfeit Christianity (he was baptized in 1980) includes this New Age view of the Lord Jesus Christ.

He says Jesus was "An example of the Western mystic" who "Integrated himself with God." [20]

Like almost all worldly roads, Peck's has a gutter!

On a cassette entitled "Further along the Road Less Traveled," he actually says this:

"Zen Buddhism should be taught in every 5th grade class in America." [21]

And,

"Christianity's greatest sin is to think that other religions are not saved." [22]

He puts *this* question to his audience: "Is Scott Peck a New Ager?" He then answers, "Yes! ... and proud to be listed as an Aquarian Conspirator."[23] Finally he states (surprise, surprise) that his,

"Foundation For Community Encouragement is very much a New Age organization." [24]

MATTHEW FOX

In a slithery little book called "**The Coming of the Cosmic Christ**" (endorsed by Peck and certainly one of Cozbi's favorites); this Episcopal priest and New Age aficionado writes,

"The Cosmic Christ is the I AM in every creature, who shows us how to embrace our own divinity." [25]

Fox declares there should be a "...shift away from the historical Jesus ... towards the Cosmic Christ."[26]

MORTON KELSEY

Episcopal priest and author of, "**Other Side of Silence: The Guide to Christian Meditation.**" His books are acclaimed by "**Spiritual Directors,**" [27] (what ever you do, stay away from *those* people); and include such gems as,

"You can find most of the New Age practices in the depth of Christianity."

And,

"I believe the Holy One lives in every soul." [28]

Could there be a better description of New Age panentheism, and its total disregard for scriptural authority and truth?

"Many are called but FEW ARE CHOSEN." (*Matt.22:14*) Only those who receive The Lord and Savior Jesus Christ by faith are called, *"the sons and daughters of God."* (*John 1:12*)

God dwells only in the "quickened spirits" (*not souls*) of those who are truly born again!
(*1Cor.15:45, Rom.8:16, 1John 3:24, 4:13, 5:12*)

HENRI NOUWEN (1932-1996)

Catholic priest, and author of "**The Return of the Prodigal Son**" – "**Here and Now: Living in the Spirit**" – "**The Inner Voice of Love,**" and many more.

In his last book, "**Sabbatical Journey,**" he wrote,

"Today I personally believe that while Jesus came to open the door to God's house, all human beings can walk through that door, whether they know about Jesus or not ... Today I see it as my call to help every person claim HIS OR HER OWN WAY TO GOD." [29] (Emphasis added)

(He obviously didn't read *Proverbs 14:12*!)

In "Bread for the Journey" he offers the following:

"Prayer is soul work because our souls are those sacred centers where all is one ... it is in the heart of God that we come to the full realization of the unity of all that is."

"Soul work?"... "Sacred soul centers?" – Listen to God's Word!

"GOD IS A SPIRIT; and they that worship Him must worship Him IN SPIRIT and in TRUTH."
(John 4:24)

"For the Word of God is quick and powerful, and sharper than any twoedged sword, piercing even to the dividing asunder of SOUL and SPIRIT..." (*Heb.4:12*)

"... shall I give my first-born for my transgression, the fruit of my body for the sin of my soul?" (*Mic.6:7*)

"But we are not of them who draw back unto perdition; but of them that believe to the saving of the soul." (*Heb.10:39*)

If the soul was a "sacred center," why would it need to be *saved?*

Only the quickened, "born-again" spirit, which God has given to those who truly belong to Christ is sacred, and acceptable to God! (*Heb.10:14*)

NOTE: The soul, or the mind/will of man is often and correctly referred to as the old (fallen) nature of Adam: therefore nothing done through the soul or flesh will ever be acceptable to God!

The soul remains in, and with the flesh, working rebellion, i.e. *"The works of the flesh."* (*Gal.5:19-21*)

Let's take a moment to look again at this vital issue, which still confuses many Christians, and has led the world into so much New Age error. Remember this was first discussed in chapter11, in the section on the body, the soul, and the spirit.

Lev.17:11 is very interesting: *"For the life of the flesh is in the blood: and I have given it to you upon the altar to make atonement for your souls: for it is the blood* (Old Testament animal sacrifice – New Covenant Blood of Christ!) *that maketh an atonement for the soul."*

So then, the *"blood is the life"* of both animals *and* men, but only men have souls with volition, which includes the ability to will or to wish.

Think now of the body as an automobile in neutral. The car is idling; it *has* fuel, i.e. a form of life (in our case blood), but it is going nowhere unless we **put in gear!** At this point, the *unsaved* driver has only one gear: – soul or reverse! His fleshly nature or "carnal mind" cannot please or reach God! (*Rom. 8:7-8, Jn 14:6*) (Hard to hear but true.) He cannot drive forward so to speak! He is a body with a soul only; he is "two in one." Spiritually, he is *"dead in trespass and sin."* (Again, that truth is found in *Eph.2:1*)

The *"quickened"* or spiritually redeemed driver however, can drive forward (in and for Christ) as well as backwards in disobedience to God's Will (in and for self!) Only the Christian has that forward gear, or the ability to *"walk in the spirit"* and please God!

How to "drive forward" consistently has been the challenge facing every Christian on planet earth since the Lord Jesus walked so perfectly before us (and *for* us) some two thousand years ago!

"... The Father hath not left Me alone; for I do always those things that please Him."

(John 8:29)

Men and women (alive *or* dead) who dare(d) to presume and teach that all men are "**inherently divine**," and that "**Christ Consciousness**" or "**One-ness with God**" is something we can earn, learn, or gain by some pagan technique; have violated the very heart of the Gospel!

"The gift of God is eternal life through Jesus Christ our Lord." (Rom.6:23)

I say again; their teaching mocks the fact that Jesus sacrificed His *ONE* and *ONLY* perfect Life on the cross to bring God's free gift to us. – *Woe unto them*!

"... The tree is known by its fruit ... O generation of vipers, how can you being evil, speak good things? For out of the abundance of the heart the mouth speaketh ... For by thy words thou shalt be justified, and by thy words thou shalt be condemned." (Matt.12:33-37)

Is it wrong to speak so badly of the departed? – **Perhaps we should ask Phinehas!**

Can you imagine all the ecumenical voices rising in protest if he were to come out of Zimri's tent today?... "**Vicious!**" "**Extreme!**" "**Judgmental!**" "**Too narrow!**" "**Why can't we all just get along?**" – Yet he received God's "*Covenant of peace.*" (Num.25:10-12)

The truth is, men like Merton and Nouwen are probably doing more damage now than they did when they were alive! Their influence (peddled through societies, internet, books, tapes, etc.) is negatively everywhere; so can any Christian doubt that those dead "*wolves*" are still devouring the "*flock of God?*" (Matt.7:15, Acts 20:27-31)

NOTE: Someone may indeed ask, "Who do you think you are to write such scathing words about these notables?" My answer is, "Absolutely nobody! But one day all Christians will stand before Christ and account for the gifts or knowledge they received; and (perhaps especially) what they did with those gifts to warn or help others! Please understand; I have not the slightest personal animosity towards any of these men or women, but once they take up a pen, or speak to wrongly influence true believers in Christ, there will certainly be "spiritual javelins" pointed in their direction!

WAYNE W. DYER

Known to his followers as the "Father of Motivation" Dr. Dyer is probably doing more to deceive people today than most of the other names I've mentioned put together. I'm sure he believes in what he says, but what he says is absolutely diabolical!

From his book, "**The Power of Intention: ...**" Dyer teaches,

"The air – regardless of its temperature or wind velocity – is the **revered air** that **is the breath of life**."[30]

And,

"A person who lives in a state of **unity with the Source of all life** doesn't look any different from ordinary folks. These people don't wear a halo or dress in special garments that announce their **godlike qualities**. ... They speak from an inner conviction that communicates their profound and simple knowing that the **Universal Source** supplies everything." [31]

And,

"They have a **consciousness of the oneness**, and therefore they make no distinctions such as '*them*' or '*those other people*' ... since they know that **all of us emanate from the same Divine Source**. ... **They point to the invisible energy that intends everything into existence and see this as their true self.**" [32]

And,

"They'll tell you that it is the Spirit that gives life, and that everyone on this planet has this Spirit within them as an **all-powerful force** for good. They believe it, they live it, and they inspire others. Death is not something that they fear, and they'll tell you, if you ask, that **they were never truly born nor will they ever die**. They see death as taking off a garment or moving from one room into another – merely a transition." [33] (Emphases added)

Is Dyer a Contemplative? *Of course!* On a radio talk show about "how to get along with your spouse," Dyer advises listeners to, "Go into the silence for guidance" when they get angry with their mate. [34]

Yet on television, he will invite his daughter to sing "Amazing Grace!"
Listen to Dyer, and you will hear from a very subtle serpent indeed!

LUANNE OAKES, Ph.D. Oakes combines Western *and* Eastern philosophies of science, spirituality, and health; and offers lectures available on compact disks with such demonically inspired titles as, **"Your Magical Divine Experiment,"** and **"Spiritual Alchemy."** In the latter, Oakes provides you with,

"Holographic technology to enhance your health, well-being, abundance, and deepest connection to the wondrous Divine Intelligence of all Creation."[35]

(You will not hear *one word* about the Lord Jesus, Who came "*that we might have* (true) *life, and that we might have it more abundantly.*") (*John 10:10*)

In "Sound Health, Sound Wealth," she teaches Eastern meditation techniques and encourages the listener to "**lie down in a magical mystery field of dreams**," and receive the "**Life force from Mother Earth**" by being "**connected to the divine intelligence.**" [36]

Her system has been embraced and endorsed by such luminaries as Deepak Chopra, John Gray ("Men are from Mars …" etc.), Tony Robbins, and Reverend Mary Murray Shelton.

Please – don't go near *any* of them!

M. Scott Peck is certainly not short of companions on the broad and immensely popular road to destruction; but enough is enough! To close out this section, let me ask the question we began with.

Are all the people named here, spiritually akin to "Balaam" or "Zimri;" i.e. are they trying to curse the Bride from outside, or trying to corrupt her from within?

Here is the simplest of tests:
To qualify as a false teacher *within* the Body of Christ, that person must truly believe and confess the following:
Jesus Christ is God come in the flesh. (*1Tim.3:16*)
He was born of a virgin and totally separate from sinners. (*Is.7:14, Matt.1:23*)
He was tempted in all points as we are; yet lived His entire Life without sin? (*Heb.4:15*)
His Blood shed on the cross was the *ONLY* atonement (sacrifice, or acceptable offering to God the Father) for the sins of mankind? (*Heb.10:10-14*)
Only through Jesus Christ can we find forgiveness, salvation, and peace with God?
(*Eph.1:7, Col.1:13-14, Rom.5:1*)

He rose from the dead on the third day (according to the scriptures); victorious over sin and death. He took the keys of death and hell from a powerless devil; and triumphed over the entire realm and power of darkness – Openly! (*1Cor.15:3, Rev.1:18, Col.2:14-15*)

Jesus alone is the Way to eternal life, and to the Father in Heaven.
(John 3:16 and 14:6, Acts 4:12)

Man is not divine! Nor in any way God! Nor will he ever be equal to (or with) God!
(Gen.1, Is.42:8, Rom.1:18-23, 2Cor.5:17,)

Man is a fallen being with the inherently sinful nature of Adam; and cannot by his own works (good deeds, rituals, or techniques) save himself, or become acceptable in God's sight.
(Is.64:6, Eph.2:8-9)

Salvation is therefore a free and unmerited gift, and is bestowed upon the elect by the Grace of God alone. *(Rom.3:24, 6:23, 9:7-18)*

If any person can *truly* believe those doctrines from the Word of God, and yet continue to teach the various deceptions and outright lies exposed earlier; then we must, by the Word of God, consider such a one as "Zimri," i.e., a brother or sister in Christ who is overtaken in a serious fault, and needs to be *"restored in the spirit of meekness; considering ourselves, lest we also be tempted."* (Gal.6:1)

Without true repentance, deceivers *outside* the "Body" will of course share the fate of Balaam, likewise perishing; (2Pet.2:15, Jude11) and, in the end, be *"judged everyman according to their works."* (Rev.20:11-13)

Obviously Satan wants to fool the entire religious world by having them believe that Christ is merely one of many "paths" leading to God; and that true Christians are utterly presumptuous in affirming Jesus as the **ONLY WAY!**

Be certain that in these perilous times, believers will be tested and retested on this all important issue, so we would do well to heed our Master's Voice.

"Behold. I come quickly: hold that fast which thou hast, that no man take thy crown." (Rev.3:11)
"And what I say unto you I say unto all, Watch." (Mk.13:37)

****

In presenting this chapter, I would like to give sincere thanks to Lighthouse Trails Publishing, and to my Christian brother Ray Yungen for allowing me to quote from his fine book, "A Time of Departing."

****

SPECIAL ADDITION

As I was searching the Internet for the address of Wayne Dyer's publisher, I came across an interesting story through the same website. It was so pertinent to all I had been writing about that I felt constrained to include it here.

Strolling through a Phoenix library back in the 1980's, a man named Jerry Hicks came across a little known book written by Jane Roberts (now deceased). With great excitement, Hicks discovered that Roberts was a spirit medium and had "channeled" the words of a non-physical personality known as "Seth" onto paper: hence the book's intriguing title, "Seth Speaks."

Afraid that his wife Esther would dismiss Robert's work as too weird or spooky, Hicks gently and gradually began sharing the book's demonic feel-good contents with her, until she was not only comfortable with the deception, but was actually desirous to learn more!

The couple then sought out a living female "channel," who invited them to ask *her* spirit guide "Theo" as many questions as time (and money) permitted. Thrilled and completely hooked, Jerry and Esther returned for another session the following day, to be told that they too would have a "clairvoyant experience," and would receive their very own "spirit guide!"

During the closing moments, Esther asked Theo what they could do to move faster toward their goals. Theo's two-fold reply was, "Affirmations" and "Meditation!"

In order for the Hicks to meet their spirit guide and become channels themselves, Theo recommended a **daily meditation of 15 minutes** with the focus on "**breathing!**" After just a few sessions, Esther described a wonderful sense of "tingling, numbness and teeth buzzing;" then, a "feeling of ecstasy," and being "suspended and not aware of anything." (Alas, husband Jerry was not to be the "chosen vessel")

During one session, Esther made this chilling statement, "It felt as though something *breathed* me."

(Clearly the conditions for demonic possession were being met!)

After nine months of daily meditation, accompanied by "waves of intense goose bumps," and "thrills throughout her body," Esther's head began moving involuntary. Then, like a human ouija board, she began spelling out letters with her nose.

"I am Abraham; I am your spiritual guide; I love you; I am here to work with you ..."

(Demonic possession complete!)

"...Almost at once Esther was moved powerfully to a typewriter, and began automatic writing!" [37]

(Just as Blavatsky, and Bailey had done long before.)

Satan, who often tries to insult God, and increase human deception by using Biblical names for evil spirit guides, made sure that this relationship (find it currently at Abraham-Hicks.com) would lead to books, speaking engagements, and public recognition.

The couple routinely travels to some forty cities per year giving question and answer workshops to thousands of people, and happily introducing them to demons named Abraham. The Hicks will also encourage you to find your own personal demonic experience, just like theirs!

(I'm sure all this is done with the utmost sincerity!)

Their latest book (based on corrupt context and a miss-quote from a promise made by Jesus to His own people in *Matt.7:7*) is titled, "Ask and It Is Given" (foreword by Wayne Dyer), and has "Abraham" dispensing all the usual "feel-good" New Age poison!

"Allow your feelings to be your guide." [38] "You are a perfect yet expanding being, in a perfect yet expanding world, in a perfect yet expanding universe." [39]

Other typical N.A. deceits found on the Hick's website include, "The essence of the Abraham-Hicks message, distilled from workshops with Abraham since 1986." [40]

Here Abraham says through Esther:

"We are many," and, "We have come to lead and guide you to expanded knowingness; to your higher, inner self ... **that you may intentionally be the creator that you have come forth to be.** We have come to awaken the total you. **We encourage all beings to look inside themselves; to access the truth within.**" [41]

Abraham goes on to say:

"You cannot die; you are everlasting life. In grace, you may choose to relax and allow your gentle transition back into your non-physical state of pure, positive energy. Your natural state is that of forgiveness. (Have fun with all of this. Lighten up! You can't get it wrong.")" [42]

May those final feel-good, but deadly lies, warn anyone who might be tempted to heed the sweet deceptions of "Abraham" (and all other demonic spirits out there)!

Without Jesus Christ as their Savior and Lord, there is no *saving* grace whatsoever! People will not only die physically, they will also perish spiritually; and be separated from God for all eternity in the *"Lake of Fire." (Rev.20:11-15)*

Tragically, on that *"great and terrible day of the Lord's judgment," (Joel 2:31, Acts 17:31)* the whole unrepentant unsaved world will discover just *how wrong* a human being can really be!

CONCLUSION

The *true* Abraham was *"the friend of God," (James 2:23)* and the *"father of God's faithful people." (Rom.4, James 2:21)* The *false* Abraham(s) of Jerry and Esther Hicks are not only despicable enemies of the Lord, but of the entire human race!

In short they are nothing more than the *"wicked, seducing spirits"* of *Ephesians 6:12*, and *1Tim.4:1*; and are themselves destined for punishment in that same eternal fire! *(Matt.25:41)*

In view of that vital revelation from Jesus Himself, know that in the last days (especially), these lying, fallen *"angels of light" (2Cor.11:14)* will do everything in their power to take down as many unsuspecting victims as they possibly can!

"Be sober, be vigilant; because your adversary the devil, as a roaring lion, walketh about, seeking whom he may devour." (1Pet.5:8)

CHAPTER TWENTY-TWO

The LION, The WITCH, and The (PURPOSE DRIVEN) WARDROBE!

The last few years have seen an explosion of interest in the writings of C. S. Lewis and the ministry of Rick Warren; but sadly, both are being used by the enemy to deceive massive numbers of undiscerning Christians in the Body of Christ.

The reasons for including both of them in this chapter should (I hope) become clear after looking into some of their statements, teachings, and philosophies.

C. S. LEWIS (1898-1963)

Clive Staples Lewis has been described as, "one of the intellectual giants of the twentieth century, and the most influential Christian writer of his day." [1]

Originally from Belfast, Northern Ireland, Lewis wrote a number of books, a few of which remain immensely popular and widely available today. Sales, according to various sources are estimated at over two million dollars annually.

His best known work, "The Lion, the Witch and the Wardrobe" (from "The Chronicles of Narnia") has been adapted for radio, television, and film. His most influential book however is undoubtedly "Mere Christianity."

To debate whether Lewis was a true born-again believer (many have and I'm sure will go on doing so) would be pointless. *"The Lord knoweth them that are His"* (2Tim.2:19)

I simply intend to reveal some of the extremely erroneous statements he has made in the Name of the Lord Jesus Christ; and as a representative of the Christian faith.

Let me say to begin with; I have a problem with any man who would title a written work, "Mere Christianity" (for whatever reason). To me it's like saying, "Merely Christ." After reading the book however, I found that the offensive title was nothing compared to some of its content!

According to Lewis, the following words were spoken to him by Jesus.

"Make no mistake, ... If you let me, I will make you perfect. The moment you put yourself in My hands, that is what you are in for. ... Whatever suffering it may cost you in your earthly life, **whatever inconceivable purification it may cost you after death**, whatever it costs Me, I will never rest, nor let you rest, until you are literally perfect – until my Father can say without reservation that He is well pleased with you, as He said He was well pleased with me." [2] (Emphasis added)

Make no mistake, ... Lewis is preaching "***another Jesus***," (see *2Cor.11:3-4*) and one who clearly teaches purgatory!

NOTE: the Catholic encyclopedia describes purgatory as a place or condition of temporal punishment for those who, having died in God's grace are not free from certain [venial] sins, and therefore must continue to pay for their transgressions.

Including purgatory in a "message from God" makes Lewis both false prophet and teacher!
Suffering after death to be made perfect is a total denial of the Lord's "FINISHED WORK" on the cross? – "*The Blood of Jesus Christ cleanses us from all sin.*" (*1John1:7*)
Believing you can pay for (or work off) sin after death is as offensive to God (and as futile) as any attempt to do so while living! (See *Eph.2:8-9*)
"***For by ONE OFFERING, He*** (the True Jesus) ***has perfected for ever them that are sanctified.***"
(*Heb.10:14*)

Christians are perfect in God's sight **NOW!** – Thanks to the precious Blood of Christ.

NOTE: "Venial" and "mortal" sins are among Catholicism's own works of fantasy, so not surprisingly, Lewis (a former Catholic) is borrowing from past masters!
The truth is; "***Any* sin (great or small) condemns us!**" (See *James 2:10*)

Next; and with all the flair of a New Age missionary, Lewis states,
"There are people in other religions who are being led by God's secret influence to concentrate on those parts of their religion which are in agreement with Christianity, and thus belong to Christ without realizing it." [3]

TRUTH: Absolutely no one belongs to Christ, and has eternal life without knowing it!
Jesus said,
"*I am the good Shepherd, and know My sheep, and **Am known of Mine**.*" (*John10:14*)
Jesus calls His own by name, and leads us: He goes before us and we follow Him, for we
KNOW HIS VOICE! (*John 10:3-4*)

Satan's whole lying New Age thrust is to convince the world that Jesus Christ is in *every* religion, and in *every* person. That way they can remain a Hindu, Buddhist, Muslim etc., and still find God!

Adding more poison to the pot, Lewis insists that,
"There are three things that spread the Christ-life to us: baptism, belief, and that mysterious action which different Christians call by different names – Holy Communion, the Mass, the Lord's Supper." [4]
(Surely only the deceived could mention those "three things" in the same breath!)

Let the Word of God proclaim the eternal truth:
"***So Christ was ONCE offered to bear the sins of many ...***" (*Heb.9:28a*)
and,
"***But this Man, after He had offered ONE sacrifice for sins for ever, sat down on the right hand of God: ...***" (*Heb.10:12*)

Lewis's claim that the vain and repetitious sacrificing of Christ in the detestable Mass, and *true* Communion are one and the same, might help to dispel some of the doubts and on-going confusion regarding his spiritual state: especially when we add another sad but convincing clue.

Referring to born again believers, Lewis suggests:

"When you have recognized one of **them**, you will recognize the next one much more easily. And I strongly suspect (but how should I know?) that **they** recognize one another immediately and infallibly, across every barrier of color, sex, class, age, and even of creeds." [5] (Parenthesis in original - emphasis added)

In other words, he is quite certain that *real* Christians recognize one another, but not being one of them, how could he be sure?

So if Lewis does not confess to be a true believer, what then are we to make of him?

The answer now seems fairly straightforward. Much of what he writes in "Mere Christianity" reeks of an old religious favorite known as "Behaviorism." This "ism" emphasizes many Christian sounding ideals or principals, but rarely (if ever) focuses on Christ Himself: His inimitable sacrifice for our sins, and our *only* way of salvation from the judgment to come!

"Mere Christianity" is then, for the most part, the C. S. Lewis version of what Christianity is, and what a Christian should, or should not do. The first three parts of the book are therefore suitably entitled, "**Right and wrong as a clue to the meaning of the universe**;" "**What Christians believe**;" and, "**Christian behavior**."

His false assertion that anyone of any faith or denomination who *merely* agrees with some of the tenets of Christianity can be called a Christian (just read his preface); *merely* reinforces the fact that **not everyone who writes a book about Christianity can be called a Christian either!**

In one of his lesser known books, Lewis first quotes a verse from the Word of God.

"Assuredly, I say to you, this generation will by no means pass away till all these things take place."

(Matt.24:34)

And then dares to write this:

"… certainly the most embarrassing verse in the Bible. The one exhibition of error and the one confession of ignorance grow side by side. That they stood thus in the mouth of Jesus himself and were not merely placed thus by the reporter, we surely need not doubt… The facts, then, are these: that Jesus professed himself (in some sense) ignorant, and within a moment showed that he really was so." [6]

How could a true believer throw such an insult in the face of God's Divine Son?

Even while He walked the earth as a man, the Lord "*Always did the things that pleased His Father.*" (*John 8:29*) Jesus *always* had the knowledge of His Father's will. He revealed it in word and in deed wherever He went!

The Lord's words are flawless, and "*forever settled in Heaven*" (*Ps.119:89*) They will never pass away! (*Matt.24:35*)

His prophecies are inevitable: they will *all* be fulfilled. – Ignorance was *not* an option!
Jesus also "*... knew all men*" and, "*... knew what was in man!*" (*John 2:24-25*)
"*Let God be true, and every man a liar!*" (*Rom.3:4*)

WHY "NARNIA" IS A NO-NO!

The works of C.S. Lewis appear to be almost "required reading" in many Christian circles these days. "Focus on the Family" (the organization headed by Dr. James Dobson) is currently endorsing and selling an audio version of "The Chronicles," and across the country, vast numbers of churches and ministries are using them as teaching aids for children's Sunday school programs.

The "Chronicles of Narnia" (by far Lewis's most famous work) is a collection of seven fantasy stories. Book one describes them as, "Your passport to a most extraordinary excursion into magical lands and enchanted happenings." Perhaps these next few paragraphs will show just how well Satan is using this so called, "intellectual giant" to further his own evil cause.

Since its 1950 publication, "The Lion, the Witch and the Wardrobe" (first of the seven fantasies) has been received and praised by countless believers as a wonderful Christian allegory. However, at no time did Lewis himself refer to his "Chronicles" as even Christian, let alone Christian parables! (And by the way, fantasies are definitely not of God!)

The Chronicles of Corruption:

In 2005, a major film production of "The Lion, the Witch, and the Wardrobe" was released by the Disney corporation in America, and went on to achieve international success.

For those who have neither read the book, nor seen the movie; the story involves four English children from the normal, every-day world, who flee war-torn London during the 1940's for the safety of a large country home. (In the equally occult chronicles of Harry Potter, someone from the normal world is known as a "muggle;" i.e. a "mug" or stupid person who doesn't understand or sympathize with Potter's world of witchcraft!) One of the children, Lucy, enters a wardrobe (while playing a game of hide and seek), and, much like Alice in wonderland, finds herself transported to a fantasy world filled with talking animals and strange mythological creatures.

Lucy is soon found in the company of a "faun," who casually invites her to take tea with him.

NOTE: In the demonic realms of pagan mythology, the faun represents any number of forest or rural deities, which possess the bodies of men, but the tail, legs, ears, and horns of a goat! "Faunus" was a Roman god of nature and fertility, and worship of him involved all manner of sexual depravity! In this and other "Chronicles," The children enter lands inhabited by gods and goddesses such as Bacchus (a.k.a. Dionysus), the god of wine and revelry. Female followers of Bacchus (known as Maenads) were commonly driven to sexual frenzies or madness during ritualistic orgies!

An evil White Witch, who is also the false Queen of Narnia, is trying to keep the land in eternal winter; and managers to persuade one of the children (Edmund) to turn traitor and join her.

Appearing in all seven stories is a talking creature named "Aslan" (Turkish word for lion), and it is this lion who is regarded by many Christian teachers as a Christ-figure or type.

(Important here is the fact that Aslan's arch-enemy is actually another mythological beast known as "Tash" who appears later in the Chronicles.)

Alright, let's suppose for a moment, that Lewis *wanted* Aslan to be a "Christ-figure." We should at least take a look to see how he measures up as a type of the Lord Jesus Christ.

Book one: In order to save the traitor Edmund from death, Aslan (using the "Deeper Magic from Before the Dawn of Time") makes a bargain with the White Witch by agreeing to give up his own life in exchange for the child's.

At first this might seem plausible, but on reflection, if Aslan *is* meant to be a type of Christ, then it is Tash, and *not* the White Witch who is a type of the devil. **Nowhere in scripture does Jesus make a bargain with Satan! – much less with one of Satan's minions!**
(Strike one!)

In book two, Aslan consorts with demons!

"The crowd and the dance round Aslan (for it had become a dance once more) grew so thick and rapid that Lucy was confused. She never saw where certain other people came from who were soon capering among the trees. One was a youth, dressed only in a fawn skin, with vine leaves wreathed in his curly hair. His face would have been almost too pretty for a boy's, if it had not looked so extremely wild. You felt, as Edmund said when he saw him a few days later, 'There's a chap who might do anything, absolutely anything.' He seemed to have a great many names – Bromios, Bassareus, and the Ram were three of them. There were a lot of girls with him, as wild as he. There was even, unexpectedly, someone on a donkey. And everybody was laughing: and everyone was shouting out, 'Euan, euan, eu-oi-oi-oi.' Is it a romp, Aslan? Cried the youth. And apparently it was. ... The boy with the wild face is Bacchus and the old one on the donkey is Silenus ... But (said Susan), I wouldn't have felt very safe with Bacchus and all his wild girls if we'd met them without Aslan." [7]

One commentator states, "The words Euan, euan, eu-oi-oi-oi are an ancient witches' chant used to invoke the power and presence of the god of drunkenness and addiction, who is named Bacchus." [8]
(Strike two!)

Towards the end of book seven, a character named "Emeth" reveals more of Lewis's confused theology and blasphemous declarations.

"... and when it began to be said that Tash and Aslan were one, then the world became dark in my eyes. For always since I was a boy, I have served Tash, and my great desire was to know more of him and, if it might be, to look upon his face. But the name of Aslan as hateful to me." Later, upon meeting Aslan, Emeth says, "Alas, Lord, I am no son of Thine but the servant of Tash." He (Aslan) answered, "Child, all the service thou hast done to Tash, I account as service done to me. ... I take to me the services which thou hast done to him, for I and he are of such different kinds that no service which is vile can be done to me, and none which is not vile can be done to him. **Therefore if any man swear by Tash and keep his oath for the oath's sake, it is by me that he has truly sworn, though he know it not, and it is I who reward him.** And if any man do a cruelty in my name, then, though he says the name Aslan, it is Tash whom he serves and by" [9] (Emphasis added)
(Strike three!)
Serve Satan – be rewarded by Jesus! ... How big a lie are we willing to swallow?

MORE CONFUSION

C. S. Lewis, and J.R.R. Tolkien (author of "Lord of the Rings") were friends as well as professors at Oxford University in England; and both shared a background of Roman Catholicism. Doubtless they believed their religion would not be at odds with hobbits, trolls, elves, fairies, witches, and magical wardrobes!

However, after freely acknowledging witches and witch-craft throughout the Chronicles, Lewis later reverses himself with a complete and erroneous contradiction.

"But surely the reason that we do not execute witches is that **we do not believe there are such things**. If we did – if we really thought that there were people going about who had sold themselves to the devil and received supernatural powers from him in return, and were using these powers to kill their neighbours or drive them mad or bring bad weather – surely we would all agree that if anyone deserved the death penalty, then these filthy quislings did." [10] (Emphasis added)

The truth is: *GOD* believes in witches, and His Word *confirms* their existence!
(Ex.22:18, Deut.18:10)

NOTE: The traditional belief that there are "black" (bad) and "white" (good) witches is simply another demonic deception. They are *all* servants of Satan; and God declares them to be an "abomination!"

Some observations

Sadly today, there are still many deluded men and women who insist that books such as "Lord of the Rings," and "The Chronicles of Narnia" are suitable, and even beneficial for Christian children!

In his book, "Harry Potter and the Bible," Richard Abanes praises Tolkien for his "masterful story telling," and "brilliant mind;" and Lewis for his "defense of Christianity." At the same time though, he attacks author J. K. Rowling for aligning her tales of "Harry Potter" with current paganism and the practice of witchcraft!

Abanes argues that the Christian theology of Lewis and Tolkien contained in their **"Godly fantasies"** is "veiled beneath the various characters" (make that *occult* characters); and that the Witch of Narnia is quite acceptable because, "... she is evil, and based on age-old and widely accepted symbols and illustrations of evil." [11] (Such are the voices of "conservative" Christianity!)

Now on the other hand:

John's just wild about Harry!

A fellow by the name of John Killinger has written a book called,

"God, the Devil & Harry Potter: A Christian Minister's Defense of the Beloved Novels."

In it, he lovingly portrays the young wizard (Potter) as a type of Christ, and practically idolizes author J. K. Rowling for her contribution to literature. (Actually, this so-called Christian minister's book is little more than a one-man public relations/advertising campaign for one of the cleverest literary seductions of modern times!)

A truly spellbound Killinger writes:

"The publication and distribution of her books has been nothing short of miraculous. To think that she was an out-of-work secretary and secondary-school teacher, lining up for her monthly assistance check when she was first writing these brilliant stories. ... the books took off like an unquenchable fire, selling millions of copies in every language. It was as if the kindling had been laid in every hearth in the world, and suddenly the magic flame ignited it, so that the *whoof* of it was astounding, was breathtaking – and we haven't begun to see the waning of the conflagration." [12]

Christians know that as an "*angel of light*," Satan is well able to perform the "miraculous;" and when he lights such a powerful "magic flame" as Harry Potter, be sure his demonic "anointing" will keep the "conflagration" burning for as long as possible!

Of course, anyone openly critical of Rowling's work is described by Killinger as (you guessed it) a mundane, stupid, non-enlightened "Muggle!" Or at the very least, a "mean-spirited, narrow-minded detractor!" [13] (This from a man who has penned two other worthless, God insulting books, which feature Christ as a woman in a modern setting!) [14]

The queen is dead – long live the queen!

Needless to say, with the staggering global success of her novels, films, and the Potter marketing-machine, Rowling has convincingly ended Oprah Winfrey's reign, and is now firmly enthroned as the satanic kingdom's, "New Age sales person of the decade" – perhaps of the century!

As the world's best selling author, she may even live to top Blavatsky, Bessant, Bailey, Tolkien, Lewis, Disney, the Beatles, and Winfrey – combined!

DIVINATION – "THE NOBLE ART?"

If any true believer still needed help discerning the gifting spirit or current power behind Rowling's "throne," this "cute and funny" little scene from "The Prisoner of Azkaban" (film version) should more than suffice.

During his third year at "Hogwarts" (school for witchcraft and wizardry), Harry and classmates (including "Hermione Granger – the brightest witch in Hogwarts") enter the classroom of witch/medium, Professor Sybil Trelawney (played by Emma Thompson).

With crystal ball at the ready, Trelawney invites her students to explore the "noble art of divination," and leads them into "Tasseomancy" (the art of reading tea leaves) to discover which of them has "the gift," i.e. second sight." Later Trelawney teaches them that, "The art of crystal gazing is in the clearing of the inner eye." Only then will they be able to see!

Rowling's books and movies are filled with similar occult practices that fly directly in the face of God's Word which has always forbidden them!

Divination, like *all* witch-craft is an "*abomination to God!*" (*Deut.18:10*) Anyone practicing or promoting it, "*does evil in the sight of the Lord, and provokes Him to anger.*" (*2Kings 17:17*)

Look at this New Testament account:

"*And it came to pass, as we went to prayer, a certain damsel **possessed** with a **spirit of divination** met us, which brought her masters much gain by **soothsaying** (Fortune-telling) ... And this she did many days. But Paul **being grieved**, turned and said to the spirit, I command thee in the Name of Jesus Christ to come out of her. And **he** came out that same hour.*" (*Acts 16:16 and 18*)

Practicing, promoting, or just *playing* with divination invites an evil spirit to take possession! How much clearer could it be? Who do *you* think was "writing" Rowling's books?

But listen once more to *Killinger's* words:

"It is unfortunate that fundamentalist Christians have been put off Rowling's novels by all the talk of witches, goblins, spells, incantations, potions, dragons, invisible capes, and magic stones, and reacted by branding **such harmless devices** as 'Satanic' and 'anti-Christian'; ..." [15] (Emphasis added)

Encouraged by such "blind guides," Christians are being taught that the demonic realm is nothing more than a "good read" or "scary movie!"

Who needs the "*whole armor of God?*" (*Eph.6:13*) Who needs "*spiritual weapons?*" (*2Cor.10:4-5*)

If Rowling's wonderful tales of "*principalities, powers, and rulers of the darkness of this world*" (*Eph.6:11-12*) are not to be taken seriously, then let's take our children back to "Dungeons and Dragons," and "Pokemon!" Let's take out the ouija board and tarot cards! After all, Killinger assures us they are merely "harmless devices" and "fantasies" provided for our entertainment!

NOTE: Thanks to medium/clairvoyant, Doreen Virtue, there is now a new Christian-friendly version of the ouija called the "**Guiding Light Angel Board**" (demons included: available on line and in stores now!) Virtue is a "spiritual doctor of psychology and a fourth-generation metaphysician who works with angels, elementals, and ascended-master realms in her writings and workshops." She believes fallen angels are merely "creations of man's fear – commonly called gargoyles." Or alternatively, "the spirits of deceased humans who are earthbound for various reasons and are sometimes referred to as ghosts."

When challenged with the Biblical view of *not* consulting with mediums and contacting the dead, Virtue replies,

"When I see people's lives heal because they have contacted a deceased love one, I don't see how that could be a sin in any way. To me, it's a process of love and forgiveness – the very properties that Jesus urged us to adopt." [16]

The lies are getting better all the time, and it becomes easier to see how "*even the very elect would be deceived*;" but thank God, Jesus will not let it end that way!

GOD OR SATAN?

It has been suggested by some that Lewis and Tolkien actually paved the way for Harry Potter; and, having already established Satan's frequent use of "gradualism," I have no difficulty whatsoever in believing it.

It is essential for believers to understand that "The Chronicles of Narnia," "Lord of the Rings," and "Tales of Harry Potter" all major on "good" and "bad" forms of the same witch-craft!

Aslan uses the "deeper magic" to beat the White witch; Gandalf and Harry use "good magic" as apposed to the evil variety of Sauron and Lord Voldermort. Together these stories form a triple flood of fantasy occult persuasion, inspired of course by one very real and supremely evil being!

Question:

Does God or Satan inspire divination, magic, and witch-craft? – there *is* no third choice!

Then there could only be *one* spiritual power behind "Rings," "Chronicles," and "Potter!"

As Christians, the *Holy* Spirit commands us to "*prove what is acceptable to the Lord*," (*Eph.5:10*)

For believers to applaud Lewis or Tolkien and condemn Rowling is simply a matter of ignorance, hypocrisy, or (more likely) a total lack of spiritual discernment!

Trying to Christianize *any* of the pagan practices inundating this entire collection is a most dangerous form of compromise and corruption. Once more the Holy Spirit tells us:

"*It is a shame even to speak of those things which are done of them in secret.*" (See *Eph.5:11-12*)

Those who would lure young Christians onto the secret and forbidden "stage" of occult darkness and deceit by claiming that their plots and props are but "harmless devises" or "fantasies" should read some of the most terrifying words found in scripture!

Jesus Himself said,

"*But whoso shall offend* (entice away or hinder from right conduct or thought) *one of these little ones which believe in Me*, *it were better for him that a millstone were hanged about his neck, and that he were drowned in the depth of the sea. Woe unto the world because of offenses!*

For it must needs be that offenses come; but woe to that man (or woman) *by whom the offense cometh."*

(Matt.18:6-7)

THE MIXED MULTITUDE

Anyone who has the time to examine the life and written works of C. S. Lewis will almost certainly be left with a conundrum. Naturally we are all imperfect fleshly beings, so none of us is qualified to *"cast the first stone"* of criticism at his personal life; but once a man of his stature puts pen to paper, and *publishes* that paper, it behooves us to take a very careful look!

From a Christian point of view, Lewis wrote some incredibly good stuff. (I don't think anyone could seriously argue with that.) But it is the really *bad* stuff that brings out the "javelin!"

When Israel finally escaped from Egyptian captivity, the scripture says, *"a mixed multitude went up also with them"* (*Ex.12:38*); and it was the *"lusting of this mixed multitude"* that caused so much trouble for the people of God. (See *Num. 11:4*)

Later of course, many Israelites willingly married *"strange"* or pagan women and, in effect, created their *own* mixed multitude by being *"unequally yoked!"* For some, the *"putting away"* of those gentile wives must have been extremely difficult; but failure to do so was to invoke the anger of a Holy God! (See *1Kings11:1-13, Ezra 9 and 10*)

As a type, that *"mixed multitude"* is to be found in the life of every single believer today!

For it is the *"flesh that lusts against the Spirit, and the Spirit against the flesh."* (*Gal.5:17*)

None of us is exempt!

One minute Peter is inspired by the Holy Ghost – the next by Satan himself! (*Matt.16:13-23*) Why would we *or* C. S. Lewis be any different?

THE LINEN, THE WOOL, AND THE WARNING!

God's priests were forbidden to wear Linen and wool while ministering to Him.

"... They shall not gird themselves with anything that causeth sweat." (See *Eze.44:17-18*)

We've already seen that *"Linen"* and *"wool"* speak of a mixture of *"Spirit"* and *"flesh;"* so wool (which causes *"sweat"*) would speak of ministry or work derived from our old sinful (often religious) nature!

The reason ministers of God should avoid these "mixtures" is summed up in *verse 23.*

"That they shall teach My people the difference between the holy and the profane, and cause them to discern between the unclean and the clean."

Every Christian man or woman who stands by faith in linen is capable of slipping into wool: hence the need for discernment! In addition, Christian parents have the responsibility, and the privilege of teaching their children to spot the difference!

So: when reading the works of Lewis, or anyone else for that matter, let's be sure to take all this into account; and consider ourselves! For one way or another, God is still using some very "woolly priests" to fulfill His ultimate, glorious and eternal purpose!

****

Now Let's take a look at the man who gave "Purpose" a whole new meaning!

(Although this account begins somewhat lightheartedly, may it not detract from the seriousness of this all-important subject. – Millions of spiritual lives are at risk!)

287

THE PROLOGUE

As you know, the "Wardrobe" was the means by which Lucy, Edward, Peter and Susan entered the imaginary world of Clive Staples Lewis. We are now about to enter the "Dream" world of Pastor Richard Warren; only this time it will be by means of the Purpose Driven Church!

RICK WARREN

Founding pastor of Saddleback Church in Orange County, California, (one of the largest "Wardrobes" in the U.S.A.). He is also the author of two extremely successful books.

The first book, a huge contradiction of terms entitled, **"The Purpose Driven Church: Growth Without Compromising Your Message and Mission"** led to the creation of **"Building a Purpose Driven Church"** training seminars. These seminars have attracted more than 400,000 Pastors and church leaders from all over "Narnia." (Soon to known as Warren's World!)

The second book was written in the form of a **"40 day spiritual journey,"** and promises to be a "blueprint for Christian living in the 21st century." [17] (Many visitors were persuaded to extend their 40 day journey, and have now made "Narnia" their permanent home!)

Since its release in 2002, **"The Purpose Driven Life: What On Earth Am I Here for"** has sold more than thirty million copies, and has been on the spiritual menu of "Wardrobes" everywhere.

My purpose is to examine some of the ingredients of this Purpose Driven recipe, and to discover why it has become the almost "forced-fed" diet of so many unsuspecting believers!

WHO'S DRIVING?

Unlike C. S. Lewis, there can be little doubt regarding pastor Warren's spiritual position. He has spoken of his salvation through a personal relationship with Jesus Christ many times, and appears to be a completely sincere and dedicated Christian brother.

Why then, should there be concern about the "Purpose Driven" ministry of Rick Warren, and its effect on so many of God's people?

To begin with, the very titles, **"Purpose Driven Church / Life"** cannot help but send out a distorted message. In the simplest of terms, the Body of Christ is not to be **"Purpose Driven:"**
it is to be **HOLY SPIRIT LED!** There is a *vast* difference between the two!
The primary warning concerning that difference came from chapters 12 and 14, but can be summed up again as follows:
  Those who reject, ignore, or limit the *full* ministry and leading of the Holy Spirit today,
     will (sooner or later) fall into other errors along the way!
Once we begin an honest reading of the "Purpose Driven Life" (PDL), the errors will not be hard to find.

NOTE: Saddleback Church is a member of the "Southern Baptist Conference." After telephoning the church, I was told by a representative that, **"The gifts of the Holy Spirit do not operate in the sanctuary, nor in any other official church meeting."**

THE WRONG "MESSAGE"

Warren claims that the PDL, "contains nearly a 1000 quotations from Scripture." [18]

Of the 773 I counted in the notes, [19] I found only thirteen from the King James Version, and three from the Amplified Bible.

The new versions quoted most freely (by my count) were –

Contemporary English Version (CEV) 47 times.
New Century Version (NCV) 55 times
Living Bible (LB) 62 times
Today's English Version (TEV) 69 times
The Message (Msg) 91 times
New International Version (NIV) over 100 times
New Living Translation (NLT) 127 times

With the exception of the NIV, "None Inspired Version" (my quote), which was copyrighted in 1973, all the rest were either published or copyrighted *after* 1990. The reason for detailing this is to show how these modern and highly suspect versions are being used to deceive millions of sincere but misguided people throughout the Body of Christ! The fact that today's WDV's (Watered Down Versions) are getting further and further from the beauty, purity and TRUTH of the King James Version, doesn't seem to bother pastor Warren one bit.

He writes,

"Read Scripture from a newer translation. With all the wonderful translations and paraphrases available today, there is no legitimate reason for complicating the Good News with four-hundred-year-old English. Using the King James Version creates an unnecessary cultural barrier ... Clarity is more important than poetry." [20]

We may see an example of this "clarity" by looking at one of Warren's "wonderful translations."

"The Message," by Eugene H. Peterson.

(Note that four of the first five Scriptures quoted in the PDL are taken from this version: one of the most erroneous, New Age friendly adaptations of modern times!)

A sample of verses from Colossians and Matthew should be enough to steer any true believer away from Mr. Peterson's book, *and* the Purpose Driven Life!

"For everything, absolutely everything, **above and below**, visible and invisible, ... everything got started in him and finds its purpose in him." (Col.1:16) [21] (Quoted on p.17 of the PDL.)
And,
"Our Father in heaven, Reveal who you are. Set the world right; Do what's best **as above, so below ...**"

(from Matt. 6:9-10) [22]

And,
"Self-help is no help at all. Self-sacrifice is the way, my way, to **finding yourself, your true self.**" (Matt.16:25) [23] (Quoted on p.19. of the PDL.) (All emphasis added.)

Every badly interpreted verse reeks of New Age deception! The phrase, "**As above, so below**" is credited to alchemist Hermes Trismegistus, and comes straight from the ancient mystery religions of Egypt!

This is supported by chief editor of the "New Age Journal."

"Thousands of years ago in ancient Egypt... Hermes Trismegistus ... proclaimed this fundamental truth about the universe: 'As above, so below; as below, so above'. This maxim implies that the transcendent God beyond the physical universe and the immanent God within ourselves are one. Heaven and earth, spirit and matter, the invisible and the visible worlds form a unity to which we are intimately linked." [24]

Stay with Mr. Peterson and you will eventually find your way to the "**God is all, all is God**" philosophies of Hinduism, and the N.A. teachings of Alice Bailey and Helena Petrova Blavatsky!
Blavatsky wrote this in her book, the "Secret Doctrine."
"Above, the Son is the whole cosmos; below, he is mankind."

After our study on Yoga (ch.20), Peterson's use of the N.A. phrase, "**Finding yourself, your true self,**" and his *misuse* of the Word of God should require very little comment.
What *God* said was,
"For whosoever will save his life shall lose it: and **whosever will lose his life for My sake** *shall find it"* (*Matt.16:25* KJV)

NOTE: Losing (giving up or surrendering) our lives for Jesus' sake, causes *His* Life to be born in us. As we continue to submit to the Lord in obedience; *His* life will grow in us, and be revealed *through* us!
*"**Christ in you**, the Hope of glory!"* (*Col.1:27b*)
Once Jesus is received by faith, "*It is no longer I* (self) **that lives, but Christ that lives in me.**" (*Gal.2:20*)
There *is* no "*true*-self!" (That term is a total contradiction – See *Jer.17:9* and *Rom.3:10*)
Self is to be "*denied*" or "*crucified daily*" (*Luke 9:23*) – **not "looked for!"**
Sacrificial works or techniques to find this "true-self"are the ways of Yogis – **not *the* Way of Jesus!**

Can thirty million Christians be wrong?

Consider this next statement from Rick Warren, which incidentally includes a verse from another of his favorite – whatever suits your point of view – "translations!"

"Because God is with you all the time, no place is any closer to God than the place where you are right now. The Bible says, 'He rules everything and is everywhere **and is in everything**'." [25]
(This pagan, pantheistic assertion is taken from the "New Century Version" of Ephesians 4:6b.)

Whether he realizes it or not; by quoting from these "New Age Bibles" in the PDL, Rick Warren is teaching (and therefore encouraging) millions of readers to embrace the "Universal Oneness of all things!"
God is omnipresent – yes! But He is certainly *not* in everything! Nor is He in everyone!
(See *Jer.23:24, 1Kings 19:11-12, Is.57:15* and *2Cor.6:14-18.* KJV)

Keep the NCV in mind as we hear from our "friendly" false Christ, the Maitreya!

"My friends, God is nearer to you than you can imagine. **God is yourself. God is within you and all around you ... I am All in All ... My name is Oneness.**" [26] (Emphasis added)

Rick Warren's total lack of discernment, or the Maitreya's pathetic lies?
(Either way, you do not want to go there!)

NOTE: In the book of Ephesians, the Apostle Paul is writing to **believers**, and makes it clear that God is in (and *only* in) those that belong to, and are in the One Lord Jesus Christ!

"There is one body, and one Spirit, even as ye are called in one hope of your calling; one Lord, one faith, one baptism, one God and Father of all, Who is above all and in you all." (Eph.4:4-6 KJV)

The ultimate mystery of God's will, and *HIS* glorious purpose is, "... *to gather together in one all things IN CHRIST, both which are in Heaven, and which are on earth; even IN HIM.*" (See *Eph.1:9-10*)

Look now at the classic New Age rendering of Ephesians 4:5-6 as presented in "The Message." Completely removing the *Lordship* of Christ, the "serpent" writes,

"You have one **Master**, one faith, one baptism, one God and Father of all, who rules over all, works through all, and is present in all. **Everything you are and think and do is permeated with oneness.**" [27] (Emphasis added)

KEY PLAYERS

As already stated, New Age deceptions are corrupting the Body of Christ like never before, and their affects are staggering! In view of the last chapter, I pray this ongoing warning will cause you to stop; think; and (as always) take a deeper look for yourself!

To better understand and therefore escape the errors of the Purpose Driven ministry, it is necessary to mention the following people, and the negative influence they have had on Rick Warren himself.

ROBERT SCHULLER
"Yes God is alive and He is in every single human being." (Hour of Power, Nov.9 2003.)

"And there's Rick Warren, a pastor who today is phenomenal. He came to our institute time after time. And in 'Christianity Today', his wife was quoted as saying, 'When we came to that institute, we were blown away'." (Hour of Power, April 4, 2004.)

Born in Iowa in 1926, Robert Schuller would (in my opinion) grow to become one of the most powerful promoters of New Age philosophies within the church today; and certainly one of the greatest threats to Biblical Christianity! Schuller's denomination is the "Reformed Church in America," previously known as the "Dutch Reformed Church," which just happens to be a founding member of the WCC! As we shall see, Robert Schuller's ministry is based in a glass-walled shrine dedicated to self-esteem, and known to the world as the "Crystal Cathedral!"

In 2006, Schuller handed over the leadership reins to his son Robert Anthony, along with some of the most erroneous theology to be found anywhere on the planet!

Here are two examples of Schuller's legacy (they are by no means the worst!)

"I contend that his (man's) unfulfilled need for self-esteem underlies every act ... over and over again that **the core of man's sin is not his depravity, but a lack of self-dignity. Self-esteem is ... the single greatest need facing the human race today.**" (From "Self-Esteem: The New Reformation,"p.15. Emphasis added)
And,

"I don't think anything has been done in the name of Jesus Christ and under the banner of Christianity that has proven more destructive to human personality and hence counter productive to the evangelism enterprise, than the often crude, uncouth, and **unchristian strategy of attempting to make people aware of their lost and sinful condition.**" (Christianity Today, Oct. 5, 1984. Emphasis added)

Unfortunately, Rick Warren sat under Schuller's ministry, and still has a tremendous regard for him. Warren's Saddle Back Church sits in the same county, and is less than twenty miles from the Crystal Cathedral. Much of what is found in the PDL can be traced back to Schuller's teachings.

In view of the seriousness of my opening statement, I'm certain you'll understand why so much of what follows has as much, if not more to do with Robert Schuller than it does Rick Warren!

Between 1969 and 1986, Robert Schuller wrote,
"You were born for a **purpose**." [28]
"God chooses us to serve his **purpose**. ... Our **self-esteem** is rooted in our divine call. **God's dream** for our life and work gives **purpose** and **pride** to our life. ... God's plan and **purpose** calls for us to succeed and not to fail." [29] (Emphasis added)
"... people who are spiritually and emotionally connected to the **Eternal Creative Force** discover their powerful potential as a creative personality and win the big prize in living." [30]
"What is the basic **driving force** in life?" [31] (Emphases added)

In 2002, Rick Warren wrote,
"You were born *by* his **purpose** and for his **purpose**." [32]
"Knowing your **purpose** motivates your life. **Purpose** always produces passion." [33]
"What is the **driving force** in your life?" [34] (Emphases added)

NOTE: Countless believers who would not give Robert Schuller's ministry the time of day have trusted Rick Warren to speak into or guide their lives without realizing the huge influence Schuller exerts upon the "Purpose Driven Church and Life!"

DR. BERNIE SIEGEL

New Age author and front-man, Bernie Siegel describes his first encounter (in 1978) with a demonic "spirit guide" named "George!"

"The Simontons taught us how to meditate. At one point they led us in a directed meditation to find and meet an inner guide. ... I didn't believe it would work, but if it did I expected to see Jesus or Moses.

Who else would dare to appear inside a surgeon's head? Instead I met George ... George was spontaneous, aware of my feelings, and an excellent adviser. ... All I know is that he has been my invaluable companion ever since his first appearance. My life is much easier now, because he does all the hard work." [35]

(It would be interesting to note how his patients would react if they knew their treatment involved the help of a demonic spirit!)

Of course, this leading New Age spokesman has written many other things; including the foreword to Robert Schuller's book, "Prayer: My Soul's Adventure with God."

Siegel writes,

"This is a beautiful book of value to all people … Robert Schuller's newest book reaches beyond religion and information to what we all need – spirituality, inspiration, and understanding. Read it and live a life of meaning." [36]

Bernie Siegel showering praise on Robert Schuller? – That much is *not* surprising; but why is this demonically inspired doctor featured in the "Purpose Driven" pages of Rick Warren?

Borrowing from one of Schuller's signature rhyming phrases of twenty years ago, "… without hope we will lose the faith that we can cope" [37] Pastor Warren presents us with this:

"Hope is as essential to your life as air and water. **You need hope to cope.** Dr. Bernie Siegel found he could predict (with the help of "George" no doubt) which of his cancer patients would go into remission by asking, 'Do you want to live to be one hundred'? Those with a deep sense of **life purpose** answered yes and were the ones most likely to survive. **Hope comes from having a purpose.**" [38] (Emphases and parenthesis added)

Why does Warren neglect to tell his readers who Bernie Siegel really is? Could the reason be that *Siegel's* own "hopes and purposes" have nothing whatsoever to do with the Lord Jesus Christ, but with the New Age "gods of Cosmic Force and Oneness?"

NOTE: Given that much of pastor Warren's book is so evidently inspired by his one-time mentor, is it not strange that Robert Schuller's name (as well as any credit for his contribution) has been completely overlooked? In all honesty, I wonder how many believers would have climbed on board, raised their anchors, and set sail on the good ship PDL, if they had known that Shadow Captain Schuller stood so frequently behind the wheel?

NEALE DONALD WALSH

Walsh's "spirit guide" (unlike Siegel's) would manifest itself under slightly more adverse conditions! …

Depressed, downcast, and apparently disgusted with life, this former radio talk show host and metaphysical seeker decided to air his complaints in the form of an angry letter, which he addressed to God!

"To my surprise, as I scribbled out the last of my bitter, unanswerable questions and prepared to toss my pen aside, my hand remained poised over the paper, as if held there by some invisible force. **Abruptly, the pen began moving *on its own*. …**" [39] (Emphasis added)

(Here Walsh is describing the form of dictation known as "**automatic writing.**" A very **common dialogue** used throughout history for conveying demonic messages!)

A soon-to-be prince among today's New Age hierarchy, Walsh would not be playing host to the likes of a mere "George," but to "God" himself!

(Satan may not have a sense of humor, but there are times when he must surely laugh out loud!)

Needless to say, "God" began a whole series of "Conversations" with Walsh, resulting in a number of best selling books; and, I suspect, a good deal more laughter from you know who!

Here is a sample of what Walsh's "god/spirit guide/angel of light" wants you to know.

"You are already a God. You simply do not know it." [40]

"The era of the single Savior is over." [41]

"You are One with everyone and everything in the universe - including God." [42]

"Returning to God is called remembrance ... This is your sole/soul purpose." [43]

"... hell does not exist as this place you have fantasized, where you burn in some everlasting fire, or exist in some state of everlasting torment. What purpose could I have in that?" [44]

"I do not love 'good' more than I love 'bad'. Hitler went to heaven. When you understand this, you will understand God." [45]

To connect the unlikely dots between this deceived New Age author and the "Purpose Driven Life," we must turn once again to Robert Schuller.

In his 1982 book, "Self-Esteem: The New Reformation," Schuller wrote,

"Theologians must have their international, universal, transcreedal, transracial standard." [46]

Walsh himself called Schuller an "extraordinary minister:" [47] but then, referring to Schuller's "universal standard," Walsh's "*god*" said this:

"Rev. Schuller was profoundly astute in his observations and incredibly courageous in making them public. I hope he is proud of himself! I suggest that such an international, universal, transcreedal, transcultural, transracial standard for theology is the statement: 'We Are All One. Ours is not a better way, ours is merely another way'." [48]

Describing "another way" as the "**New-Gospel**" or the "**New-Spirituality**" (but cleverly omitting the word "**Age**" from both), Walsh's demon (I'm tired of calling it "God") clearly implies that Schuller's brand of theology could "bridge" the gap between the New Age Movement and the Christian community!

Now here's where it gets *really* interesting!

In 2002, (one year after "9-11") Walsh published Satan's "**Five Step Plan For (world) P.E.A.C.E.**" on his "Conversations with God" website –

P ERMIT ourselves to acknowledge that some of our old beliefs about God and about life are no longer working.

E XPLORE the possibility that there is something we do not understand about God and about life, the understanding of which could change everything.

A NNOUNCE that we are willing for new understandings of God and life to now be brought forth, understandings that could produce a new way of life on this planet.

C OURAGEOUSLY examine these new understandings and, if they align with our personal inner truth and knowing, to enlarge our belief system to include them.

E XPRESS our lives as a demonstration of our highest beliefs, rather than as a denial of them. [49]

Notice that step four of the "**Plan**" calls for everyone to "**enlarge**" their system of belief. This would be accomplished by way of a global religious compromise. For Christians, it would mean "giving up on a few sacred beliefs," [50] i.e., old-fashioned, out-dated ideas such as the need to be born again, or **Jesus being the one and only Lord and Savior!** That way, we could all swim in the same Communal "Oneness" swamp of, "joint action, combined effort, and collective co-creation." [51]

On November 2nd, 2003; one year after Walsh's peace plan appeared on the internet; Pastor Rick Warren announced his own "Global P.E.A.C.E. Plan" to the members of Saddle Back Church, and to the multitudes receiving it on-line!

Using the very same acronym, Warren spelled out "**God's Dream For World P.E.A.C.E..**" ...

P lant Churches

E quip Leaders
A ssist the Poor
C are for the Sick
E ducate the next generation [52]

That "Peace Plan" is vague enough for even Walsh to be comfortable with! And by the way, the word "Church" doesn't disturb New Agers one bit!

In his book, "Deceived On Purpose," Warren Smith describes a couple from the "Church of Religious Science" who visited Robert Schuller's "Institute for Successful Church Leadership" in the early 70's.

"... they wanted to learn how to make *their* 'church' grow and become as successful as possible. After talking with them in his office, and acknowledging their New Age beliefs; Schuller opened the bottom draw of his desk and took out a copy of 'Science of Mind,' written by 'Religious Science' founder, Ernest Holmes. The woman said that Schuller seemed very comfortable showing her that he had this classic New Age text."

Warren Smith went on to say ...

"Right about the time Schuller was showing this Religious Science minister Ernest Holmes' New Age book, a young Rick Warren was reading his first Robert Schuller book on church growth and starting to put his trust in Schuller as a teacher." [53]

WHOSE DREAM? WHOSE PLAN? WHAT PEACE?

Like his second-hand "Peace Plan," Rick Warren's version of "**God's dream**" was also nothing new: it too was on loan – this time from a 1978 book by Robert H. Schuller!

"... Find a dream. Once you've got that dream and you know it's **GOD'S DREAM** for your life, then be daring. Dare to say it. **Let the redeemed of the Lord say so.** Announce to the whole world that **IT'S GOING TO HAPPEN.**" [54] (Emphasis added)

NOTE: The phrase "*Let the redeemed of the Lord say so*" appears only once in scripture as an expression of thanksgiving for God's goodness and mercy! (See *Ps.107:1-2*) It has nothing whatsoever to do with announcing "God's dream!" The expression, **"God's dream"** is found **nowhere in the entire Word of God!** Therefore the affirmation – "**It's going to happen**" comes *not* from the power of the Holy Spirit; but from the counterfeit "*power of positive thinking*!" (A New Age characteristic that Schuller is extremely well-known for.)

It's clear that Schuller himself borrowed from occultists such as Ernest Holmes and close friend **Norman Vincent Peale**; so his particular brand of pre-owned "positive thinking" is to be found in many of the New Age compatible books he has written over the years. "Move Ahead with Possibility Thinking."(1967) "Daily Power Thoughts."(1977) "Peace of Mind Through Possibility Thinking."(1977) "Discover Your Possibilities."(1978) And my own *personal* "favorite" – "If It's Going to Be, It's Up to Me: The Eight Proven Principles of Possibility Thinking."(1997)

On page 25 of his 1973 book, "You Can Become The Person You Want to Be," Schuller actually admits:

"In the Institute for Successful Church Leadership, which I conduct in Garden Grove, California, we aim to turn ministers and church leaders into dynamic Positive thinkers."

Although the total damage done by Schuller's ministry could never be fully assessed in *this* life; one *estimate* comes in the form of this Rick Warren e-mail, entitled,
"God's Dream For You – and the World."

"THIS WEEKEND, I'll begin a series of five messages on **God's dream** to use you globally – to literally use YOU to change the world! I'll unveil our **Global P.E.A.C.E. plan**, and how God has uniquely prepared you for this moment of destiny. ...The Global Peace Plan **IS GOING TO HAPPEN** ... God is going to use you, and all of us together at Saddleback to **change history**." [55] (Caps but no emphasis in original.)

With the unscriptural fantasy of "God's Dream," the "Positive Thinking" of New Age sympathizer Schuller, and a "Global Peace Plan" as flawed as the one brought forth by Walsh's "*god of this world*," Warren is preaching the **false promise** and **vain hope** of world peace at a time when mankind (and *especially* the Church) is so desperately in need of the truth!
Neale Donald Walsh claims *his* "Peace Plan" is from God – so does Rick Warren!
Compare their statements again.

Walsh: "The universe does nothing **by accident** ... you can **change the course of human history**. This is not **an exaggeration**." [56]

Warren: "You are not part of Saddleback Church **by accident** ... I say this without fear of **exaggeration** – God is going to use you ... to **change history**." [57]

Let there be no misunderstanding here: both men are prophesying a "history-changing, global peace" *for this present age*! Both are found lying against the Word of God, which is
"FOREVER SETTLED IN HEAVEN." (*Ps.119:89*)
NO ONE is going to "change history!" Any plan for true peace in *this* world will fail ...
GLOBAL PEACE IS *NOT* GOING TO HAPPEN!

As it was, so shall it be
*"Destruction cometh; and they shall seek peace, and **there shall be none**."* (*Eze.7:25*)

*"But the wicked are like the troubled sea; when it cannot rest, whose waters cast up mire and dirt. **There is no peace**, saith my God, for the wicked."* (*Is.57:20-21*)

*"And ye shall hear of **wars and rumors of wars** ... **nation shall rise against nation** ...there shall be **famines**, and **pestilences**, and **earthquakes** ... all these are the **beginnings of sorrows**."* (*Matt.24:6-8*)

God speaks fearful words to those who preach lies, and share false visions of peace.

*"Woe unto the foolish prophets, that follow their own spirit, and have seen nothing ... Therefore thus saith the Lord God; because ye have spoken vanity, and seen lies, therefore, behold, I am against you, saith the Lord God ... **even because they have seduced my people, saying, Peace; and there was no peace** ..."* (See all of *Eze.13*)

Because the vast, worldly majority will *"Not have this Man* (Jesus) *to reign over them"* (*Luke 19:14*); the only "**Global Peace**" found in these "**last days**" will be the **false peace** of the **false Messiah** as spoken of in *Daniel 8:23-25*.

*"... And through his policy also he shall cause craft to prosper in his hand; and he shall magnify himself in his heart, **and by peace shall destroy many**: he shall also stand up against the Prince of princes;* (Jesus) *but he shall be broken without hand."* (Verse 25)

The Holy Spirit speaks prophetically of this counterfeit (and short-lived) worldly peace, just prior to the Lord's return.

"For yourselves know perfectly that the day of the Lord so cometh as a thief in the night. For when they shall say, Peace and safety; then sudden destruction cometh upon them, as travail upon a woman with child; and they shall not escape." (*1Thess.5:2-3*)

How could "Global Peace" exist in this age when the Word of God emphatically denies its reality?

Christians know that the only *true* peace in this *"present world"* is the *"peace of God, which passeth all understanding."* (*Phil.4:7*) This *spiritual* peace of (and with) God is available *exclusively* through the *"strait and narrow Way"* **of a personal and saving relationship with the Lord Jesus Christ!** (*John 14:6*)

"AND <u>FEW</u> THERE BE THAT FIND IT." (Matt.7:14)

WHAT A PLAN!

Nothing would please the devil more than to see millions of "purpose driven" Christians trying to "**change the world**" with a "**Global P.E.A.C.E. Plan**" made up of "**hopes, dreams** and **affirmations**" borrowed from the "New Age Movement!" What more could we possibly do to hasten the arrival of the *"man of sin"* – the *"anti-Christ"* himself?

Just listen again to the language of one who has already claimed to be "The Christ," and is patiently waiting for the world to "call him forth."

"I am your **Purpose**. ... I am your **Hope**. ... I am your Heart. ... **God is within you and all around you**. ... My name is **Oneness**. ... I shall place before you all **the purposes of God**. ... **My Plan is God's Plan**. ... Nothing will happen **by chance**. ... Take part in a **Great Plan** which is **changing the world**.

... **My coming brings peace**." [58] (Emphasis added)

(For another look at the "Great New Age Plan," turn back to the "Great Invocation." Ch.13, page 198.)

Come out! Come out! *Whoever* You Are?

Warren's careless, and dangerous habit of quoting people without explaining who they are or what they stand for can be seen throughout the PDL. For example: Pastor Warren offers his flock the following:

"George Bernard Shaw wrote, 'This is the true joy of life: the being used up **for a purpose** recognized by yourself as a **mighty one; being a force of nature** instead of a feverish, selfish little clot of ailments and grievances ..." (PDL, p.33. Emphasis added)

And this,

"Only **shared experiences** can help others. Aldous Huxley said, '**Experience** is not what happens to you. It is what you do with what happens to you'." (PDL, p.248. Emphasis added)

George Bernard Shaw was a New Age occultist; a member of the "**Fabians**," *and* Helena P. Blavatsky's Theosophical Society! Warren doesn't seem to care that Shaw's *real* "**purpose**" was to become "**a mighty one**;" and equal in every way to the eternal "**force of nature**" he called "God!"

Believe it or not, many of New Age mystic Huxley's "**experiences**" came from taking psychedelic drugs! – Perhaps a shepherd with a flock of over twenty-thousand should have known that! – N.A. leader and writer Marilyn Ferguson certainly did!

"Huxley believed that the long-predicted religious revival in the United States would start with drugs, not evangelists." [59]

Contemplating Rick Warren

Saddest of all (for me) is Rick and wife Kay Warren's promotion of New Age Catholic mystics, such as Henry Nouwen, Richard Foster, and Brennan Manning!

On the Purpose Driven pastors.com website, Kay Warren recommends Henry Nouwen's book, "In the Name of Jesus." Mrs. Warren says, "I highlighted almost every word." [60]

I wonder if she highlighted the chapter where Nouwen wrote this: –

"Through the discipline of contemplative prayer, Christian leaders have to learn to listen to the voice of love ... For Christian leadership to be truly fruitful in the future, a movement from the moral to the mystical is required." [61]

In Nouwen's "Bread for the Journey," would Mrs. Warren have highlighted this? ...

"Prayer is soul work because **our souls are those sacred centers where all is one** ... it is in the heart of God that we come to the full realization of the unity of all that is." [62]

In his last book, "**Sabbatical Journey,**" Nouwen wrote,

"Today I personally believe that while Jesus came to open the door to God's house, **all human beings** can walk through that door, **whether they know about Jesus or not ...** Today I see it as my call to help **every person claim HIS OR HER OWN WAY TO GOD.**" [63] (Emphasis added)

(Now *there's* something worth highlighting!)

Speaking of the contemplative state, Madame Guyon said,

"**Here everything is God. God is everywhere and in all things.**" [64]

(Warren quotes *her* on page 193)

Just compare those words again with Peterson's "Message," and the "New Century Version."

"... part of the overall purpose he is working out in everything and everyone."(Eph.1:11 Msg)

"... He rules everything and is everywhere and is in everything'." (Eph.4:6b NCV)

On page 88 of the PDL, Warren actually endorses prayer techniques taught by the seventeenth century monk and "contemplative" master, Brother Lawrence! (Known for his book, "Practicing the Presence of God.")

But listen to what a former Catholic priest has to say about this so-called "Christian" brother.

"Brother Lawrence was not only traditionally Roman Catholic but also disseminated teachings that have similarities with Hinduism in the *Bhagavad-Gita*, and with many New Age writers." [65]

Unbelievably; "Breath prayers" (the occult technique already exposed in chapter 21) are also recommended *and taught* by Pastor Warren! He writes,

"The Bible tells us to *'pray all the time'*. How is it possible to do this? One way is to use 'breath prayers' throughout the day as Christians have done for centuries ... choose a brief sentence or a simple phrase that can be repeated to Jesus in one breath: ... Benedictine monks use the hourly chimes of a clock to remind them to pause and pray 'the hour prayer'. If you have a watch or cell phone with an alarm, you could do the same." (PDL, p. 89, and see also p. 299.)

If *you* "do the same," you will find yourself on the slippery slope of Christianized Eastern mysticism, Hindu mantra meditation, and major error!

Author Brian Flynn asks two far-reaching questions.

"If Rick Warren is not a promoter of the contemplative prayer movement and all that this movement entails, why was he a featured speaker at the 2004 National Pastor's Convention which offered Labyrinths, contemplative prayer sessions and yoga? And why, in 2005, did Rick Warren invite contemplative leaders from Youth Specialties to give training at his Purpose Driven Youth Ministry conferences?" [66] (Over to you Rick! ...)

KEN BLANCHARD

During his November, 2003 "Global P.E.A.C.E." message, Warren introduced New Age sympathizer Ken. Blanchard by saying,
"Ken has signed on to help us with the P.E.A.C.E. Plan. And he's going to be helping train us." [67]
Ken Blanchard says,
"I look for inspirational messages from a variety of sources besides Jesus. Our folks get to hear words of wisdom from great prophets and spiritual leaders like Buddha, Mohammed, Moses, Yogananda, and the Dalai Lama ... Buddha points to the path and invites us to begin our journey to enlightenment. I ... invite you to begin your journey to enlightened work." [68]

1. **For God's people: JESUS IS GOD'S ONLY SOURCE of "wisdom and inspiration!"**
   *"God Who at sundry times and in divers manners spake in time past unto the fathers by the prophets, **hath in these last days spoken to us by His Son** ..." (Heb.1:1 and 2a)*

2. **For God's people:** we must ask which "prophet or spiritual leader" mentioned by Blanchard is the *only* one pointing unerringly towards **JESUS CHRIST as GOD'S ULTIMATE PROPHET, SAVIOR, LORD and KING?** Listen now as the apostle Peter introduces that *true* prophet, and man of God – Moses!

*"**And He** (God the Father) **shall send Jesus Christ**, which before was preached unto you: Whom the heavens must receive until the times of restitution of all things, which God hath spoken by the mouth of **HIS** holy prophets since the world began. For Moses truly said unto the fathers, **a Prophet shall the Lord your God raise up unto you** of your brethren, like unto me; **Him shall ye hear** in all things whatsoever He shall say unto you. And it shall come to pass, that **every soul, which will not hear that Prophet, shall be destroyed from among the people.**" (Acts 3:20-23)*

3. **For God's people:** Blanchard claims that "**Buddha** points to the path of enlightenment!" But does *Buddha* point to the Lord Jesus Christ as the *Only Way* of salvation? Of course not!

As we have already discovered, Buddha points to the "**nothingness of Nirvana!**" There is no *true* light whatsoever in the so-called, "enlightened one." Buddha's way is merely another way of *darkness and death*! (*Prov. 14:12*)

Remember: Ken Blanchard is the man Rick Warren has "signed on" to help the Purpose Driven Church achieve "Global Peace!" A peace which can only be realized if world religions unite under one banner. Blanchard's presence guarantees a drive in that direction!

BRUCE WILKINSON

Pastor and well-known author of books such as, "The Prayer of Jabez," "The Dream Giver;" and "A Life God Rewards;" We'll discover that Bruce Wilkinson is as much at home in Schuller's Crystal Cathedral as he is in Warren's Saddleback Church.

In "The Dream Giver," Wilkinson parrots Schuller's "Self-Esteem" – "Big Dream" – "We are really somebodies" philosophy, [69] and presents his readers with this,
"**The Dream Giver gave me a big dream! I was made to be a Somebody and destined to achieve great things!**" [70] (Not one mention of Schuller in this book either!)

In "The Prayer of Jabez" we find Wilkinson encouraging believers to turn the "prayer" into a mantra by repeating it on a daily basis! (for even *greater* deception, try saying it in "one breath!")
The first part of the "prayer" reads, "*O, that Thou wouldest bless me indeed, and **enlarge** my coast.*" (Territory, border, or space.) (From *1Chr.4:10*)

A synoptic New Age view of both books will show pastor Bruce persuading believers to
"**enlarge** the borders of their faith by "*vain repetition.*" "**Dreaming the** (totally unscriptural) **Big Dream;**" and pressing on to achieve "**Great Things!**" (An impossible "World-Peace" for instance!)
Of course, in order to achieve "Great Things," they will have to get past the "**Border Bullies!**" (People in "The Dream Giver" who are trying to prevent "Ordinary" [a Nobody] from becoming "Somebody!") – In this case, they are Godly people trying to prevent Christians from making a terrible New Age mistake!
Let me explain.
To "**enlarge our belief system** to include new understandings of God and life" is paramount to the P.E.A.C.E. Plan of Neale Donald Walsh's spirit guide! (See part 4 of *his* Plan again.)
To "**dream the Big Dream**" of "**Oneness**" is something Schuller and friends have been recommending for decades!

Listen first to Wayne Dyer
"Who is the ultimate dreamer? Call it as you will: God, higher consciousness ... whatever pleases you ... **One dream, one dreamer**, billions of embodied characters acting out that one dream ... **your true essence is that you are part and parcel of the one big dream.** ...
You, the dreamer ... God the dreamer." [71]

Then to Robert Schuller
"Yes, God is alive and **He is in every single human being!**" [72]
"Going 'somewhere' from 'nowhere' had begun to take on a whole new meaning. I was moving further and further into a **mindset of RELIGIOUS INCLUSIVITY ...** I liked it!"
And,

"...I'm dreaming a bold impossible dream: that **positive thinking believers** in God will rise above the illusions that our sectarian religions have imposed on the world, and that **leaders of the major faiths will rise above doctrinal idiosyncrasies**, choosing not to focus on disagreements, but rather to **TRANSCEND** divisive dogmas **to work together** to bring **PEACE** and **PROSPERITY** and hope to the world." [73] (All emphases added)

Bruce Wilkinson at the Crystal Cathedral ...

"Good morning everyone. I want to talk about dreams. Of all places in the world to talk about dreams this is the place ... because I think Dr. Schuller is the Patriarch in the work about **living your dream**. ... What a touching moment it is to you and me and heaven above when men and women respond to the call of God to follow the dream that He has placed in their hearts ... Lord God, **please let me do the dream. Please let me do the dream**." [74]

Bruce Wilkinson at Saddleback Church ...

"And what Pastor Rick is going to share next week about the Saddleback global vision is right from heaven's heart. I promise. ... And I'm here to say to you as a fellow believer, you must rise up. You must fulfill the destiny that God has for this church. ... **Will you prepare for the Dream that's coming**? ... We ask you, Holy Spirit, that your **full and complete Dream** for this church and every person in this audience, that this will be the greatest living illustration in the history of the church. ... that the world is **radically transformed**." (75)

Echoing Wayne Dyer, Wilkinson told the church that one person's "dream" is connected to everyone else's, and ultimately to the "Big Dream" because it is "God's Dream!"

He also said that, **people who don't "do their dream" can negatively impact everyone else's dream for generations!** [75]

(The spiritual implications of that last statement are enormous!)

NOTE: The words, "**negatively impact**" constitute a "**curse**" imposed upon a person (or persons) as a result of another's actions (or lack thereof); and according to Wilkinson, that curse could be active for "**generations!**"

The three major manifestations of witchcraft are **intimidation**, **manipulation**, and **domination**. The first two are readily discernable in Wilkinson's threatening remark! The effect? ... Better to get with the "program" than to be guilty of negatively affecting "everyone else's dream for generations!"

Once again, expressions such as, "God's Big Dream," "Living, or doing the dream," etc., find no place at all in the Word of God! – **God does not dream!**

"Behold, He that keepeth Israel shall neither slumber nor sleep." (Ps.121:4)

Consider for one moment, the Author and Finisher of our faith at the height of His conflict in the garden of Gethsemane praying, "Nevertheless, not My Dream, but Thy Dream be done!"

No! The only dreams found in Scripture are in sleep! Not in the mind, imagination or will of man!

Regrettably, I believe what's *really* being said at Saddleback is this: if people don't play their part in the leadership's *own* vision (or version) of God's "BIG (Purpose Driven) DREAM," they will be guilty of cursing, or (at the very least) hindering and hurting everyone else!

If that sounds a little too high on the scale of extremes, look carefully at what follows.

CHANGE, LEAVE, OR DIE!

In a June, 2006 website article, Rick Warren spoke to pastors and leaders who were concerned about the time it was taking to achieve "Great (purpose driven) Things" in their churches.

"If your church has been plateaued for six months, it might take six months to get it going again. ...

If it's been plateaued for 20 years, you've got to set in for the duration! I'm saying **some people are going to have to die or leave.** ... **God killed off a million people** before he let them go into the
Promised Land. ... There may be people in your church who love God sincerely, but **who will never change.**" [76]

(Pastoral words of comfort to Christians everywhere! – Just thank God we're being "changed" or *conformed* to the image of *Christ [Rom.8:29]* – *not* Rick Warren!)

Needless to say, the "Change or die" mindset is deeply embedded in seasoned New Age practitioners. Using the New Age version of Matthew 24:14, Barbara Marx Hubbard spells out another chilling threat.

"When the word of this hope (Christ-consciousness) has reached the nations, the end of this phase of evolution will come. All will know their choice. All will be **required** to choose. ... All who choose not to evolve **will die off**." [77] (Emphasis added)

(When "Anti-Christ-consciousness" is in charge, we know *exactly* how they "will die off!" See *Rev.20:4*)

In the book "Soul Tsunami," (heavily endorsed by Rick Warren), New Age sympathizer Leonard Sweet tells us,

"It is time for a Postmodern Reformation ... Reinvent yourself for the 21st century or die. Some would rather die than change." [78]

To Suggest that believers who oppose the Purpose Driven juggernaut will share a similar fate to that of rebellious Israel in the wilderness, shows Warren has some very serious issues; not least of which appear to be delusions of grandeur; as demonstrated by his attitude and harsh reactions toward any resistance or criticism! (Characteristics which, incidentally, are shared and manifested by cult leaders the world over!)
Here are just two examples:
One of the books Warren uses to "train the church" is called, "Transitioning: Leading Your Church Through Change," by motivational expert, Dan Southerland.
With Warren's full approval, our "loving brother" Dan wrote,

"Not all of our traditional backgrounded Christians have been critical – just the ornery ones... Again, not all traditional church pastors – just the meaner ones."

Southerland now likens any "mean" (make that spiritually discerning) pastor to a hateful enemy of God! ...

"Sanballat is Nehemiah's greatest critic and number one enemy. Let me put it plainer than that. Sanballat is **a leader from hell**. We all have some Sandballats in our churches ... **You cannot call this guy a leader from hell to his face** – but you could call him Sandballat." [79] (Emphasis added)
(Warren sells this book on his website, which means the spiritual "lines" are now truly "drawn!")

A book intended be a glowing account of Rick Warren and his ministry was blasted and publicly discredited by Warren! Why? – Perhaps in part because the author, George Mair (who at one time attended Saddleback church) made the following observation:
"Saddleback distinctly bears the stamp of Reverend Norman Vincent Peale."

Peale was a 33rd degree Freemason, *and* (wouldn't you know) one of the founders of the **church-growth movement!**

In "A Life with Purpose," Mair made the mistake of telling his readers that Robert Schuller's old friend and mentor encouraged the "unification of psychology and religion;" and that,

"Many of Peale's uplifting affirmations originated with an 'obscure teacher of occult science named Florence Scovel Shinn'." [80]

At Saddleback's 25th anniversary in 2003, Warren made it clear that he would do, "Whatever it takes" to accomplish his purpose driven goals. [80] Given that his main goal is to implement a false and unscriptural "Global Peace Plan," he now has no alternative but to employ false New Age methods to achieve it!

There was a time when words like "ignorant," "accidental," "naive," or just plain old "undiscerning" were used to describe (or excuse) Warren's N.A. tendencies; but that time has long gone! No one could possibly be "in bed" with so many New Age leaders, teachers or sympathizes and not know it!

In "Quantum Spirituality: A Post Modern Apologetic," Leonard Sweet writes,

"The church is fundamentally one being, one person, a comm-union whose cells are connected to one another within the information network called the Christ-consciousness." [81]

Sweet thanks New Agers **Mathew Fox, M. Scot Peck, Ken Wilber** (take a look at *that* guy's website!), and **Willis Harman**. – Yet Warren *still* endorses Sweet's books!

CASUALTIES OF WAR

Across the country and around the world, countless so-called Christian "pillars" are falling for the contemplative "We Are One" seduction.

In "Cure for the Common Life," **Max Lucado** claims,
"We all have a Divine spark."
(Lucado's endorsement is on the back of Warren's "Purpose Driven Life!")

In "Speaking My Mind," **Tony Campolo** declares,

"A theology of mysticism provides some hope for common ground between Christianity and Islam. Both religions have within their histories examples of ecstatic union with God. ... Could they (the Sufis) have encountered the same God we do in our Christian mysticism?"

And,

"[W]e are to work with Christ to ... bring about global peace." [82]

NOTE: A mystic, contemplative, New Age bridge between Christianity and Islam; so that Christ-consciousness can bring about global peace is the only possible interpretation of Campolo's statements!

Calvary Chapel pastor **Chuck Smith Jr.**, offers this,

"More and more Protestant churches – and we are way behind the Roman Catholics on this score – are discovering a new, yet old way of reading the Bible: Lectio Divina." [83]

("Lectio Divina," [sacred reading] is yet another Contemplative mantra technique, which calls for the repetitious reading of a page or passage of scripture until it is reduced to a single word or phrase.)

MORE BAD NEWS

Chuck Colson (Prison Ministry Fellowship) has teamed up with Rick Warren, and is now endorsing Henry Nouwen!

Not long ago, the "**Salvation Army**," and "**Assemblies of God**" introduced Contemplative prayer techniques to their churches, and many more protestant denominations are opening their doors to mystic-New-Age-peddlers such as Catholic monks, Thomas Keating, and Wayne Teasdale!

In 2006, the **Thomas Nelson Publishing Company** (thought by many to be a bastion of the Christian faith) published the book by Susan Bordenkircher entitled, "Yoga for Christians: A Christ-Centered Approach to Physical and Spiritual Healing Through Yoga."

Marilyn Ferguson claims that 31 percent of New Agers she interviewed said it was "**Christian mysticism**" that got them involved! [84]

GOOD NEWS! The Calvary Chapel organization (founded by Chuck Smith Sr.), declared recently that it has rejected the "**Emerging Church**" and other Contemplative movements, and has ceased all support and use of Purpose Driven materials! – **PRAISE THE LORD!**

EPILOGUE (or return from "Narnia")

As already stated, placing C. S. Lewis and Rick Warren in the same chapter was no accident. Warren quotes Lewis at least six times in the Purpose Driven Life (more than anyone else), which means Pastor Rick is no stranger to Lewis's "enchanted land!"

Like Lewis, Warren writes some good stuff; including this passage tucked away on page 172 of the PDL. ...

"Let me be absolutely clear: You will never become God, or even *a* god. That prideful lie is Satan's oldest temptation. Satan promised Adam and Eve that if they followed his advice, '*ye shall be as gods*'. Many religions and New Age philosophies still promote this old lie that we are divine or can become gods."

How can a man who writes *that* on one page, promote "breath-prayers" on another? Also, how can Warren *still* be associated with the likes of Ken Blanchard, Leonard Sweet, Henry Nouwen, Robert Schuller (H. *or* A!), Dan Southerland and the rest?

Such confusion can only lead to more trouble!

THE WARDROBE IS STILL WIDE OPEN!

If present trends continue, the New Age "Contemplative–Interspiritual–Oneness movement" could easily become the largest "*mixed multitude*" ever assembled on earth!

By allowing such influences to enter and work within the heart of the Purpose Driven community, Rick Warren is clearly adding *his* multitudes to that number, and preparing the way for even greater deceptions to come!

He may not have sold as many books as J. K. Rowling, but no one is doing a better job of selling New Age compromises to the Church than "Dream Pastor Rick!"

One thing is inevitable: before the "Dream" is over, and the "Wardrobe" is finally closed, more and more purpose driven people will continue to be deceived and hurt at increasingly deeper levels!

There is no knowing what the final results will be.

Warren Smith put it this way,

"We may all 'dream' of peace, but a peace built upon the unbiblical dream theology of Robert Schuller is definitely *not* God's solution for a troubled world. Massive good works will never bring any real glory or honor to the Lord if He and His teachings are compromised in the process. ...The church must not give in to the teachings of a "New Spirituality" that promises world peace but may ultimately cost you your soul." [85]

Post Script

Many caring believers have already exposed some of the deceptions outlined here. They have called upon Rick Warren and leaders of Purpose Driven churches to repent, renounce their errors, and forsake the movement; but so far those warnings have had no tangible effect. I am simply adding my voice to theirs.

My special thanks, and deepest appreciation to Mountain Stream Press, and brother Warren Smith for information contained in his book, "Deceived On Purpose;" and to Brian Flynn for his work in, "Running Against the Wind."

Above all, to David and Deborah Dumbrowsky at Lighthouse Trails Publishing, who not only published Brian's book, but amongst other things, set up one of the bravest anti-Purpose-Driven websites in Christendom!

THE LAST "STRAW"

Not long after completing this chapter, I learned that Pastor Rick Warren had become a member of the **Council on Foreign Relations**. With that in mind, we would do well to take a brief look at the CFR: especially with regard to *its* ultimate "Purpose!"

WORLD GOVERNMENT

In his book, "The Creature from Jekyll Island," E. Edward Griffin gives us the following details.

"**The Fabians** (*remember G.B.Shaw?*) were an elite group of intellectuals who formed a semi-secret society for **the purpose of bringing socialism to the world** ... the word socialism was not to be used. Instead, they would speak of benefits to the people such as welfare, medical care, higher wages, and better working conditions. In this way they planned to accomplish their objective without bloodshed and even without serious opposition. They scorned the Communists, not because they disliked their goals, but because they disagreed with their methods. To emphasize the importance of gradualism, they adopted the turtle as the symbol of their movement. ... their crest portrayed a wolf in sheep's clothing." (Pp.87,105-6)

And then ...

"The brain trust for implementing the **Fabian plan** in America is called the **Council on Foreign Relations** (CFR). ... it is important to know that almost all of America's leadership has come from this small group. That includes our presidents and their advisers, cabinet members, ambassadors, board members of the Federal Reserve System, directors of the largest banks and investment houses, presidents of universities, and heads of metropolitan newspapers, news services, and TV networks. It is not an exaggeration to describe this group as the hidden government of the United States. CFR members have never been shy about calling for **the weakening of America as a necessary step toward the greater good of building world government**." (P.110) (Emphases added)

In short, CFR members and other leaders of *this* country are determined to weaken the United States (economically, militarily, politically, and of course, religiously) until she is ready and willing to give up her independence/national sovereignty, and become a part of their long awaited, "New World Order."

...Way-to-go Rick!

CHAPTER TWENTY-THREE

HOW FREE IS A "CHRISTIAN" FREEMASON?

The large sign outside our Fellowship building read as follows:

"SATAN IS THE GOD OF FREEMASONRY, SO WHY WOULD ANYBODY WANT TO BE A FREEMASON?"

This was no frivolous or unfounded statement, but one based on the words of Albert Pike (1809 -1891); the once "Supreme Pontiff of Universal Freemasonry."

Pike admitted,

"The Masonic religion should be, by all of us initiates of the higher degrees, maintained in the purity of the Luciferian doctrine ... **Yes, Lucifer is God**, and unfortunately Adonay (Jesus) is also God. For the eternal law is that there is no light without shade, no beauty without ugliness, no white without black, for the absolute can only exist as two Gods: darkness being necessary to light to serve as its foil as the pedestal is necessary to the statue, and the brake to the locomotive ... The doctrine of Satanism is a heresy; and the true and pure philosophic religion is the belief in Lucifer, the equal of Adonay (Jesus); but Lucifer, God of Light and God of Good, is struggling for humanity against Adonay, the God of darkness and evil." [1] (Emphasis added)

Needless to say, the sign made a lot of Freemasons very angry; including some who call themselves Christians! One mason wrote the following letter to a local newspaper, which I thought might be of interest.

"... Not being an expert on astrophysics, nuclear energy and many other disciplines, I do not expound on their merits, unlike the **expert academic** who runs a church in Lindale. But as a past master of Masons in Florida, I am well versed in the Masonic fraternity and its contributions to the world. George Washington, most of his generals, one third of the Continental Congress, and 13 other presidents were Masons. Other Masons included Gen. Douglas MacArthur, Frederick the Great, Winston Churchill, Roy Rodgers and Red Skelton. If the reverend who authored the signs questioning Freemasonry would like to address our local lodge at his convenience, we would love to hear from him. **We do support 18 children's hospitals without cost to anyone, and many other charities. If I am going to hell with my brothers, you can be assured that I will be in good company.**" [2] (Emphasis added)

How a sign exposing Freemasonry could possibly qualify me as an "expert academic in astrophysics, nuclear energy and many other disciplines" is completely beyond me! But then again, some of the things people say when under conviction of the Holy Spirit have probably surprised you too! That writer's only hope of avoiding hell (like so many) is to propound the good but spiritually "dead works" of self-righteous human achievement! Whoever coined the phrase,

"The way to hell is paved with good intentions," spoke the truth!

Incidentally, I never did receive an official invitation to speak at the gentleman's lodge (all attempts to contact him proved fruitless), but I live in hope!

Because of reactions to the Freemason message, an open meeting was arranged to invite questions or comments from any interested party. In spite of the initial uproar, only one relatively new Freemason (a one year member, and professing Christian) attended. Naturally, and with all sincerity, he wanted to know what, if anything was wrong with Freemasonry.

The rest of this chapter provides an in depth account of that meeting; with a prayer that the Holy Spirit would open the door to all those who knock, and are willing to explore the truth behind the "Ancient and Accepted Order of Freemasons."

"Secrecy is indispensable in a Mason of whatever degree." [3]
(Albert Pike)

The first and most vital piece of information needed to solve the Freemasonry puzzle would be this. Any *spiritual* wisdom or knowledge sought, but not revealed by the Holy Spirit (through the Word of God, see *Deut.29:29*) is counterfeit, forbidden, (*Gen.2:17*) and automatically deceptive.

Secondly: Any organization or group claiming secret revelations (mysteries which only an inner circle or privileged elite could possibly know or understand) is occult! And will therefore always degenerate from a human to a demonically controlled movement!

Thirdly: all such movements and societies are bound together (directly or indirectly; knowingly or unknowingly) as though in one giant, worldly cauldron: heated, stirred, and watched over constantly by the "*father of lies*" – Satan himself! (*John 8:44*)

This is why the New Age movement trumpets the phrase, **"Unity in Diversity,"** and includes within its ranks every false religious manifestation from Babylon to Blavatsky; Pharaoh to Freemasonry; Astrology to the anti-Christ!

"... If therefore the light that is in thee be darkness, how great is that darkness!"
(Jesus, *Matt.6:23b*)

Freemasonry teaches that *all* non-masons (including Christians) exist in **spiritual darkness**, and part of any lodge initiation is for the candidate to be brought out of this darkness and into the light of Masonic truth! [4]

Wait a minute! How could any *true* Christian swallow such a lie?

Does he not realize that this is a gigantic and blasphemous insult to the only true Light of the world, the Lord Jesus Christ?

Jesus said, "*I Am the Light of the world: he that followeth Me shall not walk in darkness, but shall have the light of life."* (*John 8:12*)

Any spiritual light apart from Christ is a demonic counterfeit provided of course by the "*angel of light*" (a.k.a. the "*prince of darkness*"), and should instantly be considered "*anathema*" (a curse) to all discerning believers!

If that were not enough, consider the following:

a) Freemasonry is for **men only** – Christ died for all! (*2Cor.5:14-15*)

b) It is for **reputable men** – Christ died to receive and save sinners! (*1Tim.1:15*)

c) It is for the **whole and healthy** – Christ came for the sick and maimed! (*Luke 7:21-23*)

d) **All gods** (religions) **are accepted and given equal status**, but in the end, only the "Great or Grand Architect," the god of Freemasonry is to be worshipped.

e) "Freemasonry is not *a* religion, it *is* religion – a worship in which **men of *all* religions may unite.**"

   (J.F. Newton)

f) To become an "Entered Apprentice" (known as the First Degree) **the initiate must take a blood-curdling oath of secrecy, which if taken seriously is an illegal murder pact!** If not, it is an extreme fantasy, supported by deluded men who have little or no idea of what they are getting involved in! [5]

Here is a summary of the oath as I first discovered it in England circa 1982.

"I, _____ most solemnly and sincerely promise and swear, that if the least trace of any letter, character or figure may become legible or intelligible to anyone in the world, or any secret of Freemasonry should become known through my unworthiness, I accept no lesser penalty than that of having my throat cut across, my tongue torn out from its roots, and my body buried in the sand at low-water mark, or by the less hurried, but no less effective punishment of being branded as one void of all moral worth and totally unfit to be received into this Worshipful Lodge." [6]

(That oath has varied little over time: here in the U.S. it is virtually identical.)

You saw just how much of God's Word has to be disregarded in order to go from letters **a)** through **c)**? Now look at **d)** through **f)**

"*All* gods are accepted" rejects the first commandment! (*Ex.20:3*)

"Men of *all* religions may unite." Ecumenical unity in the face of *John 14:6, and 1Cor.6:14.*

"Swearing oaths of secrecy" totally defies the Words of Jesus ..."*In secret have I said nothing.*" (*John 20:18*) And, "*Swear not at all ... let your communication be, yea, yea; nay, nay: for whatsoever is more than these cometh of evil.*" (*Matt.5:34-37*)

SO WHY *WOULD* ANYBODY (especially a Christian) **WANT TO BE A FREEMASON?**

To understand why so many Christian men get involved with, and continue on in Freemasonry (some for a life time), we must read the words of Manly Palmer Hall; described by the "Scottish Rite Journal" in September 1990 as, "Masonry's Greatest Philosopher."

"Freemasonry is a fraternity *within* a fraternity ... an *outer* organization concealing an *inner* brotherhood of the elect ... it is necessary to establish the existence of these two *separate* and yet *interdependent* orders, the one *visible* and the other *invisible*. The visible society is a splendid camaraderie of 'free and accepted' men enjoined to devote themselves to ethical, educational, fraternal, patriotic, and humanitarian concerns. The invisible society is a secret and most august fraternity whose members are dedicated to the service of a mysterious *arcannum arcandrum*." (secret or mystery) [7] (Emphasis added)

Albert Pike had something else to say about those in the "visible" society.

"Masonry, like *all* the Religions, *all* the Mysteries, Hermeticism, and Alchemy, *conceals its secrets* from all except the Adepts and Sages, or the elect (the worthy) and uses *false explanations* and *misinterpretations* of its symbols *to mislead those who deserve only to be misled; to conceal the truth*, which it calls light, and draw them away from it. *Truth is not for those who are unworthy.*" [8] (Emphasis added)

Once more – "**False explanations and misinterpretations ... to mislead those who deserve only to be misled.**"

That's the contempt Albert Pike and other top masons have for their lesser, unenlightened "brethren!" The vast majority of these outer (visible), and lower degree Freemasons have no idea that an "invisible inner core of elect brothers" exists; or that they are ruled over and guided by them towards Freemasonry's ultimate purpose.

Clearly then, it is the "ethical, educational, fraternal, patriotic and humanitarian" aspects of Freemasonry that attract well-meaning Christians.

For example; the Christian brother who came to our meeting, wanted to become a member of the "Shriners" (an offshoot of Freemasonry), simply to help children; but he could not become a Shriner without first joining the Freemasons! (The Shriner organization is well known for its support of hospitals dedicated to the treatment of young people; often without charge.)

With love and respect, he was asked, "But why would you need to join an occult society in order to help children?" He told us how much more effective he thought he could be in a movement already equipped to do such good things; and so far, as a Christian, he hadn't found any spiritual conflict with Freemasonry. He told us that in *his* lodge, he was actually allowed to pray in the Name of Jesus (extremely rare), and that if he ever *did* find conflict; he would certainly leave the lodge, and the movement with all speed!

FIG LEAVES AND FILTHY RAGS

For many drawn to Freemasonry, the desire (or temptation) to be identified as honorable men of "good works" is incredibly strong. The often unrecognized sense of "feel-good pride" and "self-righteousness" that goes along with such a desire however, is far more subtle and difficult to discern! (See *Is.64:6* and look again at that mason's letter.) Apart from attacking me; the whole letter was a **how great we are** chant, for and on behalf of Freemasons! Christians should have no place or part in that!

No single definition of Freemasonry is available, which means that like its mother, "*Mystery Babylon*," it offers something for everyone.

In his Encyclopedia of Freemasonry, Albert G. Mackey offers the Grand deception, and speaks to each and every Mason without fear of contradiction:

"**All unite in declaring it to be a system of morality, by the practice of which its members may advance their spiritual interest, and mount by the theological ladder from the Lodge on earth to the Lodge in heaven.**" [9]

Mackey describes Freemasonry as,

"**... That religious and mystical society whose aim is moral perfection on the basis of general equality and fraternity.**" [10]

Chief Masonic "blind guides," Joseph F. Newton and Henry W. Coil are also willing to reveal a secret or two:

"Masonry is the realization of God by the practice of Brotherhood." [11]

"Freemasonry … is a system of morality, and social ethics; a primitive religion and a philosophy of life … incorporating a broad humanitarianism … it is a religion without creed, being of no sect but finding truth in all. … **It seeks truth but does not define truth.**" [12]

If you are a Christian Freemason and happen to be reading this, doesn't a certain Scripture come to mind? Surely these men are,
"Ever learning, and never able to come to the knowledge of the truth!" (2Tim.3:7)
Ironically, it is possible for non-masons to discover far more about the inner workings (secrets or mysteries) of Freemasonry than masons themselves! We now know the reason for this: lifelong secrets (kept even from wives) which prevent them from discovering the truth until (like Scientology) they are so bound to the deception that **they will believe almost anything to be where they *think* they are!**

No one seriously expects a practicing Freemason to agree with anything an outsider (like myself) has written so far, but as a result of gathering information from a variety of Masons, the following scenario should be all the warning a Christian needs.

A blindfolded Muslim male (for example) kneels during his initiation: he must believe in, and acknowledge (confess to) the existence of a "Supreme Being." (No one can become a Freemason without this belief.) In the Muslim's case, the supreme being and god he confesses is *Allah*. The Hindu has the choice of countless gods: the Christian has the true God, but remember, Freemasonry neither cares nor makes a distinction between any of them!

As the Muslim completes his vows of initiation, he is welcomed into the Masonic fraternity and declared a **life-long brother!**

According to Freemasonry, this **bond of brotherhood** between men of all faiths within the Order is stronger than – and superior to – any without! In other words; a Christian Freemason is duty bound to help or place his Muslim brother above a non-Masonic Christian!

According to the Bible, such intimate fellowship between Christians and unbelievers (anyone outside the Body of Christ) is absolutely forbidden!
"Be ye not unequally yoked together with unbelievers: for what fellowship hath righteousness with unrighteousness? and what communion hath light with darkness? And what concord (unity or agreement) *hath Christ with Belial? or what part hath he that believeth with an infidel?"*(Non-Christian) (2Cor.6:14-15)

"ALL HOPE ABANDON YE WHO ENTER HERE"
(Inscription at the entrance to hell, from "Dante's Divine Comedy.")

How could any Christian possibly accept and hold to such a brotherhood? Simple!
With its subtle ploy of not offending those from different faiths, Freemasonry seeks to gradually convince the Christian Church that the universal (New Age) fatherhood of God, and the universal brotherhood of man has made all men (Hindus, Buddhists, Taoists, Mormons, Muslims, Jews, Christians, etc.,) equal and accepted in the sight of God! … Bottom line?

For Freemasonry to succeed, all other faiths must eventually be abandoned!
Once again, and especially to all "visible" Freemasons: the only god this ancient and deadly cult recognizes is the "Grand" or "Great Architect:" better known as the *"god of this world"* (2Cor.4:3-4)
Manly P. Hall gives us more from this perspective:

"When a Mason learns the key to the warrior on the block is the proper application of the dynamo of living power, he has learned the mystery of his Craft. **The seething energies of Lucifer are in his hands,** and before he may step onward and upward, he must prove his ability to properly apply energy." (13)

(Emphasis added)

This demonic message is both loud and clear! ...
"The true disciple of ancient Freemasonry has given up forever the worship of personalities ... As a mason his religion must be universal: Christ, Buddha or Mohammed, **the names mean little,** for **he recognizes only the light and not the bearer** (the personality). **HE WORSHIPS AT *EVERY* SHRINE, BOWS BEFORE *EVERY* ALTAR,** whether in temple, mosque or cathedral, realizing with his truer understanding **the oneness of all spiritual truth. ... No true Mason can be narrow, for his lodge is the divine expression of all broadness. There is no place for little minds in a great work."** (14)

(Emphasis added)

Albert Pike spells out this "great work" and proclaims Freemasonry's ultimate goal.
"The world will soon come to us for its Sovereigns and Pontiffs, we shall constitute the equilibrium of the universe, and be rulers over the masters of the world." (15)

(Freemasonry will just have to get in line: Satan has so many other anxious "customers" who can't wait to rule the world!)

THE BIG PICTURE

In all seriousness, the accuracy of Pike's statement cannot be denied. Since 1723, England's Royal families have been riddled with Freemasonry.

Frederick, Prince of Wales, Dukes of Montague, Kent and Sussex: George 3rd (first Grand Master of English Freemasonry) and his six sons. More recently, George 6th followed by his son in law the Duke of Edinburgh. (1952, Navy Lodge No.2612)

Queen Elizabeth (the Duke's wife) is Grand Patroness of Freemasonry, but is forbidden to enter a Masonic Lodge! Her cousin, the Duke of Kent became Grand Master of English Freemasonry in 1967. (Its 250th anniversary) So far, Prince Charles (the Duke of Edinburgh's son) has resisted membership (he does not want to join *any* secret society)! Albeit, the Prince has been extremely busy with other New Age activities (saving this or that), not to mention partaking in séances to reach his dead uncle, Lord Mountbatten! Of course, if Charles ever becomes King, Masonic pressure to "sign him up" will be enormous!

There is a terrible price to pay for any Masonic involvement, let alone a Royal one that goes back to 1723!

Even though today's English Royals have no real outward or visible political power, their Masonic connections more than compensate by giving them powerful international friends, allies, and hidden worldwide influence.

We may never know (in this life) the full extent of Masonry's "*curse* and effect," but one thing is certain:
"Sovereigns have certainly come to Freemasonry."

In the world's most powerful country, Pike's words have become far more ominous!
It's been said that only two of America's forty-three Presidents have totally resisted Masonic bondage (that is, full or affiliated membership): they are Abraham Lincoln and John F. Kennedy. Some fifteen,

312

including Ronald Reagan and Gerald Ford, have been outright Freemasons. Notables include George Washington, Andrew Jackson, Theodore Roosevelt, Franklin D. Roosevelt, and Harry Truman.

In 1987, Masonic Senators, Strom Thurmond and Alan Simpson openly declared that Masons constituted – Forty-one members of the Federal Judiciary.
Half the membership of the Senate Judiciary Committee.
Eighteen Senators, including Bob Dole and Robert Byrd (both 33rd degree), Jesse Helms and John Glenn.
Seventy-six members of the House of Representatives. [16]

NOTE: As of 1990, U.S. Masons numbered four million, while their membership stood at only six million worldwide! [17]

A glance through directories of famous or celebrity Masons (several available on line) will reveal anyone from John Wayne and Clark Gable, to Henry Ford and Winston Churchill. Incidentally, that same list, proudly entitled, "Men of Character and Integrity Join the Freemasons," [18] included the names of **29 Supreme Court Judges** and **14 Baptist Ministers!** [18]

The names of some *infamous* Masonic "Men of Character and Integrity" (not included in any masonic list I could find) read like the "royal family" of witchcraft and satanism!

Aleister Crowley (33rd degree) Leading Satanist, self-proclaimed "Beast" and "wickedest man alive!"

George Pickingill (Grand Master) Warlock of 19th century England, and leader of the Pickingill Covens!

Dr. Wynn Westcott (Master Mason) of the "*Societas Rosicruciana in Anglia*" and founding member of the occult "Hermetic Order of the Golden Dawn," the most powerful magic society of the 19th and 20th centuries.

Dr. (Albert K.)Theodore Reuss (33rd degree) Crowley's predecessor who established a "Masonic Academy" known later as the Ordo Templi Orientis. (OTO)

Annie Besant (see p.194) Leader of the occult Theosophical society and **Co-Masonic** hierarch.

Alice Bailey (see p.194) Founder of the New Age organization, "**Lucis** (formerly Lucifer) **Trust.**" [19]

(Female relatives are permitted within Co-Masonic Orders such as "Eastern Star," "Rainbow," and "Job's Daughters.")

I've mentioned just a few of these "Christ-haters" in order to ask all "Christian-Masons" this question:
Why belong to an organization, which welcomes people such as these from *any* false religious affiliation on earth, and then teaches you to call them "BRETHREN?"

****

Oaths of secrecy (or any other kind) **violate** the Word of God. Anything more than "**Yes**" or "**No**" comes from evil, or the evil one, i.e. **SATAN**.

"Swear not at all." (*Matt.5:34-37*)
Fellowship with unbelievers is absolutely forbidden! *"Come out from among them."*
(*2Cor.6:14-18*)

"Don't even talk about the things done by them in secret; **rather REPROVE** (expose) *THEM!"*
(*Eph.5:11-12*)

****

The four million or so Masons in America make up a meager 1.4% (approx.) of the overall population; yet their nation-wide influence is huge and obviously out of all proportion to that number! The *natural* explanation would be that since the country's founding, many Masons have sought for, and occupied strategic positions of power and authority; predominantly in government, politics and commerce.

The darker, and more sinister reality however, is that the hidden spiritual *"principalities and powers"* ruling over Freemasonry were (and still are) promoting, guiding, watching and waiting!

New Age leader and occult high priestess **Alice Bailey** was intimately acquainted with the "Ascended Tibetan Master," Djwhal Khul: his utterances formed the bulk of Bailey's written works. Under dictation from this demonic spirit guide she wrote the following.

"The Masonic Fraternity ... is ... the home of the Mysteries, and the seat of the initiation ...

It is a far more occult organization than can be realized and is intended to be the training school for the coming advanced occultists ..."

Bailey/Khul goes on to say,

"... Mysteries will be restored to outer expression through the medium of the Church and the Masonic Fraternity ... When the Great One (anti-Christ) comes with His disciples and initiates, we shall have the restoration of the Mysteries ..." [20] (Parenthesis added)

Freemasonry teaches that *all* faiths and *all* religious writings lead to the same God.

In Masonic Lodges, vague prayers to the Great or Grand Architect of the Universe (GAOTU) are part of the rituals.

This quote is taken from the Masonic Belief Statement.

"... (B)y the very honor which Masonry pays to the Bible, it teaches us to revere every book of faith by which men find help for today and hope for the morrow, joining hands with the man of Islam as he takes oath on the Koran, and with the Hindu as he makes covenant with God upon the book that he loves best."

NOTE: A ludicrous, yet well-known reality is that the United Nations General Assembly routinely begins its deliberations with prayers. Those U.N. prayers, which could so easily be heard in any Masonic lodge around the world, begin with, **"TO WHOM IT MAY CONCERN ..."**

(The New Age Movement likes to cover *all* its bases!)

In the seven volume "History of Freemasonry," Albert Mackey describes various heathen gods and the people who worshiped them. Among the pagan deities revealed are **Ashtaroth, Abraxas, Vishnu, Dagon, Nergal** and **Baal**. The text states:

"They were all Characters of human origin in the Mythologic ages designed as the **Saviors of Men**, each one emphatically the representative Christos, or Christ of his particular Nation; and the religious system designed to restore the lost and fallen race of Man."

In the same paragraph, Mackey shamelessly identifies the men who worship these gods.

"Now as Masons we decide not between these, but take all in as our Brethren, and the One God as our Heavenly Father, revealed to us as such in the Great Light of Masonry." [21] (All emphasis added)

WHY IS IT, that in spite of the massive amounts of information (readily available), which exposes the utterly deceptive and satanic nature of Freemasonry; sensible, well-educated men (especially Christians) chose to remain loyal Freemasons?

Supreme Pontiff, Albert Pike gives us the best explanation of all.

"The Blue Degrees are but the outer court or portico of the Temple. Part of the symbols are displayed there to the initiate, but <u>he is intentionally misled by false interpretations</u>. It is not intended that he shall understand them, but it is intended that he shall imagine he understands them. Their true explanation is reserved for the Adepts, the Princes of Masonry ...It is well enough for the mass of those called Masons, to imagine that all is contained in the blue degrees; and <u>whoso attempts to undeceive them will labor in vain</u> ... Masonry is the veritable Sphinx, buried to the head in the sands heaped round it by the ages." [22] (Emphasis added)

(If Alice Bailey wrote by demonic means, how much more do leading Freemasons?)

With all the pride and contempt of Satan himself, Pike discards the possibility of having even one of the lowly "masses" of Freemasonry plucked from its serpentine grip!

Imagine (and rejoice in) Lucifer's pain and impotent fury when the Lord Jesus Christ, moved as always by compassion and grace, stands Sovereignly before Masonic "tombs" around the world, and thunders,

"FREEMASON: COME FORTH!"

Here for God's glory, and to close this chapter, are the testimonies of two English Freemasons who did precisely that!

"The extraordinary popularity of Freemasonry and it's imitators here in America – whose love of Secret Societies exceeds that of any other country except China – can be attributed to the fact that Americans are extremely friendly, outgoing and will join anything! I think partly out of a subconscious desire to escape the matriarchal influence, so much stronger here than in my homeland, and partly perhaps to the absence of the glamour of pageantry of royalty and hereditary titles, and your less colorful and historic ceremonial in connection with government, nation and municipal occasions ...

In dealing with the complex subject of Freemasonry, I feel we should examine the background of the organization. I remember well, as a young boy, cycling in my home county of Yorkshire in England. I used to make trips over to the other side of Leeds, still in Yorkshire, to a place called Temple Newsom; perhaps the name or place is unfamiliar to you, but this is 'Bronte' country.

Temple Newsom was on a hill, hidden in the woods, just the place for us boys to play Robin Hood and the Knights of the Crusades. I remember as if it was yesterday, climbing in among the graves of the Knights, trying to decipher the names and seeing strange markings on each and every tombstone. The Knights, if you know English and Middle Ages history, came to England and Scotland, having been banished from the continent, Spain in particular, and settled in Britain in the 14th century.

It was not until 20 years later; at my initiation as an Entered Apprentice, in a Masonic Lodge, near Downpatrick, in Northern Ireland, that I was taken aback to see displayed on top of the open Bible, on the altar, the symbols I had seen on those gravestones in England. But, here they were displayed as instruments of Freemasonry. They were the legs of a man overlapping the woman in the sexual position of the Square and Compass! I can tell you, I was shattered!

It was not this revelation alone that jolted me, because I KNEW, within the first ten minutes into the first degree, that I had broken most of God's commandments! I made no pretense in those days of being a Christian. However with my Church of England background, I knew enough of the Bible to know that the blood oaths I was required to swear, in fact any oaths are against God's Holy Law. Just making an oath, not knowing what it is about, is against any national constitution; and we had the Magna Carta!

I leave you with this. Even after I had returned to the faith of my youth and had come out from among the darkness of Eastern Mysticism; and left behind the Quran and its teachings of Mohammed; and the Bhagavad of Hinduism; I was still in a spiritual battle for my life. My standard was now the Holy Bible and Jesus Christ. I knew that there was no other way to God, but there was no fullness to my walk. I read one day where Jesus said: '*You call me Jesus, your Savior, your Lord - yet you practice things I have not taught you. Depart from Me, I never knew you, you workers of evil*' (*Matthew 7: 21 - 23*). I had not found that yearned for one-on-one walk with Jesus even though I had asked for advice from almost everyone I knew. I had no answers. I finally got down on my knees and asked Jesus what was wrong. One word came back to me, as though shouted from heaven, '**Masonry!**' I knew I was still in trouble with the real God. As if I needed confirmation, a letter came from our daughter in London. In it, she said, '**You have to get out of Masonry, Daddy! You know it is evil and you'll never walk with God until you do.**' That was the day I burned all my Masonic regalia. Everything was burnt to ashes before me. After all my wanderings and searching, I was finally able to separate myself from the spirits of darkness, to ask God's forgiveness and repent before Him of the evil in which I had been a participant. And He heard my cry, for I felt the weight of all that evil lift off me, and for the first time in my life, I knew I was FREE ...

For any Mason, who calls himself a Christian, to lie about the Compatibility of Freemasonry and Jesus Christ, is paving the road to Hell, unless he repents. **I KNEW** as a non-Christian that what I was doing was evil. Those Masons who use the name of Christ to defend Freemasonry are committing blasphemy, in my opinion. I suppose it depends on what sort of a Christian you are!" [23] (Emphasis added)

A Final word and a Fond Memory

Some time after writing a tract on Freemasonry in the early eighties, I received a letter from a man whom I had never met: (nor have I to this day) but his words assured me that we would one day meet in Heaven!

Dear brother in Christ,

Having read your tract, "Freemasonry: the Truth Behind it," and its challenge to all Freemasons, I decided to explore and try to discover the truth behind it for myself. As a result, I have renounced my Masonic oaths, and have destroyed all my paraphernalia!

After delving into the Craft, I was appalled to learn that Masons were actually being led to entertain, revere, and finally worship the Light-Bearer-Lucifer. None other than Satan himself!

I discovered that this was in fact, the so-called "great light" or secret of Freemasonry. Nothing less than "Witch-Craft!" Regrettably, the only Christian presence in the Lodge is found in those deluded brothers still trapped inside! Praise God, as an ex-Freemason turned Christian, I can now declare the glorious truth: if the Son therefore shall make you free, ye shall be free indeed!

(John 8:36)

The Holy Spirit, speaking through the Apostle John, said,

"I have no greater joy than to hear that my children walk in the truth." (*3 John 4*)

May this Scripture be fulfilled for you, in Jesus' Name.

CHAPTER TWENTY-FOUR

SO WHO *REALLY* FOUNDED AMERICA?

Because of renewed Christian interest, and to confirm just how strong and pervasive the Masonic -Deistic-Theistic influence has been throughout American history, this chapter explores the growing conflict over the nation's Christian, or non-Christian foundations.

In view of the country's consistent moral decline, a growing number of frustrated and disillusioned Christians (encouraged by leaders of movements such as Reconstructionism), began rallying to the cry of, **"Let's Reclaim America for Christ!"**

Reclaim means to "retrieve," "recover," or "take back;" and of course the phrase implies that America once belonged to Christ; was lost to Him, and somehow has to be regained! (Strange in light of *Ps. 24:1*)

Immediately I think of the great perennial call to, **"Put Christ back in Christmas!"**

No one doubts the sincerity of those making that redundant statement year after year (after year!), but somewhere along the way, the truth has to be faced:

Christmas is a deception, and Christ was never there to begin with!

If God wanted us to celebrate the birth of His Son on a particular day, He would surely have given us the **TRUE DATE!**

Back in chapter 11, the question was, "If the world hates Christ, (*John15:18*) why does the world love Christmas?" The answer is simply this. –

Christmas has nothing to do with Christ (or the truth), therefore it in no way offends the unsaved!

Let me put it another way: if Christmas *was* true, and Christians celebrated it *"in spirit and in truth,"* – **the world wouldn't touch it!**

Obedience to God's Word is the real issue here: without obedience we might as well play the religious game, and make it up as we go along!

Jesus said, *"If you love Me, keep My commandments."* (See *John 14:15,and 15:14*)

Question: Did Jesus ever command us to celebrate His birth? **NO!**

He told us to remember His death! (*Luke 22:19, 1Cor.11:25-26*)

God is a Spirit – Jesus is The Truth – Christmas is a lie: so Christians cannot possibly celebrate it in *"Spirit and in truth."* (*John 4:24*)

Nevertheless they still try!

NOTE: The worst-case scenario regarding Christmas is that millions of unbelievers consider themselves Christians because they celebrate it too! After all; if Christians do it, it *must* be right!

Christmas (Christ's Mass) is, and always will be,

FALSE SENTIMENTAL ATTACHMENT TO A "FEEL GOOD," CHRISTIANIZED PAGAN FESTIVAL; VERSES THE WORD AND WILL OF GOD!

Now with the Christmas lie in mind, let's see if we can "Reclaim America for Christ!"

First: A strong command from the Word of God to *every* believer …
"And whatsoever ye do in word or deed, DO ALL IN THE NAME OF THE LORD JESUS, giving thanks to God and the Father BY HIM." (Col.3:17)

If Bible believing Christians had written the two most important documents in the history of this nation ("The Declaration of Independence," and "The Constitution of the United States"), surely the Name of the Father and the Son would *have* to appear in at least one of them! Right? Alas …
They are found nowhere in either!
Consider this short rewrite of the Constitution –
Giving thanks to God in the Name of our Lord Jesus Christ, God the Son and only Savior of mankind; we His People of the United States, in Order to form a more perfect Union, establish justice, insure domestic Tranquility, …etc., etc.

If such an opening statement *had* been made, who could possibly deny America's Christian heritage? Why then was God the Father, *and* His Son Jesus, the *"Name above all names"* so blatantly excluded by our "Christian" founding fathers?

Let's go back to a tale of two beginnings.
Although Sir Walter Raleigh had twice failed to colonize American land, he was actually responsible for naming part of it Virginia. (In honor of England's so-called "virgin queen" Elizabeth)
In 1606, a group of English businessmen (the London based Virginia Company) was granted a charter from Elizabeth's successor, king James 1st for colonial settlement in the new world.
On May 14th, 1607, the first settlers arrived at Jamestown (named in honor of King James), and began forming what was undeniably the first permanent American Colony in Virginia.
One account of their arrival, reads as follows:
"Among the first settlers to begin the Jamestown settlement in 1607 was the Reverend Robert Hunt. As the first colonists landed on Virginia soil, one of their first acts was to join Rev. Hunt in a communion service; yet the lives of these earliest colonists lacked a strong Christian commitment. Their squabbling, pride, arrogance, and greediness almost wrecked the settlement. The earliest colonists had no room for God in their personal lives and certainly had no concern for evangelizing the Indians. Disease, famine, and later, Indians, began to take their toll. In the earliest years of the settlement, nine out of every ten colonists died. As more colonists arrived from England, the problems multiplied, and the death count mounted." [1]
The settlement *did* survive however; helped much by the growing and selling of tobacco, which became Virginia's most lucrative crop! On July 30th, 1619, the the first legislature of elected representatives in America, known as the House of Burgesses met in the Jamestown Church.

Their first law was to set a minimum price for the sale of tobacco!

(Initially, King James opposed the smoking of tobacco, but quickly saw the benefits of taxing it rather than suppressing it!)

Here are two other examples of gracious "Christian" laws introduced into the community at that time.

"No man shall blaspheme God's holy name upon pain of death, or use unlawful oaths, taking the name of God in vain, curse, or bane; upon pain of severe punishment for the first offense so committed, and for the second, to have a bodkin (a large blunt needle) thrust through his tongue; and if he continue the blaspheming of God's holy name, for the third time so offending, he shall be brought to a martial court and there receive censure of death for his offense."

And,

"Every man and woman duly, twice a day upon the first tolling of the bell, shall upon the working days repair unto the church to hear divine service upon pain of losing his or her day's allowance for the first omission; for the second to be whipped, and for the third to be condemned to the galleys for six months. ... As also every man and woman shall repair in the morning to the divine service and sermons preached upon the Sabbath day in the afternoon to divine service and catechizing, upon pain for the first fault to lose their provision and allowance for the whole week following; for the second to lose the said allowance and also to be whipped; and for the third to suffer death." [2] (Parenthesis added)

So much for the *first* founding, and so much for "Life, liberty, and the pursuit of happiness!"

The second group involved in America's modern "Christian founding" included some English religious "Separatists," better known as "Puritans;" who (depending on which version is believed) came to these shores in 1620 to –

A) Escape hostility, lack of religious freedom, and persecution from the church and government of England.
B) Escape from an *excess* of religious freedom, and create a stricter regime of their own: hence the name "Puritans!"

Which version is correct? The following may help you decide.

On November 11th, 1620, much like the earlier Jamestown settlers, another "*mixed multitude*" arrived in the "New World" on board a vessel named the Mayflower. They landed, not in Virginia as was intended, but in present-day Truro, Cape Cod, Massachusetts (the result of being blown off course). Records indicate that the Puritans, or "Pilgrims" as they became known, made up only one third of the Mayflower's passengers (35 of 102): the rest on board were anything but separate, and as such were labeled "Strangers!" [3] Now although the Puritans gained overall control of the group, their legal charter or patent with the "London Company" was invalid outside of Virginia; so before landing, they drew up another agreement, signed by forty-one men (many of whom were "strangers" as no women were included), creating a form of government based on the will of the majority. It would become known as the Mayflower Compact....

"IN THE NAME OF GOD, AMEN.

We whose names are underwritten, the loyal subjects of our dread sovereign Lord, King James, by the grace of God, of Great Britain, France and Ireland king, defender of the faith, etc., having undertaken, for the glory of God, and advancement of the Christian faith, and honor of our king and country, a voyage to plant the first colony in the Northern parts of Virginia, do by these presents solemnly and mutually in the presence of God, and one of another, covenant and combine ourselves together into a civil body politic, for our better ordering and preservation and furtherance of the ends aforesaid; and by virtue hereof to enact, constitute, and frame such just and equal laws, ordinances, acts, constitutions, and offices, from time to time, as shall be thought most meet and convenient for the general good of the colony, unto which we promise all due submission and obedience. In witness whereof we have hereunder subscribed our names at Cape-Cod, the 11 of November, in the year of the reign of our sovereign lord, King James, of England, France, and Ireland the eighteenth, and of Scotland the fifty-fourth. Anno Domine 1620."

NOTE: Many people *talk* of "God," and of being "Christian," but here once again the Name of Jesus is totally excluded! The only "sovereign lord" mentioned is king James!

In December of 1620, the Mayflower sailed into Plymouth Harbor: once ashore, the settlers established the Plymouth Bay Colony. Nine years later, they were absorbed into the more powerful Colony of Massachusetts Bay. It was not until the "Articles of Confederation of the United Colonies of New England" were drawn up on May 19th 1643, that I was able to find the first mention of the Name Jesus!

"The Articles of Confederation between the Plantations under the Government of the Massachusetts, the Plantations under the Government of New Plymouth, the Plantations under the Government of Connecticut, and the Government of New Haven with the Plantations in Combination therewith: Whereas we all came into these parts of America with one and the same end and aim, namely, to advance the Kingdom of our Lord Jesus Christ and to enjoy the liberties of the Gospel in purity with peace ..." [4]

(To claim that, "we *all* came into these parts of America with one and the same end and aim" was completely untrue; but at least the Name and Lordship of Jesus is finally acknowledged!)

Like Jamestown, church attendance in Massachusetts was compulsory, and church membership was required in order to vote or hold public office. By the 1630's, the settlers had chosen to be called Congregationalists, and the church had become the focal point of all social and political life. The Church *was* now the state!

Here we go again!
Sadly, Non-Congregationalists, such as Baptists and Quakers (the Society of Friends) were regarded with hostility: they were restricted, and even persecuted by the new colonial church government!
Does that sound like true Christianity, or religion simply repeating itself?
Perhaps the Puritans really did want a "stricter regime!" (So much for non-conformists "enjoying the liberties of the Gospel in purity and peace!")

Over the next one hundred years or so, the colonial population rose dramatically, but was still firmly under the control of the British crown. By 1760 however (the reign of George 3rd), the crown was desperately short of money! So, in keeping with many other normal, greedy, self-indulgent little kings, (see *1Sam.8:11-18*) George decided to help himself to a much larger slice of the ever growing "American pie!"
Existing taxes were increased, and new ones imposed; not to mention even greater restrictions and burdens placed upon his already disgruntled British subjects! But let it be said that none of those

burdens were as heavy as the ones the Pharaohs placed on their Hebrew subjects during four-hundred and thirty years of Egyptian captivity!

George's subjects revolted! Why didn't Pharaoh's?

For some, the answers will come as no surprise.

First: The Hebrews were *God's chosen people*, and were kept waiting by the Lord Himself for His promise of deliverance to be fulfilled! (*see Ex.3:7-10*)

Second: The Hebrew "settlers" in Egypt did not find in their leadership the mind and spirit of rebellion that the British settlers in America did! (See *Num.12:3*)

The issue briefly stated was this.

When faced with the burgeoning demands of the British monarchy, the colonialists did not continue to intercede and *"pray for the king,"* (*1Tim.2:1-3*) or *"submit to him."* (*1Pet.2:13-17*) Neither did they wait for the Lord *"to deliver them,"* (*Ps.37:7*) if that was His will. **NO!**

They appealed; they complained; they protested (Boston Tea Party); **they listed their grievances** (Declaration of Independence); **and then revolted!**

NOTE: religious people are not expected to obey or submit to the **whole Counsel of God!** – Only *true* Christians are called to do that!

But to understand just how the seeds of the revolution were sown, we must cross the Atlantic again to England, where earlier, a demonic movement of Christ-less, humanistic philosophy was sweeping through Europe; known (ridiculously enough) as the **"Age of Enlightenment."**

Briefly stated, Age of Enlightenment thinkers believed in, and relied wholly upon the power of human reason! They reasoned that through proper education, humanity could be changed for the better. Great esteem was given to the discovery of "truth" by the observation of nature rather than the study of authoritative sources such as the Bible. Man's hopes (they believed) should not be placed on the *next* life, but exclusively on the means of improving *this* one!

Worldly happiness and fulfillment was placed before all (including salvation), and nothing was attacked more ferociously than the Christian faith!

Will the *real* author of the "Constitution" please stand up!

One of the head chefs of this satanically enlightened stew was an Englishman by the name of John Locke (1632-1704), who founded the Deistic **"School of Empiricism"** (meaning, recognition of a Creator, but through reliance on observation and reason; especially in the natural sciences).

Locke taught the following lies:

1 All persons are born good. (For truth see *Ps.51:5* and *Rom.3:9-12*)
2 All men are created independent and equal. (See *Acts 17:22-28* and *Rom.9:6-16*)
3 There is no Divine right of kings. (See *Rom.13:1-7, and 1Pet.2:13-17*)
4 Sovereignty resides in the state not with God. (See *Ps.3 and Ps.62:11*)
5 The state is supreme. (See *Ps.8 and Ps.47*)
6 Revolution is not only a right, but often an obligation. (See *1Sam.15:23 and 1Pet.2:13-17*)
Locke taught that government should comprise three branches:

Legislative – Executive – Judicial
(Sound familiar?)

He also believed that the state should be bound by natural, not spiritual laws. Years later, the influence of Enlightenment thinkers (especially John Locke) would have a profound effect on two rather well-known and well-placed individuals, who wasted no time promoting this Christ-less, rebellious movement in their own right – **Benjamin Franklin and Thomas Jefferson!**

Strong confirmation of this comes from author/editor Norman Mackenzie.

"It was not in France however but in America that the ideas of the 'Enlightenment' were translated into action and **MADE THE FOUNDATION FOR A SYSTEM OF GOVERNMENT** as the Declaration of Independence and U.S. Constitution clearly show." [5] (Emphasis added)

Brief bio's of three Founding Fathers

BENJAMIN FRANKLIN (1706-1790) helped draft and then signed the "Declaration of Independence" in 1776. Founder of the "American Philosophical Society," he became a **FREEMASON** in 1731, and was soon Grand Master of Pennsylvania!

Franklin was a **DEIST**. (Someone who believes in moral good, and in a supreme being who created and ordered the universe, but now has no direct involvement in the affairs of men.) Deists speak merely of God's "**general providence**" and totally reject the special and intimate fellowship the *true* God enjoys with His own people through His Son Jesus Christ!

Franklin's Deism stands (rather falls) **by the following deceptions:**
"There is no special providence: no miracles or other divine interventions violate the lawful natural order....

Men have been endowed with a rational nature, which alone allows them to know truth and their duty when they think and choose in conformity with this nature. ...

The natural law requires the leading of a moral life; rendering to God, one's neighbor, and one's self what is due to each. ...

The purest form of worship and the chief religious obligation is to lead a moral life. ... God had endowed men with immortal souls. ...

After death retributive justice is meted out to each man according to his acts. **Those who fulfill the moral law and live according to nature are saved to enjoy rewards; others are punished.**" [6]
(Emphasis added)

On February 14th, 1778, having already obtained loans and grants from Louis XVI, Franklin negotiated the "Treaty of Commerce" and a defensive alliance with France (the turning point of the American Revolution). Seven months later, he was appointed First Minister *Plenipotentiary from the U.S. to France.

In 1783, some six years after the American Revolution; and as a dignitary of one of the most distinguished Freemason Lodges in France, Franklin had the opportunity of meeting with (and greatly influencing) numbers of New Age philosophers and leading political figures in that country. Consider for a moment, that the French Revolution – one of the greatest "blood-baths" in European history – took place just six years later!

Once again the words of John Locke:
"Revolution is not only a right, but often an obligation."

Exactly why so many religious charlatans would like to us to believe that Benjamin Franklin and friends were Christians is a question discussed towards the end of this chapter; but for now, let's move on to other "Founding Fathers."

* "A person, especially a diplomat who is invested with the full power of independent action on behalf of their government." (Oxford English Dictionary; 11th edition)

THOMAS JEFFERSON (1743-1826) was also a Deist; the apparent author of the Declaration of Independence, and a drafter of the Constitution. One of the most brilliant exponents of the "Enlightenment," Jefferson was perhaps one of John Locke's most successful students: certainly in the sense that both the Declaration, and Constitution were unmistakably created in the "image and likeness" of Locke's Deistic religious philosophy! Although there is no historic proof concerning Jefferson's *direct* ties to Freemasonry, he was (and still is) lauded by Freemasons around the world. This tribute is somewhat typical –

"Jefferson may not have been a card-carrying Mason, but his philosophy and actions certainly paralleled Masonic ideals and practices ... Freemasons such as Thomas Paine, Voltaire, Lafayette, and Jean Houdon were some of his closest associates in Europe. Masons whom he admired in America included George Washington, Benjamin Franklin, Dr. Benjamin Rush, John Paul Jones, James Madison, James Monroe, Meriwether, Lewis and William Clark. ... he had all of the prerequisites for membership in the Craft. His life could serve as a role model for all Masons; ... he fulfilled the obligations of our Fraternity." [7] It is certainly not my desire to attack or even comment on the personal life of Thomas Jefferson (much of that is readily available to the interested enquirer), but his sacrilegious pronouncements and writings should be revealed and known to any and all who might still consider this man a Christian. **"The day will come when the mystical generation of Jesus, by the Supreme Being as his father, in the womb of a virgin, will be classed with the fable of the generation of Minerva in the brain of Jupiter."** [8] And referring to John Calvin, Jefferson wrote, "His religion was demonism. If ever a man worshiped a false god, he did. The being described in his five points is ... a demon of malignant spirit. It would be more pardonable to believe in no God at all, than to blaspheme him by the atrocious, attributes of Calvin." [9]

The absolute essence of Jefferson's contempt for Christianity is found in a despicable little book he wrote called, **"The Jefferson Bible: The Life and Morals of Jesus of Nazareth."** This foul offensive work is an attempt to remove every trace of Christ's Divine birth and identity; His miraculous life and ministry; His atoning death and glorious resurrection! One need only look to the close of Revelation (a book that Jefferson utterly rejected) to realize this man's dreadful plight.

"... if any man shall take away from the words of the book of this prophecy, God shall take away his part out of the book of life, and out of the Holy City, and from the things which are written in this book." (Rev.22:19)

"Spiritually Blind" Jefferson preferred the darkness of natural sight and reason to the light of spiritual revelation. (*John 1:5 and 3:19*) He confused the truth of Christianity with man-made religious deception, and because of the corruptions he saw in both (no argument there), he went to "war." Thus he fulfilled the Scripture, and found himself, *"fighting against God." (Acts 5:39)* – and this man "founded" America!

GEORGE WASHINGTON (1732-1799) Commander-in-Chief of the Revolutionary army, and America's first President was Grand/Worshipful Master of the Alexandria Lodge of Freemasons in Virginia!

Washington, like Jefferson, was a Deist and a slave owner. Tobacco made him one of the wealthiest men in Virginia. One of the most enduring tributes to this man (after the dollar bill and the city named Washington, D.C.) is the Masonic obelisk known as the "Washington monument." Obelisks were (and are) blatant phallic symbols originally created in ancient Babylon and Egypt for sun worship and fertility rites! The Washington monument is 555 feet tall, and is capped by *two* pyramids! (Freemasonry was birthed in the ancient, mystery religions of both Babylon and Egypt.)

In Alexandria, Virginia, the plaque outside his Memorial building records Washington's own words:

"Being persuaded that a just application of the principles on which the Masonic Fraternity is founded must be promotive of private virtue and public prosperity, I shall always be happy to advance the interest of the Society and to be considered by them as a Brother."

The Memorial Hall contains a 17 ft. high bronze statue of Washington wearing his Masonic apron as the Charter Worshipful Master of Alexandria Lodge No. 22. To which office he had been elected in 1788, and still held at the time of his election to the Presidency of the United States in January, 1789. The statue was presented to the Memorial by the Order of DeMolay for Boys in 1950, and unveiled by President Harry S. Truman, who was Past Grand Master of Missouri!

NOTE: The Order of DeMolay (Knights Templar) is named after Jacques DeMolay, Grand Master, of the 14th century Order of the Temple, who was executed in 1314 A.D. [10]

"The apron and sash worn by George Washington, together with the trowel he used, are today preserved in the Alexandria-Washington Masonic Lodge. George Washington, a member of the Masons since 1752, Master Mason, Past Master, and President of the United States had personally participated in the laying of the U.S. Capitol's cornerstone. He did so as a Freemason and President."[11] Anyone who has believed that a Christian spirit or voice prevailed at the founding of the U.S.A., should read Article 11 of the "Treaty with Tripoli," written and ratified while Washington was still President.

"The government of the United States is not in any sense founded on the Christian religion ..." [12]

(Washington's signature appears on the document)

Over the years, many have tried (some very dishonestly) to prove that Washington was a Christian. This effort has been based almost entirely on the fact that he attended an Episcopal Church and had served as a vestryman. In a letter dated Fredericksburg, August 13, 1835, a certain Colonel Mercer wrote to Bishop William White (who had been one of the rectors at Washington's church), asking if Washington, "Was a communicant of the Protestant Episcopal church, or whether he occasionally went to the communion only, or if ever he did so at all? ..." White sent Mercer this reply. "In regard to the subject of your inquiry, truth requires me to say that Gen. Washington never received the communion in the churches of which I am the parochial minister. Mrs. Washington was an habitual communicant.... I have been written to by many on that point, and have been obliged to answer them as I now do you." [13]

Washington's inaugural speech contained the classic Deistic names for God, and actually included the title, "Great Author." (Only the title, "Great Architect of the Universe" is used more frequently by Masons.)

"... it would be peculiarly improper to omit in this first official Act, my fervent supplications to that Almighty Being who rules over the Universe, who presides in the Councils of Nations, and whose providential aids can supply every human defect, that his benediction may consecrate to the liberties and happiness of the People of the United States, ... In tendering this homage to the **Great Author** of every public and private good ...

No People can be bound to acknowledge and adore the **invisible hand**, which conducts the affairs of men more than the people of the United States. Every step, by which they have advanced to the character of an independent nation, seems to have been distinguished by some token of **providential agency**. ... Since we ought to be no less persuaded that the propitious smiles of Heaven, can never be expected on a nation that disregards the eternal rules of order and right, which Heaven itself has ordained ... I shall take my present leave; but not without resorting once more to the **benign parent** of the human race, in humble supplication that since he has been pleased to favour the American people." [14] (Emphasis added)

In Washington's "Farewell Address" (1796), just three years before his death; Washington departed with more vague and empty Deistic words ...
"Religion" – **"religious principle"** – **"national morality"** – **"providence,"** and the **"Almighty."**

From beginning to end – not *one* mention of Christianity or the Lord Jesus Christ!

Finally: Testimony from other leading citizens (some known to Washington personally), which confirms his true spiritual condition.

"Sir, Washington was a Deist." (Dr. James Abercrombie) [15]

"Every child is familiar with the story of Washington praying at Valley Forge ... but it is false. Intelligent Christians are ashamed of it." [16]

"Zealous efforts have been made by **priestly falsifiers** to make the 'Father of his Country' something he was not. They represented him, while at the head of the army, frequently going aside to pray. This is wholly false, as is the hatchet and cherry-tree story told by Elder Weems." [17] (Emphasis added)

The Rev. Dr. Wilson affirmed that,
"The founders of our nation were nearly all Infidels ...George Washington, John Adams, Thomas Jefferson, James Madison, James Monroe, John Quincy Adams, and Andrew Jackson ...not one had professed a belief in Christianity."[18]
In one sermon Dr. Wilson gives us this amazing revelation.
"When the (Revolutionary) war was over, and the victory over our enemies won, and the blessings and happiness of liberty and peace were secured, the Constitution was framed and **God was neglected.**
He was not merely forgotten. He was absolutely voted out of the Constitution. The proceedings, as published by Thomas, the Secretary, and the history of the day, show that the question was gravely debated whether God should be in the Constitution or not, and after a solemn debate, he was deliberately voted out of it." [19] (Emphasis added)

"My researches do not enable me to affirm that Washington, on his death-bed, gave evidence of Christian belief." (Rev. Dr. Miller) [20]

"In several thousand letters the name of Jesus Christ never appears, and it is notably absent from his last will." (Gen. A. W. Greely) [21]

TO CONSPIRE OR NOT TO CONSPIRE!

Overwhelming historical evidence credits John Locke (helped of course by his European Enlightenment friends) with the lion's share of composing both Declaration and Constitution; and proves that the loudest voices (or quills) employed at America's founding were not those of born-again, Bible believing Christians; but of **Deists, Theists** and **Freemasons!**

The Founders may have been deceived, but they were certainly not stupid. They possessed great oral and literary talents; if they had wanted to declare the country a Christian nation, they would have left us in no doubt whatsoever! Instead, these religious, New Age, Enlightenment free-thinkers, **"deliberately voted God out of the Constitution,"** and laid a sandy foundation of rebellion, which in turn paved the liberalistic broad-way towards such abominations as Central Banks, including the Federal Reserve System, abortion, and legalized homosexual marriage!
    Supreme-court judges have not misinterpreted the Constitution: they are fulfilling exactly what the original founding "father of lies," and "god of this world" had in mind!

All told, it was **Thomas Paine** (another Freemason) who best summed up the anti-Christ spirit and New Age philosophy found within the majority of the founding fathers.
    "The opinions I have advanced... are the effect of the most clear and long-established conviction that **the Bible and the Testament are impositions upon the world,** that the fall of man, the account of Jesus Christ being the Son of God, and of his dying to appease the wrath of God, and of salvation by that strange means, **are all fabulous inventions,** dishonorable to the wisdom and power of the Almighty; that **the only true religion is Deism,** by which I then meant, and mean now, the belief of one God, and an imitation of his moral character, or the practice of what are called moral virtues – and that it was upon this only (so far as religion is concerned) that I rested all my hopes of happiness hereafter. So say I now – and so help me God ...
    I do not believe in the creed professed by the Jewish church, by the Roman church, by the Greek church, by the Turkish church, by the Protestant church, nor by any church that I know of. **My own mind is my own church.** All national institutions of churches, whether Jewish, Christian, or Turkish, appear to me no other than human inventions set up to terrify and enslave mankind, and monopolize power and profit." (Thomas Paine, from the "The Age of Reason") (Emphasis added)

Because the Revolution was so contrary to Holy Scripture, it caused a great rift within the "Church of England." As George 3rd was its nominal head (Bishops and priests were sworn to his allegiance), those ministers in favor of independence were forced to re-write the Anglican "Book of Common Prayer," in which prayers for the ruling monarch were offered....

"Beseeching God to be the king's defender and keeper, and giving him victory over all his enemies."

Maryland would give an example of how easily religion flows with the tide of popular opinion, political pressure, or in this case, national insurgence!

From Maryland's *Revised* Book of Common Prayer...

The Maryland Convention voted on May 25, 1776 ... "That every Prayer and Petition for the King's Majesty, in the book of Common Prayer . . . be henceforth omitted in all Churches and Chapels in this

Province. The rector of Christ Church (then called Chaptico Church) in St. Mary's County, Maryland, placed over the offending passages strips of paper showing prayers composed for the Continental Congress. The petition that God 'keep and strengthen in the true worshipping of thee, in righteousness and holiness of life, thy servant GEORGE, our most gracious King and Governour' was changed to a plea, 'that it might please thee to bless the honorable Congress with wisdom to discern and integrity to pursue the true interest of the United States.'" [22]

NOTE: Of the fifty-six signers of the "Declaration," nine have definitely been identified as Freemasons, with another ten being possible members. As stated previously, many more were Deists or *Theists.

Of the thirty-nine signers of the Constitution, nine were known Masons, 13 exhibited evidence of Masonic membership, and six more later became Masons. If a Christian voice of testimony or protest was raised at any time during the "birth" of America, it came, and sadly went away; un-heard and un-heeded!

"...There were ultimately five dominant and guiding spirits behind the Constitution – Washington, Franklin, Randolph, Jefferson and John Adams. Of these, the first three were active Freemasons, but men who took their Freemasonry extremely seriously – men who subscribed fervently to its ideals, whose entire orientation had been shaped and conditioned by it. And Adam's position, though he himself is not known to have been a Freemason was virtually identical to theirs. When he became president, moreover, he appointed a prominent Freemason, John Marshall, as first Chief Justice of the Supreme Court ... **it is in the Constitution that the influence of Freemasonry is most discernible...**" [23] (Emphasis added)

Again the question comes: why would "priestly falsifiers" (then and now) deliberately lie about the spiritual condition of the Founding Fathers?

Ambitious and corrupt men have always known that the most effective way to manipulate the masses is to present them with a cause. A cause which at first would seem to offer the people great hope and security for the future; but alas, one which routinely allows the leadership to satisfy their lust for wealth, power (preeminence), and glory.

The most powerful and corrupted causes of all time have been **religion** and **politics**; and to combine the two has been the desire of dictators and tyrants from as far back as Nimrod (the rebel, and hunter of souls before the Lord, see *Gen.10:8-10*), to a multitude of despots who clearly posses that same spirit today! The number of worldly, religious leaders who sought to join Church to State, did so invariably to enforce their own authoritarian version of the scriptures; thereby gaining a two-handed grip on the throats of the people! I strongly suspect that that is why their American counterparts wanted the Founding Fathers to be Christians; and why they now want to "Reclaim America for Christ!" After all, their expressed goal has always been to run the country – and eventually the world – on His behalf! Sadly, as I shared in chapter 16, it would not be on behalf of Jesus, but on behalf of Moses and Old Testament Law!

We should also know that if ever such men *did* rule with the law of Moses, the "life, liberty, and pursuit of happiness" – certainly regarding any other *religious* practice or persuasion – would ultimately cease to exist!

*Theism: a belief in the existence of at least one god; usually termed a "supreme being."

Although (thankfully) the false *"counsel or work"* of Reconstructionism will come to naught; those who *"watch"* (*Luke21:36*) are beginning to see a far more powerful and effective conspiracy taking shape on planet earth!

Of course, there are many who still refuse to believe in *any* such religious or political schemes: the next chapter is hardly for them. Soon however, even hardened skeptics will be forced to acknowledge that for years, the "Mother" of all conspiracies has been quietly taking over the world's central stage. And all the while in front of a largely ignorant and unsuspecting audience!

"The mystery of iniquity doth already work:" (2Thess.2:7)

What follows should prove just how well the Founding Freemasons and others have played their part in that ongoing mystery.

CHAPTER TWENTY-FIVE

"HE WHO OWNS THE GOLD (thinks he) MAKES THE RULES"

"The rich rule over the poor, and the borrower is servant to the lender."

(*Prov. 22:7*)

"Allow me to issue and control the money of a nation, and I care not who writes its laws."

(Mayer Amschel Rothschild)

Take a look at a U.S. bank note (any denomination): you will see the words, "**Federal Reserve Note**," and, "**This note is legal tender for all debts, public and private.**"

If you've ever asked why these bank notes are not from the Government and Treasury of the United States; the answer is this. The Federal Reserve System is a huge **private corporation.** (Also known as America's "Central Bank.") It does not belong to Government, or to the American people. – It *controls* them!

This extremely private corporation is in partnership with many other central banks already controlling their own governments around the world; including England, Sweden, Italy, Japan, Germany, and France.

One financial expert explains:

"The monetary system of the United States is in the hands of a few very wealthy and powerful individuals who control virtually *every* aspect of our economy. What this means is that **the power of the Federal Reserve exceeds and supersedes that of our President and Congress.** The Federal Reserve is not accountable to them. They have never published an annual report and their meetings are often not reported to the public until six months after they have made a monetary decision.

Have you ever considered why Americans cannot forgive themselves the interest on the federal debt? ...

'We the people' don't owe it to the Treasury!" [1] (Emphasis added)

In his book, "Tragedy and Hope," Dr. Carroll Quigley (Bill Clinton's mentor at Georgetown University), wrote,

"The powers of financial capitalism had another far-reaching aim, nothing less than to create a world system of financial control in private hands able to dominate the political system of each country and the economy of the world as a whole. This system was to be controlled in a feudalistic fashion by the central banks of the world acting in concert, by secret agreements arrived at in frequent private meetings and conferences. The apex of the system was to be the Bank for International Settlements, a private bank owned and controlled by the world's central banks which were themselves private corporations." [2]

"Ten times a year, the heads of the world's major central banks ... meet at their supranational second home, the **B.I.S.** (Bank of International Settlements) at Basel. ... They are '**INTERNATIONAL FREEMASONS**,' possessing a natural second allegiance to the often lonely interest of international monetary order..." [3] (Emphasis added)

The Bank of International Settlements functions on a global level; working with the central banks of each country to create the changes in domestic laws necessary to fulfill its international One World agenda (New World Order).

Not surprisingly, since its conception, the B.I.S. has gained more and more power, and now controls most (if not all) of the world's financial systems.

We now know that many of the world's financial "Barons" are Freemasons, or that they belong to other occult secret societies.

Manly P. Hall (33rd degree mason) puts some of the pieces together.

"For more than three thousand years, secret societies have labored to create the background of knowledge necessary to the establishment of an enlightened democracy among the nations of the world ... Men bound by a secret oath to labor in the cause of world democracy decided that in the American colonies they would plant the roots of a new way of life. Brotherhoods were established to meet secretly, and they quietly and industriously conditioned America to its destiny for leadership in the free world ..." [4]

SHOW ME THE MONEY!

The following illustrations from a web site entitled, "The Masonic Seal of America," show that Freemasonry has always been in control of the "almighty dollar!" [5]

The "Great Seal" printed on every dollar bill contains the most amazing detail of Freemasonry's vision for their "Novus Ordo Seclorum"(New World Order.)

The most familiar symbols of Freemasonry are the "set square" and "compass."

One of the most powerful symbols of witchcraft is the hexagram.

Simply extend the lines of the setsquare and compass: place what is now a hexagram over the pyramid on the Great Seal;

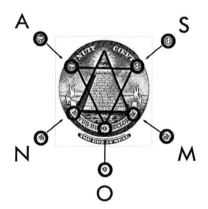

and see what happens –

**Now: guess who runs
the Federal Reserve System!**

The hexagram is seen in Masonic rituals around the world and is the symbol used especially in the "Royal Arch" degree. By the way, if anyone thinks those letters might have been spelled out by accident (what would be the odds of that?), consider the fact that every symbol and number contained in the Great Seal plays a vital role in the "sacred geometry" of both ancient and modern Freemasonry.

The five points spell out **MASON**; the sixth crowns the pyramid (the all-seeing "Eye of Horus" from Egyptian [occult] mysticism), and points Masons to the "Great Architect" above.

NOTE: The cap (including the "eye") is presently separated from the pyramid itself, i.e., floating above. When the New World Order is realized, the cap will be lowered, thereby making the pyramid one!

The words **"E Pluribus Unum"** (**One out of many**) can be seen on the banner held in the eagle's beak.

"The emblem was placed on the back of the Great Seal of the United States in 1789, and hidden from the public view until Henry Wallace convinced President Roosevelt it should be displayed on the back of the dollar bill. Both Wallace and Roosevelt were 32nd degree Masons. Wallace was also involved in other occult activities. [6]

We know now that Freemasonry is, among many other abominations, an Egyptian based, pagan fertility cult. The sexual or phallic symbolism of the **setsquare** and **compass** however is not so well-known, but is described here by someone once deeply schooled in the "black arts." ...

"When the male triangle penetrates the female triangle, it produces the six pointed crest of Solomon, or hexagram, the most wicked symbol in witchcraft." [7]

How **"International Freemasons"** and friends got their "Seal" on U.S. currency is not a mystery: again, M. P. Hall spells it out.

"On the reverse of our nation's Great Seal is an unfinished pyramid to represent human society itself, imperfect and incomplete. Above floats the symbol of the esoteric orders, (those few with specialized inside knowledge or information) the radiant triangle with its all seeing eye ... There is only one possible origin for these symbols, and that is the secret societies, which came to this country 150 years before the Revolutionary War." [8] (Parenthesis added)

All true Christians delight in the knowledge that God's Word will be fulfilled in due season.
(2Pet.3:8-10)

We also know that God is allowing the devil to run his evil course on earth for the purpose of separating "*the wheat from the chaff.*" With that in mind, I offer a summary of what these International Financiers, and their banker friends are really up to in these last days.
"*For we must not be ignorant of Satan's devises.*" (*2Cor.1:8*)

"WAKE UP AMERICA!"

For nearly 100 years the **Federal Reserve System** has been eating away at the heart and soul of our society until the American people are little more than government tax slaves who continue to feed, serve, and pay homage to this "monster" through an illegal act passed in 1913.

The "**Federal Reserve Act**" insidiously violated the Constitution of the United States by taking the "Power to coin money, and regulate the value thereof," away from government and, "We the people," and placing it into the hands of ruthless men who cared nothing for America, nor any *other* country for that matter; but only for their own agenda of profit and planetary control!

The **Federal Reserve Act** established the **Federal Reserve Corporation** with a Board of Directors to run it. The United States was then divided into 12 Federal Reserve Districts. (A simple ploy to avoid the appearance of a monopoly!) This Law removed from Congress the right to "coin money," or to have any real control over its regulation; by giving that power to some of the most greedy and corrupt men on earth!

NOTE: Less than 1 in 100 of those I interviewed knew that the Fed. is *not* "**FEDERAL**." (That title is pure deception.) It has always been a **private cartel** of international bankers, protected by federal law. It has no "**RESERVES**" (other than the debts of its victims!) It prints and makes counterfeit paper currency (known as fiat money) out of thin air! **It has never paid taxes, nor has it ever been audited!**
The word "**SYSTEM**" is just another word for banks!

This is how it works. ...
When our "*Servant*" government spends more than it has taken from its citizens in taxes, it must borrow more from its "*Master*." Because the Fed. is a **private corporation,** it demands interest. It also demands collateral!

SUPPOSE THE GOVERNMENT NEEDS $700 BILLION

It goes to the Fed. and promises to repay the loan with interest. It must also produce $700 billion worth of collateral; but as the government can no longer print money, the collateral must be in the form of "Bonds, Certificates," etc. The "Fed." then prints the $700 billion (their cost is merely the price of paper, ink, etc.), and the exchange is made. The government has now indebted the country to the sum of $700 billion – on which, "WE THE PEOPLE" must pay the interest! Are you ready for this? ...

THE I.R.S. EXISTS SOLEY AS A COLLECTION AGENCY FOR THAT DEBT!

Incidentally; Did you know that through income/sales taxes etc., and the **hidden tax of inflation**; most Americans already spend much of the year just working to pay off government/our debt?
Hundreds of thousands of these "debt-money" transactions have taken place since 1913, and the total amount the government has borrowed from the Fed. (as well as other sources) has risen to well over **$10 TRILLION!** (That's right ...$10 trillion! [2008] This figure is commonly referred to as – **The National debt!**) An estimated **$500 billion** is required by the "Fed." every year, just to service the loans to *our* government: the principle will *never* be paid back! Of course, the "Fed." doesn't *want* it to be: – they just *love* that interest! (Raising and lowering their interest rate keeps the "game" going!) Which means of course, they want our children and future generations to keep paying, and therefore *serving* this tyrannical "System" forever!

The Federal Reserve System is the world's greatest SCAM!
Congress unleashed the "monster" – Congress has the power to destroy it!
(But people must know the truth before their votes could even begin to make that happen!)

Pastor Sheldon Emry writes,

"The Federal Reserve is in close cooperation with similar organizations in other countries, which are also disguised as 'governments'. Some we are told are friends. Some we are told are enemies. 'Enemies' are created through international manipulations, and used to frighten the American people until billions more dollars are borrowed from the Bankers for 'military preparedness' – 'Homeland Security' – 'foreign aid' – 'minority rights' etc. U.S. Citizens, who are deliberately confused by brainwashing propaganda, watch helplessly while politicians give our food, goods, and money to banker-controlled alien governments under the guise of 'better relations' and 'easing tensions'! Our government has taken our finest and bravest sons and sent them into foreign wars, where tens of thousands are murdered, and hundreds of thousands are crippled. Other thousands are morally corrupted, addicted to drugs, and infected with diseases, which they bring back to the United States. ...

When the 'wars' are over, we have gained nothing, but are left scores of billions of dollars more in debt to the Bankers, which was the reason for the 'wars' in the first place!

The 'almost hidden' conspirators in politics, religion, education, entertainment, and the news media are working for a banker-owned United States, in a banker-owned world, under banker-owned world governments!" [9]

A FEW OUTSPOKEN VOICES FROM THE PAST

CONGRESSMAN LEWIS T. McFADDEN: (speaking to congress) "... the most corrupt institutions the world has ever known. I refer to the Federal Reserve Board and the Federal Reserve Banks ... They are *not* government institutions. They are private monopolies which prey upon the people of the United States for the benefit of themselves, and their foreign and domestic swindlers; rich and predatory moneylenders. ... **there is not a man within the sound of my voice who does not know that this Nation is run by the International Bankers.**"

PRESIDENT WOODROW WILSON: "We have come to be one of the worst ruled, one of the most completely controlled and dominated Governments in the world – a Government controlled by the opinion and duress of small groups of dominant men. ... **I have betrayed my Country**." (Referring to the Federal Reserve Act he signed while President of the United States.)

CHARLES A. LINDBERG Senior: "This (Federal Reserve) Act establishes the most gigantic trust on earth. When the President signs this Act, an **invisible government** by the power of money (proven to exist by the Money Trust Investigation) will be legalized. The new law will create inflation whenever the trusts want inflation. **From now on depressions will be scientifically created.**"

SIR JOSIAH STAMP: (President of the Bank of England in the 1920's, the second richest man in Britain): "Banking was conceived in iniquity and was born in sin. ... **The Bankers own the earth.**"

HENRY FORD: (Founder of the Ford motor company) "It is well enough that the people of the nation do not understand our banking and monetary system; for if they did, I believe **there would be a revolution before tomorrow morning!**"

NAPOLEON BONAPARTE: "When a Government is dependent upon bankers for money, they and not the leaders of that Government control the situation ... Money has no Motherland; **financiers are without patriotism and without decency: their sole object is gain.**"

There is an old saying ...**"THE PEOPLE GET THE GOVERNMENT THEY DESERVE."**
The only reason the Federal Reserve's "counterfeit paper" (which we are *forced* to use), and the entire country's "debt system" exist at all, is because people still have "**faith**" in their Government!

(A Government that has cheated, lied, and sold out its people continually; and must go on covering its tracts with deceit!) – Yet every four years, the people "**hope**" things will change! Some actually "**believe**" Barack Obama will make a difference! How could he? For one thing, Obama has chosen Timothy Geithner to be his Treasury Secretary! (As well as being a member of the **C.F.R.**, and **B.I.S.**; Mr. Geithner is currently President of the New York Federal Reserve Bank!) Fed. Chairman Bert Bernanke, and President Obama are both Freemasons; and with men like Secretary Geithner in place, it will not be long before the American people are forced to adjust another well known saying:

"The new boss isn't the *same* as the old boss – he's a whole lot worse!"

Did you ever imagine that **the loathsome I.R.S. was the government's collection agency for a PRIVATE BANK?** No Congressman or Senator could fail to know what is being done to the American people, yet these politicians stand by (like the puppets they have always been) posturing, and doing **NOTHING!**
Now we know why. – Financiers and Federal Reserve bankers are pulling their strings; so in the end they just do as they're told! – Doesn't it all make perfect sense now?

Also remember, that the three most powerful manifestations of witchcraft are
Domination, Manipulation, and Intimidation.
With **Deception** running a close fourth, we should readily discern what the world's financial "kings" are up to, and just where this country, and the *whole world* is heading!
As central banks dominate and squeeze their governments, so governments dominate and squeeze the people. Well orchestrated cycles of "boom and bust," and more recently, a so-called "Global Financial Crisis" are creating the fear and insecurity needed to bring about a unified world currency. The surrendering of national sovereignty will of course be requisite. Europeans have taken the lead; others will surely follow. Today, in the new "Egypt," financiers are Pharaohs; politicians are their task-masters; and populations merely the slaves, whose tax bricks are already building the ultimate social-democratic-totalitarian state!

ONE WORLD HERE WE COME

Although nothing will change the coming "One World" scenario, Christians can obviously use the knowledge gained here to promote and powerfully share the Gospel message; and to convince more and more lost souls (in bondage to the bankers, and *even worse*, to their leader Satan) that Jesus is the Only One Who can deliver them from *both*!
In the long run, knowing the names of banks and organizations involved – IMF/World Bank, the Fed., B.I.S., G7, G10, G20, G???, Council on Foreign Relations, Club of Rome, Trilateral Commission, U.N., etc., etc.; or the scoundrels who control the money that controls the world (be they Freemasons or not) – will matter little.
What *does* matter is how Satan is using them all to bring about his **"NOVUS ORDO SECLORUM"** (New World Order, or United States of the World), and his ultimate leader and false Messiah –
"The man of sin; the son of perdition" (2Thess.2:3) The anti-Christ himself!
And even if these love-of-money "*kings*" become the human power tools Satan uses to form his last-ditch, end-time revolution against God; they will still be carrying out God's will! ...

"And the ten horns which thou sawest are ten kings, which have received no kingdom as yet; but receive power as kings one hour with the beast. These have one mind, and shall give their power and strength unto the beast. ... For God hath put it in their hearts to fulfill His will, and to agree, and give their kingdom unto the beast, until the Words of God shall be fulfilled."

"... These shall make war with the Lamb, and the Lamb shall overcome them: for He is Lord of lords, and King of kings; and they that are with Him are called; and chosen, and faithful."

(Rev.17:12,14 and 17)

Thank God in Christ Jesus, we're on the winning team!

CHAPTER TWENTY-SIX

MIRROR, MIRROR ON THE WALL ... THE FAIREST HARLOTS OF THEM ALL!

In 1948, a young, and as yet uncompromising Billy Graham said,
"The three gravest menaces facing Christianity today are Roman Catholicism, Communism, and Muhammadanism."

Those "isms" were, and still are, three of the largest and most powerful anti-Christ cults ever conceived by their spiritual mother "Mystery Babylon!" Not surprisingly, all of them have spewed forth since the founding of the True Church some 2000 years ago!

Let's begin with the youngest.

COMMUNISM

"I wish to avenge myself against the one who rules above."(Karl Marx 1818-1883)

This twentieth century "harlot" was fully "birthed" in October 1917 when "Bolsheviks" (a majority faction led by Vladimir Lenin; motivated by the philosophies of Karl Marx, and financed by New York investment firms such as *Kuhn, Loeb, and Co., J.P.Morgan, and John D. Rockefeller) overthrew the existing provisional government and established the first Soviet socialistic regime.

(The last Tsarist autocracy was overthrown in February of that same year.)

Today, Communist organizations or parties exist in over 80 countries, and continue to dominate approximately one quarter of the world's population!

The purpose of this brief study is to prove conclusively that Communism is not primarily a political, social or economic system; but,

A SATANICALLY INSPIRED; GOD HATING; HUMANISTIC RELIGIOUS MOVEMENT!

** Communism (having quietly changed its "spots" to Social-Democracy) is very much on going; in spite of the fall of the Soviet Union in 1991-92. **It is still bent on undermining and destroying the U.S.A., as well as every Godly principle on earth!**

Richard Wurmbrant quotes a statement from the Soviet newspaper "Vechernaa Moskva," which confirms one of Satan's main objectives.

"We do not fight against believers, and not even against clergymen. We fight against God to snatch believers from Him." [1]

GOD HATERS

From the book, "Philosophy of Communism" comes rebellion, and the mockery of God's Word.

"Our enemy is God. Hatred of God is the beginning of wisdom." [2]

Mikhail Bakunin, Russian anarchist and Marx' partner during the "First International" wrote,

"In this revolution we will have to awaken the devil in the people, to stir up the basest passions. Our mission is to destroy, not to edify ..." [3]

* Proof that leading Wall Street banks financed the communist revolution in return for great economic rewards has been well documented. The reader is again encouraged to consult such works as, "Tragedy and Hope" by Dr. Carroll Quigley, and "The Creature from Jekyll Island," by G. Edward Griffin.

** Modern Internationalist Financiers are *all* Social Democrats. Of the many U.S. Presidents they have chosen, nurtured and controlled, I believe Barack Obama was to be their "Golden Child!"

With words that could easily have been written by Satan himself, Karl Marx declared:

"So a god has snatched from me my all, in the curse and rack of destiny.
All his worlds are gone beyond recall! Nothing but revenge is left to me!
I shall build my throne high overhead, cold, tremendous shall its summit be.
For its bulwark – superstitious dread, for its Marshall – blackest agony
And the Almighty's lightning shall rebound from that massive iron giant.
If he bring my walls and towers down, eternity shall raise them up, defiant." [4]

And...

"With disdain I will throw my gauntlet full in the face of the world,
And see the collapse of this pygmy giant, whose fall will not stifle my ardor.
Then will I wander godlike and victorious through the ruins of the world,
And, giving my words an active force, I will feel equal to the Creator." [5]

Hater of God *and* mankind (for reasons still largely unknown), Marx' demonic statements were taken so seriously by the Soviets, that in their early years they adopted the slogan, "Let us drive out the capitalists from earth, and God from heaven." [6]

No evidence has ever been found to suggest that Marx cared one iota about human beings (including his own family), which explains how the communist movement has spawned some of the most evil men on earth!

Lenin: who murdered his way to power, and later destroyed hundreds of thousands of Cossacks. Joseph Stalin: responsible for the slaughter of an estimated 20 to 30 million people.

Mao Tse Tung: for as many – or as few as – 40 million!

Not forgetting Ho Chi Minh, who sent 850,000 Vietnamese to their graves in "education camps!"

It was Stalin who once said,

"A single death is a tragedy, a million deaths is just a statistic."

(Joseph Stalin was Prime Minister of Russia, and Communist dictator from 1929-1953)

NOTE: Although somewhat curtailed, the demonic spirits motivating those earlier monsters continue to operate in communist leaders today. Among them, Fidel Castro (Cuba), Kim Jong-il (North Korea), and Tran Duc Luong (North Vietnam). All have their own hideous crimes to answer for!

According to the "Victims of Communism Memorial Foundation:"
"The Communist holocaust has exacted a death toll surpassing that of all of the wars of the 20th century combined, and has been the deadliest mass killing force ever visited upon the human race! In less than 100 years, Communism has claimed more than 100 million lives!" [7]

Liberation Theology

"We will present Marxism as a kind of religion: religious men and women are easy to convert and win, and so will easily accept our thinking if we wrap it up in religious terminology." (Lenin)

Younger sister of the communist "harlot;" Liberation Theology was born in the 1950's, and has often been described as "Communism's religious arm." It began essentially as a new form of communistic infiltration among both Protestant and Catholic churches; primarily in South (Latin) America. (Obviously the communist leadership wanted to get as close to the U.S as possible)

This carefully planned movement was designed to promote radical changes (Marxist style) in the religious, political and economic institutions of that region. This is how it happened.

Top Communists had long known (as did the Romans), that in order to break a country's back, they would first have to corrupt or destroy its religious faith!

"We must recruit them (the clergy) … to educate them in the spirit of our programme, and not to permit an active struggle against it." (Lenin)

During and after the second world war, many third world religious leaders were faced with overwhelming poverty, hunger, disease, political injustice, etc., and began turning from the Bible (which [they said] had failed to meet modern social needs). They began seeking other standards of "Christian" living in the hope of putting an end to the suffering of millions.

The results: communists began winning "useful idiots" (their term) among church leaders who would prostitute themselves and preach Marxist/Lenin ideologies disguised in Christian language. Liberation Theology (L.T.) contained all the elements that excite modern third world cultures, i.e. Nationalism, hatred of the U.S.A.(and her allies), and violent revolution.

In short, L.T. teaches that Jesus Christ was a COMMUNIST REVOLUTIONARY who encouraged his followers to revolt; and who justified murder in the name of freedom!

If all the twisted and perverted ideologies of L.T. were condensed into one single affirmation, we would read these words:
"CAPITALISM IS SATAN – COMMUNISM IS GOD"
Even the phrase, "Liberation Theology" is utterly deceiving.

"Liberation" does not mean scriptural freedom from sin by the shed Blood of Jesus Christ on the cross: it is a term for Marxist revolutionary socialism, which uses Christ's Name to commit horrifying acts of torture, violence, and terrorism in order to achieve its demonic goals!

"Theology" is not the pursuit of God through the study of His Word, but merely social analysis of prevailing conditions as viewed through the eyes of Marxism itself! It follows therefore, that while retaining a whole variety of Christian words and expressions, L.T. has given them an entirely different meaning! Nowhere is this more evident than in its description of,

"COMRADE JESUS"

L.T. states:	**Bible Truth states:**
1. Jesus died a martyr in the struggle against oppression: victim of the capitalistic bourgeoisie.	Jesus died as *"our sin Bearer."* (*1Pet.2:24*) *"All of us have sinned!"* (*Rom.3:23*)
2. He endorsed violence and revenge.	*"Avenge not yourselves"* (*Rom.12:19-21*)
3. He taught that man is capable of self-redemption.	*Only Jesus can redeem mankind!* (*Heb.9:11-12*)
4. That truth is relative to the current situation, and there are no fixed points of doctrine.	*"God's Word is forever settled."* (*Ps.119:89*)
5. Jesus taught that social change by revolution is a Christian principle.	*"Let every soul be subject to higher powers."* (*Rom.13:1-7*)

An English clergyman actually said,
"Communism is in origin, a movement for the emancipation of man from exploitation by his fellow man ... As members of the Body of Christ, we must come in simple penitence, knowing that we owe a deep debt to every communist." (Paul Oestreicher)

"A Mexican Jesuit wrote,
"The Ten Commandments are Marxist ... I believe that the Communists too belong to the church.
I believe the true church includes many who don't perceive themselves as Christians, even those who consider themselves atheists ..." (Jose Miranda) [8]

"As for me, I am not ashamed of the revolution, for it is the power of the people unto salvation ... Every time I see a guerilla, I see Jesus Christ." (The late Caanan Banana, one time President of Marxist Zimbabwe, and ordained Methodist Minister. Former official of the World Council of Churches.)

"Every Christian must be a revolutionary. Jesus was a revolutionary. I am a revolutionary ... the Jews must suffer ... there will be no sympathy for the Jews when the blacks take over." (Archbishop Desmond Tutu)

"Jesus and Marx would have got on like a house on fire ... true comrades in the struggle."
(Cedric Mayson, former Methodist Minister)

The following statements are attributed to Nelson Mandela.

1. "Long live the Cuban Revolution. Long live comrade Fidel Castro. ... Cuban internationalists have done so much for African independence, freedom, and justice. We admire the sacrifices of the Cuban people in maintaining their independence and sovereignty in the face of a vicious imperialist campaign designed to destroy the advances of the Cuban revolution. We too want to control our destiny... There can be no surrender. It is a case of freedom or death. The Cuban revolution has been a source of inspiration to all freedom-loving people ..."
2. "We consider ourselves to be comrades in arms to the Palestinian Arabs in their struggle for the liberation of Palestine. There is not a single citizen in South Africa who is not ready to stand by his Palestinian brothers in their legitimate fight against the Zionist racists ..."
3. "We communist party members are the most advanced revolutionaries in modern history."

"Idolized" and considered a "hero" by millions, Mandela's views have invariably been anti-American, and pro-Communist. In 1958 he wrote,

"...the people of Asia and Africa have seen through the slanderous campaign conducted by the U.S.A. against the Socialist countries. They know that their independence is threatened not by any of the countries in the Socialist camp but by the U.S.A., who has surrounded their continent with military bases. The Communist bogey is an American stunt to distract the attention of the people of Africa from the real issue facing them, namely, American imperialism." [9]

HUMANISM?

At first glance, communism appears to be nothing more than a form of militant Humanism. The notable exception being that Marx was not an atheist – he hated God! (How could he hate someone he didn't believe in?)

Secular Humanism is also a "religion," but one which puts "faith" in man as the supreme authority of life; "believing" that man's abilities alone can solve all human problems.

Humanism defined briefly: –

Denies or rejects the existence of God. And *all* Divine purpose or providence.

Believes in evolution. Man is the highest animal and is therefore free from any moral code, save that which he himself determines.

Deifies man. Man is "self-centered" (that much is true), "self-sufficient," "self-actualising," and "unlimited in potential and goodness."

Believes that science is the way of salvation, and the ultimate provider for mankind.

The gospel according to Humanism, Socialism, and Environmentalism states that genetic engineering will one day produce **a more uniform, and manageable population!** (Include in that a population managed by abortion, genocide, ethnic cleansing, and enforced euthanasia!)

Humanism is an old but tireless "harlot," and naturally one of "Bab's" most successful daughters!

FINALLY:

If anyone thinks the collapse of the U.S.S.R. put an end to the communist threat, they should take a good look at a 1922 speech given by Lenin, in which he predicted,

"First we shall take Eastern Europe, then the masses of Asia. After that, we shall surround and undermine the U.S.A., which will fall into our hands without struggle; like an over-ripe fruit."

Remember that the Communist revolution was actually paid for by Wall Street financiers; including "Internationalist" members of the Federal Reserve System! (But for their *own* world-dominating socialistic agenda of course.) In grateful response to that help from the Fed., Lenin said,

"The capitalists of the world ... will labor for the preparation of their own suicide."

(So much for the plans of foolish little men!)

Infinitely more important – *God's* prophecies concerning Russia are clearly revealed in chapters 38 and 39 of the book of Ezekiel!

One of the great "end time" battles involves the invasion of Israel by, "*Gog* (mighty one) *in the land of Magog* (land of the mighty one), *the chief prince of Meshech and Tubal ...*" (*Eze.38:2*)

Meshech: known later as Mushki, then Muskovy, and finally **Moscow**.

Tubal: known later as Tobolsk, the old capital of Siberia.

With him will come, "*a great company ... Persia, Ethiopia, Libya ... Gomer and ... Togarmah of the north quarters ...*" (*Eze.38:5-6*)

All of them will come to spoil Israel in the latter days. (*Eze.38:8-16*)

Persia (present day Iran) was pro-western until becoming an Islamic republic in 1979.

Today, Iran finds its greatest support coming from China, and of course, Russia! Iran is 98% Muslim.

Ethiopia: pro-western until a coalition of communist forces took over in 1991. Currently, 45-50% of the county's population is Muslim.

Libya: pro-western until its king (Idris1) was deposed in 1969 by Colonel Muammar al-Qadhafi, (also spelt Gadaffi) who then became its dictator. Libya's political system is a Gadaffi mix of socialism and Islam, known as "the Third Universal Theory."

Libya was the first of the three to turn against the West, but all are now fiercely opposed to Israel and the U.S. Libya is 97% Muslim.

Gomer: Areas of Eastern Europe allied to, or under the influence of Russia.

Togarmah: a region of Eastern Turkey (Armenia) around the Caucasus mountains. Turkey is 99.8% Muslim.

The Bible makes it clear that this Communist/Islamic threat to Israel will reach its climax in the last days. (*Eze.38:16*) As of now, Israel is surrounded on all sides by enemies, with little support except from the U.S.A. The day will come however, when God's natural people will stand utterly alone. Then, during that great conflict, God Himself will fight for them, and gain a complete and glorious victory!

He will, "*magnify and sanctify* (glorify) *His Name, and make Himself known in the eyes of many nations.*" (See *Eze.38:18 – 39:8*)

****

Now the second "menace to Christianity" ...

MUHAMMADANISM or ISLAM

Islam's founding "prophet" Muhammad, also spelt Mohammed (570?-632 A.D.) was born in or near the city of Mecca, in what is now Saudi Arabia. At about the age of forty, he began to receive "divine revelations" from a "spiritual being"(said to have been the angel Gabriel), who commanded him to recite the instructions given, and record them in what has since become known as the most sacred book of Islam – the Qur'an or Koran. The word Islam means, "submitted to God" and a Muslim is someone "who submits" to this "god." Belief in one god is basic to Islam and is known as "Tawhid." To become a Muslim, one must first utter – "Sincerely and with true intention" – the following confession:

"I bear witness that there is no god but God (Allah), and that Muhammad is the prophet (messenger) of God." (parentheses added)

Officially, "Allah" is Arabic for "the god." Unofficially, Allah refers to a pagan "moon god," which is why all Muslim countries or strongholds display the "crescent moon" on their flags, monuments and buildings.

Islam's "holy book" the Qur'an (meaning recitation) is similar in length to the New Testament, and contains 114 chapters (Suras) and 6236 verses.

ANTI-SEMETIC

Muslims claim descent from Abraham (whom they say was a Muslim) through **ISHMAEL**; and, as such, call themselves the "true sons of God." They actually believe that Abraham offered Ishmael, and not **ISAAC** as a sacrifice to God on Mount Moriah. They also accuse Christians and Jews of distorting the Old and New Testaments in order to hide the predictions of the coming of Muhammad.

In view of those things, it will not be surprising to learn that Arab and other Muslim nations are among the most anti-Semitic on earth! (A study of *Gen.17:19-21, 22:1-2, Rom.9;6-9,*and *Gal.4:22-31* offers the undistorted truth!)

Islam has for a long time labeled Israel "Little Satan," while branding America (currently chief supporter of Israel) with the supremely insulting title of "Great Satan!"

It is no exaggeration to state that increasing numbers of Muslims (thanks to their leadership) will not be satisfied until every single Jew is eradicated from the face of the earth!

The awful reality is that any act of violence against Jews or other "infidels" (non-Muslims) *has* to be tolerated by the Islamic community because Muhammad himself ordained retaliation or aggression against them! ... **"Fight and slay the infidels wherever you find them, and seize them, and beleaguer them, and lie in wait for them with every stratagem of war."** [10]

In other words; although some Muslims may not hold with "suicidal (make that *homicidal*) bombings," or other satanically inspired horrors such as "911," they would be wise not to speak out against them (at least publicly!) After all, according to the Qur'an, anyone resisting Islam's message or commands is to be punished with, **"... execution, or crucifixion, or the cutting off of hands and feet from the opposite sides; or exile from the land."** [10]

Or at the very least: **"Whosoever disobeys Allah and his messenger (Muhammad) have gone astray into manifest error."** [12]

Few people on earth have been so intimately acquainted with the curse of spiritual, mental *and* physical bondage, as are the people of Islam!

STRONG DELUSION

Tragically, Muslims also subscribe to the world's greatest deceptions. They are taught that Jesus Christ is *not* the only begotten Son of God!

"The Messiah, son of Mary is nothing but a messenger." [13]

Equally tragic, they do not believe that Jesus died on the cross for the sins of the whole world.
"They (the Jews) did not kill him and did not crucify him, but he was counterfeited for them ..." [14]

(Now remember: "Gabriel, the angel of the Lord," *told* Muhammad those things!)

Islamic teachers ("Imams" or "Mullahs") and other scholars, argue over the real meaning of that passage: some say, "A substitute was crucified." Others like Sayyid Ahmad Khan affirm that, "Crucifixion itself does not cause the death of a man ... after three or four hours Christ was taken down from the cross, and it is certain that at that moment he was still alive."

One thing however is certain:

No Muslim believes that God the Son died on a cross for the sins of the whole world, and rose from the dead on the third day!

Muslims believe that men must suffer and pay for their own sins, but that eventually, all of them will be rescued from "purgatory" by the intercession of Muhammad!

Such is the mixture of Islamic confusion, Roman Catholic error, and pagan superstition that Muhammad stated,

"Paradise lies at the feet of mothers."

And,

"He who ends the day weary from the work of his hands, ends the day forgiven of his sins."[15]

Most Muslims believe that only Roman Catholics are true Christians, but rebuke them for worshipping God, Mary, *and* Jesus! Muslims regard the worship of any god but "Allah" as the "unforgivable sin," bringing with it eternal damnation and torment. They are of course fiercely anti-Trinitarian: i.e. the belief in, and worship of the Father, Son and Holy Ghost.

But nowhere are the delusions of Islam more clearly seen than in the doctrine of "good works."

This error lies at the heart of all false religions, and has the Muslim vainly striving for "paradise" by making his "good deeds" outweigh the bad. However, should a Muslim die in "Jihad" (holy war), Islam promises that he will –

1) Have all past sins forgiven, and enter paradise immediately.
2) Receive 70 mansions and 70 black-eyed virgins.
3) Be given rivers of wine, and a white stone.
4) Have 70 members of his family join him there – without going through purgatory first!

This legal bondage (working for salvation) is condemned throughout the entire Bible; yet by such errors, Muslims go on proving (and insisting) they are, *"Children of Hagar, the Bondwoman."*

(See *Gal.4:21-25*)

Today, with over one billion followers worldwide, and anywhere between three and six million in the U.S. alone, Islam poses a far greater spiritual and physical threat than could possibly have been envisaged by Dr. Graham some 60 years ago!

BINDING THE STRONG MAN

No other faith (including Judaism) is more resistant to the Gospel message and conversion to Christ than Islam. It must be understood that terms such as SIN – SALVATION – THE CROSS – THE SON OF GOD etc., have entirely different meanings to Muslims; so that once again, only the Spirit of God could possibly bring the revelation needed to free them from such powerful deception. ...

"For the weapons of our warfare are not carnal but mighty through God to the pulling down of strongholds." (*2Cor.10:4*) ...The victory is always in Christ!

Jesus Himself taught that binding the *"strong man"* plays a vital part in bringing deliverance to such "captives" (*Matt.12:22-29*); and also how some of the really strong demons can only be cast out after a time of prayer and fasting. (*Matt.17:14-21*)

The (exceptionally) "strong man" of Islam is the "*SPIRIT OF ANTI-CHRIST.*" (*1John 2:18-19, and 4:3*) "anti-Christ" in this case means literally, "instead of Christ," or a "substitute for Christ."

For Muslims, Muhammad replaces Christ, and their "substitute" (false hope) has always been "dead works!"

V.I. Muslims are convinced that their god Allah holds himself aloof from men, and is therefore both unknowable and unreachable. The New Testament reveals God as a loving Heavenly Father, so Muhammad could *never* introduce them to the true God: ONLY JESUS CAN! By grace, born-again believers know Almighty God personally and intimately through Christ: they also know the wonder of being in fellowship with Him on a daily basis. *This* is the reality that Muslims need so much to see, hear, and recognize in our lives!

TRUST

Conversion to Christianity has very grave consequences for most Muslims; so we must be aware of the price many of them pay to identify with Jesus Christ, and to find their place in His true Church! Suspicion is an integral part of the fear motive that governs Islamic society; and Muslims need to know they can trust us! Prayer, Bible study, and a sound knowledge of Scripture will answer many of their questions: sharing our testimony, along with meaningful Bible verses will be of great help. There are none better than Romans chapters 9 and 10, the Sermon on the Mount, (*Matt.5-7*) the Gospels of John and Luke, and much of the book of Hebrews.

Our third "ism" and oldest "menace:"
ROMAN CATHOLICISM!

Throughout the Bible's inspired account of history, there has never been a more colorful, dramatic, and obvious description of end-time religious rebellion, than is found in the book of *Revelation, chapters 17 and 18.* It is there we see the full-blown manifestation of "*Mystery Babylon*" (as outlined earlier in chapter 14 of this book). We also see that the visible expression or appearance of that rebellious system is likened to a, "*woman sitting on a scarlet colored beast;*" and that the "*seven heads*" of the "*beast*" are the "*seven mountains on which the woman sits.*" (*Rev.17:9*)

The woman symbolizes "*that great city, which reigns over the kings of the earth*" (*v.18*), and since only one city has been recognized world-wide as, "the city that sits on seven hills," it is there where our study begins.

ORIGINS

According to ancient mythology, Rome was named after its founder Romulus in 735 B.C.

By 275 B.C., after centuries of striving and bloodshed, this once diminutive city/state (by now a Roman Republic led by elected Consuls, and a council known as the Senate) had gained control of all Italy! By the reign of Octavian (who ruled as Caesar Augustus from 27 B.C.-14 A.D.), the Romans had established a vast, ungodly kingdom; yet it was so that in the "*fullness of God's time,*" in a small and insignificant province of Rome's mighty empire, the Lord God and Savior Jesus Christ was born among men; lived as a man; was crucified, and buried in a tomb; only to rise and defeat death on that third (most glorious) day!

Later, He would ascend into heaven, and send forth the Holy Spirit to build His New Testament Church on earth; giving His followers (then and now!) the power to turn the pagan world completely, "*upside down!*" (*Acts 17:6, Mark16:15-20*)

COMPROMISE OR DIE!

Christianity clashed immediately with Rome, as early believers flatly refused any compromise or yoking with its heathen beliefs. Interestingly enough, Rome allowed, and even welcomed other religions, *and* their gods; but only as long as Caesar was revered as "god" over all!

Refusing to bow before Rome's emperors naturally brought great persecutions against the early church. Christians found themselves betrayed, falsely accused of various crimes, and (with satanic enthusiasm) thrown to wild animals for "sport." Many were even wrapped in oil soaked rags and burned alive as "human candles" for Roman garden parties!

Of course, this type of persecution only served to make the Church stronger and more separated from the world. It also scattered many believers, which in turn helped to fulfill the Word of God!

"Go ye into all the world, and preach the Gospel to every creature." (Mark 16:15)

THE SLIPPERY SLOPE

Sadly, as the years passed, certain church leaders (who loved to have the preeminence) began rising up as, *"lords over God's people."* Instead of being led by the Holy Spirit, and relying solely upon Him, they quenched the Spirit with *"worldly philosophies, traditions, and vain deceits."*(Col.2:8)

In addition, Satan (who had utterly failed to destroy the Church through fear and carnage) would soon begin to employ one of his favorite Old Testament axioms, "If you can't *beat* them – *join* them!"

Shortly after the dawn of the fourth century A.D., Emperor Constantine (280-337 A.D.) "professed" conversion to Christianity. Imperial orders went forth bringing an end to the persecution of saints (New Testament believers). Suddenly, Satan's "window of opportunity" was wide open! The Church began receiving fashionable, worldly recognition, and Pastors or Bishops who surrendered to the state received favor and prestige. For his munificence, the Emperor was elevated to "Head of the Church," and soon his title "Papas" (Father or Pope) would be adopted by all of Rome's future political / religious rulers.

Compromises with Roman (hence Babylonian) paganism were inevitable; thus instead of being separated from the world, the "church" grew to become part of the world's system. Needless to say, the degeneration of Christianity continued until virtually every area of life was affected!

There is no doubt whatsoever that this ancient union between the apostate church and heathen Rome, produced the organization known today as the Roman Catholic Church.

NOTE: Official persecution of Christians ended with the Edict of Milan, signed by Constantine and his co-emperor Licinius. Although this did not make Christianity the official religion of the empire (that happened under Emperor Theodosius in 381 A.D.), it did grant it legal status.

THE QUEEN OF HEAVEN (BY ANY OTHER NAME)

Goddess worship in ancient Rome was nothing new: it too originated in Babylon where the "Mother goddess," Queen Semiramis (said to have given birth to the "divine child" Tammuz) was worshipped as the "Queen of Heaven," and "Mother of god!" (This carefully woven "goddess" myth was designed merely to give the queen tighter control over her gullible subjects!)

When the people of *"Babel were scattered"* (Gen.11:8-9), they simply took this "mother worship" with them; which explains why many nations worshipped a mother and child (in one form or another) centuries before God would bring forth His Son and Savior Jesus Christ into the world!

Language was also scattered ("confounded") at Babel, and so the mother goddess became known by many different names.

The Chinese revered her as "**Shingmoo**" (holy mother).

The Germans worshipped the virgin "**Hertha**."

The Etruscans fell down before "**Nutria**."

Druids worshipped and adored the "**Virgo-Patitura**" (mother of god).

In India she became "**Indrani**," or "**Isi**" with her child "**Iswara**," "**Devaki**," or "**Krishna**."

To the Greeks she was "**Aphrodite**," or "**Ceres**."

Let's not forget Egypt, were "**ISIS**" reigned as "nature's creator and goddess of fertility."

To the Romans she was "**Venus**," or "**Fortuna**" with divine child "**Jupiter**."

In Asia the mother and child were "**Cybele**," and "**Deoius**."

Regardless of the name or place, history records Semiramis as the wife of "Baal;" the virgin queen of heaven said to have born a divine child through union with that particular "god!"

MEANWHILE; BACK AT THE FORUM

It follows that as more and more unconverted pagans joined the apostate Roman church (and wanted to continue their heathen rites and customs); adjustments needed to be made which would "Christianize" the "mother goddess and child" so popular throughout the ancient world.

But who could possibly replace the great "mother goddess" of Babylon?

The obvious and most logical choice would prove satisfactory to all concerned – *especially* Satan! Why not let the pagans go on worshipping the mother goddess and child in the form of Mary and the baby Jesus?

With one masterful stroke, inspired by the prince of darkness himself, worship that had been associated with the heathen mother was now transferred, and one of the greatest deceptions in history was underway!

The Catholic Encyclopedia admits:

"The doctrine of Devotion to Our Blessed Lady is not contained, at least explicitly, in the earlier forms of the Apostles' Creed, and there is perhaps no ground for surprise if we do not meet with any clear trace of the cultus of the Blessed Virgin in the first Christian centuries." [16]

Today, millions of sincere and devout Catholics are taught that Mary is the "Queen of Heaven," "Divine Mother," etc., etc., but they are wrong! The truth can be found in the book of Jeremiah, where the children of Israel are seen worshipping and praying to Semiramis well over 600 years before Christ!

*"The children gather wood, and the fathers kindle the fire, and the women knead their dough, to make cakes to the **queen of heaven**, and to pour out drink offerings unto other gods, that they may provoke Me to anger. Do they provoke Me to anger saith the Lord: do they not provoke themselves to the confusion of their own faces?" (Jer.7:18-19)*

UNCEASING CONFLICT

We come now to comparisons between the teaching and dogma of the Catholic Church, and the absolute truth of God's Word – the Bible.

The spiritual conflict between Catholicism and Christianity is real and unending: the errors of Catholicism so numerous that only a few key issues can be dealt with here.

May each revelation become a powerful weapon in the hands of those who are (and will be) called to reach out to Catholic souls wherever and however the Holy Spirit leads.

The following information was taken (for the most part), from "The Doctrinal Teaching of the Catholic Church," by Quentin De La Bedoyere, from the Library of Catholic Knowledge.

ON MARY

1) Catholic teaching states that Mary (unlike the rest of humanity) "was preserved exempt from all stain of original sin," and that she remained sinless during her entire life: hence the "dogma" (emphatic doctrine) of her "immaculate conception" (established in1854)

First the Bible states that, *"All have sinned and come short of the glory of God."* (*Rom.3:23*)

Then: part of Mary's utterance in the Gospel of Luke (known to millions as the "magnificat") tells us she was well aware of her sinful condition.

> *"And Mary said, my soul doth magnify the Lord, and my spirit hath rejoiced in GOD MY SAVIOR ..." (Luke 1:46-47)*

Inspired by the Holy Spirit, Mary could not have known God as her "*Savior*" if she had not first known of her sin!

To make Mary "immaculate" would make her equal with Christ, and therefore with God!

Which of course is why she receives sincere but erroneous prayers from Catholics, "Both now, and at the hour of death."

2) Catholics are taught that Mary remained a "**PERPETUAL VIRGIN.**"

After the virgin birth of Jesus, scripture reveals Joseph and Mary to be the parents of sons and daughters through **normal marital relations!** (Jesus' half-brothers are actually named: "*James, Joses, Simon and Judas*"[Jude] – *Matt.13:55-56*)

3) The "Assumption of Mary" became dogma on November 1st, 1950; i.e. that Mary "rose bodily" after death, and is now the Catholic's representative directly involved in her Son's work!

The Bible speaks of only four people who rose physically to heaven: Enoch, Elijah and the two witnesses in *Rev.11:3-12*. To claim Mary as a fifth is simply a lie told to give strength to the "queen of heaven" myth!

Also to claim she is an intercessor between God and men is nothing short of blasphemy!

Catholics believe that Jesus is too high, distant or holy to deal with men directly; thus the need for a gentle, loving mother to be a mediator.

"When we pray to her (Mary) we are in fact praying to God through her intercession." [17]

The Bible thunders out against that gross error:
> *"For there is one God and ONE MEDIATOR between God and men, THE MAN CHRIST JESUS." (1Tim.2:5)*

AND,
> *"This Man (Jesus) is able to save them to the uttermost that come unto God BY HIM seeing HE ever liveth to make intercession for them" (Heb.7:25)*

V.I. – If Catholics are praying, "Holy Mary, Mother of God, pray for us sinners now and at the hour of death;" how can they possibly be calling on Jesus?
> *"The Only Name under Heaven given among men whereby we must be saved." (Acts.4:12)*

May God open eyes to the truth – "***blessed among women***" and "*favored*" – **YES!**

BUT: Mary *was* not; *is* not; and *could* not be more than the Creator chose her to be. – "A young virgin who would conceive and bear a Son Who's Name would be called Immanuel." (God with us!) (*Is.7:14*)

ON THE POPE

As we have already seen, the words "Papas" and "Pope" mean father; but that would not be enough for religion's *leading* men: after all, *every* Catholic priest is called "Father!"

Satan would soon delight in seeing many more "hallowed" titles including, "Holy Father," and even "**Most** Holy Father" being bestowed upon fallen, sinful human beings!

Although it's impossible for us to imagine the number of blasphemous insults the devil has perpetrated against our Heavenly Father since time began, those titles must surely be high on the list! The sacred utterance, "***Holy Father***" is spoken only **once** throughout the entire Bible (by Jesus Himself), and comes during the "Lord's Prayer" in the Gospel of John.

"*And now I am no more in the world, but these are in the world, and I come to Thee.* **Holy Father**, *keep through Thine own Name those whom Thou hast given Me, that they may be one as We are One.*" (*John 17:11*)

Earlier in His ministry, Jesus addressed this very issue! His command was obviously not directed towards *natural* fathers, but to those who would be tempted to use the term religiously.

"AND CALL NO MAN YOUR FATHER UPON THE EARTH: FOR ONE IS YOUR FATHER, WHICH IS IN HEAVEN." (*Matt.23:9*)

Other titles given to Popes such as, "Supreme teacher of the church" – "Pontiflex Maximus" (Chief Bridge Builder) – "Supreme Pontiff (head) of the Universal Church" are so utterly grievous that I offer no response other than the purity and truth of God's Word!

"*But the Comforter, which is* **THE HOLY GHOST**, *Whom the Father will send in My Name,* **HE SHALL TEACH YOU** *all things whatsoever I have said unto you.*" (*John 14:26*)

"I AM THE WAY, THE TRUTH AND THE LIFE, NO MAN COMETH UNTO THE FATHER, BUT BY ME." (*John 14:6*)

"CHRIST IS THE HEAD OF THE CHURCH." (*Eph.5:23*)

Popes claim to be direct descendants or successors of the Apostle Peter; whom (they say) was the "first Pope." We may examine this in the light of Scripture.

1. **PETER WAS MARRIED!** (*Matt.8:14, 1Cor.9:5*)
   Popes must vow celibacy! (More on this subject at the end of the chapter.)

2. **PETER REFUSED TO BE BOWED DOWN TO, OR WORSHIPED!** (*Acts 10:25-26*)
   Popes are flagrantly bowed down to, and their rings and feet routinely kissed! (This is a form of worship, and absolute idolatry.) Before my conversion I actually toured the Vatican, and saw a

large bronze statue of Peter just inside the main entrance. "Peter" was seated, and his proffered foot was badly worn down by the kisses and adorations of untold numbers of penitents!

Sometimes even the Pope will kiss Peter's foot; and on such special occasions the statue is seen wearing rich papal robes as well as a three-tiered papal crown!

There are of course, many photographs of these well-publicized events; as well as those taken of a Pope actually kissing the Qur'an! (For any discerning person, the case against Catholicism could rest right there!)

3. IN *THIS* LIFE, PETER NEVER WORE A CROWN!

The only "*crowns*" Peter mentions are those glorious ones promised to *all* faithful elders of the true Church.

"*And when the Chief Shepherd* (Jesus) *shall appear, ye shall receive a crown of glory that fadeth not away.*" (*1Pet.5:4*)

There are also "*crowns of righteousness*" for *every true believer* who is longing for the return of the Lord Jesus! (*2Tim.4:8*) No true Christian (including Peter) would ever settle for a temporal or worldly, religious crown!

In short, Peter was *not* a Pope! He never *dressed* like a pope, never *spoke* like a Pope, never *wrote* like a Pope, never *acted* like a Pope, and above all, never allowed anyone to *approach* him as a Pope!

On the Catholic Church

The Catholic church claims "**Seven Doors**" (sacraments) to salvation:

Baptism - Confirmation - Eucharist - Penance - Anointing of the sick - Holy orders - Matrimony.

The Word of God declares, **HEAVEN HAS ONLY "*ONE DOOR.*"** (*John 10:7-9*)

No other way or "door" will *ever* lead to eternal Life. (*John 14:6*)

Here are **seven** reasons why!

BAPTISM

Catholics are taught that when adults or babies are baptized, they become "born-again children of God." (Large numbers of Anglicans/Episcopalians also believe and teach this lie) However, Jesus said, "*Repent ye, and believe the gospel.*" (*Mark 1:15*) Paul said, "*Believe on the Lord Jesus Christ, and thou shalt be saved.*"(*Acts 16:31*) Peter said, "*Repent and be baptized ...*" (*Acts 2:38*)

Babies who are sprinkled (aspersion), or more recently have "holy water" poured on them (affusion), cannot possibly believe *or* repent: yet the Catholic Church goes on insisting:

"Holy Baptism is the basis of the whole Christian life, the gateway to life in the Spirit (vitae spiritualis ianua), and the door which gives access to the other sacraments. **Through baptism we are freed from sin and reborn as sons of God; we become members of Christ**, are incorporated into the Church, and made sharers in her mission: Baptism is the sacrament of regeneration through water in the word." [18]

(Emphasis added)

TRUTH

The Lord Jesus Christ is the only "basis" or Foundation of the Christian life (*1Cor.3:11*), and **HE ALONE** is the "Gateway" or "Door" to eternal life!" (*John 10:7-9 and 14:6*)

CHRIST'S *BLOOD* (not baptism) **washes away our sins!** (*Heb.9:12-14, 1John1:7*)

"*Unto Him that loved us, and washed us from our sins in His Own Blood.*" (*Rev.1:5*)

Once and for all:

Baptism is an act of obedience by someone **ALREADY REDEEMED** through faith in Christ! Having declared my anger against the sprinkling farce, let me say for the last time:

INFANT BAPTISM IS A DEMONIC DOCTRINE, AND COUNTS FOR NOTHING!

It is a "dead work," religiously acted out by well-meaning parents on behalf of an unwitting child. For without the knowledge of sin there can be no repentance: without *true* repentance there is no salvation: without salvation, there is no "life in the Holy Spirit!"

CONFIRMATION

Millions more Catholics *and* Protestants are led to believe that *this* door confirms the grace they received at baptism; by allowing them to receive the gift of the Holy Spirit. In reality, they become no more than official members of "false religious clubs!" (I should know – I was one of them!)

At the age of twelve, about twenty of us were "confirmed" by an Anglican Bishop who anointed us with oil, said some things in Latin, and then told us we had just received the Holy Ghost! Most of us thought that receiving a "ghost" was a bit spooky, and laughed it off as a joke; but we had to go through with it in order to receive Eucharist (in the high churches), or Holy Communion (elsewhere).

You see, none of us knew (nor really cared) what was going on; but after confirmation we suddenly became "adult members" of the church, which meant we were able to act like grown ups, and drink real (watered down) wine at the altar rail!

EUCHARIST

As in all the sacraments ("real actions of Christ") Catholics believe that Christ is present, (albeit invisible) but it is in the Eucharist that these heretical teachings reach a climax.

"There on the altar of the Mass **LIES THE BODY AND BLOOD OF JESUS**; still looking like bread and wine, but in outward appearance only." [19] (Emphasis added)

Transubstantiation – The magical transformation of wafer and wine into the real, physical presence of Christ is perhaps the most blasphemous deception ever perpetrated by the Roman Church! Certainly it is one of Satan's most devious, and successful religious works!

Based on a total misuse of Jesus' words in *John 6:54*, Catholics are convinced that by eating the literal flesh and blood of Christ, they are receiving eternal life.

To uncover this dreadful error, we must once again go back to Babylon, and to the damnable religious practices that came forth from there.

A major aspect of ancient pagan worship was the offering of **HUMAN SACRIFICES!**

Certain gods demanded the shedding of human blood ("Molech," and "Baal" for examples), but in addition to satisfying these voracious demons, human priests would consume the flesh and blood of victims on their behalf!

It is from the land of Canaan where Baal was a ruling deity, that the word cannibal (from "Cana-Baal" i.e., a priest or worshipper of Baal) finds its origin!

During the Roman conquest or absorption of Christianity, many Canaanite pagans (accustomed to, and still desiring human sacrifice) were seduced into the "church" by the stunningly simple act of transforming the symbols of "bread and wine" into the literal "flesh and blood" of the Lord Jesus Christ! Today, "human sacrifice" continues throughout the Catholic community (in the form of the Mass), and every member who partakes of the Eucharist, unknowingly promotes the ancient and abominable sacrament of "Cana-Baal!"

NOTE: In the face of torture and certain death, the martyrs of the Reformation continued to deny the heresy of transubstantiation by flinging simple but God inspired logic back at their accusers –

"If Christ be real upon your altar; how can He be at the right hand of God the Father?"
or,

"If He is present in your Mass, (Christ had but one body) then how can He be down the road in another Mass at the same time?"

(Praise God for such testimonies handed down to us through such volumes as "Five English Reformers," and "Fox's Book of Martyrs!")

PENANCE

The sacrament of Penance (also known as Confession) gives a priest the power to become God and forgive sins! But there is still a problem:

"Absolution (a priest's forgiveness) takes away sin, but it does not remedy all the disorders sin has caused. Raised up from sin, the sinner must still recover his full spiritual health by doing something more to make amends for the sin: he must 'make satisfaction for' or 'expiate' his sins." [20] (Parenthesis added)

The tragedy of Penance is that no Pope, Cardinal, Bishop or priest can forgive the sins we have committed against God! (They can only forgive the wrongs done to them!)

Doing anything to "make satisfaction" or amends for sin, and calling it a sacrament (door) to salvation, is a travesty of the Lord's glorious **once-and-for-all-time sacrifice!** (*John 19:30*)

Christ's "finished work" has bolted the door of Penance, and no "dead-work" will ever *open* it!

ANOINTING OF THE SICK

Formerly known as "Extreme Unction" or "Final anointing," the anointing of the sick was originally coupled with a prayer for healing. (*James 5:14-15*) When the vast majority failed to recover, it conveniently became a sacrament referred to as the "Last Rites!"

"If a man is too sick to do penance, this anointing will give him health of soul by forgiving him his sins." [21]

There is even an anointing which takes you straight to Heaven.

"By Extreme Unction, a man is prepared for immediate entry into glory." [22]

(This door appears to evade the now unfashionable trip to "purgatory!")

HOLY ORDERS

At every Mass, "Holy Orders" give a bishop or priest the power to "**Make present** the victim of our sacrifice" [23] so that, "The work of redemption is **continually accomplished** in the mystery of the Eucharistic Sacrifice." [24] (Emphasis added)

In other words, Catholic redemption is never complete! These men repetitiously conjure up their "physical Christ," in order to sacrifice him – drink his blood, and eat his flesh – again and again and again! They can offer nothing more than an ongoing counterfeit salvation!

The only thing these priests ever "make present" is an obscene mockery of the Word of God!

TRUTH – *"CHRIST WAS OFFERED ONCE FOR SINS."* (*Heb.9:28*)
"For by ONE OFFERING He hath perfected forever them that are sanctified."
(*Heb.10:14*)

NOTE:

Have you ever considered why the Host is a perfectly round wafer; and that until quite recently, only the priests were allowed to touch it? (It was always placed on the tongues of Catholic recipients.)

The Host has always been a symbol of the sun god Baal, whose priests were the only ones allowed to prepare and handle sacrificial human flesh!

Today, one only has to visit the Vatican to be made shockingly aware of Catholicism's pagan roots, and especially its Baalistic sun worship!

MATRIMONY

Catholic teaching states:

"In the moment of their union with each other, they (the Catholic couple) are taken up into Christ's redeeming work (along side Mary perhaps?), and their children are not merely members of the human race, but future members of the Mystical Body of Christ." [25] (Parentheses added)

This last sacramental presumption merely reinforces the vain hope and total lack of eternal security that orthodox Catholics around the world have always manifested: particularly as they approach the "hour of death."

TRUTH – JESUS CHRIST is the ONLY DOOR; HIS CROSS the ONLY KEY!

We are saved (redeemed or born again) the moment we exercise faith in His atoning blood sacrifice; and receive Him as Lord and Savior of our lives! (*John 1:12*)

"Christ died for our sins." (*1Cor.15:3*)

We become involved in the "redeeming work" of Christ the moment we share His Gospel of salvation with others. (*Matt.28:19*) Marriage does *not* equal redemption, nor ever will!

Having viewed this "seven-door" vicious-circle from birth to death, and (for the living who continue to pray for those in purgatory) even *beyond* death: the Catholic deception is, for the most part complete! However, we need to understand that generations of "faithful" followers have been trapped behind these seven religious doors by one evil, and all consuming lie!

"It is only through the Roman Catholic Church that a man may be saved." [26]

Pope Innocent III said in 1208,

"By the heart we believe and by the mouth we confess the one Church, not of heretics but the Holy Roman, Catholic, and Apostolic (Church) outside which we believe that no one is saved."[27]

In 1302, an "infallible utterance" by Pope Boniface VIII stated,

"...We declare, say, define, and proclaim to every human creature that they by necessity for salvation are entirely subject to the Roman Pontiff."[28]

Pope Pius IX, said in 1863,

"... But, the Catholic dogma that no one can be saved outside the Catholic Church is well-known; and also that those who are obstinate toward the authority and definitions of the same Church, and who persistently separate themselves from the unity of the Church, and from the Roman Pontiff, the successor of Peter, to whom 'the guardianship of the vine has been entrusted by the Savior', cannot obtain eternal salvation." [29]

"...There is no salvation outside the Church." [30]

Pope John Paul II

With those quotes in mind, we should be aware that one of the principle characteristics of any cult member is the fear he or she has of leaving or being excommunicated from the "Family" or "Flock!"

NOTE: Recently, an increase of liberalism, and ecumenical pressure has prompted a softening of the Church's doctrinal position on salvation. It seems that non-Catholics, or "separated brethren" have been granted the possibility of being saved outside the "Mother Church!"

Isn't *that* a relief? (May the Pope make us *truly* thankful, amen!)

IS CATHOLICISM A CULT?

Walter Martin once defined cultism as, "... any major deviation from orthodox Christianity relative to the cardinal doctrines of the Christian faith." [31]

Sadly, he never once (to my knowledge) applied that definition to Catholicism!

Traditionally, the word "cult" has been used to describe the "usual suspects," such as Mormons, Jehovah's Witnesses, Seventh Day Adventists, Moonies, Scientologists, Hare Krishna, etc., etc.

In reality, the term "religious cult" applies to *any* group, sect or organization, which believes and declares the following aberration.

1 That it is the only institution on earth being led by (or correctly applying) God's will.
2 That it *alone* holds the key to the correct interpretation of Scripture.
3 That its leader (or leadership) is inspired by God, and therefore uniquely qualified to govern and direct the members.

(Certain other cults; Communism and Humanism for example, fail to meet the above criteria – the obvious reason being – they are currently at war with God!)

The Roman Catholic Church however, affirms all three!

Why is it then, that even today, very few Christian voices are declaring the cultic nature of the Catholic Church? I believe there are two main reasons.

First: The Catholic Church is a huge and immensely powerful organization, and one that has been around for a long, long time. Most of the unsaved world believes it to be the true Church, so who would dare take it on?

Second: One of the most seductive spirits of this age is unquestionably the religious (lying) spirit of "Ecumenical Unity" (a.k.a. "Unity in Diversity"), with the claim that, "All world faiths are valid, and all share common truths which will take us to God."

This ecumenical spirit is moving on the Body of Christ like never before, and defies anyone to expose it with the truth; labeling them critical or judgmental. (Speaking of Jesus as the Only Way is naturally regarded as extreme or intolerant!)

So who dares to rock this giant ecumenical boat?

Thankfully, more and more Christians have entered the arena, and are fighting the *"good fight"* against these Catholic and Ecumenical "Leviathans:" among them is Dave Hunt.

"To deny that Roman Catholicism is a cult is to repudiate the Reformation and mock the millions of martyrs who died at Rome's hands, as though they gave their lives in vain. ... Paul Crouch, head of the largest Christian TV worldwide network, demeans the martyrs by calling the issues they died for mere semantics; and he makes a mockery of the Reformers by declaring orthodox the heresies that sparked the Reformation." [32]

Having heard several ecumenical messages by Paul Crouch, I can agree wholeheartedly with brother Hunt's assessment: further more, I believe we are seeing the "spirit of unity" not only loosed, but rapidly gaining strength throughout the entire Trinity Broadcasting Network!

THE NINE COMMANDMENTS

In bringing this chapter to a close, let me to share two seemingly unrelated, but equally important revelations. The first involves the Ten Commandments. *(Ex.20)*

Imagine if you will, an organization totally given over to idolatry; i.e. the kissing and worshipping of *"graven images"* such as statues, pictures, icons and relics; and the "extreme reverence" (disguised worship) given to a human being, i.e. Mariolatry.

Now imagine that same organization actually *removing* one of the Ten Commandments in order to allow for, and continue with, those pagan practices!

Take a careful look at God's **second Commandment**, and note that it reads as follows:

"Thou shalt not make unto thee any graven image, or any likeness of anything that is in heaven above, or that is in the earth beneath, or that is in the water under the earth: thou shalt not bow down thyself to them nor serve them ..." (Ex.20:4-5a)

Now take a look at any official *Catholic* version of the Ten Commandments.

See that this second Law (condemning idolatry) has been **completely removed**, and replaced by dividing or corrupting Commandment number Ten!

"Thou shalt not covet thy neighbor's house, thou shalt not covet thy neighbor's wife, nor his manservant, nor his maidservant, nor his ox, nor his ass, nor anything that is thy neighbor's." (Ex.20:17)

Catholic bible versions have split the tenth and last commandment, and have created two!

Commandment number 9 reads – "Thou shalt not covet thy neighbor's wife."
Commandment number 10 reads – "Thou shalt not covet thy neighbor's goods."

If by any chance you happen to be reading or "seeing" this for the first time, it may take a while before the enormity of the corruption sinks in. Even now it is difficult for me to express the amazement, anger and sorrow I felt after first discovering such blatant (and willful) violations of scripture. How many orthodox Catholics will ever fully grasp the implications of this one deception alone; or the fearful judgments pronounced upon all those who, "... *take away from, or add to, God's Prophetic Word?" (Rev.22:18-19)*

In taking away the second Commandment, and adding to (doubling) the Tenth, Roman Catholicism shows us once again that it's entire foundation is built on paganism, fabrications, errors, and bold-faced lies! Who would knowingly remain subject to the bondage and darkness of the Catholic system in light of so many proven indictments? May God give Catholics everywhere, eyes to see and ears to hear. In Jesus' Name.

Finally, and as promised, I share from a tract written some years ago in answer to the scandalous events arising from homosexual activity within the Catholic priesthood. The tract was originally titled, **"What's Happening to the Catholic Church?"**

My purpose was and still is, to address the *spiritual* implications and the errors of celibacy – not to criticize or condemn any individual.

CELIBACY AND THE CATHOLIC PRIESTHOOD

"*...And Peter's mother-in-law was taken with a great fever; ...*" (*Mark 1:30, Luke4:38*)

"*Nevertheless, to avoid fornication, let every man have his own wife, and let every woman have her own husband.*" (*1 Corinthians 7:2*)

Having established that the Apostle Peter was neither a Pope nor celibate, we can now discover the truth behind the doctrine (or in this case law) of celibacy, and why it came into being.

Here are two definitions:

"Celibacy is the state of not being married; or the state of one bound by vow not to marry." [33]

Former Catholic priest, A.W.R. Sipe defines it as,

"... a freely chosen dynamic state, usually vowed, that involves **an honest and sustained attempt** to live **without direct sexual gratification** in order to serve others productively for a spiritual motive." [34]

(Emphasis added)

TRUTH

Biblical celibacy is a "*Gift from God,*" (*Matt.19:11-12, 1Cor.7:7*) and one that is *EXTREMELY RARE!*

True celibacy is **not** obtained through man-made vows of abstinence, or through "an honest and sustained attempt ..." etc.

It is the Divine gift of being able to live, and minister comfortably without the desire (or need) **for** *any* **sexual contact or gratification whatsoever!** (Direct *or* indirect!)

(How in the world does anyone receive "**indirect**" **sexual gratification**, and still stay truly celibate?)

TRUTH

To vow (for any reason whatsoever) is forbidden by Jesus Himself!

"*But I say unto you, **swear not at all**; neither by heaven; for it is God's throne: nor by the earth; for it is His footstool ... but let your communication be yea, yea; nay, nay: **for whatsoever is more than these cometh of evil.**" (See Matt.5:34-37)*

According to the Word of God, anything more than a simple "Yes" or "No" comes from evil (or the evil one); we should therefore understand more readily the dreadful prospects facing anyone trying to live out such a powerful and illicit vow as celibacy.

THE TWIGHLIGHT ZONE

The men and women who *do* give up the right to marry and take this vow, submit themselves to an unscriptural law established over one thousand years ago; but to find the origins of celibacy among priests and priestesses, we must go back even further in time to yet another pagan source!

To the,

"... yellow-capped Lamas of Tibet, the ascetic hermits of Egypt, the virgin priestesses of Thebes, the Astorte cult of Syria, the primitive worshippers of Dodona, the Vestal Virgins of ancient Rome, and the temple priests of the Aztects." [35]

"One does not approach the altar and consecrated vessels with soiled hands" was the hypocritical pagan view, which would later become the keystone for Catholic celibacy. [36]

Jesus condemned this same hypocrisy in Israel's religious leaders:
"... *Now do ye Pharisees make clean the outside of the cup and the platter; but your inward part is full of ravening and wickedness." (Luke 11:39)*

Another key factor in the promotion of celibacy was (surprise, surprise) "economic development" (a.k.a. old fashioned GREED!) According to David Rice, **"legitimate children of priests could inherit and deprive the church of its land!"** [37]

(In those "dark ages," under common law, **illegitimate offspring** could not inherit, and, as such, posed no threat to the church!)

KNIFE'S EDGE

To really appreciate the struggle Catholic priests have, and the reasons for the devastation caused by their failure to live up to their vows, we must reinforce the following.

1   **A law forbidding marriage to priests, nuns** (or anyone else for that matter) **is absolutely contrary to the Word of God!**

    In fact the Bible calls such a law, *"A doctrine of demons!"* (See *1 Tim. 4:1-3*)

2 **Celibacy is a supernatural gift from the Holy Spirit!**

    Without it, the man or woman who commits to celibacy as a way of life is living on a knife's edge – **no matter how sincere he or she may be!**

NOTE: A.W. R. Sipe suggests that nearly 50 percent of Catholic priests break their vow of celibacy by engaging in some form of sexual activity. He estimates that 6 percent of priests have sexual contact with youngsters, 2 percent with children under 10 years, and 4 percent with adolescents. Sipe goes on to say, "sexual abuse of minors is only part of the problem. Four times as many priests involve themselves sexually with adult women, and twice the number of priests involve themselves with adult men." [38]

Some complex surveys indicate that only 2% of all priests are completely true to their vows of celibacy during their lives as priests.) [39]

TO MARRY OR NOT TO MARRY

As hard as this is to hear, it must be said: outside of marriage, men and women can only satisfy their sexual needs in an ungodly and sinful way!

The Bible clearly teaches that "lusts of the flesh" i.e., fornication, masturbation (self-gratification prompted by impure or lustful thoughts), adultery and homosexuality are *all* sins in God's sight.

(See *1 Cor. 6:9, 2 Tim. 2:22*)

It's been suggested that mankind's sexual drive is the second most powerful force on earth: bested only by the power of God's Holy Spirit! One thing we know for sure is that the temptation (and willingness) to commit some form of sexual sin is common to virtually every human being on the planet!

In addition to that, place men or women in institutions where they have no lawful access to one another (certain prisons for example) and the worst expressions of sexual sin can become manifest!

Without realizing it, Catholic priests as well as nuns have willingly entered a "spiritual" prison, so it should not be surprising that their lack of liberty in the realm of marriage has resulted in tragic sexual failures; not only in terms of recent scandals, but throughout the long history of the Catholic Church. Add to this the sad fact that alcoholism runs rampant among the priesthood, and you have a much greater idea of just what these unfortunate people are up against.

THE FINAL CALL

With paganism as her foundation, and false doctrines permeating every part of her structure; the Catholic Church moves slowly and irrevocably towards God's judgment!

Once again God's final call is given to any and all who are trapped anywhere inside Mystery Babylon's evil domain.

"Come out of her, My people, that ye be not partakers of her sins, and that ye receive not of her plagues." (*Rev.18:4*)

With well over a billion Catholic souls in jeopardy, the prospect of reaching out them through evangelism may seem somewhat daunting, especially as they (along with many others) think of themselves as Christians already!

Nevertheless, *"the Lord knows those that are His:"* Praise God for Catholics who are indeed "coming out," and entering into real salvation, and the *True* Church though faith in His Son, and only Savior, the Lord Jesus Christ.

V.I. Pray that more and more laborers will be raised up to work in Catholic "fields;" equipped with knowledge of the truth, and with the desire and ability to approach them in love, gentleness, meekness and faith. (*2Tim.2:24-26*) And let's never forget, *"Joy shall be in Heaven over one sinner that repenteth, more than over ninety and nine just persons, which need no repentance."* (*Luke 15:7*)

Amen.

PART FOUR

THE BRIDEGROOM COMETH

"And there shall be signs …"

CHAPTER TWENTY-SEVEN

THREE GREAT – LATE FEASTS

*"Blessed, happy, fortunate and to be envied, are the people who know the joyful sound, **who understand and appreciate the spiritual blessings symbolized by the feasts**; they walk, O Lord, in the light and favor of Your countenance." (Ps.89:15 Amp. Version)*

Earlier in our travels (ch.10) we looked at the first four of the *"Seven Feasts of the Lord."* Now as our journey draws closer to the end of the age, and in order to better understand the unfolding of God's eternal purpose, we must turn the spiritual spotlight onto the last three of those remarkable celebrations: "Trumpets," "Atonement," and "Tabernacles."

Let's quickly look back, and remind ourselves that all of the Feasts carry with them a three-fold revelation.
The natural – old Israel's actual (physical) Feasts.
The prophetical – seen as types, pointing to (and being fulfilled in and by) the Lord Jesus Christ.
The experiential – to be embraced the by Church, and observed (spiritually) by faith!

THE FEAST OF TRUMPETS

"...In the seventh month, in the first day of the month, shall ye have a sabbath, a memorial of blowing of trumpets, an holy convocation. Ye shall do no servile work therein: but ye shall offer an offering made by fire unto the Lord." (Leviticus 23:24-25)

In Leviticus, only those two short verses describe this fifth remarkable Feast, which was celebrated on the first day of the seventh month (Heb. Tishri) as a *"memorial"* (remembrance), and a *"holy convocation"*(gathering) for the whole of Israel. The day of Trumpets was a sabbath of rest with an offering made by fire, but absolutely no *"servile"* or laborious work was to be done by anyone.
For greater insights regarding the blowing of trumpets, we should go to *Numbers 10:1-10.*
Two silver trumpets were made, and used for specific purposes:

For the calling of the assembly, and for the journeying of the camps.*(Num.10:-2-3)*

First and foremost, trumpets were blown to rouse, gather, and move the nation (*"assembly"*) already redeemed by God! Throughout the Church Age, "Gospel trumpets" (inspired by the Holy Spirit) have been sounding out in exactly the same way!

Not for routine or stagnant gatherings, but for assemblies of life, unity, and movement, i.e. a working or functioning body! (Just look at chapters *12-14 of 1Corinthians*, and *Eph.4:11-16*)

The *"journeying"* of Israel now speaks of the Church moving forward into growth and maturity. As seen for instance in *Heb.6:1-3* ...

"Therefore leaving the principles of the doctrine of Christ, let us go on unto perfection; not laying again the foundation of repentance from dead works, and of faith toward God, of the doctrine of baptisms, and of laying on of hands, and of resurrection of the dead, and of eternal judgment. And this will we do if God permit."

One trumpet was blown to gather the *"princes"* (leaders) of Israel together. (*v.4*)

God shows us clearly that united leadership was an essential part of His guiding the children of Israel on their travels; first through the wilderness, and then in order to possess and finally occupy the Promised Land. However, jealousy and prideful ambition would lead some two hundred and fifty princes to rebel against God's ordained leaders (Moses and Aaron), which in turn brought swift and severe Divine judgment! (See *Num.16*)

Today, Church leaders are plagued by the same spirits of ambition, envy, and pride; not to mention those of greed, suspicion, insecurity, independence, and fear! *Proverbs 13:10a* states that pride is the *only* cause of *"contention"* (strife, quarrels and division).

Just listen to the trumpet's call in *1Cor.1:10.*

*"Now I beseech you brethren, by the Name of our Lord Jesus Christ, that you all speak the same thing, and that there be **no divisions** among you; but that ye be perfectly joined together in the same mind and in the same judgment. For it hath been declared unto me of you brethren, by them which are of the house of Chloe, that **there are contentions** among you. Now this I say, that every one of you saith, **I am of Paul; and I of Apollos; and I of Cephas; and I of Christ. Is Christ divided? was Paul crucified for you? or were you baptized in the name of Paul? ...**"*

Yet in spite of that, the contention between Paul and Barnabas (over John Mark) was so strong, they departed asunder one from the other! (See *Acts 15:36-39*)

Such verses also prove unequivocally that the spirit of pride has been responsible for the countless denominations (which are nothing more than "broken bones") formed within the one true body of the Lord Jesus Christ!

The world reads any lack of unity among Christians as confusion and discord. In other words, why would an unsaved person follow Jesus Christ if we can't agree about Him ourselves??

Little wonder Satan has had so much success with that spirit; he is after all, *"a king over all the children of pride."* (*Job 41:34, Eze.28:17*)

(To revisit the study on the nature and spiritual significance of "broken bones," see page 132.)

Sounding the alarm for war! (*Num.10:9*)

Much later, God would emphasize the importance of this verse through His prophets, including Isaiah (*58:1*), Jeremiah (*4:5*), Hosea (*8:1*), Zephaniah (*1:14-18*).

Hear now from Joel and Amos:

"Blow ye the trumpet in Zion, and sound the alarm in My Holy Mountain: let all the inhabitants of the land tremble: for the day of the Lord cometh, for it is nigh at hand." (Joel 2:1)

"Shall a trumpet be blown in the city, and the people not be afraid? shall there be evil in a city, and the Lord hath not done it? surely the Lord will do nothing, but He revealeth His secret unto His servants the prophets. The lion hath roared, who will not fear? the Lord God hath spoken, who can but prophesy?" (Amos 3:6-8)

This world is heading for disaster: (*Ps.9:17, Rev.11:18*) the Church must find its prophetic voice. Spiritual warfare is unavoidable, especially in these last days; (*Eph.6:10-18*) and the Gospel is most definitely a "call to arms!" The people of God are to *"fight the good fight"* of faith, *"overcome the world,"* and through Christ, triumph over all the wiles of the wicked one. But we are also called to *"sound the alarm"* to a world of lost souls that God's Kingdom (salvation) *and* His judgments are at hand!

In the day of your gladness, and in your solemn days *(Num. 10:10)*

By the grace of God, trumpets would not only sound for journeys, alarms and wars, but for joyful days of celebration and rest. When seen in terms of the New Testament, this verse becomes a glorious celebration of all that Jesus has accomplished for us.

"Rejoice ever more. Pray without ceasing. In everything give thanks: for this is the will of God concerning you." (1Thess.5:16-18)

"Giving thanks unto the Father, which hath made us meet (fit) *to be partakers of the inheritance of the saints in light: Who hath delivered us from the power of darkness, and hath translated us into the Kingdom of His dear Son: in Whom we have redemption through His Blood, even the forgiveness of sins." (Col.1:12-14)*

"Rejoice in the Lord always: and again I say rejoice." (Phil.4:4)

"My brethren, count it all joy when ye fall into diverse temptations (various trials); *knowing this, that the trying of your faith worketh patience. But let patience have her perfect work, that ye may be perfect* (mature) *and entire* (complete), *wanting* (lacking) *nothing." (James 1:2-4)*

Those *"solemn"* or appointed days of old can now be seen as special leadings of the Holy Spirit involving individual or corporate periods of *"prayer and fasting"* when deemed necessary; (*Matt. 17:14-21*) and extending even to the temporary (and voluntary) sexual abstention between husband and wife. (*1Cor.7:1-6*)

Trumpets to be blown in the beginnings of your months ...and over your burnt offerings and the sacrifices of your peace offerings *(Num.10:10)*

For the Israelites, the seventh month was the *last* month of feasts, and the one determined by God to hold all three of these increasingly important celebrations. Tishri was however (and still is) the *first* month of Israel's civil new year (Rosh Hashanah): making it a truly symbolic "first and last" month with obvious Messianic implications! (see *Rev. 1:8*)

In honor of the perfect sacrifice made by the Lord Jesus Christ, and through the empowering of the Holy Spirit, Christians now have the wonderful privilege of offering continual spiritual sacrifices of praise, worship, thanksgiving, service and sharing.

"By Him therefore let us offer the sacrifices of praise to God continually, that is, the fruit of our lips giving thanks to His Name. But to do good and to communicate (share) *forget not: for with such sacrifices God is well pleased." (Heb.13:15-16)*

"I beseech you therefore, brethren, by the mercies of God, that ye present your bodies a living sacrifice, holy, acceptable unto God, which is your reasonable service." (Rom.12:1)

"If I then, your Lord and Master, have washed your feet; ye also ought to wash one another's feet. For I have given you an example, that ye should do as I have done to you." (John 13:14-15)

"...And for a memorial" (*v.10*)

Just as trumpets were so often blown to remind God's Old Covenant people of His will and purpose (by Law), so now the Holy Spirit fulfills their type by gently and continually reminding God's New Covenant people of all that Jesus said, did – and does still – by Grace!

*"But the Comforter, which is the Holy Ghost, Whom the Father will send in My Name, He shall teach you all things, and **bring to remembrance**, whatsoever I have said unto you. ... He shall glorify Me: for He shall receive of Mine, and shall show it unto you." (See John 14:26 and 16:13-15)*

"For the Law was given by Moses, but grace and truth came by Jesus Christ." (John1:17)

SUMMARY

The Apostle John was in the Spirit on the Lord's day (Sunday), and heard behind him a *"great voice, as of a trumpet ..."* (*Rev.1:10*) That *"great voice"* belongs to none greater than our Lord and Savior Jesus Christ, Who is calling His Church to move forward in faith, and *"into the unity of the Spirit, in the bond of peace." (Eph.4:3)*

The natural trumpets of Israel were made of silver, (*Num.10:2*) which can readily be seen as a type of redemption, freedom and hope! (*Ex. 30:11-16* and *38:25, Num.3:40-49, Lev.25:8-10*) This tells us that the Lord Jesus is also sounding out to an unbelieving world (through His Church), that He is the One and Only Way of salvation!

"Neither is there salvation in any other: for there is none other Name under Heaven given among men, whereby we must be saved." (Acts 4:12)

There can be no question or doubt regarding God's ultimate will and purpose:

*"That in the dispensation of the fullness of times He might gather together **IN ONE** all things **IN CHRIST**, both which are in Heaven, and which are on earth; **EVEN IN HIM**." (Eph.1:10)*

"This is My Beloved Son, HEAR YE HIM." (*Luke 9:35*)

We know that in Spirit, and to the degree that faith has allowed; believers throughout the church age have been able to celebrate and experience *all seven* of the *"Feasts of the Lord;"* but speaking directly of the last days, Jesus Himself said,

*"And this Gospel of the Kingdom shall be preached in all the world for a witness unto all nations; **and then the end shall come**."* (*Matt.24:14*)

So today, by the Word of the Lord, and perhaps more than ever before, the Church has the responsibility, the privilege, and the blessing of keeping the Feast of Trumpets: for in doing so, believers will be boldly announcing the Good News of God's Kingdom on earth; proclaiming His Majesty and Grace; and above all, sounding out His unfathomable Love and mercy in reconciling the world to Himself through Christ!

****

For those wishing to go a little further into "Trumpets," the following scriptures offer some interesting comparisons.

1. The call for gathering, preparation and warning. (*2Pet.3:3-14, Rev.1:9-11*)
2. Sabbath of rest for the people of God. (*Heb.4:9-11*)
3. Memorial of blowing of trumpets. (*Ps.20:7, 2Pet.1:12-21, 2Pet.3:1-2, Jude5*)
4. Holy Convocation (gathering). (*Eph.1:10 -14, 2Pet.2:5 -10*)
5. No servile (fleshly) work. (*Gal.5:16-21, Col.3:16-17 and 23*)
6. An offering made by fire. (*Rom.12:1-2, 1Pet.3:12-14*)

****

THE DAY OF ATONEMENT (*Lev.23:26-32*)

*"Also on the tenth day of the seventy month there shall be a Day of Atonement: it shall be an holy convocation unto you; and ye shall **afflict your souls**, and offer an offering made by fire unto the Lord. ... Ye shall do **no manner of work** ..."* (*Lev.23:27, 31a*)

Observed on the tenth day of the seventh month (Tishri) as a day of corporate or national cleansing; the *"Day of Atonement"* (Heb.Yom Kippur) is regarded by many commentators as the most important day of Israel's year. Christians however, should recognize "Atonement" as another spiritual step (the sixth) toward understanding God's glorious and unfolding revelation of the *"Seven Feasts of the Lord;"* which, through the finished work of Christ, He has graciously given to His New Covenant people.

By way of background, let me say here that although the Day of Atonement was counted among the Feasts of the Lord, it was definitely not a "feast" for God's people!

"No manner of work" was a commandment intended to create an atmosphere of prayer and meditation; and *"afflicting the soul"* refers to the "humbling" or "chastening" of each individual. An explanation, and confirmation of this can be found in two Psalms written by King David.

"... I humbled myself with fasting; ..." (Ps.35:13)
"... I wept and chastened my soul with fasting, ..." (Ps.69:10)

A detailed description of *"the Day of Atonement"* is given in *Leviticus chapter 16*, but as I have already shared some of its wonders (ch.9), please forgive a small amount of repetition.

The chapter opens with a sobering reminder of the folly of Aaron's sons, Nadab and Abihu, in offering to God, *"strange (unholy or profane) fire"* in their censers, *"which He commanded them not."* (See *Lev.10:1-2*)

The severity of their punishment must be discerned in light of the fact they obviously knew that only coals of fire taken from *"the altar before the Lord"* were to be used in offering incense.

(*Lev.16:12*)

"Strange fire" forever stands as a symbol of fleshly works, or worldly gimmicks offered to God in any form of ministry; be it prayer, praise, worship, or service!

"God is a Spirit: and they that worship Him must worship Him in sprit and in truth." (*John 4:24*)

No fleshly endeavor is pleasing to God (*Rom.8:8*), even when done in the Name of Jesus!

The flesh must (and will) die! Consider this New Testament example:

In the early church, many who possessed lands or houses sold them, and brought the proceeds to the apostles who shared them with the needy. (*Acts 4:32-37*)

"But a certain man named Ananias, with Sapphira his wife, sold a possession, and kept back part of the price, his wife also being privy to it, and brought a certain part, and laid it at the apostle's feet. But Peter said, Ananias, why hath Satan filled thine heart to lie to the Holy Ghost, and to keep back part of the price of the land? While it remained, was it not thine own? And after it was sold, was it not in thine own power? Why hast thou conceived this thing in thine heart? Thou hast not lied to men but unto God. And Ananias hearing these words fell down, and gave up the ghost:..." (See *Acts 5:1-11*)

Caught with the "strange fire" offering of wanting fleshly recognition, or of *"loving the praise of men more than the praise of God,"* (*John 12:43*) Ananias and Sapphira were both smitten, and died before the Lord for their transgression!

These scriptures, and many others, confirm that the closer the manifestation of God, the more powerful are His corrective measures!

Now see how other types and shadows of Leviticus 16 come alive!

Once a year as high priest, Aaron was given limited, lawful access (through a material veil) to God's earthly throne (the Mercy Seat) within the Holy of Holies. (v.2)

Through the veil of Christ's flesh (and by pure grace), believers now have unlimited spiritual access to God's Heavenly throne.

"Let us therefore come boldly unto the throne of grace, that we may obtain mercy, and find grace to help in time of need." (*Heb.4:16*)

"For Christ is not entered into the holy places made with (human) hands, which are the figures of the true; but into heaven itself, now to appear in the presence of God for us." (*Heb.9:24*)

"Having therefore, brethren, boldness to enter into the holiest by the blood of Jesus, by a new and living way, which He hath consecrated for us, through the (torn) *veil, that is to say His flesh; and having an High Priest over the house of God; let us draw near with a true heart in full assurance of faith, having our hearts sprinkled from an evil conscience, and our bodies washed with pure water."(Heb.10:19-22*; see also *Eph.2:4-18)*

Before making atonement for Israel, Aaron was commanded to offer a bullock as a sacrifice for his own sins as well as those of his household. (*vs.3, 6, and 11*)

The sinless Christ however, would need only to offer *Himself* (once and for all) as the complete and perfect sacrifice for the sins of the whole world!

"Not yet that He (Jesus) *should offer Himself often, as the high priest entereth into the* (most) *holy place every year with blood of others* (animal sacrifices); *for then must He often have suffered since the foundation of the world: but now once in the end of the world hath He appeared to put away sin by the sacrifice of Himself." (Heb.9:25-26)*

"For such an High Priest became us, Who is holy, harmless, undefiled, separate from sinners, and made higher than the heavens; Who needeth not daily, as those high priests, to offer up sacrifice, first for his own sins, and then for the people's: for this He did once, when He offered up Himself." (Heb.7:26-27)

No human priest could ever take away sins – only our heavenly High Priest could!

Aaron's righteousness was external: i.e. ceremonial, ritualistic and temporary. (*v.4*)
In other words, his offerings could never take away sins nor impart true righteousness.

"But in those sacrifices there is a remembrance again made of sins every year. For it is not possible that the blood of bulls and goats should take away sins." (See *Heb.10:1-18*)

Christ's righteousness is internal, i.e. actual, life-changing, and eternal!
The moment we are given faith to believe in Christ, and receive Him; (*John 1:12-13*) God's righteousness is imputed or attributed to us!

"How much more shall the Blood of Christ, Who through the eternal Spirit offered Himself without spot unto God, purge your conscience from dead works to serve the Living God?" (Heb.9:14)

"For He (God) *hath made Him* (Jesus) *to be sin* (sin offering) *for us, Who knew no sin; that we might be made the righteousness of God in Him." (2Cor.5:21)*

"IT IS FINISHED." (John 19:30)

"Two goats for sin, and a ram for burnt offering." (*vs. 5, and 7-10*)
Could Aaron possibly have known that it would take all the sacrifices of the Old Testament (and so much more) to even begin to paint the canvas that our Lord and Savior would one day so wonderfully complete? On that *ultimate* Day of Atonement, God's lot would fall unswervingly upon Jesus; first as the sin offering to die for our sins, (*1Cor.15:3*) and then as the *"scapegoat"* to bear them forever away! (*John1:29*)

If you ask, "Why goats for the sin offering, and not sheep or lambs?"

The answer is, *"For God so loved the world"* that Jesus would die for *all* men; *(1Tim.4:10)* even those who would despise and reject Him! *(Is.53:3)*

The ram was offered as a burnt offering for "acceptance." (*Lev.1:4*)

Typically the burnt offering was voluntary, *(Lev.1:2)* and of course in truth, Jesus would become the ultimate Volunteer! *(Heb.9:14)* It is also true that only those that are chosen to accept the "Ram" (the King of Sheep – Christ Jesus) as their "burnt offering" will be "accepted" by His Father in Heaven!

*"According as He hath chosen us in Him before the foundation of the world, that we should be holy and without blame before Him in love: having predestinated us unto the adoption of children by Jesus Christ to Himself, according to the good pleasure of His will, to the praise of the glory of His grace, wherein **He hath made us accepted in the Beloved.** In Whom we have redemption through His blood, the forgiveness of sins, according to the riches of His Grace; ..."*

(Eph.1:4-7)

Aaron took coals of fire, and sweet incense beaten small within the veil so he would not die.

(vs.12-13)

Holy fire together with sweet incense made a cloud of fragrance, which would not only cover the Mercy Seat but also the smell of Aaron's flesh!

As we've seen, fire was to be taken only from the *"altar before the Lord,"* and the incense was to be made exclusively by and for the priests. Any one found making counterfeit incense would be *"cut off"* or expelled from God's people Israel! *(Ex.30:34-38)*

NOTE: One of the *"blemishes"* which prevented any descendant of Aaron from ministering to the Lord *"within the veil"* was a *"flat"* or "blunt"(perhaps broken) nose; which naturally speaks of not being able to smell the difference between genuine and counterfeit incense. (See *Lev.21:16-24*) One of the greatest needs in the Body of Christ today is the ability to discern between the holy and the profane; the clean and the unclean; the Spirit and the flesh! (See *Eze.22:26*) – We should *all* pray for a "sharper nose!"

Also of particular interest here is the fact that priests would die *"before the Lord,"* only for disobedience! In complete contrast, Jesus would surrender to death only as the result of absolute obedience to His Father's will! *(John 8:29, Luke 22:42)*

Christ's whole life of obedience and love was as *"sweet incense"* before the Father: He took the *"coals of fire"* as the trials sent from God's hand, and willingly accepted them for our sakes; making His sacrifice perfect in every way. And let's never forget that His fragrance came from being *"beaten very small."*

"But I am a worm, and no man; a reproach of men, and despised of the people." (Ps.22:6)

"Yet it pleased the Lord to bruise Him; He hath put Him to grief: when Thou shalt make His soul an offering for sin, ..." (Is.53:10a)

"Let this mind be in you, which was also in Christ Jesus: Who, being in the form of God, though it not robbery to be equal with God: but made Himself of no reputation, and took upon

Him the form of a servant, and was made in the likeness of men: and being found in fashion as a man, He humbled Himself, and became obedient unto death, even the death of the cross." (*Phil.2:5-8*)

The sin offerings: Aaron first took some of the blood from the bullock and then from the goat, and sprinkled it with his finger *seven times* before the Mercy Seat (*vs. 14-16*)

The cross or tree upon which the blood of Jesus was sprinkled *seven times* before the Father (from head, side, hands, feet and back) becomes the believer's "spiritual altar." It is there for all time that sin was dealt with and mercy received. Like the *"rock"* in the wilderness; Christ only needed to be smitten *once!* *"For by **one offering** He hath perfected forever them that are sanctified."*(separated or made holy) (*Heb.10:14*)

Years ago, I came across a copy of "The New Panorama Bible Study Course." (Published by Fleming H. Revell.) In it, the various dispensations, or progressive stages of God's dealings with mankind are beautifully laid out in picture form. I had enjoyed looking through the book a number of times, but then, one day I "saw" it! **The first** dispensation (Edenic or innocence) ended in judgment upon Adam and Eve as they were expelled from the garden. **The second** (Antediluvian or Conscience) ended with the flood, and judgment upon mankind. **The third** (Postdiluvian or Human Government) ended with judgment on Babel, and a scattered human race. **The fourth** (Patriarchal or Promise) ended with God's judgment upon Israel and their bondage in Egypt. **But the fifth** (Legal or Mosaic) dispensation would end, **not in judgment upon mankind; but upon sin itself in the Person of God's Only Beloved Son, Jesus Christ!**

That dear reader, was the "**DAY OF ATONEMENT!**"

No man would be with Aaron in the Tabernacle until the atonement was completed, and he came out! (*vs. 17-19*) We know now that Jesus had to be alone until His atoning work was *"finished."*

*"**Smite the Shepherd, and the sheep will be scattered** ..." (Zech.13:7)*

*"Behold the hour cometh, yea, is now come, that **ye shall be scattered**, every man to his own, **and shall leave Me alone**: and yet I am not alone, because the Father is with Me." (John 16:32)*

After His inimitable atoning sacrifice; after His death and descent into the *"lowest parts of the earth;"* (*Eph.4:9*) after His glorious resurrection, and finally after His ascent into heaven where He presented His Own Blood before the Throne of His Father; Jesus came out from the heavenly Holy of Holies as the almighty conquering King! *"Which in His times He shall show* (manifest), *Who is the blessed and only Potentate, the King of kings and Lord of lords; ..." (1Tim.6:15) "I AM Alpha and Omega, the Beginning and the End, saith the Lord, which is, and which was, and which is to come, the Almighty." (Rev.1:8)*

Aaron laid both his hands upon the head of the scapegoat Year after year, the high priest would confess the sins of Israel, and place them vicariously, albeit symbolically on the head of the live goat; which would then be led away by the hand of a *"fit man"* into the wilderness. (*v.20-26*)

Remember the title put on the cross by Pilate?

"JESUS OF NAZARETH THE KING OF THE JEWS"

Pilate had it written in *"Hebrew, and Greek, and Latin" (John 19:19-20)* ; but did he realize that those translations (almost certainly written in mockery) would nevertheless reveal a staggering truth?

The truth being, that those three languages would encompass, and therefore represent

every single human being on earth!

Hebrew: the religious, or "covenant" language of Jewish Law, through which God made Himself known to men. **Greek:** the intellectual and international language of culture, representing human wisdom (reason), art, exploration, and commerce. (See *1Cor.1:22*) **Latin:** the official language of the Roman Empire (at that time, the known world); representing human achievement, power and conquest. (Not to mention greed and corruption!) So then, it has never been a question of whether "Jews" or "Romans" crucified Christ. In reality, *each and every one of us* born with the fallen nature of Adam, and under the curse of sin (*Gen.5:3, Rom.5:12*) would collectively drive the nails into Christ's Body on that tree! (*1Pet.2:24*) On God's great Day of Atonement, every man, woman and child who ever lived would "lay their own hands" on Jesus, the "*Lamb of God:*" Who in gracious and selfless love would bear away the sin of the whole world! (*John 1:29, 1John 2:2*) However, because each of us put Jesus on that cross; each of us must believe, and "*receive Him*" as Lord and Savior in order to obtain God's forgiveness, and be saved from the judgment to come! We must each "*confess with our mouths that Jesus Christ is Lord, and believe in our hearts that God raised Him from the dead!*" (*Rom.10:9*) **This is the Way of salvation!**

NOTE: As almost all the information shared on the remaining part of Leviticus 16 can be found in pages 118-121, I feel nothing would be gained by repeating it here; so please allow me to close this study with the following synopsis.

The Hebrew word for atonement is "Kaphar," which means – to cover, expiate, placate, cancel, pardon, purge away, appease, cleanse, disannul, forgive, put off, make reconciliation, and to be merciful! Although kept by Israel naturally every year (*vs. 29-31*), Christians can now see this day as completely fulfilled in Christ; and applied by faith whenever sin is committed and sincerely confessed. (*1John 1:9*)

The Day of Atonement is therefore bestowed upon the Church as the "gift of repentance."

(1Tim.2:24-25)

Knowing also that it was Israel's day of corporate or communal cleansing, means that before the Church can enter into the "spirit" of that day, true believers (especially those in leadership) must begin to overcome carnal barriers or divisions within the "Body," such as denominational labels, independent attitudes, man made traditions, resentment, unforgiveness, rivalries, and so on.

(Perhaps by first *really listening* to the "Trumpets!")

Obviously the Body of Christ coming together before God in repentance, and "*in the unity of the Holy Spirit*" has to be a *spiritual* reality; for unlike natural Israel, "Christ's nation" couldn't all be in the same physical place at the same time! True Christian unity however, will always shine forth when genuine brokenness and humility allow us to love and accept one another **unconditionally**. But it will always be brought about by a deepening love for **Jesus**; inspired of course by the Holy Spirit Who is totally dedicated to performing God's will on earth, and bringing about the fulfillment of Christ's High Priestly prayer,

"That they may be one." (*John 17:11, 21, 22, and 23!*)

The actual word "ATONEMENT" (it may help to see it as "**at-one-ment**" with God) is found **80 times** in the Old Testament, (K.J.V.) but *only once* in the New!

"For if, when we were enemies, we were reconciled to God by the death of His Son, much more shall we be saved by His life. And not only so, but we also joy in God through our Lord Jesus Christ, by Whom we have now received the atonement." (Rom.5:10-11)

Surely even *that* fact speaks of Jesus as the New Testament believer's *one* and *only* "Day of Atonement;" and His Gospel (passed on from one generation to the next, *vs. 31-34*) as the means by which that atonement is imparted to a sin-sick and dying world!

****

THE FEAST OF TABERNACLES

"And the Lord spake unto Moses saying ... The fifteenth day of this seventh month shall be the Feast of Tabernacles for seven days unto the Lord ... with offerings made by fire ... the first day shall be an holy convocation: ye shall do no servile work therein ...on the eighth day shall be an holy convocation unto you. ..." (See *Lev.16:33-44*)

We now approach the seventh and final Feast of the Lord, which took place on the fifteenth day of Tishri (seventh month) and lasted for eight glorious days! (See *Lev.23:33-44*)

But first let me share this – In *Deuteronomy 16:16*, the Lord divided the seven feasts into three groups:

The Feast of Unleavened Bread (including "Passover" and "First Fruits.") – 1 The Feast of Weeks (Pentecost) stands alone. – 2 The Feast of Tabernacles (including "Trumpets" and "Atonement.") – 3

The way I've laid them out here, may give us a better understanding of God's Divine plan and purpose for His New Covenant people.

Feast of Passover – Redemption or justification (getting us out of "Egypt," i.e. this world.) Unleavened Bread – Sanctification or separation (getting "Egypt" out of us!) First Fruits – His Resurrection Life in us (includes baptism in water.) Pentecost – Holy Spirit Baptism (empowering the spiritual life already received.) Trumpets – Proclaiming (sharing the Gospel.) Atonement – Preparing (individual/corporate repentance.) Tabernacles – Celebrating and uniting (the ultimate goal!)

As the seven feasts are already fulfilled in Christ Jesus, the Feast of Tabernacles becomes the absolute fulfillment of God's purpose for those **IN** Christ.

*"Having made known unto us the mystery of His will, according to His good pleasure which He hath purposed in Himself: **that in the dispensation of the fullness of times He might gather together in one all things in Christ**, both which are in heaven, and which are on earth; **even in Him.**"* (Eph.1:9-10)

Here are a number of natural or historical aspects of "Tabernacles" together with thoughts on their spiritual application within the Body of Christ.

A FEAST OF INGATHERING (*Ex.23:14-16, Lev.23:39*)
"When ye have gathered in the fruit of the land ..."

Shadow

The harvest of spring began in the first month (Abib) with "the *Feast of First fruits,*" and ended fifty days later with the celebration of "*Pentecost.*"

"*Tabernacles*" (also known as the Feast of Harvest) was the climax of the sacred year (seventh month), and a feast to celebrate the autumn harvest of fruits.

Both harvests are confirmed in *Deut.11:14.*

"*That I will give you the rain of your land in his due season, the first rain and the latter rain, that thou mayest gather in thy corn, and thy wine, and thine oil.*"

(Not until autumn would both harvests be reckoned as "*gathered in.*")

Substance

After Jesus fulfilled the Feast of First Fruits, the great in gathering or "spring harvest" of souls would begin! (*John 4:35*) The Holy Spirit would confirm this "*first rain*" on the day of Pentecost, as He empowered an already established church: (*Acts 2: 1-4*) but the "Bride of Christ" will only experience the "autumn harvest" or *complete* fulfillment and celebration of Tabernacles when the Lord finally calls us all to be with Him!

"*For the Lord Himself shall descend from heaven with a shout, with the voice of the archangel, and the trump of God: and the dead in Christ shall rise first: then we which are alive and remain shall be caught up together with them in the clouds, to meet the Lord in the air: and so shall we ever be with the Lord.*" (*1Thess.4:16-17*)

A FEAST OF TEMPORARY DWELLINGS (*Lev.23:42*)

"*Ye shall dwell in booths seven days; all that are Israelites born shall dwell in booths ...*"

Shadow

Upon their arrival in the Promised Land, God commanded His people to take the branches of certain trees - *Olive, Pine, Myrtle, Palm* (*Neh.8:15*); and use them to build "*booths*" or temporary dwellings on the roofs of their houses. This was to be a permanent reminder of how God took care of the nation during its forty years of wandering in the wilderness.

"*That your generations may know that I made the children of Israel to dwell in booths, when I brought them out of the land of Egypt: I am the Lord your God.*" (*v.43*)

Substance

God's people have always been "*strangers and pilgrims on the earth*". (*Heb.11:13*) Believers are "*in the world,*" but they are not "*of the world:*" (*John 17:16,18:36*) we are simply passing through!

Abraham looked for, "*a* (heavenly) *city which hath* (eternal) *foundations, Whose builder and maker is God.*" (*Heb.11:10*)

Speaking of his approaching death, Peter wrote,

"*Yea, I think it meet, as long as I am in this tabernacle,* (temporal body) *to stir you up by putting you in remembrance; knowing that shortly I must put off this my tabernacle, even as our Lord Jesus Christ hath showed me.*" (*2Pet.1:13-14*)

And who could improve on Paul's summation?

"For I reckon that the sufferings of this present time are not worthy to be compared with the glory which shall be revealed in us." (*Rom.8:18*)
And,
"Behold, I show you a mystery; we shall not all sleep (die), *but we shall all be changed, in a moment, in the twinkling of an eye, at the last trump: for the trumpet shall sound, and the dead shall be raised incorruptible, and we shall be changed."*(glorified) (*1Cor.15:51-52*)

Characteristics of the spiritual life can even be found in the types of trees used to build those tempo-rary dwellings.
V. I. They all emanate from Christ!

"Olive" Its oil speaks of the Holy Spirit's anointing, and Christ's illumination of our lives while in these temporary "tabernacles." (*Ex.27:20-21, Matt.5:14-16*)

"Pine" Speaks of fullness, richness, beauty, and (lasting) endurance. (*Is.60:13, Jn.1:16, 2Cor.8:9, James1:12*)

"Myrtle" Speaks of purity and fragrance. (Its snow white flower has a perfume more exquisite than the rose.) (*2Cor.2:15, Eph.5:2*)

"Palm" Speaks of uprightness, fruitfulness, and victory. (Its branches were often used to welcome Royalty!) (*Ps.92:12-14, John 12:12-13, Rom.8:37, Rev.7:9*)

A FEAST OF REJOICING (*Lev.23:40, Deut.16:14-15, Neh.8:17*)

"... and ye shall rejoice before the Lord your God seven days. ... thou and thy son, thy daughter, ... manservant ... maidservant, and the Levite, **the stranger***, the fatherless, and the widow, that are within thy gates."*(*Deut.16:14*)

Shadow
Those sheltering within the gates of Israel were graciously invited to "Tabernacles!"
The *"stranger"* in this case was a Gentile who had come to trust in the God of Israel, had entered into the covenant of circumcision, and was therefore accepted as a permanent member of the chosen nation.

NOTE: Neither *"foreigners"* (mere lodgers) nor *"hired servants"* (temporary paid workers) were allowed to partake of the Passover lamb; but as far as God was concerned, the stranger who was circum-cised was the same as one born in the land.

"One law shall be to him that is home born, and unto the stranger that sojourneth among you."

(See *Ex.12:43-48*)

In other words, the blessings of the seven feasts, including God's provision, protection, mercy, and love were given to the "abiding stranger" as well as to the natural born Israelite!
***All of them* could dwell in booths!**

Substance

Neither the "*foreigner*" (religious visitor) nor the "*hired servant*" (those relying on good works) will partake of any of the "*Feasts*" – or the eternal blessings of God!

Today, by the grace of God, any "home born" Jew, or Gentile "stranger" who sincerely "*calls upon the Name of the Lord* (Jesus) *will be saved*;" (see *Rom.10:9-13*) and will find eternal shelter within the "spiritual gates" of God's "*holy nation*"(*1Pet.2:9*) – the true church, or the "*Israel of God*." (*Gal.6:16*) **Everyone of us must be "Born again!"** (*John 3:3*)

"*For there is no difference between the Jew and the Greek* (Gentile): *for the same Lord over all is rich unto all that call upon Him.*" (*Rom.10:12*)

Of course, circumcision is *still* required to enter God's Kingdom, but it is now the New Covenant circumcision of the *heart* (spiritual separation by grace), *not* the Old Covenant separation of flesh by letter of the law! (See *Rom.2:28-29*)

Once in Christ, Gentiles cease to be Gentiles; Jews cease to be Jews. *Both* share "booths" and "tabernacle" together as "new creatures in Christ!" (See *2Cor.5:17* and *Eph.2:11-19*.)

"*For as many of you as have been baptized into Christ have put on Christ.*" (*Gal.3:28-29*)
"*Where there is neither Greek, nor Jew, circumcision nor uncircumcision, Barbarian, Scythian, bond nor free: but Christ is all in all.*" (*Col.3:11*)

How wonderfully all this answers to Noah's prophecy in *Genesis 9:27*.

"God shall enlarge Japheth, and he shall dwell in the tents of Shem."

The fact that Japheth, (speaking of Gentiles) would one day share the same "*tents*" or "temporary dwellings" as Shem (speaking of Jews) was a mystery hidden deep in the mind of God, and kept from mankind until "*the fullness of time.*" But from the very beginning God had purposed to bring believing Jews and Gentiles together eternally (as one) in Christ Jesus. This was indeed, "*the mystery which was kept secret since the world began, but now is made manifest by the scriptures of the prophets,*" (*Rom.16:25-26*) "*That the gentiles should be fellow heirs, and of the same body, and partakers of His promise in Christ by the Gospel:* (*Eph.3:6*) "*Christ in you the hope of glory!*" (*Col.1:27*)

(No wonder God wanted them to rejoice!)

A FEAST FOR THE GLORY OF GOD (*Lev.23:43, Deut.16:12*)
"*...That your generations may know ... and thou shalt remember ...*"

Shadow

In *2Chronicles 7:1-10*, God caused the Feast of Tabernacles to coincide with the dedication of Solomon's Temple.

"*Now when Solomon had made an end of praying, the fire came down from heaven, and consumed the burnt offering and the sacrifices; and the glory of the Lord filled the house. ...*
And on the three and twentieth day of the seventh month he sent the people away into their tents, glad and merry in heart ..." (vs. *1* and *10*)

The Temple of Solomon was naturally the most glorious, and extravagant expression of God's blessings upon Israel. The crowd attending its dedication and the accompanying celebration of Tabernacles was huge! (See *2Chr.7:5-8*)

Nothing in Israel's history would eclipse the glory of that Temple, for it stood for or proclaimed the very heart of God's Old Testament message: that His people should "*know*" and "*remember*" Him, and continue to glorify Him throughout all their generations!

Not because God was insecure and needed their support, but because He knew (for Israel's sake) that forgetting or departing from Him would be the cause of the nation's downfall, and its eventual destruction!

A remarkable verse in the book of Nehemiah states that the Feast of Tabernacles had not been celebrated correctly (in its entirety) from as far back as the days of Joshua to the return of God's people from captivity in Babylon! (*Neh.8:17*)

So even at the Temple dedication, the feast was not performed according to the expressed will of God!

Substance

We may now see Solomon's Temple as a type of God's "*spiritual house,*" which is the Church being built with "*living stones*" by the Holy Spirit. (See *1Pet.2:5*)

(Remember the stones used to build the *natural* Temple were "*great and costly;*" but they were, "*not to be seen.*" (*1Kings 5:17, 6:18*) This is surely God's evaluation of us, and also His desire for the *whole* Body of Christ – great and costly, but hidden in His Son!

That "huge crowd" celebrating tabernacles was nothing less than a type of that "*great multitude, which no man could number, of all nations, and kindreds, and people, and tongues, clothed in white robes and celebrating with palms in their hands before the throne of God, and before the Lamb*" in heaven itself! (*Rev.7:9*)

The fact that the Feast of Tabernacles was rarely (if ever) celebrated according to the perfect will of God, tells us (sadly) that the Church here on earth has likewise failed to come together in "*the unity of the Spirit and in the bond of peace.*" (*Eph.4:3*)

There were of course, many separate "*booths.*" (*Neh.8:16*) Physically the Church has many members: we cannot all live in the same booth! Nevertheless, if we are in Christ we are one!

In *this* age, Tabernacles must surely express a collective manifestation of Psalm 133.

"*Behold, how good and how pleasant it is for brethren to dwell together in unity! It is like the precious ointment upon the head, that ran down upon the beard, even Aaron's beard: that went down to the skirts of his garments; as the dew of Hermon, and as the dew that descended upon the mountains of Zion: for there the Lord commanded the blessing, even life for evermore.*"

Jesus Christ is the Divine fulfillment of the Feast of Tabernacles, and those of us who are born again abide or dwell in Him. (*John 15:4-10*) Though the ultimate manifestation of the Feast of Tabernacles is found *after* the millennium, (*Rev. 21:1-4*) many believers in this age are joyfully celebrating this, and all the other feasts of the Lord –

BY FAITH!

NOTE: The temple described in the book of Ezekiel (*chapters 40-47*) is certainly not the Temple of Solomon. The measurements of Ezekiel's temple differ greatly from that of Solomon's, or any other for that matter, including the one rebuilt by Zerubbabel after the Babylonian captivity.

The Temple of Ezekiel's vision may well prove to be the millennium temple located in Jerusalem, where, after the "great tribulation," a remnant (survivors) from *all* nations, "*shall even go up from year to year to worship the King, the Lord of hosts, and to keep the Feast of Tabernacles.*" (See *Zech.14:16*)

The Bible makes no mention of those Gentile nations keeping any of the other feasts during the millennium. Why? Because Jesus will be the Living, Reigning Lord, Who will actually dwell or tabernacle with men on the earth! His very presence will make the first six feasts unnecessary.

In light of that glorious reality, even the "Ark of the Covenant" will be remembered no more ...

"*And it shall come to pass, when ye be multiplied and increased in the land, in those days, saith the Lord, they shall say no more, the Ark of the Covenant of the Lord: neither shall it come to mind: neither shall they remember it: neither shall they visit it: neither shall that be done any more. At that time they shall call Jerusalem the Throne of the Lord; and all the nations shall be gathered unto it, to the Name of the Lord, to Jerusalem: neither shall they walk any more after the imagination of their evil heart.*" (*Jer. 3:16*)

CHAPTER TWENTY-EIGHT

FRIEND OR SERVANT?

"...It is given unto you to know the mysteries of the Kingdom of Heaven, but to them it is not given." (Matt.13:11)

Several years have passed since the Trade Towers were destroyed by the Islamic terrorist group known as al-Qaeda. – A large and growing volume of evidence suggests that "911" was in fact allowed (therefore aided and abetted) by the Bush/Cheney Administration as an excuse for (amongst other things) the invasion of Iraq, Afghanistan. Certainly, those on the "inside" know the truth: it has always been that way!

As I began writing the final part of this book, another terrorist faction known as Hezbollah, crossed into Israel from Lebanon; kidnapped two Israeli soldiers, and at the same time began firing rockets into northern sections of Israel itself. Two stories emerged ...

1) Israel's retaliation was appropriate. 2) Israel's response was "Overly aggressive," "Heavy-handed," or "Extreme!" It didn't take long before poor little Hezbollah (financed directly by Syria and Iran; and supported by virtually every other Arab nation) was being portrayed everywhere as the little hero underdog fighting bravely against big bad Israel! (Well, what did you expect? – Satan owns a lot of media outlets!) There is currently a fragile cease-fire, but in reality, things are just getting started!

NOTE: The word Hezbollah is also correctly spelt Hezb Allah, and means literally – the party or people of the moon god. (Remember the "crescent moon" has always been Islam's main symbol.)

Back in 1946, Hezbolla, al Qaeda, Taliban, etc., did not exist. Very few had heard of Syria, Iran or Iraq, let alone Palestine! (Israel was not yet a nation). How many knew then of radical Islam's dark ambitions to take over the "infidel's world," and destroy every Jew on the face of the earth!

After the ravages of World War II, this "Humpty Dumpty" world just wanted to put itself "back together again!" The cry was "Peace, peace!" but there would be no peace!

"Destruction cometh; and they shall seek peace, and there shall be none." (Eze.7:25)

Today, the eyes of the whole world are on the Middle East! Even people who have no idea what the Bible teaches about the "last days" are instinctively aware that something monumental is brewing there! More and more are convinced it's only a matter of time before the "ticking Arab bomb" goes off!

Long ago, Jesus spoke privately to His disciples of such a time.

*"Take heed that no man deceive you. For many shall come in My Name, saying I am Christ; and shall deceive many. And ye shall hear of wars and rumors of wars: **see that ye be not troubled: for all these things must come to pass**, but the end is not yet. For nation shall rise against nation, and kingdom against kingdom: and there shall be famines, and pestilences, and earthquakes in divers places. All these are **the beginnings of sorrows**." (Matt.24:4-8)*

Jesus also said,

*"**Ye are My friends**, if ye do whatsoever I command you. Henceforth **I call you not servants; for the servant knoweth not** what his lord doeth: but **I have called you friends**; for all things that I have heard of My Father **I have made known unto you**." (John 15:14-15)*

Jesus is telling us that His "friends" may know the inner workings of God's plan for the ages (including end-time events), but His "servants" may not! It follows then that much of what is written in the scriptures is hidden from the eyes of servants, but can be readily discerned by friends!

Look at the first fourteen verses of *Matthew, chapter 24* for example, and realize that the Lord is speaking primarily to His friends. In verse14 He tells us that *"the end"* will come only after the Gospel has been preached, *"...in all the world for a witness unto all nations."*
But suddenly in verse15 He begins to speak to His servants.
*"When ye therefore see the ABOMINATION OF DESOLATION, spoken of by **Daniel the prophet**, stand in the holy Place, (let the reader consider this:) ..."*
The *"abomination of desolation"* could only mean something to Jews familiar with the history of their temple, and its desecration by Seleucid ruler Antiochus IV Epiphanes (175-163B.C.), who commanded swine to be sacrificed on the temple's brazen altar! (*Dan.11:31*)
This was foreshadowing a time (still to come) of even greater blasphemy and abomination, when the *"anti-Christ"* himself will sit in the temple of God, and actually claim to be God! (*2Thess.2:4*)

Food for thought: Jesus called Daniel *"a prophet"* (much of his book is prophetic); so perhaps we shouldn't separate it from the "other twelve!"
To confirm that the Lord is speaking to servants (Jews who will face the *"great tribulation"*); Jesus says in verses 20-21,

*"But pray that your flight be not in the winter, **neither on the Sabbath day**: for then shall be great tribulation, such as was not since the beginning of the world to this time, no, nor ever shall be."*

The law of Moses prevents the orthodox Jew from traveling more than two thirds of a mile (approx.) on a Sabbath day. (See *Acts 1:12*) No *"friend"* (born again believer) would be concerned with such a law! (Just one more reason why the Church will *NOT* go through the "great tribulation!")

"For God hath not appointed us to wrath, but to obtain salvation by our Lord Jesus Christ!"
(*1Thess.5:9*)

Along with that, did you know that, *"**the first fruits were not to be burned on the altar**?"*
(*Lev.2:12*)

However, before that longed for *"day of Christ"* comes, and the church is *"caught up,"* or *"gathered together unto Him;"* (see *1Thess.4:16-17,* and *2Thess.2:1-4*) two things must happen.

*"Let no man deceive you by any means: for **that day shall not come**, except there be a **falling away first, and that man of sin be revealed**, the son of perdition ..."*

1. A general *"falling away"* (world-wide religious departure from the Word of Truth).
2. The appearance of the *"man of sin"* (anti-Christ), *"the son of perdition."*

Who could argue that we are already experiencing prophecy number one?

The second confirms that believers (still living) will be here when the anti-Christ is revealed!

Of course Jesus has not even told His "friends" exactly when the catching away of the church, or His "second coming" will occur: *"no man nor angel knows the hour or the day."* (*Matt.24:36*)

But we *do* know that the *"wrath of God"* comes down upon the already established *"seat* or kingdom *of the beast"* (*Rev.16:10*) during the *second half* of the great (seven year) tribulation!

So then, as *"we are not appointed unto wrath,"* we should look forward to the "rapture" taking place some time during the first three and a half years!

The period known as the *"great tribulation,"* or *"Jacob's trouble"* (*Jer.30:7*) begins with the anti-Christ *"confirming* (making) *a covenant* (treaty of peace) *with many for one week* (seven years)."

(See *Dan.9:27* Amp.)

This covenant will most certainly involve Israel and the Arab nations, but it is only when he breaks it (after three and a half years), that *"the wrath of God"* is progressively poured out upon his "kingdom" and the whole unbelieving world!

Jesus said of that time,

*"except those days should be shortened, there should no flesh be saved: but **for the elect's sake** those days will be shortened."* (*Matt.24:22*)

The elect here does not refer to the Bride of Christ (born again believers), but to those who will *"...come out of great tribulation, and **will wash their robes and make them white** in the Blood of the Lamb. Therefore they are **before the throne of God** and serve Him **day and night in His Temple**: ..."*

(from *Rev. 7:9-15*)

Do you see it?

First: these saints *"wash their robes ..."* as they are being put to death by anti-Christ for refusing to *"worship him or his image, or receive his mark."* (See *Rev.14:12-13,* and *20:4*)

Christ has already washed His bride (*1Cor.6:11. Rev.1:5*), and given her robes of *"fine linen, clean and white."* (*Rev.19:8*)

In other words, during the church age, Christ died for His Bride. – Those who are saved *"out of great tribulation"* will (literally) have to die for Christ!

Second: they are *"standing **before** the throne of God ..."* (*Rev.7:9 and 15*) – Where is the Bride?

"IN CHRIST" – "SITTING IN HIS THRONE," – "AT GOD'S RIGHT HAND!" (*Rom.12:5, Eph.1:20-23, 2:5-6, Col.3:1, Rev.3:21*)

Third: *"they serve Him **day and night in His Temple**."* – The Bride will be in the *"New Jerusalem."* (*Rev.21:27*) – There is **NO TEMPLE** there! Nor is there any **NIGHT!** (See *Rev.21:22-25*)

Some insist the church must go through the great tribulation in order to be purified or perfected, but that would deny both the Word of God, and the finished work of Christ!
    *"**For by one offering He has perfected forever them that are sanctified**."* (*Heb.10:14*)

Some say that through the centuries (especially the early ones) Christians suffered dreadfully; so why should today's saints (or tomorrow's) get off so lightly?
    This argument fails when we consider that the Body of Christ has never been (nor ever will be) plagued or judged by the wrath of God!
    Jesus said in *John 16:33*, *"In the world you will have tribulation ..."* (persecution, tests or trials).
    That's normal for *"any who will live Godly in Christ Jesus,"* (*2Tim.3:12*) but the *"**great** tribulation"* is something altogether different!
    God shows us that His purpose for this great (end-time) tribulation is three fold.

1 To judge the world, and especially the *"great whore!"* (See *Rev.6:15-17, 16:1-7, 19:2*)
2 To *"**purify** (prepare) **the sons of Levi**,"* and to bring the remnant of Israel to repentance, and a knowledge of the true Savior, Jesus Christ. (See *Mal.3:3, Zech.12:10, 13:8-9*)
3 To offer salvation to as many will receive it. (See *Rev.14:6-13*)

1 There has not been a planetary judgment since the days of the great flood. Because of this, many unbelievers and "servants" make light of the judgment to come.

"... there shall come in the last days scoffers (mockers), *walking after their own lusts, and saying, where is the promise of His coming? for since the fathers fell asleep, all things continue as they were from the beginning of the creation ..."* (*2Pet.3:3-4*)

Nevertheless, friends know ...

"The Lord is not slack concerning His promise, as some men count slackness; but is long-suffering to us-ward, not willing that any should perish, but that all should come to repentance." (*2Pet3:9*)

When God's wrath finally falls on this world, the chaos and devastation will surpass anything currently imaginable to the human mind!

"In those days men will seek death and not find it!" ... They will hide in caves and among the rocks of the mountains: they will say to the mountains, "Fall on us, and hide us from the face of Him that sits on the throne, and from the wrath of the Lamb: ..." (*Rev.9:6, 6:15-17*)

*"...**Woe, woe, woe, to the inhabiters of the earth** ..."* (*Rev.8:13*)

As far as the false "one-world" religious system, or *"great whore"* is concerned; her judgment is to come in a single day!

"For her sins have reached unto Heaven, and God hath remembered her iniquities. ...
How much she hah glorified herself, and lived deliciously, so much torment and sorrow give her: for she said in her heart, I sit a queen, and am no widow, and shall see no sorrow. Therefore shall her plagues come in one day, death and mourning, and famine; and she shall be utterly burned with fire: for strong is the Lord God Who judgeth her." (See *Rev.18:5-8*)

Judgment is surely coming! Only the grace of God in Christ has held it back this long!

2 Friends know that *"blindness in part is happened to Israel, until the fullness of the Gentiles be come in."* (*Rom.11:25*) ... they also know not to *"be wise in their own conceits!"* – Why? Because, *"if God spared not the natural branches, take heed lest He also spare not thee!"* (*Rom.11:21*)

Paul tells us that through Israel's fall, *"salvation is come unto the Gentiles, for to provoke them to jealousy. Now if the fall of them be the riches of the world, and the diminishing of them the riches of the Gentiles; how much more their fullness?"* (*Rom.11:11-12*)

The prophecies of Zechariah give a truly heartbreaking account of just what the "fall" of Israel will mean in the last days.

"For I will gather all nations against Jerusalem to battle; and the city shall be taken, and the houses rifled, and the women ravished; and half the city shall go forth into captivity, and the residue of the people shall not be cut off from the city...And it shall come to pass, that in all the land, saith the Lord, two parts therein shall be cut off and die; but the third shall be left therein.. And I will bring the third part through the fire, and will refine them as silver is refined, and try them as gold is tried: they shall call on My Name, and I will hear them: I will say, it is My people: and they shall say, the Lord is my God." (See *Zech.13:8, 14:1-2*)

Failure to believe the Word of God and embrace their true Messiah Jesus Christ will cause the Jews untold suffering during the great tribulation; but just as it was throughout the entire Old Testament, God will not forget or forsake His natural people! At the height of their persecution, and when all hope is seemingly gone, the *"remnant"* of Israel will be miraculously delivered, and will finally see and recognize the glorious, *"King of kings and Lord of lords!"*

On that great day God will,

*"Seek to destroy all the nations that come against Israel, and will pour out upon the house of David, and upon the inhabitants of Jerusalem, the spirit of grace and supplications: and **they shall look upon Me Whom they have pierced**, and **they shall mourn for Him**, as one mourneth for his only son, and shall be in bitterness for Him, as one that is in bitterness for his first-born ... and the land shall mourn ..."* (See *Zech.12:10*)

NOTE: The same process of "refining," extends to the *"the sons of Levi,"* and is God's way of restoring and preparing His natural priesthood (and nation) for their millennial ministry on the earth.

"That they may offer unto the Lord an offering in righteousness. Then shall the offering of Jerusalem be pleasant unto the Lord, as in the days of old, and as in former years." (*Mal.3:3-4*)

3 Among the vast majority of Christians, the great tribulation is viewed almost exclusively as "God's fearful judgment upon the world." (Many are nervous when the book of Revelation is mentioned, let alone read or taught!) With that in mind, the third facet of this short end-time study brings some balance to the much tilted scale of judgment, horror, wrath, and woe! – Certainly there is all of that, and more; but while the "*sun is being darkened*;" the "*stars of heaven are falling*,"(*Rev.6:12-13*) and "*the sea is turning to blood*," (*Rev.8:8*) the "amazing grace" and love of God continues to reach out to a world of lost souls with the message of salvation!

*"And I saw another angel fly in the midst of heaven, having the **everlasting gospel** to preach unto them that dwell on the earth, and to **every nation**, and kindred, and tongue, and people, saying with a loud voice, Fear God, and give glory to Him; for the hour of His judgment is come: and worship Him that made heaven, and the earth, and the sea, and the fountains of waters."*
(Rev 14:6-7)

The mercy of God offers the only hope of forgiveness for mankind in the Person of Jesus Christ; but the righteousness of God demands justice! The generation that receives God's *final* demand will pay the price for man's rebellion and lawlessness from the beginning of time!

*"... And he that sat on the cloud thrust in his sickle on the earth; and **the earth was reaped.** ... For her grapes are fully ripe. ... And the cities of the nations fell: and **great Babylon came in remembrance** before God, to give unto her the cup of the wine of **the fierceness of His wrath**."*
(See *Rev.14:16-18, and 16:19*)

God's love is infinite – His patience is NOT!

What is almost beyond belief, is the fact that in spite of the plagues of torment and suffering being poured out upon mankind (to bring them to repentance), the hearts of men will grow harder, and ever more set against the Creator!

*"And men were scorched with great heat, and **blasphemed the Name of God**, which hath power over these plagues: and **they repented not** to give Him glory. ... And the rest of the men which were not killed by these plagues **yet repented not** of the works of their hands, that they should not worship devils, (demons) and idols of gold, and silver, and brass, and stone, and of wood: which neither can see, nor hear, nor walk: **neither repented they** of their murders, nor of their sorceries, nor of their fornication, nor of their thefts."* (See *Rev.16:9-11, and 9:20-21*)

What more can God do? He gave His only begotten Son that we might be saved from the wrath to come; but to those whose must go through the tribulation, He graciously answers the prayer of Habakkuk.

"... in wrath remember mercy." (Hab.3:2)

To continue with this chapter's theme, "friend or servant?" I'd like to move on into the realm of illustrations, literal warnings, and parables spoken by the Lord in connection with the last days.
    During the tribulation period, Jesus specifically tells certain people to beware of false Christs or prophets who will be able to deceive many with "*great signs and wonders*." (Matt. *24:23-24*)

"*Even the elect* (the saved out of great tribulation) *would be deceived if it were possible!*" (*24:24*)

I know that what I'm about to say will be difficult for some to hear; but from *Matthew 24:15* to the end of *chapter 25*, Jesus is actually speaking to "servants" and not to "friends!"

Certainly there are principles shared there, which the body of Christ can benefit from, but His message is literally for those who will be "left behind" after the church has gone!

Let me explain:

in the parable of the fig tree, (type of Israel, *Matt.24:32*) "*tender branches and the putting forth of leaves*" tells the Jews that summer is near. Likewise, the generation that lives to see the "*signs of the end*" prophesied by Jesus, "*shall not pass, till all things be fulfilled.*"

That would include Israel, and *all* the Gentile nations i.e., "*the fig tree, and **all** trees.*"(*Luke 21:29*)

On earth, there will be no doubt whatsoever as to the glorious appearing or return of Christ.

"*Immediately after the tribulation of those days shall the sun be darkened, and the moon shall not give her light, and the stars shall fall from heaven, and the powers of the heavens shall be shaken: and then shall appear the sign of the Son of man in heaven: and then shall all the tribes* (nations) *of the earth mourn, and they shall see the Son of man coming in the clouds of heaven with power and great glory.*" (*Matt.24:29-30*)

Those verses are indelibly linked to these:

"*And I saw heaven opened, and behold a white horse; and He that sat upon him was called Faithful and True, and in righteousness He doth judge and make war. ... And He was clothed with a vesture* (robe) *dipped in blood: and His Name is called The Word of God.*"

(See *Rev.19:11-13*)

Now look back at *Matthew 24:30*
"*And He shall send His angels with a great sound of a trumpet, and they shall gather together His elect from the four winds, **from one end of heaven to the other.**"*

Finally go back to *Revelation.19:24:14*
"***And the armies which were in heaven** followed Him upon white horses, clothed in fine linen, white and clean.*"

By the end of the tribulation, everyone who is in heaven is gathered together, and those "*armies*" return to earth following the Lord.

Those on earth will either be ready or totally surprised!

Suddenly – the flood came and took them all away! (*Matt.24:39*)

Suddenly – one shall be taken, the other left! (*24:40*)

Suddenly – the thief came! (*24:43*)

In *verses 45-51*, the "*faithful and wise servant*" who is taking care of the Lord's "*household*" (other servants) is rewarded for his good works when Christ returns.

The "*evil servant*" who is not looking for the Lord's return, and abuses his position of trust will be "*cut asunder,*" and cast away!

This is a warning – *not* a parable!

The parable of the ten virgins (*Matt.25:1-13*) has also nothing to do with the "Church!"

These "*virgins*" are "bridesmaids" – *not* the "Bride!"

Five of them were "*wise,*" or ready when the Lord ("*the Bridegroom*") arrived (Second Coming), and five were not!

Here Jesus is emphasizing what the Word of God has been saying all along; that during the "church age" (and through the tribulation), unsaved Jews and Gentiles are "asleep!"

"*They ALL slumbered and slept.*" (*Matt.25:5. See also Mark 13:35-37 and Eph.5:14*)

And,

"*Blindness in part is happened to Israel, until the fullness of the Gentiles is come in.*

But finally:

"*ALL ISRAEL* (the chosen ones, both Jews *and* Gentiles) *SHALL BE SAVED.*" (*Rom.11:25-26*)

The five wise who "*took oil in their vessels with their lamps*" were those invited in as late as "*midnight*" to "*the marriage.*" (Today we might say, "At the eleventh hour!")

The five foolish cried, "*Lord, Lord, open to us,*" but were denied access by the Bridegroom.

One day Jesus will say to them, and to *all* such religious pretenders,

"***Depart from Me, I never knew you!***" (See also *Matt.7:21-23*)

The "wise" with additional "oil" could only refer to those "*servants*" who are kept, and saved from ultimate judgment – though not from great tribulation – by the Holy Spirit's anointing and grace.

The parable of the "talents" (*Matt.25:14-30*) should now be much more discernable.

"*For the kingdom of heaven is as a man traveling into **a far country**, who called **his own servants**, and delivered unto them his goods.*" (*v.14*)

These "*servants*" see the "*man*" (the Lord Jesus) as being *far away* in another country; but Jesus told His friends,

"*I will never leave thee, nor forsake thee.*" (*Heb.13:5*)

And,

"*Lo, I am with you always, even unto the end of the world.*" (*Matt.28:20*)

And,

"*For where two or three are gathered together in My Name, there am I in the midst of them.*"

(*Matt.18:20*)

Our Lord is not in a "far country" – He is right here with us!

God gave His servant Israel – "***His goods,***" "***The oracles*** (Word) ***of God,***" (*Rom.3:2*) "***The Law,***" (*Ex.24:12*) "***The Covenants of promise,***" (*Eph.2:12*) "***Treasures old and new.***" (*Matt.13:52*)

When Jesus returns, His question will be, "**What have you done with what I gave you?**"

Remember: "*the Law was a schoolmaster to bring the Jews to Christ.*"(*Gal.3:24*) Those who come to Christ are "*redeemed from the works, and curse of the Law.*" (*Gal.2:16, and 3:13*)

Those who don't receive Christ will be judged by their works! (*Rev.20:12*)

Faithful servants "*traded with their talents*" (a type of works), and upon Christ's return were rewarded with the words, "*Well done thou good and faithful servant; thou hast been faithful over a few things, I will make thee ruler over many things: enter thou into the joy of thy Lord.*"

What they <u>did</u> with what they were given was the basis of their reward!

Not so the *"Bride of Christ."*
*"For by grace are ye saved through faith; it is the gift of God **not of works**, lest any man should boast." (Eph.2:8-9)*

Those *"wicked and slothful servants"* who *"digged in the earth and hid their Lord's money"* had no knowledge or understanding of Christ's compassionate nature, or His Divine purpose on the earth! Neither did they *want* to know! And because they did nothing with what they were given, Jesus measures out to them a judgment equal to that of the "foolish virgins!"
*"... **Depart from Me.** ... **Cast ye the unprofitable servant into outer darkness: there shall be weeping and gnashing of teeth.**" (v.30)*

The judgment of the nations (*Matt.25:31-46*) is definitely not a parable; though it *is* reminiscent of the *"wheat and the tares."* (*Matt.13:24-30*) Again, this judgment has nothing to do with the body of Christ: we will be there as witnesses!

NOTE: this "judgment of *all* nations" should not be confused with the judgment of those standing before the *"great white throne"* at the end of the millennium. (*Rev.20:11*)
There the dead from *every* age will be judged for all eternity! Here all the *living* nations are judged to determine who will go through into the millennium kingdom on earth.

*"When the Son of man shall come **in His glory**, (Second Coming) and all the holy angels with Him, then shall He sit upon the **throne of His glory**: and before Him shall be gathered **all nations**: and He shall **separate them** one from another, as a shepherd divideth his **sheep from the goats**." (Matt.25:31-32)*

This *"Throne of Christ's glory"* will be in Jerusalem: on Mount Zion to be precise! (See *Ps.2:6, and Is. 24:23*) On that day, *"the Lord shall be King over all the earth: in that day shall there be One Lord, and His Name One!"* (*Zech.14:9*)

Those who are gathered before Him on earth are survivors of the Great Tribulation from all nations of the world. As He divides them, the Lord *"sets the sheep on His right hand, but the goats on His left."* (*v.33*)

The *"sheep"* are blessed of the Father, and will be given *"the kingdom prepared for them from the foundation of the world."*(*v.34*) – Why?
Because they *"**fed the Lord** when He was hungry." "When He was thirsty **they gave Him drink**." "He was a stranger, and **they took Him in**." "When He was "naked, **they clothed Him**:" "When He was sick and in prison, **they visited Him**."* (*Matt.25:34-36*)
The *"sheep"* have no idea that Jesus is the recipient of their "good deeds!"
Their overall response is, "Lord, when did we do such things for You?" (See *vs.37-39*)
Jesus replies,
*"Verily I say unto you, inasmuch as ye have done it unto one of **the least of these My brethren**, ye have done it unto Me."* (*v.40*) The key to understanding this statement is found in the words, *"**My brethren**."*
In *Mark 3:31-34* and *Luke 8:19-21*, Jesus reveals two kinds of *"brothers"* – natural *and* spiritual.

"There came then his brethren and His mother, and standing without, sent unto Him, calling Him."

When Jesus heard that they were outside, He said, *"Who is My mother, or* ***My brethren****?"*

Turning to the multitude *within* He said,

"Behold My mother and My brethren! For whosoever shall do the will of God, the same is My brother, and My sister, and mother."

Clearly then, only those who do the will of God are Christ's *true* "relatives!"

And what *is* the will of God?

The work or the will of God is for us to believe on the One He sent! (*John 6:29* and *40*)

Natural relationships are extremely temporary; those in Christ are eternal!

"For both He that sanctifieth and they who are sanctified ***are all of one****: for which cause He is not ashamed to call them brethren"* (*Heb.2:11*)

"These My brethren" are therefore those that belong to Christ *spiritually*, and are the persecuted and martyred believers who have endured the great tribulation!

In showing a measure of kindness to these *"brethren saints,"* the *"sheep"* are now spared, blessed, and given the millennium kingdom as a reward.

The opposite is true of the *"goats;"* they did *nothing* to help Christ's brethren, and so were condemned.

"Depart from Me, ye cursed, into everlasting fire, prepared for the devil and his angels."
(*Matt.25:41*)

This of course, points irrefutably to a judgment of *works*! A far cry from the Bride's "salvation by *grace*!"

Also worth considering is the fact that the *"lake of fire"* was *originally* created for Satan and the demonic realm! Sadly, in *Isaiah 5:14*, God reveals that,

"Hell hath enlarged herself, and opened her mouth without measure ..."

People, who through pride and unbelief have rejected God's mercy forgiveness and love, will one day follow the *"devil and his angels"* into the eternal and inescapable torment of smoke, fire and brimstone! (*Rev.14:9-11, 19:20, 20:10, 14* and *15*)

NOTE: In spite of making it through the tribulation, the privileged remnant (*"sheep"*) who go on to repopulate the earth during Christ's millennial kingdom will *not* be born again. They will still retain the old Adamic nature of sin and rebellion (though greatly subdued), and for a thousand years will continue to pass that nature on from one generation to the next!

For proof of this, let's look briefly at the following events.

When Jesus returns to earth in glory at the end of this age, His first order of business is to deal with the *"beast"* (anti-Christ)," the *"false prophet,"* and the rebellious armies fighting on the plain of *"Megiddo"* in Israel. This war, described in the Bible as, *"the battle of that great day of God Almighty"* is better known to Christians as the "battle of Armageddon!" (See *Rev. 16:14-16* and *19:19-21*)

At the very height of that conflict,

"... the beast was taken, and with him the false prophet that wrought miracles before him, with which he deceived them that had received the mark of the beast, and them that worshiped his image. ***These both were cast alive into a lake of fire burning with brimstone.****"* (*Rev.19:20*)

NOTE: because of the seriousness of their crimes against God and His people, (*Rev13:5-10*) the "*beast and false prophet*" are the only ones condemned to suffer in the "*lake of fire*" until Christ's one thousand year reign on earth is over!

After slaying the "*remnant*" of Armageddon's armies with the "*sword of His mouth*" (His Word!) Jesus has Satan (remember him?) "*...bound with chains in the bottomless pit **for a thousand years**. ... that he should deceive the nations no more until the thousand years should be fulfilled: and after that he must be loosed for a little season.*" (See *Rev.20:1-3*)

Can you imagine? No demonic activity on the earth for a thousand years! No wars! No crippling diseases! No abortion nor infant mortalities! No unpunished crime!
"*There shall be no more thence an infant of days, nor an old man that hath not filled his days: for **the child shall die a hundred years old**; ... For as the days of a tree are the days of my people, and Mine elect shall long enjoy the work of their hands. ...*
They shall not hurt nor destroy in all My holy mountain, saith the Lord."
Yet there will still be sin!
"*... **but the sinner being a hundred years old shall be accursed.**" (See *Is.65:20-25*)

Due to Christ's reign of righteousness, life expectancy throughout the millennium is literally compared to "*the days of a tree;*" and may also be likened to the days of "*Methuselah,*" who lived for nine hundred and sixty-nine years! (*Gen.5:27*)
Anyone dying at the age of one hundred ("*accursed*" or "*cut off*" because of willful sin) will be considered a mere child!
Of course, no open rebellion or lawlessness will be tolerated, but the hidden rebellion in the hearts of men will continue to fester until the time appointed for Satan's release!

SATAN'S LAST HURRAH

"*And when the thousand years are expired, Satan shall be loosed out of his prison, and shall go out to **deceive the nations** which are in the four quarters of the earth, Gog and Magog, to gather them together to battle: the number of whom is as the sand of the sea.*" (*Rev.20:7-8*)

As a prelude to the eternal separation of mankind, Satan (still blinded by pride, and by his all consuming hatred of God) will be allowed to orchestrate one final, massive wave of human rebellion!

"*And they went up on the breadth of the earth, and compassed the camp of the saints about, and the beloved city: ...*"

With Divine poetic justice, and drama eclipsed only by God's supreme and glorious triumph, the final conflict ever staged will be fought over God's chosen, beloved and holy city Jerusalem!
Once again, and for the last time, God will intervene.

"*... And fire came down from God out of Heaven, and devoured them.*" (*v.9*)

From those tragic opening scenes in the "*garden*" long ago, to God lowering the curtain on time itself, Satan will continue to act out his vile, yet necessary role in our Heavenly Father's grand design. Then, just as the devil had deceived and discarded billions of souls during his "*short time*" here on earth, so God will simply, and unceremoniously discard him!

"... And the devil that deceived them was cast into the lake of fire and brimstone, where the beast and the false prophet are, and shall be tormented day and night for ever and ever." *(Rev.20:9-10)*

With the counterfeit "trinity" of devil, beast, and false prophet consigned to their appropriate places, other climactic events begin to unfold! Events so vividly described by the Apostle John, and so well known to us, that any additional comments would be completely unnecessary!

"And I saw a great white throne, and Him that sat on it, from Whose Face the earth and the heaven fled away; and there was found no place for them. And I saw the dead, small and great, stand before God; and the books were opened: and another book was opened, which is the Book of Life: and the dead were judged out of those things which were written in the books, according to their works. And the sea gave up the dead which were in it; and death and hell delivered up the dead which were in them: and they were judged every man according to their works. And death and hell were cast into the lake of fire. This is the second death. And whosoever was not found written in the Book of Life was cast into the lake of fire."

(Rev.20:11-15)

I'd like to go back for a moment here, and re-emphasize the difference between the **"Day of Christ,"** *(2Thess.2:2)* and the **"Day of the Lord."** *(Joel 2:31, Zech.14:1, 2Thess.1:7-8)*

The **"Day of Christ"** is expressly the day in which the dead *in Christ* shall rise (be resurrected) first; and those who are still alive will be caught up with them *"in the twinkling of an eye"* to meet the Lord **IN THE AIR!** (See *1Thess.4:16-18*) I.e. raptured **BEFORE** the wrath of God is poured out upon the world!

(For more details of this glorious transformation, see *1Cor.15:35-58*.)

The **"Day of the Lord"** occurs at the end of the **"great tribulation"** when Jesus returns to the earth in power and great glory during the **"battle of Armageddon ... with all His saints with Him!"** I.e. the "Second Coming." *(Zech.14:5, Matt.24:29-31, Rev.19:11-21)* – *Both* occur during this present age. (Believers are not omnipresent – we have to go up before we can come back down!)

Consider the following types of "raptured" and "tribulation" saints.

Only two men throughout the entire Old Testament were caught up bodily into Heaven:
Enoch and Elijah.
"And Enoch walked with God: and was not; for God took him." (See *Gen.5:23-24*)

At the then relatively young age of *"three hundred and sixty-five,"* Enoch silently, and instantly disappeared! God took (translated) him straight to Heaven!
Elijah was also taken up or translated, but this time in a *"whirlwind."* (See *2Kin. 2:1-11*) Not – as is often taught – in a *"fiery chariot."*

Enoch (caught up before the flood/wrath of God) may well be seen as a type of raptured believer; whereas Elijah (the persecuted prophet), a type of those who will *"come out of great tribulation."*

(Rev.7:14)

How could believers identify with Enoch, or find "*comfort*" in Paul's words concerning the rapture of the Church, (*1Thess. 4:13-18, and 5:1-11*) unless they knew the catching away took take place *before* the "great tribulation?"

> "*For God hath not appointed us to wrath, but to obtain salvation by our Lord Jesus Christ.*"
> (*1Thess.5:9*),

In other words:

> The "*Grace of God*" keeps the "*friends of God*" from the "*wrath of God!*"

> "*Blessed and holy is he that hath part in the first resurrection:* (rapture) *on such the second death hath no power, but they shall be priests of God and of Christ, and shall reign with Him a thousand years.*" (*Rev. 20:6*)

The first death is merely the end of physical, or natural life. The "*second death*" is the lost soul's eternal separation from heaven, and from the presence and glory of God!

This **endless living death** means not only the burning agony of the "*lake of fire,*" but also the constant, tormenting awareness (memory) of every vile and sinful thing ever done by those who rejected God's supreme gift of love in the Person of the Lord Jesus Christ!

> "*He that **overcomes** shall not be hurt of the second death.*" (*Rev.2:11*)

> "*For whatsoever is born of God **overcomes** the world: and this is the victory that **overcomes** the world, even our faith. Who is he that **overcomes** the world, but he that **believes** that JESUS IS THE SON OF GOD.*" (*1John 5:4-5*)

V.I. Look at *Luke 16:19-31* again and remember; this is not a parable! Hell is merely a place of waiting for the *ultimate* judgment to come! (See *Rev.20:11-15*)

One day, all those in hell will find out what it *really* means to, "jump from the frying pan into the fire!" (*Rev.20:14*)

May this inspire us to reach out to the lost whenever, wherever, and however we can!

Final thought:

"A glimpse of hell may do more to win souls, than a week spent in Heaven itself!"

CHAPTER TWENTY-NINE

TOGETHER FOREVER!

"But blessed are your eyes, for they see: and your ears, for they hear." (*Matt.13:16*)

Well, we've come a long way together: both the end and the beginning are now clearly in sight! Let's recap for a moment, and at the same time fill in some gaps.

While the *"wrath of God"* is being poured out upon the unbelieving world, those who have been *"caught up"* to be with the Lord will experience at least two major events in heaven.

FIRST: *"… we must all appear before **the judgment seat of Christ**; that everyone may receive the things done in his body, according to that he hath done, whether it be good or bad."*

(*2Cor.5:10*)

Things we have done on earth (as believers) will determine the rewards of *"gold, silver and precious stones,"* which may well be acts of *"faith, hope and love."* On the other hand, the loses or burnings of *"wood, hay, and stubble"* may simply be works of flesh, flesh, and more flesh!

Also, any tears shed at *"the judgment seat of Christ"* must not be confused with the tears wiped away after God's *"great white throne"* judgment at the end of the millennium. (*Rev.21:4*)

There is a thousand year difference between the two!

The **"judgment seat of Christ"** is for believers only! The **"great white throne"** (one thousand years later) concerns God's judgment upon *all* men, resulting in eternal life or death! (*Rev.20:14-15*)

This final judgment leads to a **"new heaven, and a new earth,"** (*Rev.21:1*) which will never pass away!

Physical human beings who are to populate the *"new earth"* will never die; (*Rev.:20:14*) although *"Leaves from the Tree of Life"* (in the New Jerusalem) will provide for their *"healing."* (*Rev.22:2*)

The scriptures also tell us that the *"saved from all nations"* (and from all ages) who live on the new earth, *"will walk in the light of the new jerusalem,"* (*Rev.21:24-27*) which is the ultimate home of the *"Bride of Christ"* – His Body and Church! (*Rev.21:9-10*)

SECOND: *"Let us be glad and rejoice, and give honor to Him: for **the marriage of the Lamb** is come, and His wife hath made herself ready. … And he said unto me, Write. Blessed are they which are called unto the **marriage supper of the Lamb**."* (*Rev.19:7 and 9*)

In the New Testament, only one verse refers directly to the "*marriage of the Lamb.*" A few others (mostly in the form of parables) point to it, and to the subsequent "*marriage supper.*" However; what the Holy Spirit reveals in types and shadows should be more than enough to whet our spiritual appetites, and make us thoroughly "home-sick" for heaven!

The union of the "*Lamb*" (Jesus) and His "*wife*" (the church, or "*the Israel of God*" *Gal.6:16*) takes place in heaven sometime towards the end of the great tribulation, (see *Rev.19:1-9*) and is the complete fulfillment of God's purpose for the church in this age. Or, as we saw in chapter 27, the Old Testament mystery now revealed in and through the "*Feast of Tabernacles.*"

As the "*marriage of the Lamb*" and "*marriage supper of the Lamb,*" are two completely different subjects, let me begin with

THE MARRIAGE SUPPER

Jesus said of the man who was chosen to prepare the way before Him (*Is.40:3, Mal.4:5*),

"*... Among them that are born of women there hath not risen a greater than John the Baptist: notwithstanding he that is least in the kingdom of heaven is greater than he*" (*Matt.11:11*)

Obviously the Lord was making a distinction between Old and New Testament believers: a distinction confirmed by John himself.

"*He that hath the bride is the Bridegroom: but the friend of the Bridegroom, which standeth and heareth Him, rejoiceth greatly because of the Bridegroom's voice: this my joy therefore is fulfilled.*"
(*John 3:28-29*)

Only the "*bride*" marries the "*Bridegroom;*" but as the "*friend of the Bridegroom,*" John could well represent all the Old Testament believers who are invited first to the marriage, and afterward to the "*marriage feast*" or "*supper.*"
Take a look at the parable in *Matt.22:2-14*, and compare with *Luke 14:15-24*, where Jesus said,

"*The kingdom of heaven is like unto a certain King, which made a marriage for His Son. And sent forth His servants to call them that were bidden to the wedding: and they would not come ...*"

God first sent His prophets to call Old Testament Israel to the marriage. Some "*made light*" of the invitation; others treated the prophets, "*spitefully and slew them.*" (*v.6*)
In righteous anger, the King "*sent forth His armies, and destroyed those murderers, and burned up their city.*" (*v.7*) Clear reference to Israel's ongoing persecution; including the past and future destruction of Jerusalem. (See *Matt.24:2, Zech.13:8-9, 14:1-2, Rev.11:13*)

As "*... they which were bidden were not worthy,*" (*v.8*) the King sent other servants, "*... into the highways, and gathered together all as many as they found, both bad and good: and the wedding was furnished with GUESTS.*" (*vs.9-10*)

How important is it for "*friends*" to know that the marriage between the King's Son and His "*bride*" (*v.2*) was in fact determined and established by God before the "*foundation of the world;*" (*Eph.1:3-12*) and everyone else who is invited – **comes as a guest?**

Many in the church have been taught wrongly, that since the Jews rejected Jesus, God sent His *"servants"* out into the *"highways, streets, lanes, and hedges"* to bring in *"the poor, the maimed, the halt, and the blind"* – to marry His Son! (see *Luke 14:21-23*)

To all Christians: the fact that we are *"in Christ"* makes us His *"friends."* This is not a cause for boasting or self-righteousness, but for humble rejoicing, and gratitude for the grace and love of God, *"Who chose us and accepted us in the Beloved."*(*Eph.1:4 and 6*)

Of course *"friends"* also serve; (*Jn.13:14, Gal.5:13*) but if Christians have been made to feel like *"servants"* or *"guests,"* it's no wonder so many believe they can lose their salvation! (*"Servants"* cannot possibly enjoy the same assurance as *"friends."*)

Once and for all: the Kingdom of Heaven (God's House, *Matt.22:10, Luke 14:23*) will be filled with Old Testament ***"guests"*** (the poor, the maimed ..., servants, bridesmaids, souls under the altar etc.), but they will not be marrying the King's Son!

FINALLY: *"...When the King came in to see the <u>GUESTS</u>, He saw there a man which had not on a wedding garment: and He said unto him, Friend* (here the term "Friend" is God's way of saying, "Hey you!") *how camest thou in hither not having a wedding garment? And he was speechless."* (*Matt.22:11-12*)

Here was an intruder, wearing his best Sunday suit (remember *"FIG LEAVES"*), who was convinced (as so many are) that religious practices, and self-righteous acts would cover or hide his *"nakedness"* before God!

NOTE: In our society, it's fairly common for people with enough nerve, to "gate-crash" certain parties or exclusive events knowing full well that their names are not on the "guest list." If discovered, they may only have to face the embarrassment of being manhandled by security, and put out onto the street! However, down through the ages, countless religious men and women from *all* societies have tried in vain to gate-crash God's exclusive *"marriage feast."* One day, many of the world's "best dressers" will have their nakedness uncovered by God Himself, and themselves ejected from His kingdom!

What those people face will be infinitely worse than embarrassment. ...

"Then said the King to the servants, Bind him hand and foot, and take him away, and cast him into outer darkness; there shall be weeping and gnashing of teeth. For many are called, but few are chosen." (*Matt.22:13-14*)

Not long after becoming a Christian, I spent some time with an ageing minister who belonged to the "United Reformed Church" (the joining of Congregational and Presbyterian denominations in England). During one conversation I asked him if he knew he was saved and going to heaven.

His reply completely floored me. With all the confidence in the world he said, "Young man, I am perfectly prepared to stand before God and find acceptance on the basis of my life's work and service to Him. Being born again is not for all of us you know, but I'm delighted you've had such an experience."

I can remember exactly what went through my young spiritual mind at that moment: "This man is either very brave, or incredibly stupid!" (The truth is, he was simply deceived!) I shared with him what little I knew of the Gospel, but to no avail. A few weeks later both he and his wife died in a dreadful head-on automobile accident. – Did they make it?

Who on earth can say? – *"The Lord knoweth them that are His."* (*2Tim.2:19*)

But what we *can* say is that immediately after death, all pretences and deceptions will forsake us; all castles of self-righteousness and self-worth will come crashing down; all of us will know the truth. **"*White robes*" for heaven – "*fig leaves*" for hell!**

THE MARRIAGE OF THE LAMB

We know now that the "*marriage of the Lamb*" was in the heart and mind of God before the heavens and the earth were ever brought forth. We also know that from beginning to end the Bible declares God's wonderful three-fold purpose.

Above all, to glorify His Son Jesus: (*Heb. ch.1*) to reveal Him to us in the fullness of time: (*Gal.4:4*) and finally, to bring Him into eternal union with His spiritual bride, His Church. (*Eph.1:10*)

"That He might present it to Himself a glorious church, not having spot or wrinkle, or any such thing; but that it should be holy and without blemish." (See *Eph. 5:22-32*)

In linking *Eph.5:30-32* with *Gen.2:23-24*, the Holy Spirit immediately take us back to the "*garden of Eden*," and reveals a mystery involving the first marriage on earth.

"For we are members of His body, of His flesh, and of His bones. For this cause shall a man leave his father and mother, and shall be joined unto his wife, and they two shall be one flesh. This is a great mystery: but I speak and concerning Christ and the church."

God said in *Gen.2:18*,
"It is not good that the man should be alone; I will make him an help meet for him."

Since the creation of Adam and Eve, God has shown us by many wonderful types and shadows, that His will was – and still is – focused on the greatest wedding of all time!

For me, the most beautiful picture looking toward the "*marriage of the Lamb*" is found hidden in **Genesis 24**. By the grace and revelation of God the Holy Spirit, we may unearth some of the spiritual treasures buried in this amazing chapter.

A BRIDE FOR ISAAC (*Gen. 24*)

Abraham was "*old and well stricken in age:*" – surely a type of God the Father or "*the Ancient of days.*" (See *Dan.7:9,13, 22*)

Abraham made a covenant with his "*eldest servant*" **Eliezer** (*Gen.15:2*) who "*ruled over all that Abraham had.*"

As a type of the Holy Spirit, Eliezer is sent to find, and bring back a wife for Abraham's beloved son Isaac.

Isaac, who must wait until his wife appears, may now be seen as a type of God's beloved Son, the Lord Jesus Christ; who graciously waits until *His* wife is ready! (*Rev.19:7*)

V.I. Remember (from pages 122-123) that it was the Holy Spirit Who was sent to build God's "*living temple*," and eventually bring back a "*bride*" for Christ (our "heavenly Isaac!")

Verses 3 and *4* make it clear that the bride would not be taken (or chosen) from the daughters of "this world" (the Canaanites born of Ham), but from Abraham's "*own kindred*" (God's chosen people, born of Shem). (See *John 8:23*, and *15:19*)

Two more profound truths are revealed in *verses 5-8*. First the mystery of free will.

"Peradventure the woman will not be willing to follow me unto this land: must I needs bring thy son again unto the land from whence thou camest?"

Throughout history the question has been raised; if God is Sovereign, and chooses or determines everything according to His Own will; then how could man possibly have free-will?

If on the other hand, man *has* free-will; how then can God be the absolute sovereign?

I've already pointed out that even though everything in the universe is ruled by the will of God, He will still righteously judge those who have ignored or rejected that will. God has given all men enough "light" to make them accountable!

Abraham's reply to Eliezer was, *"If the woman will not be willing to follow thee, then thou shalt be clear from this my oath:* **only bring not my son hither again.**"

Surely our spirits must recognize the significance of those seven words; for in failing to heed them, Moses was forbidden to enter the Promised Land!

Remember that instead of simply speaking to the *"Rock"* (the second time), Moses struck it; and by so doing brought God's Son *"hither again"* – to be smitten twice!
Christ died for sins ONCE : God would not send His Son to die a second time!

The revelation continues as Eliezer takes, ***"Ten camels** of the camels of his master, and departed; for **all the goods of his master were in his hand** ..."* (*v.10*)

"Ten" often speaks of the O.T. *"tithe"* (tenth or 10%), which is another shadow pointing directly to the substance.

*"Now He which stablisheth us with you in Christ, and hath anointed us, is God; Who hath also sealed us, and given us **the earnest of the Spirit** in our hearts." (2Cor:1:22)*
And,
*"That we should be to the praise of His glory, who first trusted in Christ. ... In Whom also after that ye believed, ye were sealed with that Holy Spirit of promise, which is **the earnest of our inheritance until the redemption of the purchased possession**, unto the praise of His glory."*
(Eph.1:12-14)

When we realize the word *"earnest"* means a pledge (down payment), or the amount given as security until the possession is fully redeemed; we may rest in full assurance of our salvation! After all,
*"...**He that began a good work in you will perform it until the day of Christ.**" (Phil.1:6)*

Eliezer traveled though *"Mesopotamia"* (a land of two rivers or ways), and came to the *"city of Nahor at the time of evening when women go out to draw water."* (*vs.10-11*)

His intercession and answered prayer is a glorious reflection of the ministry of the Holy Spirit, and what He is looking for in the bride of Christ.

"O Lord God of my master Abraham, ... let it come to pass, that the damsel to whom I shall say, Let down thy pitcher, I pray thee, that I may drink; and she shall say, Drink, and I will give thy camels drink also: let the same be she that Thou hast appointed for Thy servant Isaac." (*vs.12-14*)

Before Eliezer had finished praying, Rebekah (a virgin who's name means to "fetter," or "capture by beauty") came to the well to draw water; and, *"she was very fair to look upon."* (*v.16*)

Eliezer approaches her with a question which takes us straight to *John 4* where Jesus first asked the woman at the well for a drink; and then, in return, offered her the *"living water"* of eternal life! Here too in *Gen. 24* we are watching the Gospel message unfold!

Rebekah's response is immediate: she not only gives the man a drink (calling him *"Lord"*) but runs again, and (I'm certain), again and again to water his camels! (I'm told that each animal could drink up to forty gallons!) – That girl had a "servant's heart!"

Again: we may be *"friends"* but we are still called to serve! Ministering to the needs of others is a gift of the Holy Spirit, (*Rom.12:6-7*) and Jesus made it a priority in the kingdom of God. (*Luke 22:27, John 13:2-17*) We could *all* learn from Rebekah's example!

By the time the camel's have stopped drinking, the issue is settled – Rebekah is the one!

Eliezer now gives her a taste of things to come, *"a golden earring of half a shekel weight, and two bracelets for her hands of **ten shekels** weight of gold."* (*v.22*)

(Another glimpse of the *"earnest of our inheritance"* from the *"goods"* [or gifts] of *our* Master!)

In verse 23, Eliezer provides us with the loveliest of all the Holy Spirit's questions,

*"Is there room in thy father's house **FOR US** to lodge in?"*

Those of us who are *"born again"* know we have received not only God the Son and Savior Jesus Christ, but God the Father, and God the Holy Spirit also! (See *John14:17-23, 2Tim.1:14, 1John 4:13-16*)

And Jesus said, **"I WILL NEVER LEAVE THEE, NOR FORSAKE THEE!"** (*Heb.13:5*)

Now, thanks to Christ's victory on the cross, the FATHER, SON, and HOLY GHOST don't just *"LODGE"* with us – They *"ABIDE"* with us *"FOR EVER MORE!"*

Long ago, God had told Abraham (then Abram) to *"leave his country, his kindred, and his father's house."* (*Gen.12:1*) and, given the Hebrew meaning of the names of Abraham's relatives, one can quite understand why!

Abraham's father *"Terah"* ... a *"desert place,"* or *"wilderness."*

His brother *"Haran"* ... *"lacking;"* *"idle;"* *"state of the dead."*

His brother *"Nahor"* ... *"snoring"* (as one asleep.)

His nephew *"Lot"* ... *"wrapped up,"* or *"covered with a veil."*

Nahor's wife *"Milcah"* ... *"a queen."*

Nahor's son *"Bethuel"* ... *"destroyed of God!"*

NOTE: In *"leaving his* (pagan) *country,"* Abraham would become the father, as well as a type of all those who are called to leave *"this world,"* and follow Christ by faith! (*Gal.3:7*)

"Leaving father's house" means letting go of all dead religious traditions, including sentimental observances and attachments; as well as the bondage of man made philosophies, or deceits! (*Col.2:8*)

The fact that Rebekah (type of believer) was the daughter of Bethuel, should give all of us a sobering view of our roots; not to mention the old natures, habits and characteristics that God has called us to leave behind! (*Rom.6:20-22, Eph.5:8, Phil.3:13-14*)

When Rebekah's brother Laban (Jacob's future "deceitful" uncle, (see *Gen.31:1-7*) hears of her good fortune, and sees the gold jewelry now adorning his sister; he makes a grand outward gesture to Eliezer:

"Come in thou blessed of the Lord; wherefore standest thou without ..." (*v.31*)

Once inside, and after sharing the details of his mission, (*vs.33-48*) Eliezer comes straight to the point.

"*... Now if ye will deal kindly and truly with my master, tell me: and if not, tell me; that I may turn to the right hand or to the left.*" (*v.49*)

Rebekah's father and brother sum up the attitude of many relatives who prefer to sit on the fence rather than make a full and genuine commitment to the Lord.

"*The thing proceedeth from the Lord: we cannot speak unto thee bad or good. Behold Rebekah is before thee, take her and go, ...*" (see *vs.50-51*).

Sadly, their words have a familiar ring to so many (including myself) who have been redeemed amidst unbelieving relatives.

"If this is what you want, all well and good, but we're happy the way we are. We go to church when we want to: we have our own Jesus thank you very much. Do as you will, but please leave us alone!"

I recall my sister's light hearted, yet pointedly mocking response to my conversion:

"Good for you; you really needed to be saved!"

Bethuel and Laban's neutrality however, was a sure sign of Eliezer's success!

He immediately, "*... brought forth jewels of silver, and jewels of gold, and raiment, and gave them to Rebekah: he gave also to her brother and to her mother precious things.*" (*vs. 52-53*)

If silver and gold speak of hope and faith, could not this raiment be a type of the "*clean, white robe of righteousness*" (*Rev.19:8*) given by the grace of God to all that are called and chosen in Christ?

The fact that Rebekah's family also received precious things suggests the unconditional overflow of God's blessings upon our loved ones, regardless of their eternal destination!

The next morning, (*v.54*) Eliezer is ready to leave; but now suddenly, mother and son are singing a different tune!

"*Let the damsel abide with us a few days, at the least ten; after that she shall go.*"

It would be nice to think that Laban and his mother wanted the "*earnest of the Spirit*" for themselves; and that their desire to delay Rebekah was therefore a Godly one. Alas – not so!

I believe the main reason for their wanting her to stay "*at least ten more days,*" was to see if perhaps a few more "*precious things*" would come forth from the hands of this generous man!

Eliezer's reply came in the form of a firm, no nonsense rebuke!

"*Hinder me not, seeing the Lord hath prospered my way; send me away that I may go to my master.*" (*v.56*)

He knew these relatives were being used by Satan to stand in the way of God's purpose (through greed or whatever other motive), and would have none of it!

Faced with the unyieldingness of Abraham's servant, the two of them could only bring Rebekah forth in order to ask her personally, "*...wilt thou go with this man?*"

Could the entire heavenly host be more joyful, or inspired to give praise to God, than in the hearing of this chosen one's reply? – "*I WILL GO!*"

Jesus Himself said, "*... Likewise joy shall be in Heaven over one sinner that repenteth, more than over ninety and nine just persons, which need no repentance.*" (*Luke 15:3-7*)

SATAN ...this is going to hurt!

NOTE: regarding *verse 59*, there are positively no female angels mentioned anywhere in Scripture (no plump flying baby cherubim either), so we cannot make Rebekah's *"nurse"* a type of angelic being!

"Strong's Concordance" gives the Hebrew meaning of the word *"nurse"* as "one who gives milk" (as in a nursing mother): so spiritually speaking, this nurse might represent someone who helps bring a "modern" Rebekah through to the Lord by nurture (sharing and teaching the Word), or by intercessory prayer.

In regard to *verse 60*, some of the most profound and powerful words spoken in the Bible came from the lips of bona fide unbelievers! For example: Balaam (the false prophet) was hired by Balak to curse God's people in *Numbers 22*; but by the time God had finished with him, he was bringing forth some of the greatest prophecies ever uttered concerning Israel and their coming Messiah, the Lord Jesus Christ! (See the whole of *Num.24*)

When speaking of Rebekah, Laban is given a similar privilege:

"...Thou art our sister, be thou the mother of thousands of millions, and let thy seed possess the gate of those which hate them."

How could Laban have known that his sister would become the literal mother of *"Jacob,"* who would one day be known as *"Israel,"* the father of God's chosen nation?

How could he have known that the true church (*"the Israel of God"*) would one day be numbered in *"thousands of millions;"* and that together, both Jews and Gentiles would become the body, and the everlasting *"bride of Jesus Christ?"*

How could he have known that *"forty two generations"* later, (*Matt.1:17*) Jesus would say of *"Rebekah's seed,"* and that very same church He Himself would build,

"THE GATES OF HELL SHALL NOT PREVAIL AGAINST IT ?" (Matt.16:18)

Obviously Laban could *not* have known, but our Heavenly Father knew; and now (by His grace) so do we!

*"And Rebekah arose, and her damsels, and they rode upon the camels, and followed the man: and **the servant took Rebekah, and went his way.**"* (*v.61*)

Only the Holy Spirit can lead us into God's Way! Jesus (Who *is* God's Way) sent the Comforter to *"teach us all things, and guide us into all truth."* (*John 15: 26*)
But first,
WE MUST "SEE" JESUS! (*John 12:21, Acts 4:12*)

*"And Isaac came from the way of **the well Lahai-roi**; for he dwelt in the **south country**. And Isaac went out to meditate in the field at the eventide: and **he lifted up his eyes, and saw**, and behold, the camels were coming. ..."* (*vs. 62-63*)

The *"well Lahai-roi"* or *"Beer-lahai-roi"* means literally the "Well of the One Who Lives, and Sees me," It was given this name by Hagar (Sarah's Egyptian handmaiden, and mother of Ishmael) in honor of God Who *"saw her"* and later had mercy on her and her son. (See *Gen.16:13-14, 21:9-21*)
This well was in the *"south country"* where Isaac dwelt, yet the Bible makes it clear that God inhabits the North! (See *Ps.48:2* and *Eze.1:4*)

Once again a beautiful picture of the Lord Jesus, Who in Heaven saw us, and chose us "*before the foundation of the world.*" And even though "*He was with God, and was God,*" (*John 1:1-3*) He came down from His Throne, His Kingdom and His Glory to this lowly "*south country*" world in order to dwell with us, redeem us, and show us the way home!

"Isaac lifted up his eyes ... and saw."

*"And Rebekah lifted up her eyes, and **when she saw Isaac**, she lighted off the camel. For she had said unto the servant, **What man is this** that walketh in the field to meet us? And the servant had said, It is my master: therefore she took a veil, and covered herself." (vs. 64-65)*

From a distance Isaac had seen Rebekah: but while it is true that Rebekah also got a glimpse of Isaac; at that point she could only ask, "*What man is this?*"

She had no real idea who Isaac was until Eliezer revealed him as her future husband! (It's one thing to see with our natural eyes, but quite another to have them truly "opened.")

In confirmation of this, the scriptures tell us that the disciples constantly failed to recognize Jesus! Even after seeing Him calm a storm on the Lake, their vision was still extremely limited. Their question was strikingly similar to Rebekah's. "*What manner of man is this?*" (*Matt.8:27*) The two disciples on the Emmaus road could not "see" Him until the moment He broke bread with them (as only He had done): then, "*their eyes were opened, and they knew Him.*" (*Lk.24:31*)

Later, when Jesus appeared to them all in the "upper room," they thought He was a "*spirit*" or a ghost! (*Lk.24:37*) It follows that just as Eliezer opened the natural eyes of Rebekah to behold his master Isaac, so the Holy Spirit must open our spiritual eyes to reveal our Divine Master, Husband and Savior, Jesus Christ!

*"And this is the will of Him that sent Me, **that everyone which seeth the Son**, and believeth on Him, may have everlasting life ... **No man can come to Me, except the Father which hath sent Me draw him**: and I will raise him up at the last day." (John 6:40 and 44)*

"Blessed are your eyes for they see ..." *(Matt.13:16)*

"And when she saw Isaac, she lighted off the camel ..."
Taking the step from pride to humility has often been described as, "Getting off one's high horse!" An expression that came readily to mind as I pondered Rebekah's action upon seeing Isaac.

As if it were yesterday, I remember being given the Pocket Testament of John by someone I had only known for a day or two. My initial reaction was, "Please: I know all about this stuff! I was a choir member in the Anglican Church: I don't need anyone to tell me about God!"

"Just read it," was the challenging reply; "What have you got to lose?"

With a polite yet condescending smile – plus the lie of promising to look it over – I left it at that!

Wouldn't you know? The following evening I found myself in the strange and unusual position of having absolutely nothing to do! (Funny how God will clear your calendar when He wants to make a Divine appointment!) Well, rather than face a night of baseball, or re-runs on television; I picked up the tiny Gospel of John, and began to read ...

Some thirty years have passed, but I can instantly recall how my heart "burned within me" as I seemed to "behold the face of Jesus!"

How tears of repentance and joy sprang from my eyes as I felt His love reaching out to me from the pages of that precious little book! For the first time in my life, I "saw" Him!

The stubbornness and pride which had resisted Christ for a life time was swept away in an avalanche of gratitude and surrender. I practically leaped off my camel!

"Rebekah took a veil and covered herself."
The natural custom of an ancient time; and sadly, one long removed from our western society. Nevertheless; a lovely portrayal of the chasteness and modesty that by grace extends to everyone *"born of the Spirit of God;"* and certainly the instinctive spiritual attitude of all those who find themselves standing in the presence of Jesus!

"And the servant told Isaac all things that he had done." (v.66)

Upon returning home with Rebekah, Eliezer gave Isaac (and no doubt Abraham also) the details of his successful mission. What a time of rejoicing it must have been?
Surely everything here looks forward to a time when the Holy Spirit will reveal all that has been accomplished in gathering together the Saints of God, and in uniting them with their heavenly Bridegroom! Can you imagine seeing and hearing (first hand) the glorious revelations of *"all that Jesus began to do and teach?"* (*Acts 1:1*) And to discover, and enjoy throughout all eternity what the Holy Spirit declared long ago through the Apostle John ...

> *"And there are also many other things which Jesus did, the which, if they should be written every one, I suppose that even the world itself could not contain the books that should be written. Amen."*

"And Isaac brought her into his mother Sarah's tent, and took Rebekah, and she became his wife; and he loved her: and Isaac was comforted after his mother's death." (v.67)

Joy and sadness are mingled together in this last climactic verse. Joy for the love Isaac had for Rebekah, but sadness in a son's need for comfort after the loss of his beloved mother Sarah.
To put the final piece or *"fragment"* of this remarkable parable into its place, we need to "see" the natural death of Isaac's mother Sarah (Abraham's wife) as a heartbreaking symbol of the spiritual loss of God's beloved nation Israel.
The Bible frequently refers to Old Testament Israel as God's *"wife;"* and to God Himself as a devoted and *"jealous"* husband! (See *Is.54:5, Jer.3:1,14, 20. Hos.2:16-20*)
Nothing in all of scripture depicts the compassionate nature of our Savior more vividly than His sorrow over those (His own) who rejected Him, and would in turn be lost forever!

> *"O Jerusalem, Jerusalem, which killest the prophets, and stonest them that are sent unto thee; how often would I have gathered thy children together, as a hen doth gather her brood under her wings, and ye would not!"* (*Luke 13:34*)

> *"And when He was come near, He beheld the city, and wept over it, saying, If thou hadst known, even thou, at least in this thy day, the things which belong unto thy peace! But now they are hid from thine eyes. For the days shall come upon thee, that thine enemies shall cast a trench (an embankment) about thee, and compass thee round, and keep thee in on every side, and shall lay thee even with the ground, and thy children within thee; and they shall not leave in thee one stone upon another; because thou knewest not the time of thy visitation."* (*Luke 19:41-44*)

"He came unto His own, and His own received Him not." (*John 1:11*)

After the tragic loss of natural Israel ("*only a remnant will be saved*," *see Rom.9:27*); Jesus will take a "*neither Jew nor Gentile, new creation bride*" unto Himself; and find comfort in those (truly His own) who have been chosen to enter "Sarah's tent," and have a burning desire to "love, honor, and obey Him" throughout all eternity!

"*And the Spirit and the bride say, Come. And let him that heareth say, Come. And let him that is athirst, come. And whosoever will, let him take of the water of life freely.*" (*Rev.22:17*)

Even so, come, Lord Jesus.
The grace of our Lord Jesus Christ be with you all. Amen.

END NOTES

Chapter 4 – All Sin Leads to a Noah

1 "Mormon Doctrine" by Bruce McConkie, p.109, 114, 343. See also "Journal of Discourses" vol. 7:290. (Remarks by Brigham Young reported by G.D.Watt)
2 "Mormon Doctrine" 477, 527-28, and 109. 1966 original edition, (changed in the current edition)
3 "Mormonism: Shadow or Reality." Jerald and Sandra Tanner. Utah Lighthouse Ministry Publishers, 1978. See also Fraser's Magazine, 1973, p.229.
4 "Doctrine and Covenants," Joseph Smith. Section 130:22

Chapter 11 – Are We deceived?

1 From a personal conversation with Carl Strader, Carpenter's Home Church, Florida.
2 Edward A. Powell and R.J.Rushdooney, "Tithing and Dominion." Also found in "God and Government" by Gary Demar. Vol. 2, p.108.
3 "Catechism of the Catholic Church." 2nd ed.1997, pt. 1, sect. 1, ch. 2, art. 2, III #100.

Chapter 13 – Fickle Folk and Shifting Sands

1 "Golden book of the Theosophical Movement" 1925. Helena P. Blavatsky
2 "Nine Departed Leafy Friends" by Marc Dadigan, (Rome Georgia News-Tribune staff writer, May 10, 2005)
3 "Principles of Theosophy," taken from the Theosophical Society's website.
4 Ibid.
5 "Isis Unveiled," Blavastky, vol. 1, p.62.
6 'Triangles in Education'. http://freespace.version.net/caduceator.clh/trined.htm
7 Ibid.
8 Ibid.
9 From "The Magical Work of the Soul:" lecture given by Sarah McKechnie, [current president of Lucis Trust] at St. James' church in London, on Feb. 2nd, 2004. (comment in parenthesis, and emphasis mine)
10 Alice Bailey, and from "The Doctrine of Avatars – Eastern Teaching," Lucis Publications.

11 Ibid.
12 Ibid.

Chapter 14 – The Whore Raises Her Cup

1   Ted Scott, is Archbishop of the Anglican Church in Canada, and Moderator of the W.C.C. Central Committee. See the 'Fundamental Evangelistic Association's website @ http://www.fundamentalbiblechurch.org/
2   (Click on 'Tracts & Literature On-Line')
3   Ibid.
4   W.C.C. Central Committee Press release, Aug.26, 2003. CC moderator:
5   Interreligious dialogue an ecumenical priority. E-mail: media@wcc-coe.org
6   Ibid
7   Full speeches available through the W.C.C.'s website
    http://www.oikoumene.org/en/home.html

Chapter 16 – Christian Reconstruction

1   "Changing of the Guard" by George Grant. Published by Dominion Press, Ft Worth Texas 1987, pp. 50-51
2   "The Sinai Strategy: Economics and the Ten Commandments" by Gary North. Published by Dominion Press 1986
3   "Institutes of Biblical Law" by R.J. Rushdoony. Published by Nutley, NJ: Craig Press 1973
4   "In the Shadow of Plenty" by George Grant. Dominion Press 2002.
5   Public Eye Magazine, vol.8 #1&2, March/June –1994. On line at http://www.publiceye.org/

Chapter 17 – Transcendental Meditation

1   From T.M.'s official website, http://www.tm.org
2   From "Doug Henning and the Giggling Guru," by Martin Gardiner. Skeptical Inquirer Magazine, May/June, 1995
3   "Beacon Light of the Himalayas" Maharishi [Bala Brahmachan] Mahesh Yogi, [Maharaj] 1955)
4   "T.M. and Cult Mania," by Michael A. Persinger. 1980
5   See Malnak v. Yogi. Civil action No. 76-341, District of New Jersey: decision upheld in U.S. Court of Appeals.
6   "Golden Book of the Theosophical Movement." H.P. Blavatsky
7   Dennis E. Roark, TM-EX Newsletter. Go to http://minet.org/TM-EX/index.html (click on spring 92 and scroll down to "Roark letter.")
8   "Maharishi International News." Winter 1988.
9   http://www.vedicknowledge.com/Maharishieffect.html
10 For more information, go to http://www.freedomofmind.com/resourcecenter/groups/t/tm/ (click on German Study.)
11 From "Beacon Light of the Himalayas." For more details, go to … http://www.trancenet.org/law/denarot.shtm
12 For the complete interview, (Shank 1-5) go to …
    http:/www.freedomofmind.com/resourcecenter/groups/t/tm/shank1.htm
13 See http://www.trancenet.org/start/money.shtml

14 To find Joe Kellet's excellent site, "**Falling down the Rabbit Hole: How Transcendental Meditation really works, a critical opinion.**" (Also with great links) go to ... http://www.suggestibility.org/

Chapter 18 – Scientology

1   Quoted from a story in the Los Angeles Times. Aug.27, 1978.
2   Hubbard: Philadelphia Doctorate Course lecture 18, "Conditions of Space-Time-Energy."
3   Interview in Penthouse Magazine, June 1983.
4   "Scientology: The Cult of Greed," Time Magazine, May 6, 1991.
5   L.R.Hubbard, "Dianetics: Evolution of a Science," Astounding Sci-Fi Magazine, May 1950, p.66.
6   "Bare Faced Messiah," by Russell Miller. 1987, pp.112-120.
7   "Magic in Theory and Practice," Aleister Crowley. 1929, reprinted 1976.
8   Ibid., p.24
9   L.R.H. "What Your Donations Buy," Sci. Church Pamphlet.
10 "Magic in Theory and Practice," pp. 146-7.
11 "Dianetics: The Modern Science of Mental Health," p.340
12 "L. Ron Hubbard, Messiah or Madman?" by Bent Corydon and L.R. Hubbard Jr., p.305
13 "Bare Faced Messiah," p.355
14 L.R.H. Philadelphia Doctorate Course, Lecture 20, 1952.
15 "The Hubbard is Bare," Essay by Jeff Jacobson. On-line at http://www.clambake.org
16 L.R.H. Taped messages HCOPI9 March 1972 MS OEC 384
17 Confidential taped briefing, re the enormous income to be made from "Scientology Missions International." From "L.R.H. In His Own Words," quoted on line at http://www.thingy.apana.org.au/-fun/scn/demo/leaflets/lrhquote/html
18 Time Magazine, August 23, 1968.
19 "E-Meter Essentials," by L.Ron Hubbard. 1961
20 "The Hubbard is Bare," J. Jacobson.
21 "Dianetics," P.24
22 Ibid P.228
23 Ibid P.24
24 Ibid P.18
25 "The Hubbard is Bare," J. Jacobson
26 "A Piece of Blue Sky," by Jon Atack, 1990
27 "Ability," No. 81 1959.
28 L.R.H. H.C.O. Bulletin, May 11 1963 A.D. (After Dianetics)
29 Ibid.
30 "Admissions of L.Ron Hubbard," assembled and presented by Gerry Armstrong (former C.of S. member) currently on line at http;//www.lermanet2.com/reference/Admissions: pdf
31 "The Hubbard is Bare," J. Jacobson
32 Adapted from an essay by Bob Minton at http://www.xenu.net/archive/otlll-scholar/minton-essay.txt
33 Ibid.

Chapter 19 – Martial Arts

1   "The Black Belts of the Screen are Filling the Dojos," by Glen Rifkin. New York Times, Feb. 16 1992, p.10
2   "Enter the Dragon: Wrestling with the Martial Arts Phenomenon, Part 1," by Erwin Castro, B.J. Oropeza, and Ron Rhodes. Christian Research Institute.
3   "Martial Arts." http://en.wikipedia.org
4   Ibid.
5   "Addressing Christian Concerns: a practical definition of Chi." http://www.orlandokuntao. com
6   "Martial Arts," Wikipedia.
7   Ibid.
8   Probe Ministries. "The Origins and Popularity of the Martial Arts," www.probe. org/content/view/749/169/
9   Gospel Martial Arts Union. http://Pastornet.au/response/articles/6.htm
10 http://www.karateforchrist.net/technique.html E-mail soke@karateforchrist.net
11 Bob Orlando. Je Du-Too School of Martial Arts, Denver, Colorado. http://www.orlandokuntao. com/
12 "Stand Your Ground," by Kaleghl Quinn, original Publisher, Orbis 1983.
13 "Hand Fighting Manual," by Fred Neff. Lerner Pub. 1977.
14 "Enter the Dragon: Wrestling with the Martial Arts Phenomenon, Part 1."
15 Probe Ministries "The Origins and Popularity of the Martial arts."

Chapter 20 – Yoga

1   "Structural Yoga Therapy," by Mukunda Stiles. Published in 2000 by Samuel Weiser, p.7
2   Ibid., p.27
3   Ibid., p.29
4   "Patanjali's Vision of Oneness: An Interpretive Translation," by Swami Venkatesananda. II 29
5   Ibid. I 27, I 28
6   "Yoga Life Magazine," Spring 1996, The Yogi, Portraits of Swami Vishnu-Devananda (Mantra Initiation)
7   "Yoga Meditation of the Himalayan Tradition," by Swami Jnaneshvara Bharam.
8   Sri Sankaracharya, International Sivananda Yoga Vedanta Centers.
9   "Yoga Life" Spring 1996. 'Portraits …'
10 David Frawley: American Institute of Vedic Studies. (Hinduism, Santana Dharma and Yoga)
11 "Kundalini Demystified." Yoga Journal, issue 64, Sept./Oct.85, p.43
12 "Baba Beleaguered," Yoga Journal, issue 63, July/Aug.1985, P.30
13 "Hinduism Today Magazine," Oct.-Dec., 2003 (Insight Hinduism)
14 Ibid. (Insight Hinduism) "A Splendorous Lotus with Four Superb Petals." Also April-June, 2005.
15 Ibid.
16 Ibid.
17 "Yoga Life" Autumn 2003.
18 Ibid.
19 Ibid.
20 Ibid.
21 Ibid.

22 Ibid.

23 Ibid.

24 David Frawley: American Institute of Vedic Studies.

25 "Yoga Life Magazine" Spring 1996, "Portraits ...'

26 "Guru and Divine Grace," by Swami Rama: from "Sacred Journey: Living Purposefully and Dying Gracefully."

27 Ibid.

28 Ibid.

29 "Does Hinduism teach that all religions are the same?" A Philosophical Critique of Radical Universalism, by Dr. Frank Gaetano Morales Ph.D. Dec. 2004.

30 "Yoga and the West," in Psychology and the East, Carl G. Jung. (R.F.C. Hull Translation, Princeton University Press, 1987, p.81)

31 "The Osgood File" (CBS Radio Network) 4/11/03, 8/18/03.
    Susan Bordenkircher, Christian Yoga Instructor, Jubilee Shores United Methodist Church, Fairhope, Alabama.

Chapter 21 – Alternative Christianity

1   "Kundalini Energy and Christian Spirituality: A Pathway to Growth and Healing," by Philip St. Romain. Published by Crossroad, 2002. (chapter 6 summary)

2   Ibid. (Foreword by Thomas Keating)

3   Ibid.

4   Ibid.

5   Ibid.

6   Ibid. (After word by James Arras)

7   "Finding Grace at the Center," M.B. Pennington – T. Keating, T.E. Clarke. Published by St. Bede's, Petersham, Mass. 1978, pp.5-6.

8   "Conjectures of a Guilty Bystander," by Thomas Merton. Doubleday, N.Y.1989, pp.157-8.

9   "The Wisdom of the Desert: Sayings of the Desert Fathers," compiled by Thomas Merton. Shambala Publishing, Boston, Mass. 1970. Author's note, P.IX.

10 Ibid.

11 "Yoga and Christianity," by Justin O'Brien Ph.D. Himalayan International Institute, Honesdale, Pa. 1978, p.25

12 "Thomas Merton's Life and Work." W.L. Lyons Brown Library, Thomas Merton Center, Bellarmine University.

13 Book of the Year, Reader's Poll. "Christianity Today," April 5, 1993, p. 26.

14 "Celebration of Discipline," by Richard Foster. 1978 edition, p.15.

15 "Finding the Heart's True Home," Foster, p.122.

16 "Meditative Prayer," Foster, Intervarsity Christian Fellowship. 1983.

17 "Devotional Classics," Richard Foster and James Bryan Smith. Harper, San Franscico, Ca.

18 "The Road Less Traveled," by M. Scott Peck. Simon and Schuster Inc. New York, N.Y. 1978, p.283.

19 Ibid., p.309

20 "A World waiting to be Born," M.S. Peck. Bantam Books, N.Y., N.Y. P.21.

21 "Further Along the Road Less Traveled," Peck. Simon and Schuster Audio Works 1992.

22 Ibid.

23 Ibid.

24 Ibid.

25 Matthew Fox, "The Coming of the Cosmic Christ." Harper and Row, San Franscico Ca. 1988, pp.154, 232.
26 Ibid.
27 "In the Spirit of the Early Christians." Common Boundary Magazine, Jan./Feb 1992, p.19.
28 Ibid.
29 "Sabatical Journey." Henry Nouwen. Crossroad Pub. Co. N.Y. 1998, p.51.
30 "Power of Intention: Learning to Co-Create Your World Your Way," by Wayne W. Dyer. Hay House Pub. 2004, from chapter 15.
31 Ibid.
32 Ibid.
33 Ibid.
34 AM Northwest Morning Talk Show, KATU Channel 2 Portland OR. Interview with Wayne Dyer, March 27,1997
35 Nightingale-Conant Presents: "Spiritual Alchemy ™ The New Technologies for Abundance, Health, and Harmony," by Luanne Oakes Ph.D. (On 8 compact disks)
36 "Sound Health, Sound Wealth." Oakes (on 4 C.D's 22991cd)
37 From the C.D. or tape: "Introduction to Abraham." Abraham-Hicks Publications. www. abraham-hicks.com
38 "Ask and it is Given." Abraham-Hicks, Hay House Pub. Oct. 2004, ch. 13.
39 Ibid., ch.15
40 Abraham-Hicks.com (website) "Abraham's Teachings in Brief."
41 "Introduction to Abraham," C.D. from Abraham-Hicks Pub.
42 Abraham-Hicks.com (Look for "Abraham's Teachings in Brief.")

Chapter 22 – The Lion, The witch, and The Purpose Driven Wardrobe.

1 "Mere Christianity," by C. S. Lewis. HarperCollins Edition 2001. 10 East 53rd Street, New York, N.Y. 10022. (From back cover)
2 Ibid., p. 202
3 Ibid., p.109
4 Ibid., p.61
5 Ibid., p.223
6 C. S. Lewis, "The World's Last Night and Other Essays," pp 98-99.
7 "Chronicles," Book two, "Prince Caspian," pp. 131-133. The Macmillan Company. 866 Third Avenue, New York, N.Y. 10022.
8 Last Trumpet Ministries Beaver Dam, WI 53916 USA. http://www.lasttrumpetministries.org
9 Chronicles, book seven, "The Last Battle," pp.153-154, 156. Macmillan Company, N.Y.
10 Mere Christianity," p.14
11 Richard Abanes, "Harry Potter and the Bible." Camp Hill, Pennsylvania: Horizon Books, 2001, pp.241, 271. Quoted from the introduction to, "God, the Devil, and Harry Potter," by John Killinger. St. Martin's Press, 175 Fifth Avenue, N.Y.N.Y. 10010
12 Ibid. From the introduction p.12.
13 Ibid. pp.2 and 11.
14 Ibid. Inside back-cover. "Jessie, and The Night Jessie Sang at the Opry."
15 Ibid., p.39
16 "About Doreen Virtue, Ph.D." http://www.angeltherapy.com/about.php
17 "The Purpose Driven Life," by Rick Warren. Pub. by Zondervan Grand Rapids, U.S.A. Inside back cover

18 Ibid., p.325

19 Ibid., .327

20 Rick Warren, "The Purpose Driven Church: Growth Without Compromising Your Message and Mission." Grand Rapids, Michigan. Zondervan, 1995. P.297.

21 Eugene H. Peterson, "The Message: The New Testament in Contemporary Language." Colorado Springs, Colorado: NavPress. 1993, p.415.

22 Ibid., Matt.6:9-10, from pp.21-22

23 Ibid., Matt.16:25, from p. ?

24 Ronald S. Miller, New Age Journal. "As Above So Below: Paths to Spiritual Renewal in Daily Life." Los Angeles: Jeremy P. Tarcher, Inc. 1992. P.XI.

25 Purpose Driven Life, p.88, and citing the "New Century Version," Dallas, Texas. Word Publishers, 1991.

26 Messages from Maitreya the Christ: One Hundred Forty Messages. 1992, pp.88, 23, 203.

27 The "Message" p.400

28 "Be Happy You Are Loved:" Robert H. Schuller. Thomas Nelson Publishers, Nashville, Tennessee. 1986, p.65.

29 "Self-Esteem," Schuller: The New Reformation. Word Books, Waco, Texas, 1982, p.19.

30 "If It's Going to Be, It's Up to Me," Schuller. 1997. Pub. by ?????

31 "Self Love," Schuller. Jove Books: New York. Berkeley Publishing Group, 1969, p.16.

32 "Purpose Driven Life," p.17.

33 Ibid., p.33

34 Ibid., p.27

35 "Love, Medicine & Miracles," by Bernie Siegel. HarperCollins Publishers: HarperPerennial, New York. 1998, from pp.19-20

36 "Prayer: My Soul's Adventure with God: A Spiritual Autobiography," Schuller. Published by Thomas Nelson Inc., Nashville, Tennessee. 1995, opening page.

37 "Self-Esteem: The New Reformation," Schuller,. 1982. Quote from author Rene Dubois.

38 "Purpose Driven Life," p.31

39 "Conversations With God: An Uncommon Dialogue." Book 1, by Neale Donald Walsh. G.P. Putnam's Sons, New York. 1996, p.1.

40 Ibid., p. 202

41 "The New Revelations: A Conversation with God." Walsh. Atria books, New York. 2002, p. 157.

42 Tomorrow's God: Our Greatest Spiritual Challenge." Walsh. Atria Books, 2004, p.311.

43 "Conversations With God: ..." Book 1. Walsh, p.28.

44 Ibid., p.40.

45 Ibid., p.61

46 "Self-Esteem: The New Reformation." Schuller. Word Books, Waco, Texas. 1982, p.38.

47 "The New Revelations: ..." Walsh, p.282.

48 Ibid.

49 "The Five Steps To Peace," Conversations with God website. http://www.cwg.org/5steps/5stepstopeace.pdf (Page 1)

50 "The New Revelations: Walsh, p.175

51 Ibid., p. 157

52 Weekend Message Application Guide: "Our Global P.E.A.C.E. Plan, Nov. 1-2, 2003. http://www.saddleback.com/maturity/fullstory.asp?type=238 Page 2

53 "Deceived On Purpose," by Warren Smith. Mountain Stream Press, P.O. Box 1794, Magalia, CA 95954-1794. Second Edition 2004, pp.101-102.

54 "Discover Your Possibilities," Schuller. New York: Ballantine Books, 1978, p.100.

55 Rick Warren, Saddleback Church e-mail, October 27, 2003.

56 "Tomorrow's God: Our Greatest Challenge," Walsh, p.1X.

57 Saddleback Church e-mail, Warren. Oct. 27, 2003.

58 "Messages from Maitreya the Christ: ..." pp. 123, 23, 123, 88, 203, 183, 218, 45, 44, 150.

59 "The Aquarian Conspiracy: Personal and Social Transformation In the 1980's," by Marilyn Ferguson. J.P Tarcher. Inc. Los Angeles. 1980, p.375.

60 Purpose Driven pastors.com (If you have difficulty finding her comments, try typing in - *Kay Warren and Henry Nouwen*, and just look around - you'll be amazed at what comes up!)

61 "In the Name of Jesus," by Henry Nouwen. Crossroad Pub. Co., New York, 1989, pp.31-32.

62 "Bread for the Journey," Nouwen. Harper, San Francisco, 1997, Jan.15 and Nov.16.

63 "Sabbatical Journey," Nouwen, Crossroad Pub. 1998, p.51.

64 "The Search for the meaning of Life," by Willigis Jager. Ligouri, MO, 1995, p.125

65 "The Adulation of Man in the Purpose Driven Life," by Richard Bennett. Berean Beacon website http://www.bereanbeacon.org/articles/rick_warren_purpose_drivenhtm,accessed6/2005.
Ci.ted from "Running Against the Wind," by Brian Flynn. Lighthouse Trails Publishing, Silverton, Oregon, p.199 (second edition).

66 Ibid., p201

67 Sermon video clip concerning Ken Blanchard is available at http://wwwlighthousetrailsre-search.com/pressreleasevideoclip.htm

68 "What would Buddha Do at Work?" Ken Blanchard and Frank Metcalf. Berkeley, Ca: Seastone, imprint of Ulysees Press, 2001, foreword.

69 "Reach Out for New Life," Schuller. Hawthorn Books Inc: New York. 1977, p.51.
And "Self-Esteem: The New Reformation," Schuller, p.102

70 "The Dream Giver," by Bruce Wilkinson. Multnomah Publishers, Sisters, Oregon, 2003, p.15.

71 "You'll See It When You Believe It: The Way to Your Personal Transformation," by Wayne Dyer. Avon Books, New York, 1989, pp.96-97.

72 Robert Schuller, "Hour of Power," November 9, 2003.

73 "My Journey: From an Iowa Farm to a Cathedral of Dreams," Schuller. HarperSanFrancisco, San Francisco. 2001, pp. 492 and 502.

74 Recorded telecast of the "Hour of Power," Bruce Wilkinson, program # 1760, "Living Your Dream." Oct.26, 2003.

75 Internet broadcast from Saddleback Church, October 26, 2003.

76 "What Do You Do When Your Church Hits a Plateau?" June 14, 2006. Purpose Driven Pastors. com website. (And from Lighthouse Trails Research. com.)

77 http:// www.lighthousetrailsresearch.com/resistersdieorleave.htm

78 Ibid.

79 Ibid.

80 Ibid. (Also look for an interview with George Mair.)

81 "Quantum Spirituality," by Leonard Sweet. United Theological Seminary. 1991, p.122.

82 "Speaking My Mind," by Tony Campolo. West Pub.Group. Div. of Thomas Nelson, Nashville, TN.2004, pp.149-150.

83 "The End of the World as we Know It," Chuck Smith Jr., Water Brook Press, Colorado Springs, Co., 2001, p.103

83 "The Aquarian Conspiracy," Marilyn Ferguson, p.419.

84 "Deceived On Purpose," by Warren Smith, pp.78 and180

Chapter 23 – How Free is a Christian Freemason?

1   Albert Pike: A.C. De La Rive, "La Femme et L'enfant Dans La Franc-Maconnerie Universelle," p.588. Lady Queensborough, "Occult Theocracy," pp.220-221. Addressing the 23 Supreme Councils of the World on July 14, 1889

2   James Sender: Letter to "Rome Forum," (Rome Tribune, Ga.) Sept 12, 2005.

3   Albert Pike: "Morals and Dogma of the Ancient and Accepted Scottish Rite of Freemasonry." (Charleston, S.C.: The Supreme Council of the 33rd Degree for the Southern Jurisdiction of the U.S. 1906) pp.106-107.

4   Malcolm C. Duncan: "Masonic Ritual and Monitor," (New York: David McKay) p.29.

5   "Masonry: The Truth Behind It," Circa 1983. Upper Room Tracts, Gt. Yarmouth, Norfolk, U.K.

6   Ibid. Compare with "The Secret Teachings of the Masonic Lodge: A Christian Perspective." John Ankerberg and John Weldon, Moody Press, Chicago, 1990, p.81.

7   Manly P. Hall. "Lectures on Ancient Philosophy: An Introduction to Practical Ideas." Hall Pub. L.A. Ca. First Published 1929, p.433.

8   Pike: "Morals and Dogma," p.109 (3rd Degree)

9   Albert G. Mackey's "Revised Encyclopedia of Freemasonry." Revised and enlarged by Robert I. Clegg. (Richmond-Macoy 1966, Vol. 1, p.269.

10   Ibid.

11   Joseph Fort Newton: "The Religion of Freemasonry: An Interpretation." Richmond-Macoy, 1969, p.116.

12   Henry Wilson Coil, "A comprehensive View of Freemasonry." Richmond-Macoy, 1973, p.234.

13   Hall, "Lectures on Ancient Philosophy," Philosophical Research Society Inc., 1984.

14   Hall, "The Lost Keys of Freemasonry," Macon Pub. and the Masonic Supply Co. Inc., Richmond Va. 1976, pp. 64-65.

15   Pike, "Morals and Dogma," (XXX Degree) p.533.

16   Congressional Record, Senate, Sept. 9, 1987: S11868-70. From "Secret Teachings of the Masonic Lodge," pp. 23-24.

17   Ibid., p. 323

18   Thomas S. Hughes. No. 574 – "Famous Freemasons: Alphabetical Listing." 10/15/2004. On-line go to, http://lodges.gl-mi.org/tshughes574/FamousMasonsAlpha.html

19   On-line, Freemasonry: The Witchcraft Connection. (Article by William J. Schnoebelen).

20   "The Externalization of the Hierarchy," by Alice Bailey, p.511.

21   "History of Freemasonry." A.G. Mackey. Vol. 6, p.1721

22   Pike: "Morals and Dogma" (Knight Kadosh - XXX Degree) pp.533-534.

23   Mick Oxley, "In His Grip Ministries," Route 1, Box 257, Crescent City, Fla. 32112 On-line at http://www.saintsalive.com/freemasonry/fmworld.htm

Chapter 24 – So Who Really Founded America?

1   From "Glimpses Bulletin" #19: "Christianity in Jamestown: England's First Permanent Colony." Christian History Institute, http://chi.gospelcom.net/GLIMPSEF/Glimpses/glmps019.shtml

2   American History 1 Notes. On-line at http://housatonic.net/faculty/ABALL/US1Notes003.htm Click on, Go to Excerpt

3   Columbia Encyclopedia Sixth Edition, 2001-5. "Pilgrims" Columbia University Press.

4 The Articles of Confederation of the United Colonies of New England; May 19ᵗʰ 1643. (Courtesy of Yale Law School)

5 "Secret Societies," edited by Norman Mackenzie. Aldus Pub. 1968, pp.168-169.

6 "Dictionary of the History of Ideas," volume 1, P.647. Electronic Text Center, P.O. Box 400148, Charlottesville, Va.

7 James Beless, (33ʳᵈ Degree) writing in the Scottish Rite Journal, "Freemen and Freemasons," vol.3 No.2, March 1997.

8 Thomas Jefferson – Letter to John Adams, April 11, 1823. Quoted from "Breaking the Last Taboo," by James A, Haught, 1996.

9 "Works." Jefferson, 1829 edition vol. 4, p.322. Quote from Franklin Steiner.

10 The Masonic New World Order, "Masonic Foundations of the U.S." http://watch.pair.co_m/mason.html

11 "The Age of Washington," by George W. Nordham. Chicago: Adam's Press, 1989, pp.142-143.

12 "Treaties and Other International Acts of the U.S." Edited by Hunter Miller, vol. 2, U.S. Government Printing Office, 1931, p.365.

13 "Six Historic Americans," by John Remsberg. Crown Rights Book Co., reprinted 2001, Part 1, pp.103-104.

14 Washington's Inaugural Speech. (1789) From classbrain.com (Source: National Archives and Records Administration)

15 "Six Historic Americans," Part 1, pp.119, 122.

16 Ibid., pp.134-135.

17 Ibid., p.146.

18 Ibid., pp.119-120.

19 Ibid., p.120

20 Ibid., p.147

21 Ibid., p.148

22 "Book of Common Prayer," England: John Baskerville, circa. 1762. (Washington National Cathedral Rare Books Library [95])

23 "The Temple and the Lodge," Michael Biagent and Richard Leigh. NY: Arcade Pub., 1989. See pp. 239-260

Chapter 25 – He Who Owns the Gold ...

1 Joan Veon: worldnetdaily.com (2002)

2 "Tragedy and Hope," by Dr. Carroll Quigley. (G.S.G. and Assoc. 1975)

3 "The Confidence Game," by Steve Solomon. Pub. by Simon and Schuster, 1995, p.28.

4 "The Secret Destiny of America." M.P.Hall. Philosophical Research Society Inc., L.A., Ca. 1944, p.72.

5 "The Masonic Seal of America." http://www.geocities.com/endtimedeception/seal.htm

6 "Spiritual Policies," McLaughlin & Davidson, op. cit., p. 249. See also: "Scarlet and the Beast," op. cit., p. 174, and 26, 29-30, taken from "Brotherhood of Darkness," by Dr. Stanley Montheith. Hearthstone Publishers, Oklahoma City, Ok.

7 Quote from David J. Meyer; from "Dancing with Demons: the Music's Real Master," by Jeff Godwin. (Chino, Ca: Chick Publications, 1988, p.312)

8 "Secret Destiny of America," Hall, p. 17

9 Full article available on-line at http://www.jesus-is-savior.com (Scroll down to "Billions for the Bankers, Debt for the People.")

Chapter 26 – Mirror, Mirror on the Wall ...

1   "Marx and Satan," by Richard Wurmbrant. Living Sacrifice Book Publishers, 1986

2   "Philosophy of Communism." Charles Boyer (introduction) Fordham University Press., Jan.1, 1952.

3   Roman Gul, Dzerjinski, Published by the author in Russian. (Paris,1936) P.81. (Taken from "Marx and Satan" – Wurmbrant.

4   "Invocation of Despair," by Marx. "A Book of Verse," Inter. Publishers, 1975 Marx/Engels' collected works.

5   "Menschenstolz." (Human Pride) Marx. Ibid.

6   "Marx and Satan." Wurmbrant, ch.2.

7   "Victims of Communism Foundation," on-line at http://www.victimsofcommunism.org/history_communism.php

8   "Marx and the Bible," by Jose Miranda.

9   "The Struggle is My Life," by Nelson Mandela. Published by London: International Defense and Aid Fund for South Africa. (1986) P.76.

10 Qur'an sura 9:5

11 Ibid., sura 5:33

12 Ibid., sura 33:36-38

13 Ibid., sura 5:79/75

14 Ibid., from sura 4

15 Quotes from "Islam," by Richard Tames.

16 "Catholic Encyclopedia," vol.15, p.459.

17 "Doctrinal Teaching of the Catholic Church," Quentin De La Bedoyere: Library of Catholic Knowledge.

18 "Catechism of the Catholic Church," 1997, part 2, article 1.

19 "Doct. Teaching of the C.C.," Bedoyere.

20 "Catechism of the C.C." (1459)

21 "Doct. Teaching of the .C.C.," Bedoyere.

22 Ibid.

23 Ibid.

24 "Catholic Code of Canon Law" (Canon 904).

25 "Doct. Teaching of the C.C." Bedoyere.

26 Ibid.

27 Denzinger's Enchiridion Symbolorum (sources of Catholic Dogma) 30th Edition, para. 423.

28 Ibid., para. 469.

29 Ibid., para. 1677.

30 Pope John Paul II at L'osservatore Romano, 10.12.'81.

31 "Rise of the Cults," by Walter Martin.

32 "A Cult is a Cult," by Dave Hunt. Reaching Catholics for Christ, P.O. Box 7019, Bend, OR, 97708. On-line at www.reachingcatholics.org

33 "Webster's Dictionary."

34 "A Secret World: Sexuality and the Search for Celibacy," by A.W. Richard Sipe. Brunner-Routledge Publishers, p.58.

35 Ibid., p.35.

36 "Shattered Vows," by David Rice. Original Publisher, Triumph Books (p.161)

37 Ibid.

38 "Sex, Priests, and Power: Anatomy of a Crisis," by A.W.R. Sipe. Brunner and Routledge, Publishers, April 1995.

39 "Celibacy is the Issue," a thesis by Thomas G. Lederer, M.A. 1992.

****

ADDENDUM

Open letter from "Evangelicals at Vancouver."

(Sixth Assembly of the W.C.C. July 24 – August 10, 1983)

Many evangelicals from all over the world are present at the 6ᵗʰ Assembly of the World Council of Churches as delegates and observers, advisers and visitors, speakers and press representatives. Many are members of churches within the WCC framework.

A number gravitated together and frequently shared impressions and matters of common concern during these days. This statement represents our deep desire to bear witness to what we believe God sought to say to us through the Christians we encountered, the words we heard and the official actions taken at Vancouver. We do not claim to speak on behalf of our churches, or of all the evangelicals at the Assembly.

The theme of Vancouver is "Jesus Christ – the Life of the World." **We are impressed anew with the rich diversity and complexity of the worldwide Christian movement.** We found the exploration of this theme a stimulating experience, especially because the Assembly sought to call Christians everywhere to be more faithful to their threefold task– the pastoral, the prophetic and the apostolic. As a result, its on going concern is that the churches be spiritually renewed (the pastoral), that they become socially responsible (the prophetic) and that they display diligence in their holistic witness to the Gospel (the apostolic).

As we pressed deeper into days crowded with presentations, reflection and interaction, it became apparent that Vancouver 1983 marks significant progress over the last two Assemblies (Uppsala 1968 and Nairobi 1975) in its overarching spiritual and Biblical orientation. This was apparent in the following ways:

1. The dimension of worship was both central and spiritually refreshing. At plenary sessions and in the daily worship services, **we enjoyed warm communal fellowship** as we reached out to God in prayer and praise.
2. The wider space given to Bible exposition and the affirmation of basic Biblical themes in plenary sessions represent unmistakable loyalty to the historic rootage of our Christian faith.
3. Biblical messages on the nature and mission of the church under such key themes as Jesus Christ, life and the world, prepared the way for earnest efforts to relate these truths to the problems facing Christian today.
4. The Orthodox with their trinitarianism, their spirituality, and their participation in group discussions at all levels reminded us of some of the church's non-negotiable treasures, while other segments of the worldwide church called us to face the urgencies of today.

5. We entered into deeper anguish over the terrible injustices currently perpetrated against the poor, the powerless and the oppressed throughout the world. We perceived anew that the issues of nuclear disarmament and peace could become a preoccupation and divert attention from the equally urgent issues of deprivation, injustice, human rights and liberation.

6. We found ourselves standing with the many who refused to believe that the powers of oppression, death and destruction will have the last word on human rights and liberation.

7. Finally, and most important of all, representatives from all segments of the church called the Assembly to accept the reality that Jesus Christ is indeed the life of the world. Women spoke alongside men. The youth and the disadvantaged were heard. Even the children. And the ordained clergy made no attempt to dominate the ministry of the Word of God.

Ever since the WCC was formed in 1948 at Amsterdam, each successive Assembly has been unique. Vancouver was no exception. In its study papers, group discussions and personal conversations, we could readily discern several concerns:

1. That Christians must rigorously eschew any docetic understanding of the Gospel. The church can only be renewed today if it faces courageously the relation of Jesus Christ to the totality of human need and experience. We see one-sidedness in a preoccupation with "contending for the faith" while ignoring a world going up in flames.

2. That as the church presses deeper into the '80's, all agreed that Christians shall increasingly be drawn in their Biblical reflection and theologizing to focus on the plight of the poor – those whom Christ particularly singled out as the ones to hear the good news of the kingdom (Luke 4:18,19).

3. That increasingly, the church being reinforced in its perception of the demonic dimensions of structural evil. They are as offensive to God and as destructive to people as any personal evil.

   One WCC official spoke for many when he related the poor to "the church's most important missiological issue – the centrality of Jesus Christ "Christ alone is the life of the world and He alone can deal with the problem of evil. But He must be proclaimed to all peoples. And the majority of those who have not heard the Gospel are the poor.

4. That the dominant issue before the church today is the inter-relation of it's concerns for justice and peace. They cannot be separated. We note that this issue has both vertical and horizontal implications. Moreover, the Biblical vision of justice with peace through Jesus Christ, the life of the world, was not posed as one of several options for those who could follow Him, but the only option.

We were moved to join hundreds from the United States and Central America who covenanted together to seek a better understanding of the issues involved in the present conflict in Central America as a positive step toward the achievement of peace with justice throughout the area.

As evangelicals we rejoiced that the Assembly did not simply confine itself to the prophetic task of the church. The nurture of Christians and their witness to the unbelieving world were also included. But we could not be true to our evangelical convictions were we merely to endorse the positive affirmations made at Vancouver. **We were troubled by occasional statements which implied that apart from Jesus Christ the world can have life. Not every address reflected high Christological and soteriological perspectives. On occasion we wanted to rise up and call the WCC to be consistent with it's own basis**: "A fellowship of churches which confess the Lord Jesus Christ as God and Savior according to the Scriptures and therefore seek to fulfill together their common calling to the glory of the one God, Father, Son and Holy Spirit." We would assert that WCC leadership has the solemn responsibility to uphold this confession in all it's public programs. True, none of us wants to judge the Assembly by the input of some of the speakers. Nevertheless, at the end of the second week of deliberations we would like to make the following observations:

1. Although the WCC Central Committee had approved (1982) an illuminating and thoroughly evangelical study: Mission and Evangelism – an Ecumenical Affirmation, we were disappointed that it wasn't referred to in any plenary address. We were gratified that the Affirmation received strong support in the Assembly's Message to the Churches. No ecumenical document has been so welcomed by evangelicals. Actually, the evangelical counsel was widely sought in it's preparation. Furthermore, the Assembly did not give central place to the shameful fact that at this late hour in the history of the church, more than three billion have yet to hear the Gospel of Christ – despite Christ's mandate that it be proclaimed to all peoples. We did not feel that the Assembly adequately treated either Gospel proclamation or the invitational dimensions of evangelism.

2. On occasion terminology became fuzzy and theology worse. For example, while the Assembly frequently heard that sin brings social alienation, little was said about spiritual alienation – from God Himself. As a result, the redemptive dimension of Christ's suffering on the Cross was not particularly stressed. Moreover, while larger issues of social ethics were frequently treated, more personal ethical concerns rarely surfaced.

In sum, there were times when we wished that evangelical voices in the churches were given the prominence accorded some theological mavericks. Fortunately, in the issue and discussion groups, we heard evangelical men and women participate whose evident concern was to remind fellow delegates of the Biblical authority and witness to the issues under review. Evangelicals are convinced that if Jesus Christ is the life of the world. His claim that His words are spirit and life (John 6:63) should not be downplayed.

All of which brings us to raise the crucial question: What should be the evangelical response to the many signs of growth and renewal we discerned in the Assembly? Should evangelicals seek more direct involvement in the ecumenical process?

At Vancouver, some evangelicals were adamant in their stand against any participation in the WCC. We were saddened to come upon a few zealous Christians distributing scurrilous anti -WCC literature. We deplored their tactics and hung our heads in shame over their sweeping denunciations. Their actions, in our judgment, constituted false witness against their neighbors.

At the same time, should evangelicals see significance in the growing effectiveness of the Orthodox contributions to the WCC alongside the growing WCC challenge to the Orthodox to extend their mission into the world? **Is there not the possibility that evangelicals have not only much to contribute but something to receive through ecumenical involvement?**

Do evangelicals not also share the obligation along with other Christians to seek to overcome the scandal of the disunity and disobedience of the churches that the world might believe? (John 17:21) Should evangelicals not seek to receive all who confess Jesus Christ as Lord, even though they may seriously disagree on theological issues apart from the core of the Gospel? There is no Biblical mandate to withdraw from those who have not withdrawn from Christ. Should not Christians gladly receive all those whom God has manifestly received? Are not the alternatives – religion or indifference – totally incompatible with the Apostle Paul's affirmation that Christ is not divided (1 Cor.1:13)?

Our experience at Vancouver challenged stereotypes some of us have had of the WCC. And our involvement in WCC processes and programs made us realize anew the distortions in the popular evangelical understanding of them. Hence, we felt pressed to declare publicly our determination to be more actively involved in all efforts seeking the unity of the church. Because we have seen evidence of God at work here, we cannot but share our growing conviction that evangelicals should question Biblically the easy acceptance of withdrawal, fragmentation and parochial isolation that tends to characterize many of us. Should we not be more trustful of those who profess Christ's Lordship? Should we not be more concerned with the peace, purity and unity of the people of God in our day? And if God thereby grants the church renewal for which many pray, shall this not forever demolish that all too **popular evangelical heresy** – that the way to renew the body of Christ is to separate from it and relentlessly criticize it? (Emphasis added)

****

Praise God for the "**few zealous Christians**" handing out so-called "**scurrilous anti-WCC literature**" (then and now!). Praise God for those who cry out for true believers to separate themselves from any and all involvement with this vile ecumenical "harlot!"

By the way; "**scurrilous**" means slanderous, libelous, outrageous, or defamatory, and obviously implies that the literature exposing the WCC was heretical and false. However, to understand *real* heresy, and how it applies to the WCC and its affiliates, here are a few offerings from the book "No Longer Strangers," published in June 1984 by the Lutheran World Federation, the World Council of Churches, the World Student Christian Federation, and the World Young Women's Christian Association (YWCA).

Written as a "guideline to worship," the book exhorts us to use the following names for **GOD** during times of devotion:

The Source – Lady of peace – Lady of wisdom – Lady of love – Lady of birth
Lord of stars – Lord of planets – Mother – Home – Baker woman – Presence –
Power – Essence – Simplicity.

Is there anything more "**scurrilous**" or blasphemous than these insults to God from the WCC ?
Since when was God a "**lady**," or a "**baker woman**," or a "**mother?**"
Throughout this entire publication, God is described and addressed in female terms!
Consider a few more sickening examples:

TEACH US TO KNOW & LOVE YOU

O God of a thousand names and faces, Mother and father of all life on earth –You who live in the cells of all life, – Teach us to know and love you – Lady of peace, of love, of wisdom, Lord of all the stars and planets, – Best consoler, inward guest, – Teach us to know and love you.

BLESSING THE BREAD

In the beginning was God - In the beginning, the source of all that is – In the beginning, God yearning, God moaning, God labouring, God rejoicing – And God loved what **SHE** had made – And God said, "It is good." – Then God, knowing that all that is good is shared, held the earth tenderly in **HER** arms – God yearned for relationship God longed to share the good earth – And humanity was born in the yearning of God – We were born to share the earth. (Emphasis added)

"Mystery Babylon the Great" is the "**Mother** of harlots," and the "**goddess**" of the entire New Age Movement! (*Rev.17*) Satan is her "husband," and is the "**god** of this world," the "**father** of lies," and of *all* "harlots!" Together they reign over the WCC, and over every other false religious organization on planet earth!

A PARTING BLOW
(DEALING WITH CURSES, UNFORGIVENESS, AND FEARS.)

OCCULT CHECK LIST (From chapter 4)

Part A) Involvement with Magic – Astrology – Spiritualism – Satanism

Have you ever consulted a
- medium/spiritualist?
- witch?
- clairvoyant or fortune-teller?
- palm reader?
- spiritual healer?

Have you ever practiced
- astral travel?
- levitation?
- placing curses or spells?

Have you used or dabbled with
- ouija boards?
- tarot cards?
- pendulums/divining instruments?
- horoscopes?

Have you ever watched, attended, or taken part in
- séances?
- coven or black magic rites?
- Halloween parties?
- satanic films?
- pornography?

Have you ever been aware of
- psychic powers?
- voices speaking forcefully in your mind?
- any curses or spells against you?

Have you read books by authors such as
- Stephen King, Dennis Wheatley,
- J. K. Rowling (Harry Potter)

- C.S. Lewis (Chronicles of Narnia)
- Jean Dixon, Edgar Cayce?

Do you know if your parents, grandparents, great grandparents (or any other family members or close friends) have, or have had, a strong connection to any of the above?

Through prayer, the Holy Spirit will often reveal names or events long forgotten in order to bring about deliverance and freedom. (See prayers at the end of this section)

Part B) Involvement with other potentially dangerous activities

Have you ever consulted
- Hypnotists?
- Homeopaths?
- Gurus?

Have you been influenced by, or taken special interest in
- Re-incarnation?
- ESP/telepathy/mind control?
- Yoga/Transcendental Med?
- superstitions?

Have you ever been involved with
- Mysticism or Eastern Religions?
- A religious sect?
- Freemasonry or any other secret society?

Have you ever practiced
- Pre-marital sex?
- Homosexuality or
- Lesbianism?

Have you ever used mind altering drugs such as
- Amphetamines?
- Marijuana/cannabis?
- Cocaine/heroin, LSD, etc.?

Have you been or are you addicted to
- alcohol, tobacco?
- prescription drugs?
- gambling?

Have you ever possessed occult jewelry, or objects such as
- Charm bracelets?
- Italian horns?
- Egyptian ankhs?
- Horseshoes?
- Lucky coins or mystic medals?
- Star of David or *any* religious symbol?
- African masks, idols, etc?
- Dolls?

Can you remember any other powerful act, incident or experience still making you feel ashamed, guilty, or frightened?

V.I. - Are you aware of any UNFORGIVENESS or RESENTMENT towards ANYONE?

NOTE: that questionnaire and the following information are only **general guides** to revealing areas of spiritual bondage. A person may need to seek mature counseling and/or deliverance ministry for help with more complex issues.

Addictions are the results of consistent sinful habits or practices (sometimes passed on to infants while still in the womb!)

The drink, cigarette, bet (or other drug) is merely an outward expression, or a "leaf" on the addict's "tree." The "root" of all addictions however is a dependence on something (or someone) other than God Himself! – **All addictions are therefore rooted in IDOLATRY!**

These demonic strongholds will begin to surrender and depart when "*the axe is laid at the root;*" (*Luke 3:9*) i.e. when the **sin of idolatry** is acknowledged, *truly* repented of, and renounced in the Name of Jesus. The following prayers have proved to be extremely effective in personal deliverance, but are intended for born again believers only.

> **Heavenly Father,**
> **In the Name of Jesus, I confess my involvement with _____**
> (name anything on the check list which applies; and of course anything else that the Holy Spirit reveals)
> **I acknowledge, repent of, and renounce all these occult practices, sinful habits, and IDOLATRIES (or addictions) that have given the devil a legal right to oppress, demonize or enslave me. I break the power of the spirit (s) of_____**
> (Again, *name specific sins* and command them to leave in the Name, and by the blood of Jesus Christ.)
> **I sever the cords (soul ties) that have bound me to _____**
> (name anyone you know who may have brought occult bondage into your life)
> **and I claim my freedom from all demonic subjection. In the Name of Jesus Christ, I forbid any further access or hold, and all legal rights given to the enemy are now to be removed, broken and destroyed. Through Christ's blood I am free! I stand by faith on the Word of God, and from now on, neither Satan nor any demon has a legal right *to* me, a place *in* me, or power *over* me!**
> **In Jesus' Name, Amen.**

****

BREAKING CURSES

(Be prepared for the Holy Spirit to reveal the source of any curse; past or present)

Curses come in so many forms: If believed or received they often become an open door for demonic access! Some common **self-imposed** curses are as follows:

"Cross my heart and hope to die," – "I was frightened to death!" – "I wish I was dead!" – "Over my dead body!" etc., etc., etc. Be aware; **those are Death wishes!**

"Seven years bad luck" – "Wishing on a star" (or chicken bone) – "Any reference to good or bad luck" – "Fingers crossed" – "Knocking on (or touching) wood" – "Throwing rice or confetti" (fertility

rites) – Throwing salt (for good luck) – "Walking under ladders" – "Broken mirrors" – "Black cats" – "Friday 13ᵗʰ" etc. …**All Come under the heading of Witchcraft!**
   Other common curses imposed on individuals; especially children.
   "You're so stupid" – "You'll never amount to anything" – "You're so ugly (fat, dumb, careless, retarded etc.) – "You're as stubborn as a mule" – "You're a born loser" – "You eat like a pig," and (when used negatively) – "You're just a chip off the old block."

> **BONDAGE CURSES** can and do come through **blood covenants** (e.g. friends who cut themselves and share their blood to become "blood brothers or sisters" for life).
> **Having ears or other body parts pierced** – this produces occult "soul ties" with whoever does the piercing.
> **Tattoos** – indelible skin markings with ink often "blessed" in pagan rites before use.
> **Receiving or owning evil things** – photographs, clothing, or objects rooted in witchcraft.
> **Being related or involved** with anyone in witchcraft, religious cults, or secret societies such as Druids, Freemasonry (Shriners) etc.
> **Sexual perversions** such as bestiality, incest, homosexuality, lesbianism, and un-Godly sexual acts.
> **All pornography** – 'soft' or 'hard core'.
> **Abortion** – performing or receiving … also the curse put upon unwanted or illegitimate children, (see *Deut.23:2*)
> **Adultery – fornication – Lying – Theft …**
> There are many, many more!

A prayer for deliverance from such curses

Heavenly Father,
   I come to You sincerely in the Name of Jesus. I desire to be free from all curses and their effects. Through the precious blood of Christ, I confess all my sins, and the sins of my ancestors. _____(be as specific as you can) **I repent of those sins, and renounce every demonic curse allowed through my own sins or passed down from my forefathers.**
   Through the blood of the Lamb, and the word of my testimony, I break the power of any and all negative words and statements (vocal curses) **put upon me by my family, friends or ancestors. I sever all occult connections, unions and soul ties with _____ _____ and renounce the demonic domination or control of _____** (name anyone involved and known to you; alive or dead).
   In Jesus' Name, I take back all ground legally given to the devil through ignorance, sin or these curses in my life. I command every evil spirit which came in through any curse to go now!
   I claim my freedom, and stand in the blessings of God from this moment on!
   Thank you Lord Jesus for setting me free.

****

UNFORGIVENESS

Unforgiveness has always been one of the most serious issues within the Christian community!

All sins are "transgressions," (*1John3:4*) but unforgiveness is described as *"wickedness!"* (See *Matt.18:21-35*) The man who would not forgive was called a *"wicked servant"* and was delivered to the *"tormentors"* until his debt was paid!

In *Matt.6:15*, Jesus spells out His Father's attitude towards this unwarranted condition:

"But if ye forgive not men their trespasses, (sins) **NEITHER WILL YOUR HEAVENLY FATHER FORGIVE YOURS!"** (See also *Mark 11:25-26*)

To be sent to the *"tormentors"* (or torturers) by God is a most fearful thing! The tormentors are evil spirits who delight in their work of inflicting physical, mental and spiritual pain.

Unforgiveness allows these spirits to rob us of peace, joy and contentment; and put us in bondage to heaviness, stress, sickness and fear! In light of all that Jesus has forgiven in us,

HOW DARE WE HAVE UNFORGIVENESS TOWARD ANYONE?

Someone may say, "But I don't feel I can forgive such and such a person."

The good news? Forgiveness is not a *feeling* – it's an act of your *will*!

If you *WILL* forgive others – your Heavenly Father *WILL* forgive you!

Make up your mind or will to forgive **anyone** you have anything against! Anyone who has ever wronged you! The consequences of unforgiveness can be very grave!

Not too long ago, a woman with **severe migraine headaches** asked the Lord why she could not receive healing. The Lord showed her that for years she had hated **king Henry VIII** (that's right – Henry VIII!) She began hating him primarily because of the way he treated his wives; now she was in the hands of the "tormentors!" (Migraine headaches, arthritis, depression, anxiety, etc., are common to those who will not forgive!) A person may not always manifest those full-blown symptoms, but if they have unforgiveness, they are heading down that road! Resentment is usually the starting place.

A prayer to avoid the "tormentors."

Heavenly Father,

In the Name of Jesus, I confess my sin(s) of unforgiveness (resentment, bitterness or hatred) **towards** _____ (Let the Holy Spirit search your heart; and then name each person)

I *will* **forgive them. Help me to be willing to forgive** *any* **and** *all* **in light of Your forgiveness toward me. Lord Jesus, You said of me, and all mankind,** *"Father forgive them, for they know not what they do."* **Please help me to do the same. Let me not be given to the tormentors; but let me live in the freedom of Your love, joy and peace. Forgive my sins Father, as I forgive those that sin against me.**

In Jesus' Name,
Amen.

******

UNGODLY FEARS

"The fear of the Lord, that is wisdom ..." (*Job 28:28*)

All other fear is contrary to faith! – *"Whatsoever is not of faith is sin."* (*Rom.14:23*)

And, *"...Without faith it is impossible to please God."* (*Heb.11:6*)

Therefore we cannot please God if we are living in fear! It is a sin to be afraid!

Look at it this way:

If fear is *not* a sin, we could be stuck with it for the rest of our lives!

But if we are willing to acknowledge ungodly fears as sins, we can confess them, renounce them, and claim our victory and freedom in Jesus' Name!

NO MORE BUMPS IN THE NIGHT!

I was only eleven years old when I saw my first horror film: it was called "The Curse of the Mummy's Tomb!" Looking back, it was the kind of silly "B" movie that the grown ups laughed at; but for me – it was the scariest thing I'd ever seen! The Mummy *always* came at night, so for weeks afterward I needed the bedroom light on before I could even think of going to sleep!

As I grew up, the Mummy faded from my mind, but a fear of the dark remained. (A spirit of fear doesn't care how old you are!) Twenty-one years later, as a very young Christian, I happened to be staying in a small, secluded English village. (Typically the kind with narrow wooded country lanes, and no street lighting whatsoever!) One night I was walking home alone, and – you guessed it – that old Mummy fear was suddenly right there!

I was thirty-two years old; tall and powerfully built; it was embarrassing! I whistled and sang choruses, but I was still scared! A verse in the Bible said,

"For God hath not given us the spirit of fear; but of power, and of love, and of a sound mind." (*2Tim.1:7*)

Well if God didn't give me *"the spirit of fear"* – someone else surely did!

When I asked the Lord why I was so afraid of the dark, He took me straight back to the cinema where the spirit had entered! I saw myself watching the "Mummy's Tomb" and realized, amongst other things, I was there **illegally**! (In those days, sixteen was the minimum age for watching such a film, so naturally I had lied, and purchased a ticket by pretending to be five years older.)

The price of that admission was twenty-one years of fear!

Another scripture verse spoke to me,

"There is no fear in love; but perfect love casts out fear: because fear hath torment. He that feareth is not made perfect in love." (*1John 4:18*)

As I began confessing my sin and rebuking the fear, God's perfect love began casting it out! Ground that I had given away was now taken back. All that remained for me to do was to confirm and proclaim the victory!

I headed for the darkest places: basements, woods, passages, alleyways etc., and always at night. In each place I confessed my victory over the fear in Jesus' Name!

Praise God; no more fear of the dark!

"Thou shalt not be afraid for the terror by night; nor for the arrow that flieth by day; nor for the pestilence that walketh in darkness; nor for the destruction that wasteth at noonday." (*Ps.91:5-6*)

(My fear of heights went a short time later in exactly the same way!)

Since then I've had the privilege of seeing the Lord deliver many of His people from spirits of fear.

One sister (unable to face baptism due a fear of water) confessed her fear and began to overcome it by regularly immersing her head in the bathroom sink! After a week of confessing her victory, she was baptized in the ocean not far from her home!

Another sister was equally afraid of spiders! After confessing this fear as a sin, she stopped running away, or crushing them automatically as she always had, and began picking them up on pieces of paper or cardboard. She would then discard them elsewhere – unharmed!

Within a month she was actually able to hold one in her hand! You've never seen anyone more victorious – or blessed!

One brother learned by the word of knowledge, that a spirit had gained access while he was still in his mother's womb! Her fall down a flight of stairs resulted in his life-long fear of heights!

After prayer that spirit was cast out!

No matter what the fear or phobia might be, it has a name; but the Name of Jesus is above *every* name! At the Name of Jesus, *every* knee must bow! Including spirits of fear and all other demonic powers! Remember that any fear (other than a godly *"fear of the Lord," Job 28:28*) is sin!

A prayer to overcome fear(s)

Heavenly Father,
    I acknowledge that all ungodly fear is sin. I confess my fear(s) of _____ ___ and repent. I confess my own sins, and any of my forefather's, which gave spirit(s) of fear access into my life. I believe Jesus died and rose again to deliver me from the power of darkness, and all fear. In His mighty Name, which is above every name, I renounce every fear that has bound or tormented me, and I call upon the Lord Jesus Christ to set me free!
    I command the spirit(s) of _____ to leave me now and never return! I take back the ground given, and I am willing to proclaim my victory over any fear as the Holy Spirit leads.

****

MAINTAINING DELIVERANCE
*"Finally, my brethren, **be strong in the Lord**, and in the power of His might. **Put on the whole armor of God**, that ye may be able to stand against the wiles of the devil." (Eph.6:10-11)*

It is essential to recognize that freedom from any and all demonic bondage is only possible in the strength and power of God's might! *"The battle is the Lord's" (2Chr.20:15)*
    Jesus said, *"... **for without Me ye can do nothing**." (John 15:5)*
    However, God's Word also says, *"We can do all things through Christ Who strengthens us."*
(Phil.4:13)

It is therefore in the power of Christ's strength and victory alone, that we *"**put on the whole armor of God**."* Only then can we stand against all the wiles of the devil!

First: God's strength! Second: God's armor!

The whole armor of God is seven fold
The Belt of **TRUTH**
The Breastplate of **RIGHTEOUSNESS**
Feet (our walk) prepared (to advance) with the **GOSPEL of PEACE**
The Shield of **FAITH**
The Helmet of **SALVATION**
The Sword of the Spirit, which is the **WORD OF GOD**
Prayer **IN THE SPIRIT**

Girding our loins with God's Truth (His Word) is the central and vital action in maintaining our freedom. Jesus said, "I AM THE WAY, **THE TRUTH**, and THE LIFE." (*John 14:6*)
We might well see the belt of truth as Jesus being constantly wrapped around us!

Remember: the amount of truth/light we walk towards is the amount of deception/darkness we leave behind!
Learning to confront the "*father of lies*" with the "*Word of Truth*" on *every* level of temptation is the key to victory. If Jesus did it, (*Matt.4:1-11*) how much more should we?
"*Submit yourselves therefore to God. Resist the devil and he will flee from you.*" (*Eph.4:27, James 4:7*)

The breastplate of righteousness protects our new heart; but like all the other "*armor,*" it must be worn on a daily basis! The breastplate is there to promote the rightness of godly character (integrity), and conduct.
"*The* (old natural) *heart is deceitful above all things and desperately wicked: who can know it?*" (*Jer.17:9*) That's why God gave us a new one! (*Eze.36:26*) Of course, Christ is our breastplate, and our *only* righteousness; but before He can guard the door of our hearts and bring forth His Life in us, we must give Him the keys! Then only that which is of God will be allowed to reach our innermost being.

"*Keep your heart with all diligence; for out of it are the issues of life.*" (*Prov.4:23*)

Feet shod
Biblically speaking, there is no such thing as a "Christian Retreat." The next time you hear it described that way, please tell somebody,
"It should be a CHRISTIAN ADVANCE!"
The Gospel is marching onward! Our feet are prepared for war! "*The gates of hell shall not prevail against us.*" And always be aware:

THERE IS NO SPIRITUAL ARMOR FOR THE BACK!

In ancient times, Roman soldiers wore special shoes (called caligae) when advancing towards their enemies. Likewise, the believer's feet should be moving forward – not slipping back!
"*...shod with the preparation of the Gospel of peace.*"
One rendering of that phrase implies "a willingness or readiness to advance towards spiritual enemies, and take the fight to them!" Clearly then, whenever the Gospel message is shared with others,

we not only help to break *their* "chains," but we also encourage ourselves in the Lord, and build strength to overcome those spiritual enemies in our own lives!

"How beautiful are the feet of them that preach the Gospel of peace, and bring glad tidings of good things." (Is.52:7, Rom.10:15)

***Above all, taking the shield of faith** wherewith ye shall be able to quench all the fiery darts of the wicked." (Eph.6:16)*

After any measure of deliverance we may expect evil spirits to attack with renewed vigor seeking to bring us into bondage once again.

"Above all." Faith is our primary defense against all the *"fiery darts* (assaults or temptations) *of the wicked one."* *"Taking the shield"* implies its continual daily use!

Remember: *"**Faith cometh by hearing, and hearing by the Word of God.**" (Rom.10:17)*
Immersing oneself in the Word of God is the key to *"quenching"* enemy onslaughts.
Listening to the *"God of Heaven"* will bring strength, freedom and victory!
Listening to the *"god of this world"* will bring weakness, bondage and defeat.
Hold your shield up high!

*"...**The people that do know their God will be strong, and do exploits.**" (Dan.11:32b)*

The helmet of salvation
In the natural realm, there is only one reason for wearing a helmet: to protect the head!
In the spiritual realm, the believer's helmet protects the MIND!
God's salvation in Christ provides all that we need to resist and overcome demonic forces, but it is not automatic. We must arm ourselves through faith!
Humanly speaking, the battle for salvation begins with *"repentance,"* i.e., a change of mind.
It is in the mind that virtually every ensuing conflict will take place!
In a very real sense, the mind is the Christian's war zone: often described (and rightly so) as a
"MIND – FIELD!"

Remember: the body is neutral. Its members act or move only in accordance with the directions of the mind or will. If the will is submitted to the Holy Spirit, the members move forward in obedience and righteousness. If the will resists or rejects the Spirit of God, the members move backwards in disobedience and sin.

If the mind is overcome, the rest of the body becomes vulnerable to attack.

There is no better place to find evidence of this mental battle ground, and our need to wear the *"helmet of salvation,"* than in the 6th, 7th, and 8th chapters of the book of Romans.

Chapter 6 **RECKONING** with sin (key verses 11-16, esp. 13 and 16).
Chapter 7 **WARRING** against sin (key verses 14-24, csp. 15, 18, and 23).
Chapter 8 **OVERCOMING** sin (key verses 1-14, esp. all 14!)

*"**Thou wilt keep him in perfect peace, whose MIND is stayed** (fixed or set) **on Thee:** because he trusteth in Thee." (Is.26:3)*

The Sword of the Spirit, which is the Word of God
This "Sword" is the Believer's only weapon, and there is none mightier!
Notice that the putting on of God's armor begins and ends with the *"Word of God:"* and because the *"Sword"* is always carried on the soldier's "Belt," we can see that God's Word is to be used offensively as well as defensively.

"The Word of God is quick, and powerful, and sharper than any two-edged sword, piercing to the dividing asunder of soul (mind) *and spirit, and of the joints and marrow, and is a discerner of the thoughts and intents of the heart." (Heb.4:12)*

In all of life (not just in deliverance), victory gained, and liberty maintained will always be in direct proportion to the believer's faith in – and dependence on – the *"Sword of the Spirit!"*

A beautiful picture of this is found by looking at one of King David's men:

*"... and Eleazar ... arose, and smote the Philistines until his hand was weary, and **his hand clave unto*** (became one with) ***the sword**: and the Lord wrought a great victory that day!"(2Sam.23:9-10)*

Be persistent: if we hold fast to the *"Sword,"* God's victory will come!

Jesus said, *"If a man love Me, he will keep My words, and My Father will love him, and We will come unto him, and make Our abode with him." (John 14:23)*

Loving and keeping he Word of God opens the door to God's presence; while at the same strengthening us against demonic influence!

Praying in the Spirit

Although not always counted among the actual *"armor of God,"* praying in the Spirit is nevertheless an integral part of our warfare. As we saw in chapter 12, to pray in the spirit is to pray with other tongues, *(1Cor.14:14-15)* and is altogether necessary when *"wrestling against demonic powers"* whose names are unknown to us.

On pages 152 -154, we explored five scriptural reasons for speaking in tongues:

Interpretation – Intercession – Spiritual warfare – Praise and worship – Edification.

However, in the context of maintaining deliverance, let me close this study by re-emphasizing the fifth.

The Holy Spirit said through Paul,

*"**I would that ye all spake*** (spoke) ***with tongues**" (1Cor.14:5a)*

And,

*"**He that speaketh in an unknown tongue, edifieth himself.**"(1Cor.14:4)*

To *"edify"* means to **INSTRUCT**; to **CONFIRM**; to **STRENGTHEN**, and to **MAKE BOLD.**

All concerning our **WALK of FAITH!**

So then, it is no surprise that the devil would stop at nothing to prevent us from speaking with other tongues!

*"But ye beloved, **building up yourselves on your most holy faith, praying in the Holy Ghost,** keep yourselves in the love of God, looking for the mercy of our Lord Jesus Christ unto eternal life." (Jude 20-21)*

Finally:

After exhorting us to put on *"**the armor of light**,"* the Apostle Paul goes on to say,

*"**But put ye on the Lord Jesus Christ, and make not provision for the flesh, to fulfill the lusts thereof**" (Rom.13:12,14)*

This of course confirms that putting on the armor of God is nothing less than putting on the Lord Jesus Christ Himself!

The Holy Spirit was sent to "*reveal*" the things of Christ; and to "*empower*" His people: (*John 16:14-15, Acts 1:8*) so the more we surrender (submit) to the power of the Holy Spirit, the stronger the Word of God becomes in our lives!

Never forget:

The Holy Spirit seeks to reveal, and through faith drive out anything that is not "*Christ in us;*" and He will do so by the power of **Confession** (*Rom.10:10, 1John1:9*) – **Repentance** (*2Cor.7:10, Rev.2:5* and *3:19*) – **Renunciation** (*2Cor.4:2*) – **Resistance** (*James 4:7*) – **Humility** (*Prov.16:5, James 4:6*) – **Forgiveness,** (*Matt.18:21-22, Mark11:25-26*) and above all – **Love** (*1Cor.13, 1John 4:18*).

May it be so for you, in Jesus' mighty Name!

****

ABOUT THE AUTHOR

K ole Eremos is an Evangelist, Speaker, Bible teacher and musician.
Some years ago, while ministering in the realm of spiritual warfare, he was led by the Holy Spirit to write dozens of articles and tracts exposing a variety of religious and occult deceptions. By the grace of God, circulation of those tracts has helped many people around the world to escape from the powers of darkness, and find light and life in the Kingdom of God's only begotten Son!

Before his conversion, Kole was a member of two successful British musical groups, and appeared regularly on television, radio, and stage; but like so many other entertainers, he would find "no satisfaction," nor meaning in that way of life.

His love for the sea, combined with a desperate longing for peace and fulfillment would lead him to purchase a sailing yacht, and cross the Atlantic Ocean in search of the truth.
(Two years later, the "TRUTH" would find him!)

Soon after his conversion in America, God began using Kole's earlier show business experience by allowing him to appear in many similar arenas; only this time as a witness to the glorious life-changing Gospel of Jesus Christ!

In this, his first full-length book, the author "gathers up the fragments" of over thirty born again years in order to equip today's saints for "the work of the ministry," and for their own *personal* victory in the many spiritual battles yet to come!

Contact the author by e-mailing koleeremos@ymail.com

nited States
2BB/3/P

9 781607 913931